D0224464

ARCHAEOLOGY OF NATIVE NORTH AMERICA

Dean R. Snow

Pennsylvania State University

Prentice Hall

Boston Columbus Indianapolis New York San Francisco Upper Saddle River
Amsterdam Cape Town Dubai London Madrid Milan Munich Paris Montréal Toronto
Delhi Mexico City São Paulo Sydney Hong Kong Seoul Singapore Taipei Tokyo

VP, Editorial Director: Leah Jewell
Editor in Chief: Dixon Musslewhite
Publisher: Nancy Roberts
Project Manager Editorial: Vanessa Gennarelli
Editorial Assistant: Nart Varoqua
Director of Marketing: Brandy Dawson
Senior Marketing Manager: Laura Lee Manley
Marketing Assistant: Pat Walsh
Managing Editor: Maureen Richardson
Project Liaison: Shelly Kupperman
Senior Operations Supervisor: Nick Sklitsis
Operations Specialist: Cathleen Peterson
Cover Designer: Margaret Kenselaar
Manager, Visual Research: Beth Brenzel
Photo Researcher: Francelle Carapetyan
Manager, Rights and Permissions: Zina Arabia
Image Permission Coordinator: Debbie Latronica
Manager, Cover Visual Research & Permissions: Jayne Conte
Senior Media Editor: David Alick
Full-Service Project Management/Composition: DeAnn Montoya, S4Carlisle Publishing Services
Printer/Binder: Hamilton Printing Co.
Cover Printer: Lehigh-Phoenix Color Corp.
Cover Art: Art Resource/Field Museum of Natural HistoryArt Resource/Field Museum of Natural History
Text Font: Sabon 10/12 pts

Credits and acknowledgments borrowed from other sources and reproduced, with permission, in this textbook appear on pages 363–364.

Copyright © 2010 Pearson Education, Inc., publishing as Prentice Hall, 1 Lake Street, Upper Saddle River, NJ 07458. All rights reserved. Manufactured in the United States of America. This publication is protected by Copyright, and permission should be obtained from the publisher prior to any prohibited reproduction, storage in a retrieval system, or transmission in any form or by any means, electronic, mechanical, photocopying, recording, or likewise. To obtain permission(s) to use material from this work, please submit a written request to Pearson Education, Inc., Permissions Department, **Prentice Hall, 1 Lake Street, Upper Saddle River, NJ 07458.**

Many of the designations by manufacturers and seller to distinguish their products are claimed as trademarks. Where those designations appear in this book, and the publisher was aware of a trademark claim, the designations have been printed in initial caps or all caps.

Library of Congress Cataloging-in-Publication Data

Snow, Dean R.,
  Archaeology of Native North America/Dean Snow.
    p. cm.
  Includes bibliographical references and index.
  ISBN-13: 978-0-13-615686-4 (alk. paper)
  ISBN-10: 0-13-615686-X (alk. paper)
1. Indians of North America—Antiquities. 2. North America—Antiquities. 3. United States—Antiquities. I. Title.
E77.9.S565 2010
970.01—dc22

                         2009027301

10 9 8 7 6 5 4 3 2 1

Prentice Hall
is an imprint of

www.pearsonhighered.com

ISBN-10:   0-13-615686-X
ISBN-13: 978-0-13-615686-4

For Jan

Contents

3 THE PEOPLING OF AMERICA   41

8 POSTCLASSIC MESOAMERICA   172

9 THE MISSISSIPPIANS   195

10 THE NORTHEASTERN FORESTS   218

13 THE WEST COAST   278

14 THE ARCTIC AND SUBARCTIC   304

15 WORLDS IN COLLISION   321

Special Features

Ningunos Príncipes de España jamas ganaron tierra alguna fuera della, slavo agora que vuestras Alteza tienen acá otro mundo [Princes of Spain have never gained possession of any land outside of their own country, until now that your Highnesses have here an other world].

Christopher Columbus,
journal of the third voyage

I have spent the latter part of my childhood and all of my adult life studying the "other world" we now call North America. I have traveled across most of it at one time or another, almost always in the company of my family or colleagues. The lives of real American Indians have been interwoven with those of my ancestors for the dozen generations that my line of Snows has been here, and studying the archaeology of the continent has been my life's work.

There are many books in print on this subject, some of them very good ones. I have been lucky enough to be involved in the production of books such as the *Mysteries of the Ancient Americas*, which was published by Reader's Digest, a series of books and maps by the National Geographic Society, the *Atlas of Ancient America* with Michael Coe and Elizabeth Benson, and some other works under my own authorship. I made my first attempt to synthesize the native archaeology of this continent in 1976, with the publication of my first book, *The Archaeology of North America*. Several other book projects followed.

Two things are new and different about this book. First, it covers all of North America, including Mesoamerica, not just the United States and Canada. Second, it is organized around the themes of evolution and ecology. I believe that it is important to explain the past in terms of scientifically valid conclusions. To that end I have done my best to avoid the conceit of merely finding clever new ways to state the obvious, or to simply string together pretty pictures and basic descriptions.

This book is about the continent before it was dominated by the United States, before epidemics devastated its native inhabitants and it lapsed into wilderness, before

it was the America familiar to us from history books. This is also a book about the archaeology of a continent, not a book about how to do archaeology. Many readers will want to know more about how I have reached a particular conclusion, or more importantly how to solve specific problems themselves. Accordingly I have supplied a series of "how to" boxes, inserting them where I think the reader is most likely to want them to appear. They can be read out of order and applied in many situations. Readers can also refer to the many good books on archaeology as a discipline to find out more about how we apply both archaeological science and the several related sciences upon which archaeologists depend. E. O. Wilson, whose quote begins the first chapter, is profoundly right. "Without the instruments and accumulated knowledge of the natural sciences . . . the world is too remote from ordinary experience to be merely imagined." There is no substitute for the scientific method in archaeology, even though there may be many good supplements to it provided by literature and the arts. Many such contributions enhance the central themes of this book.

There are many ways to organize a book like this one. While its organization attempts to make it possible for readers to jump around and follow their own paths, even read the chapters out of order, it is nonetheless constrained by decisions I have made about how best to tell the story of Native America. We could start with the most recent and thus the most securely known part of that story and work backward in time from there, but the river of time flows in the opposite direction and pushing upstream against it would make it nearly impossible to explain the evolutionary processes that unfolded over the course of time. Only in part of Chapter 13 did I use this technique, in that case because I judged that the reader needed to first have a clear understanding of the end-points of the evolutionary trajectories of the Northwest Coast.

I could also have let facts speak for themselves, as some authors have, writing heaps of boring description that would leave readers able to remain awake with few clues about the bigger picture. I have chosen to avoid that option as well, mostly leaving out pottery types, point types, and local sequences that fill site reports, technical articles, and many regional syntheses. Readers wishing to find out more about these details are encouraged to refer to paragraphs on further reading at the ends of the chapters, and to follow the parenthetical references in the text to the references at the end of the book. Those sources, typically peer-reviewed books and journal articles, will lead the reader stepwise to other more obscure sources that might answer specific questions. I hope that questions that go unanswered will lead at least some readers into the professional pursuit of archaeological science.

I am mindful that in addition to the big picture many people will want to know more about that projectile point they found in the garden last year, or that archaeological site just down the road. To make that possible I have tried to reference the most recent and the most reliable sources available, but readers must be aware that important ones will come out after this book is published. In some cases I have not used a very recent source because it is still controversial, and I judge that we should wait for subsequent debate in journals to settle matters. Some sources are not listed because they are misleading or just plain wrong; others are not listed simply because there is not enough room to mention all the best work in an introductory volume. However, I regard those that I have listed as trustworthy, and they in turn should lead to most or all of the reliable works available in major research libraries. Many journal articles are now available on the Web, and one often needs only to enter a few key words to find the full text of a reliable peer-reviewed article. There is also plenty of junk science on the Web, and readers must take care to exercise their critical skills on everything they find there.

Articles that have been published in recent years and are available through research libraries are almost invariably in high-quality peer-reviewed journals and therefore trustworthy. Books are another matter because quality depends upon the nature of the press. University press publications are peer reviewed and usually trustworthy, but some commercial presses are no more trustworthy than tabloid newspapers. That is what happens when the desire to make money overtakes other motives. Reviews in professional journals usually help one evaluate books. Finally, it is wise to remember to beware the person of one book, no matter what book that may be, including this one.

My maternal grandmother, who died in 1995 just eight days short of her 101st birthday, knew me well. I was her oldest grandchild, the one who was fascinated by time and words even at a young age, and I have never forgotten that most of my genes relevant to those traits came from her. My mother, who died too young, and my father, who still sometimes seems more like an older brother, gave me the freedom and resources to pursue an unlikely career. Their love and kindness extended even to the protracted suppression of their astonishment when I actually proved able to make a living as an academic. My sisters have forgiven the occasional meanness of childhood, share my wacky sense of humor, and along with their husbands and siblings-in-law on my wife's side—are my informal council of advisors. My paternal grandfather pinned his hopes and part of his legacy on me in blind faith that as the only son of his only surviving son I would be worthy of it all. There have been a wise uncle, admiring aunts, and an enduring cheering section of cousins, nieces, and nephews. In a perfect world everyone would have such a family.

For their efforts reviewing part or all of the manuscript and generously sharing their ideas with us, I gratefully acknowledge Pearson's editorial reviewers:

Don E. Dumond, University of Oregon

Michael A. Glassow, University of California–Santa Barbara

Ted Goebel, Texas A&M University

Mark J. Hartmann, University of Arkansas–Little Rock

Robert L. Kelly, University of Wyoming

David J. Meltzer, Southern Methodist University

Jerald T. Milanich, University of Florida

George R. Milner, Pennsylvania State University

Gerry Schaefenberger, Monmouth University

Bill Schindler, Monmouth University

Joseph A. Tiffany, University of Wisconsin–La Crosse

Richard F. Veit, Monmouth University

I especially thank my now adult children, Kate, Barb, and Josh. I value them each and all more than my own life. They have tolerated archaeological vacations, countless museum visits, sunburns, tortured humor, Spartan accommodations, blood-sucking insects, and life-threatening illnesses far from home, often for my sake. Scattered by careers and marriage, we are still kept close by unqualified love, the joy of grandchildren, and rare adversity. In a perfect world every father would have such children.

Most of all I thank my wife, Jan, whom I have known since childhood and loved for more than five decades. She has been and will always be my constant partner, the mother of my children, my editor, my confidant, my traveling companion, my most valued critic, my best friend, and more. In a perfect world every husband would have such a wife.

Dean Snow

ACKNOWLEDGMENTS

One cannot have a productive career in any field without the direct or indirect support of innumerable people. In one way or another a book project like this one draws upon all of these many interactions. A few of them always stand out as having been especially important, sometimes crucial, to the success of this project. I thank those people now with the hope that I have not inadvertently omitted any, and with silent thanks to all those who have helped me, sometimes without realizing it, along the way.

Kenneth Ames, Linda Cordell, Don Dumond, Susan Evans, Michael Glassow, Ted Goebel, Robert Kelly, David Meltzer, Jerald Milanich, George Milner, Madonna Moss, Bruce Smith, Joseph Tiffany, and David Webster all read sections of the book at various points in its development and made many valuable comments and corrections. Roy Hammerstedt and Douglas Gonzales, experienced scientists in other disciplines, read the manuscript and provided invaluable advice for its improvement. Janet Snow read everything, sometimes multiple times, and provided invaluable help with its organization and continuity. Of course, I remain solely responsible for any lingering errors. Nancy Roberts and Vanessa Gennarelli provided editorial guidance and practical help for Prentice Hall. Anonymous reviewers they chose provided cogent criticisms of the book's first draft.

I acquired the background needed to complete this book as an undergraduate at the University of Minnesota, a graduate student at the University of Oregon, as a beginning professor for 3 years at the University of Maine, in my 26 years at the University at Albany, and in my first 13 years at Penn State. I am indebted to colleagues, students, and friends at all of these institutions. I am also indebted to many unnamed people, many of them still good friends, who assisted me in many ways while I carried out research in various parts of the United States, Canada, and Mexico. I am especially grateful to Penn State for a one-year sabbatical leave, 1995–1996, during which I was able to complete a first draft of this book. Dumbarton Oaks Research Library, an institute of Harvard University, hosted me as a senior scholar during the fall 2005 semester. I am particularly indebted to Edward Keenan, Joanne Pillsbury, and Jeffrey Quilter for their generosity and support during my stay there. Jai Alterman, Peter Haggerty, Elizabeth Boone, John Verano, Leonardo López Luján, Laura Filloy Nadal, Saburo Sugiyama, Scott Hutson, and Jeffrey Splitstoser were invaluable colleagues during my stay there. While I was in residence in Washington I also had help from Tim Beach, Bruce Smith, Tobi Brimsek, Francis McManamon, and Terry Childs.

There are over 300 illustrations in this volume, many of which required help of various kinds. Those people who went out of their way to provide me with more than incidental assistance include Herbert Alexander, Richard Alley, David Anderson, Timothy Babcock, Larry Benson, John Blitz, Kenneth Block, Bruce Bourque, Janine Bowechop, Ian Brown, Tricia Buckingham, Rebecca Carr, Theresa Carstensen, Robert Clouse, Michael Coe, Richard Collier, Michael Collins, Jon Czaplicki, Janet Davis, Tom Dillehay, Glen Doran, Penelope Drooker, David Dye, Alicia Egbert, Tom Elliott, Dolores Elliott, Rich Friedman, Bridget Gazzo, Jon Gibson, Al Goodyear, Campbell Grant, David Grove, George Hamell, Michelle Hill, Kenneth Hirth, John Hoffecker, Gordon Hull, William Iseminger, George T. Jones, Joe Joseph, Miguel Jorge Juárez Paredes, Anne Juergensen, John Kelly, Maureen King, Ashley Koebel, Michael Kunz, Vincent Lafond, Larry Lahren, Gene Mackay, Joyce Marcus, Lisa Marine, Bruce Masse, Jerry McDonald, Jerald Milanich, George Milner, Claire Milner, John Neikirk, Jill Neitzel, Lee Newsom, Keely Parker, Robert Pearce, Richard Pirko, Mary Pohl, Nelly Robles Garcia, Hilda Sánchez Villanueva, William Sanders, Joe Saunders, Thad Schurr, Molly Scofield, Lynne Sebastian, Peter Siegel, Sergei Slobodin, Sovati Smith, Anna Sofaer, Arthur Spiess, Lou Stancari, Meridith Stanton, Lynne

Introduction

Without the instruments and accumulated knowledge of the natural sciences—physics, chemistry, and biology—humans are trapped in a cognitive prison. . . . [T]he world is too remote from ordinary experience to be merely imagined.

E. O. Wilson

BIOLOGICALLY MODERN HUMANS HAVE ROAMED the earth for tens of thousands of years, but it was not until around 14 millennia ago that a trickle of humanity leaked across the land bridge connecting Siberia and Alaska. Small human populations expanded from Siberia to North America, where they slowly multiplied, expanded, and eventually spread to all corners of the American continents. Like people everywhere at the time these earliest of all Americans were hunter-gatherers, but from that time forward their histories diverged from the rest of the earth's peoples. Their descendants lived in almost complete isolation from the rest of humanity until a mere five centuries ago, yet the trajectory of their long independent cultural evolution in the Americas paralleled those of other peoples on other continents. That this should be so is at once surprising and reassuring (Figure 1.1).

The long preliterate history of the American Indians and its remarkable parallels with developments elsewhere in the world have seized the imaginations of many people over the years. But it takes more than imagination to explore this saga. It takes careful application of archaeology and related natural sciences, and that is what this book is about. The pages that follow introduce the ways in which native North American cultures evolved and adapted to changing environments

Figure 1.1 A full-scale diorama at the New York State Museum depicts a band of hunter-gatherers as they might have looked 14,000 years ago.
Source: Courtesy of the New York State Museum.

and to the changing opportunities afforded by their own technological and social innovations. Just as important, they explore the ways in which archaeological science reveals those ancient developments.

Why It Matters

The archaeology of North America matters to those who live on the continent today because it is embedded in the landscape we all share. It is part of our common heritage simply because this land is ours. Like the forests, grasslands, birds, mountains, and streams all around us the evidence of the past gives context to our lives. The growing popularity of public archaeological **sites** as tourist destinations is clear evidence of public appreciation for the past (Figure 1.2).

Archaeology and the evidence of the past that archaeologists study have special importance to anyone of Native American descent because it is even more directly their past and their heritage. The resurgence of American Indian cultures during the twentieth century revived broader appreciation for their role in the history of the continent and underscored the connection between the archaeological past and living cultures.

Quite apart from the meaning North American archaeology has for the living residents of the continent, American Indian or otherwise, it is important to science because it provides an independent laboratory for the study of the evolution of human societies from simple bands of hunter-gatherers to large urbanized state societies having all the gaudy trappings we have come to think of as defining civilization. Without the Americas we might never have been sure that the explosive growth in the size and complexity of human society was not a single unique phenomenon, a combination of singular lucky happenstance followed by wholesale imitation. But the appearance of cities, literacy, technology, organized religion, and state polities in North America occurred with little if any influence from South America and none at all from the rest of the world. American archaeology reveals that all of these traits were latent in the biologically modern but thinly scattered hunter-gatherers that made up the world's human population 15 millennia ago.

The forces of continental drift that previously separated the Americas from the rest of the world's continents over the course of millions of years thereby produced a laboratory for an American control group in the great human experiment of which we are all a part. More than three decades ago Peter Farb (1978) described it in a deliberately cumbersome book titled *Man's Rise to Civilization: The Cultural Ascent of the Indians of North America*. He did not live long enough to write more books that might have celebrated the cultural ascent of other peoples on other continents. Fortunately, other authors have (Trigger 2003).

The Americas were so isolated from the rest of the world until the last five centuries that it is unreasonable to think of the various forms of American Indian agriculture to have been anything but an independent development. The ancient Sumerians, Egyptians, Greeks, and Chinese have long been held up as crucial founders of civilization in Eurasia and Africa, the implication sometimes being that without them civilization would have been at least different and perhaps impossible. But the existence in 1492 of American civilizations that were utterly disconnected from analogues in the Eastern Hemisphere shows that seeds of civilization were inherent in human beings everywhere a dozen millennia ago. The American Indians' gift to the world is the assurance that complex human societies arose independently in the past and that even after some future global catastrophe they would do so again so long as modern humans survived as a species.

Archaeological Science

While acknowledging the many different meanings American archaeology may have for us as individuals, this book is about archaeological **science**. At the

Figure 1.2 The major modern nations of North America.

foundation of scientific thought lies the certainty that there is a correct answer to any question, even though the available evidence might allow for only the uncertainty of multiple possibilities. Scientists are comfortable with uncertainty and revision but they are also driven to find ways to exclude possibilities, thus increasing the probabilities for the alternative explanations that remain. Scientific opinion tends to converge over time as the collective effort disposes of alternatives. But absolute certainty is rarely approached, and therein lies the fundamental difference between science and religion, for religion begins with the certainty of faith and resists revision with a brittleness that produces fracturing over time. In contrast, science is above all a procedure for figuring things out from the evidence, and as a consequence it is subject to constant revision as new evidence comes in.

E. O. Wilson has said that "the world is too remote from ordinary experience to be merely imagined," and this applies to archaeology as much as it does to particle physics. The American world before 1492 lies too far beyond the ordinary experience of anyone alive today to be merely imagined, but archaeological science is the lens through which we can begin to understand it. Thus archaeological science is our primary access to the history of North America prior to 1492 and an indispensable adjunct to our understanding of what came after that date.

According to a recent survey, 93% of Americans think that archaeology includes the study of dinosaurs. It does not; paleontologists study dinosaurs. The largest dinosaurs became extinct millions of years before evolution produced the first humans, so it is hardly surprising that they fall to different areas of science. The confusion about who studies what is a harmless misconception compared to many beliefs that are simultaneously widely held and demonstrably wrong, but it provides additional inspiration to archaeologists to write books like this one. **Archaeology** is the scientific study of historic or prehistoric peoples by analysis of their material remains. **Pseudoarchaeology,** and there is lots of it, is the description of the past that claims to be based on fact but is actually fictional or a deliberate distortion of observations for some nonscientific purpose. Examples are dealt with in various places in the chapters that follow.

Archaeological science, like any science, is a process for the development of principles and procedures for the systematic development of **theory,** which involves the recognition and formulation of problems, the systematic collection of data through observation and experience, and the formulation and testing of **hypotheses.** Theory is indispensable, and we all use it all the time. If I point to something and say it is a bus, I am not making a factual statement so much as I am using my perceptions along with a theoretical model of what a bus is in order to make sense of those perceptions. We all do this easily all the time, and we have generally agreed that we will treat such observations as factual, at least until we disagree. If someone says that what I am pointing at is not a bus but rather a truck and we both have time on our hands we might argue about it. Fortunately, most of the time we can take each other's word for it. Most of the time if I use my archaeological experience to say that something is a projectile point, a hearth, a burial mound, or a ball court my judgment will be taken at face value. But it is in the nature of science to provide a means to argue about propositions that are more complicated than bus identification, and to provide a means to force choices between alternative propositions that are mutually exclusive.

Thus science is not a philosophy or a religion, but rather a process for eliminating wrong answers that scientists exercise according to a well-developed set of rules and procedures. What we end up with are current propositions that have survived repeated testing but which may yet fail to survive some future test. That is why any science is a dynamic thing that is comprised of theories and hypotheses that have survived so far. Some theories, such as those involving planetary motion and biological evolution, have generated so many hypotheses that have been tested so many times that their central features are no longer doubted by reputable scientists, but technically all such propositions remain potentially disprovable.

Perhaps the most important rule is that a theory, if it is to be worth spending time on, must be able to generate testable hypotheses. If the theory is not testable in that way it will not interest a scientist. What is unsettling about this for many people is that no matter how many thousand times a theory is scrutinized and hypotheses about it are tested, it is never and can never be proven. It remains only the best currently known explanation for some particular set of phenomena, always subject to disproof in light of new data. As I write this the best available evidence for the first appearance of human beings in North America has them arriving around 14,000 years ago. In 2005 the *New York Times* reported that human footprints were found in Mexican volcanic ash that dated to 40,000 years ago, a discovery which if true would force revision of this book. More recently geologists reported their discovery that the ash layer was 1.3 million years old, not 40,000 years old as previously thought. Either the prints indicated that people evolved in North America over a million years ago, or the features were not human footprints at all. By the end of the day everyone but the producers of supermarket tabloids had decided that they were not footprints at all, at least not human ones. The example points out some other requirements of the scientific method, which are thorough documentation and publication of findings in peer-reviewed journals. It is a much slower process than reporting a story on the evening news, and it does not often make for breathless headlines or titillating talk shows, but the process almost always produces the most correct answers currently available.

Coping with Incomplete Information

A big problem for archaeological science is that it often has to make do with very spotty and incomplete data, connecting the dots to produce a recognizable picture. If all that is known about an object is when and where it was made, and when and where it was deposited in the ground, the archaeologist has no choice but to use broader theoretical understandings about how things move through space and time to describe the object's most probable history. Much of what we do is connecting the dots in this way, and that explains why theory

Box 1.1 HOW TO EVALUATE A THEORY

What a theory is depends upon who you ask. The popular definition of "theory" usually contrasts it with "fact," implying that it is clearly inferior. Indeed, the electronic thesaurus in the word processing program I am using to write these words provides the following alternatives: conjecture, speculation, assumption, premise, presumption, supposition, and guess (there is another that I will save until the end of this little essay). Little wonder that the average person has a low opinion of theory. But none of those definitions has anything to do with how scientists define "theory" or how they are expected to employ it.

The National Academy of Sciences defines scientific theory as a "well-substantiated explanation of some aspect of the natural world that can incorporate facts, laws, inferences, and tested hypotheses." Thus a scientific theory is a body of principles that is designed to explain a related set of phenomena and that is capable of generating testable hypotheses. Good examples are the planetary theory of Copernicus and Newton, electromagnetic theory, Einstein's relativity theory, and Darwin's evolutionary theory. There are many more, but I have mentioned four that are particularly robust. Without them much of what we take for granted in our daily lives would not exist. Hypotheses based on them have been tested so often and so rigorously that they have become the bedrocks of their respective sciences.

A hypothesis in turn is a proposition inspired by some combination of evidence and theory that is potentially disprovable. One cannot prove a hypothesis; one can only disprove it. This leads to several observations that might be unsettling to the scientifically uninitiated.

- The best current hypothesis might be only the least incorrect one, given that not all of the relevant evidence is known.
- Every hypothesis should be regarded as a temporarily acceptable working hypothesis.
- While it is a fundamental principle that all people are politically equal, it is not necessarily the case that their ideas are of equal validity.
- Because we can never prove but only disprove hypotheses, scientists are comfortable with uncertainty.
- While imagination is an important source of new hypotheses, it is no substitute for the scientific method.

Unfortunately, even first-rate scientists often use the term "theory" in two confusing ways. First, many lapse into using the term by its popular definition. About half of the 11 authors in one of the edited volumes I have cited in this book have done that, and I cringe every time I see it used that way. The proposition that, say, a society collapsed because the climate got hotter and drier over time might be a testable hypothesis, but it is not a scientific theory. The error is common, and it weakens scientific efforts to persuade the public that a scientific theory is not just a lot of guesswork.

The second way in which even good scientists muddy the water is by referring to some interpretive frameworks that do not generate testable hypotheses as theories. Much social theory, including Marxism, is of this type. A school of thought should be honored with the theory label only if it can generate testable hypotheses. And as a sad footnote, "hypothesis" is one of the words my computer tells me is a synonym for "theory."

is so important to archaeological science. The elements of human culture are mutually contingent and theory specifies those contingencies. Popular Sudoku puzzles are a good analogy. Sudoku publishers provide us with 81-cell tables and provide numbers for two or three dozen of the cells. The task is to fill in the remaining blank cells with numbers that are all contingent upon each other and those already present. If enough cells are already filled then filling the rest is easy. Sudoku puzzles like that shown in Figure 1.3 are difficult because fewer than 30% of the cells are already filled, but there is only one possible solution. An archaeologist is lucky to get even that much information, so any picture of the past that is based on known data and theoretical contingencies is likely to resist solution. If a half-dozen numbers were removed from the Figure 1.3 puzzle there would be more than one possible solution and no way to choose between them. This is often the case for archaeological puzzles. For the archaeologist the task is often to acquire more data through excavation or to reduce the scope of the problem so that it becomes solvable. The alternative is to be content with the uncertainty of two or more alternative hypotheses, to accept that there may be two or more mutually exclusive explanations and no way to force a choice between them.

The beauty of science is that it is self-correcting. Human beings are uniquely gifted with the ability to learn not only from their own mistakes but also from the mistakes of others. Science is just a formal means for doing that. Because it takes training and experience, most mistakes are found and corrected by other scientists. There is no shortage of young archaeologists willing to reexamine old solutions to archaeological puzzles in order to either confirm or improve upon them. It may be disappointing to have ones conclusions replaced because of new information or new methods, but that is how any scientific discipline evolves over time.

Although our imaginations are a good source for new testable hypotheses, they are no substitution for the scientific method, as E. O. Wilson said in the quote found at the beginning of this introductory chapter. If imagination were enough we could shut down NASA and let George Lucas guide our understanding of the universe. While I enjoy his work as much as the next person, I am sure that Lucas would agree that the universe is too remote from our everyday experience to be merely imagined.

The Use and Misuse of Evidence

Empirical archaeological science requires evidence, and negative evidence simply will not do. Perhaps in religion and politics one can get away with the view that an absence of proof is not proof of absence, but one cannot get away with such a statement in science, or for that matter in a court of law. This is a serious and seemingly unreasonable constraint in some instances. When rising sea levels are likely to have destroyed all evidence of early coastal sites it is logical to argue that while there is nothing there now, there was probably once much evidence of human settlement along the coast. That might be true, but in the long run skepticism about negative evidence prevents science from being overtaken by fantasy, just as in law it forestalls convictions in the absence of evidence. One of the most astounding examples of an author's failure to avoid the trap of negative evidence can be found in Jeffrey Goodman's *American Genesis* (1981). Here the author interprets the absence of any biologically premodern human remains in the Americas as (negative) evidence to support the absurd notion that biologically modern people evolved in the Americas and later spread to other continents. This hypothesis is easily disproven. I have done my best to avoid this kind of trap in this book, and I have tried to be explicit on those occasions when logic must take some accounting of negative evidence.

It is also the case that an open mind allows for ideas to be tested and rejected, whereas dogged advocacy of a particular wrong idea too often leads others to reject not just the idea but its advocate. Goodman's mistake was that he came upon a proposition that he

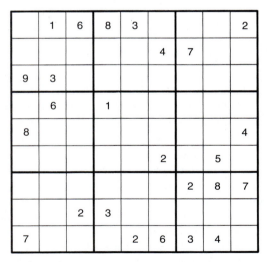

Figure 1.3 Sudoku puzzle. Place numbers 1–9 in the empty cells so that when the grid is full every column, row, and nine-cell block contains all the numbers from 1 to 9 with no repeats.

found attractive for some reason, then set about gathering evidence to support his thesis. Once he set his mind to it rejection of the proposition in light of the evidence ceased to be an option. This is a popular way to argue a position, but it almost always proves to be no way to conduct research. It is found much more often in nonscientific disciplines than among scientists. The scientist's approach is to list all of the reasonable alternative propositions as hypotheses, then to try to find tests that will disprove them one at a time until only the most correct one is left. If all the hypotheses fail testing then the researcher must come up with some more of them. If two or more mutually exclusive hypotheses resist disproof then we must live with the situation until someone comes up with new data or a new test that can force a choice between them.

By taking the very different approach of seizing upon a single hypothesis and promoting it as a thesis, the researcher in effect makes himself rather than a hypothesis the thing that must be tested and discarded by others if found wanting. The advocate strategy of research has littered the history of some disciplines with many failed advocates. The casualty rate is high, and this kind of approach to research is thus inefficient at best because single-minded advocates perish as a result of their errors rather than learning from them. But this is how many people unfamiliar with the scientific process still think that research is or should be carried out.

I have brought this up because many popular books and articles on North American archaeology have resulted from the advocate approach. Colossal stone heads along the Gulf Coast of Mexico do indeed look superficially African, but there is no supporting archaeological, linguistic, or genetic evidence to support the proposition that they portray African immigrants who there arrived three millennia ago. A Norse rune stone turned up a century ago in Minnesota, but there is no supporting archaeological, linguistic, or genetic evidence to support the proposition that a crew of Norse adventurers presaged the settlement of the region by later Norwegians. Besides, in this case the people who faked it later admitted to it.

Mistakes and Fakes

Another example is the **sasquatch** or bigfoot mythology, that fetid stew of legend, hoax, and overripe imagination. The silliness of sasquatch enthusiasm is revealed if one does nothing more than consider the minimum size necessary for any mammalian population to sustain itself over the long run. Some optimistic ecologists cite 500 as the minimum viable population size, others

1,000, but it might be 10 or 20 times that. Even if it is only 500, there would have to have once been many more than a handful of sasquatches running around the woods of northwestern America for there to be even a single one to have survived into the twentieth century (Culotta 1995). If there had been at least several hundred sasquatches living at any moment over the last 10,000 years or so, then we should expect to have found plenty of skeletal evidence by this time. That there is none at all should prompt skepticism from even the most gullible among us. It takes little effort to come up with a plausible alternative explanation for each bit of imagined or faked evidence advanced by sasquatch advocates.

Roman coins, fake inscriptions, superficial resemblances, religious innovations, and endless wishful thinking have all contributed to the nonsense that is mixed in with reputable North American archaeology on the shelves of libraries and bookstores (Mainfort and Kwas 2004). Disappointed advocates will continue to complain that professional archaeologists are narrow-minded, hidebound, and unwilling to consider alternative viewpoints. And they will continue to publish the occasional new imaginary revelation. So it is up to everyone to do their own sorting through the contradictory literature and to apply the scientific method to separate sense from nonsense. The "how to" sections in this book are guides. Also recommended are Kenneth Feder's (2002) exposé of frauds and myths regarding Danish, Egyptian, Chinese, Greek, Norse, Phoenician, Roman, and other purported influences in pre-Columbian America.

The Difference between Biological and Cultural Evolution

The theory of **evolution** is the single most important established scientific theory needed to understand what follows in this book. Other perspectives are included where they are appropriate, and in this sense the book takes a broad view of the past. The "New Archaeology" of the 1960s and 1970s spawned several theoretical perspectives, including evolutionary ecology, behavioral archaeology, and Darwinian archaeology. An ecological perspective dominates in this book because it is the easiest way to both describe the long story of North American prehistory while at the same time explaining why and how it all unfolded as it did. It is, in the jargon of the time, a "processual" approach to the subject, and the perspective that currently dominates in professional journals like *American Antiquity*.

Box 1.2 HOW TO TEST AN ARCHAEOLOGICAL HYPOTHESIS

This book contains many hypotheses, some of them paired and mutually exclusive. In at least these latter cases it is more satisfying to force a choice between competing hypotheses than to let them both stand as equally possible. Sometimes one lacks either enough information or the analytical means to force a choice and the alternative propositions must be allowed to stand untested at least for the time being. In any case, even repeatedly tested hypotheses should be thought of as always temporary, the best explanations given the current state of knowledge, and thus potentially falsifiable. But hypotheses, like opinions, are not equal, and authoring one that stands the test of time and repeated testing is undeniably satisfying.

Consider two habitual hypothesis testers, physicians and auto mechanics. Physicians work on human bodies, natural systems resulting from biological evolution, and auto mechanics work on systems designed by engineers. In neither case is it true that if you have seen one you have seen them all. Individual people and individual cars vary within their populations. Nevertheless, experience on one individual does provide some useful information to apply to the next case. I want an experienced surgeon to operate on my knee and an experienced mechanic to work on my antique Morgan.

Both physicians and mechanics often begin with multiple working hypotheses, testing the most probable ones first and moving down the list until the right one is found. A good way to observe this process at a safe distance is by listening to *Car Talk* on National Public Radio (NPR) on Saturday morning. The Magliozzi brothers do their best to diagnose problems with cars, winnowing hypotheses with various indirect tests, mainly questions asked of car owners having problems. Call-in shows featuring physicians typically involve the same process, and lead to the same only partially satisfying conclusions. Both mechanics and physicians so removed from their subjects usually can offer only the most probable explanations, not conclusive ones.

An important difference between the radio show and a real repair garage is that the mechanics do not have the option of testing hypotheses on the problem auto. Worse, they are dependent upon the often inept descriptions of symptoms provided by inexperienced car owners. In a clinical setting both physicians and mechanics have the opportunity to conduct test after test of each of several hypotheses until they (usually) zero in on the one that cannot be disproven.

Archaeological hypothesis testing is more like call-in show diagnosis than clinical testing. Our subject is far removed in time if not in space, and we can typically observe only the scanty physical remains of systems long dead. The evidence comes to us in fragmentary and garbled form, filtered by the destructive forces of time much as telephoned information about malfunctioning cars is filtered by the ignorance of inexperienced callers. Archaeologists cannot run repeated tests on a functioning system to see how it works, they can only use the surviving evidence and living analogies to make inferences about extinct systems. That means that like the Magliozzi brothers they can usually do no more than list a series of possible hypotheses and indicate which is the most probable. That, following the advice of William of Occam, is usually the one that explains all the known facts most simply. But this is where experience comes in to play. Like the Magliozzi brothers archaeologists substitute repeat observations of similar problems in different cases for repeating trials on the same case in a clinic. If the process boils down to two or more equally plausible hypotheses and there is no information to force a choice between them, one can either take comfort in knowing that there are countless other hypotheses too silly to have survived even that much testing, or one can design a research program to acquire the information necessary to break the deadlock.

A shift by some archaeologists to a more historical and humanistic approach in the last two decades of the twentieth century led to a broadening of perspectives and many fine studies. Unfortunately, the identification of this as a shift to "postprocessual" archaeology created a theoretical linkage with the philosophical fad known as "postmodernism." Postmodernist philosophy influenced archaeology only briefly, and had little impact beyond a legacy of prose too clever to be understood. In fact the mainstream of archaeology in recent years has been and continues to be what Michelle Hegman has called "processual-plus," an expanded continuation of the best that processual approaches have brought to the discipline (Hegmon 2003).

To understand the long pageant of humanity over time and space we must distinguish between the different processes of biological and cultural evolution. The two often work together, cultural forces stimulating biological changes and vice versa (Durham 1991; Shennan 2000). But they are conceptually different, and to truly understand how they interact one has to understand how each often acts alone.

The Principles of Biological Evolution

Biological evolution operates by means of four simple principles, each of which is intuitively obvious.

- First, members of any **breeding population** vary in both outward appearance and genetic makeup. A quick glance around a room full of people is sufficient to confirm this observation. Identical twins are often regarded as exceptions, but even these may exhibit minor differences.

- Second, whether it is plant or animal, most of any organism's makeup is inherited from its parents. Characteristics are heritable, so individuals tend to look like their parents. Bisexual reproduction leads to genetic recombinations that make even siblings somewhat different from each other, but no one doubts that genetic inheritance is an important determinant in any breeding population.

- Third, all breeding populations produce more offspring than necessary for simple population replacement. This was formerly true of even those populations (species) that have eventually dwindled to extinction because of changing circumstances in their environments. We can be grateful that flies suffer high mortality rates, or we would be buried under them. As some African nations have recently discovered, even elephant populations will boom if predators (including human ones) are restrained.

- Fourth, individuals that are less well adapted to the environments in which they live will reproduce less successfully than those that are better adapted. This does not necessarily imply wholesale death and universal mayhem, of course. Pandas, as lovable as they are, are simply finding it hard to reproduce effectively in a shrinking environment; Neanderthals, an early form of *Homo sapiens,* dwindled when they could not compete with our direct ancestors for resources in Ice Age Europe.

That is all there is to biological evolution, four basic principles that are individually irrefutable, and that have together provided science with one of its most durable and robust theoretical structures. The principles were pulled together by Charles Darwin over a

century and a half ago and published in 1859 (Darwin 1959). The maintenance of variability in a breeding population is crucial. Bisexual reproduction and random mutations do the job. While most mutations are deleterious, even fatal, every so often a rare one is advantageous in current or emerging environmental circumstances. In such a case the adaptive new trait is selected for, and the offspring of the organisms having it are advantaged, with the result that they in turn reproduce more effectively than the general population.

To gain acceptance Darwin's theory had to overcome a series of false preconceptions, some of which could be refuted only by advances in other fields of science. One objection was that the earth was too young for evolution to have had enough time to produce the modern spectrum of life. Physicists and geologists overcame that objection by showing conclusively over a century ago that the earth has been around for billions, not thousands, of years. Geneticists have more recently discovered the mechanisms of inheritance so critical to the validity of Darwin's second principle. Biologists also had to refute the notion that evolution necessarily meant progress, or the related notion that we humans were somehow the wonderful goal at which evolution was aimed. Earlier notions that biological change occurred by means of a series of catastrophes, or that the universe was created in its present form suddenly in one magical moment, or that the variable individuals in any populations were but flawed approximations of some essential ideal type all fell in the face of evidence and logic (Mayr 1972). Attempts to revive some of these discredited notions, such as the absurd arguments for a young earth or origin by intelligent design, still surface from time to time, but among reputable scientists the debate has been over for more than a century.

The Principles of Cultural Evolution

Cultural evolution is another matter, not least of all because it applies exclusively to humans. Here the basic principles facilitate its much more rapid evolutionary change.

- First, there is variability in any cultural population, and more of it can be generated rapidly. The analogue of the biological gene is the cultural **meme,** which can be defined as an idea, notion, or innovation. Human capacity for inventing both good (adaptive) and bad (maladaptive) memes would appear to be nearly limitless.

- Second, traits (memes) are not bound within individuals like genes, so they can be conveyed easily between individuals. Offspring benefit from memes accumulated by their parents during their lifetimes. They are not limited to those memes that their parents were born with; even better they are not limited to *only* those memes that are available from their biological parents. Here is the difference that makes cultural evolution potentially such a rapid process when compared to biological evolution.

- Third, unlike biological evolution, the potential of cultural evolution is *not* dependent upon the overproduction of individuals, because individuals do not have to be weeded out by natural selection for the population to evolve culturally. In other words, biological evolution depends upon endogenous overproduction so that natural selection has a surplus from which to do its selecting, but cultural evolution is not limited in this way. It is the memes that are selected for or against in cultural evolution, and individuals can acquire or discard them like baseball cards. That is not to say that cultural groups do not grow endogenously by exuberant reproduction, for they often do; but such growth is not strictly necessary for cultural evolution to work.

- Consequently, the fourth point is that because cultural reproduction can be supplemented through (or in extreme cases even replaced by) recruitment, memes can become very popular or disappear without respect to the lives of their human carriers. Differential survivorship of individuals is not required for cultures to evolve.

Stubborn people sometimes know better and are rewarded accordingly while others just as stubborn die young as a consequence of being wrong, but most humans have the capacity to recognize their mistakes and learn from them. Better yet, we can learn from the mistakes of others. Consequently, while we cannot change our genetic constitutions, we can rather easily change our cultural constitutions; individuals can transform themselves culturally if not genetically. Thus just as in biological evolution the unit of selection is the individual human being (Snow 2002). But beyond that observation the basic principles differ because individuals can change culturally. Instead of being well-bounded breeding populations, the social groups in which cultural evolution works are numerous, not often well bounded, overlapping, and highly variable. Individual humans form cultural groups of many sizes, of highly variable permanence, and for many purposes. There is cultural variability within any of these, just as there is biological variability from one individual to another;

whereas one might define an individual culture as, say, a group that shares a particular language, such a group is usually neither as well bounded nor as permanent as a biological breeding population.

An advantage to the study of cultural evolution is that biological evolution is more difficult to observe because its process is usually so slow. The time scale on which biological evolution plays out is typically nowhere near the scale of individual human experience, which is one of the reasons that so many people imagine that it does not occur at all. There are exceptions, of course, and it is possible to point to naturally emerging new species. New flu strains evolve very rapidly, and in those cases significant evolutionary change can sometimes occur in a matter of weeks. Fortunately, many more cultural processes evolve rapidly, and are easy to track. Chain letters are a good example, for they mutate rapidly as the result of copy errors and are subject to severe selection (Bennett et al. 2003).

An important principle to bear in mind when thinking about biological evolution is that it is a population that evolves, not the individuals that constitute it. The population evolves as less-well-adapted individuals leave it and better-adapted individuals are added through reproduction. This principle often gets lost when we talk about evolutionary phenomena of many kinds. In 2005 a television newscaster explained that a large dust cloud was moving toward the Gulf of Mexico as the result of a huge dust storm in the Sahara Desert. He mentioned that the dust particles were getting smaller as the cloud moved west. Millions of viewers probably imagined that the particles were shrinking individually due to some unspecified process. What he should have said was that the average size of the particles was going down as the cloud moved west because the largest particles drop out first and only the smallest stay in suspension for a long time. The distinction is an important one because it also characterizes a common misunderstanding of the dynamics of individual elements in evolving populations. When a population of plants or animals evolves it does so because individuals join and leave the population. For breeding populations this is exclusively through reproduction and death. The population does not evolve because the individuals change as individuals, but because the mix of individuals changes over time.

For cultural groups, populations of many possible sizes, membership can be quite fluid. Individuals can often join or leave a hunting band almost at will. Individuals can also transform themselves culturally, through religious or cultural conversion and the like. Some groups, like Amish communities, are quite exclusive, allowing few if any new members by any means other than birth. More usually, people can belong to many groups simultaneously, some of which are subsets of others, and they will assert membership in any or all of them situationally. For example, religion is just one possible category, yet an individual might be simultaneously Catholic, a Mohawk Indian, a member of a particular parish, a member of the church lacrosse team, a member of the choir, and any number of other nested affiliations. Group affiliations can range from very permanent memberships such as gender to very temporary ones such as an airline passenger list. It might be nearly impossible for the average modern citizen of the world to inventory a complete list of such memberships, for one might simultaneously be formally or informally affiliated with dozens or even hundreds of exclusive, inclusive, nested, or overlapping social groups, from the very permanent to the very temporary, from the very public to the very secret. Just how many any individual can identify is a measure of the overall complexity of the social network(s) that individual lives in.

This leads us to the problems raised by complexity and the idea of progress. Any evolutionary adaptation, whether biological or cultural, is an improvement in the sense that it allows the population to survive more successfully in its environment. That is progress of a sort. But what if the forces changing an environment to which a population is adapting reverse themselves and return to some approximation of a prior state? Then the forces of natural selection might prompt the population to evolve back to a previous form as well. This too is evolution, and Darwin was at great pains to dissuade people from the notion that evolutionary change is necessarily progressive. His problem at the time was that in the nineteenth century almost everyone but Mark Twain thought that humans were God's greatest work, the pinnacle of a great chain of being, the creatures for whom all the universe was created. If evolution occurred, they thought, it must have been with the goal of humankind as its objective, or at the very least all evolution was progressing toward intelligent life. The popular preconception of progress caused Darwin to play down the undeniable fact that early single-celled organisms were simpler than later multicelled ones in order to argue that evolution did not necessarily move breeding populations toward greater individual complexity, because to many people at the time increasing complexity was the same thing as progress.

Early attempts to adapt evolutionary theory to human culture ended badly because scholars like Lewis Henry Morgan (1818–1881) could not let go of the notion of progress (Morgan 1985). In the hands of political

opportunists this line of argument ended in the ideological excesses of Communism, Nazi eugenics, and racism (Pavelka 2002). This in turn gave the study of cultural evolution a bad name. It has even been argued in recent years that cultural evolution is a myth created by nineteenth-century Europeans to justify colonial exploitation (Diamond 1974). However, it is simply not true that cultural evolution is a theory that is inescapably colonialist or racist (Trigger 2003:41). Stripped of smug notions of cultural or biological progress and superiority, evolutionary theory provides us with our best means to understand human change over time.

Unlike biological evolution, cultural evolution is clearly marked by a trend toward increasing complexity. As human populations grow in size so do they grow in complexity as measured by the number of their constituent social groups and the complexity of social networks. A hunter-gatherer from 20,000 years ago plunked down in Tokyo would probably be no less intelligent or less capable than the average modern Japanese person, but he or she would have no trouble recognizing that modern society is more complex than that of 20 millennia ago.

Basic Concepts for the Study of Cultural Evolution

Our basic anthropological vocabulary includes the hierarchical terms "band," "tribe," "chiefdom," "state," and "empire" that I use to classify **polities** that evolved in North America over the last 14 millennia (Service 1962). This theoretical construct is a progression of forms from small to large, simple to complex. Size matters, but size ranges overlap. This is mainly because a larger and more complex form such as a chiefdom can suffer misfortune, shrink in population, but still retain the organizational complexity of a chiefdom. A boatload of castaways familiar with the formal characteristics of state organization may well retain them on an island refuge rather than revert to simpler band organization. On the other hand it is next to impossible to retain a tribal form of sociopolitical organization if the population rises into the thousands. One solution is for a supersized tribe to split into two or more new manageable tribes. But if competition for space from other surrounding societies make this impossible then innovations leading to chiefdom organization become imperative. Economics might also drive an evolution to more complex organization, even in the absence of rising population density. Examples are societies that enjoy abundant seasonal foods that must be stored and redistributed, or develop large irrigation systems that must be maintained, either of which in turn require centralized authority and management that they can acquire only by moving to the next level of organization.

Special care is required when using "band" and "tribe." Canadian law refers to all native nations as "bands" regardless of their organizational structures. United States federal law uses "tribe" in the same way because of that term's specific use in the Constitution. These are terms having legal definitions that do not conform to anthropological usage. Readers must be mindful of the distinctions and employ context to decide which definition a particular document is using.

Table 1.1 lists some but not all of the characteristics of each societal type in very simplified form. It is important to remember that the individuals involved and their everyday lives are equally complex regardless of the complexity of the society in which they happen to live. One can choose to live a simple life in a complex state, or alternatively a complex life as a member of a small band.

Specialists will quibble about the specifics in Table 1.1, but most will agree with the basic outline. It allows the use of standard terms without having to repeatedly define or characterize them. The most important thing is that the sociocultural evolution implied by Table 1.1 occurred many times around the world. Figure 1.4 shows the rough distribution of these sociopolitical forms in North America around 1500 CE, the time of first contact with Europeans (Sanders and Price 1968:50).

Figure 1.5 depicts forms of sociopolitical integration in a very simplified shaded hierarchy. Population levels, shown on the vertical axis, are not precise and authoritative opinion about specifics will vary. The important thing to note is that the population scale is logarithmic such that values increase by powers of 10 (orders of magnitude). There is not much doubt that a **band** can shrink to no fewer than a single person before it ceases to be a band. Small bands are at great risk of extinction simply because they are so vulnerable to random events (Wobst 1974). The weakest bands, those

Table 1.1 Some characteristics of five levels of social complexity, simplified.

	Band	Tribe	Chiefdom	State	Empire
Settlement Type	Mobile	Mobile/Fixed	Fixed	Fixed	Fixed
Settlement Size	Camp	Village	Town	City	City
Social Organization	Kin	Kin	Kin/Rank	Rank	Rank
Social Stratification	No	No	Usually	Yes	Yes
Leadership	Informal	Big Man	Formal	Formal	Formal
Bureaucracy	No	No	Simple	Complex	Complex
Standing Army	No	No	Yes	Yes	Yes
Languages	1	1	1	1+	2+
Formal Religion	No	No	Yes	Yes	Yes
Food Production	No	Sometimes	Usually	Yes	Yes
Trade and Exchange	Reciprocal	Reciprocal	Redistrib.	Redistrib.	Redistrib.
Public Architecture	No	No	Yes	Yes	Yes
Writing	No	No	No	Yes	Yes

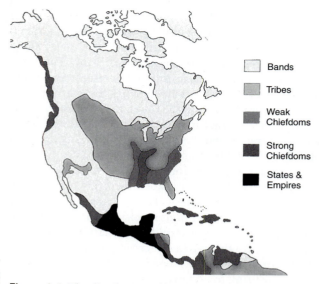

Figure 1.4 The distribution of bands, tribes, chiefdoms, states, and empires around 1500 C. E.

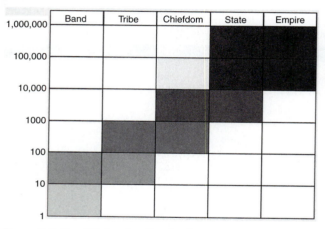

Figure 1.5 Simplified scale of levels of sociopolitical integration.

having populations of 10 or fewer, are shown as a lighter gray. There are cases of bands that exceed 100 people, but these are rare and unstable.

Above 100 there is a strong tendency for a population to acquire the organizational characteristics of a **tribe.** A group smaller than that might adopt tribal characteristics even in the absence of population pressure to do so if its members are familiar with other tribes and they perceive benefits to doing so. An unlucky tribe might lose population yet cling to tribal characteristics such as food production and village life. There are remnant tribes known to have populations as low as 25 (Hays 1998). In both cases these are weak tribes, shaded a lighter gray in Figure 1.5. Tribal

societies start to show signs of instability when populations exceed 1,000 and few remain intact beyond 2,000. There are only rare cases in a worldwide sample of tribes that reach 3,000 (Hays 1998).

There is a strong tendency for large tribes to adopt the characteristics of **chiefdoms,** including social ranking and the storage and redistribution of food. As in the case of tribes, copycat chiefdoms can form when tribes are in contact with chiefdoms and competition or perceived benefits prompt them to adopt the chiefdom characteristics even in the absence of other pressures to do so. Also as in the case of tribes, chiefdoms in reduced circumstances may cling to ranking and other customs rather than reverting to tribal modes of operation. There are known cases of chiefdoms having maximum community sizes as low as 200. Most are much larger, ranging up to a maximum of 10,000 (Hays 1998). Weak chiefdoms are represented by the lighter cell in Figure 1.5 (Earle 1991).

Populations above 10,000 tend to acquire complex bureaucracies, standing armies, and the other characteristics of **states.** The upper size limit for states has not yet been reached. Figure 1.5 stops at 1 million, but modern China is a thousand times bigger and still counting. States can also arise spontaneously through imitation or be spun off by colonial empires (Smith 2004). Large states can become small ones through misfortune. Whatever the case, smaller, weaker states are shown as a lighter shade in Figure 1.5.

Empires are typically multiethnic superstates that grow by conquest. They can fragment easily into independent states, as the British Empire and later the Soviet Union did so spectacularly in the second half of the twentieth century. Alternatively, they can sometimes evolve into large, well-integrated state organizations.

Implicit in Figure 1.5 is the observation that, generally speaking, each of the five societal types is subordinate to those (if any) that are to the right of it and dominant over those (if any) to its left. Occasionally a strong chiefdom can dominate a weak state, at least temporarily. The same exception is true in the other three cases of adjacent columns. The pastoral nomads of Eurasia used military and technological advantage to intimidate the more complex societies of Europe and China several times, but the absence of large domesticated animals in North America prevented the development of this dramatic exception to the general rule here until the colonial period. In the end there was too little time and too many epidemics to allow pastoralists to develop and become a significant threat to states in North America.

The theory represented in Figure 1.5 is simple and imperfect but serviceable and testable. Hypotheses derived from it can be tested against ethnographic data available from several sources (Ember 1963; Hays 1998; Murdock 1962; Murdock and Provost 1973; Naroll 1956). In practice it is important to define types of societies according to the criteria summarized in Table 1.1, then scale them by population size in order to avoid the circularity inherent in simply naming them according to their sizes. North American archaeology affords many examples of each of the five types, and each has its own evolutionary history.

Other Basic Concepts

Three other key concepts that will be mentioned in later chapters are the threshold of 500, connubia, and circumscription. Five hundred is both the approximate minimum number of people needed to maintain a viable social system and the maximum number of personal contacts maintained by the average human being (Hunn 1994). Bands typically number fewer than 100 individuals, so they must maintain close interactions with other bands. Overlapping networks called connubia met this need (Williams 1974). A **connubium** is thus an abstract concept, a unit made up of a band and its neighboring bands, each of which is also the center of its own connubium. This is something that humans adjust to very easily. Each of us is the center of a network of relatives and friends, and we are comfortable with the fact that those networks are rarely identical but that they overlap considerably. But it makes a big difference in daily life if one lives among fewer than 500 people or more than that number.

Circumscription constrains physical expansion and forces growing populations to increased density, which in turn leads to the organizational innovations of tribes, chiefdoms, and states. Societies can be circumscribed by geography, as in the case of islands or valleys, or by other societies of either like or unlike kinds. Without circumscription growing societies would simply expand into unoccupied space and thereby defer the organizational innovations of more complex levels of sociopolitical integration (Carneiro 1970).

Ecological Approaches

Ecology helps explain the past for archaeologists, but it is also relevant to the future, particularly now that we are all increasingly concerned with how we are going to adapt to the changing world we live in, even as our own activities increasingly drive that change. We are interested in past environments partly because we worry about future ones and the best way to understand them

is over the course of long-term change. We are also interested in how we as human beings came to be who we are. The past is discoverable, but only imperfectly, just as the future is only imperfectly predictable.

Not long ago a synthesis of North American archaeology was typically presented as merely a simplified summary of descriptive regional culture histories, which were in turn summaries of local ones. Modern archaeological synthesis requires much more than that, and that is why ecology has been adopted as a perspective of this book (Butzer 1982; Dincauze 2000). This approach demands analysis of processes that play out at very large scale. This is difficult because of the small-scale and often parochial nature of archaeological research projects, the resulting heavy dependence archaeologists have on each other's data, and the scattered nature of those data. Fortunately, many dedicated archaeologists have risen to this challenge in recent decades, pulling together scattered data in order to work out the big evolutionary picture of native America. Jill Neitzel's edited volume comparing the Southwest and the Southeast at grand scale is just one excellent example (Neitzel 1999).

Generally speaking, climate change over time has driven environmental change in North America, and this in turn has been the context for evolving human adaptation. Multiple lines of evidence have allowed researchers to reconstruct the timing and extent of past climatic changes with increasing accuracy. The last 11,600 years, the millennia since the close of the **Pleistocene,** are particularly well understood. Cores of ice from the Greenland ice cap show annual layers of ice that each trap the conditions of the year in which it was deposited. Concentrations of the beryllium-10 isotope in annual layers vary with the amount of solar radiation in those years. Years in which solar radiation was down also saw lowered production of the carbon-14 isotope in the upper atmosphere, and this is recorded in the annual growth rings of ancient trees. In the North Atlantic, cores from the sea bottom contain annual layered sediments of a different type. Particle sizes in them vary with annual fluctuations in temperature and ice debris. The result of all of this evidence is that we now have a climate curve for the past 12,000 years that shows why it is that human populations are always slightly off balance in their evolutionary efforts to settle on an ideal adaptation. The conditions to which they were adapting were always a moving target, sometimes moving more quickly than at other times.

The curve in Figure 1.6 begins on the left with the end of the Younger Dryas episode around 11,600 years ago (Bond et al. 2001:21, 32). The Pleistocene had come to a false finale about 14 centuries earlier, but disruption

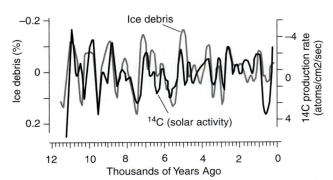

Figure 1.6 Climate fluctuation over the past 12,000 years.

of ocean currents caused average temperatures to plunge to Ice Age levels once again during the Younger Dryas. The cold episode switched off again in a matter of just a few years around 11,600 years ago and this time the **Holocene** came to stay. There were still variations, and the history of the Holocene has been punctuated by cool episodes at a frequency of about 1,500 years, give or take a few centuries. Figure 1.6 shows that there have been nine such cool spells over the last 12 millennia.

Warm episodes between the cold cycles have sometimes been very hot and dry. A series of three peaks between 7000 and 3500 **BCE** have often been referred to as the **Altithermal** period within the Holocene. The three peaks were separated by relatively mild cool cycles, so the entire 3,500-year period was a time of unusually hot and dry conditions that turned parts of North America into uninhabitable deserts and put severe stresses on human adaptations to many other parts of the continent (see Chapters 4 and 12). In some other regions the conditions of this long climatic episode actually made life a bit easier for bands of hunter-gatherers.

Around a thousand years ago Europe and North America were in the midst of the **Medieval Maximum,** an extended spell of warm conditions that made life for some people harder but also opened up possibilities for farmers in regions where it had been previously too marginal to take root. This was followed by the Maunder Minimum, popularly known as the **Little Ice Age,** a cool period that lasted roughly from 1430 to 1850 **CE.** We are now in a new episode of rapidly increasing warmth, this one caused by humans, mainly our burning of hydrocarbons.

These long-term cycles have consequence for human populations, albeit consequences that are not often perceived as they are happening. Individual human memory is simply too short to take account of changes

that occur on a scale of centuries. Episodes having shorter cycles, such as the El Niño phenomenon, are scaled much more noticeably to human lifetimes. El Niños occur every two to eight years, and cores from lakes in Peru indicate that this has been going on for the last five millennia. Curiously, they were weaker and much rarer before that (Rodbell et al. 1999).

Human beings adjust to change with varying success, often depending upon how stubbornly they cling to responses that have worked in the past. The hard truth is that if 5% of a population perceives a new opportunity and acts upon it, the other 95% can die off, leaving the prescient 5% as the founder population for a new adaptation. This is the cultural equivalent of speciation in biological evolution, something that might not happen very often but produces a sea change in the archaeological record when it does. There is no shortage of interest in societal collapse and other forms of catastrophic change (Diamond 2005). Such episodes produce discontinuities in the archaeological record that are hard to miss even with our impaired hindsight. These are the tipping points between boom periods of well-being and bust periods of misery that produce a ratchet effect in human adaptation over the long term (Figure 1.7).

There are thus two sides to human adaptation, one conditioned by environmental forces and the other driven by potential for innovation and organization that resides within us all. It is clear that the natural environment sets limits to human adaptation, but it also provides opportunities. Some anthropologists argue that this is the key to understanding cultural evolution, while others counter that the approach amounts to environmental determinism. The latter group often favors an approach that emphasizes endogenous self-organizing

Figure 1.7 Modern ecozones of North America between the Arctic and Mesoamerica.

explanations for innovations and new patterns of culture (Pauketat 2001; Sassaman 2005:81). Regrettably these debates often become polarized and an important principle gets lost. Discussion of these points by archaeologists seems to end too often in a false dichotomy, with opposing arguments advocating one over the other approach to understanding the past. The important underlying principle is that each of the two sides of human adaptation is necessary but by itself insufficient to allow a clear understanding of the whole.

Another important principle is that both culturally endogenous (internal) and exogenous (external) factors have to be considered in any complete explanation. Human behavior is much more than just adaptation to changing environments, for innovation often combines with individual or collective ambition to produce cultures that go way beyond what is necessary for simple survival. Culture is **emergent** in the scientific sense that it generates large patterns from the interactions of simple basic principles. Environment constrains and conditions that process but it does not determine it in any strict sense. The highly synchronized movements of schools of fish or flocks of birds are similar emergent phenomena in which simple rules followed by many individuals produce large patterns over time and space.

Apart from small artificial exceptions and the wonders of modern transportation, there are no orange groves in North Dakota, no caribou in Arizona, no manioc in British Columbia, no wild rice in Guatemala, and no lobsters in Missouri. It also makes a difference to human adaptation whether resources are abundant and come all at once or are relatively scarce but spread out over the year. It makes a difference whether people can make a living by staying in one place or have to relocate their residences from time to time. It makes a difference whether plants can reproduce themselves or have been so modified by human use that they can no longer survive without the aid of farmers. These are all exogenous constraints, forces that are largely outside the bounds of human culture.

Within environmental constraints there are many options, and this is where the human capacity for organization and technology comes into play. Environment made Las Vegas impossible until recently, but advances in electrical generation, transportation, and associated technology reset limits and constraints. Thus although environment constrains human populations, human innovations can overcome those constraints. Neither environmental factors taken alone nor cultural factors taken alone can explain why there are human footprints on the moon, why Gulf Coast cities were flattened and drowned in September 2005, or why the ruins of Las Vegas are likely to seem singularly improbable to future archaeologists.

Because of the complexity of past climate change, the unexpected ways in which that change can affect environment, and the unpredictable cleverness of people, adaptations of humans to their environments is a tricky thing to understand. The chapters that follow will sometimes distinguish between **focal adaptations**, such as the single-minded dependence of mounted nomadic Plains Indians on bison herds, and **diffuse** (broad or generalized) **adaptations** like that of Great Basin hunter-gatherers. Similarly, settlements can range from highly nucleated to highly dispersed. Because density varies, the physical size of the community can vary independently of the number of inhabitants, although density does tend to remain constant within a given culture.

Intensive adaptations, which are usually focal, tend to remain that way as long as they can. But focal adaptations are subject to catastrophic collapse because they lack diversification. Extensive (diffuse) adaptations tend to either remain so or to shift toward intensive over time. This is probably a fundamental principle similar to the observation that societies tend to become more complex rather than less complex when faced with adaptive challenges. That is, generally speaking societies tend to opt for intensification when the opportunity to do so arises. The problem with increased complexity and/or increased intensity is that both tend to involve (focal) specialization. This in turn can mean fatally maladaptive solutions in the long run. If the bison herds disappear, or extended drought wipes out the maize crop year after year, or a landslide ends salmon runs, focal adaptations that depend upon them will collapse as well. When conditions change, more extensive (diffuse) adaptations are favored, and cultures facing them sometimes have to scramble to readapt. It is not always possible for them to do so, particularly if important technology needed for a more generalized adaptation had long since been abandoned, forgotten, or never developed in the first place. Stable environments are necessary for intensive, focal, and specialized adaptive systems to emerge and persist, and the long histories of all the regions of North America document the usually cautious evolution of conservative societies in that direction as their environments stabilized over the long term. The potential for catastrophe also explains why generalist hunter-gatherers persisted for so long, particularly in regions where resources have never been abundant or invariably predictable (see Chapter 12) (Whitlam 1983).

It is important to remember that human beings are generally wise, and wise people do not take unnecessary risks. But life is a chess game in which it is not possible to predict things more than a few moves in advance. No matter what people did in the past it seemed like a good idea at the time. Hindsight allows us sometimes to know better, of course, but that does not bestow superior intelligence upon us. Some intensive adaptations carry within them the seeds of their own eventual demise. Irrigation systems can work well for a long time, then collapse because of the long-term buildup of salts. Herds can sustain hunters for decades, then dwindle quickly when their human predators increase slightly in numbers and harvest just a few too many for a few years. Shifting to an alternative adaptation is often painful and sometimes impossible. Societies, sometimes whole regions, have collapsed and their populations have dispersed or disappeared over time in North America. There are lessons here worth remembering even in a global economy, with its built-in buffers, fall-back positions, insurance policies, and other means of compensation over time.

Generally speaking, the larger the scale the less risky the long-term prospects. A band of two dozen people is at high risk of extinction simply because it is so small and vulnerable. A state organization of millions has much better odds for long-term survival simply because of its size and internal adaptability. At the same time, the extinction of a small band is not likely to leave a major discontinuity in the archaeological record, but the collapse of a state society is, to say the least, a large-scale event that is likely to alter the course of history in a profound way. Examples of both appear in this book.

North America and Human Potential

That brings us back to the prior question: How and why did human cultural evolution develop as it did in North America, independent from but along tracks that paralleled those of Eurasia and Africa? The answer to this question probably lies not in finding what triggered the intensity of food gathering that eventually led to agriculture in so many places, but rather in finding what prevented it from happening earlier. Biologically modern humans evolved in Africa perhaps 70,000 years ago, spread across much of Eurasia and as far as Australia by 40,000 years ago. By 14,000 years ago they had reached the Americas and the cold corners of Eurasia. The capacity for all the human achievements that followed must have been latent in all of these early *Homo sapiens sapiens*, so what took them so long? What held them back until the last several millennia? The answer appears to be the hostile and unpredictable climates of the Pleistocene.

The glacial climates of the Pleistocene epoch were dry and low in atmospheric CO_2, even in regions well away from the vast ice sheets. Worse, they were unpredictably variable over short time spans. Under these conditions humans could not respond to their own population pressures by intensifying the production of food plants, a first step toward domestication. Conditions prohibited such intensification. When this constraint disappeared at the end of the Pleistocene it did so worldwide, and the intensification of food production took off wherever suitable plants existed (Richerson et al. 2001).

In crude terms, more food allowed for larger populations, yet there were always constraints, as Thomas Malthus explained long ago (Malthus 1798). Carrying capacity always puts a cap on maximum population size; misery and premature death always arise when that cap is approached. At times, particularly in recent millennia, human innovations or rapid climate changes raised the cap quickly and dramatically allowing populations to grow almost unrestrained for a time, a scenario made clear by Esther Boserup (1965). Favorable environmental changes or highly adaptive technological changes can raise the bar and unleash cultural innovations that may last centuries. But all such cycles are followed by population increases that slow as they approach the new higher carrying capacity, and elaboration inevitably slows accordingly.

When the constraints described by Malthus are relaxed by innovation or changing environmental conditions, a population can grow, expand, and increase in complexity. Such circumstances often produce cultural elaborations that attract archaeological attention. Many examples follow in the chapters of this book. New constraints are inevitably reached, and a new equilibrium develops. This cycling produces a ratchet effect over the long term, which we can often detect as periods of cultural stability separated by short episodes of rapid growth and change (Wood, J. W. 1998). Even the flood of modern innovations in the second millennium CE has not removed the caps on expansion, which can often be defined in terms of some critical resource. The cap might be set by water availability or by the crowd tolerance of the average human, and it has clearly already been reached in some places in our own time.

If the end of the Pleistocene allowed agriculture and settled life to arise around the same times and in many of the same ways in several parts of the world, it is reasonable to ask how often and where it happened. The current answer is that there may have been at least nine such hearths (Diamond 1997). There were at least three in the Americas, in Mexico, Peru, and the Eastern Woodlands of the United States.

Geography and Basic Terms

The continents we call the Americas split the world's vast ocean into its Pacific and Atlantic divisions with a combined landmass of around 38,900,000 km² (15,000,000 mi²), about a third of the earth's habitable land area. In the fifteenth century the Americas were inhabited by millions of people who knew nothing of the Eastern Hemisphere and who were in turn just as utterly unknown to the rest of the world. It truly was the "other world" that Cristóbal Colón (Columbus) said it was in his account of his third voyage, a hemisphere that was completely unexpected by Europeans, just as the peoples of America had no reason to expect that what we call the "Old World" existed.

The other world that would soon be explored by the Spanish and other Europeans presented them with many things that dashed the constrained certainties of their most cherished beliefs. Their discoveries unlocked the intellectual prison that had been built by strict Christian dogma. Here was a world in which outlandish and completely unanticipated things like hummingbirds, turkeys, poison ivy, monkeys that could hang by their tails, coyotes, chocolate, rattlesnakes, maize, and birch bark canoes (to name just a few) abounded. The natives of America were just as shocked by the things the hairy pale men from Europe brought with them: iron, horses, gunpowder, sails, smallpox, and pigs (again to name just a few). These and other things were the currencies of an interchange that would play out over the course of the centuries that followed (see Chapter 15).

All parts of the world contributed to the interchange, a complex history of exotic contributions that probably can be seen most easily in national cuisines. Medieval diets in Europe were particularly bland, and it is not hard to understand why spices from India and Indonesia captured the interest of European cooks. Tomatoes from the Americas and pasta from Asia are signature components of Italian cooking today, although tomatoes were not added to that cuisine until well into the seventeenth century. It seems impossible to imagine a world today without chocolate, maize (corn), beans, pumpkins, or avocados, yet all of these were American crops that were unknown elsewhere until after 1492.

An early explorer who was at the time even more famous than Columbus wrote to Lorenzo de Medici that "not one of all the ancients had any knowledge of it, and the things which have been lately ascertained by us transcend all their ideas" (Davis 1992:73). He was right. The wisdom of the ancients, which most Europeans depended upon almost entirely at the time, was not equal to the task of explaining the larger world that opened up in the age of discovery. The explorer lucky enough to have Medici as his patron was Amerigo Vespucci, who traveled more than once to what he called "the fourth part of the world," but whose inclination to exaggerate his accomplishments diminished his reputation later on. In 1507 Martin Waldseemüller rewarded Vespucci's insight by naming the unexpected continents "America" on his map titled *Cosmographiae Introductio*. He removed it from later editions, but by that time it was an established usage for better or for worse. Although the name stuck, naming something falls far short of explaining it.

North American Geography

This book includes all parts of the North American continent, including Mesoamerica (central Mexico to western Nicaragua), Greenland, and the Greater Antilles. While most other books on North American archaeology stop at the Rio Grande, this one does not. Geographic accuracy means that some of the references cited will be in languages other than English. But that is a small price to pay given that the archaeology of North America cannot be fully understood in amputated form. Mesoamerica especially was a cornucopia, the fruits of which nourished the majority of people living in all of North America in 1492. Whereas ecologists put most of North America into the **Nearctic** ecozone, coastal and southern Mesoamerica are considered part of the **Neotropic** ecozone.

Including Greenland and the islands around the Gulf of Mexico, North America covers about 24.5 million km² (9.4 million mi²). Canada is the largest country in the Americas and the United States is only slightly smaller. Greenland is a huge island, but only its fringe is inhabitable. The rest is covered by an ice cap, at least for now. Mexico is smaller than Greenland, and its northern deserts are excluded from our definition of Mesoamerica. The rest of Mexico is included in that definition, along with the other Central American countries listed in Table 1.2. Perhaps not all of Honduras should be included and a corner of Nicaragua might be.

Terms are defined as they are introduced and a glossary list at the end of each chapter provides definitions for specialized terms for which a standard dictionary might not suffice. Some terms are used rather loosely in order to facilitate communication. Archaeologists often use the word **complex** when naming a specific tool industry. The term **culture** can imply that we know more about our subject than we do. Nevertheless,

Table 1.2 Modern political units of North America.

	Square Miles	Square Kilometers	% of North America
Canada	3,849,674	9,970,656	40.8%
United States*	3,664,099	9,490,016	38.8%
Greenland	840,000	2,175,600	8.9%
Mexico	756,066	1,958,211	8.0%
Guatemala	42,042	108,889	0.4%
Honduras	43,433	112,491	0.5%
Belize	8,867	22,966	0.1%
El Salvador	8,124	21,041	0.1%
Caribbean	233,018	603,517	2.5%
Total	9,445,323	24,463,387	100.0%

*Excluding Hawaii.

"culture" is used more often because it is handy and widely understood. If, for example, the Nenana complex is narrowly defined as such we can still assume that its carriers had something broader that we can reasonably refer to as "Nenana culture," and not get hung up on details.

Calendric Conventions

This book follows the convention of discussing the earliest part of the story in terms of years before present. This usage is limited mainly to Chapters 2 and 3, where the discussion involves geological time prior to the end of the Pleistocene (Ice Age) around 11,600 years ago. Once the story comes to focus on the arrival of humans in North America, references to past time switch to BCE (before the common era) and CE (common era), which are equivalent to the older, more culture-bound BC and AD (*anno domini*) usages. Chapter 4 begins 9000 BCE (before the common era), which is identical in usage with the more traditional BC (before Christ).

Except where noted otherwise only calendar dates are used in this book. That means that all radiocarbon dates have been calibrated, preferably by the investigators who paid for them, published the results, and best

understand their associations with archaeological remains. Calibration should make understanding easier for most readers. When archaeologists say "years ago" their point of reference is 1950 CE, as it is for radiocarbon age determinations, so 10,000 **BP** (years before present) converts to 8050 BCE. "Before present" can be abbreviated to "BP," and it has the same meaning as "YA" (years ago). However, one must be alert to the difference between uncalibrated radiocarbon dates, which deviate from calendar years, and calibrated radiocarbon dates that have been made consistent with calendar years. Geologists tend to prefer uncalibrated dates because they are internally consistent and avoid potential errors that might be introduced by calibration programs. Archaeologists tend to prefer calibrated radiocarbon dates because calendars and other dating techniques keyed to them become more and more important as one approaches the present in North American archaeology. The difference is made clear in this book, but it might not be at all clear in many of the sources cited.

Some publications use "(cal) BP" to report calibrated calendar years before 1950 CE, while others simply use "BP" and mention in a footnote or introduction that calendar years are intended. Other publications, particularly geological ones, often use "BP" to report uncalibrated ages without mentioning that they are uncalibrated. These differences in usage can be very confusing and such variations in convention explain some apparent inconsistencies between sources that often turn out on close examination to not be inconsistent at all.

Other Conventional Terms

The names we give things matter at the time, often turn out later to be inappropriate, but in time take on their own new meanings such that their origins become mere curiosities. Names are also sometimes charged with unintended meanings, banished from the generally accepted vocabulary, insisted upon for political reasons, and so forth. A brief discussion of the name game is important because archaeologists habitually name things and because names have consequences in broader contexts (Figure 1.8).

When speaking of North American Indians only "North" has some chance of not being controversial. In some sense America did not exist until 1507, when Waldseemüller used it to honor Amerigo Vespucci. Columbus reached the islands of the Caribbean in 1492, but he thought that he had landed in the East Indies. The mistake led him and later writers to refer to the people of the Americas as "Indios," in English "Indians." Thus the human subjects of this book are known as American Indians because of some combination of deceit and error committed over five centuries ago. Most modern American Indians shrug all this off and few that I know prefer the "Native American" label invented in the twentieth century. Most of them often use specific national names instead, but these often carry their own sometimes bizarre baggage.

Many American Indian cultures acquired names that resulted from mistranslations, mistakes in pronunciation, or deliberate insults. The Mohawks and the Sioux were both given names that stuck by enemies that did not like them very much. One nation was given a name meaning "what?" in their own language when the first Spanish to visit them could not make themselves understood. Tongue-twister names in unfamiliar languages ensured that even honest attempts by Europeans to call groups by the names they used for themselves often failed. One result is that in several cases modern American Indian nations are asking that the rest of us call them by more appropriate names (see especially Chapters 6 and 13). It is a small and reasonable request, but it can confuse readers trying to use both recent and older sources when the two use different names for the same people. The best solution in specific cases is to refer to various volumes of *The Handbook of North American Indians,* where most terminological confusion is sorted out.

Archaeologists tend to name sites after landowners, but not exclusively. Late sites sometimes have the names they had when people were still living on them, but naming a site according to one found in a historical document carries with it the assumption that one has correctly identified the site. There is risk in that assumption and there are many cases of sites that have been inappropriately named. This is an especially significant problem for many sites that were named in the nineteenth century, when enthusiasm raced far ahead of caution in the name game. Sites still known as Aztalan, Montezuma's Castle, and Toltec in the United States are a few of the more egregious examples. All three were named according to mistaken identification with Mexican cultures.

The Smithsonian Institution advocated a system for naming U.S. archaeological sites before the advent of computerized databases. An example is the 4-Butte-1 site in Butte County, California. The initial number identifies the state (California is fourth in alphabetical order). The county is named and the following number identifies the site in a listing of all those known for the county. Some states adopted this system, but many others did not. Canada has a national alphanumeric system. For example, the Draper site in Ontario is AlGt-2 in that system. Both systems have information that archaeologists considered important embedded in their site numbers. Computerized databases made such embedded

Figure 1.8 Naming things is only one step in the scientific process.
Source: DILBERT: ©Scott Adams/Dist. by United Feature Syndicate.

information unnecessary. In fact both the U.S. and Canadian systems involve designations that computers do not handle easily, and it is likely that they will both fall into disuse. Sites in Mexico and the countries of Central America do not have elaborate alphanumeric designations, and shorthand numbers tend to be specific to the publications in which they are mapped and described.

Whole archaeological cultures are often named for their type sites. These are often equivalent to or subdivided into developmental **phases.** A temporal series of related phases can be strung together as a named **tradition.** The older archaeological literature sometimes contains terms such as "branch," "focus," or "aspect" that are no longer used.

Projectile point **types** and pottery types are often named after locally significant place-names or geographic features, supplemented by some descriptive term. Often their names are the same as the sites on which they were initially defined. The results are names like "Steubenville Stemmed" points and "Red Mesa Black-on-white" pottery. These names tend not to be controversial. Perhaps unfortunately, there is no central authority for the approval and registration of type names. That means that a single projectile point type might have two names, one in each of the two adjacent states in which it is found. Or a single type might have different names depending upon which archaeologist is authoring a publication mentioning it. Anyone can name a point or pot type, and whether it becomes generally accepted or not depends upon precedent, the authority of the publication, and the prestige of the author. This was much more important in an era when key types were necessary for **cross dating,** but it is much less important today because radiocarbon and other independent techniques for dating have largely replaced cross dating.

It is also the case that the products of cultural evolution cannot be classified hierarchically in the same way that the products of biological evolution can be. A. L. Kroeber (1948:260) long ago depicted the difference in terms of the trees seen in Figure 1.9. The origins of new species through biological evolution produce hierarchical branches in the tree that remain separate forever, gradually growing and splitting further into new branches. Species diverge over time and never reconverge or swap traits. That is why the phrase "**ontology** recapitulates **phylogeny**" was applied to the classification system first devised by Linnaeus for biology. The classification system, if it is done correctly, accurately depicts the evolutionary history of the species classified. No such branching model can be used to illustrate cultural evolution because the

Figure 1.9 A. L. Kroeber's models for biological evolution (left) and cultural evolution (right).

endpoints can be the result of many recombinations of elements. Cultural evolution allows for both reconvergence and swapping, so a branching model is often inapplicable. The difference is that while biological evolution is a mindless process, cultural evolution is the result of the usually rational choices made by intelligent human beings. Thus the names used by archaeologists are not as rigorously managed as those used by biologists because doing so would not serve an important purpose.

A consequence of the differences between biological and cultural evolution is that there is no right answer to the problem of archaeological classification in the same sense that there is inherently a right answer in biological classification. Because of that there is no basis upon which to argue in archaeology that one classification scheme is inherently better for all purposes than another. For this reason archaeological types are not tightly controlled and classifications are allowed to vary according to the needs and purposes of specific research programs.

The Special Place of Rock Art

Many North American archaeologists have traditionally avoided the study of rock art, yet this is often the most visible evidence of the American Indian past. Many rock art sites are open to the public, and people unfamiliar with anything else relating to the archaeology of the continent more often than not find rock art to be fascinating. Interest in it appears to be high at least in part because while it is physically accessible, the intellectual accessibility of rock art often seems to lie tantalizingly just beyond our reach.

This simultaneously explains why rock art is so popular and why so many professional archaeologists have avoided it, at least until recently. Rock art is typically separate and disconnected from the deposits archaeologists excavate, and unassociated with the specimens and samples archaeologists use to date and understand their finds. As examples in the chapters that follow will show, rock art often cannot be related to the historic cultures of the same region (see Chapter 12). In cases where a link can be demonstrated the interpretation of rock art too often depends upon tenuous oral tradition. Only rarely have archaeologists been able to relate rock art to historic culture in a more satisfyingly complete way (see Chapter 10).

However, some sites have begun to yield more reliable evidence that can be used to tie rock art more securely to the broader domain of archaeology. Careful excavation can sometimes relate rock art to datable deposits containing other kinds of archaeological evidence. Paint from rock art can sometimes be dated directly. The symbols that turn up in rock art can sometimes be directly related to relevant ones in the ethnographic record. This is good news because although most archaeological deposits are the unintentional or inadvertent results of past human activity, rock art was certainly intentional in its own right. The maker of any example of rock art surely had some intended meaning in mind, however poorly we might perceive it today (Keyser and Whitley 2006).

Rock art comes in two basic forms, which are only rarely combined. **Petroglyphs** are pecked or engraved on rock faces. **Pictographs** are painted on rock surfaces. Both forms occur by the thousands across the North American landscape, common in some regions but rare in others. Recording and preserving rock art has become part- or full-time activity for many researchers. These are more often volunteers than professionals. However, a growing rock art interest group within the Society for American Archaeology is increasingly bringing professional and avocational archaeologists together to focus on the protection and interpretation of sites.

Many impressive rock art sites are now protected in public parks. Nearby American Indian tribes often have a hand in preservation, even when the rock art sites lie off reservation lands. Unfortunately, many rock art sites are at remote locations, where they are subject to vandalism. This is particularly the case with sites in the West. However, volunteer organizations are doing much to preserve and protect even sites that are remote and difficult to access. Rock art is increasingly an important public face for North American archaeology (Loendorf et al. 2005).

Oral Tradition

The history of American Indian cultures is largely undocumented except by archaeology, but the oral traditions of their living descendants can sometimes supplement and enrich the story. The problem with archaeology, of course, is that its evidence is extremely fragmentary and silent about some of the topics we might wish to understand much more than we can. Oral tradition can sometimes flesh out details and meanings that would otherwise remain unknown, but there is risk in this. Oral tradition typically exists to support current political and religious positions, not to provide historical documentation. For example, tribal elders of one nation reported two centuries ago that their political system dated to only a few decades before the arrival of Europeans. Their descendants, the elders of today, insist that the same institution is a millennium old, contradicting the elders of yesteryear. In another case a medicinal remedy that an herbalist insists was used for centuries before Columbus turns out to depend upon alien plants that arrived only with European colonists. The message is that oral tradition shifts and changes over time for a variety of reasons. What is today sincerely believed to be ancient and unchanging wisdom can often turn out to be neither (Mason 2006).

Despite the hazards, oral tradition can be useful if it is used carefully and honestly. For example, the interpretation of petroglyphs in Chapter 10 would have been impossible without nineteenth-century Abenaki oral tradition. At the very least, oral tradition presents archaeology with an additional source for testable hypotheses. Good science cannot allow oral traditions to trump alternative hypotheses, of course, and propositions derived from oral traditions have to be tested as rigorously as any others. Occasionally native oral tradition produces a viable hypothesis that might not otherwise have occurred to the archaeologist. Some of the best examples of this phenomenon have resulted from the research carried out at the site of Ozette, discussed in Chapter 13.

The demand for alternative testable hypotheses is the best argument for diversity in the population of researchers that make up any scientific discipline. There is as yet not enough such diversity among North American archaeologists. A healthy science requires an endless stream of new ideas, and a diverse array of energetic practitioners to generate them. It is my hope that the chapters that follow will help recruit the next generation of American archaeologists.

Summary

1. The archaeology of North America reveals that civilization arose independently more than once.

2. Archaeological science is one of the natural sciences.

3. There are important differences between biological and cultural evolution, but the unit of selection is the individual in both cases.

4. The hierarchy of terms used to classify polities includes "band," "tribe," "chiefdom," "state," and "empire."

5. The threshold number 500 is important to the functioning of human societies.

6. A central theme of this book is ecological.

7. North America includes Mesoamerica for the purposes of this book.

8. Conventional terms facilitate the discussion of North American archaeology.

9. The study of rock art was outside mainstream archaeology for many years but is increasingly part of what North American archaeologists study.

Further Reading

Jared Diamond's *Guns, Germs, and Steel* provides an excellent worldwide context for the ecological approach taken in this book. Several textbooks provide a more detailed introduction to the methods and techniques used in archaeological research. Fagan's *Ancient Lives: An Introduction to Archaeology and Prehistory*, Sharer and Ashmore's *Archaeology: Discovering Our Past*, and Renfrew and Bahn's *Archaeology: Theories, Methods, and Practice* are all comprehensive introductions. A good way to become familiar with North American rock art is through *Discovering North American Rock Art*.

Note: Various sources that are cited in the text provide excellent expansions on the points made briefly in each chapter. Refer to the "References" section at the back of this textbook for publisher details.

Glossary

Altithermal: A long series of high-temperature climatic episodes, 7000–3500 BCE.

archaeology: The scientific study of historic or prehistoric peoples by analysis of their material remains.

band: The smallest human society, egalitarian and typically fewer than 100 people in size.

BCE: Before the common era, equivalent to BC.

BP: Before present, which is set by convention to 1950 CE.

breeding population: Any set of individual plants or animals that is sustained by internal reproduction.

CE: A date in the common era, equivalent to AD.

chiefdom: A society of 1,000–10,000 people, characterized by social ranking and permanent leadership.

circumscription: Constraint on population growth imposed by surrounding populations of similar type.

complex: A set of artifact types that typically occur together in excavated assemblages.

connubium (pl. connubia): An abstract social unit consisting of a band and related surrounding bands.

cross dating: The inferential dating of a deposit at one site to the age of a similar deposit at another site by means of shared artifact types.

culture: A coherent way of life shared by members of a population that often speak the same or related languages.

diffuse adaptation: A human adaptation that is focused on a broad array of resources.

ecology: The study of the interrelationship of organisms and their environments.

emergent: Produced by the bottom-up formation of large, complex patterns from simple, fundamental rules.

empire: A multiethnic superstate, typically created by the conquest of one or more subordinate states by a dominant state.

empirical: Based on evidence and observation.

evolution: Change in a reproducing population resulting from differential reproductive success.

focal adaptation: A human adaptation that is focused on a narrow range of resources.

holocene: The last geological epoch, which began 11,600 years ago and continues today.

hypothesis (pl. hypotheses): A proposition inspired by some combination of evidence and theory that is potentially disprovable.

Little Ice Age: A cool period that lasted approximately 1430 to 1850 CE.

Medieval Maximum: An episode of climatic warming that peaked around 1000 CE.

meme: The smallest unit of culture, analogous to the biological gene.

Nearctic: One of the world's eight ecozones, covering most of North America.

Neotropic: One of the world's eight ecozones, covering Mesoamerica, the Caribbean, and Central and South America.

ontology: The systematic organization and classification of things.

petroglyph: Rock art made by pecking or engraving.

phase: An archaeological culture, limited in space and time, and often one of a developmental series.

phylogeny: The branching relationships between species resulting from biological evolution.

pictograph: Rock art made by painting.

Pleistocene: The geological epoch lasting from 1.8 million to 11,600 years ago, popularly known as the Ice Age.

polity: A general term for a political unit of any size or complexity.

pseudoarchaeology: The selective use of archaeological evidence to promote nonscientific accounts of the past.

sasquatch: A modern mythological primate thought by some to roam the forests of the Pacific Northwest.

science: A set of principles and procedures for the systematic development of theory, which involves the recognition and formulation of problems, the systematic collection of data through observation and experience, and the formulation and testing of hypotheses.

site: An archaeological location containing a concentration of remains.

state: A society numbering over 10,000 people, having social ranking, permanent leadership, bureaucracy, and a standing army.

theory: An internally consistent and well-substantiated explanation of some aspect of the natural world that is capable of producing testable hypotheses.

tradition: A series of two or more phases representing a developmental continuum over time.

tribe: A society of two or more bands, having impermanent leadership and a population typically between 100 and 1,000.

type: A named class of artifacts.

Eurasian Origins

Scientists cannot use jargon to communicate to the public even though one word may describe where an artifact was found, in what era, and in what condition. The general public needs information to be clear without it being too complex.

Jean Auel

THIS CHAPTER TRACES THE MOVEMENTS OF early human beings from their origins in Africa to the threshold of America in the far-off reaches of northeastern Siberia. Humans evolved in Africa, expanding to Europe and Asia at least three times. Modern *Homo sapiens* expanded farther than earlier forms could, adapting to cold conditions and reaching northeastern Siberia around 15,000 BCE. Domesticated dogs joined human bands around that time. Genetic, dental, and linguistic evidence is all consistent with the archaeological evidence that humans crossed through Beringia into North America soon thereafter. The Siberian Ushki Lake complex is related to the Nenana complex in Alaska, but it might be too young to have been its ancestor. The Siberian complex known as Dyuktai appears to be ancestral to the similarly later Denali complex in Alaska. By at least 12,000 BCE the ancestors of the American Indians were living in Beringia and were unknowingly poised to expand southward across two continents on which humans had never before walked.

Introduction

It took a long time for us to get our turn at life on this earth, and as much as we might not like to admit it, everything that went before was not just a prelude for humanity. The earth is about 4.6 billion years old and for all but the last sliver of that time it got along just fine without humans. But the human past is what archaeologists study so it is that last sliver that is our focus here. The human past in North America is an even smaller sliver of the longer saga of human evolution.

Geologists have long since blocked out the major eras, periods, epochs, and stages of geological time. By the nineteenth century the geological sequence had been divided into four great eras, the Primary, Secondary, Tertiary, and Quaternary. It was later discovered that the first two covered immense periods of time that were much longer and more complicated than was generally appreciated at first, so they were dropped. The Tertiary and Quaternary were recast as shorter "periods," and the longer eras were given new names that reflected their dominant forms of life as shown in Table 2.1. The Cambrian period became the earliest period of the Paleozoic (Ancient Life) era. Everything earlier was at first simply "Pre-Cambrian." Later generations would put everything in Table 2.1 into the Phanerozoic eon, and add earlier eons not shown here. For the time being the absolute ages of these great building blocks of geological time were unknown. The geologists of the nineteenth century had to be content with a relative chronology, one that had all the pieces in the right order from oldest to youngest, but that lacked dates.

The discovery of radioactive elements around the beginning of the twentieth century made it possible to create an absolute chronology for the geological sequence. The results astounded some physicists but delighted most biologists. Darwin had said that immense time was needed for biological evolution to work, but many nineteenth-century physicists had argued that the earth was too young to accommodate it. The new dating techniques showed that there was more than enough time for life to have evolved as Darwin had said. They also revealed that in geology as in written history

Table 2.1 Recent periods of geological history. Everything here makes up the Phanerozoic eon.

Eras	Periods	Epochs	Stages	Began	Ended
Cenozoic	Quaternary	Holocene	Recent	11.6 tya[1]	0 tya
		Pleistocene	Late	128 tya	11.5 tya
			Middle	750 tya	128 tya
			Early	1800 tya	750 tya
	Tertiary	Pliocene		5 mya[2]	1.8 mya
		Miocene		23 mya	5 mya
		Oligocene		37 mya	23 mya
		Eocene		55 mya	37 mya
		Paleocene		65 mya	55 mya
Mesozoic	Cretaceous			140 mya	65 mya
	Jurassic			200 mya	140 mya
	Triassic			250 mya	200 mya
Paleozoic	Permian			280 mya	250 mya
	Carboniferous			345 mya	280 mya
	Devonian			395 mya	345 mya
	Silurian			435 mya	395 mya
	Ordovician			500 mya	435 mya
	Cambrian			543 mya	500 mya

1. Thousand years ago.
2. Million years ago.

those events closest to us in time are known in greatest detail. Mammals did not dominate until the onset of the Tertiary, which began a mere 65 million years ago, but we know that period well enough to divide it into five epochs. The **Quaternary** period began only 1.8 million years ago, but we have divided it into the Pleistocene and Holocene epochs, further subdividing the Pleistocene into three stages. Most of what this book covers is relegated to the Holocene, but the roots of the human presence in the Americas go back to the Late Pleistocene, sometime prior to 11,600 years ago.

The Evolution of Modern Humans

There can no longer be any doubt that we humans, all of us, descend from ancestral populations that evolved over the course of millions of years in Africa. It was there that evolutionary adaptation slowly selected for the unique traits that make us human: upright posture, loss of body hair, skin pigmentation, opposable thumbs, large brains, speech, and various other traits. Early populations of mammals were scurrying underfoot in a world dominated by dinosaurs well before the wholesale extinctions of 65 million years ago, but humans and dinosaurs never coexisted. Tree shrews had already differentiated from primates, and like them the ancestors of other major subclasses of mammals were already distinct breeding populations (Kumar and Hedges 1998).

The Pleistocene epoch was the setting for the evolution of modern human beings, and it was during its final stages that people finally reached North America. The climate history of North America has always set the moving parameters of environmental conditions to which people have had to adapt. The environments that result from the interactions of climate, physiography, vegetation, animal species, and latitude do not determine human adaptation so much as they set limits to it.

The single most dominant feature of the North American landscape prior to 11,600 years ago (9650 BCE) was glacial ice. Vast dynamic Pleistocene ice sheets spread out of the north and down from the Rocky Mountains, carrying along pulverized earth and rock like a slow-motion conveyor belt, spewing torrents of meltwater from their leading edges, depressing the landscape hundreds of meters under their enormous weight, forming vast glacial lakes, and casting a chill upon the land. The depression of the landscape, and the rebound that occurs after glacial ice disappears, is called **isostatic** change.

The coastlines of North America and other continents moved seaward during the Pleistocene as more and more of the earth's water was locked up in glacial ice. The balance of snowfall and melting was shifted by cooling climate so that year after year snow accumulated and compacted into glacial ice in the far north and in the higher mountains, in some places to thickness measurable in kilometers rather than meters. At the same time sea levels lowered to 100–150 meters (or 328–492 ft) below their current levels because so much water was locked up as ice on the land. Eventually the weight of accumulation in the ice caps forced ice to flow slowly out from the centers of accumulation, creating dynamic moving lobes of ice, some of which moved southward until they reached warmer regions where melting balanced the rate of advance. There the debris carried by the advancing ice accumulated in large end deposits that can still be recognized today. New York's Long Island is one such **moraine** deposit. Others stretch westward from there to the Midwest, marking the lines where the margins of the great ice sheets stood for long periods.

The largest North American ice sheet was the Laurentide sheet, which formed over what is now north-central Canada (Figure 2.1). Another, the Cordilleran ice sheet, formed over the Rockies and the other major mountain ranges of western North America. This sheet expanded eastward out of the mountains until it collided with the Canadian Laurentide sheet advancing from the east. On its western side tongues of the Cordilleran sheet advanced down mountain valleys to the Pacific, often pushing out across a continental shelf laid bare by lowered sea levels. The last major advance along the Northwest Coast was the Fraser advance, which peaked 14–16,000 BCE. Melting rates overtook rates of ice advance by 12,000 BCE, and by 10,000 BCE most of the coastline of the Northwest Coast was no longer under glacial ice. By 7500 BCE Cordilleran ice was almost entirely confined to the mountains. Similar dates mark the peak and retreat of the Laurentide sheet.

The Pleistocene climate did not come to a graceful end. Its last gasp was a 14-century return to frigid conditions called the **Younger Dryas**. The episode lasted from 10,850 to 9550 BCE, a span that turns out to have been contemporary with some of the early evidence of human movement into the Americas. The Younger Dryas was followed by the Holocene epoch, which with a long series of warmer and cooler cycles has persisted until today. We have come to another warm episode in the post-Pleistocene history of America, perhaps the warmest of them all, abetted this time by our production of greenhouse gases. Remaining mountain glaciers are melting at a rapid rate, spewing out artifacts, plants, animal carcasses, and even human bodies trapped frozen in the ice for millennia (Kaiser 2002). It is a short-term boon to archaeologists who scour the

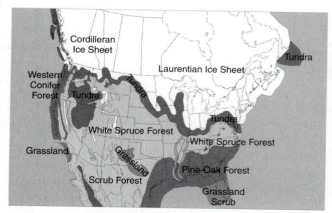

Figure 2.1 Pleistocene ice sheets of North America at their maximum extent.

melting margins of glaciers to find the latest treasures released from icy bondage. But the current global warming could entail another ironic twist. The sudden switch that turned off a warming trend and plunged the Northern Hemisphere into the Younger Dryas 10,850 BCE could be thrown again. It seems illogical, but given the complex of natural forces at work, the current warming trend could even precipitate the beginnings of a new Ice Age (Calvin 2002).

Out of Africa

Humans originated in Africa during the Pleistocene, later spreading out from there, first along the tropical fringe of southern Asia and into Europe. *Homo erectus*, the direct ancestor of *Homo sapiens*, evolved in Africa around 1.7 million years ago. These people looked like us in most respects, but their skulls were more robust and their brain cases were smaller. It is likely that they

Box 2.1 HOW TO USE RADIOCARBON DATING

Carbon is one of the basic building blocks of all living things. Animals exhale carbon dioxide and plants take it up. It is also abundant in petroleum, natural gas, coal, limestone, marble, and various other inorganic materials. It is everywhere, and its most common isotope is carbon-12 (^{12}C). About a hundred times less common is another isotope, carbon-13 (^{13}C). The third naturally occurring isotope of carbon is carbon-14 (^{14}C), which was discovered by Willard Libby in 1941.

Carbon-14 interested Libby because, although it was rare, it appeared to be an isotope that should not exist at all. The half-life of carbon-14 appeared to be only a few thousand years, much shorter than any of the isotopes used in geological dating. How could this be? Even an isotope like beryllium-10, with a half-life of over a million and a half years, had long since disappeared from the earth. Clearly there had to be some source of new carbon-14.

It turned out that ^{14}C is constantly being produced from nitrogen-14 (^{14}N) by cosmic ray bombardment in the upper atmosphere. It behaves chemically like the other isotopes of carbon, so all are taken up by plants and by the animals that feed upon them. The half-life of ^{14}C is currently set at 5,730 years, meaning in that much time half of a sample of ^{14}C of any size will decay once again to ^{14}N. Libby realized that he could use the known decay rate to calculate the age of any organic material, back perhaps to as much as 50,000 years ago. Any specimen that age or older would have too little ^{14}C left to be measured, but younger samples should be datable. He tested the technique by using ancient samples of known age, well-dated Egyptian artifacts and the like, to see how much smaller the fractions of ^{14}C in them were as compared to the constant proportion in very recent samples. This involved converting a sample to pure carbon, then measuring the number of decay events with a Geiger counter.

Laboratories that produce radiocarbon dates for archaeologists customarily report them as "radiocarbon years" with error estimates. For example, when I received an age estimate of 7135±200 BP (SI-2638) in the late 1970s, I knew that this was sample 2638 run by the laboratory at the Smithsonian Institution. The numbers also told me that the experience of that laboratory was such that it estimated that there were about two chances in three that the true age of the sample was within 200 years of 7,135 radiocarbon years before present. The age was stated in radiocarbon years, which were close to but not necessarily identical with calendar years. Finally, I knew that "before present" meant prior to AD 1950, which had been set as the standard reference point by all radiocarbon laboratories. The error was expressed in terms of the standard statistical "1-sigma" range of error, but it is important to realize that it was not based on repeated analyses of the same sample. In other words, the measure was not arrived at by direct statistical means; it was instead based upon the lab's general experience with samples over several months or years of operation. The error might have been reduced slightly by leaving the sample in the counter longer. However, in the 1970s samples had to be left in counters for hours, tying up expensive laboratory time, so practical costs always limited precision to some degree.

There has been more fine-tuning of the radiocarbon technique over the last quarter century. Careful comparison of dates taken from different kinds of organic materials revealed that some plants and animals preferentially take up the isotopes of carbon in slightly different proportions, enough to throw off dates by as much as a few decades. The development of direct measurement by accelerator mass spectroscopy (AMS) to replace indirect Geiger counter measurement has allowed the use of much smaller samples in recent years.

did not have language as we know it, for their tools were simple, crude enough to have been made by people who learned by simply mimicking one another. But they probably cooperated with each other, driven to it for mutual support in the millennia before they evolved from a prey species to a predator species (Brooks et al. 2005). They might have been able to control fire and they were adaptable enough to spread out of Africa to other warm parts of the Eastern Hemisphere. This expansion of the *Homo erectus* population was an adaptive radiation that carried them into southern Europe and across southern Asia to the Indonesian archipelago. The first *Homo erectus* skull found was the famous Java man but others have since been found elsewhere across southern Europe and Asia (Figure 2.2).

The zones of climate and vegetation of Asia tend to be east–west bands that facilitate movement in those directions by animals adapted to them. Even today moving north or south more often requires greater adaptation than moving east or west. For humans these may be largely cultural, but some biological adaptations were also entailed in the distant past. Moreover, adaptation to new environments by early human populations was harder the farther they penetrated into the higher latitudes. Because virtually all of Asia lies north of the equator the higher latitudes were mostly northward.

The Expansion of Modern Humans

Based on current evidence it is most likely that our branch of *Homo sapiens* evolved in Africa over 100,000 years ago. Another early branch of *Homo*

sapiens, people popularly called Neanderthals, evolved in cold Pleistocene Europe, from an earlier human population already there (Figure 2.3). The Neanderthals were equipped with at least better tools and minimally adequate clothing, and as in Africa they evolved from the older *Homo erectus* population. Our branch probably had the additional adaptive advantage of language, and a capacity for symbolic thought. Our ancestors could communicate easily with each other, empathize, and even anticipate each other's actions, probably more effectively than the Neanderthals. They collaborated, created friendships with nonrelatives, shared food, and in short did all those things that today set humans apart from all other living species.

Our ancestors were more often prey than predators, and they faced adaptive pressures that nearly drove them to extinction (Hart and Sussman 2005). Instead of killing them off, the pressures pushed the population to evolve rapidly to our biologically modern form. Genetic data indicate that perhaps only 25,000 individuals survived a period of severe selection that occurred around 74,000 years ago, passing through what demographers call a population bottleneck (Harpending et al. 1993). Some say that the number of survivors was less than a tenth of that. The near-fatal episode led to the rapid evolutionary selection for language and the other traits just mentioned, and positioned them for a new adaptive expansion (Elena et al. 1996).

The earliest art known dates to this time and place. The adaptive advantage of a gene or small set of genes that produce this and other capabilities was so extraordinary that it must have spread rapidly, both as people having it bred with those lacking it and as populations

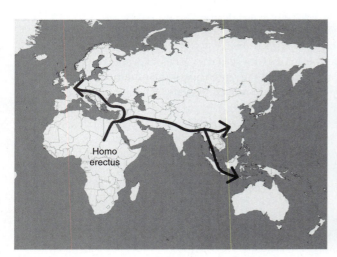

Figure 2.2 *Homo erectus* expanded out of Africa to Europe and southern Asia after evolving in Africa.

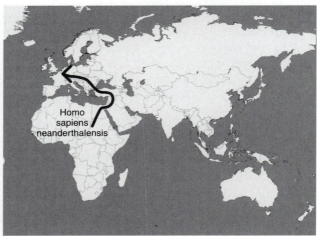

Figure 2.3 Neanderthals appeared about 85–60,000 years ago and spread to Europe.

having it expanded and displaced the comparatively hapless *Homo erectus* populations. No new feature arises *for* anything, so like birds, which evolved flight based on feathers that evolved for other reasons, we got lucky when random mutation made a tiny but key change in some remote ancestor's brain.

Another byproduct of our ancestors' new capacity for language was technological. By around 50,000 years ago hunters were making small projectile points that could be used to tip spears that could be launched at game or human enemies, a terrific advance over heavier thrusting spears (Brooks et al. 2005). Spear throwers were still being used in the Americas when Europeans arrived. Aztec soldiers used them to launch torrents of spears against the Spanish invaders, so the weapon is well understood by modern archaeologists. The spear thrower (called "atlatl" by the Aztecs) is typically a wooden shaft about as long as a forearm. At one end there is a handle or perhaps a couple of finger loops. At the other end is a hook designed to fit loosely into a socket at the end of a spear. The hunter (or warrior) holds the spear loosely in the same hand that holds the spear thrower, with the butt of the spear set against the hook (Figures 2.4 and 2.5). The spear is thrown with

Figure 2.4 A time-lapse series showing how a spear thrower is used to launch a small spear or dart.

Figure 2.5 The author trying his hand with a spear thrower.

the same motion that one serves a tennis ball, except that as the spear thrower whips through the air the spear is released so that it is propelled by the far end of the spear thrower, which (like the head of a tennis racket) is moving at a much greater speed than the hunter's hand. Once launched the spear is flying faster than the fastest javelin because of the boost provided by the spear thrower. It was a formidable weapon, and it eventually gave our ancestors as much advantage over *Homo erectus* people and the Neanderthals of Europe as guns would later give the Spanish over the Aztecs. Even better, our early ancestors had an improved intuitive grasp of the geometry of landscape and their three-dimensional world, a legacy shared today by all of us (Dehaene et al. 2006).

Spear throwers were made of perishable materials, so they are rarely found by archaeologists. The oldest one known probably dates to no more than 18,000 years ago (16,050 BCE), so the arguments in favor of its invention thousands of years earlier is inferential and based on the sizes of the stone projectile points that are preserved. Small points would make no sense on heavy thrusting spears. However, there is a weight limit for those used on the lighter spears, sometimes called **darts,** that were launched with spear throwers. The impact of a thrown spear was a product of its weight and velocity, so clever people could increase impact by significantly increasing velocity, even if weight was reduced somewhat. The same principle was followed in the late twentieth century, when military rifles were redesigned to fire smaller bullets but at supersonic velocities.

Genetic Evidence

Modern genetic evidence indicates that our ancestors expanded and broke up into a series of further expanding populations. These founder populations expanded out of Africa into Europe and Asia, where they displaced earlier populations, pushing them into marginal habitats and eventual extinction. Those expanding into Europe, where they are commonly referred to as Cro-Magnon, soon displaced the Neanderthals already resident there, squeezing them to extinction (Figure 2.6).

The genetic distance between Neanderthal DNA and modern human DNA was substantial, so great that it is unlikely that they could have interbred successfully when they came into contact with each other in Europe. It is unlikely that the genes of Neanderthals were added to our branch of humanity when they came into contact in Europe sometime after 50,000 years ago. The Neanderthals dwindled and disappeared, not necessarily killed off by modern humans, just outcompeted by them.

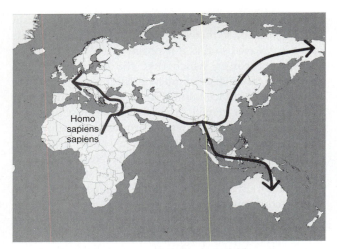

Figure 2.6 After a close brush with extinction, our *Homo sapiens* ancestors spread out of Africa and across the tropical and temperate parts of Eurasia, reaching Australia by 40,000 years ago and Siberia by 15,000 years ago.

Recent experimental research has shown that learning to make the tools used by Neanderthals can be accomplished without the mediation of language. Not so those made by Cro-Magnon people. Biologically modern humans needed language to teach each other how to make their more complex tools (Tattersall 2001).

The population grew and spread eastward as well, rapidly outcompeting the older *Homo erectus* populations in Southeast Asia and pushing their remnants to remote locations (Macaulay et al. 2005). In 2004 we were all astonished by the discovery of one of these on the island of Flores in Indonesia. During the Late Pleistocene the sea level was about 125 m lower than today and many islands were connected by land that is today covered by shallow seas. New Guinea was connected to Australia and many Indonesian islands were then parts of larger island masses, but there were still straits of deep water that impeded human expansion. Flores was part of one such larger island, and it was there that a *Homo erectus* population managed to hang on until as recently as 18,000 (16,050 BCE) years ago. The remnant population evolved into micropygmies, as did several other animal species that shared their island, a common evolutionary outcome in island environments (Diamond 2004). Modern *Homo sapiens* took over much of the rest of the region, crossing various water barriers, including the one to New Guinea and Australia, by around 45,000 years ago (Chappell et al. 1996).

The human expansion northward and eastward toward America depended upon cultural adaptation to colder regions, new technology, and clever use of it.

Just when and how this happened continues to be the focus of current archaeological research. No evidence exists for any premodern humans in the Western Hemisphere. Most archaeologists agree that people did not reach the Americas until well after 45,000 years ago and thus well after modern *Homo sapiens* had emerged and earlier human forms had all but disappeared. Only modern humans had the cultural capacity to expand into and live in the cold reaches of northern Eurasia, the only route to the Americas for people lacking advanced seagoing boats. The Americas had lain well over the horizon and far beyond the theater of human evolution until near the end of the last Ice Age. Every human alive today descends from common ancestors that lived not very long ago in the grand scheme of things. So the first Americans for the most part looked like us, talked like us, and thought like us.

Lines of Evidence from Living American Indians

Archaeology reveals much about the past, but allied scientific disciplines often provide important independent lines of evidence. Archaeology has benefited especially by genetics, the study of teeth, and linguistics (Meltzer 1995).

The Evidence of DNA

Genetics, particularly evidence from **mitochondrial DNA** and **Y-chromosome DNA,** has helped clarify the origins of modern American Indians. We all carry loops of mitochondrial DNA (mtDNA) in our cells in addition to the nuclear DNA that encodes our physical makeup (phenotype). We inherit the mtDNA strands from our mothers. The strands are more abundant than nuclear DNA and thus easier to extract and study. Rare mutations over the long term have created different lineages of mtDNA, which can be used to trace descendant populations back to their geographic origins. The genetic variants or **haplotypes** that define the lineages are relatively few and very useful for this purpose.

Haplotypes in mtDNA cluster into a handful of diagnostic **haplogroups** (A, B, C, D, and X) that are found in varying proportions in sample populations drawn from the Americas and Asia. The proportions found in American Indian populations are most similar to those of central Asia. Another form of haplogroup X is present in certain European populations, and it appears to be 35–13,000 years old (Schurr 2000). The haplogroup X variant is diverse, though, and the

American variant is distinct from the European one (Merriwether 2002). However these details are eventually resolved, it is clear that the genetic evidence confirms the Siberian origins of American Indians.

There are also two useful haplogroups (C and Q) on the Y-chromosome, a nuclear chromosome carried only by men and inherited through the male line. These too point to American Indian origins in northeast Asia.

Geneticists are able to date the ages of haplogroups because they can estimate the rate of mutations that produced them. That is how they estimate that haplogroup X is at least 13,000 years old. The formation of American haplogroup B emerged between about 17,700 and 13,500 years ago (15,700–11,500 BCE), but the other three American haplogroups (A, C, & D) emerged earlier, at least 23,500 years ago. This genetic differentiation could have occurred before the descendants of any of the Asian populations expanded into North America, or the estimated ages might be too old, as some recent research suggests (Kemp et al. 2007). Whatever the timing, haplogroup B is most frequent in northern North America, indicating that it was carried to America soon after it emerged as a distinctive haplogroup. Had all of the haplogroups been carried to the Americas in a single migration after, say, 11,000 BCE, we would expect the proportions to be more similar across both North and South America (Schurr 2000). Thus the genes of American Indians tell us that they have been here for at least 13,000 years. To set an *upper* limit on the peopling of the Americas we must look to other lines of evidence.

The Evidence of Teeth

Human teeth are much more variable than most of us think, and distinctive dental characteristics also point to Siberian origins for the American Indians. We are all aware that many people lack some or all of their third molars, or wisdom teeth. But molars also can vary in the number of cusps or roots they have. A supernumerary root on lower first molars (3RM1) is common in northeast Asia, present in 6% of Native Americans, but very rare or absent in modern and prehistoric Europeans. Incisors can vary by the degree to which their back (lingual) sides have shovel-shaped ridges (Figure 2.7), also common in northeast Asia and the Americas but absent elsewhere. These and other sometimes more subtle dental features indicate that the ancestors of American Indians originated in Siberia, and that small numbers of them expanded by way of Alaska no more than 15,000 years ago (13,000 BCE) (Turner 1989, 2002). The patterns of dental variation within the Americas supports the hypothesis that there were three discernable waves of expansion from Siberia, one being ancestral to most living American Indians, a second being ancestral to the Nadene speakers of western North America, and a third being ancestral to the speakers of Eskimo-Aleut languages in the American Arctic. Some of the details of these findings have been challenged on statistical grounds, and some researchers believe that the three-wave hypothesis is too simplistic, but these criticisms have not cast doubt on Siberian origins (Powell 1993).

The Evidence of Languages

Languages also inform us about the human past because historical linguists are able to not only show how they split and multiplied over time but to even reconstruct parts of extinct ancestral languages. There were probably about a thousand distinct languages being spoken in the Americas in 1492. Of these perhaps 400 were being spoken in North America (Figure 2.8).

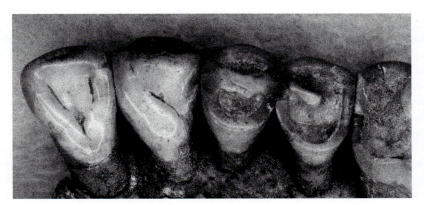
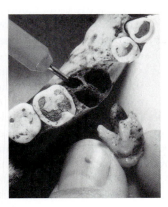

Figure 2.7 Left: Incisor to the left shows pronounced shoveling. Right: Pen points to the socket of a supernumerary third root on the lower first molar (3RM1).
Source: Images courtesy of Christy G. Turner III.

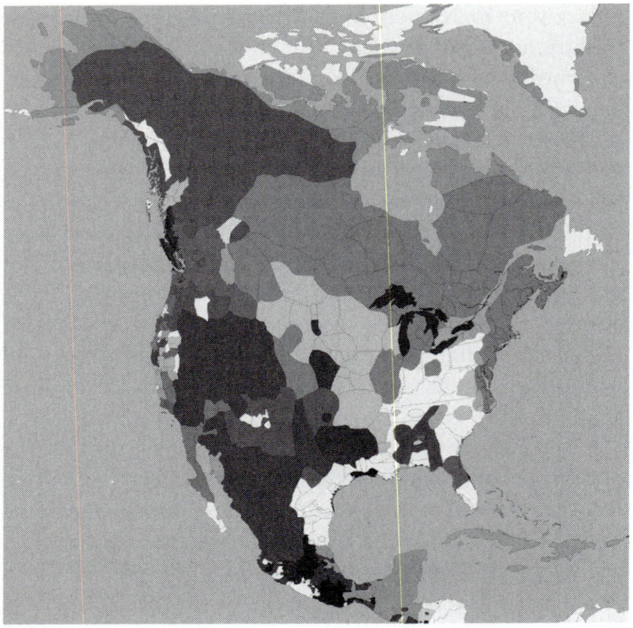

Figure 2.8 Language families of North America at the time of European contact.

of New Guinea, where there are many languages. The reverse is found in eastern subarctic Canada, where thin, mobile populations have existed for centuries. In this case a single language, Cree-Montagnais-Naskapi, has persisted for a long time over a large region because tiny mobile bands have stayed linked to one another. Easy communication persisted over the long run between adjacent bands, but a Naskapi person from the east and a Cree person from the west would have some difficulty communicating if they were suddenly thrown together. In this case the language is so variable over space that some linguists refer to it as a language complex, and it is clear that if something caused the complex to split into two or more isolated populations, separate and mutually unintelligible languages would form. But because population density is low, mobility is high, distances are great, and isolation is low, the Cree-Montagnais-Naskapi language complex persists.

By studying language structures and vocabularies, linguists have been able to group most American Indian languages into families. Related languages can be shown to descend from common ancestors called **protolanguages.** Linguists can even reconstruct parts of the vocabularies of protolanguages from the vocabularies of the daughter languages based on known rules of sound change over time. This kind of analysis has been verified many times by reference to language families that have long histories of writing. Thus the English word "hound" is **cognate** with the German word "hund" and the sound changes that occurred in both after the breakup of their common protolanguage can be traced with considerable accuracy. Many such cognates exist between related languages, but occasionally they are replaced by completely different words over time, sometimes words borrowed from other languages, sometimes internally generated neologisms. Thus "hound" has taken on a narrower usage in English and the **semantic** equivalent of the German "hund" is now "dog" in English. "Dog" originally referred to a particularly powerful breed in Old English. If for some reason our descendants all come to prefer the Spanish word "perro" future linguists will have to dig even deeper. It is not just word replacements and sound changes that plague linguists; semantic shifts (changes in meaning) can push a word to a corner of the vocabulary where it might not be noticed. For example, one might conclude that the Spanish word for horse (*caballo*) did not derive from earlier Latin roots until one realizes that it derived from a Latin word for "nag" that replaced the Latin term for horse (*equus*) over time.

Notice that the ancestral form of the cognates "hound" and "hund" is not necessarily intermediate

These seem like very large numbers until it is remembered that about 800 languages are being spoken today just on the island of New Guinea. The propagation of new languages is something that occurs naturally as populations expand and fragment. Related speech communities become isolated from one another over time, and when this happens the languages drift apart due to their own internal evolutionary dynamics.

The rate at which languages drift apart can be measured in terms of the half-lives of words. This is the amount of time required for there to be a 50% chance that a word will be replaced by a new word. For most words the half-life is about 2,000 years, but for a few very conservative words it might be greater than 10,000 years (Gray 2005). A problem is that even though a word might survive for thousands of years it will change as sound systems evolve, making them recognizable only to experienced linguists. Thus the linkages between related languages are often very difficult to trace after a few thousand years. This severely limits the usefulness of languages in tracing more ancient origins, but their discussion is included here because of recent and well-known attempts to use them in that way (Cavalli-Sforza and Cavalli-Sforza 1995; Greenberg 1996).

The process of language diversification is amplified by increasing population density, decreased mobility, the rise of political barriers, and geographic isolation. All of these apply to the agricultural groups between those two words because both have evolved over time from the form taken by their common ancestor. The same principle holds for the later forms produced from common origins by both biological and cultural evolution. For example, the common ancestor of humans and chimpanzees almost certainly did not look like some cross between the two modern species. The search for so-called intermediate forms in either linguistics or biology is a fool's errand because an ancestral form should not be expected to be necessarily intermediate between descendant forms.

The Northern Iroquoian language family is an informative case. There are over a dozen Northern Iroquoian languages known, some of them still spoken. The differences between them are about as pronounced as the differences between the closely related Romance languages of Europe, which include Spanish, Portuguese, French, Italian, and some others. Thus the time depth since the breakup of the Northern Iroquoian protolanguage is probably about equivalent to the time it has taken the Romance languages to emerge from various colonial forms of Latin, more than one but less than two millennia. Some other American Indian language families have constituent languages that are as closely related as the Northern Iroquoian languages are, but others do not hold together nearly as well, usually because they broke up longer ago. Linguists still debate whether the Penutian language family of the far west really holds together, and those that think it does argue that the common protolanguage was probably spoken more than 6,000 years ago (Nichols 2002:280). In addition there are isolates, some of which cannot be easily classified with any other languages. Cherokee is the only surviving example of Southern Iroquoian, related to Northern Iroquoian to be sure, but without close sister languages. Tsimshianic and Zuni are both small isolates that might or might not be distantly related to the Penutian family, depending upon which linguist one consults. Similarly, Beothuk, the native language of Newfoundland, might or might not be related to the Algonquian language family. Some isolates that are now extinct will probably never be linked to other languages because we lack the necessary information. Others will be linked by way of ancient connections only after much more research.

We know that people have been in the Americas for at least 12,000 years, so it is no surprise that we have many language isolates and little consensus among linguists about how language families were connected in deep time. A few, most notably Joseph Greenberg, have been willing to assume that most American Indian languages descend from the same very ancient protolanguage, excluding only the Nadene languages and the Eskimo-Aleut languages brought by later waves of migrants from Siberia (Greenberg 1996; Greenberg et al. 1986). But this leaps over problems of classification rather than specifying solutions for them. For example, how did the "Macro-Indian" phylum break up into descendant families and languages? Most linguists take a bottom-up empirical approach, preferring to establish language families as sets of demonstrably related languages before moving on to link families into larger units. Lyle Campbell and Marianne Mithun listed no fewer than 21 families and many unclassified isolates that they could have listed as the sole survivors of still more families (Campbell 1979). Most archaeologists have followed this cautious approach (Coe et al. 1986). Volume 17 of the authoritative *Handbook of North American Indians* inventories no fewer than 62 language families and isolates (Goddard 1996:4–8). This number could be reduced if 1 of the families turn out to be members of a still-tentative Penutian superfamily and if 10 others turn out to be members of a Hokan superfamily. But the number families accepted by most linguists will remain larger than the 3 proposed by Greenberg: Amerind, Nadene, and Eskimo-Aleut.

If a protolanguage can break up into, say, 10 daughter languages over the course of a millennium, then it would be easy for many more than the 400 or so known languages to have resulted in the time available since the first peopling of North America. In fact, such a rapid rate of new language formation would predict that there were many languages and even some language families that must have appeared and then gone extinct over that much time. If the rate of language splitting can be measured we have another dating technique, but attempts to gauge rates of linguistic change are notoriously inaccurate. **Glottochronology,** which uses standard rates of word replacement in vocabularies as a means to estimate the age of the split between any two related languages, works convincingly only some of the time and only for closely related languages.

It is clear that comparative linguistics has difficulty finding connections between languages that have been separate for more than a few thousand years. Even the most optimistic linguists set the limit at $8,000 \pm 2,000$ years (Dunn et al. 2005). The good news is that using language structure, sound systems, and grammar rather than vocabularies might allow historical linguists to extend the time depths at which languages can be linked. At least for now archaeology provides the best reliable means for dating the peopling of the Americas. Like genes and teeth, languages help us understand where the first Americans came from better than they tell us when they arrived.

Languages also define speech communities, the networks of individuals that normally interact with one another and think of themselves as both related to one another and different from the foreign others that reside beyond the barrier of easy communication. The speech community is a handy concept because it typically approximates the concept of archaeological culture that is used in this book. Archaeological cultures are defined by tool complexes and inferred ecological adaptations that probably correspond to extinct speech communities. In other words, there is an implied linguistic component to the concept of an archaeological culture, one that corresponds to language or protolanguage and has the potential to help researchers sort out the histories of American Indian languages that are or were until recently still spoken across the continent.

Box 2.2 HOW TO MANAGE THE DIMENSIONS OF TIME AND SPACE

People pressed northward into northern Siberia crossing invisible lines of latitude as they did. They could not have known that those following the coastline would find it bending farther and farther eastward and eventually southward again as they followed it. They had to expand northward to about 62° north latitude in order to pass over the watery threshold of the Pacific Ocean and into the northwesternmost portion of North America. The scales of time and space involved in this process are mind-boggling, especially considering the severity of the climate in which they were played out. The only way to fully grasp it is to bring it into human scale.

Degrees of latitude are divided into 60 minutes, giving us (360 × 60) = 21,600 minutes of arc to encompass the earth. By definition each minute of arc covers 1 nautical mile along the circumference of the earth, which means that circling the globe requires one to travel 21,600 nautical miles. The terrestrial mile that is commonly used in the United States is slightly shorter, so a nautical mile equals 1.1508 of our terrestrial miles (mi) or 1.852 kilometers (km). That means that for every 5° northward people expanded in Siberia they traveled (5 × 60 × 1.852 =) 555.6 km (or 345.24 mi). That seems daunting until we factor in the time it took for them to cover that ground. Use the following simple equation to try out a variety of possibilities:

$$\frac{D \times 111}{Y} = K$$

Where D = degrees of latitude
Y = years of elapsed time
K = kilometers moved per year

With a little high school algebra one can estimate any two of these variables and derive the third. If people expanded northward from 55° to 60° north latitude over the course of 10,000 years, they did so at an average rate of only 0.0555 km (55.5 m or 182 ft) per year. Running backs are expected to do better than that in a single football game. The point is that the hunter-gatherers of Siberia expanded northward without knowing they were going anyplace. Their average movement per year was far less than their normal hunting range. One has to change one or more variables by an order of magnitude, multiplying or dividing it by 10, to produce a noticeable effect. Moving 50° rather than 5° would have taken them to the North Pole and well beyond it, but they could have done it moving only 555 m a year. Cutting the time from 10,000 to 1,000 years has a similar effect. Expanding northward 5° in only a millennium would have required moving only 555 m per year, still a trivial amount measured against a normal hunting range.

These numbers bring the human ecology of ancient Siberia into a human scale that we can understand intuitively, but they also throw light on another feature of archaeological logic. If all I knew about you as a person was your place of birth, your age, and your current location I would have to conclude that you spent your life (so far) moving from point A to point B at some ridiculously slow speed. It is ridiculous because real people actually zigzag through space and time, frequently retracing their steps, putting mileage on cars equal to circling the earth several times yet often selling them within a few kilometers of where they purchased them. What this tells us is that population expansion and conscious migration are very different things. While individuals are not even aware of the first, they undertake the second quite deliberately.

Crossing Beringia

People first expanded into Siberia from the south, lured by the game that roamed there but constrained by the limitations of their technology. Siberia is a bleak place today, but it was an even more challenging environment in 15,000 BCE. Vast continental ice sheets in western Eurasia and North America locked up much of the world's water, exposing continental shelf and land bridges that today lie covered by shallow seas. The Bering Strait did not exist then, but the term "land bridge" misrepresents what archaeologists today call **Beringia.** The isthmus connecting Siberia and Alaska was actually 1,600 km (1,000 mi) across, hardly a narrow bridge. Small ice caps existed here and there, but for the most part the regions of northeastern Siberia and western Alaska that made up much of Beringia were parts of a single, largely unglaciated, landmass the size of Australia. Figure 2.9 shows the approximate location of the Pleistocene shoreline of Beringia and the locations of sites mentioned in this chapter.

Researchers have made a strong case for boat travel in the Late Pleistocene. After all, by 15,000 BCE people had long since made it to New Guinea, Australia, and nearby islands, something that they could not have done without at least crude boats, even though they could have seen their destinations on the horizon. But ocean crossings were another matter. The Pacific Ocean was a forbidding obstacle, and even hardy boaters would have stayed near the fringe of land. The more distant islands of Oceania or for that matter Madagascar would not be found and settled for thousands of years. For the human populations of eastern Asia 15 millennia ago the Pacific was a vast obstacle that could be overcome only by expansion northeastward through Beringia or along its Pacific coast. Of course, nobody knew that Beringia was there, or that two unoccupied American continents laid beyond it.

Just as important, the slow expansion toward America was not intentional in the sense that they anticipated expansion into the Americas. The horizons of the hunter-gatherers of Siberia were limited to the scope of their personal experience and the information they could pick up from their relatives in other bands. Their decisions were short-range ones, conditioned by the opportunities and capabilities that they had at hand, but collectively those short-range decisions drew them farther and farther afield as their capabilities improved.

Archaeological sites show that modern humans peopled southern Siberia 43–38,000 BCE (Goebel et al. 2008). Further expansion into the Siberian subarctic and eventually the arctic took longer, especially because in the Late Pleistocene the ecological zones of Eurasia were displaced much farther south than they are today. The ecozones of the north lie approximately in bands across the region, with the tundra band farthest north and the steppe farthest south.

During the Late Pleistocene southern Siberia was a patchwork of these zones, with tundra on elevations and treeless steppe in the valleys. Northward was mostly a glacial environment often referred to as mammoth steppe, a biome that supported mammoths and other large herd animals but was very cold, lacked edible plants for humans, and was short on wood for fuel and shelter. Not surprisingly, the earliest sites left by modern humans are south of 55° north latitude (Figure 2.10). They are, for the most part, open sites on bluffs or terraces, looking out over broad floodplains. Hearths at the centers of larger rings of stone indicate that these people were living in skin tents. Their stone tools included **bifaces** and long, slender blades struck from cores of fine-grained **chert,** a family of hard stones that includes flint. The chert bifaces were probably used as knives, with ivory, bone, and antler points used to tip spears launched by spear throwers. The blades were often worked further into end scrapers,

Figure 2.9 Beringia, showing the Pleistocene coastline relative to the modern one, as well as some key archaeological sites.

Table 2.2 Ecozone bands of northeastern Siberia arranged north to south.

Ecozone Name	Type
Tundra (Arctic)	Tundra
Taiga	Boreal Forest
Forest-Steppe	Park Grassland
Steppe	Grassland

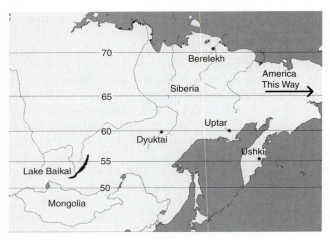

Figure 2.10 Lines of latitude in eastern Siberia. Early hunters had to be able to live as far north as 62° before they could expand across Beringia into North America.

side scrapers, **burins,** and points. Other tools were made from bone, antler, and ivory. These must have included needles, for the cold climate of even southern Siberia would have required tailored clothing (Goebel 1999:213–214; Madsen 2004).

Siberian sites are old enough to have been ancestral to all Native Americans almost regardless of how early one thinks they arrived (Goebel and Aksenov 1995). These people were generalized hunter-gatherers, taking Mongolian gazelles, argali sheep, horses, woolly rhinoceros, reindeer, steppe bison, and Siberian mountain goats as opportunities arose, but they undoubtedly gathered edible plants as well (Goebel 1999:215–216).

The rising human tide in eastern Asia carried the earliest American populations eastward out of Siberia. But the process was slow because the skills required to survive in northeastern Siberia were not easy to come by. Thin human populations expanded northward on to the northern steppe of Siberia, then fell back again more than once before reaching a latitude that would allow them to spill eastward into America. The oldest known site north of 70° north latitude dates from more than 25,000 BCE, the Yana Rhinoceros Horn site (RHS) in the lower Yana Valley (Pitulko et al. 2004). However, there is still no evidence that people expanded eastward into Beringia that early.

Larger numbers of southern Siberian people expanded northward on to the mammoth steppe during the colder conditions that prevailed 24–17,000 BCE, mostly occupying land up to about 60° north latitude, almost but perhaps still not quite far enough northeast to allow the population to expand into the American part of Beringia. What enabled this adaptive expansion remains uncertain. It might have been nothing more than better clothing, or improved knowledge of the environment and its resources. By this time they were clearly harvesting the full range of available fur-bearing animals, and downy birds, and even killing the occasional mammoth (or at least dining on one found already dead).

It was a Sisyphean task taken up unknowingly by hunters just trying to make a living, attracted by the possibility of game or food plants just over the next hill. On a conventional map, with north at the top, the rim of the Pacific looks like a hill to be climbed, but it is no more so than a high pressure "ridge" on a weather map. Yet the analogy is apt, for the barriers of geography and climate held back a rising tide of humanity for millennia, and even then allowed only a relative few to pass.

It is important to remember that there were also technological and social constraints on the expansion. No band could afford to move too far from related bands, on which they depended for information, assistance, marriage partners, and trade (Moore and Moseley 2001). Sources of fine chert were left far behind in some cases, and trade in high-grade materials was necessary to keep hunters supplied. If recent hunter-gatherers are good analogies, then this was probably couched as gift giving, an activity that reinforced the other linkages between related bands.

The peak of glaciation in the Late Pleistocene came around 16,000 BCE. The number of archaeological sites on the mammoth tundra declined sharply around that time as the human population dwindled, retreated, or both. People were almost completely driven out of Siberia around this time. One site contains hearths in which people were burning combustible shale, an indication that wood was probably in short supply with the return of colder climate (Goebel 1999:218,222). Game was still plentiful, but the fuel shortage might have been the critical factor limiting the expansion of human bands.

Traveling Companions

Dogs are the oldest domestic species, unless we count ourselves. The mitochondrial DNA of domesticated dogs indicates that they all descend from a common origin in a single gene pool (Savolainen et al. 2002). Until recently most investigators concluded that dogs had evolved separately from up to four subspecies of wolves, but that argument is not supported by the genetic evidence (Morey 1984; Vilá et al. 1997). Put another way, the evidence available until recently made multilinear evolution of dogs the most probable hypothesis, but new evidence has disproven that hypothesis and made a single origin for dogs the most likely hypothesis. Larger genetic variation in eastern Asia suggests that this was the region in which the early population of dogs evolved, probably around 13,000 BCE. Several maternal lineages were present in the population of domesticated dogs that diverged from wolves, and several of them persisted in the population that expanded with humans into the Americas. One of them is unique to the Americas, indicating that it arose through mutation after dogs arrived in North America. This would probably not happen without long geographic isolation, so it is further evidence that dogs came with the first humans, already hunting companions, camp cleaners, and sentinels.

The unique American **clade** of domesticated dogs never spread back into Eurasia. It is also the case that it is largely absent from modern dog breeds in America, indicating that colonists from Europe discouraged breeding between their imported breeds and native American dogs (Leonard et al. 2002).

Dogs and humans communicate very well, better in fact than great apes (our closest relatives) and humans do. Puppies whine like human babies and have other behaviors that ingratiate them to humans. They are also very good at reading human cues, signals that help them find food in test situations or carry out commands that lead to food rewards. These abilities, which are present even in puppies who have had little human contact, are absent in wolves, even those that have been raised by humans. That means that there was strong selection for social and cognitive abilities during the course of dog domestication (Hare et al. 2002). That does not necessarily mean that dog domestication was an intentional process on the part of Asian hunters in 13,000 BCE. It might have been fortuitous, emerging from chance associations between humans and a few unusual mutant wolves that happened to have the mental skills that preadapted them to cooperate with people. So far the oldest archaeological evidence for domesticated dogs in eastern Siberia appears to be the 10,650-year-old dog burial at Ushki-1 (Dikov 1996:24; Morey 2006:160).

Archaeological Traces in Siberia

The background presented thus far in this chapter is context for the scattered and sometimes confusing archaeological traces of humans in Siberia on the eve of their expansion into America (Figure 2.11). The Pleistocene waned and the climate of Siberia slowly warmed after 15,000 BCE, but it did so in long fits and starts

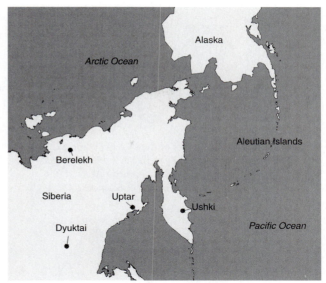

Figure 2.11 Siberian sites mentioned in the text.

separated by short reversals. People recolonized the areas that had been abandoned, but this time with more advanced technology. Wedge-shaped cores and **microblades** of chert were new additions to the technology, which archaeologists see appearing first in the Lake Baikal region. Microblade technology is sophisticated and difficult to master, but mastery of the new technology was worth the effort given the effectiveness of composite tools and the difficulty of acquiring high-quality cherts (Yesner and Pearson 2002).

Yuri Mochanov has defined the Dyuktai complex (also transcribed as "Diuktai," "D'uktai," or "Dyukhtai") based on his excavations at Dyuktai Cave. The complex is characterized by microblades, wedge-shaped **microblade cores,** burins, many flake tools, and a minority of bifaces. Reliable radiocarbon dates indicate that complex is well dated around 12,050–10,050 BC (Yi and Clark 1985).

Craftspeople made clever composite tools from multiple materials, such as bone points with stone microblade edges set into slots, which in turn had been carved using specialized burins. Curiously, several sites show evidence of hunting specialization, a risky choice that one might think they could not afford (Figures 2.12 and 2.13). Reindeer bones dominate one site assemblage, mountain goat another, red deer another, and bison still another. Mammoths appear to have been more often scavenged than hunted, and hares were perhaps more important in the long run.

Unlike earlier people living in the Siberian subarctic, the makers of the Dyuktai complex did not use a

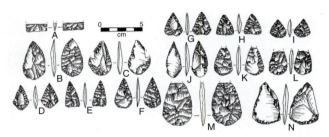

Figure 2.12 Bifaces of the Nenana complex. *Source:* From Hoffecker et al. 1993:49. Reprinted with permission from the American Association for the Advancement of Science.

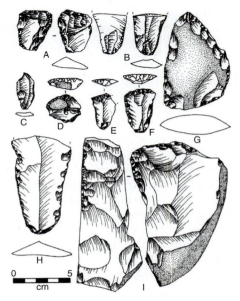

Figure 2.13 Other Nenana complex tools: (A) *pièce esquillée* (wedge), (B and H) retouched blades, (C) graver, (D–F) end scrapers, (G) side scraper, and (I) plane. *Source:* From Hoffecker et al. 1993:49. Reprinted with permission from the American Association for the Advancement of Science.

combination of larger base camps and smaller short-term camps. Instead archaeologists see evidence of a different strategy, one that emphasized small, temporary camps and highly mobile bands (Goebel 1999:223). This was a strategy that, with a modest population growth rate, would have allowed rapid expansion of a hunter-gatherer population without risk of it becoming too thin for interband connections to be maintained.

Nikolai Dikov found a series of sites along the shoreline of Ushki Lake on the Kamchatka Peninsula. The people responsible for them might have expanded into the area from farther south along the eastern side

of Asia. The Ushki complex is comprised of small, stemmed bifacial points, bifacial knives, and stone and ivory beads, all found on the floors of substantial houses (Goebel et al. 2003). Unlike the Dyuktai complex, this one lacked microblades and burins. The people who lived at Ushki Lake subsisted by exploiting both salmon runs and large terrestrial mammals. Unlike the Dyuktai complex, the Ushki Lake complex resembles the earliest known (Nenana) assemblages in central Alaska in the view of some archaeologists.

Swan Point

The earliest reliable archaeological evidence from eastern Beringia comes from the central Alaskan Swan Point site (Goebel et al. 2008). The artifacts found at Swan Point date to around 12,000 BCE and they resemble artifacts from Dyuktai and several other northeast Siberian sites. Most notably the Swan Point assemblage includes microblades and burins. Following this the picture becomes more complicated.

The Nenana Complex

Seven sites in the Nenana Valley document this tool complex, which is dominated by bifacial projectile points (Powers and Hoffecker 1989). Other stone tools include scrapers, burins, *pièces esquillées*, and some blades, but like the Ushki complex Nenana lacks microblades.

The Nenana Valley was a strange environment by modern standards but not too unlike the mammoth steppe of Siberia. Calibrated radiocarbon dates from several sites put the age of the Nenana complex at 11,500–9500 BCE (Figure 2.14). Nenana is not too young to have been the source for Paleoindian cultures farther south in North America, and a growing number of archaeologists conclude that indeed it was (see Chapter 3). Nenana complex must have been carried by people that were similar in a general way to the hunter-gatherers of Siberia around that time (Goebel 1999). These were very mobile people who did not use large base camps, just the sort of folk who could expand rapidly in numbers and across space if presented with a vast new landscape that was both attractive and wide open for human occupation.

Apart from timing, the issue is whether such an important technological advance as microblade manufacture would have been dropped by the Beringian descendants of the earlier Siberians that had it. Another possibility is that Nenana derived from some remnant of the people who lived in Siberia prior to 16,000 BCE

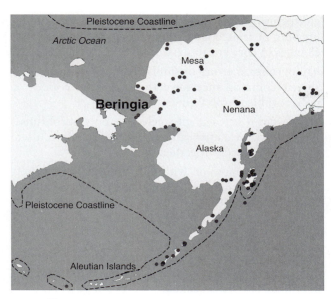

Figure 2.14 Alaskan sites mentioned in the text.

and whose technology did not yet include microblades. The Yana RHS site shows that this is a possible scenario. That possibility even suggests the further one that some people made it into Beringia before the general Siberian retreat southward around 16,000 BCE, but that archaeologists have not yet detected them.

The Ushki complex was subsequently replaced on Kamchatka by bearers of the Dyuktai complex. These people still later pushed on through Beringia, eventually also into Alaska. There the Dyuktai derivative is known as the Denali complex, which became widespread in eastern Beringia. More on this complex appears in Chapter 3.

The First Americans

Looked at from Siberia, although they could not have been aware of it, Asiatic people were finally poised to spill eastward into America in 13,000 BCE, but probably not earlier than that (Bever 2006:811). These mobile hunters-gatherers were accompanied by dogs whose curved tails and tractable dispositions set them apart from wolves and advantaged their human partners. In their hands the humans carried spears and spear throwers that made them lethal at a distance, particularly to game that had never before experienced such a skilled predator. They wore cleverly tailored clothing, and carried complex tools made of multiple materials and designed for mobility. And in their minds were stored the strategies, traditional knowledge, and skills necessary to survive, even thrive, on the great mammoth steppe of Beringia. Like any other well-adapted species these

early people were not necessarily on their way to being something else or somewhere else. They could have had no idea that they were on the threshold of a continent, that great things awaited their descendants, or that they had within them the capacity to demonstrate the potential of humans to thrive on their own in a new world. Over the succeeding 14,000 years, the children of these few founders would demonstrate as no other branch of humanity could that the potential for the development of complex societies has been in all of us all along.

Summary

1. The earth is about 4.6 billion years old, but the history of modern *Homo sapiens* is confined to the last 85–60,000 years.

2. Modern humans expanded out of Africa, replacing *Homo erectus* and Neanderthal populations in Europe and across Eurasia.

3. Genetic, dental, and linguistic evidence supports archaeological evidence indicating a Siberian origin for the ancestors of all American Indians.

4. People expanded northward into and through Siberia as Pleistocene conditions allowed, a few small bands making it through Beringia and into Alaska sometime after 13,000 BCE.

5. Dogs were domesticated around the same time and probably accompanied the first human bands into North America.

6. Among the earliest archaeological traces in Siberia are those at the Yana RHS site, which dates to 25,000 BCE.

7. The Ushki complex is related to the Nenana complex found in Alaska, but perhaps too young to have been ancestral to it.

8. The Dyuktai complex of Siberia is different from both Ushki and Nenana, but probably ancestral to the Denali complex found in Alaska.

9. By 12,000 BCE the ancestors of the American Indians were established residents of the northwesternmost corner of North America and poised for their subsequent expansion.

Further Reading

There are many well-reasoned and well-written summaries of the first peopling of North America, but research has been so intense in recent years that such sources become out-of-date very quickly. The vast area involved and the spotty nature of the archaeological evidence also makes for contentious disagreements over particulars. An excellent place to start is with Nina Jablonski's *The First Americans: The Pleistocene Colonization of the New World*. David Madsen's *Entering America* is a more detailed recent accounting of the environmental and cultural conditions that shaped the expansion of humans across Beringia. Beyond that readers should look to the professional articles cited at various places in this chapter. Because of the high current interest in the peopling of the Americas articles also emerge frequently in popular magazines such as *Scientific American*, *Natural History*, and *Archaeology*. These are for the most part trustworthy but likely to be made quickly obsolete by new discoveries.

Glossary

Beringia: the broad Pleistocene isthmus joining Alaska and Siberia, today largely under water.

biface: a flat chipped-stone tool having two faces.

burin: a chipped-stone tool made from a blade and used to chisel bone, antler, and ivory.

chert: a glassy cryptocrystalline stone material that is well suited for making chipped-stone tools.

clade: a taxonomic group of organisms consisting of an ancestor and all the descendants of that ancestor.

cognate: a word in one language that is related to a word in another language by virtue of the two words having derived from a single ancestral word in their common protolanguage.

dart: a small spear, larger than an arrow, used with an atlatl.

glottochronology: the estimation of the timing of the breakup of related languages by measurement of changes in core vocabulary.

haplogroup: a group of similar haplotypes that share a common ancestor with a single nucleotide polymorphism? (SNP) mutation.

haplotype: a set of single nucleotide polymorphisms (SNPs) that are statistically associated; in effect, a set of genes that occur together.

isostatic: having to do with the rise and fall of the landscape due to the presence or absence of heavy sheets of glacial ice.

microblade: a small sliver with parallel sides, struck from a prepared core.

microblade core: a wedge- or tongue-shaped nodule of chert having long, parallel scars produced when microblades were detached.

mitochondrial DNA: genetic material inherited by all animals from their mothers.

moraine: deposits of ground-up rock laid down along the sides and especially at the leading edges of glaciers.

pièce esquillée: a stone wedge, probably used to split antler, bone, and ivory.

protolanguage: an extinct language reconstructed on the basis of evidence found in living descendant languages.

Quaternary: the geological period containing the Pleistocene and Holocene epochs.

semantic: pertaining to meaning in language.

Y-chromosome: a chromosome that determines male characteristics and is inherited by males from their fathers.

Younger Dryas: the last cold cycle of the Pleistocene.

The Peopling of America

How do you know where to dig?

Anonymous visitor to an archaeological site

La chance ne favorise que l'intelligence préparée. (Chance favors only the prepared mind.)
Louis Pasteur

THIS CHAPTER SUMMARIZES WHAT IS KNOWN about the earliest inhabitants of North America and the principal controversies surrounding their interpretation. There are and probably will always be an assortment of sites for which very early dates are claimed, but few stand up under close examination. The Paleoindian period spanned at least the centuries from 11,100 to 9900 BCE. Clovis was the first widespread Paleoindian culture and it appears to have derived from Nenana culture in Beringia. Nenana (Chapter 2) is even old enough to have predated the controversial Monte Verde site in Chile. Claims for a few scattered and possibly older sites elsewhere in both North and South America are hotly debated.

Clovis culture was the foundational Paleoindian culture for most of North America, but there is little support for the alternative hypothesis that its distinctive technology came from Europe. Paleoindians might have been partly responsible for the extinctions of many large game animals. The Paleoindian period ended as the Holocene began, the geological epoch we are still in.

Introduction

The earliest Americans traveled light, were few in number, and left only the faintest traces on the archaeological landscape. Theirs was a generalized adaptation, one suited to an environment that was unstable and changing more rapidly than later would be the case

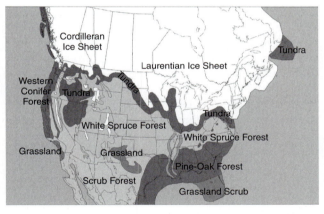

Figure 3.1 Ice Age North America. Archaeologists debate when and how people first got past the Pleistocene ice sheets.

after the close of the Pleistocene (Figure 3.1). Large game animals, many of which would be extinct before long, might seem to us to have been the most obvious resource to these early nomadic hunter-gatherers, but they also exploited plants and smaller animals when and where they could (Barton et al. 2002).

Was Clovis Culture First?

Clovis was the first widespread culture of the Paleoindian period, and it is well established that it was widespread across much of North America approximately 11,100–10,850 BCE (Waters and Stafford 2007).

Anything presented as older than that raises red flags and draws the critical attention of archaeologists who have been fooled before by false claims and want to avoid being fooled again. Thus the debate over who were the earliest Americans often hinges on the question of whether or not some particular site or artifact is evidence of pre-Clovis people.

There is a logic inherent in archaeological science that puts the burden of proof on any claim that something is older than previously thought. Time flows in one direction, and in human experience it does not reverse itself. Finding something that is younger than expected can be explained in either of two possible ways: Either it is representative of a late survivor or it is something that was picked up and introduced into a later context by some natural process. If it is well established that several examples of something are, say, 11,000 years old then it is hardly news when other examples are found that are around that age or younger. But an older example, one dating to say 15,000 BCE, is bound to make headlines. It is also bound to attract the critical scrutiny of skeptical scientists, for we revise established knowledge only after fair and rigorous review. While the popular press is prone to excited announcements about the oldest whatever yet found, specialists are more inclined to skepticism, and with good reason. Few archaeologists who have been in the profession for a few decades have not regretted accepting claims for antiquity that were later discredited. A book like this one, originally written in 1976, reported four very early sites that taken together at the time indicated that humans were in northern Canada by 27,000 years ago, California by 24,000 years ago, Mexico by 23,000 years ago, and Peru by 20,000 years ago. The scenario was neat, internally consistent, widely accepted at the time, and dead wrong (Snow, 1976). Each of the dates and sites on which that scenario was based failed to stand up under subsequent close scrutiny and redating after the book was published. Many other early claims had been refuted in the years prior, and many more have been refuted in the years since. There should be little wonder that experienced archaeologists are hard to convince given that track record. Ironically the demand for more and better evidence is greatest for this initial period of human presence in North America, when the supply of it is likely to be the least.

Empirical science by definition demands evidence, yet the special circumstances of the peopling of the Americas have made evidence especially hard to produce. In any plausible scenario of that process the founding population is invariably tiny and its members'

possessions few. Vast tracts of continental shelf where these people might have lived and traveled along are out of reach below modern sea level. Valleys where they might have hunted and camped lie deeply buried under the accumulated sediments of the last dozen millennia. The longer something is in the archaeological record the less likely it is to survive, so the oldest things are always in the shortest supply. In short, the evidence we need was meager to begin with, subject to destructive forces, possibly under water, and in any case scattered thinly on the landscape of a huge continent.

Based on the evidence presented in Chapter 2 there can be little doubt that the roots of modern American Indian populations snake back to eastern Asia (Schurr 2000). There may have been complications, but it is reasonable to start with the premise that Siberia set the scene for the peopling of the Americas. We should not expect to find evidence of people in the Americas prior to the date when human populations were able to expand northeastward across Beringia, that broad, now half-submerged intercontinental bridge that once included Alaska and northeastern Siberia. No wonder then that a site in Brazil (of all places) for which excavators have claimed human occupation dating back 48,000 years has created such a furor.

Dubious Claims for Pre-Clovis Sites

The Pedra Furada site is a huge Brazilian rock shelter with pictographs, very deep deposits containing charred wood, what might be hearths, and what might be crude stone tools. Most archaeologists reject the claims (Meltzer et al. 1994; Roosevelt et al. 2002), but the French and Brazilian archaeologists who have by now made very significant investments of time and money in the excavations fiercely defend their interpretations of their findings, which include the claim that they are as much as 48,000 years old (Guidon et al. 1996; Parenti et al. 1995).

The case of Pedra Furada shows why an empirical approach is necessary but insufficient for the solution of the problem of Native American origins. Empirically the biggest questions are these: Are the concentrations of charred wood deep in the site human hearths or the remains of ancient forest fires? Are the crude flaked pebbles human tools or rocks that fell from the top of the high shelter and fractured naturally? It is in the interests of everyone (except perhaps the excavators) to err on the conservative side of these questions, but there is more. Is there a means by which *Homo sapiens*, only recently emerged from Africa, could have expanded to Brazil at

Box 3.1 HOW TO APPLY THE LOGIC OF ARCHAEOLOGICAL DATING

Archaeologists use stratigraphy and other techniques to determine relative ages of deposits or individual artifacts. For any site having three superimposed occupations that are separated stratigraphically, the uppermost of them is necessarily younger than the other two, the second one intermediate, and the lowest one oldest. In addition to relative dating within sites, we frequently use key artifact types for cross dating between sites in the absence of an independent means to obtain absolute dates, such as radiocarbon dating. A key artifact type that was sufficiently short-lived allows one to infer that a stratum containing an example of it in each of two sites indicates that the sites were simultaneously occupied at around the same time regardless of what might have been deposited at either site before or after the time in which the key artifact was in wide use. The problem is that some artifact types were manufactured for long periods of time while others were manufactured only briefly, but were so highly valued that they stayed in circulation for a long time. Still others might have been independently invented at different times or revived after long periods of disuse.

Even if these problems with cross dating can be controlled, one has to keep in mind the implications of the comings and goings of key artifact types over time. Artifacts and absolute dating techniques are both used to establish the *terminus post quem* (time after which) and the *terminus ante quem* (time before which) of a site or artifact assemblage. The *terminus post quem* is the date after which a site was occupied or an assemblage was deposited. The *terminus ante quem* is the point in time before which those things must have occurred. The logic of one is quite different from the other, but thinking about them clearly is often necessary in the absence of good associated radiocarbon dates.

If we know that a given artifact type was first made and used in, say, 1200 CE then its presence in an assemblage must mean that the assemblage is at least that old. Fragile everyday things might be discarded quickly whereas very valuable artifacts might stay in circulation for a long time, so there is a variable rate much like the half-life decay in radioactive materials at which objects fall out of circulation and into the archaeological record. That half-life might be very long for the most valuable objects but very short for common and easily broken ones. In any case it is not possible for any object to have been used before it was invented, so the presence of the object establishes a *terminus post quem*, a point in time after which the assemblage it is in must date. For example, George Ravenscroft invented crystal by adding lead to glass around 1676, so no deposit containing it can predate that year, the *terminus post quem* of English lead crystal. The exceptions are cases where frauds or later artifacts are accidentally or deliberately inserted into early sites, strata, or assemblages. Logically there can be no coin with a BC date on it, and finding one should immediately send the finder in search of a hoaxer.

The *terminus ante quem* is logically different because it is set by the absence of artifact types that one could reasonably expect to be present if the age of a site or assemblage is equivalent to the expected diagnostic object(s). In other words, like it or not determining the date before which a site was abandoned requires the careful use of negative evidence. One can be sure that an assemblage predates, say, 1200 CE only if common items that date to that year and later are missing. Thus the period of occupation of any site is bracketed by a *terminus post quem* (an initial date) and a *terminus ante quem* (an ending date), but the two are determined by very different logical means.

such an early date? Is it plausible that an early population of *Homo sapiens* could have become established in South America 48,000 years ago but then have been so unsuccessful that it left no later evidence over the course of dozens of millennia? These are not empirical questions but rather questions that require the application of theory based upon what we know about *Homo sapiens* more generally and how human populations behave over time and space. When theoretical questions are added to the argument the likelihood that Pedra Furada is what its excavators claim it is becomes vanishingly small.

Another site in South America, Taima-taima in Venezuela, has attracted interest for many years, and it is often cited as a very early mastodon kill site (Bryan et al. 1978). But the radiocarbon dates are inconsistent, the samples are probably contaminated, and the mastodon bones lack clear artifact associations. Similarly, the Calico site in southern California received a gush of attention when the already famous Louis Leakey visited it and pronounced it authentic in 1968 (Leakey and Simpson 1968). But the Calico specimens turned out to be naturally fractured pseudoartifacts unassociated with anything human other than the excavators.

The list of pre-Clovis candidates that were taken seriously for a while but then failed one test or another is a long one. Those just mentioned, along with names like Pendejo, Lewisville, and Old Crow, are on the list, but so are many others not mentioned. The only reason to list them all here would be to head off the criticism that they have not been given a fair hearing. There may be attempts by others to revive interest in one or another of these sites, both named and unnamed, and claims for new sites not yet published as of this writing will surely crop up in the future. But there is no good reason to spend time and space on a review of discredited evidence.

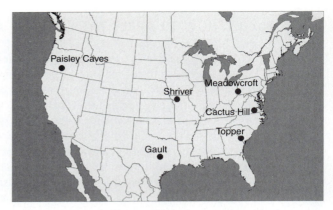

Figure 3.2 Probable pre-Clovis sites mentioned in the text.

More Likely Claims for Pre-Clovis Sites

The jury is still out on some other candidates. At Cactus Hill, Virginia, there is a Paleoindian component in a sand dune overlying older deposits of unknown age containing blades and cores. The Gault site in Texas clearly contains an extensive Clovis **stratum** with older human-made tools well below it (Collins 2002). The Shriver site in Missouri similarly produced blades in a stratum below a Paleoindian level containing fluted points (Reagan et al. 1978). The Topper site in South Carolina has a clear Paleoindian component, beneath which there are also undated deposits containing blades and cores in a Pleistocene-age deposit (Goodyear 2004), but the older materials could have been produced naturally (Figure 3.2). Similarly, the Meadowcroft site in Pennsylvania, surely one of the most carefully excavated of sites, produced evidence in levels below Paleoindian, but critics claimed that the radiocarbon samples could have been contaminated by ancient carbon (Adovasio et al. 1990; Roosevelt et al. 2002:175–177). Further analysis showed that the deposits were not contaminated in this way (Goldberg and Arpin 1999).

There is a curious pattern to many of these sites. Convincing Paleoindian strata have often undated strata containing (usually) a few blades under them. In the absence of independent dates for these mysterious earlier strata, the best course is to conclude for now that they represent what some researchers refer to as the "pioneer" phase of colonization, which one should expect to have low visibility as compared to the later "residential" phase represented by Clovis culture (Adovasio and Pedler 2005:49; Housley et al. 1997). The skimpy bits of evidence found beneath the more diagnostic Clovis levels need not have been substantially older, say on the order of millennia rather than centuries. At least we should not assume that they were in the absence of compelling evidence.

Research in the Paisley Five-Mile Point Caves in south-central Oregon has produced more convincing evidence. Here human coprolites containing tell-tale A2 and B2 haplogroups have been dated to 1,000 years earlier than the earliest generally accepted dates for Clovis (Gilbert, Jenkins, et al. 2008). Because the DNA and the radiocarbon dates both come from the same samples there appears to be little or no justification for doubting this evidence that people were in North America a millennium before the appearance of Clovis culture.

An exception to the largely dismissed claims for South American sites is the remarkable case of Monte Verde, an early site in far-off Chile. But before examining the implications of that site for North American archaeology we turn to a summary of what is generally known about North American Paleoindians and their origins.

The Paleoindian Period

There have been many pre-Clovis claims, and many sites that probably belong to the Paleoindian period, but the number that measure up to modern dating standards are few. A stroll through the older literature reveals dozens of sites once taken seriously that failed one test or another and are no longer mentioned (Bryan, 1969, 1986; Krieger, 1964; Willey and Phillips 1958). Anna Roosevelt provides a summary of those sites whose credibility has survived until recently (Roosevelt et al. 2002). Roosevelt applies the most rigorous standards to demonstrate validity (or the lack of it) in each of these cases. To pass muster the empirical data from candidate sites must (1) have suites of radio-carbon dates exhibiting low standard error, which were (2) run on single, clean, and taxonomically identified carbon samples that were (3) in undisputed primary association with diagnostic artifacts. Furthermore, (4) the results must have been published in peer-reviewed publications. These are tough but sound standards. Popular outlets such as magazines, newspapers, and the Internet are, after all, rife with bogus science of all kinds. Only a few candidates pass these stringent but necessary requirements. At the time Roosevelt wrote her review, only five of the many Clovis period Paleoindian sites in the western part of North America met all of them: Lehner, Murray Springs, Domebo, Dent, and Anzick. This is a good place to begin (Figure 3.3).

The Paleoindians were certainly established in North America by 11,100 BCE, but their possible earlier presence is a question that remains open. Before 1927 few American archaeologists thought that the archaeology of North America had much time depth. Geologists using crude techniques to estimate when the Pleistocene ended were starting to zero in on around 8000 BCE, but nothing in the known archaeological record at the time suggested that people were around when Canada was largely under ice and Ice Age mammals roamed the rest of the continent. Then in the summer of that year researchers from the Denver Museum of Natural History followed up on a discovery made 18 years earlier by a cowboy named George McJunkin in eastern New Mexico. The site near Folsom produced the bones of an extinct form of bison, and lodged between the ribs of one of the animals was an exquisitely made chipped-stone projectile point (Meltzer et al. 2002). The Folsom point, as it has been called ever since, later turned up at many other sites as well, often in Late Pleistocene or early Holocene contexts.

Folsom points are bifacial and **lanceolate** in shape, lacking either barbs or stems. They tend to be finely made from high-grade material, carefully chipped and ground along their lower edges to keep them from cutting through the lashing that would have been used to haft them to handles, spear shafts, or foreshafts (Figure 3.4). The most striking feature of the Folsom points was a single, long flake removed from each flat side. These were so pronounced that archaeologists called them **flutes** after the channels carved on fluted columns. It would be decades before researchers were able to experimentally reproduce the flutes by striking long channel flakes from the sides of bifaces after preparing tiny striking platforms on their bases. Flutes made Folsom points much thinner, actually biconcave in cross section, presumably to facilitate their hafting in split shafts or foreshafts. Occasionally fluting on one side made the point so thin that a second flute could not be struck from the opposite side without breaking the point, so it was left with a single flute. Actually the flutes do not contribute much to the hafting properties of the points, and some archaeologists have suggested

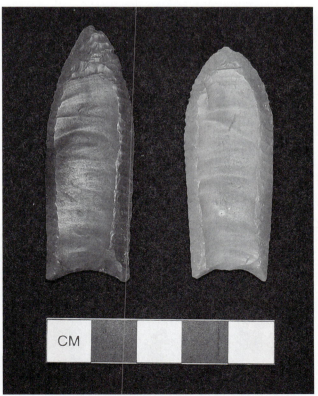

Figure 3.4 Folsom projectile points, probably the finest fluted lanceolate points ever made.

Figure 3.3 Key well-dated Clovis culture sites.

that the skilled artisans who did the **knapping** (called knappers) were mainly just showing off their skills.

Eminent archaeologists visited the Folsom site, rubbed their chins, and declared it authentic. The find was unprecedented and quite unlike the contents of other clearly later American Indian sites with which they were all familiar. There had been other claims of great antiquity for a few sites in North America, but these had not panned out despite the hopes of some archaeologists that the Americas would prove to be as rich in Paleolithic remains as the Eastern Hemisphere had proven to be. Now, at last, they had clear evidence of humans in America as long ago as the Late Pleistocene. Over time these very early Americans came to be called "Paleoindians."

It was not long before archaeologists began recognizing other Paleoindian sites. The Blackwater Draw site near Clovis, New Mexico, produced lanceolate projectile points similar to but larger than Folsom points. The Clovis points were also fluted, but they often had more than one channel flake removed from each side (Figure 3.5). Stratified sites eventually showed that Clovis points were older than Folsom points, and the discovery of many additional isolated finds and dozens of site excavations showed that whereas Folsom points were restricted to the Plains and Rocky Mountains, Clovis points occurred all across the lower 48 United States, northern Mexico, and parts of Canada that had become free of glacial ice near the end of the Pleistocene. David Anderson and Michael Faught's (1998) inventory of 11,257 Paleoindian projectile points found up through 1997 shows that a preponderance of them were found east of the Mississippi River, confirming a pattern already suspected over four decades ago (Mason 1962). The total is now over 13,000 and still growing, but the West is where they were first found and where the best dated finds are located (Figure 3.6).

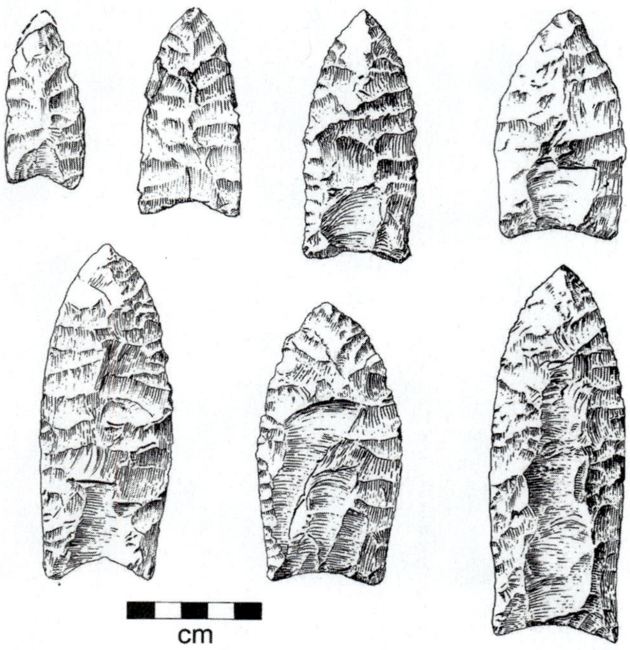

Looking at only these most reliable radiocarbon dates, from the securely dated sites of Lehner, Murray Springs, Domebo, Dent, and Anzick, Roosevelt and others argue that the Clovis components at these sites most likely date 11,100–10,850 BCE after **calibration** (Roosevelt et al. 2002:170). Other investigators argue that the true time range for Clovis is even narrower (Waters and Stafford 2007). Either of these options is considerably younger than the range advocated by some archaeologists (Fiedel 1999; Taylor et al. 1996:523). For now it is prudent to take a conservative approach.

Resolution of the dating of Paleoindian sites containing Clovis points is important because this is the most prominent and widespread of Paleoindian phenomena. It is also important to discover how it fits with the last gasp of the Pleistocene, the Younger Dryas cold spell (see Chapter 2). Generally colder conditions returned for about 13 centuries, calibrated to 10,850–9550 BCE. The spell began and ended abruptly, each time perhaps over the course of just a handful of years. But while it lasted it was an episode that conditioned human adaptation in ways that we do not yet fully understand (Alley et al. 2003; Taylor 1999). Clovis culture appears to have flourished during the warm episode just before the Younger Dryas, perhaps lasting into the early years of the cold spell. If one or the other of the younger ranges is correct then the rapid spread of Clovis culture across North America was something that occurred just before Younger Dryas began. This makes sense ecologically, for one should expect Clovis to have flourished when the climate was warming, not during a presumably more difficult cold episode. But we do not yet understand either the Younger Dryas or Paleoindian adaptation well enough to be sure.

Figure 3.5 Clovis fluted points from the Lehner site, Arizona, earlier and much more widespread than Folsom points.
Source: From Haury 1959:17. Reproduced by permission of the Society of American Archaeology from *American Antiquity* 25(1), 1959.

cm

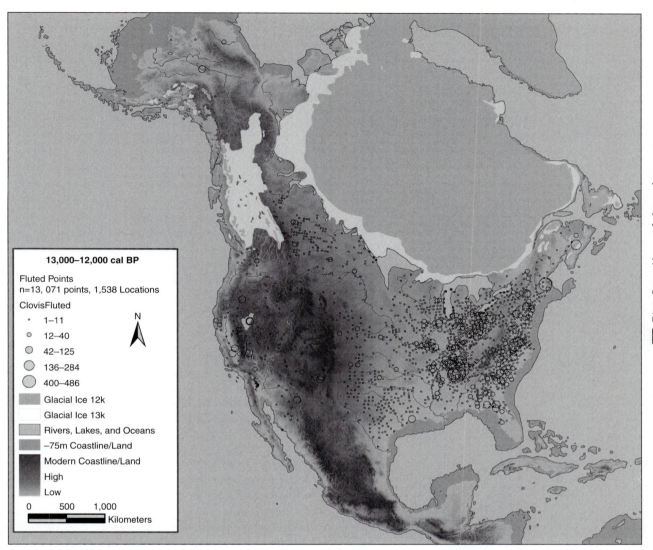

Figure 3.6 The distribution of Clovis points per 2,590 km² (1,000 mi²) in the United States.
Source: Courtesy of David Anderson et al (2005).

Tracking Paleoindians from Beringia

The origins of Clovis culture are the focus of archaeological attention because this is the first fully attested Paleoindian culture, and a crucial problem is how it might have descended from the early cultures of Beringia. Even though it is still not unequivocally dated at a large fraction of the sites where it has been found, Clovis culture is established as an archaeological phenomenon in the early human history of North America. Alternative hypotheses to explain how it might have derived from the early cultures of Beringia have been subject to contentious debate for many years. It was long thought most likely that population expansion southward from Beringia occurred after the Laurentian and Cordilleran ice sheets had melted back far enough to open a corridor through western Canada. This might have happened as early as 12,000 BCE (Hoffecker et al. 1993). Although the recently deglaciated landscape would have been a bleak place with many cold glacial lakes and just the beginnings of reforestation, this would have been early enough to accommodate the ancestors of Clovis Paleoindians.

Box 3.2 HOW TO VISIT PALEOINDIAN SITES

Most Paleoindian sites are on private or public lands that are closed to public access in order to protect their archaeological resources. A few are accessible on a scheduled basis and a few others are open to the public while excavations are in progress. The best way to find them is through your favorite Internet search engine.

Paleoindian sites are usually not much to look at. A few offer spectacular views of the surrounding countryside because they were situated where hunters could observe the movements of game animals. But even these sites contain few photogenic features. Artifacts are typically removed and on display in museums. The modern environment is almost never very much like that which Paleoindians were adjusting to when they selected a site, so going there will not often give the modern visitor a clear sense of place or purpose. Nevertheless, if the visitor works hard at it a visit to a Paleoindian site can yield useful insights. The following is a list of Paleoindian sites that are worth a visit:

- The Blackwater Locality No. 1 site is open to visitors April through October. It is located at 508 Highway 467, about eight miles north of Portales, New Mexico, one mile north of the Oasis State Park highway exit.
- The Topper site has been open to volunteers through the South Carolina Institute of Archaeology and Anthropology, but it is on private land and not open on a drop-in basis.
- Russell Cave in Alabama is a national monument that is maintained by the National Park Service. It is open daily year-round. The cave has yielded evidence of repeated occupations from the Paleoindian period down to the appearance of European settlers.

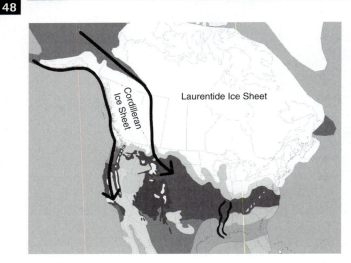

Figure 3.7 Possible migration routes from Beringia.

However, many archaeologists now argue that migration along the Pacific Coast (Figure 3.7) was also possible and perhaps a more likely scenario than expansion through a more hostile interior ice-free route (Ames and Maschner 1999:63; Busch 1994; Erlandson 1994, 2002). A major difficulty is that it is hard to find much archaeological evidence for coastal expansion because of rising post-Pleistocene sea levels.

There were pockets of unglaciated landscape along the Northwest Coast even at the height of Cordilleran glaciation. These were biological refugia, where plants and animals were isolated for centuries or even millennia.

The northern Queen Charlotte Islands and Prince of Wales Island of British Columbia were one such **refugium** (Warner et al. 1982). In addition, portions of the coastline along the Gulf of Alaska were deglaciated and probably supplied with driftwood by 12,000 BCE (Mann and Peteet 1994).

Some archaeologists have argued that an interior ice-free corridor would have afforded less wood and food than the coastal route. However, the speed at which the landscape around Mount St. Helens recovered after its 1980 explosion suggests that trees could have become established in the admittedly harsher ice-free corridor in a matter of a few centuries (Dale et al. 2005).

People elsewhere in the world had boats by this time, and the earliest Americans might well have had them as well. Yet a coastal route would not have been without its hazards. Malaspina glacier is an immense mountain glacier that still extends all the way to the ocean, where it stands as a 70-km-wide icy barrier to anyone trying to move south along the coast. Yet with sea levels substantially lower than today, boats presumably available, and stretches of unglaciated landscape for camps scattered along the coast, expansion along that route would have been possible.

The Nenana Complex Revisited

The Nenana complex in central Alaska is the current best candidate ancestral culture for Clovis culture, and its oldest sites are old enough to predate Clovis if the

Table 3.1 A very simplified comparative chronology for understanding the relationships between the complexes of Beringia and interior North America.

Years Ago (BP)	Years BCE	Climate	Beringia	Interior North America
10100 to 10000	8150 to 8050	Holocene	Denali	Folsom and other Late Paleoindian Cultures
10200 to 10100	8250 to 8150			
10300 to 10200	8350 to 8250			
10400 to 10300	8450 to 8350			
10500 to 10400	8550 to 8450			
10600 to 10500	8650 to 8550			
10700 to 10600	8750 to 8650			
10800 to 10700	8850 to 8750			
10900 to 10800	8950 to 8850			Clovis Culture (Early Paleoindian)
11000 to 10900	9050 to 8950			
11100 to 11000	9150 to 9050			
11200 to 11100	9250 to 9150			
11300 to 11200	9350 to 9250			
11400 to 11300	9450 to 9350		Mesa	
11500 to 11400	9550 to 9450			
11600 to 11500	9650 to 9550			
11700 to 11600	9750 to 9650	Younger Dryas		
11800 to 11700	9850 to 9750			
11900 to 11800	9950 to 9850			
12000 to 11900	10050 to 9950			Various Possible Pre-Clovis Sites
12100 to 12000	10150 to 10050		(uninhabited)	
12200 to 12100	10250 to 10150			
12300 to 12200	10350 to 10250			
12400 to 12300	10450 to 10350			
12500 to 12400	10550 to 10450			
12600 to 12500	10650 to 10550			
12700 to 12600	10750 to 10650			
12800 to 12700	10850 to 10750		Nenana	
12900 to 12800	10950 to 10850			
13000 to 12900	11050 to 10950			

11,100–10,850 BCE date range for Clovis is correct. Central Alaska was eastern Beringia when Nenana culture existed. The Nenana people made both triangular and lanceolate bifaces, but none of them were fluted (see Chapter 2).

Fluting is a diagnostic trait for Clovis and related Paleoindian points, and archaeologists have long sought an origin for it elsewhere. Curiously, a single fluted point is reported for the Uptar site near Magadan in Siberia. The point lacks the fine detail of most fluted Paleoindian points (Figure 3.8) and it is associated with other artifacts that as a group do not fit well with any of the other known tool complexes from Beringia. A single radiocarbon date is young compared to either Nenana or Clovis, so if anything the Siberian specimen is evidence of a flow of technology from America back to Siberia rather than evidence for a Siberian origin for fluting (King and Slobodin 1996). The longer we go without finding fluting in Siberia that

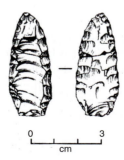

Figure 3.8 Fluted point from Uptar site, Siberia.
Source: From King and Slobodin 1996:635. Reprinted with permission from the American Association for the Advancement of Science.

predates Clovis, the more it looks like fluting was indeed an early American Indian innovation.

The Mesa Site

The Mesa site is located on the north slope of the Brooks Range, far to the northwest of the Nenana Valley in Alaska. Here another complex of bifaces, gravers, and scrapers provides further evidence of an early Paleoindian presence (Figure 3.9). The bifaces are lanceolate with concave bases, and while they are often thinned at their bases fluting is missing here as well. The radiocarbon dates for the Mesa site indicate that its occupation occurred mostly during the 1,430-year-long span of the Younger Dryas period from 10,850 to 9550 BCE, although part of the occupation predated that climatic episode. (Table 3.1) Dates from the Nenana complex in the Tanana Valley fall similarly into the time of the Younger Dryas, but dates from the Nenana complex in the Nenana Valley are older, similar to the older Mesa remains (Bever 2006). Thus the Nenana people might have been as much driven as attracted southward during the early years of the Younger Dryas, laying the foundation for Clovis culture far to the south. Environments offer both carrots and sticks, and over the long term the early human populations of Beringia necessarily responded rationally to both (Kunz and Reanier 1994).

Accommodating the Monte Verde Site

The derivation of Paleoindian technology from the Nenana complex of Beringia seems clear, but assumptions and conclusions of many kinds have been reopened by the Monte Verde site, the only early South American site to have achieved some measure of acceptance from archaeological critics (Dillehay 2008). The implications of Monte Verde are those of that rarely found single site that changes the way archaeologists understand the past. Tom Dillehay worked on the site for many years, excavating the remains of pole-frame huts that are preserved in the boggy sediments along Chinchihuapi Creek (Figure 3.10). Wet sites preserve wood, bone, fiber, and other materials that would normally decay by preventing oxygen from reaching them. Of course, stone tools and other more durable artifacts are also preserved. Downstream from the huts Dillehay found mastodon bones, animal skin, worked wood, and the remains of plants used for food and medicine. There was much more, and the richness of the site

Figure 3.9 Projectile points from the Mesa site. *Source:* From Kunz and Reanier 1994:661. Reprinted with permission from the American Association for the Advancement of Science.

would have made news in the archaeological world no matter what its age. However, when Dillehay (2000) started receiving unexpectedly early radiocarbon dates from dating labs there was more than the usual amount of interest.

A dozen senior archaeologists traveled to Monte Verde in 1997 to take a hard look at the site and the evidence, just as another team had done decades earlier at the Folsom site. The team remained skeptical about any claim for more ancient human occupation, but most team members agreed that an age of about 10,500 BCE for the site appeared to be supported by the evidence (Gibbons 1997; Meltzer 1997).

The evidence from Monte Verde has to be considered in light of what we know about the demography

Figure 3.10 The Monte Verde site.
Source: Courtesy of Tom D. Dillehay.

of hunter-gatherer bands. It is clear from everything we know about how human beings behave that migration to the Americas could not have been accomplished by a small number of people moving far and fast. Bands of hunters require connections with related bands if they are to find suitable marriage mates and maintain lifelines to other bands through periods of food shortage (Anderson and Gillam 2000, 2001; Moore and Moseley 2001). We can infer from archaeological evidence alone that the bands that moved into Alaska sometime around or before 12,000 BCE were not large, and their economy probably forced them to live as dispersed from each other as their vital but attenuated mutual connections would allow. Simulations have shown that left alone a band of a few dozen people will tend to dwindle to extinction in a matter of a few centuries (Moore and Moseley 2001; Wobst 1974). The lucky ones have more girl babies than boys, a ratio that favors long-term survival, but even lucky bands do not remain lucky forever. As the accidents of birth and death played out, bands split, joined, waxed and waned, repackaging as circumstances required. Thus even an expanding population of hunters and gatherers that multiply band numbers when large bands split or daughter bands hive off will not expand too far or too fast for connections between them to be too attenuated or even severed. The closest thing to long-term security was preserved in those connections (MacDonald and Hewlett 1999). So how can we explain the appearance of hunters at the Monte Verde site in South America before the rise of Clovis culture in North America?

In a new environment with plenty of food, even small hunting bands can realize rapid growth. Under favorable conditions populations can easily double every century. Such an increase will produce population densities that cannot be sustained for long by a hunting and gathering population, so there will always be pressure for bands to spread out farther and farther while maintaining at least some mutual contacts. Population growth at the center of an expanding population will often produce leapfrogging, as bands move though occupied territory to unoccupied (by humans) lands (Anderson and Gillam 2000). Because there were no competing human bands to resist this process in America 14 millennia ago, the process could have been steady and rapid even though it must have lacked the frenzied character of historic land rushes.

We can be reasonably certain that Nenana and other complexes were present in central Alaska at least a thousand years earlier than a 10,500 BCE occupation of Monte Verde (Bever 2006:611). Is it plausible to conclude that expansion of that founder population could have filled two continents in only a thousand years? Under favorable circumstances a population of hunter-gatherers could double every generation, that is, every 20–30 years. But such a rapid rate of expansion might not be sustainable over the long term, even under the most favorable circumstances, like a warming continental landscape empty of other humans but teeming with naïve game. Let us assume then that the population doubled only once a century. It turns out that even at that modest rate a founding population of only 100 people would expand to over a million in only a thousand years.

But what about the available space? Would an expanding population of Paleoindians distribute themselves evenly across two continents, like gas escaping into a vacuum? The answer is that they would certainly not do that for reasons just reviewed. They would continue to cluster in small bands in which the bonds of marriage, parenting, and mutual support were strong. New bands that formed as numbers grew, old people died, and old bands split usually would have stayed in close enough contact to allow emergency support, occasional cooperative hunting, exchange of goods, access to marriage partners, and so forth. Even the small mobile bands that moved into Beringia from Siberia required such minimal social networks. But here again even if the number of bands doubled only once a century there would have been over 10,000 of them in a millennium, and the limited availability of resources would have forced them to spread out.

Monte Verde (Figure 3.10) is over 15,000 km south, which seems like a daunting distance even today. But that amounts to only 150 km (93 mi) per century. Put that way distance too seems to be within range of the possible. Nevertheless, archaeologists who take

Monte Verde's 10,500 BCE date seriously find themselves drawn to the Pacific Coast alternative when the subject of routes comes up. If the earliest population expansion was adapted to a coastal environment, then a rapid spread of humans southward along first the edge of North America and then South America makes Monte Verde seem much less far-fetched. Paleoindians could have reached southern South America before they expanded into the interior of North America.

Interest has also been stimulated by the work of linguists who have found languages scattered all around the Pacific rim that share some fundamental traits. Some have also found connections between languages at much deeper time levels by studying sound systems and grammar rather than comparative vocabularies (Dunn et al. 2005; Nichols 2002; Nichols and Peterson 1996). This may be further evidence for an early founder population that spread southward along the Pacific Coast, but archaeologists accustomed to hard data and rigorous radiocarbon dating are skeptical of linguistic evidence.

Archaeologists continue to argue over the details (Anderson and Gillam 2000, 2001; Moore and Moseley 2001), but few appear to be particularly troubled in principle by the dating of the Monte Verde site in Chile to 10,500 BCE (Fiedel 1999; Haynes 1999).

Sites on the California Coast

The evidence from Daisy Cave, California, suggests that early Paleoindians had seaworthy boats that were sufficient to allow them to get around barriers (Rick et al. 2001). Daisy Cave is on San Miguel Island, one of the Channel Islands off the coast of southern California. San Miguel was an island even during the Late Pleistocene, when sea levels were lower, but not low enough to provide a bridge to the mainland. To reach the closest of the Channel Islands one must cross at least 19 km of open ocean, and San Miguel lies even farther out. Daisy Cave (Figure 3.11) was occupied by people exploiting the rich maritime environment 9550–6550 BCE, so the site tells us that boats and fishing were in use at least that long ago.

Coastal environments also offer the best of the terrestrial and marine worlds. They are typically rich environments, offering offshore fishing, migratory fish runs in estuaries, sea mammals, large bird populations, terrestrial game, plant foods, and shellfish to name just the most obvious resources. The residents of Daisy Cave took more than half their diet from fishing, and their gear included the earliest evidence known for

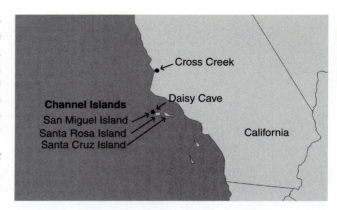

Figure 3.11 Early archaeology on the southern California coast.

hook-and-line fishing. The evidence clearly shows that early North Americans already had seaworthy boats, nets, fishhooks, leisters, and other sophisticated technology for exploiting the rich maritime resources of the West Coast (Rick et al. 2001:609).

North of San Miguel Island, on the mainland California coast, the Cross Creek site contains evidence of a maritime economy dating to 8350–6700 BCE. It boasts the oldest known mainland shell midden on the West Coast, as well as milling stones and food remains that point to a gathering economy. The excavators argue that it is very unlikely that Cross Creek could have been the site of interior hunters who readapted quickly to a coastal environment. It is much more likely that the site is further evidence of an earlier spread of maritime people down the Pacific Coast (Erlandson and Colten 1991; Erlandson et al. 2007; Jones 2002).

Clovis Culture

At least some of the people who descended from Nenana culture probably expanded from interior Alaska through the ice-free corridor sometime after around 12,000 BCE. By that time birch and other trees were colonizing recently deglaciated interior landscapes. The transition from Nenana to Clovis required only the innovation of the fluted point (Goebel et al. 1991; Hoffecker et al. 1993). This might have occurred as an adaptation to big game hunting, but archaeologists are hard put to demonstrate that fluting was a technologically significant innovation. Experiments have revealed that it confers no particular advantage in either hafting or killing power (Adovasio and Pedler 2005). Thus fluting may well have been produced not as a technological response to environmental conditions, but as a function of that other side of human adaptation, the human capacity for and love of the impractical.

Clovis points were often made of high-grade cherts that came from quarries far distant from the locations where the finished points fell into the archaeological record. For example, Clovis points made from bright red eastern Pennsylvania jasper, a form of chert, were found 250 km to the north on the West Athens Hill site in New York's Hudson Valley. The lack of chipping debris of the same material at West Athens Hills tells us that they were brought in as finished points, not made there from imported raw jasper (Funk 2004). Similarly, Clovis points found on the Shoop site in central Pennsylvania were made from high-quality Onondaga chert from central New York State.

Clovis knappers generally made points from the finest materials they could obtain, knapped them with care, supplied them with flutes that were at once unnecessary and almost impossibly difficult to produce, and valued them highly. Perhaps we can understand what was going on only by referring to analogies among modern human cultures, including our own. What we are seeing in this case is evidence of the human pursuit of excellence, the production of highly valued objects, and their use as both tools and gifts. Hunter-gatherers living in mobile bands typically couch exchange as gift giving rather than trade. People living in small-scale societies often share food and other resources freely, for in the long run there is much greater advantage in sharing than in hoarding, although the specific mechanisms are more complex than that statement might imply (Hawkes 1993). Moreover, gifts constantly renew social bonds, as anyone ever invited to a wedding knows. A gift given or a favor done today might not be reciprocated for years, but it creates the kind of obligation that holds societies together.

It is not possible to say where the fluting innovation occurred, but Clovis points are more numerous east of the Mississippi than west of it, further evidence that it is probably not an idea imported from Siberia. The sudden appearance of Clovis culture around 11,100 BCE, and its rapid adaptive radiation across much of interior North America might need no more complex explanation than that, except that a secondary question remains. Did fluted points spread as the population of people making them grew and expanded across the continent, or did the technique spread independent of population spread, as knappers trained each other in the technique? It is revealing that modern knappers that have rediscovered and mastered the difficult technique of fluting are very proud of their work, and that their points sell for high prices. In fact it is

Figure 3.12 One of the first models proposed for Clovis expansion was Paul Martin's wave advance hypothesis. Martin assumed that the Clovis population grew and spread rapidly, wiping out Pleistocene game as it advanced across the continent.

likely that a fairly large percentage of the fluted points in the antiquities market are modern fakes. Most archaeologists appear to have not thought about this question very much. Instead many of us have silently assumed that the Clovis points spread as the population carrying them fanned out across the continent. This might be due to the durable influence of Paul Martin's wave advance hypothesis (Figure 3.12) of the peopling of North America by Clovis hunters (Martin 1967, 1973). This hypothesis is at least consistent with the sudden appearance of Clovis points. But the widespread distribution of Clovis points and the brief four-century period in which they were made seems more consistent with the second hypothesis. Clovis points have all the attributes of a fad, probably America's first really big one. It was gloriously impractical, as many of the most interesting human accomplishments often are, and so was its replication in the late twentieth century. But if the second hypothesis were the better one we would expect to see evidence of preexisting cultures taking up the new fad, and that is not what we see in the archaeological record (Figure 3.13). The debate remains unresolved (Meltzer 1995).

The rest of Clovis culture reveals that Clovis people did much more than make beautiful projectile points (Frison and Bradley 1999; Haynes 2002). The weapons they tipped were often complicated composite spears that were designed to be both efficient and deadly. The Anzick site in Montana produced a burial that was accompanied by beveled foreshafts that were designed to hold fluted points and to fit atop longer, heavier spear shafts. If they were detachable (and it is not certain that they were) the hunter could have

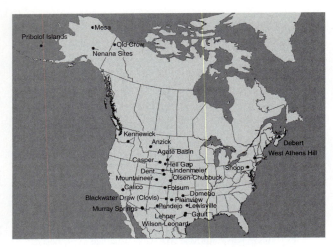

Figure 3.13 Paleoindian sites mentioned in the chapter.

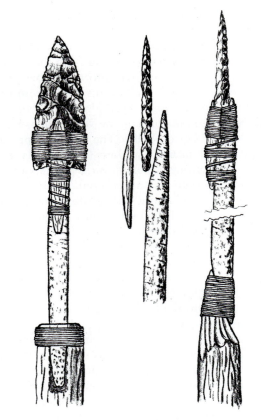

Figure 3.14 Reconstructed foreshaft and projectile point composites from the Anzick site, Montana.
Source: From Lahren and Bonnichsen 1974:149, Fig. 3. Reprinted with permission from the American Association for the Advancement of Science.

carried several foreshafts, each with a fluted point firmly lashed in place (Figure 3.14), which he could then use to reload a used spear. If that was the tactic, then the points and foreshafts were designed to stay inside a wounded animal while the spear was refitted and reused. Even the relatively light spears (or darts) used with spear throwers were heavy enough to limit the number a hunter could carry easily, so being able to use them repeatedly was an advantage. Detachable foreshafts would have improved upon this by allowing the hunter to carry more points without having to increase and perhaps even decrease the load of heavy shafts (Lahren and Bonnichsen 1974).

But contrary to that interpretation is the observation that all lanceolate points lack barbs to hold them inside a wounded animal. Perhaps lightly equipped mobile hunters wanted to be able to wound an animal and recover the entire spear, foreshaft, and point quickly in order to use the weapon again.

Their subsistence included hunting, but they were not exclusively big game hunters. Everything about them suggests that these were people who were doing their best to stay as flexible as they were mobile in a period of rapid and dramatic environmental change (Tankersley 1998). The type site at Blackwater Draw established that Clovis hunters exploited mammoths at least some of the time. Protein residues on Clovis weapons found in southern Alberta reveal that they were also using them to hunt horses and either bison or muskoxen (Kooyman et al. 2001). Clovis people camped at the Debert, West Athens Hill, and Shoop sites in the Northeast were probably intercepting herds of caribou. But these were only their most obvious subsistence activities. They also must have hunted many smaller animal species such as rabbits and hares, and harvested a limited range of plants they were familiar with (Cannon and Meltzer 2004). The Gault site in Texas has revealed that they were using birds, turtles, frogs, and antelopes as well as large game. Not all viable food resources are obvious, and some that may seem to be are poisonous. It would take many centuries for the environment to stabilize and for the descendants of Paleoindians to learn how best to use everything it had to offer.

A rare foundation ring, 5 m (16 ft) in diameter, at the Mountaineer site in Colorado, shows that later Paleoindians sheltered in temporary structures capable of holding more than just single families (Stiger 2006).

Labor was probably divided much as it typically has been among more modern hunter-gatherers, largely along lines of sex and age. Everyone had a range of skills and tasks, and the band's survival depended upon a complementary mix of individuals. Tailored skins, without which no one could survive even the milder winters, required slender needles and clever tanning techniques. Needles were made from bone or antler, which in turn had to be worked using specialized *pièces esquillées,* gravers, burins, and scrapers to split, wedge, and carve the tough materials. These in turn required deft knapping techniques and sources of good-quality cherts.

Fire was a tool that these people undoubtedly controlled, and it might have been used in ways that are hard to appreciate today. Deliberate firing of the landscape often produces new growth of edible plants that can be consumed directly by people but that also attract large herbivores. Fire can also be used to drive game over cliffs or into wetlands where they can be killed more easily. Use of fire at such a large scale was common in the last millennium and there is no reason to think that Paleoindians did not employ it as well. The general warming and drying of the environment would have made fire easier to use if not easier to control than previously, and there is some evidence for it in the cores pulled from lake and bog sediments by palynologists (Kerr 2003). All of this means that by 9000 BCE the landscape of North America was already starting to become an **anthropogenic** one, shaped in part by human activity, and it has been so ever since. The brief historic episode of wilderness that separates the widespread epidemic depopulation of some regions of the continent from their repopulation by Euroamerican settlers was a short-term anomaly (Anderson and Blackburn 1993). The wilderness that we love and protect today is in many cases new to America since 1492.

Clovis bands lived in almost every part of North America south of the glacial ice and north of highland Mexico. Fluted points and other diagnostics of Paleoindians occur in interior California, but they occur only very rarely along the coast (Jones et al. 2002:227). While older sources speculate that the Milling Stone culture of California evolved out of some variant of Clovis culture, it now seems more likely that it goes all the way back to the arrival of California's earliest coastal inhabitants.

In the East they pushed all the way to the coast, and probably beyond its current stand to shorelines now deeply submerged. The Debert site of Nova Scotia lies so far north that its occupants would have felt the chill of air spilling down the face of the retreating glacier only a few kilometers distant. Far to the south other Clovis people were enjoying the warmer climes of what was then a much broader west coast of Florida. It was a successful adaptation, but as always in human history it was a temporary one, and things were about to change.

Pulling back to view Clovis culture at broader scale, one can see that there was a structure above the band level, but that it was not one that would be familiar to modern political scientists. Bands interacted with neighboring bands, exchanging prized artifacts, providing marriage partners for each other, cooperating in collective hunts, and bailing each other out of trouble in hard times. For any particular band there were probably on average about six surrounding bands that were closely related and with whom members of the home band interacted from time to time. We can use the term "connubium" (see Chapter 1) to refer to this larger social unit (Williams 1974).

Consider Figure 3.15, which shows an imaginary landscape having 16 bands. Each band is the center of its own connubium, although only 7 connubia are shown here as large circles. Notice that band A has band B within the orbit of its connubium. However, band B has its own connubium along with 6 other bands. Band A is one of them, but there are also 3 other bands in band B's connubium that are outside the ring of band A's connubium. Similarly, band A had connections with 3 bands that band B might never contact. The point here is that larger Paleoindian social units were overlapping abstractions, not bounded mutually exclusive things. Were it not for mountain ranges and large rivers the fabric of this kind of thin indivisible landscape of social connectedness could have extended all across North America during the Paleoindian period. It persisted for as long as the population remained thin and mutual interdependence remained indispensable.

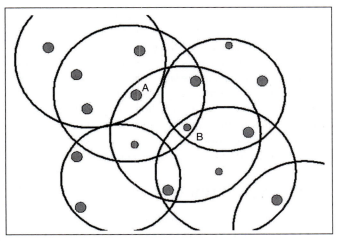

Figure 3.15 Bands and connubia.

The Atlantic Alternative

The Atlantic Alternative is an old and largely forgotten hypothesis for Clovis origins that has recently been revived by Dennis Stanford. He argues that Clovis points and other tools in the Clovis complex could have derived from the Solutrean culture of Upper Paleolithic France and Spain. The two tool complexes are remarkably similar, and it is tempting to speculate about a possible connection, but the evidence arrayed against the hypothesis is formidable. Dental, genetic, and linguistic evidence all point to northeast Asia, not Europe. If Solutreans made it to North America they left no clear genetic mark on American Indian heritage.

Solutrean founders would have had to come by sea across the Atlantic, something no one else accomplished until the Norse a mere thousand years ago. Although we now know that humans must have had boats of some sort by 14,000 BCE, there is no evidence that they had oil lamps and other advanced technology that they would have needed to skirt the vast northern Atlantic ice pack. The more recent Inuits survived in such an environment, but only because they had the means to hunt sea mammals and to render their blubber for heat, light, and cooking.

If Solutreans followed the currents on a more southerly route, like Columbus, at least some of them also would have landed in the Canary Islands. The archaeology of those islands yields nothing to indicate that people have lived there for more than a few thousand years.

Solutreans would also have needed a time machine, for which there is also no evidence. They thrived in southwestern Europe 22–17,000 BCE, evolving into something else more than 5,000 years before the advent of Clovis. This is a gap even harder to leap than the Atlantic. Bifaces similar to Clovis and lacking only flutes were made in Beringia just before Clovis, and in Siberia just before that. We need look no farther afield to find the hypothesis that is both more economical and covers all the known facts.

What the similarities between Solutrean and Clovis really tell us is that there are only a limited number of ways to make effective chipped-stone points for spears that are designed to be propelled by spear throwers. It also reminds us that human ingenuity is such that good ideas can occur more than once when circumstances favor them, and indeed they often do (Straus et al. 2005).

The Great Extinction

Several dozen genera of **megafauna** went extinct at the end of the Pleistocene, some around the time that human hunters added themselves to the ecological equation, and researchers have debated the possible role of human hunters for several decades. No scientist doubts that there was an episode of wholesale extinctions in America at the end of the Pleistocene. Seventy-three percent of the large herbivore species present during the Late Pleistocene went extinct by the early Holocene, and many researchers have long suspected Paleoindians to have been the culprits. The archaeological evidence is scanty; only a few sites show conclusively that humans were hunting species that subsequently dwindled to extinction. A hard-nosed empirical approach to the problem, coupled with standard scientific skepticism, has led many leading archaeologists to doubt that Paleoindians could have been the major factor in Late Pleistocene extinctions. However, new evidence and computer simulations have swung opinion back and forth in recent years (Fiedel and Haynes 2004; Grayson and Meltzer 2003; Martin 1999).

Most of the reliably dated extinctions in Table 3.2 occurred before or during the Younger Dryas, and probably during the heyday of Clovis or later Paleoindians. There are a few sites that show that Paleoindians were hunting mammoths, horses, bison (extinct form), mastodons (Figure 3.16 & 3.17), and giant tortoises, in addition to prey species that still survive, but that evidence alone is not sufficient to make a strong case for humans having been responsible for their extinction. On the other hand, we should not expect to easily find lots of sites showing clear evidence of Paleoindians killing large mammals that are now extinct. The problem is finding a way to avoid arguing from negative evidence.

Hunters nearly drove the modern bison (Figure 3.18) to extinction by the twentieth century, reducing them from around 30 million to fewer than 1,000 (Isenberg 2000). There are photographs of great heaps of their skulls and others of landscapes strewn with their corpses, but a millennium from now there might be little in the archaeological record to document the carnage. Because archaeological preservation can be so spotty, situations like this require the application of generally accepted theory, and the development of computer simulations that can mimic the playing out of processes like continental extinctions at large scale. They also require the organization of data, as in the online Faunmap database, as well as careful dating.

Paul Martin (1967, 1973) was the first to attempt to model the impact of Clovis people on the megafauna of North America at large scale. His 1973 article outlined a scenario in which an expanding wave of Clovis bands advanced across North America, its human population concentrated along the wave front that obliterated large game animals as it advanced. Expanding out of southern Canada it reached an arc connecting

Table 3.2 Extinct Late Pleistocene mammalian genera in North America. (Grayson 1991:195, 208; Martin 1967) Most recent calibrated reliable radiocarbon dates where known. All dates are 1 sigma ranges, in some cases covering multiple intercepts, expressed as calendar years BCE. Some mammoths held out longer on certain islands. (Guthrie 2004)

Order	Family	Genus	Common Name	Extinction Date (BCE)		
Xenarthra	Dasypodidae	Pampatherium	Southern pampathere			
		Holmesina	Northern pampathere			
	Glyptodontidae	Glyptotherium	Simpson's glyptodont			
	Megalonychidae	Megalonyx	Jefferson's ground sloth	12522	–	11840
	Megatheriidae	Eremotherium	Rusconi's ground sloth			
		Nothrotheriops	Shasta ground sloth	10087	–	9283
	My lodontidae	Glossotherium	Harlan's ground sloth	23371	–	22046
Carnivora	Mustelidae	Brachyprotoma	Short-faced skunk			
	Canidae	Cuon	Dhole			
	Ursidae	Tremarctos	Florida cave bear			
		Arctodus	Giant short-faced bear			
	Felidae	Smilodon	Sabertooth cat	11324	–	10896
		Homotherium	Scimitar cat			
		Miracinonyx	American cheetah			
Rodentia	Castoridae	Castoroides	Giant beaver			
	Hydrochoeridae	Hydrochoerus	Holmes's capybara			
		Neochoerus	Pinckney's capybara			
Lagomorpha	Leporidae	Aztlanolagus	Aztlan rabbit			
Perissodactyla	Equidae	Equus	Horses	10803	–	9761
	Tapiridae	Tapirus	Tapirs	11326	–	10218
Artiodactyla	Tayassuidae	Mylohyus	Long-nosed peccary			
		Platygonus	Flat-headed peccary			
	Camelidae	Camelops	Yesterday's camel	11326	–	10218
		Hemiauchenia	Large-headed llama			
		Palaeolama	Stout-legged llama	11023	–	10840
	Carvidae	Navahoceros	Mountain deer			
		Cervalces	Elk-moose			
	Antilocapridae	Capromeryx	Diminutive pronghorn			
		Tetrameryx	Shuler's pronghorn			
		Stockoceros	Pronghorn			
	Bovidae	Saiga	Saiga			
		Euceratherium	Shrub ox			
		Bootherium	Harlan's musk ox			
Proboscidea	Mammutidae	Mammut	American mastodon	10630	–	10128
	Elephantidae	Mammuthus	Mammoths	10922	–	9887

modern San Francisco, Denver, and Minneapolis in 180 years (Figure 3.12). It reached northern Mexico and the Gulf Coast after another 170 years, passing down the funnel of Mesoamerica and into South America after just another 220 years. The less dense human population behind the wave front mopped up the surviving remnants of megafauna, and it was all over in less than six centuries. This neat scenario was greeted with the usual skepticism from professional archaeologists.

John Alroy (2001a) more recently carried out a more sophisticated computer simulation of the effects of human predation on 41 prey species. He assumed slow human population growth and hunting pressures that were both random and low in intensity. The simulation correctly predicted the rapid extinction or survival of 32 out of the 41 species included in the study. His findings were criticized on archaeological grounds by Donald Grayson (2001), and on technical grounds by Richard Slaughter and Joseph Skulan (2001), but Alroy countered all of the criticisms and stands by his findings. Revisions to the simulation program that were prompted by the criticisms actually improved the results, leading Alroy to conclude that "standard ecological theory shows that these factors lead inexorably

Figure 3.16 Mastodons.
Source: Courtesy of the New York State Museum.

Figure 3.17 Przewalski's horses. These Asian horses, which probably resemble extinct American horses, are now all but extinct in the wild.
Source: (c) Image by © Han Chuanhao/XinHua/Xinhua Press/CORBIS. All Rights Reserved.

Figure 3.18 Modern bison.
Source: Courtesy of the New York State Museum.

to strong apparent competition, and therefore to mass extinction" (Alroy 2001b:1462).

Alroy's simulation accurately predicted the fates of 78% of the 41 species he considered. The 9 that the simulation missed include 6 that it predicted would survive but did not, and 3 that it predicted would go extinct that actually have survived.

We have known for a long time that the larger animals were more vulnerable to extinction than smaller game like deer and elk. It is no surprise that simply pre-

dicting that any species having an average weight over 180 kg (397 lbs) would go extinct predicts 73% of the known extinctions, a record almost as good as Alroy's complex simulation.

It turns out that while animals larger than us are scary, they are vulnerable to multiple risks. Environmental factors drive extinction risk for species whose individuals weigh less than 3 kg (7 lbs), but larger ones are at risk for both environmental and various inherent reasons (Cardillo et al. 2005). For example, consider the risk a large, slowly reproducing species would face if a new predator were able to selectively remove vulnerable young members of the herd. Repeated removal of the next generation is how nineteenth-century hunters drove passenger pigeons to extinction; they chopped down the trees in which the gregarious pigeons concentrated their nests, harvesting thousands of flightless squabs for the restaurant market. Killing off the next generation year after year extinguishes the whole population even if no adults are killed; the adults simply all die of old age and there are insufficient younger ones to take their places. It is not impossible that such a fate befell some of the large Pleistocene game.

Some large animals managed to survive longer than others, and in at least one case they did so by rapidly evolving to smaller sizes. Pygmy mammoths survived for a time on the Channel Islands (Santarosae) off southern California, miniaturized by evolutionary forces as species confined to islands often are. This might suggest that the islands were connected to the mainland by a land bridge when Pleistocene sea levels were at a low level and that the mammoths got trapped there when the water rose. But the absence of other common terrestrial animals on the islands and the depth of the water around them indicate that no land bridge to them ever existed. Because elephants are known to swim long distances, a better inference is that the ancestors of the pygmy mammoths swam across to the islands, a distance never less than 6.5 km (4 mi)(Johnson 1978, 1980). There they remained until either with human predation or without it they expired.

Mammoths were extinct on mainland Alaska by 9300 BCE, although stranded individuals persisted on the Pribolof and Wrangel Islands until around 2000 BCE, when much later people carrying the Arctic Small Tool tradition might have reached them (Guthrie 2004).

No one doubts the coincidence of the appearance of humans and the extinction of large animals in North America (Barnowsky et al. 2004:71). The problem is that it was also coincident with rapid climate change, which also must have been a factor. To counter that argument the overkill proponents tell us to consider all the other similar coincidences around the world, many of which happened at times when climate was not changing. Australia's large animals disappeared about 46,000 years ago, very near the time that people showed up (Miller et al. 2005; Roberts et al. 2001). Large animals disappeared abruptly from islands such as Cyprus, Madagascar, New Zealand, and the West Indies coincident with the arrival of humans regardless of long-term climate trends (Diamond 1997:42–47; Steadman 1995).

The bottom line is that empirical scientific archaeologists accustomed to working from site-specific data remain skeptical of the hypothesized role of humans in the widespread extinctions of large animals. Ecologists who work at larger scale, often with complex computer models, are much more inclined to see the hand of humankind in the extinctions (Flannery 2001).

Even while the debate drives some of the participants to polarized opinions, a more nuanced explanation is beginning to emerge. Several lines of evidence coming together now indicate that humans contributed to extinctions in many places but were not solely responsible for it everywhere. Extinctions took place regionally and at different times, the result of both climatic stresses and the effects of humans as an invasive species (Barnowsky et al. 2004). For example, the Beringian steppe bison was declining in numbers 37,000 years ago, 10,000 years before any human hunters reached its habitat. It may be that people delivered the *coup de grace*, but that is not the same as attributing the extinction to them alone (Shapiro et al. 2004). Similarly, horses were under stress and declining in average body size before extinction in some regions, quite independent from human predation (Guthrie 2003).

Further research on extinctions will probably take new and unexpected directions, and it will likely not focus on forcing a choice between two oversimplified hypotheses. For example, the microscopic spores of a fungus that was adapted to live in mastodon dung disappear from bog sediment cores just as microscopic charcoal flecks sharply increase (Kerr 2003). Is the charcoal evidence of deliberate human firing of the landscape or the natural consequence of lighting in a warmer and drier postglacial environment? Questions like this one will drive future research.

Paleoindian Skeletal Evidence

The number of individual Paleoindians found to date is small, but even this meager sample indicates that they did not necessarily look like modern American Indians. There are about a dozen and a half sites that have yielded skeletal remains of anonymous Paleoindians or their early descendants, and more that are still being evaluated. Table 3.3 provides a simplified listing and sources that can be consulted for more complete descriptions.

Various studies have been carried out on different sets of remains from the list in Table 3.3. Some of the studies also include more recent remains from other sites. These studies have repeatedly noted that Paleoindians were physically similar to some modern populations in eastern Eurasia, but that they were not as similar to modern American Indians as many had expected. The ancestors of Paleoindians might have

Table 3.3 Paleoindian Skeletal Finds That Are Generally Accepted as Authentic

Site	State/Prov.	Number of Individuals	Reference
Anzick/Wilsal	MT	2	(Steele and Powell 1993; Taylor 1969)
Arlington Spring	CA	1	(Protsch 1978)
Brown's Valley	MN	1	(Jantz and Owsley 2001; Myster and O'Connell 1997)
Buhl	ID	1	(Green, et al. 1998)
Fishbone Cave	NV	1	(Orr 1974)
Gordon Creek	CO	1	(Swedlund and Anderson 1999)
Horn Shelter	TX	2	(Young 1985, 1986; Young, et al. 1987)
Kennewick	WA	1	(Chatters 2001)
Marmes Rockshelter	WA	10	(Sheppard, et al. 1987)
Mostin	CA	1	(Young 1986)
Sloan	AR	1	(Morse 1997)
Spirit Cave	NV	1	(Dansie 1997; Jantz and Owsley 1997, 2001)
Sulphur Spring	AZ	2	(Waters and 1986)
Warm Mineral Spring	FL	21	(Doran 2002:33; Lien 1983)
White Water Draw	AZ	2	(Steele and Powell 2002)
Wilson-Leonard II	TX	1	(Weir 1985)
Wizards Beach	NV	1	(Dansie 1997; Jantz and Owsley 1997, 2001)

been from local Siberian populations that did not yet have the Asian characteristics of modern American Indians. Alternatively, later gene flow could have altered the American population, just as evolutionary forces might have. These problems remain unresolved (Jantz and Owsley 2001; Steele and Powell 2002).

It is important to remember that ancestry doubles with every generation, and while every person alive today has an extremely large number of ancestors, any individual who lived long ago may have either many descendants or none at all. The founder effect is a biological phenomenon wherein those lucky enough (or well adapted enough) to leave many descendants thereby determine the makeup of the descendant population. Those who were unlucky or less well adapted and consequently left no descendants contributed no genes to the descendant population. The founder effect is one of several factors to be kept in mind when comparing ancient skeletal remains to presumed modern descendant populations.

The skeletal differences between most Paleoindians and modern American Indians leapt into the news with the discovery of the Kennewick skeleton in 1996. Because it lacked some classic American Indian features, James Chatters initially thought the remains might have been those of a Euroamerican settler. Only later when radiocarbon dating indicated that the remains dated to around the end of the Paleoindian period did Chatters realize that his tentative identification had been in error. By that time the newspapers had declared the remains to be "Caucasian." Popular logic led many readers to conclude that Europeans had been present on the Columbia River before 6000 BCE. A less exciting but more likely conclusion is that Kennewick was an early American Indian, who like most others before 5000 BCE did not look like a typical modern American Indian.

The End of the Paleoindian Period

Clovis culture and the Folsom culture that descended from it both came and went quickly. Until recently the precise dating of Clovis and more recent Folsom sites has been difficult because the relevant radiocarbon dates fell beyond the limits of calibration. Now that even these dates can be calibrated it appears that Clovis culture not only spread rapidly, it waned even more quickly. Clovis culture probably came and went in only four centuries, and the transition from Clovis to Folsom might have taken only a century or even less. If the calibrated dates for Folsom are correct, this late Paleoindian variant came and went around 10,900–9900 BCE, overlapping the earlier Clovis time span (Taylor et al. 1996).

The ecological **niche** that was occupied by Clovis culture was broadly defined. Their adaptation was a general one compared to what came later, exactly what we should expect for a human culture adapting to an environment that was at once unfamiliar and still changing. As Clovis bands became more familiar with their local environments they began to differentiate from one another. This must have pervaded all parts of their culture, from language to technology. Where we can observe it, of course, is mainly in the durable parts of their technology that have survived in the ground. Fluted points diversified from standard Clovis forms to a variety of regional types, which archaeologists have given names like Cumberland, Neponset, Nicholas, and Folsom.

Folsom points are the most famous of the derivative fluted points. They are confined to the Great Plains and probably best known at the Lindenmeier site in Colorado. Folsom culture persisted until around 9900 BCE, a few centuries before the Younger Dryas cold spell ended and the Holocene began. The pattern of monsoonal rains that had watered the Plains changed with the onset of the Holocene, disrupting established human adaptations (Lovvorn et al. 2001; Mann and Meltzer 2007). Complex patterns of air circulation and precipitation produced other results in other areas, but on the High Plains generally warmer conditions caused Paleoindians to split into two adaptive modes. Those living in the foothills of the Rocky Mountains soldiered on, surviving over the long term by diversifying their subsistence to exploit plants and what animals remained after the largest of them became extinct. Those living on the open plains were dependent upon bison herds after the extinction of other large mammals. Bison kills declined after 6000 BCE and human habitation of the High Plains nearly ended between then and 3000 BCE except for summer forays from the margins of this forsaken landscape (Lovvorn et al. 2001; Meltzer 1999).

Elsewhere across North America other Late Paleoindian cultures that were derivative from Clovis also appeared as Holocene climate became established. Fluting was dropped as a knapping technique in most areas, although the production of finely made lanceolate points continued (Figure 3.19). Several unfluted lanceolate point types, such as Plainview and Agate Basin, are often lumped together and called Plano points. In other areas knappers shifted to stemmed forms, all changes that probably say as much about fashion as technology.

The Agate Basin and Plainview are named after key type sites having the same names. There are many other interesting sites dating to this era, but they are too numerous to mention more than a couple here. The Casper site in central Wyoming is a bison kill site in which Hell Gap points predominate (Frison 1974; Gibbon 1998:356). South of Casper in southeastern Colorado, the Olsen-Chubbock site documents the mass killing of nearly 200 individuals of a now extinct form of bison. The animals were stampeded into an

Figure 3.19 The distribution of late unfluted Paleoindian point types.
Source: From Meltzer et al. 2002:42.

arroyo, where the panicked creatures trampled each other to death while hunters picked off the survivors from above. No hunting band could make use of that much meat, and analysis of their butchering techniques revealed that only the choicest cuts (especially tongues) were removed from the carcasses at the bottom of the heap. Even so, nearly 25,000 kg (55,000 lb) of meat were carried away (Wheat 1972).

The Laurentian ice sheet retreated to a point at which the Laurentian lakes piled up along its southern margin drained catastrophically through the Hudson Strait into the North Atlantic around 6250 BCE. The event triggered cold, dry, and windy conditions on the Great Plains. The cooler conditions did not last, but the dryness did. A few centuries later the region was both hotter and drier than today. Monsoonal rains returned after around 5850 BCE, breaking the long drought. The intense dryness of this episode altered plant communities, the animal populations that depended upon them, and the humans who depended upon both. Little wonder that the High Plains were virtually abandoned in favor of safer adaptations to the foothills to the west and the milder prairies closer to the Mississippi to the east of them during the long, dry period. Both the bison herds and their human hunters avoided the harsh High Plains for a long time (see Chapter 12) (Lovvorn et al. 2001).

Back in the distant North, the Denali complex (Figure 3.20), which had derived from the Siberian Dyuktai complex, spread throughout Beringia mainly after the Younger Dryas, replacing the Mesa and Nenana complexes. But Denali did not spread farther east than the Yukon territory, and it never spread very far southward through the interior. It is tempting to associate this expansion with the appearance of the Nadene language family in northwestern North America, but that

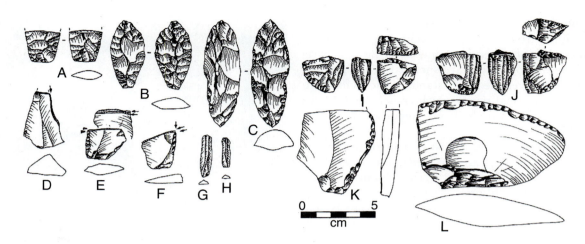

Figure 3.20 Artifacts of the Denali complex. Note the micro-blades (G and H) and wedge-shaped microcores (I and J).
Source: From Hoffecker et al. 1993:50. Reprinted with permission from the American Association for the Advancement of Science.

hypothesis like so many others is likely to prove to be too simple (see Chapter 14). Indeed, the probable relationships between the major complexes of eastern Beringia are the subjects of much current debate (Bever 2006). Some archaeologists even argue that some or all of them might have been produced by the same cultures, depending upon season, location, and other adaptive variables (Yesner and Pearson 2002).

None of these changes were either simultaneous or universal across the continent. When we knew little about Paleoindians it was easy to think in terms of broad generalizations, but the accumulation of new evidence invariably generates more complexity. Archaeologists used to talk about the end of the Paleoindian period and the beginning of the following "Archaic" period(s) as if the transition took place suddenly and simultaneously everywhere. But it is clear now that the long-gone early American Indians did not organize themselves for the convenience of later archaeologists. At the Wilson-Leonard site in Texas a stratum containing stemmed Wilson points, nominally Archaic in character, is overlain by a later one containing Plano points, which is in turn overlain by other Archaic and still later strata. The best explanation is that there were a variety of cultures that shifted back and forth across the southern Plains around 8000 BCE, leaving behind a more complex record than we might have hoped for (Bousman et al. 2002).

That being the case, there is no empirical means to pinpoint the end of the Paleoindian period in Texas, let alone across the entire continent. The best way to end this chapter and move on to the next is to set its close at a convenient round number and be done with it. For that purpose 9000 BCE will serve for the time being. One thing that archaeologists can agree on is that American Indians were certainly on the continent in substantial numbers by that date, and the foundation of their long and complicated evolution into an array of hundreds of contrasting cultures was set. Like any moment in time it was both an end and a beginning.

Summary

1. The study of the earliest North Americans is made more difficult by the scarcity of their archaeological remains and the tendency for evidence to disappear over time.

2. The oldest well-attested Paleoindian culture is Clovis culture, which was widespread 11,100–10,850 BCE, appearing around the beginning of the Younger Dryas, the last gasp of the Pleistocene that lasted from 10,850 to 9550 BCE.

3. Claims for older pre-Clovis remains are scattered and hotly debated.

4. Several claims for very early remains in South America cannot be supported, but the Monte Verde site in Chile is an exception, which in turn suggests an early spread of maritime people southward along the Pacific Coast.

5. Clovis culture probably derived from Nenana culture in Beringia, but its hallmark fluted point style was probably a North American invention.

6. Clovis technology is superficially similar to earlier Solutrean technology in Europe, but few archaeologists conclude that there could have been a connection.

7. Many large game species went extinct around the time of the Paleoindian expansion, but while the earliest Americans might have contributed significantly to their demise they were not the only factor.

8. Surviving skeletons of Paleoindians appear different from those of modern American Indians, indicating that the connections between Siberian donor populations and early migrations were complex.

9. The Paleoindian period ended by around 9000 BCE and the founding population of later American Indian cultures broke up into regional adaptations to a changing Holocene environment.

Further Reading

Fagan's *The Great Journey* summarizes what was known about the peopling of the Americas in 1987 with a 2003 update. Less comprehensive but more up-to-date is Nina Jablonski's *The First Americans*, which contains assessments by leading scholars. Most current is Meltzer's *Search for the First Americans*.

Glossary

anthropogenic: Created in part by humans.

calibration: Specifically radiocarbon date calibration. The use of tree rings and other materials of precisely known age to calibrate age determinations to the modern calendar.

flute: The long, concave scar left by one or more flakes detached from the side of a fluted biface.

knapping: Tool manufactured by means of flaking and chipping using percussion and pressure techniques.

lanceolate: Lance shaped. Usually applied to a projectile lacking notches or stems.

megafauna: Very large animal species.

niche: As used in ecology, the specific part of an environment to which an organism is adapted.

refugium (pl. refugia): A region where plants and animals survived during periods when conditions elsewhere were too hostile for them.

stratum (pl. strata): A depositional layer in an archaeological site, often one of several strata, the oldest at the bottom and the youngest at the top.

Archaic Adaptations

Science is at no moment quite right, but it is seldom quite wrong, and has, as a rule, a better chance of being right than the theories of the unscientific.

Bertrand Russell

THE PASSING OF THE PALEOINDIAN PERIOD WAS followed by a long period of Archaic adaptations, 9000–3500 BCE. These unfolded according to the special circumstances of each of the continent's many local and regional environments, which were all in flux because of changing climatic conditions. But underlying these details were some common themes and a move toward plant domestication that was similar to other contemporaneous cases elsewhere in the world. The forests of North America changed their compositions and shifted their locations because of both natural and human forces. Human populations became generally more dense, less mobile, and more diverse, as expressed in a myriad of projectile point types. Social and political boundaries appeared where none had existed previously. Two major centers of crop domestication emerged in areas where people were lucky enough to find appropriate plants, the Eastern Woodlands and Mesoamerica.

Introduction

Paleoindian adaptations were followed by many derivative ones that archaeologists have long referred to as "Archaic cultures." This term gained wide usage in the middle of the twentieth century as a handy way to refer to the evidence of societies that existed after Paleoindians but before the advent of ceramics, agriculture, and permanent settlements. Although many archaeologists have also long used "Archaic" as a period name, usually breaking it up into Early, Middle, Late, and Terminal

Archaic periods, these are unsatisfactory today because they carry different dates in different regions and thus actually impede our ability to make broad regional comparisons at large scale. This became a problem as radiocarbon dating clarified local and regional chronologies.

The Hazards of Cross Dating

A half century ago archaeologists depended upon the use of key projectile point types to identify the stratigraphic components of various Archaic sites and arrange them chronologically by means of cross dating. This was popular in part because most of the many distinctive projectile point types found across North America were made by Archaic knappers rather than earlier (Paleoindian) or later people. The cross dating technique was similar to the use of index fossils to cross date geological deposits around the world. The problem for archaeologists was that we work on a much shorter time scale, and projectile points are highly variable over both time and space. Nevertheless, archaeologists became adept at glancing at an assemblage of artifacts and saying with reasonable certainty that it was "Early Archaic," "Middle Archaic," or "Late Archaic" based on their knowledge of a few key sites where similar artifacts had been roughly dated by radiocarbon. Notice, however, that this technique creates a rigid Cartesian framework of compartments for projectile points and associated artifacts. All lines are either horizontal or vertical in such a framework, not because the time–space relationships are observed to be

Table 4.1 The use of three diagnostic types (A, X, and G) to cross date strata found at three different Archaic sites.

	Site I	Site II	Site III
L. Archaic	Type A	Type A	
M. Archaic	Type X	Type X	Type X
E. Archaic		Type G	Type G

such but because the technique assumes that they are, as Table 4.1 shows for three imaginary sites and three imaginary point types.

Projectile points did not evolve like species because their forms were determined by human knappers rather than by biological processes. There is considerable variability even within well-defined types. Their forms were mediated by human intent, and their shapes often changed over the courses of their useful lives before they were discarded. Resharpening or conversion from one kind of tool to something used for quite different purposes sometimes occurred. Add to this the tendency for some types to persist much longer than others and for types to be earlier in some regions and later in others and it should be clear that the tidy matrix of Table 4.1 must only rarely reflect archaeological reality.

The development of advanced radiocarbon dating techniques should have changed archaeological practice, for it has reversed the relationships between what we can observe and what we can infer from those observations (Snow 1978). It is expensive, but we can usually date sites and strata within sites directly, making it unnecessary (and sometimes misleading) to assume that their ages correspond to those defined for similar

artifacts at other sites of known age. Many archaeologists still use index types to get a first approximation for recently discovered artifacts or sites, but precision requires independent dating using radiocarbon or some other independent technique for any serious analysis.

Defining the Archaic

The term "Archaic" is used here to refer to Holocene hunter-gatherers as a broad culture type rather than as part of various period names. The use of Archaic time periods is avoided and an effort has been made to use calendrical references to millennia and centuries as much as possible when locating Archaic cultures in time. Eleven thousand years ago was a good point at which to end the previous chapter, so it is also a good point at which to begin this one. However, having left the Pleistocene behind with the end of the Younger Dryas 9550 BCE, we entered the Holocene epoch, in which it is more convenient to scale events according to the calendar that is in general use today.

Holocene Adaptations

The Holocene release at the end of the Pleistocene allowed human societies to gradually master their environments, not just in North America but everywhere. Soon they were managing plant and animal species with accumulating skills such that the subsistence strategy we call agriculture arose not once but several times and in several regions of the world. The American cases occurred in isolation from the rest of the world and more than once, a circumstance that makes answering the question "why" a more profound challenge than it would otherwise be (Figure 4.1).

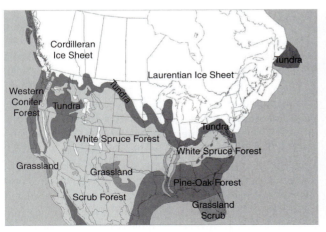
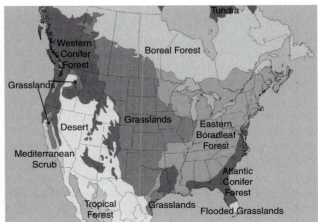

Figure 4.1 The ecozones of North America (left) at the height of the Pleistocene and (right) today. Most of the change and thus most of human readaptation occurred during the Holocene.

There is no evidence that people were suddenly smarter than they had been before the Holocene, just as there is no evidence that they are smarter in one region than in another. Furthermore, while people everywhere probably had the intellectual capacity to develop agriculture earlier, it arose nowhere for thousands of years preceding the Holocene. Yet once the Holocene began cultural evolution toward agriculture played out more or less independently in many places at roughly the same time.

Before the nature of the shift from Pleistocene to Holocene conditions was understood as well as it is today researchers worked mainly with three possible hypotheses to explain the rise of agriculture. These were (1) climatic stress, (2) the pressure of population growth, and (3) the internal dynamics of cultural evolution. However, each of these taken alone fails to explain the phenomenon for one reason or another, and together they do not do much better. Yes, one can point to climatic stress around the time that agriculture was emerging in (for example) Southwest Asia, but why did a dozen other similar stressful episodes not lead to the same development?

Second, population pressure is a plausible driving force, but it had been a factor for thousands of years of *Homo sapiens* history without producing a move toward agriculture. Why would it suddenly become a relevant force in the early Holocene? In the end, and despite much tinkering, it is not easy to make the pressure of population growth work as a driver.

The third common way of thinking about the development of agriculture has been in terms of technological and organizational innovation, dynamics internal to cultural systems. To the extent that innovations allow for an increase in carrying capacity they can spur increases in population sizes and densities, which in turn will allow for increases in complexity of various kinds that people find desirable. But here again, the opportunity for innovation had been present since the emergence of *Homo sapiens*, tens of thousands of years before the emergence of agriculture. What took us so long to get started?

In short, if people were so clever all along, why did it take them all that time to get around to exercising their cleverness? Put another way, why would agriculture not develop at all for say 30,000 years and then develop independently at least twice and more likely several times here and there around the world in just a matter of a few millennia? Peter Richerson and his collaborators argue that the answer is that the Pleistocene made the development of agriculture impossible, but the new conditions of the Holocene made it inevitable. They argue that the explanation is that the abrupt climatic changes that mark the beginning of the Holocene changed conditions worldwide from ones that made agriculture impossible to ones that made it possible in many places. The new conditions included generally warmer conditions, increased rainfall, a reduction of CO_2 in the atmosphere, and perhaps most importantly a reduction in ecologically disruptive short-term variability. Conditions were favorable for agriculture in large part because they had become sufficiently predictable for humans with good memories, and that is just about everybody (Richerson et al. 2001:404).

Periodic climatic stress, the constant pressure of population growth, and human ingenuity were there all along, so it was the advent of the Holocene that made agriculture possible. But if conditions ripened 11,570 years ago, why was the development of agriculture prompt in some places but delayed in others? If the sequence of tending, cultivating, domestication, and intensification of production were all inevitable, why did they unfold at different times and at different rates in the regions where they arose? It turns out that it arose first where conditions were demonstrably most favorable, later where conditions were more difficult, and still later where people were most challenged by the environment. Of course agriculture did not arise at all in parts of the world where it was simply impossible.

Table 4.2 provides a listing of seven regions where agriculture probably developed independently. There is little doubt that the Americas were completely isolated from Eurasia and Africa while this was going on, but we can be less certain about the possibility of stimulating influences moving between regions within each of these hemispherical domains. There might have been as many as three separate developments in Sub-Saharan Africa, and perhaps the two in China should be considered as one.

To understand the reasons why the move to food production started at different times and went at different paces where it was able to begin at all we must look to the details of the climatological record as well as to variations in opportunity. When the Younger Dryas ended about 9550 BCE it did so abruptly, perhaps over only a few years and certainly within the lifetimes of many perplexed hunter-gatherers alive at the time (Alley et al. 2003). The Holocene that followed, and which continues today, was less variable than previous interglacial periods. That is not to say that it was all smooth going until the recent human-induced episode of global warming. That certainly was not the case. But the variations that have produced devastating droughts, cold episodes, long-term variations in precipitation, and so forth have not been as drastic as they

Table 4.2 Selected regional centers of agriculture with approximate dates BCE.

Hemisphere and Region	Intensive Foraging	Initial Plant Domestication
The Americas		
Central Mexico	10,000	8000
Eastern United States	6000	3000
South Central Andes	5000	5000
Amazonia	9000	8000
Eurasia and Africa		
Southwest Asia	12,000	7500
North China	9600	5800
South China	10,000	6500
New Guinea	10,000	10,000
Sub-Saharan Africa	7000	2000

Sources: Duarte, et al. 2007; Highsmith 1997; Richerson, et al. 2001:400; Smith 2001c:203; Smith 2007; Zeder, et al. 2006.

were during the Pleistocene. This has made human dependence upon agriculture possible, if still sometimes episodic and precarious, and inevitable given the constant pressure of population growth.

Paleoclimatologists have been able to track the rise and fall of average annual temperatures using two independent lines of evidence that generally confirm each other (Figure 4.2). Sediment cores from the North Atlantic reveal variations in the debris falling from melting glacial ice. Ice cores from the Greenland ice cap reveal variations in the production of ^{14}C as the result of changes in solar activity. The two curves match each other closely, giving us a general understanding of climatic variation over the last 12,000 years. The upward spike of the Medieval Maximum around a thousand years ago, followed by plunge into the Little Ice Age and then the current episode of rapid global warming are all apparent near the right end of Figure 4.2. A dozen or more similar peaks and valleys preceded these over the millennia that followed the end of the Younger Dryas. As jagged as this record appears to be, it is smooth compared to the Pleistocene climate record.

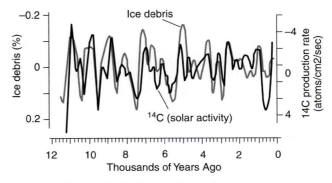

Figure 4.2 Holocene climate fluctuations.

Yet the history of Holocene climate was not just a long relatively smooth trend toward modern conditions. The 3,500-year-long period from 7000 to 3500 BCE saw three very high peaks in average temperatures, separated by mild cooler cycles. This period as a whole is often referred to as the Altithermal in the older archaeological literature. The 35-century climatic roller-coaster ride heated and dried some parts of North America so severely that they became uninhabitable deserts. Human adaptation in many other areas was made more difficult overall and critically so in centuries that were particularly hot and dry. Of course there were other parts of the continent where warmer and drier conditions were locally more rather than less advantageous for hunter-gatherers. Chapters 5 through 14 touch on many specific cases where past climatic cycling has changed local and regional adaptations.

The Roots of Domestication

Environmental constraints on opportunity relaxed but did not disappear with the beginning of the Holocene. The very existence of agriculture in pre-Columbian America means that given the Holocene release of people everywhere from the adaptive constraints of the Pleistocene it was inevitable that they would refine their techniques for acquiring more and better food. Large low-hanging fruits and large sluggish animals are easy to take but rarely encountered. Generally speaking, there is more food available from less obvious sources, but it is also less easily obtained, even when it is close at hand. For example, there is more meat per **hectare** running around the woods of Pennsylvania in the form of small rodents than in the form of whitetail deer; the problem is figuring out how to hunt and consume such an alternative resource (Kennett and Winterhalder 2006).

Most plant foods are like mice, seemingly difficult to harvest in quantity and once harvested often difficult to convert into palatable food or store for future consumption. But human beings are not merely good at exploring environmental details, they are also inclined to tinker with them. The result is that hunter-gatherers construct their own niches as they learn more and more about their environments (Smith 2007).

The forests and grasslands of eastern North America are full of potentially nutritious plants, but they are also full of dangerous ones. A popular field guide to edible wild plants in North America warns of about 9 that can cause severe dermatitis, poison ivy being the best known (Peterson 1978). No fewer than 90 species are poisonous, and 24 of them are known to have caused fatalities. Some things, like acorns, are not listed as being poisonous, but only because in this case acorns can be turned into human food if one knows how to leach the tannins from them. The wild ancestors of modern watermelons and potatoes were unpalatable too, and it must have taken both time and luck for their potential to be realized.

Caraway and wild carrot look alike and both are nutritious. But both also look very much like fool's-parsley

and poison hemlock, at least one of which is lethal (Figure 4.3) (Britton and Brown 1923, vol. 2:625–659). Some mushrooms are tasty whereas some others are deadly, and it takes an expert to tell the difference. Examples could go on like this for pages but the point is that hunter-gatherers could not simply settle into a region and exploit the available animal and plant resources without going through a long and complicated learning process. We can only speculate about how this took place, how many times a desperately hungry gatherer took a chance on what turned out to be a poisonous plant. Estimates in print generally underestimate the time required given the many plants available and the natural caution of any pioneer gatherer. However the specifics played out, and some of them must have been tragic, the people of North America like people everywhere else slowly became better and better at using the plant and animal resources they found around them. Given the natural variation in those resources from one region to another it is no surprise that they became regional specialists, that cultures and languages began to specialize and diverge from one another as a result, and that in a few cases they took the first steps toward domestication.

Figure 4.3 Edible and poisonous plants that look alike. Caraway and wild carrot (top) are nutritious while fool's-parsley and poison hemlock (bottom) are poisonous. *Source:* Adapted from Britton and Brown 1923, vol. 2:625–659.

The emergence of domesticates was not a conscious process for gatherers, at least not in the beginning. The process led to interactions between plants and gatherers that led in turn to unconscious artificial selection. Gatherers tend to harvest the plumper juicier berries or the larger tastier tubers. Discarded seeds might grow into unusually healthy plants in the garbage deposits surrounding campsites, leading to still more careful selection by gatherers. Fruits that are bigger, or less bitter, or sweeter will be favored. Gatherers might even discourage competing plants. Over the long term they will favor plants that grow quickly, are easy to harvest, easy to store, and easy to convert into food. The selective process will also favor self-pollinating plants, as opposed to those that depend upon cross-pollination, because self-pollinators pass on their own desirable genes unchanged and respond more quickly to selection.

But how, one might ask, does this process lead to better food plants if the best are constantly selected out for consumption rather than being allowed to reproduce? The answer is that the people doing the harvesting inadvertently propagated desirable plants in patches where they would not otherwise reproduce naturally, like garbage middens. They eventually knew enough to encourage the mutant strains that had heightened food value.

It did not necessarily have to be a conscious process. For example, if a gatherer unconsciously favored those plants that retained their seeds rather than releasing them, the selected plants came to depend upon humans for their reproduction. Plants that disperse their seeds easily when they mature will tend to be seedless by the time a human gatherer comes around, so those that hold their seeds longer and more tightly stand a better chance of being gathered, threshed, and winnowed. Over time the human gatherers will inadvertently select for plants that produce bigger more tightly bound seeds, plants that are less efficient at reproducing in the wild but more desirable to gatherers. Thus over time humans and their domesticated plants have developed a strong mutual dependence.

The Luck of Good Location

The other variable that determined the possibility and timing of domestication was geographic luck. One class of plants that was particularly well suited for eventual domestication was made up of the large-seeded grass species. There are about 56 of these worldwide. Thirty-two of them (57%) are found only in and around the Fertile Crescent of southwest Eurasia. Little wonder that this was the region where cereal crops were first

domesticated, for it was where the opportunities were most numerous. East Asia and Africa had six and four respectively, and domestication there emerged later on. Similarly North America had nine, five of which were confined to its Mesoamerican region Table 4.3.

Animal Domestication

Potential animal domesticates were also much more numerous in Southwest Asia than in North America and elsewhere, with similar consequences. Good candidates for domestication were mammals that weighed more than 45 kg (100 lbs), had appropriate diets, grew quickly to adulthood, would breed in captivity, had tractable dispositions, were not subject to fits of panic, and were comfortable in herds. Even those that were successfully domesticated sometimes emerged as lucky mutants from wild populations in which other individuals were for the most part intractable. Domesticated horses, for example, may well all descend from a single unusual individual that a lucky herder happened to encounter in central Asia. Most wild horse species, including all the zebras and Przewalski's horses, are very resistant to domestication. The Przewalski's horses seen in wild animal parks appear even less inclined to be tamed than zebras. Perhaps a rare mutant might have changed the course of human history in North America, but horses became extinct here during the Paleoindian period, making the question moot.

In other cases some other key difference made one mammal population a good candidate for domestication while another very similar one was not. Wild sheep are found in both North America and Eurasia. Opportunities for domestication must have presented themselves on both continents, yet while the Eurasia sheep was domesticated early on the bighorn sheep of North America never was. The critical difference is not found among the human populations on the two continents but sheep species themselves. That difference is that Eurasian sheep have a social system that causes subordinate individuals to behave submissively to dominant ones, a trait that allows for large herds. North American bighorn sheep lack that trait, so they will not form large herds under dominant leaders, let alone under human shepherds trying to substitute themselves for the dominant leaders. Confining and selectively breeding bighorn sheep was simply not an option for early agriculturalists in North America.

Of 148 mammalian candidates for domestication, 72 occurred in Eurasia and only 24 in the Americas. Thirteen of the 72 Eurasian species eventually proved to be suitable for domestication. Only one of the 24 American species, the llama, made the cut and geography

Table 4.3 Approximate dates at which certain key traits were introduced in selected centers in Eurasia and North America.

Fertile Crescent	China	Europe	Mesoamerica	Eastern Woodlands	Approx. Date
					1500 CE
					1000
		States			500
		Writing	Copper/Bronze		0
	Iron	Iron	State Animal Domesticates	Chiefdoms Villages	500
Iron			Writing		1000
	Writing		Chiefdoms Villages	Copper/Bronze	1500
	States Copper/Bronze	Copper/Bronze			2000
		Chiefdoms	Pottery	Pottery Plant Domesticates	2500
Writing		Villages	Plant Domesticates		3000
States		Pottery Animal Domest. Plant Domest.			3500
Copper/Bronze	Chiefdoms				4000
					4500
					5000
Chiefdoms					5500
					6000
					6500
Pottery					7000
	Pottery Animal Domest. Plant Domest.				7500
Animal Domesticates	Villages				8000
Plant Domesticates					8500
Villages					9000 BCE

prevented it from spreading northward from its native South America to North America until after 1492.

Apart from dogs there were no potential animal domesticates in North America 10,000 years ago. Horses were extinct or nearly so. Surviving **camelids** were confined to highland South America, far beyond a long tropical isthmus they could not transit. Bison had none of the qualities of wild cattle, which had never been part of the North American landscape. Bighorn sheep, mountain goats, peccaries, and javalinas (the American relatives of Eurasian sheep, goats, and pigs) all lacked one or another of the qualities needed for domestication.

Humanizing Environments

Holocene reforestation played out with the participation of humans, who modified the outcome. No environment stands still, so the Archaic peoples of North America had to adapt to a landscape that had always been diverse but at the same time had always been changing. The great ice sheets of the Pleistocene compressed the ecozones arrayed south of them in what are now the 48 lower United States. Figure 4.1A, which shows a simplified version of forests at the height of the Pleistocene, reveals how limited grasslands were at that time. But every forest and grassland of that epoch was also different in type from anything familiar to us today. The mix of each forest type was different from today, both in constituent species present and their relative frequencies. The several forests I have lumped here as "western conifer forest" were unlike any variant of today's western conifer forest, just as the white spruce forest that was spread across much of what are now the central and eastern United States was similar to but not identical with the modern boreal forest of Canada. The history of the evolution of the North American forests from the Pleistocene pattern in Figure 4.1A to the modern one in Figure 4.1B is a long with many strands (Bonnicksen 2000).

The shapes of landmasses and the locations of mountain ranges also make a big difference. While the east–west environmental bands of Eurasia have always facilitated the spread of plants, animals, and humans there, the north–south trending mountain ranges of the Americas have been more constraining because they are aligned across rather than parallel with lines of latitude. Living things have to adapt more as they move if they change latitude at the same time, as any gardener familiar with North America's growing zones knows (Diamond 1997:183–186). A plant can spread easily from Europe to China, but the same plant cannot spread as easily from Mexico to Canada. Ironically, the same geographic contrast doomed some European plants that still survive in North America. Sweetgums, tuliptrees, magnolias, hemlocks, and cedars were all squeezed to extinction in Europe when expanding glacial ice forced them up against the wall of the Pyrenees and Alps and the shores of the Mediterranean. In North America they all had southern refugia where they persisted until the glaciers retreated, and they are common here today.

Even though the band of Pleistocene tundra lay along the cold margins of the ice sheets or in areas made equally cold by altitude, the latitude was low compared to the modern Arctic tundra. There was no midnight sun and no perpetual winter darkness on the tundra of southern Minnesota during the Pleistocene. As a result, the low-latitude Pleistocene tundra had more animals and larger animals than any high-latitude tundra that has existed since. But whether or not they were partly responsible for the declining numbers of game animals, the Archaic people adapting to post-Pleistocene environments necessarily had fewer large species to hunt than did their Paleoindian ancestors because the thinning animal populations shifted northward with the retreating tundra.

Palynology

Some tree species that are common today retreated to comparatively small refugia during the Pleistocene. The onset of the Holocene allowed them to expand out of their refugia, changing the mix of the spreading and evolving forests. These shifts are tracked by scientists who study **palynology** (called palynologists), who often extract long cores from the bottoms of bogs, lakes, and ponds in order to detect the constituent species of extinct forests over time. Each core is sliced like a salami and the pollen grains in each slice are counted by genus, and if possible by individual species. Some of the slices are dated by radiocarbon so that the core can be scaled according to years before the present. The work is tedious, and it is complicated by several factors. Some plants produce large amounts of pollen while others, particularly those pollinated by insects, produce only small amounts. Some pollen grains can travel long distances in the wind whereas others fall out quickly. Despite the complications, pollen tends to preserve well in wet sediments and palynologists are able to reconstruct extinct forest environments for the areas they sample.

Palynologists have tracked many tree and other plant species as they shifted over time and space in the course of the Holocene. Some surprises have been encountered along the way. For example, the deglaciation of New England was followed by the spread of cold-tolerant trees into the region. Spruce trees were among the first to become established on what was initially a treeless tundra. Pine began to appear after the first spruce trees were established and palynologists initially noticed an unexpected decline followed by a second surge in pine after several centuries. Pine pollen grains all look pretty much alike and at first the palynologists were content to count grains in their samples at the genus level, lumping all the species of pine together. They later found ways to distinguish the grains of one pine species from those of others, and when they did they discovered the reason for the strange two-phase surge in pines over time. The first pines into the region were jack and red pines. The decline occurred when these species moved farther north and the second surge was caused by the arrival of more slowly spreading white pines. It might seem like a small point, but such shifts were important to early hunter-gatherers.

The Humanized Forest

Native Americans were constrained by their environments, but they were not slaves to them, for the Archaic Indians also had technological innovation going for them. Some of these were small-scale innovations. For example, once they developed the basic technique for removing tannin from acorns, people had a new source of protein and fat, and the expanding oak forests took on a whole new meaning for them.

But the Archaic Indians also had fire in their tool inventory. In the absence of people and fires pioneer species like grasses, birches, tamaracks, pines, and aspens are the first to occupy disturbed ground. They grow rapidly and live relatively short lives. Some are well adapted for growth on recently deglaciated soils having few nutrients. Settler species like maples, beeches, hemlocks, and firs expand by infiltrating into stands of pioneer species, where they appear later, grow more slowly, but eventually replace the smaller, short-lived trees. Native Americans redirected this natural process with fire. Human firing changed the character of forest environments because it selected out mature settler tree species and repeatedly encouraged pioneer species even as general climate change was reworking the makeup of shifting Holocene forests.

The arrival of humans accelerated the frequency of fires. Consequently, since the beginning of the Holocene there have never been as many mature old-growth forests on the continent as there would have been had humans not been in the picture. Grasslands and pioneer tree species have had their fortunes promoted by humans for at least the last 10 millennia; the landscape of America has been in large part anthropogenic for all of that time. To take it a step further, there are many parts of the continent that have never looked as they would have looked had humans not been present because before people arrived, climatic conditions were very different and after they arrived they changed everything with fire. Some scientists even argue that deliberate burning probably initiated global warming thousands of years before the industrial age, perhaps even heading off what otherwise would have been a cyclical return to Pleistocene conditions (Ruddiman 2003).

Eastern Woodlands

Each region of North America experienced its own series of vegetation changes over the course of the Holocene. The open spruce forests of the East had been home to both mammoths and mastodons. They shared the forest by not competing with each other, the mammoths being grazers and the mastodons browsers who preferred leaves to grass. Both dwindled and disappeared as the spruce forests gave way to first other conifers and then to broadleaf trees expanding out of their refugia. At the same time white spruce were in the vanguard of pioneer species invading the tundra as the glaciers melted back.

The spruce forest migrated even though individual spruce trees remained as rooted to their spots as they do today. As the two great ice sheets retreated from each other in western Canada the spruce forest spread up in the gap between them, a finger of vegetation in an ice-free corridor 2,000 km (1250 mi) long. In the East the spruce trees spread into Canada and up the slopes of the Appalachian Mountains, where they survive today. Hardwood trees followed the conifers into the Appalachians and the deglaciated Northeast through the course of the Holocene. Oaks arrived early but hickory trees were slow to spread and did not reach New England until around 5,000 years ago. Both species depend on rodents and birds to spread their seeds.

Other forces independent of climate change and human intervention sometimes affected the evolution of the forests. Eastern hemlocks spread widely across the Appalachians and the Northeast, then the hemlock population crashed. Up to 80% of the hemlocks died off in a few decades around 2800 BCE, possibly from a fungal disease, and it was 2,000 years before a resistant strain evolved and the species recovered. American chestnut trees expanded slowly out of a refuge in the lower Mississippi Valley, reaching New England around 0 CE. The chestnut flourished throughout its eastern range after that, probably advantaged by burning and clearing carried out by human farmers. It was dominant in the eastern forests until the twentieth century, when a blight all but exterminated the species (Bonnicksen 2000:45).

Ten thousand years ago the forests of the Southeast were similar to those of the Northeast today. The flooded grasslands of southern Florida of today were sand dunes covered by scrub growth when Paleoindians first ventured there.

West Coast

In the West the frigid conditions of the Pleistocene had kept trees largely below the 600-m (2,000-ft) line in the mountains of the northwestern part of the continent. This compressed subalpine forests into narrow bands, and pushed some species into refugia where they all but expired. The Douglas fir might have survived mainly on the exposed continental shelf, where the Pacific kept conditions mild enough for it to flourish. The giant redwoods of the California coast were also protected by the Pacific Ocean, growing where they are found today but also far out on to the exposed continental shelf. Western hemlocks and Sitka spruces probably made it through the Ice Age similarly, in pockets here and there where conditions were tolerable for them (Bonnicksen 2000:24–26).

As the Holocene began the jet stream no longer pushed moisture into the interior Great Basin but directed it instead at the Northwest. Sitka spruce and western hemlock were becoming established there at the beginning of the Holocene and the modern forest dominated by those giants was more or less established by 4000 BCE. The third giant, red cedar, was slower to spread, and did not become an important component of that forest until 3,000 years later. The process was even slower away from the Pacific, which was still much lower than its current level. Hemlocks were not abundant in eastern Washington until 500 BCE or in Idaho until around 500 CE (Bonnicksen 2000:46–47).

Greater Southwest

The Pleistocene jet stream, redirected by the massive sheets of ice to the north, pushed moist air into the Southwest, where it rarely appears today. Forests of pygmy conifers and oaks flourished in areas that support desert cacti today. Piñon and juniper trees were widespread at the beginning of the Holocene, but they crept up the mountainsides and abandoned the lowlands to desert scrub. At the same time ponderosa pines expanded out of their refuges and spread through much of what is now the western conifer forest.

Many plant species, and the animal species that are adapted to living amongst them, died out at lower altitudes and found new ranges higher up. There was an upper limit to this, of course, and where the mountains were not high enough various species simply died out. As the Holocene wore on people had to adapt more and more to mobile exploitation of the relatively limited resources of an expanding desert and remaining islands of more productive resources in the mountains above.

Great Plains

The Great Plains, that vast sea of grass that is an iconic backdrop for the popular image of the American Indians, was all but nonexistent in the Late Pleistocene. White spruce forest covered most of what is now grassland. Two somewhat different islands of grassland survived the big chill, one on the Llano Estacado of Texas and New Mexico and the other on the Edwards Plateau of central Texas. From these two islands of grass and smaller patches scattered around the middle of the continent grew the prairies and high plains so familiar to us today. The spruce trees that had dominated the Great Plains during the Pleistocene were gone from the central part of the region by 11,300 years ago, seared by the warmer drier conditions and blackened by more frequent fires. Some stands survive, most notably in northwestern Montana and the Black Hills of South Dakota. Those in the Black Hills share their refugia with more dominant ponderosa pines and wildlife species long isolated from their relatives elsewhere (Bonnicksen 2000:9–40).

Consequences for Human Adaptation

The point of all of this is that Holocene forests were complex, dynamic, and shifting, their compositions determined in part by human activity, especially firing. The patterns we see today have evolved over the last 10,000 years and they continue to evolve as our changing climate forces species to shift their distributions. The living environment is always in flux, but as complicated and pervasive as those changes were over the course of the Holocene, they were gradual enough to allow people to settle into long-term adaptations. Their investments in new knowledge about local environments and new technology for extracting food from them led gradually to the domestication of a few plants, and a shift from foraging and gathering to food production (Wolverton 2005).

Hallmarks in Stone

Archaic projectile points made by Archaic people and the **debitage** (waste material) produced in the course of their manufacture are often the only obvious evidence found in the sites of the long period from 9000 to 3500 BCE. What were once tools for ancient hunter-gatherers become tools of a different sort for archaeologists. The points that tipped Archaic spears, darts, and knives come in a wide variety of forms that are often diagnostic for specific regions or time periods. This characteristic was more important prior to the advent of reliable radiocarbon dating than it is today, but people still use point typology for initial assessment of finds. Noel Justice (1987) has compiled an inventory of point types for the midcontinental United States. His inventory includes 41 types for just the period covered by this chapter in that region (Table 4.4). To make that number more manageable Justice has grouped them into 15 clusters, sets of types that hang together because they are similar and in some cases occur together repeatedly in archaeological sites.

One could portray the Archaic cultures of North America in a long narrative, describing each of the many point types and putting them in their time–space contexts. There was a time when a book like this one typically did just that, but such a long descriptive portrayal would be impossibly boring. We are long past the point in the history of archaeology where we can pretend to let such data speak for themselves. They never did, and now that there are hundreds of named types to choose from it makes even less sense to pretend otherwise. Yet point types still have their uses. Figure 4.4 shows four basic forms.

One purpose for continued interest in typology is that it allows the archaeologist to define a tool or complex of tools as the hallmark(s) of a particular cultural adaptation. The regional context of such a tool type or complex can be examined once the time-space distribution of a set of known examples is worked out. Perhaps they tend to cluster in a particular ecological setting. Perhaps they are older in one part of their range than across the rest of it, and persist longer in one place as compared to others. It is often useful to use sets of specimens this way, as members of type populations (admittedly not breeding populations), for it is at the population level rather than the level of

Table 4.4 Point types and type clusters for the midcontinental United States, 8050-3500 BCE.

Type Clusters	Point Types
Dalton	*Beaver Lake* *Quad* *Dalton* *Greenbriar* *Hardaway Side Notched*
Hi-Lo Scottsbluff	*Scottsbluff* *Eden*
Hardin Barbed Thebes	*Thebes* *St. Charles* *Lost Lake* *Calf Creek*
Large Side Notched	*Graham Cave Side Notched* *Kessell Side Notched* *Raddatz Side Notched* *Osceola*
Kirk Corner Notched	*Kirk Corner Notched* *Stilwell* *Palmer Corner Notched* *Charleston Corner Notched* *White Springs*
Benton	*Benton Stemmed* *Pine Tree Corner Notched* *Decatur*
Kirk Stemmed	*Kirk Stemmed* *Kirk Serrated*
Rice Lobed	*Rice Lobed* *MacCorkle Stemmed* *St. Albans Side Notched*
LeCroy	*LeCroy Bifurcated Stem* *Lake Erie Bifurcated Base* *Kanawha Stemmed* *Fox Valley Truncated Barb*
Stanly Stemmed	*Stanly Stemmed* *Neville Stemmed*
Eva	*Eva I* *Eva II*
Morrow Mountain	*Morrow Mountain I* *Morrow Mountain II*
White Springs	*Sykes* *Elk River Stemmed*

Source: From Justice 1987:35–114.

the individual artifact that interesting problems more often reside.

In the analytical process it is important to be able to say whether two similar artifacts are **homologs** or **analogs**. Two stemmed points, one from California and one from New Jersey, may look alike but they are almost certainly analogs, similar points that originated separately. There are, after all, only a limited number of ways to make points that will serve the purpose of providing durable sharp tips for projectiles. Two stemmed points, both from Missouri, which are made from the same raw material, appear to have been produced by the same knapping techniques, and were found in the same area, are almost certainly homologs, specimens that have a common cultural origin. Because we are typically interested in sets of artifacts that were made by individual knappers in bounded cultures, it is important to be reasonably certain that the specimens we study are homologous and not merely analogous to each other. A display of stemmed points that some collector put together a century ago may be pretty, but if they are all analogs that he or she picked up here and there while traveling, measuring them to compute average dimensions would be a waste of time. On the other hand, an assemblage of homologs excavated carefully from a single site, or collected systematically from the surface of a small area form a population, and average measurements might be useful in the solution of particular problems.

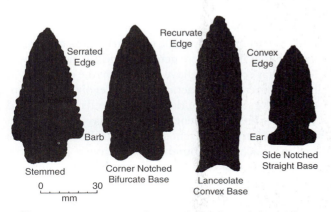

Figure 4.4 Basic projectile point forms. From left to right: stemmed, corner notched, lanceolate, and side notched. *Source:* Justice 1987:37, 64, 83, 87.

Box 4.1 HOW TO CLASSIFY PROJECTILE POINTS

Just as ornithology is not merely the physical description of bird species, archaeology is not merely the physical description of artifact types. Nevertheless, as a bird watcher I want to know how to identify a species in the wild, and I expect that readers of this book will want to be able to name distinctive point types.

Projectile point types often provide a first approximation for the cultural identity of a site or a stratum within a site, particularly for the Archaic cultures that evolved across North America after 8050 BCE. There are regional guides, such as Justices's (1987) survey of types in the midcontinent. In addition there are other regional or state guides, usually available from state museums or state or provincial archaeological societies. These can be found online or in catalogs.

Start with basic point form. Paleoindian point types were generally lanceolate, lacking stems, barbs, or notches. Some were also fluted, but this feature disappeared near the end of the Paleoindian period. Lanceolate forms persisted in some areas after 8050 BCE, but points made after that date were increasingly side notched, corner notched, or stemmed. Corner notching facilitated the production of barbs on some points. Points may or may not be thinned at their bases, and their lower edges may or may not be blunted by grinding.

Figure 4.4 provides a basic vocabulary of common terms used to describe projectile point types. Type descriptions might also indicate that a type is relatively large or small, thick or thin, biconvex or plano-convex in cross section, or typically made from some particular raw material.

The use of specific terms may vary. What appears to be a stemmed point to one specialist might be described as "corner notched" or "corner removed" by another. "Bifurcate base," "basal notching," and "lobed" are all terms that might be used to describe the second point from the left. Be aware of these inconsistencies and use the guide that is most relevant to the region from which the specimens to be typed came. Points that lack locational contexts (provenience) often defy classification. Even in cases where points are well provenienced it is often the case that a significant percentage cannot be convincingly classified.

Major Adaptive Trends in the Holocene

Human adaptations are always dynamic, even when the environment is stable or nearly so, but human life spans are so short that individuals often do not perceive the evolutionary changes of their cultures. The environmental changes of the Holocene unfolded slowly, so slowly that most of the time people would not have known that it was a moving target for their adaptations. Most abrupt changes were local or regional, an enormous fire here or a landslide there. If there were abrupt widespread climatic changes like the sudden one that ended the Younger Dryas we have yet to detect it.

Most people even today gauge their options and make their decisions over the short term. One has to get one's family through the winter and make decisions according to that short-term goal. Why plan for a rare event, the likes of which the elders do not remember and which will probably not occur? Yet if killer winters occur once a century they are frequent enough to be taken seriously. Unfortunately, such risks could not be assessed in the absence of modern record keeping, and oral tradition was not up to the task. Even if they had the capacity to anticipate low probability episodes it is unlikely that they would have done much to prepare themselves. Consider what happened to New Orleans in 2005, or our own behavior at the gas pump. Even today people tend to plan mainly for the short term.

Despite the fickle and sometimes brutal constraints of the environment, Archaic adaptation was not simply at its mercy. There were general trends in cultural evolution that could only have come from the dynamics of human potential interacting with the evolving environment. Brian Hayden outlined these trends in 1981, and they are still an excellent summary (Hayden 1981).

The 10 trends sketched by Hayden in Table 4.5 are striking, each a profound shift specifying part of the human potential that was released by the coming of the Holocene. What is striking about Table 4.5 is that the very same trends can be observed for Eurasia and Africa in the same time frame. Wherever these trends were possible they were actualized, something

Table 4.5 Trends of change from Paleoindian to Archaic.

Paleoindian	Archaic
1. High mobility and nonpermanent habitations	1. Seasonal sedentism and scheduling of annual movements
2. Little midden accumulation around sites	2. Midden accumulation due to specialization in resource rich areas
3. Relatively simple technology	3. Relatively complex technology with ground stone tools, fishing equipment, bow and arrow, and food boiling
4. Limited resource base of medium to large game	4. Resource diversification to more and smaller game species
5. Low population density with marginal habitats unpopulated	5. Increased population density with expansion into marginal areas
6. Egalitarian social organization	6. Competition and ranking in social organizations
7. Exchange of high-grade exotic lithic materials	7. Use of local lithic materials
8. Little environmental modification	8. Increased environmental modification through burning
9. Relatively large band ranges	9. Reduced band ranges
10. Little food storage	10. Increased importance of food storage

Source: From Hayden 1981.

that cannot be explained by reference to environmental change alone. That is not to say that there is no material explanation for them, for the pressure of human population increase was an important driver, and human intelligence was an important supplier of innovations. But no amount of intelligence or population pressure led to the 10 trends prior to the close of the Pleistocene, so again it must have been the interaction of population pressure, innate human potential, and new environmental conditions that let it all happen.

The 10 Holocene trends amount to a settling in process that took centuries to unfold. Hunter-gatherers live on what they can find. Those who live in poor environments tend to practice conservation and hunt communally more often than those who live in naturally rich environments. In all cases the availability of dietary fat is an important restriction. There are other limiting factors too, some of them not at all obvious. As a result it is not easy to assess the carrying capacity of any particular landscape for hunter-gatherers. What may appear at first glance to be a very productive environment might be short of some critical resource for a brief period each year, and even short-term starvation can keep numbers small over the long run.

Insights from Ethnography

The ethnographic study of people who were still living by hunting and gathering in the last two centuries has allowed archaeologists to make general statements about their way of life that are relevant to our understanding of Archaic cultures that have been long extinct. Periods of hunger were most frequent in regions where there was not much food, little variety of food, or both. There was always upward population pressure and thus always a desire to accommodate more and more hungry mouths by producing more and more food rather than by letting starvation reduce the number of mouths. Being clever, humans have consistently tried to artificially increase the density, diversity, and reliability of their food resources whenever possible. For the simplest hunter-gatherers this might mean nothing more sophisticated than setting fire to dry forest once in a while to encourage grasses and the game animals that feed on them. The difference between this and modern industrial agriculture is, at the most general level, just a matter of degree.

Men tended to specialize in hunting and women in foraging, so there was a natural division of labor. Both tended to go after the most abundant, most obvious, or the most easily acquired resources, but such a simple statement conceals the important complication mentioned earlier. The most abundant protein source in a given environment might be tiny rodents, but the difficulty in acquiring them caused people to concentrate instead on scarce large game. Similarly, there could have been tons of food available in the form of the tiny seeds of certain grasses, but harvesting problems forced people to look for larger but rarer tubers instead. Both cases illustrate that technology is an important component; better mousetraps and better winnowing devices can make huge differences in the success of hunter-gatherer populations (Gremillion 2004).

Hunter-gatherers typically spend two to five hours a day acquiring food, and 40% or more of any local population often produces no food at all. Today we live in a society where most adults younger than 65 years on average work twice as hard as the typical hunter-gatherer, and we sometimes might wonder where we went wrong. The answer, of course, is that Archaic hunter-gatherers had very limited material wants, and they necessarily lived at much lower densities than most of us would find comfortable. They were also at much higher risk of periodic starvation and death from exposure.

Nomadism also required more energy than sedentism, so if faced with a choice most hunter-gatherers stayed put. Transportation costs kept efficient foraging within 8 km (5 mi) of a base camp. Hunters ranged farther, but they too reached a point of diminishing returns 16–24 km (10–15 mi) from the base camp. A pedestrian hunter-gatherer band could not exploit a range of much more than 2500 km² (965 mi²) (Hayden 1981).

Managing Mobility

Mobility was driven by the need to maximize the chances of encountering food resources as well as the need to maximize contacts with other bands in a connubium. Thus under conditions where food resources were scarce, the overall population was broadly and thinly distributed over a large territory. In the absence of transportation, bands remained highly mobile as much to maximize contact with each other as to maximize encounters with food resources. Band moves were optimized in the sense that the expense of a move was judged against its perceived benefits. Moves were often delayed until it was clear that the benefits of moving outweighed the benefits of remaining. This inertia resulted from caution in the assessment of risk. Considering all of this one can see why there was a trend from high mobility and very temporary habitations to

Box 4.2 HOW TO USE THE LOGIC OF TIME'S ARROW

The flow of time is unidirectional, and that puts the burden of proof on any claim that something is older than established knowledge would have predicted. We implicitly recognize this in our everyday lives, taking notice when the dawn of human artistic impulse is pushed back another 10,000 years or when some domesticate is found to be a millennium older than previously thought. No one gets very excited when an age is merely confirmed by additional research, or when more recent examples of some phenomenon are found to be commonplace. Because of this, attention, funding, and criticism tend to be focused on cases that are, or are claimed to be, older than expected.

The discoverers in such cases are often severely conflicted. On the one hand they often find themselves stuck with unexpected discoveries, scattered artifacts under a stratum containing Paleoindian remains or a radiocarbon date that is millennia older than predicted. They worry that they might have made a mistake or that the finding will not be well received. On the other hand they often have invested much time and money leading up to the discovery, and they are hard pressed to let their own skepticism or that of others toss all that effort aside. The best they can do is to conduct their work as carefully and as thoroughly as they can, as Goodyear has done at the Topper site and Adovasio has done at Meadowcroft, and let the process of criticism and peer review play out. That process will uncover hoaxes, as it did in the case of the Holly Oak pendant (Custer et al 1989; Griffin et al 1988; Lewin 1988, 1989), or correct errors as it did in the case of the Old Crow flesher (Irving and Harington 1973; Irving 1987). It will also keep discoverers hopping long after they have moved on to other research projects, as Goodyear and Adovasio can testify.

The logic of time's arrow forces us to be more skeptical of claims that are older than expected than we are of claims that are younger than expected. Related to this is the requirement of evidence, for the burden of proof rests more heavily on the unexpected than the expected. It took excavation of a substantial amount of evidence at L'Anse aux Meadows, Newfoundland, to convince archaeologists that the Norse had established an outpost there a millennium ago. It takes far less to convince anyone that there were Norwegians in Minnesota a century ago. But the two are related because the presence of people of Norse descent in modern America has increased enthusiasm for scattered claims of early Norse exploration and has even led to some elaborate hoaxes. Just as we must remain very skeptical of any claims for a Norse presence earlier than those at L'Anse aux Meadows, we must also remain similarly skeptical of any claims for a Norse presence at unlikely American sites distant from Newfoundland.

seasonal scheduling and longer-term camps. As Archaic peoples got better at extracting food from their environments their populations went up. As population density rose the need to keep moving in order to stay in contact with neighboring bands declined.

Mobile hunter-gatherers buffered food shortfalls by their mobility and by sharing with other members of their connubia. The lack of clear linguistic or social boundaries made it impossible to exclude "others" from the group within which people were willing to share. There was a preference for sharing with consanguinal (blood) relatives, but any individual was hard put to refuse any other a helping hand because of long-term reciprocal obligations. Food storage was regarded in this context as antisocial hoarding. Food storage displaced consumption either spatially or seasonally. It was possible only when a group was able to (or forced to) abandon much of its mobility and exclude hungry neighbors. It was therefore related to increased population size, more permanent camps, the establishment

of social boundaries, and internal social innovations for maintenance and redistribution of stored food. Archaeologists see this happening during the long period of Archaic adaptation. Camps became larger and more permanent, resulting in midden accumulations around them. Evidence of long-term food storage began to turn up in Archaic sites, something that would have been possible only if the connubia were beginning to crystallize into bounded sets of related bands. Archaic hunter-gatherers shifted from an economy that focused on a small number of obvious food resources to a broader array of less obvious ones. The array of plant and animal species in the emerging diffuse economy was both richer (more species) and more even than the earlier economies of Paleoindians.

Low-density, low-intensity foragers tend to marry distantly, while later high-density, highly invested cultivators tended to marry locally (Fix 1999). To understand these changes we have to define specific kinds of mobility. Permanent **migration** is not cyclical and by definition it is not reversible. **Territorial mobility** refers to shifting territoriality, which might cycle with a periodicity of decades but which we should not refer to as migration. **Residential mobility** refers to the relocation of the local band within a known territory. **Logistical mobility** refers to the temporary dispatch of task groups to specific locations, usually for purposes of specialized hunting, fishing, or gathering activities. All of these can be varied in terms of frequency, duration, and in the case of logistical moves the makeup of the task group. Some researchers distinguish between **foraging** behavior, which involves moving residential or logistical camps to food resource areas, and **collecting** behavior, which involves bringing food resources back to the base camp (Binford 1978). In short, Archaic cultures lowered their overall mobility and distinguished between more specific kinds of it.

For lack of a better means to define regional boundaries for the Archaic, archaeologists have often resorted to using the boundaries of major river drainages (Coe et al. 1986:40). The assumption is that travel and communication are easier within such units than across the heights of land that separate them. This has worked reasonably well, but the accumulation of new survey and excavation data has allowed us to do better in recent years. For example, Archaic sites in the coastal Southeast, the Carolinas, turn out not to cluster by watersheds. Instead they are scattered across the landscape in ways that varied seasonally according to the availability of wild foods, and the locations of high-quality stone quarries. Thus the availability of good stone for knapping was an important consideration, one that caused Archaic peoples to keep quarries in mind as they moved from one harvesting location to another through the course of their seasonal movements (Daniel 2001).

The Magic Number 500 and the Redefinition of Sharing

The threshold of 500 reminds us that perhaps the simplest and easiest way to scale human societies is demographically. Martin Wobst (1975) long ago showed through simulation that human breeding populations below 500 are often too unstable to survive in the long run. Moore and Moseley (2001) have made a similar argument more recently. Interestingly, 500 appears to also be about the maximum number of face-to-face relationships that the average person can maintain easily, regardless of the size of the society he or she lives in? Individuals in successful breeding populations must

maintain enough face-to-face contacts to assure long-term success, even when the size of the local band might be as low as a dozen people. On the other hand, most individuals living in large urban societies are not comfortable trying to manage thousands of face-to-face contacts.

But 500 is not just the average number of face-to-face relationships an individual has and not just the minimum number of individuals in a viable human population. It is also the average number of words for plant and animal species, colors, and specific place names in any language. The range of specific place names is 200–900, but the average is around 500 (Hunn 1994). All of this suggests that we can set 500 as the minimum aggregate size a collection of Archaic bands had to reach before they could end their connubial relationships with other surrounding bands, set up social boundaries, begin to store food for exclusive future use, and defend their territory against intruders. These were momentous changes for the people living through the transition.

The size of a local population is determined by the carrying capacity of the environment given the technology and social organization of that population. It would be nice if archaeologists could easily assess the prevailing mode of subsistence, the specific characteristics of a particular hunter-gatherer adaptation, and compute the carrying capacity for that adaptation in a particular environment. But it turns out that carrying capacity is not a concept that archaeologists have been able to apply effectively (Bayliss-Smith 1978). As it happens, all primates, humans included, for the most part live far below the objective carrying capacities of their environments. There is usually upward population pressure, and the misery predicted by Malthus can arise from time to time regardless of a culture's adaptive strategy. But there are too many variables for us to predict it accurately before it occurs and much of the time too many for us to even account for it after the fact.

Even though we may remain unable to specify the details, we still model the processes in a general way. Small bands clearly face extinction in the long run, and larger ones have better chances to survive and grow. But subsistence and mobility demands put limits on how large bands can grow. There are also what statisticians call **stochastic** variables, the lucky or unlucky breaks that affect smaller populations more greatly than bigger ones. A band that has been doing well for generations might experience a run of male babies that leaves it fatally short of females 20 years later. A band that has for centuries been able to fall back on rabbits when other game is scarce, finds out the hard way that rabbit populations cycle from low levels to highs 25 times higher than the lows. If a low point in the rabbit population happens to coincide with the kind of killer winter that comes along every few decades, the results could be fatal for such a band.

Because of these factors averages are misleading in the world of hunter-gatherers, for it is the extremes that are lethal and death is a one-way door. Thus of all the bands that were alive and well in, say, 8000 BCE, many shrank and had to join with others, many others simply dwindled to extinction, while only a relative few left living descendants. The cycles of boom and bust explain why there is so much variability in the projectile point styles they left behind, and why there is so often evidence of change over time in the archaeological record when we are unable to specify the reasons for it. Most of the drama of the ancient past was played out by individuals at a scale too small over either space or time for archaeology to detect it.

Those groups lucky enough to live in parts of North America where natural abundance was sufficient to allow them to grow into the size range of tribes (100–1,000 people) eventually reached the threshold size of 500 where it was no longer necessary for them to share with nearby tribes in exchange for possible future reciprocity when their own circumstances turned to misfortune. Hoarding and the exclusion of distant neighbors became adaptive; group self-reliance meant that long-distance relationships were no longer needed for insurance against hard times, or for the acquisition of marriage mates. Thus the emerging tribal societies of the long Archaic settling in turned inward looking, **endogamous,** and exclusive. Tribal boundaries, language barriers, and mutual intergroup estrangement were inevitable features of this process, and we can see it in the multiplicity of Archaic projectile point styles.

The Great Basin Laboratory

Archaic adaptation was not one thing, but a theme with many variations, and the Great Basin, which lies between the Rockies and the Sierra Nevada, has been a favorite region for the archaeological study of hunter-gatherers for decades. Hunter-gatherers living an Archaic lifeway survived there until only a century ago, and both cultural anthropologists and archaeologists have found it to be an excellent laboratory for the study of relatively simple adaptations. They were only simple relative to the more complex societies of the continent; the scientific analysis of their supposedly simple adaptations has proven to be very complex and difficult.

Jesse Jennings (1957) excavated Danger Cave (Figure 4.5) and the site has been generally recognized as a key site for understanding the long-lived Desert Archaic. The lowest stratigraphic level in Danger Cave is beach sand left by Lake Bonneville when it stood 34 m (110 ft) above the current level of the Great Salt Lake (Figure 4.6). Radiocarbon dates on mountain sheep dung and wood found atop this lowest level showed that human occupation of the cave began over 12,000 years ago. The archaeological deposits above that foundational stratum were 4.3 m (14 ft) deep. Jennings divided them into five **stratigraphic** zones. Excavators found over 2,500 chipped-stone artifacts, over 1,000 grinding stones, lots of bone refuse, and many fiber artifacts. Dry conditions in the cave ensured that many items that would have disappeared in wetter environments were well preserved.

Lacking good English terms, archaeologists often call the large grinding stones **metates** and the hand stones used to grind on them **manos.** These Spanish terms are commonly used in the Southwest and across Mesoamerica, but they crop up in other parts of North America as well.

Modern archaeologists use many different lines of evidence to test hypotheses about how varying kinds of mobility were actually deployed by Archaic hunter-gatherers. One team used trace element analysis to identify the quarry sources of finished tools found all over the Great Basin (Jones et al. 2003). They then used information about quarry sources to define band territories across the Great Basin. By linking tools in camp sites to their quarry sources they were able to show that there were five large band territories, each with its own diagnostic set of favored types of obsidian. The territories were mostly large oblong regions as much as 400 km (250 mi) across (Figure 4.7). Chapter 12 offers more on the Great Basin.

The Northeastern Archaic

A widespread series of related Archaic cultures emerged across the Great Lakes region and along the Northeast coast after 5000 BCE. They are recognized by specific projectile point types, as well as spear thrower weights (bannerstones) and **semilunar** slate knives. In the upper Great Lakes craftspeople of this widespread culture learned to fashion points and other artifacts from nuggets of native copper, found mainly on the Keweenaw Peninsula of northern Michigan. This variant is often referred to as "Old Copper" culture. Working copper nuggets required the development of a whole

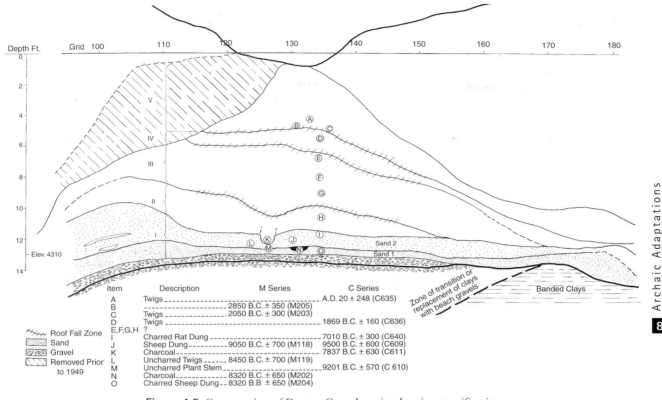

Item	Description	M Series	C Series
A	Twigs		A.D. 20 ± 248 (C635)
B		2850 B.C. ± 350 (M205)	
C		2050 B.C. ± 300 (M203)	
D	Twigs		1869 B.C. ± 160 (C636)
E,F,G,H	?		
I	Charred Rat Dung		7010 B.C. ± 300 (C640)
J	Sheep Dung	9050 B.C. ± 700 (M118)	9500 B.C. ± 600 (C609)
K	Charcoal		7837 B.C. ± 630 (C611)
L	Uncharred Twigs	8450 B.C. ± 700 (M119)	
M	Uncharred Plant Stem		9201 B.C. ± 570 (C 610)
N	Charcoal	8320 B.C. ± 650 (M202)	
O	Charred Sheep Dung	8320 B.B ± 650 (M204)	

Roof Fall Zone
Sand
Gravel
Removed Prior to 1949

Elev. 4310

Figure 4.5 Cross section of Danger Cave deposits showing stratification.
Source: Reproduced by permission of the Society of American Archaeology from
American Antiquity from Danger Cave, Memoir 14, 1957.

Figure 4.6 The lower terrace shown in this photo marks the beach line
of Lake Bonneville above modern Salt Lake City.

new set of techniques that were not at all like those used to chip or grind stone tools (Figure 4.8). The same copper source was also important to later mound builder cultures (see Chapter 5).

An unusual coastal adaptation emerged from this widespread tradition along the coast from Maine north to Newfoundland after around 5000 BCE. This culture is usually referred to as the Maritime Archaic, although their use of red ocher (iron-rich hematite) caused them to be known as the "Red Paint People" in the popular literature of the last century (Figure 4.9). They used heavy ground stone **celts,** axes, gouges, and adzes as woodworking tools to construct large dugout canoes and perhaps other things now long since decayed to dust. We know that they were at least building substantial canoes because swordfish were one of their favorite targets.

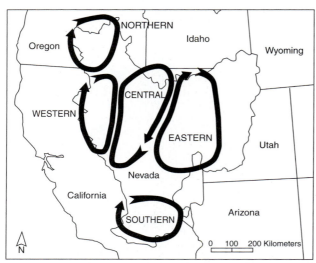

Figure 4.7 Band territories in the Great Basin.
Source: From Jones et al. 2003:31. Reproduced by permission of the Society of American Archaeology from *American Antiquity* 68(1), 2003.

Figure 4.8 Old Copper culture points made from beaten nuggets, mainly from sources in northern Michigan.
Source: Courtesy of the National Museum of Natural History, Smithsonian Institution.

Figure 4.9 Four Maritime Archaic gouges, ground stone tools used in heavy woodworking. The largest is 28 cm (11 in) long.

Figure 4.10 Slate bayonets from a site near Bangor, Maine.

These large ocean fish do not come near shore, but occasionally basked on the surface of the Gulf of Maine. Swordfish rostra (swords) were fashioned into engraved bayonet-like spears and daggers, then later left behind in shell middens along the coast. The rostra and the tasty flesh of the swordfish could only have been acquired at some risk by hunters in canoes operating on open water.

Slate bayonets (Figure 4.10) that mimicked the rostra were also made, but it is hard to say how these fragile artifacts might have been used. They turn up with woodworking tools, points, fishnet sinkers (plummets), and other distinctive artifacts in ocher-lined graves in cemeteries near estuaries and streams in Maine, the Maritimes, and Newfoundland (Snow 1975, 1980:187–222). Long-distance trade was revived too, as evidenced in Maine sites by elegant projectile points made from an exquisite smoky quartzite known as Ramah Chert, found only in Labrador (Figure 4.11).

The soils are very acidic in this region and human bone does not preserve well in it. For a long time archaeologists were not even certain that the caches of distinctive tools on red ocher were burials. Tooth enamel and the occasional fortuitously preserved bone make it clear that they were Native American graves, and they are now treated accordingly. Some of them were originally dug into natural gravelly hillocks known as glacial **kames** or long sinuous glacial features called **eskers.** In either case people were making use of natural mounds, turning them into memorials for the deceased.

The Maritime Archaic was once thought to have been a brief flash in the pan, lasting only a few centuries at most. However, it now appears to have been a cultural theme with variations scattered broadly in the region and over millennia rather than centuries. These were sea hunters, skilled canoeists like others who come later on the Pacific Coast. There is no evidence of

Figure 4.11 Ramah chert projectile points found in Maine are evidence of trade and exchange with people nearer its source in Labrador. Opposite sides of a 96-mm-long (3.8 in) point from Grave 170, Haskel site, Maine. Collection of the R. S. Peabody Foundation.

Figure 4.12 Steatite quarries in southern New England and the Middle Atlantic coastal zone provided material for making bowls prior to the introduction of pottery. Top: steatite bowl from Truro, Massachusetts, 27 cm (10.6 in) long (Bronson Museum). Center: partial large steatite bowl with notched decoration and mending holes (Haffenreffer Museum). Bottom: steatite bowl with single lug (American Indian Archaeological Institute).

direct contact between the two coasts, yet similar strategies emerged along both, even to the parallels in slate tools. Maritime economies make high-quality bone and ivory available as materials for making attractive and durable tools. The techniques learned to work these materials are easily transferred to slate, so if that particular stone material is available tools made from it are likely to turn up in the inventory. That this happened independently on both coasts is further testimony to the importance of environmental opportunities and the irrepressible nature of human ingenuity.

Environmental change and technological innovation brought a replacement of the Maritime Archaic and related adaptations by culture(s) from the Middle Atlantic region after 1700 BCE. This intrusive culture is known as the Susquehanna tradition, from a prototype in Pennsylvania. A sudden shift in projectile point types, preferred materials, and burial mode suggests the expansion of a dominant population from the Middle Atlantic region northward. Susquehanna tradition peoples often preferred tough rhyolite to chert and cremated their dead before interment. Some made **steatite** containers that presaged pottery (Figure 4.12).

Mortuary innovations also occurred around the upper Great Lakes, where Glacial Kame culture people also used these natural features as cemeteries. Their descendants built artificial burial mounds, possibly inspired by the natural kames. Far away in the southwestern corner of the Eastern Woodlands other people began modifying the landscape with earthworks of another kind. Their sites, which date to before the third millennium BCE, were not tentative first attempts but ambitious and impressive undertakings (see Chapter 5).

Other Archaic Cultures

There are many named Archaic cultures scattered across the continent, each of them an example of the general adaptive trends that have been described in this chapter. San Dieguito and Pinto cultures evolved in southern California and western Arizona. The Cochise sequence dominated in the hot desert of southern Arizona and New Mexico and the northern reaches of Mexico. To the north Oshara culture laid foundations on which Anasazi culture would later develop.

The Arnold Research Cave in Missouri has produced among other things a long sequence of Archaic footwear. Sandals and slip-ons made from fiber and leather date to as early as 6205 BCE there (Kuttruff et al. 1998). Russell Cave, in northeastern Alabama, yielded an 8,000-year-long sequence that also illuminates the Eastern Woodland variation on the Archaic theme. There acorns were processed for food and fuel. Hickory nuts provided "hickory cream," a nutritious oil is obtained by boiling crushed nuts in water. The dried hickory mash could be used as flour and like acorn shells the hickory shells were a good fuel.

Elsewhere in the Eastern Woodlands Archaic peoples zeroed in on other food resources, maximizing them where they could. In Kentucky they scoured the rivers for freshwater mollusks, and left behind extensive middens of discarded shells. These sites are typically located in places where local resources were particularly rich. People were eating not only mussels, but also birds, fish, deer, and a range of domesticates and near domesticates that I discuss below.

Where Boston now stands they built weirs of closely set stakes to impound fish when the tide went out (see Chapter 5). Other seafoods were available here too, but most of the wild plants that had potential as domesticates were not.

Evidence of central bases occurs in situations where abundant food resources allowed a relaxation of mobility. They were also possible where transportation innovations allow relatively rapid long-distance deployment of logistical task groups. Base camps tend to contain the full range of tools and debitage produced by the band. Logistical camps (sometimes called field camps) typically contain only part of the full range of tools and debitage. The tools present in a logistical camp indicate the special activities carried out there and/or the nature of the task group. One example would be a hunting camp used only by adult men. Another would be a root gathering camp used only by women.

Canoes would have provided transportation capability for logistical teams, so archaeologists can infer their use even when the canoes themselves have not been preserved. Newnans Lake in Florida is a major exception. It has produced over 100 canoes dating from 2300 BCE to perhaps as early as 7000 BCE (Wheeler et al. 2003).

Perhaps the most remarkable single Archaic site discovery of recent years is the Windover site in Florida (Figure 4.13). This wet site dating from 6000 to 5000 BCE contained an astonishing array of materials that one would normally not expect to be preserved, even in a site a few decades old. At least 160 people were buried in the waterlogged soil at Windover, anaerobic conditions that preserved not just their skeletons but brain tissue, textiles, wooden implements, and even their last meals. One unfortunate woman was given a

Figure 4.13 The Windover site in Florida is a large wet site that was difficult to excavate but provided excellent preservation of many samples relating to Archaic diet and subsistence.

rich but ineffective medicinal concoction just before she died (Newsom 2002). Elsewhere in the site is evidence that people were using bottle gourds, grapes, prickly pears, and many other plants as foods, containers, and raw materials for tools (Tuross et al. 1994). Curiously, an analysis of the isotopes in their bones indicates that these people were concentrating on terrestrial plants and were not consuming much of the marine foods that must have been available only a short distance away (Doran 2002; Doran and Dickel 1988). Women at Windover show more dental variation than do men. This is what we would expect if these Archaic people practiced **patrilocal** postmarital residence (Tomczak and Powell 2003).

Evolving Technology

The development of a weighted flexible spear thrower was a clever technological advance in Archaic weaponry (Figure 4.14). Ground stone artifacts called "bannerstones" have been turning up for many years all across the Eastern Woodlands. These are often similar in shape and size to a computer mouse, but with a 10- to 15-mm (0.4–0.6 in) hole drilled through from side to side. Early archaeologists could not imagine what they were used for, so they fell back on the "ceremonial object" catchall term.

Fortunately, the low acidity of soils containing shell promotes preservation. Examples of bannerstones found with burials in the shell mounds of Kentucky were often arranged with bone hooks and loops that made them all appear to be parts of complex spear throwers. The shafts had disappeared even in the relatively benign shell deposits, but the other parts survived, often in the same telltale arrangements, handle or finger loops at one end, **bannerstone** in the middle, and hook at the other end (Webb 1974). Figure 4.14 shows such a composite spear thrower, compared to a simple one-piece spear thrower.

The composite spear thrower looks complicated, and it is. The handle or finger loops provide the hunter with a good grip, and the bone hook would have fit well into the socket at the base of a spear shaft. But the bannerstone at first seemed unnecessary at best, and dysfunctional at worst. A weight at the middle of the spear thrower shaft confers no practical advantage, assuming that the shaft is rigid. Furthermore, the hole in the bannerstone is usually so narrow that experimentally any rigid wooden shaft small enough to fit through it would snap on the first throw. The answer must be that the shafts of the complex spear throwers were flexible. Green ironwood (*Carpinus caroliniana*) would be a perfect material for this purpose, and it might also explain why shafts are not preserved. Ironwood decays more rapidly in the ground than most woods despite its supple hardness. Experiments with flexible spear throwers show that Archaic hunters probably discovered the benefits of flexibility, which fiberglass has brought to modern golf, pole vaulting, and other sports. The added weight flexes the spear thrower at the beginning of the throw, loading force and releasing it at the end of the throw. This results in greater velocity than would be possible with a rigid spear thrower (Palter 1976).

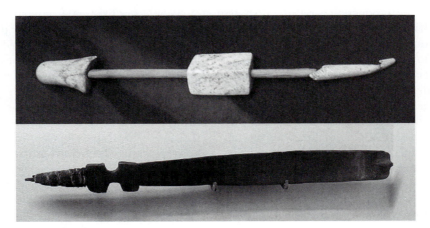

Figure 4.14 Two spear throwers. Top: composite weighted spear thrower (Mathers Museum, Indiana). Bottom: simple one-piece spear thrower Nevada State Museum, Las Vegas.

Centers of Plant Domestication

The transition to food production occurred slowly over the long term as people learned the details of their local environments and came to focus on a few plants that were productive and easy to manage. Archaic adaptations persisted for millennia in some parts of North America, in a few cases until the early twentieth century. However, in the Eastern Woodlands and in Mesoamerica the Archaic adaptations laid the groundwork for a transition from hunting and gathering to food production. As elsewhere, the Archaic peoples in these two regions of North America shifted to more diversified diets, using increasingly complex technology to exploit resources that were productive but tricky to harvest. They modified their environments, especially through the use of fire, increased food storage, and turned increasingly inward as their populations increased and their ranges shrank.

The critical difference was that in the Eastern Woodlands and Mesoamerica the plants people had close to hand were species that had potential for domestication. In neither case could early gatherers have known that. They were just trying to make a living, unaware that in the process their interactions with certain plants would yield quite unexpected results over the long run.

For many years influential archaeologists assumed that there was a sharp difference between hunter-gatherers and farmers, and that the transition to food production was so rapid and pervasive as to have been revolutionary (Childe 1951). Hunter-gatherers on the one hand and farmers on the other were regarded as very different human phenomena, and the shift from the former to the latter was perceived as an almost mystical transformation. But painstaking research in various parts of the world where food production evolved has shown that the essential characteristics of these two categories arose more from our desire for conceptual simplicity than from archaeological reality. For any particular human adaptation over the sweep of several millennia there was a mix of casually used wild species, intensively used wild species, managed species, and domesticates. Species were added to and dropped off these four lists through the course of the evolution of any culture, and at any given moment whatever the current mix was would have appeared to be a reasonably stable way to make a living. In other words, we should expect to find evidence for long periods of low-level food production in the archaeological record, not revolutionary transformations, and that is in fact what we do find. Just as importantly, it turns out that we cannot accurately characterize the level of food production by simply measuring the relative importance of domesticates in the diet, for they were only part of the picture (Smith 2001b).

Eastern Woodlands

Eastern Woodlands plant domestication may appear to have been simple, but its effects were profound. By 6000 BCE people living in the Eastern Woodlands of North America were foraging with considerable skill and a sophisticated knowledge of the plant species of their environment. They used hundreds of plants, some of them casually and some intensively. It was only a short logical step from intensive harvesting and occasionally firing of patches to protective tending, given that people's seasonal routines had already settled into a predictable round. By harvesting stands of plants around their traditional camps at the right times people inadvertently reduced plant competitors and encouraged synchronization of ripening. They were already focused on healthy stands, so the plants they were harvesting were those occurring in what for them were the most adaptive locations. It was not hard for people to take things a step further by suppressing competing plants, which were not as valued for food and which were already at a natural disadvantage relative to the favored plants.

From protective tending it was only another short step to encouraging the plants to reproduce in midden soils around camps or other places where it was more convenient for people to tend and harvest them. Selection of the most desirable plants at around the same time year after year continued to encourage synchronization of fruiting and also selected for plants whose seeds dispersed neither too early nor too late for the harvesters. Over time the plants acquired microscopic characteristics that archaeologists can detect as evidence of domestication.

People fired the environment as they had for millennia, except now it was to clear patches in the forest where the plants they desired would flourish. The practice favored fire-tolerant oaks, chestnuts, and pines in the upland forests, and reduced the frequency of other tree species (Delcourt et al. 1998).

Table 4.6 shows four species that evolved quickly through artificial selection to become true domesticates. Four more species were intensively used but in those cases there is not yet sufficient evidence to regard them as domesticates.

Squash species have been difficult to distinguish but it appears most likely that the wild Ozark gourd (*Cucurbita*) was domesticated in the Eastern Woodlands by 3000 BCE. Plants of another variant of squash were apparently domesticated in Mesoamerica much earlier and were later introduced to the Eastern

Table 4.6 Domesticates and intensively used or managed plants in the Eastern Woodlands, 6000-2500 BCE.

Scientific Name	Common Name	Status	Seeds
Cucurbita texana	Squash	Domesticate	Oily
Lagenaria siceraria	Bottle gourd	Intensively used	Oily
Iva annua	Sumpweed/marshelder	Domesticate	Oily
Helianthus annuus	Sunflower	Domesticate	Oily
Chenopodium barlandieri	Goosefoot	Domesticate	Starchy
Polygonum erectum	Erect knotweed	Intensively used	Starchy
Phalaris caroliniana	Maygrass	Intensively used	Oily
Hordeum pusillum	Little barley	Intensively used	Oily

Source: From Kay et al. 1980; Smith 1989, 2001c:224.

Woodlands as well. Bottle gourds, *Lagenaria siceraria*, were being intensively used in the Eastern Woodlands by 5000 BCE, probably as fishnet floats and containers rather than food (Doran et al. 1990; Hart et al. 2004; Kay et al. 1980). Their seeds and flesh were nearly unpalatable, but experiments show that they would have worked well as floats.

Knotweed, goosefoot, little barley, and maygrass are all high in carbohydrates. The first two produce in the fall while the second two are spring-maturing. Squash, sumpweed, and sunflower (all fall-maturing) are high in oil or fat. None of them are good sources of protein. In the absence of suitable animals for domestication the people of the Eastern Woodlands had to remain dependent upon game and fish for their protein. This would not change until thousands of years later when beans, a good plant source for protein, were introduced from Mesoamerica.

Sometimes archaeologists are tipped off by plants that turn up in sites far from their natural ranges. A fragmentary squash rind from the Sharrow site in central Maine is among the oldest known for the Eastern Woodlands but northern New England is not in its natural range (Petersen and Sidell 1996). Similarly, wild onions (*Allium canadense*) grow wild from Pennsylvania southward, yet we sometimes find them still growing in patches around Archaic sites well north of there (Barber 1977). Unlike squash, onions cannot be propagated from seed, but can be from bulbs. That means that people must have been responsible, either consciously or unconsciously, for spreading these plants beyond their natural range.

Another sunflower, *Helianthus tuberosa*, was eventually domesticated for its tubers. These can still be found in supermarkets, sold as Jerusalem artichokes. The tubers are not artichokes and the plant has nothing to do with Jerusalem. Like so many other American domesticates this one was carried to Europe in the sixteenth century, probably by Spanish merchants who referred to it as *girasol* (sunflower). This became "Jerusalem" to some Englishman with a tin ear, and the name stuck.

Many other seeds and tubers were used by Archaic gatherers once they got to know the plants and understand how to prepare them. Groundnuts (*Apios apios*), tuckahoe (*Peltrandra virginica*), and wild calla (*Calla palustris*) are all edible, but the last must be thoroughly dried and the second has to be first baked in an earthen oven. These examples show that across the Eastern Woodlands people were as engaged in intensive plant utilization and in modifying the living environment as people were anywhere else. Fortunately for them they had plants close at hand that had potential as domesticates. Unfortunately for them there were only a few plants that could become really productive domesticates.

Mesoamerica

The long transition to food production in Mexico began around 8000 BCE and continued until 2500 BCE when the first village-based agricultural economies were well established (López Austin and López Luján 2001:24; Smith, 2001b:25). The Mesoamerican example shows us that the advent of agriculture was not a revolutionary event but an evolutionary one that took over five millennia to evolve from the first plant domesticates to village farming. But the people who practiced low-level food production around, say, 5000 BCE were not living in incomplete or unstable adaptations. Instead they were reasonably well adapted to the prevailing circumstances of their time.

A few plant species with potential to become domesticates were scattered around Mesoamerica. Three that were particularly important later on in both Mesoamerica and other regions were squash, maize, and beans. Maize, called "corn" by most modern Americans, had a complicated history because it derived from teosinte, a wild plant that at first glance has little to recommend it (Bennetzen et al. 2001; Iltis et al. 1979; Wilkes 2004). So different is teosinte from domesticated maize that botanists first doubted that teosinte could be the plant from which domesticated maize sprang. But teosinte thrives in disturbed habitats, tolerates drought, is easy to harvest and store, and is curiously unappealing to insects, mice, and birds. Archaic people in Mesoamerica made good use of it, reducing it to edible form by pounding and grinding it into meal, and promoting its growth with fire. Two or more forms of teosinte contributed to the long history of hybridizing and artificial selection that eventually led to maize.

Figure 4.15 shows the likely approximate recent distributions of wild beans, wild squash, and teosinte, along with the five cave sites where archaeologists have been lucky enough to find well-preserved examples of early domesticated plants (Smith 2001c). Evidence from Guilá Naquitz Cave, which probably lies within the range of wild squash, indicates that this plant was domesticated there around 8000 BCE (Flannery 1986; Smith 1997). Domesticated maize (*Zea mays*) appears

in the same cave by around 4300 BCE, centuries earlier than it had previously been detected in Coxcatlán and San Marcos to the north in the Tehuacan Valley (Benz 2001; Long and Fritz 2001; Piperno and Flannery 2001). Teosinte had to undergo a series of mutations for it to become maize, and strong selection by humans was required for the mutations to persist. Relocation of the fruit from the top of the plant to its side, tight husks encasing larger ears, and tight binding of kernels to cobs are all major biological changes that humans preferred but that would have been lethal to the plants in the wild. The basic changes that turned teosinte into maize occurred by 4300 BCE, but we may yet find earlier evidence closer to the modern range of Teosinte.

Beans (*Phaseolus vulgaris*) were domesticated later than squash and maize, no later than around 300 BCE. Lima beans (*Phaseolus lunatus*) were domesticated separately. We may yet find earlier evidence because the natural range of wild beans is far away from the cave sites that have been excavated so far. Once domesticated, beans spread more slowly than other domesticates, probably because their fruiting is timed by the hours of daylight. It took a millennium for them to reach the caves of northeastern Mexico, although they reached the U.S. Southwest more quickly (Smith 1997, 2001a).

Other species of squash, pumpkins, beans, avocados, chilies, and even cotton (*Gossypium hirsutum*) were also domesticated once the basic process was understood. A critical feature of them all was that they could be planted, tended, and harvested with only the simplest hand tools. There were no large animals suitable for domestication in North America, so unlike Southwest Asia there was no opportunity for people in North America to develop plows and carts, or to use animal manure as fertilizer. Complex settled societies eventually developed despite these severe limitations, and three of the domesticates, maize, beans, and squash, eventually spread throughout the Southwest, the Eastern Woodlands, and the Gulf of Mexico rim, fueling complex societies there as well.

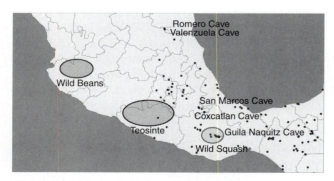

Figure 4.15 The probable locations of wild beans, squash, and teosinte. Five caves in which early domesticates have been found.

Summary

1. The Archaic was originally conceived by archaeologists as the long period of hunting and gathering between the Paleoindian period and the advent of agriculture and pottery production.

2. Agriculture turns out to have emerged gradually in multiple regions, two of them in North America, where appropriate plants happened to occur naturally.

3. Changing climatic conditions and the use of fire by early American Indians drove the complicated evolution of North American forests through the course of the Holocene.

4. Rising population densities increased local populations to above the threshold of 500, making it possible for people to establish exclusive social and political boundaries, deny resources to outsiders, and store food for future consumption.

5. The emergence of bounded cultures put an end to connubia and led to the production of hundreds of diagnostic projectile point types.

6. Decreased mobility, a shift to smaller food resources, and increased competition were only three of several general trends that characterized Archaic cultural evolution.

7. Archaeologists often study Archaic cultures in the Interior West, particularly the Great Basin, where hunter-gatherer cultures still existed only a century ago.

8. Centers of plant domestication in the Eastern Woodlands and Mesoamerica produced domesticates that were important sustainers of later developments in those regions and elsewhere in North America.

Further Reading

Jared Diamond's *Guns, Germs, and Steel* is a good popular source for anyone seeking to understand the variations in worldwide plant and animal domestication despite its occasional flaws. Colin Turnbull's *The Forest People* and Robert Kelly's *The Foraging Spectrum* are two excellent books that will introduce the reader to hunter-gatherer cultures. Margaret Scarry's *Foraging and Farming in the Eastern Woodlands* provides specifics on the region. Many books on regional archaeology in North America have detailed coverage of the Archaic cultures leading up to later (usually more complex) cultures, but these discussions tend to be technical ones dealing with site stratification and point types rather than their adaptational implications. The references for this chapter will lead to many good sources that deal with specific topics and problems. Interested readers should refer to the "References" section at the back of the book.

Glossary

analogs: Forms that are similar but do not share a common origin.

bannerstone: A ground stone artifact usually having a cylindrical hole for the insertion of a wood shaft.

camelid: A species of the camel family, including South American llamas, alpacas, vicuñas, and guanacos.

celt: A stone ax blade.

collecting: Food collecting that involves no residential relocation.

debitage: Waste flakes and chips from the manufacture of chert tools.

endogamy: Marriage within the local group; contrasting with exogamy.

esker: A long gravel ridge created when a glacier melts in place and a river bed formed within it is deposited on the landscape.

foraging: Food collecting that involves residential relocation.

hectare: A unit of area equal to a square 100 meters on a side or 2.471 acres.

homologs: Similar forms that share a common origin.

kame: A gravel mound left behind by melting glacial ice.

logistical mobility: The temporary dispatch of task groups to specific locations, usually for purposes of specialized hunting, fishing, or gathering activities.

mano: Spanish term for the hand-sized grinding stone used with a metate.

metate: A flat or concave grinding stone used with a smaller mano to grind seeds into meal or flour.

migration: For humans, the permanent relocation of an individual or group.

palynology: The study of pollen.

patrilocal: Postmarital residence in which women move in with their husbands' families.

residential mobility: The relocation of the local band within a known territory.

semilunar: In the shape of a half moon.

steatite: A soft, homogeneous mineral derived from talc. Also known as soapstone.

stochastic: Having to do with random chance.

stratigraphic: Pertaining to strata.

territorial mobility: The long-term shifting of group range due to the cumulative shifting of it constituent parts.

The Mound Builders

Of labour on the large scale, I think there is no remain as respectable as . . . the Barrows, of which many are to be found all over this country. These are of different sizes, some of them constructed of earth, and some of loose stones. That they were repositories of the dead, has been obvious to all: but on what particular occasion constructed, was matter of doubt.

Thomas Jefferson

THE CONVERGENCE OF FAVORABLE CLIMATIC conditions and innovations in food production raised the cap on cultural elaboration in the Eastern Woodlands after 5000 BCE. By 1000 BCE the tribal societies of the region were enjoying unprecedented adaptive well-being, with technology and in an environment that encouraged population growth and cultural elaboration. Sea hunters in the Northeast, hunter-gatherers in the Great Lakes region, and villagers in Louisiana were variations on a widespread theme. At the region's core the domestication of native plants provided the subsistence base for the mound building cultures. The florescence of these cultures lasted for 14 centuries, beginning with what archaeologists call Adena culture and culminating with Hopewell culture. Both were built on a base of tribal societies that came to be linked through a widespread network of trade and exchange. The hallmarks of both are thousands of burial mounds and other earthworks scattered across much of the Eastern Woodlands. Eventually the mound building tradition changed in the face of competition and spreading conflict. The construction of effigy burial mounds continued in the region's northwest, but earthworks were converted to an entirely new purpose elsewhere.

The Environment of the Eastern Woodlands

The Eastern Woodlands region is a temperate deciduous forest that lies south of the coniferous forests of central and eastern Canada, east of the Great Plains (Figure 5.1).

The environment of the region varies due to differences in latitude, altitude, soils, and proximity to the ocean. Environmental boundaries within the region tend not to be sharp, which is why archaeologists usually treat it as a single piece.

The weather systems that affect the Northeast tend to come from the west and northwest, bringing frigid air in the winters and fair skies in the summers. Winters can be very cold, and the snow deep. Areas downwind from any of the Great Lakes tend to get very heavy

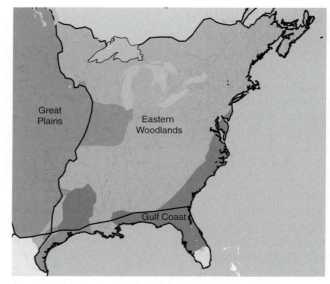

Figure 5.1 Eastern Woodlands ecozone. This chapter includes the Prairie Peninsula, and an eastward extension of the prairie portion of the Great Plains, but it excludes the Gulf Coast.

snowfalls, yet summers can be hot, humid, and productive for people reliant on plant foods.

Air masses moving west to east collide with others moving up the Atlantic Coast, producing the complex climatic conditions of most of the Eastern Woodlands, including the ferocious "Noreaster" winter storms and deluges from exhausted hurricanes in the summer. Cold fronts advancing from the Great Plains spawn random but deadly tornados, especially where there are no mountains to disrupt them.

Appalachian Mountains

The Appalachian Mountains run from southern New York to Alabama and Georgia, although some geographers include the Adirondacks of northern New York as well as the mountains of New England as part of the chain. The Appalachian forests are mixed hardwoods. To the north the forests were dominated by beech, maple, and elm trees, while oaks, chestnuts, and hickories all traditionally dominated to the south. Chestnuts and more recently elms have all but disappeared because of diseases that attacked them in the twentieth century.

The Great Lakes

The Great Lakes drain the northern interior of the Eastern Woodlands. The basins of the lakes and thousands of smaller ones were scoured by the great ice sheets of the Pleistocene. These five bodies of water were once surrounded by forests of beech, maple, and associated trees. North of the lakes birch trees provided bark for canoes, which in that part of the region were in turn the preferred mode of transportation along streams and across the chains of lakes left behind by continental glaciers. Agricultural communities eventually approached the southern shores of the Great Lakes, and even spread north of the two lowest lakes, Ontario and Erie. But short growing seasons kept agriculture from becoming established as a reliable economy elsewhere.

New England and the Maritimes

The rugged landscape of New England is an ancient geological gift from another of the earth's great tectonic plates, long ago grafted on to the North American continent. The metamorphosed bedrocks of New England do not make agriculture easy even in the southern parts, where the growing season is generally adequate for it. Maize and other imported domesticates arrived late and did not always fare well even in southern New England. Northern New England and the Maritime provinces remained in the hands of hunter-gatherers until the arrival of European settlers. The spruce and fir forests of the northern part of the region were most easily traversed in swift birchbark canoes, whereas the more temperate forests of the southern part were laced with overland trails.

Coastal Plain

The Southeastern Coastal Plain of eastern North America lies between the Appalachian Mountains and

Box 5.1 HOW TO MAKE THINGS FROM NATIVE COPPER

Nuggets of native copper can be found around the upper Great Lakes. They are concentrated on the Keweenaw Peninsula of northern Michigan, but glaciers carried many farther south as well, where they can still be found in stream beds. Many nuggets are small, bean-sized lumps that can be used to make beads but not much else. There are much larger nuggets too. A friend of mine has one that weighs over 90 kg (200 lb) hanging from a reinforced ceiling beam. Another much larger one graced the campus of the University of Minnesota when I was an undergraduate student there.

American Indians did not learn how to melt native copper or how to smelt it from copper ore. Copper has a melting point of around 1,000°C (1830°F), depending upon the amounts of impurities, too high for even the hottest fires they could manage at the time. Casting was thus out of their reach. However, native copper is malleable, meaning that it can be beaten into various shapes, but only to a point. Beating copper gradually transforms its shape but it also makes it brittle. After a time it will begin to crack and lose strength. Native craftspeople discovered that they could remedy this by heating the piece periodically between poundings and plunging it into cold water. This process, known as annealing, restored malleability to brittle copper and enabled the artisan to continue working it into the desired shape. Copper projectile points were made early on, but the craft was later used to produce copper sheets, and many copper-clad artifacts such as ear spools.

the Atlantic Coast. It begins in New Jersey and broadens to the south. The coastal lowland fringe of the Eastern Woodlands was covered by Atlantic coniferous forest in which southern pines and associated species predominated. The lowland environment was fairly rich in natural resources, particularly on or near the coast, but it was peripheral to the main developments described in this chapter.

Mississippi Valley

The western margin of the Eastern Woodlands was within the widespread region of burial mound building and long-distance trading that flourished after 1000 BCE. The cultural potential of this vast interior lowland was to culminate later with platform mound building and advanced agriculture, when Mesoamerican domesticates and the farming potential of broad floodplains combined to produce another florescence in human adaptation (see Chapter 9).

Ohio River Valley

The Ohio River Valley and the other interior drainages of the heartland of the Eastern Woodlands was center stage for the events described in this chapter. The vast hardwood forest of oak, hickory, chestnut, and associated trees provided abundant food. This was also the core area of the Eastern Agricultural Complex, the set of locally domesticated plants that emerged during the Archaic periods and underpinned the elaboration of mound building and burial ceremonialism after 1000 BCE (Smith 1989).

First Impressions

What archaeological remains represent and what early archaeologists made of them were often two rather different things. The landscape of the Eastern Woodlands was strewn with thousands of mounds and other earthworks when the first European settlers moved westward through the Appalachian Mountains, and the documentary history of those sites dates only from the era of European exploration and settlement, not before. Even the farmers among the first European settlers, who generally regarded the mounds as a nuisance, were impressed by them, and speculation about their origins was widespread. There is a lesson for us in what followed. It is that while the archaeological evidence of the past should be understood in its own terms, the prejudices and ideological agendas of later people trying to understand it can easily distort understanding.

The formidable Thomas Jefferson took note of burial mounds in the vicinity of his home in Virginia, and undertook to excavate one of them in an unusual example of early archaeology, which he wrote about sometime prior to 1782 (Jefferson 1955:97–100). His techniques were careful and his conclusions were sound (Dunham et al. 2003). He inferred from the evidence that the mound had been built in stages, and that a local American Indian community had been responsible. But popular imagination did not follow his lead in the nineteenth century. The political agendas of the time put their own spin on the earthworks of the Eastern Woodlands, while Jefferson's sober objective assessment gathered dust on the library shelf.

The Moundbuilder Myth

Most settlers typically imagined that there was no connection between the mounds and the vanishing American Indian nations of the Eastern Woodlands. Despite the precedent of Jefferson's well-reasoned conclusions there developed a body of mythology about a supposed lost race of "moundbuilders" who had been exterminated by less advanced American Indians in the centuries before Columbus (Silverberg 1968). Stories about mythological moundbuilders were harmless enough on the surface because in their simplest form they asserted only that mounds had been built by builders of mounds. But the stories were actually a cover for racist denigration of American Indians, a convenient justification for their dispossession by expanding Euroamericans that was not harmless at all.

Smallpox and other diseases had so decimated the eastern Indian nations that many areas of the Eastern Woodlands had been abandoned for decades before the first Euroamericans arrived. The park forests and fields that had been opened and maintained by the Indians for millennia had reverted to wilderness in only a few decades. Settlers arriving later typically concluded that the landscape had always looked that way, and that the remnant Indian tribes they encountered had never matched the accomplishments of the mythical moundbuilders that had been there earlier. But the wilderness that Daniel Boone explored was in fact not much more than a century older than he was, and the real mound builders were more or less than the ancestors of the remnant Indian societies he encountered.

It is helpful to remember that prior to the seventeenth century nearly all Europeans looked to ancient texts, not to empirical scientific evidence, for wisdom and truth. The great earthen mounds of the Eastern Woodlands were to them likely the remains of people more like the ancient Greeks than any more recent culture. Francis Bacon pointed out in 1605, "These times are the ancient times, when the world is ancient, and not those which we account ancient . . . by a computation backward from ourselves" (Bacon 1952:15). But Bacon was ahead of his time in grasping the ways in which contemporary views promote misinterpretation of the past. It would be centuries before a majority of Americans would abandon their belief in the superiority of ancient wisdom and embrace instead a more objective scientific point of view.

The moundbuilder myth flourished even as two intrepid archaeological surveyors explored the region on horseback and attempted to map the major earthwork sites before they disappeared under the plow. Ephraim Squier and his colleague E. H. Davis doggedly explored the woodlands before the railroads reached beyond the Appalachians, drawing maps of mounds and other structures, and describing what they saw. They were meticulous and careful to avoid speculation, particularly about mythological moundbuilders. Their primary work, published by the Smithsonian Institution in 1848, is still worth reading, and would be even if so much of what they described had not been destroyed later (Squier and Davis 1848). Their publication is all the knowledge we have left for many important earthwork sites.

Box 5.2 HOW TO VISIT MOUND BUILDER SITES

The greatest concentration of Adena and Hopewell sites is in southern Ohio and the State of Ohio has preserved several of them in parks, often with excellent on-site museum exhibits. The Miamisburg Mound is the largest Adena mound still in existence. Grave Creek Mound in Moundville, West Virginia, is also impressively large.

Hopewell mounds and earthworks at the Seip site and in Newark, Ohio, are well worth visiting. The huge circle and octagon portions of the Newark earthworks are preserved on the grounds of a modern golf course. The club has a preservation agreement with the State of Ohio and archaeological visitors are welcome. Across town another great circle with an interior moat and an eagle effigy at the center is preserved in a park. A small museum interprets the whole Newark complex, other bits and pieces of which still survive in residential neighborhoods.

Mound City, north of Chillicothe, is now a national monument, and the original Hopewell type site was recently added to its holdings. Elsewhere in rural Ohio the dedicated archaeotourist can find Tarlton Cross Mound preserved in a wayside park.

The Fort Ancient site was used by the later Fort Ancient people, but it appears now to have been built first by earlier Hopewell people. The site is easily visited, another of those Ohio sites having a fine museum on site.

The Pinson Mounds are located near Jackson in southwestern Tennessee. They date to 1–300 CE. The central mound at the Pinson site is named Sauls Mound. The mound stands 22 m (72 ft) high and, unlike most mounds of the period, it is square and has four corners that point to the cardinal directions. An earthwork enclosure 365 m (1,200 ft) in diameter sets off 6.7 hectares (16.5 acres) of ceremonial space containing the mounds. The ramped and flat-topped Ozier Mound, 10 m (33 ft) high, contains no burials and was probably used as a ceremonial platform. It is one of the oldest such mound in the Eastern Woodlands.

Serpent Mound, in southern Ohio, is worth a visit. Frederick Ward Putnam of Harvard University worked on this great effigy mound from 1886 until 1889. He raised money among the ladies of Boston and accumulated enough to buy the property and pay for site restoration. He restored the effigy as well as some nearby conical mounds. Harvard transferred ownership to the State of Ohio in 1900. Visitors can climb a tower for a better look and a small museum provides information about the site.

The effigy mounds of Wisconsin and adjacent states might have been meant to be seen from the air, but they are nearly invisible from that perspective unless forest cover is cleared and the sun is very low in the sky. They are also very difficult to photograph at ground level. The best way to see effigy mounds still is to walk around them. Effigy Mounds National Monument in northeastern Iowa and Lizard Mounds Park north of Milwaukee are excellent venues. There are many other effigy mounds in wayside parks in Wisconsin, even one intaglio (a negative mound) in Fort Atkinson, Wisconsin. Effigy Mounds National Monument and nearby Pike's Peak State Park contain impressive effigy mounds.

Early mound building extended deep into the South as well. Marksville, Louisiana, has 5 large earth rings and 8 mounds, as well as around 70 earlier small circular earthworks outside the big enclosures. The site dates from 50 BCE to 400 CE.

The Roots of Mound Building in the Eastern Woodlands

The origins of mound building are difficult to trace, as the origins of great traditions often are. Some of the ideas that led to mound building appeared first around the perimeter of the region. As elsewhere in North America, Archaic adjustments in the Eastern Woodlands focused on the intensification of the use of local resources as the environment stabilized and people became increasingly familiar with them. The continent's human population had grown rapidly during the Paleoindian period, but it stabilized and remained at about the same overall level for about six millennia, through the better part of the Holocene. There was a new upward trend after around 5000 BCE that lasted for 20 centuries or more. After a downturn it resumed its upward trend again around 2000 BCE (Milner 2004:28).

The upward bump in population after 5000 BCE appears to have been the result of favorable conditions for hunter-gatherers and their mastery of local resources, particularly in places where local plants could be domesticated or coastal resources were abundant. This was a time span that Eastern Woodlands specialists often refer to as Late and Terminal Archaic periods. Sites from this long episode of growth and apparent well-being are abundant, as are the many projectile point types that are the hallmarks of specific cultures.

It was in the context of the Late Archaic heyday that the practice of building burial mounds began in the Northeast, around the Great Lakes, and into southern Illinois. Most were piles of earth but occasionally they were heaps of stone. In either case they began to appear in disconnected parts of the East, so distant from one another that the practice seems to have arisen spontaneously in

each case. This is not surprising, because burial mound construction arose independently many times around the world. For example, burial mounds were built in central Asia recently enough to have been described by Greek travelers. The Mapuche Indians of Chile also built mounds in recent times, and they also developed the tradition independently (Dillehay 1990).

The Northerners

Far to the north along an unlikely stretch of the Labrador coast archaeologists have found what appears to be the earliest stone burial mound in the whole region. The L'Anse Amour site contains the face-down burial of a 12-year-old accompanied by an antler toggle-head harpoon, a walrus tusk, three quartzite knives, a bone whistle, and socketed bone points. A radiocarbon date indicates that the mound was constructed at least 8,000 years ago (McGhee 1976).

The later Maritime Archaic adaptation, which emerged along the coast of northern New England, the Maritime Provinces, and the Atlantic Provinces of Canada, featured lavish burials (see Chapter 4). These were often placed in natural gravelly kames, glacial features that presaged artificial mound building. Artificial mounds, even stone ones, are cheap and easy to build if the materials are close at hand, and elaborate mound building later became a major theme elsewhere in the region.

Mortuary innovations also occurred around the upper Great Lakes, where Glacial Kame culture people also used these natural features as cemeteries (Figure 5.2). Their descendants later built artificial burial mounds, which regional archaeologists have sometimes proposed were inspired by the natural kames. But far away in the southwestern corner of the

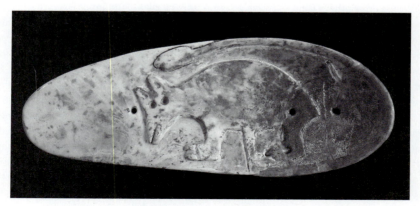

Figure 5.2 A Glacial Kame culture marine shell sandal-sole gorget from Hardin County, Ohio, 19.4 cm (7.6 in.) long. *Source:* Courtesy of the Ohio Historical Society.

Eastern Woodlands, well south of any glacial kames, other people also began modifying the landscape with earthworks.

The Southerners

The sites of Watson Brake and Poverty Point are both in Louisiana, both very old, and both very large. These sites, which date to before the third millennium BCE, were not tentative first attempts but ambitious and impressive undertakings. There are 11 earthen mounds at Watson Brake, connected around a huge oval by a low meter-high (3.5-ft) earthwork ridge. The oval is about 280 m (919 ft) in diameter and the highest mound stands 7.5 m (25 ft) high. The other mounds are lower, but as a whole the complex is imposing, all the more so because it dates to 3400 BCE (Saunders et al. 1997; Saunders et al. 2005).

The better known site of Poverty Point (Figure 5.3), now a state park, was built later, around 1600 BCE. The general layout of Poverty Point has been known for decades, but only recently has it been mapped using modern technology (Kidder 2002). There are six nested arcs of ridges, the outermost being 1.2 km (3,900 ft) in diameter. Each arc is a portion of a giant hexagon; the ends of the curved ridges of each segment are separated by gaps such that avenues radiate westward from the center. The eastern halves of the nested octagons were never built, for a bayou and swampy ground lie there. Five large stand-alone earthen mounds were built near the ridges. One is conical and one appears to be in the shape of a bird effigy. The rest are flat-topped platforms.

Figure 5.3 An artist's conception of the appearance of the Poverty Point site.
Source: Courtesy of Jon L. Gibson.

The biggest is 21 m (70 ft) high, huge even by later standards in the Eastern Woodlands. It has a long earthen ramp oriented toward the ridges.

The function (or functions) of the nested ridges at Poverty Point remains uncertain. Hearths and post molds suggest that people lived on them for at least part of the year. Golf-ball-sized lumps of fired clay, some of them fashioned into effigies, were probably used for heating food. Before they developed pottery that could stand the direct heat of a fire, people typically cooked soupy foods by dropping reasonably clean heated stones into them. In this way stews could be brought to a boil even in skin bags or bark trays. Stone boiling was consequently a popular way to heat food but it required stones, and there are precious few of them around Poverty Point. The fine alluvial soils of the lower Mississippi Valley do not contain proper pebbles, so the environment made the manufacture of artificial ones necessary.

The conditions that fostered the rise of Poverty Point changed because of a major climatic shift between 1000 and 600 BCE. High-resolution analysis in the Mississippi basin shows that changes in average temperature and precipitation upset the ecological balance there. Increased flooding led to abandonment of settlements and the demise of Poverty Point culture. The resulting abrupt cultural reorganization of the region has long been used by archaeologists to mark the time boundary between Archaic and later Woodland periods (Kidder 2006).

Elusive Origins

There are no apparent connections between the early mound builders and glacial kame users of Labrador, Maine, Michigan, and Louisiana, nothing to indicate that mound building was an idea that had a single source. As in the case of plant domestication and tool manufacture, here we have another example of human behavior that arises independently when the conditions are right.

While the earliest examples of mound building around the margins of the Eastern Woodlands faded, the impulse did not. As people readapted to changing conditions, earthwork construction gradually became a major preoccupation across much of the Eastern Woodlands, and the center of it all came to be located in southern Ohio. This is at the heart of the Eastern Woodlands, and burial mounds were the hallmarks of the cultures that arose there from Archaic roots. Human-made earthworks began to appear in southern Ohio around 1000 BCE.

Box 5.3 HOW TO EXPLAIN BIG MEN

Egalitarian bands of hunter-gatherers begin to collapse of their own weight when they grow to a hundred members and their very informal organization tends to be supplanted by part-time leaders. These cannot dominate all the people all the time, but just coordinating larger numbers of people requires that strong personalities assert themselves from time to time. If they become too assertive everyone else will vote with their feet and leave, but if no one is assertive the whole tribe will suffer. This is a precarious balancing act for natural leaders, but one that is common in tribal societies. Tribes are often described as "segmentary," in the sense that they can fragment and the pieces can easily come together again in new packages. The segments are socially as viable alone as they are together, so any large tribe is temporary, held together by forces of perceived mutual advantage that can change as quickly as perceptions change.

In male-dominated societies, there is a pronounced tendency for strong-willed men with charismatic personalities to assert themselves as big men. They seize opportunities to lead, often on behalf of their kin group, however that may be defined. In tribal societies they might have to lie low for long periods, letting the collective will prevail, but eventually some crisis or another will provide such a man with the opportunity to take the lead. This might come in the form of a communal hunt that needs to be organized, a visiting delegation of foreigners that needs to be spoken to, or a raid that needs to be repulsed.

It is human nature for big men to want to retain their hard-earned status for as long as they can, for this can bring many other benefits: better food, more wives, adulation of the young, and so forth. As tribal size approaches 1,000, the benefits of putting up with big men become more obvious to everyone else, and their status becomes more permanent than temporary. Between 1,000 and 10,000 the same forces are very likely to produce permanent chieftains.

The evolutionary explanation for big men is quite simple. Big men usually want to pass their gains on to their sons, and sons having a tendency to inherit their fathers' characteristics are often well suited to the inheritance. A big man with several wives will have many sons, so the tendency is self-perpetuating.

The down side is that societies dominated by strong-willed males tend to be fractious, a feedback loop that reinforces the temporary nature of segmentary tribes. A large village with several patrilineal kin groups will often have several competing big men. Competition between them can lead to conflict and breakup of the community. If geographic constraints or circumscription by other tribes prevent breakup and relocation of factions then one of the big men will usually rise to uneasy dominance.

Big men preside as chieftains in chiefdom societies and as kings in states. The most successful of them have many descendants. One in 10 living Irishmen appear to be direct male-line descendants of Niall of the Nine Hostages, a chieftain that lived around 500 CE. About 16 million Asian men appear to be direct male-line descendants of Genghis Khan. These examples differ from successful tribal big men only in the scale of their success.

Adena and Hopewell Cultures

The Eastern Woodlands were one of the world's hearths of plant domestication during the long evolution of North America's Archaic cultures. The cultural flowering that cultivation made possible eventually found expression in the construction of thousands of earthen mounds across the Eastern Woodlands. Most of these were conical or dome-shaped burial mounds, although there were also other expansive earthworks in a variety of shapes and sizes. All of them were made by and for ritual activity, the specifics of which we can only speculate about now. Great rings of earth sometimes defined ritual precincts, singularly important spaces that were once the scene of ceremonies that have left few archaeological traces other than the earthworks themselves. At other places earthworks enclosed burial mounds, sometimes many of them, monuments to the kin groups that built and maintained them, sometimes for centuries.

The two great early mound building cultures of the Eastern Woodlands were the Adena and Hopewell cultures (Figure 5.4). Adena was centered in Ohio and Kentucky, and named after the estate on which the type site was located. Hopewell, named for the site's owner, was centered more in southern Ohio. Adena culture lasted from 1000 BCE to 400 CE. Prior to the advent of radiocarbon dating the Adena and Hopewell cultures were thought of as dating to "Early Woodland" and "Middle Woodland" periods respectively, but we now know that the two cultures overlapped considerably in time. Indeed, Adena might better be regarded as an early regional variant of Hopewell (Railey 1996).

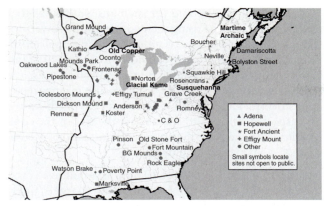

Figure 5.4 Cultures (bold) and sites mentioned in this chapter. See Figure 5.8 for the site cluster in southern Ohio and Figure 5.24 for the site cluster around southern Wisconsin.

Adena Culture

Adena is referred to here as a culture, even though the evidence for it is largely restricted to burial practices that could have been shared by several cultures that were otherwise distinctively different. Adena sites are concentrated in southern Ohio and parts of Kentucky and West Virginia, with a few outlier sites as far away as Vermont and New Jersey (Coe et al. 1986:51; Milner 2004). The earliest Adena sites were constructed by around 1000 BCE, and they were still being built in northern Kentucky as late as 100 CE, three centuries after the appearance of Hopewell culture (Webb and Snow 1974).

The economic foundation of Adena culture was the set of dependable native cultigens they inherited from their Archaic forbearers. Tropical cultigens, namely maize and tropical squash, had not yet spread north into the Eastern Woodlands from Mesoamerica, so the cultigens that spurred this growth had to be the home-grown ones native to the region. Bottle gourds were probably used initially as fishnet floats and containers (Hart et al. 2004; Hudson 2004). Native squash (*Cucurbita pepo*) was being used in a few places by 3900 BCE, and spread to other parts of the Eastern Woodlands over the following centuries. Other important early cultigens included sunflower (*Helianthus annuus*) and goosefoot (*Chenopodium barlandieri*). Acorns, hickory nuts, black walnuts, butternuts, chestnuts, raspberries, and other wild foods were harvested so regularly that they nearly became domesticates as well.

Protein continued to come from animal sources. It would be a very long time before beans, an alternative plant source of protein, would spread into the Eastern Woodlands from Mesoamerica. Although it was increasing once again, the population density of the Eastern Woodlands was still low compared to levels reached

later on. There were probably fewer than 40 people per 100 km² (39 sq mi) in Ohio 3,000 years ago, more than the 12/100 km² of historic hunter-gatherers in northern New England, yet lower than the 77/100 km² known for the later agricultural Mohawks of New York State. The regional population would climb even more later on, fueled by new plant domesticates from Mesoamerica, but for the Adena people that was still part of an unknown future. It was a time of cultural well-being, a time when revived long-distance trade relationships appear to have operated well, a time before competition for resources led to escalating warfare (Milner 2004:28).

Earthen Architecture. Adena people built simple mound earthworks in the early centuries, more complex ones later on. Many were built over places where circular buildings had previously stood. The outward-leaning posts of some early examples led archaeologists to reconstruct cupcake-shaped houses, but post mold patterns are also consistent with more familiar wigwam house style of later times (Sturtevant 1975).

Adena burial mounds tended to be built in single construction episodes. Sometimes simple clay-lined basins were first excavated to hold the ashes of the cremated deceased, then the basins and their contents were buried under the mounds. At other times elaborate log tombs were built for uncremated burials, covered up, but left accessible from the side of the mound for a long time. This was probably to make the mausoleum available for additional burials. Log tombs eventually decayed and collapsed, and their entrances were sealed.

Grave offerings included red ocher, graphite, and occasionally severed trophy heads. Many portable objects made of exotic materials such as copper, which had to have been obtained through a network of trade and exchange, were also included. Many Adena individuals exhibit deliberate cranial deformation. In analogous historical societies this was often a sign of beauty, status, or both.

Why People Build Mounds. The reasons for building burial mounds are simple. Generally speaking, cultures that do not have well-defined territorial boundaries will often have closely guarded core areas, typically main villages or centralized cemeteries. The latter probably describes the Adena pattern. Burial mounds were popular because they were prominent on the landscape and they required only the simplest engineering. They were, after all, just piles of earth. They were also surprisingly cheap and easy to construct. The volumes of burial mounds, particularly the largest of them, are impressive to anyone, and it is difficult today for us to imagine their easy construction without heavy machinery. However, a hundred adults with digging sticks and baskets, each moving a cubic meter or two (1–2 yards) of earth per day, can easily construct an impressively large burial mound in a matter of a few days. Furthermore, the construction of a burial mound requires no more complex social and political organization than does an Amish barn raising. It is something that can be accomplished easily by people who had only the weak and temporary leadership traditions of tribal society. Thus the presence of burial mounds does not necessarily imply that they were built by ranked societies, large dense populations, or people having advanced agriculture. And indeed archaeologists working in the Eastern Woodlands have not found any of those things associated with the first big wave of burial mound construction in the Adena heartland.

The Functions of Mounds. Burial mounds provided cultural centers for a dispersed society that did not have strong concepts of land tenure or political boundaries. But the contents of Adena burial mounds often reveal that some people enjoyed higher status than others, and that the possessions buried with them were sometimes luxury goods that had been imported from distant sources. It may seem contradictory at first, but even this evidence of inequality is consistent with tribal organization. The people receiving the most elaborate burials were probably clan leaders, big men who had acquired their status through lifelong effort. Grave offerings made of exotic imported materials imply a system of trade and exchange through which such things could move, which in turn was probably not much more than a network of friendships between widely scattered big men. Other people accorded lavish burials might have been shamans, religious practitioners who brought home exotic goods as evidence of long-distance pilgrimages to source locations.

Benefits to Successors. The success of any clan leader brought benefits to the whole group, not just in terms of goods that were passed along to them, but also in terms of the status and prestige enjoyed by everyone in such a group. Lavish burials were the means through which clan or family members both signaled their respect for a deceased leader and made a statement about the relative status of their group as a whole. Thus all members of a leading clan or family benefited from strong leadership and the respect shown deceased leaders; prestige accrued to the whole group. That means that the biggest mound and the most lavish burial probably went not to the most powerful or respected in a succession of leaders but rather to that person's immediate predecessor. This is because in a tribal society the most elaborate treatment is typically organized *by* big men, not *for* them.

The same can be said for shamans, so long as they were perceived to be using their supernatural powers for the general good of the community. Traditional North American shamans often claimed the ability to transform themselves into animal forms while in trances, and they typically worked their magic while in apparently transformed states. Such power was as much feared as respected, enough to ensure that the rest of the community would ensure that powerful possessions accompanied a shaman even in death.

Adena Trade and Exchange. The traits that are traditionally used to identify Adena sites are largely finely made portable artifacts, many of them made from exotic materials obtained through a large regional exchange network. Barrel-shaped, effigy, and straight cylinder tubular pipes made from fine-grained stone (Figures 5.5 and 5.6) indicate that tobacco had

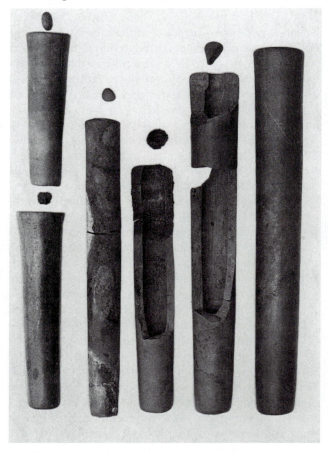

Figure 5.5 Tubular Adena pipes for smoking tobacco, some broken and including the pebble pills put at the bottoms of the tubes to prevent the tobacco from being inhaled with the smoke. Whole and fragmentary tubular pipes from the Boucher site, Vermont.
Source: Courtesy of Louise Basa.

Figure 5.6 Front and rear views of a human effigy tubular pipe from Adena Mound, 20 cm (8 in) tall. *Source:* Courtesy of John Bigelow Taylor.

A

B

Figure 5.7 The Berlin (A) and Wilmington (B) Adena tablets. The Berlin tablet is 14.3 cm (5.6 in.) long while the Wilmington tablet is 12.8 cm (5 in.) long. *Source:* Courtesy of the Ohio Historical Society.

already spread to the Eastern Woodlands from South America. This was *Nicotiana rustica,* not the comparatively mild *Nicotiana tobacum* found in modern cigarettes. Other ingredients were probably added as well. Tobacco might have come into the Eastern Woodlands by way of the Antilles. It was known in later Mesoamerica, perhaps a more logical route for the northward spread of tobacco, but smoking appears not to have been as widespread or as early there as it was elsewhere in North America, a circumstance that makes an end run through the Antilles an attractive hypothesis.

Adena craftspeople made gorgets of stone, copper, and mica, freshwater pearl beads, mica cutouts, copper bracelets, rings, and beads, bird effigy atlatl weights, and engraved tablets. The tablet might have been used to apply dye patterns to textiles, but they were more likely used for temporary body decoration and tattooing (Figures 5.7A and 5.7B).

The Adena people were also early pottery manufacturers. Early examples were crude, but later ones were better made and decorated by simple stamping. We are not sure what advantages spurred the adoption of pottery, for it represented a bigger time investment and was more cumbersome than existing bark or skin containers. It probably had to do with a more settled lifestyle and a trend toward slow cooking of porridges

and similar foods. The durability of pottery would have offered a distinct advantage under those circumstances. Adena artisans also made a variety of cloth weaves from fibers. These have sometimes preserved to the present when they were deposited in contact with copper artifacts. The copper salts protect delicate fibers from decay.

Adena Sites. Many Adena mound sites (Figure 5.8) have been destroyed and most of those that survive are simply shaped and typically attract little attention. Story Mound, for example, sits amidst residential properties in Chillicothe, Ohio. Others are more noticeable, mainly for their sizes. Grave Creek Mound still dominates a park in downtown Moundville, West Virginia. It was originally 20 m (66 ft) high and contained 70,000 m³ (91,500 yards)

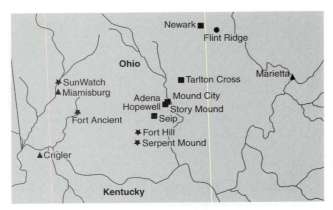

Figure 5.8 Sites in the Adena–Hopewell heartland. Many Adena (▲), Hopewell (■), Fort Ancient (★), and other (●) sites are clustered in this area. Smaller symbols locate those not open to the public.

Figure 5.9 Miamisburg Mound, Ohio.

of earth. Miamisburg Mound (Figure 5.9) is an even larger conical Adena mound in southern Ohio.

Marietta holds a more complex set of earthworks near the Ohio River. The burial mound known as "Conus" is closely surrounded like a medieval castle by a berm and a ditch (Figure 5.10). An earthen wall *outside* the ditch means that this was a ceremonial precinct, not a fortification. No military engineer would put the wall outside the ditch. A gap in the wall and an earthen ramp across the ditch give access to the mound. The mound is now preserved in a historic cemetery.

Outlier Adena sites have been found far from the heartland in New York, Vermont, and New Jersey (see Figure 5.4). These were once thought by some archaeologists to indicate migration(s) of Adena people outward from Ohio. However, the Adena burial complex appears to have been grafted on to local cultures in these instances, and there is no need to infer migration. These were probably local cultures benefiting

from their connections to the Adena exchange network, source areas for things Adena big men and shamans wanted (Grayson 1970). Early excavators also believed that Adena mounds typically contained the remains of high-status adult men, but detailed analysis of skeletons has revealed that individuals of both sexes and of a wide range of ages were buried in Adena mounds.

Hopewell Culture

Hopewell culture developed out of Adena in southern Ohio around 200 BCE, but other centers of it sprang up in Illinois and elsewhere in the Eastern Woodlands as well (Figure 5.4). Meanwhile, Adena was not replaced by Hopewell in some parts of Ohio and it continued there and in northern Kentucky, overlapping Hopewell in time for three centuries. Hopewell sites continued to be constructed in southern Ohio as late as 400 CE (Figure 5.11). Hopewell subsistence and settlement were very similar to those of Adena. They were both outgrowths of the agricultural complex that had arisen earlier in the Eastern Woodlands (Brose and Greber 1979; Dancey 2005). The difference was that Hopewell culture produced much more elaborate earthworks, its burial practices spread much farther around the Eastern Woodlands, and its trade network stretched even farther.

As with Adena culture, what we know about Hopewell has mostly to do with burials and ceremonial architecture, and it is referred to as a "culture" here only for convenience. Hopewell architects took mound building to a new level, and these practices were grafted on to a range of otherwise distinctive Eastern Woodlands cultures. Its hallmarks are vast complex earthworks and an elaborate inventory of beautiful artifacts made from exotic raw materials that were imported from great distances. Luxury goods came to Hopewell centers through a far-flung exchange network that stretched far beyond the limited reach of the earlier Adena network.

Hopewell people built burial mounds as the Adena people had, again for a wide range of individuals, but they also built large earthwork enclosures. These were often very large square, circular, even octagonal earthen ridges (Figure 5.12). Some were as large as 500 m (1,640 ft) in diameter. Sometimes they were complexes of two or more shapes, sometimes irregular, and they were sometimes connected to each other by avenues flanked by long earthen walls. In all cases the interiors of these sprawling figures were clearly intended

Figure 5.10 Marietta Mound, Ohio, from an 1840 engraving.
Source: From Squier and Davis 1848:40.

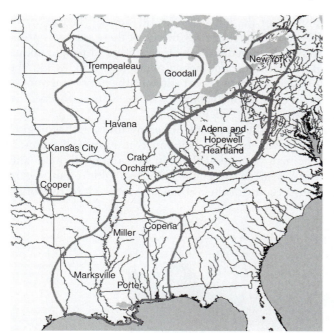

Figure 5.11 Adena–Hopewell heartland and the distribution of secondary Hopewellian mound building cultures.

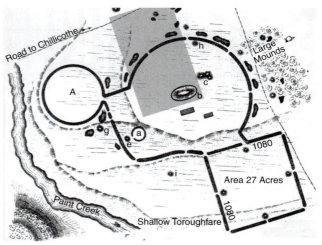

Figure 5.12 Seip site, Ohio. The shaded portion is preserved as a state park. The rest, like many Hopewell earthworks, has been leveled by modern agriculture. *Source:* From Squier and Davis 1848:56.

to be ceremonial spaces, precincts set off from the surrounding countryside for rituals now long forgotten. In some cases earthworks enclosed single burial mounds or clusters of them; in other places they are simply expansive spaces that are now flat and empty. Their earthworks were built in a variety of ways. Earth could be scooped up from the loose forest floor or taken from borrow pits. In Illinois Hopewell mounds were sometimes built at least in part by piling blocks of sod (Van Nest et al. 2001).

In many cases the individuals found in the central tombs of Hopewell mounds clearly enjoyed higher social standing than those buried in simple interments around the edges. Sometimes male burials dominated in the central tombs. At other times both males and females found in central tombs were taller than average, suggesting either that high-status individuals were better fed or that those simply lucky enough to be tall were accorded higher status.

Archaeologists once hypothesized that Hopewell societies were characterized by chiefdom organization and that dominant elite classes were supported by agriculture, but testing has invalidated this hypothesis. Extensive research has shown no evidence for the inheritance of wealth or an agricultural system capable of supporting those institutions. There is no evidence for military expansion or colonization, so the expansion of Hopewell culture must have been through trade and exchange. Some individuals were accorded more lavish burials than others, and these were probably big men in most cases, or at least the fathers of big men. Others were probably successful shamans. Much later Eastern Woodlands chiefdoms had leaders that enjoyed inherited wealth, better food, and relatively lavish lifestyles, but none of that necessarily applies in the Hopewell or for that matter the Adena cases.

Surviving Hopewell sites are today typically grassy knolls, often with mature trees growing on and around them. It is likely that they were in clearings when they were first built, and that periodic clearing, burning, and refurbishing kept them bare and more visible while they were in use. After all, the purpose of monuments is to be seen, and the purpose of ceremonial precincts is to provide open ritual space. A few excellent examples of large complex Hopewell earthwork sites still exist, most often preserved in national, state, or local parks. Many are open to the public. As large and impressive as the earthworks are, they did not require great feats of engineering. A few clever people could have laid out even the largest of them using only sticks, cordage, and an understanding of basic geometry.

Hopewell Sites

Seip Site. In addition to mounds, ceremonial earthworks could also encompass large buildings, as at the Seip site. Their foundations can still be traced using the stains left by large wall posts sunk into the subsoil. House structures inside the larger circle at Seip are 10.5–12 m (34–40 ft) long and 9–10.5 m (30–34 ft) wide. These structures were much more substantial than the residence the Hopewell people lived in. We can only speculate about the activities that went on in them inside the larger ceremonial precinct.

The Seip site was once a complex Hopewell earthwork of two large circles, a square, some other walls, and interior mounds. The great central mound and a portion of the larger circle still survive (Figure 5.13). The size and complexity of one of these sites was probably determined more by the number of people taking part in the ceremonies conducted within it and the frequency of those events than by the importance of the people buried in them. This is the pattern observed in historic cases (Dillehay 1990).

As is the case with Adena mounds, archaeologists find a wide range of individuals in Hopewell mounds. The main mound at the Seip site contained males and females in nearly equal numbers. Only infants were conspicuous for their absence, a common feature of all

Figure 5.13 The main mound at the Seip site, as seen through a gap in the earthen ring.

Figure 5.14 Mound City site, Ohio, from the west side.

ancient cemeteries. Infants were often excluded from ancient mortuary practices, and poor preservation often combines with inadequate excavation techniques to make them invisible.

Anderson Mounds. Some of the Hopewell mounds were flat-topped platform mounds rather than pointed or rounded mounds. A platform mound at the Anderson site in Indiana has a sequence of clay platforms, each deliberately covered by a layer of ash. This architectural form presaged larger platform mounds that were later common in the Eastern Woodlands (see Chapter 9) (Milner 2004:76, 91–92).

Mound City. Mound City in Ohio is a large, square earthwork enclosure containing 5.25 hectares (13 acres). Scattered within the enclosure are 22 mounds. One of these contained a large number of mica sheets laid in and around the rim of a large grave. The cremated remains of four people were accompanied by beads, teeth, galena cubes, broken pipes, and a copper head-dress (Figure 5.14).

Tarlton Cross Mound. Tarlton Cross Mound is a symmetrical cross earthwork with a circular central depression. Its shape is reminiscent of the modern Blue Cross corporate symbol.

Newark Earthworks. The largest surviving Hopewell earthwork complex is in and around the city of Newark, Ohio (Figure 5.15). The site was begun around 250 CE. Its Great Circle is 321 m (1,054 ft) in diameter, and it features a large, flat central field with an eagle effigy mound at its center. Ringing this is a large ditch and an exterior earthen embankment, both cut by an opening for level access. A gap in the exterior wall is matched by an unexcavated earthen ramp across the ditch. Elsewhere at Newark a huge earthwork circle is linked to an octagon of about the same size by an avenue flanked by two long earthen walls (Figure 5.16). The octagon is actually a

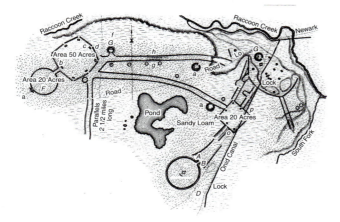

Figure 5.15 Newark Earthworks, Ohio.
Source: From Squier and Davis 1848:opposite 66.

Figure 5.16 Northwestern complex of the Newark Earthworks from the air, showing its current use as a golf course. Winter snow highlights the earthworks.
Source: Courtesy of Richard Pirko.

square with its sides pushed out such that there are two sets of angles rather than eight equal angles the corners. Each corner has a gap in the wall and a mound just inside. The octagon alone covers 18 hectares (44 acres). Careful surveying has revealed alignments with points on the horizon marking the maximum and minimum moonrises and moonsets (Lepper 2004:77).

The Pinson Site. Tennessee's Pinson site is one of several sites belonging to a secondary Hopewell development called the Miller Hopewellian, which is centered in northern Mississippi. The site is enclosed by a 365-m- (1,200-ft-) diameter earthwork. The central mound at Pinson, Sauls Mound, stands 22 m (72 ft) high. Unlike most mounds of the period it is square and has four corners that point to the cardinal directions. Ozier mound is a 10-m- (33-ft-) high flat-topped ceremonial platform, not a burial mound. It presaged a new architectural form that became widespread in the heyday of later Mississippian culture, and it is one of the oldest such mounds in the Eastern Woodlands.

The Eastern Woodlands Trade Network

Exotic Materials. Like earlier Adena ones, Hopewell artisans made use of a wide range of exotic materials when fashioning the finished artifacts that were the hallmarks of their cultures (Griffin 1967:184). Copper nuggets came from the Keweenaw Peninsula of Upper Michigan and perhaps other sources. Silver ones probably came from Ontario. Meteoric iron came from wherever it landed. Mica came from quarries in the southern Appalachians, quartz crystal from the Mohawk Valley of New York, aventurine and chlorite came from the southern Appalachians, and galena cubes came from Illinois or Missouri. Nodular flint came from deposits in Indiana and Illinois, and chalcedony from the Knife River region of North Dakota. **Obsidian** (Figure 5.17) came from the Yellowstone region of the Rocky Mountains, and grizzly bear canines were probably also of western origin. Catlinite came from quarries in southwestern Minnesota and possibly Wisconsin. Cannel coal came from any of many coal deposits in Pennsylvania and elsewhere. Cassis shell came from the Florida east coast, while *Busycon, marginella, oliva,* and *olivella* shells came from the Gulf Coast. Alligator teeth, shark teeth, marine turtle shells and barracuda jaws all came from the Gulf Coast.

The system was characterized by conspicuous consumption of valuable objects by acquiring them, giving them as gifts, and ultimately burying them,

Figure 5.17 Ceremonial obsidian artifacts from the Hopewell site, Ohio. *Source:* Courtesy of the Ohio Historical Society.

rather than by accumulating wealth. Hopewell artisans used some exotic materials to craft a wide range of finished products. Other exotic objects, such as galena cubes and grizzly bear canines, were only slightly modified treasures. By moving all of these objects through the system and into the archaeological record Hopewell consumers maintained a steady demand for more of them.

Ritual Gift Giving. Big men probably acquired both raw materials and finished artifacts through down-the-line trade, much of it couched as gift exchange between trading partners. Local big men were nodes in a widespread network of trade and exchange that had the capacity to expand as new nodes became attached. The possessions of a big man thus fluctuated as items came and went. Ritual gift giving and trading partnerships was a pattern of friendship and cooperation that transcended cultural boundaries that is frequently documented in historic American Indian tribes.

The Importance of Clans. Trading partnerships across cultural and language boundaries were traditionally facilitated by bonds of fictive kinship. These were typically established in historic times by means of shared clan totems. Someone from the bear clan in one tribe was symbolically related to someone from the bear clan in a distant and unrelated tribe. The shared identity facilitated hospitality for travelers and fraternal reasons for ritual gift exchange.

For many years anthropologists hypothesized that clans had arisen as social units to regulate marriage in societies larger than bands or small tribes. However, Elisabeth Tooker (1971) showed that their original function was to facilitate trade. Only later did marriage prohibitions with clan siblings and political innovations like the League of the Iroquois build upon preexisting clan structures. Although Tooker was unaware of the Eastern Woodlands Trade Network when she drew her conclusions about the origins of clans, it seems clear now that those origins extend back at least to Adena and Hopewell times.

Long-Distance Quests. In contrast to big men, shamans probably engaged more often in long-distance quests that took them to the magical sources of materials such as galena, obsidian, pipestone, quartz crystals, mica, and marine shell. Exotic materials from distant sources would have confirmed a successful quest and would have provided the successful shaman with a stock of powerful magic.

Trace element analysis shows that obsidian found in Ohio sites all came from Obsidian Cliff in what is now Yellowstone Park (see Chapter 12). Yellowstone obsidian was used to manufacture huge projectile points whose sizes and frequent odd shapes made them useless for any practical purpose. Some of the exotic materials probably reached the core area by down-the-line exchanges, moving through many hands before reaching their destinations. But Yellowstone obsidian had to have been acquired by more direct expeditionary means. All of the obsidian found in Ohio was deposited sometime in the century 100–200 CE, and more than half of it was found as unfinished raw material in a single grave. This was most likely the remaining stock of a shaman who managed to bring a single large shipment from Yellowstone's Obsidian Cliff, 4,000 km (2,500 mi) away (DeBoer 2004; Griffin 1967). This might seem like an impossible journey, particularly in light of the difficulties experienced by Lewis and Clark along the same route 1,700 years later. However, the big man traders that were nodes in the Hopewell trading network would have facilitated the flow of both information and travelers. Someone in Ohio with a trading partner in the galena-producing area of Illinois could have found out about Minnesota pipestone from that source. Small quantities of obsidian from Yellowstone had already passed through Minnesota (Stoltman and

Hughes 2004). People living around the pipestone quarries would have known about the Knife River chert quarries farther to the northwest in North Dakota, and these people in turn would have known about the still more distant obsidian quarries. As long as the trading network was functioning and travelers could move from node to node easily, long-distance expeditions needed only information and enough time for travel.

Copper nuggets were often beaten into sheets, then either embossed with designs or used as coverings for other objects, such as ear spools. Like earlier Old Copper craftspeople they used **annealing** to prevent the beaten copper from becoming brittle and cracking due to repeated pounding. Copper artifacts include cutouts, breastplates, embossed sheets, artificial noses, beads, gorgets, celts, axes, and adzes. Copper-clad artifacts include ear spools (Figure 5.18), panpipes, and deer horns. Meteoric iron was also collected and pounded into foil sheets. The foil was then used to cover ear spools, axes, adzes, and in one case a human arm bone. Sheets of mica were highly valued as blanks for cutouts that took the shapes of serpents, claws, human hands, human heads, swastikas, and other forms.

Hopewell potters made elaborate "zoned" vessels with incised panel designs (Figure 5.19). They also made figurines in both clay and fossil mammoth ivory that tell us much about their hair styles and clothing. Platform smoking pipes were made in simple monitor forms or more often to depict effigies of human heads, frogs, toads, water birds, raptors, ravens, bears, beavers, and the like (Figure 5.20).

Figure 5.18 A mass of Hopewell copper ear decoration. *Source:* Courtesy of the Ohio Historical Society.

Figure 5.19 Hopewell vessel from Mound City.
Source: Courtesy of John Bigelow Taylor.

Figure 5.20 Hopewell beaver
effigy platform pipe from
Bedford Mound, Illinois.
Source: Courtesy of
Gilcrease Museum.

Hopewell Artisans. Hopewell artisans also made many items that were clearly intended to be worn by shamans as parts of costumes. These include deer antlers, either real or made of copper, and masks made from the facial portions of human skulls. One buried individual, who had years before his death lost his front incisors, was equipped with the upper jaw of a wolf, carved to fit in the gap in his mouth. It was probably all part of a more elaborate costume.

Hopewell ceremonialism must have been a terrific show. Steady demand for fancy new artifacts was ensured by their ostentatious burial or perhaps even ostentatious destruction by competing groups. When the most desirable materials were in short supply lower cost materials were sometimes substituted. Thus clay beads coated with mica were cheap imitations of pearls and hard cannel coal mimicked obsidian (Milner 2004:94).

We know from ethnographic cases that the exchange of fine objects made from exotic materials was probably couched as ritual gift giving. Generosity was rewarded by enhanced prestige. Productive families thus gained status for themselves collectively and for the leaders who spoke for them and interacted with other leaders. Modest surpluses allowed large kindreds to gather periodically to collectively build the earthen monuments that were designed as permanent symbols of family success as much as tributes to successful leaders.

The Decline of Hopewell. For whatever reasons, the long-distance network of trade and exchange could not be maintained, and Hopewell declined in the face of widespread conflict and social change. Circumstances caught up with the favorable environmental and technological conditions that had made the Hopewell golden age possible. Hopewell culture and the trade network that sustained it declined around 400 CE. Hopewell soon evolved into Fort Ancient culture, which was peripheral to the Mississippian societies that later arose to the west and south. The historic descendants of Hopewell and later Fort Ancient culture, if they still exist, are uncertain.

The specific reasons for the decline of Hopewell remain uncertain and a continuing focus of archaeological debate. Generally speaking it is clear that population growth and tendency for societies to press the limits of capacity had closed the gap between adaptive reality and adaptive potential, but the details are still unclear.

Community organization changed such that earthworks were no longer highly valued. Perhaps villages became more important foci as food production and population density increased and settlements became more nucleated. Perhaps population growth approached regional capacity under the prevailing form of food production and competition reduced the general well-being. Perhaps new weapons upset the equilibrium that had been maintained for centuries. The bow and arrow appeared in the Eastern Woodlands around the same time that Hopewell culture was fading. It seems likely that growing population sizes were finally starting to produce competition for resources, and the availability of a lethal new weapon combined with those pressures to produce a wave of intertribal conflict. Archaeologists have yet to find convincing ways to force choices between these competing hypotheses. Whatever the complex of causes, the importance of centralized earthwork complexes declined and people shifted to small family burial mounds on river bluffs. These featured a greater use of stone slab crypts, more frequent bundle burials, and a decline in the burial of cremated remains. **Bundle burials** result when bodies are exposed and the bones are later gathered for burial. Both bundle burials and cremation are forms of deferred interment, something that might have been made necessary initially by a lack of accessible tombs during the cold months when frozen ground made interment impossible. Once such tombs were no longer being built and the public spectacle of cremations had waned as well, bundle burials probably became more common just as a matter of convenience.

Later Burial Mound Builders

People continued to build mounds after 400 CE, but they were smaller and accompanied by neither large earthwork enclosures nor fancy artifacts made of exotic imported materials. Population growth also continued, but without the Adena-Hopewell trade network regional cultures looked inward once again. The period from 400 to 1000 CE set the stage for major developments yet to come. Yet like many periods of human history that have not produced impressive artifacts for museum display, this one was long ignored by many archaeologists. Nevertheless, this was a time in which maize became adopted as a staple crop and large permanent towns became possible, setting the scene for the developments described in Chapter 9.

Fort Ancient Culture

Fort Ancient culture developed out of Hopewell and lasted from 1000 to 1670 CE. The site of Fort Ancient in Ohio was long thought to be the type site for later Fort Ancient culture. Figure 5.21 shows the site as it was drawn by Squier and Davis (1848:19). While it was used in later times by Fort Ancient people, the site now appears to date initially from the Hopewell period. It is on a flat hilltop, and the earthen walls follow the edge in a manner that suggests a possible defensive purpose as well as a ceremonial one. There are many gaps in the walls at Fort Ancient, often partially blocked by mounds just inside, like those at many other Hopewell sites. But in this case the walls appear to have a more defensive purpose.

Fort Ancient culture can be subdivided into at least eight phases that fall into different time periods and different areas of southern Ohio and adjacent states. There was increasing similarity between Fort Ancient

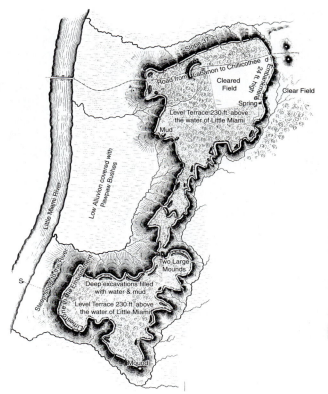

Figure 5.21 Fort Ancient, Ohio.
Source: From Squier and Davis 1848:opposite 18.

phases leading up to 1650 CE, characterized by the native artifacts and European trade goods found at the extraordinary Madisonville site.

Some archaeologists have equated Fort Ancient culture with contemporary Mississippian cultures that ranged generally south of it. However there is no evidence for an elite upper class on Fort Ancient sites. The evidence indicates that Fort Ancient leadership continued the big man tribal forms of Hopewell culture. They might even have had a system like the historic Iroquois, where the obligations of generosity left leaders to be buried with no more than others of their ages (Griffin 1992). However, the Iroquois system was based on matrilineal kinship, a special case involving large multifamily, female-dominated households that do not appear to have characterized Fort Ancient villages.

Serpent Mound. Serpent Mound (Figure 5.22) was once thought to be an Adena or even Hopewell monument, but new excavations in 1991 have dated it to the period of Fort Ancient culture. The sinuous mound winds for 411 m (1,348 ft) along a hilltop in southern Ohio. The

Figure 5.22 Serpent Mound, Ohio, from the air.
Source: Courtesy of the Ohio Historical Society.

head of the effigy looks to many people like that of a snake swallowing an egg, a mound 9 × 26 m (30 × 86 ft) in size. To others it represents a solar eclipse, to still others a comet.

Effigy Mound Culture

Serpent Mound is a unique effigy in Ohio, but many more animal effigy mounds are found in southern Wisconsin and parts of adjacent states. Effigy mound builders constructed at least 10,000 of them, perhaps as many as 30,000, mostly in the largely unglaciated "driftless" region of southern Wisconsin (Figure 5.23) and nearby portions of Minnesota, Iowa, and Illinois (Theler and Boszhardt 2006). These people continued the tradition of building small family burial mounds, but they took the practice in a new direction. Many of their mounds were laid out in the shapes of animals. While it is not yet well dated, many of the sites of effigy mound culture date from 650 to 1300 CE (Figure 5.24) (Milner 2004:106–109).

Favorite forms appear to have represented birds, serpents, wolves, elk, bears, turtles, and panthers, or at least those are the names archaeologists have assigned them. Some have been identified as lizards or other less likely creatures, and the truth is that some identifications are more than a little speculative. Many mounds continued to be simple earthen domes or stretched-out "linear" mounds. Most effigy mounds have dedicatory hearths, often where the hearts of the animals depicted would have been located. Many but not all contain burials, both extended and flexed and both **primary burials** and **secondary burials**. Grave offerings appear to have been confined to the personal possessions of the deceased.

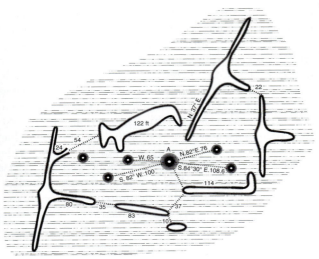

Figure 5.23 Effigy mounds along the northern bank of the Wisconsin River.
Source: From Squier and Davis 1848:opposite 128.

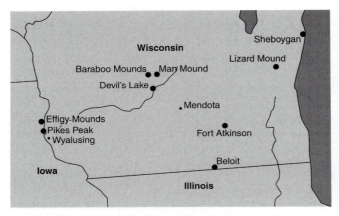

Figure 5.24 Effigy mound sites in and around southern Wisconsin. Large symbols identify sites that are open to the public.

Some bird effigies have enormous wingspans. A bird effigy mound on the grounds of Mendota State Hospital near Madison, Wisconsin, has a wingspan of 190 m (624 ft) and central height of about 2 m (6 ft). Other rare effigies are also known, including one in Wisconsin that was clearly intended to be a human effigy. Man Mound is a large prone human figure in a small park. It was once 65 m (213 ft) long, but its feet have long since been cut off by a modern road.

Effigy mounds were typically constructed in single building episodes. Usually sod was first stripped from the ground to define the outline of the effigy, then one or a few individuals were buried in the head or heart area of the effigy. Finally, earth was mounded up over the entire stripped area. Burials were sometimes primary interments, burials of fully articulated human remains in graves. At other times they were bundle burials or cremations, secondary interments of remains of people who probably had died months before burial. This suggests that effigy mounds were built during the warm months to contain the remains of family members who had died since the last mound had been built. If someone died during the summer months a mound could be constructed over a primary interment. If not, some sort of secondary burial would occur when warm weather returned.

The people of the effigy mound culture were primarily hunter-gatherers who probably cultivated only a few plants. They made pottery but probably lived at a population density lower than that of the earlier Hopewell people. Clusters of effigy mounds were probably important seasonal sites where people not only gathered to bury the recently deceased, but also conducted important ceremonies, renewed vital friendships, and arranged marriages.

Effigy Mounds National Monument. Effigy Mounds National Monument is a large and beautifully preserved site that is situated overlooking the Mississippi River valley in northeastern Iowa. There are 196 mounds in the park, 31 of which are effigy mounds. The simplest forms are domes of earth referred to as "conical" mounds. Two or more such mounds were sometimes connected by saddles of earth to form compound mounds. Some of the conical, compound, and elongated "linear" mounds here are older that the effigy mounds also found in the monument. The effigy mounds were constructed mainly between 600 and 1300 CE.

Great Bear Mound measures almost 42 m (137 ft) from nose to tail, and the mound rises over a meter above the original ground level. Nearby is the Little Bear Mound Group. Little Bear lies left side up, while Great Bear lies right side up. In the south unit of the park is a group of ten bear effigies, three birds, and two linear mounds. Most of the bears are lined up facing south, their left sides up, so modern views refer to them as the "marching bears" (Figure 5.25).

One can see these mounds clearly only by walking around on them. They do not photograph well unless they are artificially outlined by vegetation or some other material. Perhaps they were intended to be seen from above by supernatural beings, but it would have been a false hope unless the mounds were kept bare of vegetation. Today, even if the forest were removed, unless the sun is very low on the horizon the relief of the mounds is too low for the grassy mounds to stand out from the rest of the landscape when viewed from above.

Lizard Mound. The questionably named "Lizard Mound" is one of 28 effigy mounds now preserved in Lizard

Figure 5.25 Marching bears, bird effigy, and linear mounds, Effigy Mounds National Monument, Iowa.
Source: Courtesy of the National Park Service.

Mound County Park north of Milwaukee, Wisconsin. The mounds were constructed between 650 and 1300 CE. Some are in simple hemispherical (conical) or linear shapes. Two are large bird effigy mounds and seven are long-tailed animal forms usually referred to as "panther" effigies. The latter are typically depicted in profile view. The great lizard mound might have been intended to represent the same animal, whether it was intended to represent a panther or something else, but in a spread-eagle posture that shows all four limbs.

There were probably more than 60 mounds in this group in the nineteenth century. A sketch made in 1883 shows that 47 still survived at that time. Excavations in 1960 showed that the mounds were certainly funerary constructions. Flexed burials were placed in burial pits and the mounds were constructed over them. Pots, pipes, bone tools, beads, and projectile points were often buried with the dead.

Other Effigy Mounds. A roadside park near Baraboo, Wisconsin, contains several nonhuman effigies. Effigy mounds are also found on the campus of Beloit College in Beloit, Wisconsin. One effigy there, in the shape of a turtle, has been adopted as the symbol of the college. A large panther effigy, the Wehmhoff Mound near Burlington, Wisconsin, was cut in half by modern road construction (Birmingham and Eisenberg 2000; Highsmith 1997).

Rarest of all is a panther intaglio in a residential yard in Fort Atkinson, Wisconsin. Here moundbuilders created a negative mound by excavating a pit in the shape of a panther rather than piling the earth. There were once several such intaglios in southern Wisconsin, but this is the only surviving one.

The Beginnings of Platform Mounds

The Toltec mounds of Arkansas are an excellent example of a mound building culture that thrived after Hopewell but before the rise of Mississippian cultures (see Chapter 9). They are also very inappropriately named. The mounds at the Toltec site were built 600–1050 CE, and the later Toltecs of Mexico had nothing to do with them. There were eventually at least 16 mounds inside a high, curving 1,615-m (1-mi) embankment and exterior defensive ditch. The northwest side of the large D-shaped site was protected by a small lake, now called Mound Pond.

The Toltec mounds were flat-topped rectangular platform mounds arranged around two plazas, a new architectural style in the Eastern Woodlands that was only occasionally hinted at earlier at sites like Anderson Mounds. These were not burial mounds but rather they were structures designed to be elevated bases for imposing buildings. Two of the platform mounds (Figure 5.26) were once 11–15 m (38–50 ft) high, and excavations in one large mound showed that it was built in at least five construction stages. The new architectural form was very similar to the larger Mesoamerican pyramids that were being constructed at the same time (and earlier) in highland Mexico (see Chapter 7).

At least two low mounds at Toltec were used for feasting. Deer were a favorite food, as indicated by discarded bones. There were also residential areas inside the fortified settlement. This was a time in which villages and towns were replacing nonresidential mortuary centers as central places in the Eastern Woodlands. Similar developments were occurring in many areas, such as the Coles Creek phase in the southern Mississippi Valley (see Chapter 11). In southern Illinois

Figure 5.26 Platform mound at the Toltec, Arkansas, site.

and western Kentucky stone-walled hilltop enclosures were being built by the residents of villages in the valleys below. Similarly, Hopewell builders were abandoning ceremonial earthworks in favor of earthworks to defend settlements like the one at Fort Ancient. It was a major shift in focus, this move from mortuary to village-centered architecture, and one that must have been driven in large part by forces close at hand. The population was growing, and with it competition for the best land. The bow and arrow was introduced to the region by 6–700 CE, bringing with it a rise in warfare (Blitz 1988). The days of sprawling ceremonial earthworks and friendly long-distance trade were over, and the scene was set for a new era in the Eastern Woodlands.

Summary

1. The Archaic theme and all its variations led to some unusual adaptations as well as to the domestication of several native plants.

2. Eastern Woodlands plant domestication provided the subsistence base for mortuary earthwork construction and widespread trade in exotic raw materials and finished artifacts.

3. Burial mounds are quick and easy to construct and are a nearly worldwide phenomenon that arose independently in several regions.

4. Mounds are often built by people more conscious of territorial cores than boundaries.

5. The most widely recognized mound building cultures were Adena and Hopewell.

6. The most elaborate burial mounds are built by strong leaders rather than for them.

7. There is no evidence for high population levels, maize agriculture, or chiefdoms in the cultures that practiced Adena and Hopewell ceremonialism.

8. Mortuary earthwork construction faded with increasing competition and the appearance of the bow and arrow.

9. Earthwork architecture shifted from mortuary functions to defensive works and platform mounds.

10. The origins of the new architectural forms are debatable, but might have involved some inspiration from Mexico.

Further Reading

The best place to begin further reading is with George Milner's *The Moundbuilders: Ancient Peoples of Eastern North America*, which is the best general work on the topic. William Morgan's *Precolumbian Architecture in Eastern North America* and Mainfort and Sullivan's *Ancient Earthen Enclosures of the Eastern Woodlands* are good sources for readers looking for more on earthworks. The lavishly illustrated *Hero, Hawk, and Open Hand* is both an exhibit catalog and a volume of edited papers on the mound builders. Together the bibliographies of these books and the references at the end of this book will lead to many more specific sources. Volumes 14 and 15 of *The Handbook of North American Indians* contain chapters on archaeology as well as a comprehensive overview of the American Indian nations that succeeded the mound builders of the Eastern Woodlands.

An excellent source for understanding the Eastern Woodlands Trade Network is Carr and Cases' *Gathering Hopewell: Society, Ritual, and Ritual Interaction.*

Glossary

anneal: In the case of copper, to decrease brittleness by applying high heat and rapid cooling.

bundle burial: A form of secondary burial in which disarticulated remains are gathered up and bundled before interment.

obsidian: Volcanic glass, usually black.

primary burial: An interment of an intact individual. Compare *secondary burial.*

secondary burial: An interment of disarticulated, bundled, or cremated human remains.

The Greater Southwest

Although [the Seven Cities] are not decorated with turquoises, nor made of lime or good bricks, nevertheless they are very good houses, three, four, and five stories high, and they have very . . . good rooms with corridors, and some quite good apartments underground and paved.

Francisco Coronado, August 3, 1540

VILLAGE FARMERS SPREAD NORTHWARD INTO THE deserts of the U.S. Southwest and the Mexican Northwest from Mesoamerica over three millennia ago. The three major cultural traditions used different adaptations to farming in this arid region. The frontiers of farming expanded over time, but farming also spread beyond the margins of the major traditions, adopted by hunter-gatherers who made it work in even more unlikely environments. Farming later collapsed in many areas in the face of climate change, forcing widespread relocations and spawning new derivative cultures. Major tasks for archaeologists have been to determine when, how, and why farming was made to work in this environment, and why it was abandoned across so much of the region by 1200 CE.

Introduction

The hot, dry Southwest of the United States and the Northwest of Mexico seems at first glance to be an unlikely setting for agricultural villages, but maize and other tropical domesticates began appearing here 4,000 years ago, a millennium before they were carried to the Eastern Woodlands. Agriculture allowed for permanent settlements, and American Indians living in this region found that stone and adobe were durable building materials. The result was that residential architecture survived better here than in most regions on the continent, and their ruins attract many modern visitors. The challenge to modern archaeology is to determine how agriculturalists managed to adapt to this apparently hostile environment (Cordell 1997; Kantner 2005).

The region is hard to name because its identity varies depending upon whether one's perspective is from the United States, where it is called the Southwest, or from Mexico, where it is called the Northwest. Carroll Riley argues for calling it Aztlan, the Aztecs' mythological place of origin, which was so remote in the mists of time and space that they knew only that it was far to the northwest of Mexico City (Riley 2005). This was the distant region from which the Mesoamericans acquired turquoise jewels, and to which they or their intermediaries sent in exchange rubber balls, copper bells, and live macaws. This was the region where Coronado searched in vain for the Seven Lost Cities of Gold in 1540. The states of Arizona and New Mexico are at the heart of the region, but it also includes parts of all their adjoining states, including most of the Mexican states of Sonora and Chihuahua (Ericson and Baugh 1993; Foster and Gorenstein 2000; Webster and McBrinn 2008).

The Greater Southwest region straddles the continental divide, an international border, and several physiographic zones. The Colorado Plateau, where most of the landscape lies over 1,500 m (4,920 ft) above sea level, covers the northern part of the region (Figure 6.1). The rugged mountainous edge of the Colorado Plateau, the Mogollon Rim, gives way to lower desert lands to the south. There ranges of mountains interrupt the otherwise flat desert terrain.

Portions of the region west of the continental divide, mainly in Arizona, are drained by tributaries of the Colorado River. To the east of the divide the region is drained by the Rio Grande, the Pecos River, and their tributaries. Thus the eastern part of the region includes southwestern Colorado and most of New Mexico.

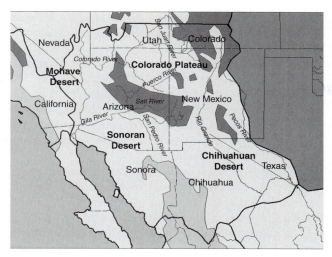

Figure 6.1 The environments of the Greater Southwest.

The region is generally dry, but it has never been devoid of edible plants and game. The deserts of the Greater Southwest come in three varieties, depending upon moisture and the amount of winter frost. The Mojave Desert includes Death Valley, seasonally one of the hottest and driest places on earth, but it is also subject to winter freezing. Its most distinctive plant is the Joshua tree (*Yucca brevifolia*). The Sonoran Desert is hottest and driest overall. Rare brief freezes eliminate some more delicate cacti but allow the huge saguaro cactus (*Carnegiea gigantea*) to prosper. The Chihuahuan Desert is high, generally above 1,000 m (3,300 ft). Its dominant plant is the lechuguilla (*Agave lecheguilla*), a kind of century plant.

What little rain falls on the western deserts comes from the Pacific, while the eastern part of the Southwest gets most of its summer rain from the Gulf of Mexico. Winter sometimes brings soaking rain, mostly to higher elevations, but most rain falls unpredictably as localized thundershowers. Whereas an upland area might get 50 cm (20 in.) of rain annually, the deserts average less than 20 cm (8 in.).

The First Farmers

Farming communities appeared in the Southwest region sometime before 1000 BCE. A major archaeological problem has long been to determine if they arose from the spread of key Mesoamerican cultigens to local bands of Archaic hunter-gatherers or if they resulted from the northward expansion of farmers who brought domesticates with them from highland Mexico. Accumulating evidence currently indicates that the latter hypothesis is more likely. The growth and spread of farming

populations was a common demographic phenomenon in world prehistory, one that led to the establishment of new dominant populations at the expense of the older thinner ones they displaced or absorbed.

Early expansion of agriculturalists northward through western Mexico was comparatively easy because there is no barrier zone separating the region from Mesoamerica. Jane Hill (2001) argues that farmers speaking early Uto-Aztecan languages found favorable locations all along the way, eventually reaching the Colorado Plateau by the first millennium BCE (Figure 6.2). Words for maize and other key agricultural terms were already present in the Uto-Aztecan protolanguage at that time, and the finding is consistent with the archaeological evidence. Not all linguists are so sure of that hypothesis explaining the origins of the Uto-Aztecans, but it is consistent with what is generally known about the usual spread of growing populations of farmers and the languages they speak.

The Cerro Juanaqueña site is in the northwestern part of the state of Chihuahua, Mexico, not far from the

Figure 6.2 The recent distribution of Uto-Aztecan languages (shaded) shows evidence of expansion from northwestern Mexico both southeastward and northwestward into and beyond the Greater Southwest.

New Mexico border. It was a residential complex having 8 km (5 mi) of terraces and evidence of cultivation. Radiocarbon dates on maize kernels show that this farming village was occupied around 1000 BCE (Hard and Roney 1998). Maize also appeared in Bat Cave, New Mexico, at about the same time. Archaeologists are currently investigating a site in west central New Mexico that has produced preliminary radiocarbon dates on maize that push its first appearance back to 4000 BCE.

The Santa Cruz Bend site was found buried under a meter of river alluvium in Tucson, Arizona. Researchers found hundreds of pithouses and storage pits containing maize kernels and other seeds dating to 800–200 BCE. Even these later dates put the site into what was previously thought to have been a preagricultural Archaic phase. The site also produced early ceramics and the region's earliest known ceremonial structure (Muro 1998).

What is certain is that by the first millennium BCE the Archaic cultures of the Southwest were being rapidly replaced by farming cultures that were the foundations of the three major traditions of the prehistoric Greater Southwest: Hohokam, Mogollon, and Ancestral Pueblo. Their Archaic roots differed, and each was a different kind of adaptation, a different combination of human ingenuity and environmental potential.

The beginnings of the Hohokam tradition were in place in southern Arizona by that time. So too were the first residents of Paquimé (Casas Grandes) in Chihuahua. Finally, the people called Oshara, or Basketmaker, were in place on the Colorado Plateau (Irwin-Williams 1979; Kidder 1927). They would eventually evolve into the communities of the Ancestral Pueblo tradition.

The farming practices that developed in the region involved what Richard Ford (1985) has called the "Upper Sonoran Agricultural Complex." The complex includes maize, bottle gourd, three kinds of bean (pinto, navy, and kidney), and squash. There was initially only one type of squash, but more varieties were added later. This was the package of domesticates that the cultural traditions in the region found different ways to produce.

Language Families

There are six native language families in the Southwest region and their distribution reflects their long complex histories (Figure 6.3). One of them, Nadene, is the family of relatively recent arrivals, the Navajo and various Apache nations. These peoples arrived only about five centuries ago, when climate change forced farmers to retreat and opened up vast areas for simpler hunter-gatherer societies. Uto-Aztecan is much more ancient

and the likely language of the first immigrant farmers. Three other language families—Keresan, Kiowa-Tanoan, and Cochimí-Yuman—all have ancient roots in the West, with connections so distant in the past that linguists still disagree about how they are related. The Zuni language might be related to California Penutian, but its origins also remain a topic of debate. All of these language families survive in the region, their languages still spoken by their modern Native American descendants of the ancient traditions.

There is a much wider context to this linguistic history. A branch of the Uto-Aztecans eventually spread farther northward out of the region, becoming hunter-gatherers in the Great Basin and beyond. Far to the south still other Uto-Aztecans spread into the central highlands from western Mexico into the central highlands. Nahuatl, the language of the Aztecs, is a Uto-Aztecan language, and it later spread farther across Mesoamerica with the expansion of the Aztec Empire (see Chapter 8). By 1500 CE there was a scattering of dozens of Uto-Aztecan languages that extended all the way from Idaho to Nicaragua. Figure 6.3 shows only a small part of the whole picture.

Regional Ecology

Archaeologists want to know how and why agriculture could spread into this environment, probably carried northward into the region by early Uto-Aztecans. Irrigation, an expensive proposition, was a farming strategy

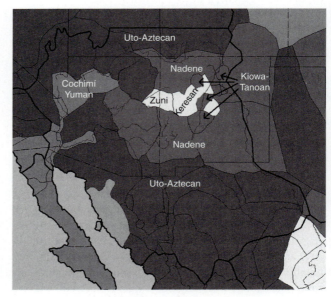

Figure 6.3 Language families of the Greater Southwest in 1600 CE.

Chapter 6

almost from the beginning because of the general dryness of the region. The simple traditional view is that demographic pressure forced people into this marginal area and they used agriculture to meet subsistence demands. A better ecological explanation may be that while population pressure might be a good explanation in stable environments, in unstable ones like the Greater Southwest it is sometimes the case that cultivation was initially taken up to buffer periodic shortfalls, then adopted more generally when its long-term benefits became apparent. Fortunately for them the Uto-Aztecan farmers that had met this kind of ecological challenge in western Mexico were preadapted to make the most of the Southwest's environment. Like the modern builders of Las Vegas they made it all work not because the environment offered so much, but because they already had the tools and domesticates to succeed despite environmental limitations.

Researchers have measured and dated swings in Southwestern climate using clues from columnar stalagmites in caves in the Guadalupe Mountains of southern New Mexico. The annual banding in them shows that the climate in the Southwest was very similar to that of today before 1000 BCE, but shifted in important ways around that time. After 1000 BCE conditions became wetter and cooler, and they remained that way until around 1150 CE, when conditions generally like those of today returned. After 1150 CE conditions were once again generally more hostile to farmers than they had been when they first began farming in the region (Polyak and Asmerom 2001).

It is not surprising that farming became widespread in the Southwest with the onset of attractive cooler and wetter conditions 3,000 years ago. It is also not surprising that they ran into trouble when conditions turned generally hotter and drier 2,150 years later around 1150 CE. After that date the climate was much like it is today except for a slightly wetter period from 1490 to 1780. Native farmers had to adapt to more difficult circumstances during most of the second millennium CE. Tree rings also reveal that more severe droughts began to plague farmers periodically after 1150 CE. Their descendants survived in places where farming was still possible, but droughts put an end to the heyday of prehistoric farming cultures across the region (Jones et al. 1999).

Hohokam

Sites of the Hohokam tradition were previously thought to be the oldest farming communities in the region, but it is now clear that they were not the first

farmers in the Greater Southwest (Figure 6.4). Hohokam villagers depended upon human-made irrigation ditches to bring water to their fields as early as 800–200 BCE, but irrigation had already been practiced farther south for centuries and maize had been in the region for even longer. The Hohokam people were the first farmers in southern Arizona, where the permanent Salt and Gila Rivers flowing through the hot Sonoran Desert made their irrigation strategy possible (Figure 6.5).

At first glance, irrigation engineering seems difficult and unlikely under premodern conditions, but it is not. Fast-flowing rivers are fast because their gradients are steep. If one taps into such a river by digging a ditch from its edge inland one can create a more sluggish canal having a less steep gradient. The ditch can be made to

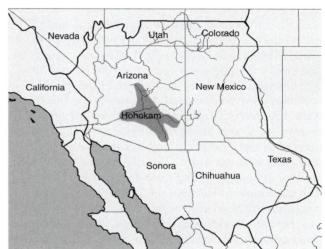

Figure 6.4 Location of Hohokam culture.

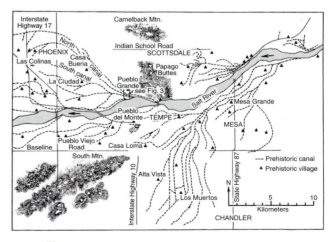

Figure 6.5 Hohokam canals in the Phoenix area.
Source: From Masse 1981:410.

veer farther and farther from the river by controlling its gradient, and letting it wind along the lower slopes of bluffs adjacent to the river's flood plain. Even a short canal allows a farmer to water crops between the canal and the river by breaching the irrigation ditch slightly uphill from the fields. Water from the ditch then flows down across the fields. As the ditch is extended and it veers farther from the faster-flowing river, more fields can be opened for irrigation agriculture (Plog 1997:75).

Digging irrigation canals was hard work, but it was feasible even through the hardpan of the Sonoran desert because water flowing in behind them softened the soil around the legs of diggers as they gradually worked their way across the flood plain, toward the flanking bluffs and away from the riverside. Digging sticks and baskets would have been enough equipment for the job. Best of all, water seeks its own level, keeping diggers from veering either too much uphill or too much downhill. A little additional digging every year eventually produced canals and secondary ditches that were many kilometers long and watered many hectares of land (Masse 1981).

Hohokam villagers also inherited the tradition of craftwork on marine shell imported from the Pacific Coast. Bracelets, beads, and pendants made from Pacific marine shell also show that regional trade networks existed in the Southwest long before the emergence of the Hohokam tradition. Tubular ground stone pipes and tobacco seeds dating to 350 BCE are evidence that tobacco smoking had also spread to the region by that time, but this was centuries later than its appearance in the Eastern Woodlands. Hohokam craftspeople also used ground stone techniques to produce elegant stone palates.

Life in a Hohokam village was comfortable, undoubtedly punctuated by the rhythm of the annual cycle of sport and ceremony that enliven such communities everywhere. The Phoenix Basin eventually had a Hohokam population in the tens of thousands. There were hundreds of kilometers of canals and thousands of fields under cultivation at the peak of this major cultural tradition.

Snaketown

The Snaketown site, located on the Gila River Indian reservation, is an important Hohokam site that was excavated by Emil Haury and crews from the University of Arizona. Snaketown was found to contain 167 houses and at least one ball court. The oval earthen ball court was built around 750 CE. Ball courts are found at other Hohokam sites as well, and there are at least 200 of them in the Phoenix Basin.

Excavators also found the bones of tropical macaws and parrots, copper bells, marine shell, rubber balls, and turquoise. The balls, tropical bird bones, and copper all indicate at least indirect trade connections with Mesoamerica to the south. The rubber balls probably came from latex-producing tropical forests in southern Mexico (Filloy Nadal 2001). The birds probably came live, perhaps in the later centuries of Hohokam passing through the trading center at Paquimé in Chihuahua, where pens for them have been found. Regionally obtained turquoise probably moved south to Mesoamerica in exchange for these goods.

Hohokam settlements tend to be strung out along irrigation canals, some of which reached lengths up to 26 km (16 mi) long. The need to maintain canals that served two or more communities probably led to the development of multivillage political systems, at least weak chiefdoms. Fractious segmentary tribes probably could not have maintained such a system for long. Some archaeological research suggests that chiefdoms were certainly present by at least 1100 CE, and that they probably developed long before that (Gregory 1991:173). However, other researchers argue that political centralization at the chiefdom level is not necessary to explain Hohokam canal systems. Yet clearly some sort of authority was necessary, and various kinds of communal organization would have served the purpose (Hunt et al. 2005). This debate illustrates the principle that generally speaking one should infer only the minimum level of social complexity needed to explain the case at hand (see Chapter 1) (Yoffee 2005).

Hohokam houses at Snaketown were shallow pithouses. Builders excavated them only deeply enough to remove loose sand and expose the hard caliche layer that occurs throughout the Phoenix Basin. This served each house as a hard floor, and deeper excavation was not needed for insulation in this hot desert. Hearths were small clay-lined basins near the doorways of the houses.

Houses like these were homes to small extended Hohokam families. Men and women worked in the fields, coaxing crops from desert soils made productive by irrigation. It is likely that men did the heavy work, particularly canal construction and maintenance. Women might have been primarily responsible for planting and tending crops. Maize, beans, squash, tobacco, and cotton were all important Hohokam domesticates. They also continued to gather wild plant foods such as the nopal cactus fruit (prickly pear), cholla, hedgehog, agave, mesquite seeds, and the fruit of the saguaro cactus. Men also hunted, for there were rabbits, deer, and bighorn sheep in the hills, and fish, waterfowl, and turtles in the larger permanent streams.

Box 6.1 HOW TO USE TREE-RING DATING

The Ancestral Pueblo tradition is the best dated of the traditions of the Southwest because of dendrochronology, or tree-ring dating. Most people have counted the annual growth rings on a tree stump at one time or another. A. E. Douglass found a way to use tree rings to date ancient logs in the first part of the twentieth century. Douglass was a University of Arizona astronomer who was interested in past climatic cycles, which he thought might be related to sun spot cycles. He hit upon the idea of using variations in tree ring widths to assess past variations in the climate of the American Southwest. Dendrochronology was an accidental by-product of this research. It was a classic case of a scientist finding something important while looking for something else.

Douglass observed in sections of living trees that the rings laid down in unusually dry years were always very narrow, and that those that grew in wet years were always wide. He found that he could determine the year of death of a dead tree by matching its ring pattern to that of a living tree that overlapped it in age. From there it was a matter of finding older and older specimens that could be overlapped to produce a single long sequence for the region. Douglass had a basic thousand-year-long "floating chronology" in hand for the Southwest by 1930.

Once the floating chronology was established, the cutting date of an archaeological sample, say a beam from a house, could be determined by matching its ring pattern to the master sequence. When a match was found, the cutting date was set at the year following the growth of the outermost ring.

Douglass needed a long-lived Southwestern tree that would provide a single long-term climate record and confirm the linkages in his floating chronology. Edmund Schulman eventually discovered such a tree, a bristlecone pine of the southeastern California desert. Bristlecone pines can provide a record of up to 5,000 years of growth. These trees have also later turned out to be crucial for the proper calibration of radiocarbon dates.

Dendrochronology is a wonderful archaeological tool for telling absolute time, but unfortunately it works well only in certain parts of the world. It works best where trees undergo widespread periodic stress from general climatic variations, as they do on the Colorado Plateau. While trees growing there respond in similar ways to widespread periodic droughts, the trees in the woodlands of eastern North America and many other parts of the world lay down annual growth rings in response to much more local and consequently highly variable events. Consequently, they are not generally useful for dendrochronology.

There are also some technical problems with dendrochronology. Some dry years produce no rings at all in some trees. Beams that have been dressed or shaved by carpenters often lack their outer rings, making cutting dates impossible to determine accurately. Ancient builders also sometimes reused beams from older structures. However, with adequate sample sizes archaeologists can overcome these problems and use tree ring dating to date many deposits to within one year.

Pueblo Grande

Pueblo Grande is a major Hohokam site that is now a city park near the eastern boundary of Phoenix. Pueblo Grande is now a national landmark, but it is only one of several large sites of its type in the Phoenix area. Mesa Grande, from which the modern city of Mesa gets its name, is another such site. Pueblo Grande features a large platform mound with retaining walls, which was once surmounted by walled structures. This massive structure contains over 20,000 cubic meters (yards) of fill. There were also many houses and at least three ball courts. People settled here by 450 CE. By 750 CE they were building ball courts (Figure 6.6), the best example of which is 25 m (82 ft) long and 12 m (39 ft) wide (Abbott, 2003 #3215; Gumerman, 1991 #3216).

Figure 6.6 Pueblo Grande ball court with its platform mound in the background.

Ball courts and traditional house forms went out of fashion after 1150 CE, about the time that climate change began to disrupt life across the Southwest. Adobe residential compounds and platform mounds replaced the earlier pithouses and ball courts at the Pueblo Grande site from then until its abandonment around 1450 CE (Wilcox 1991:262). These changes reflect the effects of intensified irrigation and widespread population movements in the region during that period.

Archaeologists infer that this and other platform mounds at large Hohokam communities are evidence of increased political and religious authority (Reid and Whittlesey 1997; Waters and Ravesloot 2001). The site lies at a point on the north bank of the Salt River where four large irrigation canals tapped into the main stream. The canals drew the water westward, two of them branching again farther to the west, serving several other Hohokam communities and watering the fields lying between them and the main course of the river. The sites of La Ciudad, Las Colinas, and others downstream along the branching canals were both incorporated into Pueblo Grande's multivillage political system by 1000 CE. As with other multivillage systems in the Phoenix Basin, these sites are spaced at regular 5-km (3-mi) intervals. Each village tended to grow northward as new canals were constructed farther and farther north of older ones in order to open up more land to cultivation (Gregory 1991:173–179). Pueblo Grande, at the key water control point, appears to have remained politically dominant.

Nonlocal pottery turns up in small quantities at Pueblo Grande, as it does in many Hohokam sites having public architecture. Exotic vessels make up only a fraction of 1% of the whole, but they typically occur as burial offerings, another indication that political leadership resided at these major sites. The largest fraction of exotic pottery at Pueblo Grande came from northern Arizona, but several other regions of the Southwest were also sources. Pueblo Grande was also a destination for California marine shell and obsidian that moved through the Hohokam trade network (Doyel 1991:230–235). All of this is evidence that at its peak Pueblo Grande was much more than just a prosperous farming community.

Hard times for the Hohokam communities around modern Phoenix began as early as 1020–1160 CE, when they experienced widespread erosion of their irrigation canals. Larger towns were partially or entirely abandoned in the face of this breakdown of their irrigation systems. Many Hohokam communities underwent significant change during the demographic disruptions that followed climate change after 1150.

Figure 6.7 Gila Polychrome vessel, an example of Salado pottery.

But settlement persisted, even grew, along some canals to as late as 1450 CE, a circumstance that indicates that archaeologists do not yet fully understand what happened to the Hohokam farmers (Ingram 2008).

Ancestral Pueblo refugees from the Colorado Plateau resettled in various places, sometimes in Hohokam communities in southern Arizona. Several local Hohokam and Mogollon cultures began making new Salado pottery styles as a result (Figure 6.7). This new ceramic tradition was founded by an amalgam of people drawn from all three of the region's major cultural traditions, many of them refugees in their own land. The late "great house" site of Casa Grande and the cliff dwelling at Tonto both document this cultural transformation.

Casa Grande

Casa Grande is one of the great house communities of the late Hohokam tradition of southern Arizona, founded around 1350 and abandoned by 1450 CE. Like earlier Hohokam communities around Phoenix this one relied upon irrigation agriculture. The central feature of Casa Grande is a large adobe dwelling, now covered by a protective roof (Figure 6.8). The outer rooms of the great house stand three stories high. The central room on the ground floor of the structure was completely filled with adobe to strengthen it and to provide stability for a fourth floor that was constructed above the central block. The builders did not have access to quality stone, so they built the walls as courses of damp adobe, each of which was allowed to dry and harden before the next was laid. The walls are thicker at their bases and taper toward the top, which gives them added strength. The horizontal cracks that define

Figure 6.8 The great house at Casa Grande.

the breaks between adobe courses can still be seen on the wall exteriors. Casa Grande has a ball court much like those found at Pueblo Grande and other Hohokam sites. It also has a platform mound like Pueblo Grande.

The great house and lower structures surrounding it were all contained within a large rectangular adobe-walled compound. The Casa Grande community was unlike the settlements of scattered houses that made up earlier Hohokam communities. The innovative architecture of this site and others like it was another result of the dynamic mix of Hohokam and Ancestral Pueblo practices brought on by the widespread population dislocations and amalgamations of the fourteenth century.

The Tohono O'Odham and the Akimel O'Odham nations are descendants of the Hohokam tradition that still live in reservation communities scattered across southern Arizona. Some people still know them better as Papago and Pima. Descendant Hohokam societies dwindled after 1450 CE. Early Spanish explorers found local Indians living in brush dwellings near the abandoned ruins of great houses. These descendants of the once flourishing farming tradition said that the builders of the impressive sites were the "ho-ho-kahm," meaning "all used up," and the name was later adopted by archaeologists. Many of them now work in the expanding modern economy of the region, but the tradition of irrigation farming remains alive and the cultivation of olive trees and other crops suited to this hot dry environment is productive.

Mogollon

The Mogollon tradition, the second major cultural tradition of the region, is comprised of a half dozen related local cultures, the earliest of which were founded around 200 BCE. The local cultures of the Mogollon tradition were Mimbres, Pine Lawn, Black River, San Simon, Forestdale, and Jornada (Figure 6.9). One dispersed as early as 1150 CE, while others hung on until 1450 CE. How their descendants melded into the historic American Indian cultures of the region remains largely uncertain, but many probably joined communities at Zuni, Paquimé, and various Rio Grande pueblos.

The earliest Mogollon sites are clusters of pithouses, often located on high ground in rugged eastern Arizona and western New Mexico where the Colorado Plateau gives way to lower deserts. The first villages appeared around 200 BCE. Each had fewer than 20 houses on high ground, some on the ridges and bluffs of the Mogollon Rim, from which archaeologists have taken the name of the tradition. The communities appear to have been located as they were at least in part for defensive purposes.

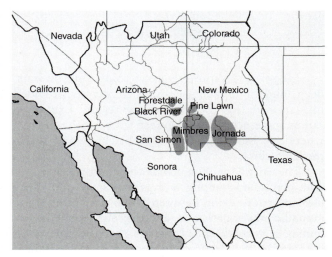

Figure 6.9 Locations of Mogollon cultures.

Box 6.2 HOW TO VISIT SITES IN THE GREATER SOUTHWEST

The states of the U.S. Southwest and northwestern Mexico have many archaeological sites that are worthy of extended visits. Many of these are accessible by car in local, state, or national parks that provide guides, trails, interpretation, and other facilities. The density of important sites is so great in this region that those that are clustered in major parks have not been separately mapped for this chapter. Mesa Verde National Park in southwestern Colorado holds many spectacular cliff dwellings, the largest of which is Cliff Palace. But there is much more, including earlier surface villages and clusters of pithouses. Hovenweep National Monument, which straddles the Colorado–Utah border, has six major Ancestral Pueblo sites. Canyonlands National Park in southeastern Utah has three major Ancestral Pueblo ruins and many rock art sites, including the Great Gallery and the All-American Man.

Canyon de Chelly National Monument is on the Navajo reservation and administered by the Navajo Nation. They provide truck tours to major sites in the canyon from their base in Chinle. Major sites include Mummy Cave, Antelope House, Standing Cow, and White House.

Chaco Canyon (Chaco Culture National Historical Park) lies at the center of a major ancient network of roads and outlying towns in what is now a remote part of New Mexico. The canyon holds several large and very impressive Ancestral Pueblo town sites called great houses. Most visitors will want to examine Pueblo Bonito, Chetro Ketl, Pueblo del Arroyo, Kin Kletso, Una Vida, and the solitary great kiva known as Casa Rinconada. Those with more time and a sense of adventure will trek to Pueblo Alto, Peñasco Blanco, Wijiji, and some of the smaller pueblo ruins. There is plenty of rock art on the canyon wall between Pueblo Bonito and Chetro Ketl.

The Chacoan road network radiated out from Chaco Canyon, connecting outlying communities to the cultural hub. The Great North Road linked the canyon to Aztec and Salmon, among others. These two sites in the northwestern corner of New Mexico are the easiest Chacoan outliers to visit.

The site of Kuaua, in Coronado State Monument north of Albuquerque, is interesting for its kiva murals and its historic visit by the Coronado expedition. Pecos, east of Santa Fe, was also visited by Coronado, and it continued to be occupied well into Spanish colonial times. The Gila Cliff Dwellings and the Mimbres site in southwestern New Mexico are interesting Mogollon sites.

Beyond those already mentioned, spectacular Ancestral Pueblo sites in Arizona include Betatakin, Keet Seel, and Inscription House, all components of the Navajo National Monument. Montezuma Castle, Tuzigoot, Wupatki, and Walnut Canyon are all Sinagua sites worth visiting in central Arizona. Pueblo Grande provides an excellent introduction to Hohokam culture in Phoenix. Tonto and Casa Grande are very different expressions of Salado culture in southern Arizona, each spectacular in its own way.

Paquimé (Casas Grandes) is a unique site located in northern Chihuahua. Although it is worth a visit, travelers should be aware that crossing an international boundary can sometimes be a lengthy process.

There are many other large sites in the Greater Southwest, scattered across four U.S. and two Mexican states. Those that are publicly owned, protected, and provided with signs and interpretation are usually worth a visit.

Mogollon pithouses were circular, knee or waist deep, and built facing east. Their depths provided insulation in this cool part of the region. Excavated ramps gave access on the east sides of the houses, where the morning sun could brighten and warm their interiors.

The early Mogollon people were part-time farmers who continued hunting and gathering as well. They lived in a zone lying between Hohokam farmers and nomadic hunter-gatherers, and they survived by maintaining a generalized adaptation that used a mix of both strategies. Part-time Mogollon farmers planted the same crops as those used by the Hohokam people,

but with only the simplest irrigation. The mountainous edge of the Colorado Plateau precluded long irrigation canals, but it provided them with enough springs and rainfall for successful crops in most years. Hunting and gathering served as a supplement in good years and a backup in years when crops failed. Like the Hohokam farmers their crops included tobacco, which they smoked in tubular clay pipes or in cigarettes made from tobacco-packed reeds.

Early Mogollon pottery was plain red ware that might have been derived from Mesoamerican prototypes. They continued to produce basketry too, and it did not decline in quality with the introduction of pottery. They also made a few clay figurines, simpler versions of those made in the far-off highlands of Mexico.

By 300 CE Mogollon cultures were expanding and their influences can be found in both Hohokam sites to the west in the southern Arizona desert and to the north in Ancestral Pueblo sites. The Mogollon tradition expanded westward into Hohokam territory around 900 CE and remained there for two centuries. They began making decorated pottery around 650 CE, often red-painted designs on brown backgrounds, their contribution to the vast range of pottery types that were produced across the Greater Southwest in the distant past and is still produced today.

Changing Architecture

Mogollon villagers lived mostly in pithouses before 1000 CE but in above-ground rooms after that. Early pithouses were round, but later ones were smaller and square, echoing the development of square surface apartment dwellings around that time. Early dwellings were large enough to accommodate extended families, but later ones were homes for smaller nuclear families. The change from round to square housing units was driven by the mechanical demands of building common walls for surface rooms. The shift to smaller quarters might have been accompanied by a shift to **matrilocal** residence, a social rather than a mechanical reason for the size change. This possibility gains support from the appearance of ceremonial **kivas** around the same time. In historic Pueblo villages kivas typically served as men's clubs and were modeled on older pithouses. They were places where male clan members could get together in a society where residences were dominated by female clan members and married male clan brothers were scattered among matrilocal households. The Raven site near Springerville, Arizona, has nice examples.

Large, square "great" kivas began to appear in some Mogollon villages after 1000 CE. These very large ceremonial structures were clearly designed to serve more than a few closely related males. Archaeologists infer that they must have served broad ceremonial purposes for whole communities. The bow and arrow also appeared by around 1000 CE, but Mogollon hunters also retained the atlatl as well for many years.

Mimbres

Mimbres was one of the Mogollon tradition cultures, best known for spectacularly decorated pottery bowls that were made late in its history, 1000–1130 CE

(Figure 6.10) (Brody 2004; Creel and Anyon 2003). Settlements in the early phases were clusters of bean-shaped or D-shaped pithouses on the tops of ridges. Like earlier Mogollon houses, entry to them was by long ramps that sloped down from the surface to pithouse floor levels. Storage was in separate storage pits and the houses might have been occupied only during winter months. But storage pits are not what have attracted modern looters.

The earliest Mimbres pottery was made between 200 and 550 CE. It was plain brown ware that was standard for all early Mogollon phases. Later types were red-slipped, and then still later decorated red on brown types. Sometime around 600 CE Mimbres potters began applying a white slip to their vessels before decorating them with red paint. Designs were more complex than they had been previously. Still later they learned to fire the vessels in reducing rather than oxidizing atmospheres, causing the red paint to turn black during firing. Around the same time the Mimbres people began to move their villages from the ridge tops down to terraces nearer streams. The newer houses were square and burials accompanied by black-on-white vessels were often placed under their floors.

Mimbres pottery reached its peak of development after 1000 CE. It is particularly appealing to modern tastes, with the consequence that many Mimbres sites have been irreparably damaged by looting. Many vessels are bowls with stylized animal figures and other designs on their interiors. Designs could be either figurative or nonfigurative, either positive or negative. Those that were used as burial offerings were symbolically killed, having holes deliberately puncturing their bottoms. While they were very well made, probably by craft specialists, there is no evidence that they were intended for use by an elite minority.

The Mimbres population grew and aggregated into larger surface pueblo communities between 1000 and 1130 CE. Larger villages had large ceremonial rooms, either above or below ground. Dependence on farming probably increased as evidenced by the growing use of check dams, canals, and reservoirs to manage water. However, the construction of new pueblos and the manufacture of distinctive Classic Mimbres pottery came to an end around 1130, when climate change afflicted the whole region (Powell-Marti and Gilman 2006).

The Mimbres population was more dispersed and perhaps smaller after 1150 CE. Their strategy was to move to smaller, more dispersed settlements. The abandonment of large villages was previously interpreted by archaeologists as evidence that they abandoned the

Figure 6.10 Mimbres bowls. (Mesa Verde National Park.)

whole Mimbres region, but that no longer appears to have been the case (Nelson et al. 2001). A few older pueblos were remodeled whereas new adobe-walled ones were founded, one on the ruins of the Galaz site.

The dwindling of traditional Mimbres pottery continued after 1300 CE. However, Gila Polychrome ceramics were added as the Mimbres people were caught up in the widespread Salado phenomenon. New Salado pottery styles resulted from the migration of displaced Ancestral Pueblo people from the northern part of the region to areas where farming was still viable. Some of them took up residence in Mimbres villages just as others had at Casa Grande.

Mimbres people lived in semisedentary communities at this time, relocating every quarter century or so. Many previously occupied parts of the area were not lived in at all anymore as the population shrank. After 1450 CE the last of the Mimbres people and the refugees they had taken in all disappeared from the area, reorganizing themselves elsewhere once again, and the landscape became home to newcomers, Apache hunter-gatherers (Nelson et al. 2006). Because migrants so often reinvent themselves as they move, archaeologists are not entirely sure where they went. But like the other peoples of the Mogollon tradition many might have ended up at Zuni, Paquimé, and various Rio Grande pueblos.

Paquimé

Paquimé, also known as Casas Grandes, is one of the largest and most complex sites in the region (Figure 6.11). It has tended in the past to receive less attention than it deserves from American archaeologists because it is located in northwestern Chihuahua in Mexico. Long-term excavations have revealed a sequence for Paquimé that began modestly in the first millennium CE then blossomed into a major spectacular regional center in the thirteenth century CE. Archaeologists thought for many years that maize horticulture was a late development and that population density was thin around Paquimé before it was founded. We now know that maize was being cultivated in the vicinity at least 3,000 to 3,500 years ago (Hard and Roney 1998). Furthermore, surveys have shown that regional population was dense enough to have allowed Paquimé to develop from local roots (Whalen and Minnis 2003).

Paquimé is related to cultures of the Mogollon tradition as well as to an archaeological culture in the vicinity of El Paso, Texas. Some archaeologists classify Paquimé as Mogollon because of this. But many others consider the site and its nearby satellites as a culture unique unto itself, or at least more central to the broader tradition that spawned Mogollon in its northern reaches (Plog 1997:173–178). Paquimé is so large and its trade connections were so widespread that it makes no sense to put it under a label meant to describe the much less complex cultures in the Mogollon Mountains (Whalen and Minnis 2003).

Turquoise was carried south from northern New Mexico, passing through Paquimé on its way ultimately to urban centers in the Mexican highlands. South of Paquimé traders also passed through the mining district of Chalchihuites, which served as another node in the long-distance trading network that connected the region to the big urban centers in highland Mexico. **Chalchihuitl** means 'jewel' in Nahuatl, the language of the Aztecs, and turquoise was one of the most desired of them. Traders at Paquimé supplied Mesoamerican exotics such as copper bells and live macaws to the Pueblo communities north of them. Macaw pens at Paquimé indicate that they even bred and raised the tropical birds there.

Ancestral Pueblo

The Ancestral Pueblo peoples developed the third and largest major cultural tradition of the region, and consequently the third major adaptation of farming to the regional environment (Figure 6.12). For decades this tradition has been termed "Anasazi," a word that means "enemy ancestors" in Navajo. It is a term that is neither accurate nor particularly appealing to modern

Figure 6.11 Rooms at Paquimé.

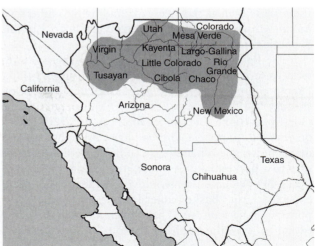

Figure 6.12 The maximum extent of Ancestral Pueblo (Anasazi) settlement. Not all areas were occupied simultaneously.

Pueblo Indians, their living descendants (Cordell 1984:58). Some people argue that it should be abandoned, and for the most part it has been here. But Anasazi is so entrenched in the literature that avoiding it without explanation would be hopelessly confusing. Like "America" it is a term that has acquired its own usefulness just as it has over time shrugged off its inappropriate origins.

The Ancestral Pueblo solution to farming was a flexible form of dry horticulture, raising maize and other crops opportunistically where rainfall and springs made productive cultivation possible. Their adaptation to the Colorado Plateau involved minimal but critically important use of irrigation (Damp et al. 2002). Seeps and springs along the cliffs of the plateau were used to supplement natural rainfall in many places. Small fields were laid out where that was possible, an intensive yet finely tuned approach to farming.

The adaptation put the Ancestral Pueblo farmers perpetually at the edge of failure. A slight drop in rainfall or a slight rise in temperature could end the productivity of most fields around a village and force its relocation. Despite the hazards of living on the edge, Ancestral Pueblo communities prospered and expanded over time, branches of the culture eventually spreading to portions of five of the modern United States (Figure 6.12). They were eventually able to support themselves on the southern Colorado Plateau, the southern Great Basin, and the upper Rio Grande Valley, regions that were variable and always challenging for farmers. Fluctuating environmental conditions forced the delicately adapted communities to abandon some areas even as they were expanding into others, so no single map can accurately portray the history of this dynamic tradition.

The Basketmaker cultures of the northern Southwest were Archaic peoples who evolved into the later Pueblo communities of the Ancestral Pueblo tradition (Kidder 1927). Basketmaker culture was defined as the oldest part of the Anasazi tradition in the 1920s, based on sites left by people who had agriculture but did not make pottery. Archaeologists initially assigned these sites to a Basketmaker II phase, in anticipation of finding earlier evidence that would allow them to define an expected earlier Basketmaker I phase not having either pottery or agriculture. That never happened, so the earlier roots of the tradition are to be found in various Archaic phases of the region.

Pottery, which derived from Mogollon prototypes, was not adopted by the Ancestral Pueblo people until around 450 CE. This adoption marked the beginning

of Basketmaker III in the old terminology. Thus the anticipated early Basketmaker never materialized and later Basketmaker culture is defined by the addition of pottery. These are circumstances that strike many archaeologists as nonsensical, but they too are part of the archaeological legacy one must be aware of to make sense of terms used in older publications.

Whatever terms are used, it is clear that one or more variants of Archaic culture evolved into the Ancestral Pueblo tradition with the addition of maize agriculture and later pottery. The cultural shift was accompanied by a physical shift in head shape that was once thought to be a major discontinuity, and probably evidence of population replacement. However, a simple switch from fiber to wooden cradleboards, not population change, apparently caused the change in head shape. The heads of infants are malleable, and the new cradleboards produced adults with rounder heads.

The early Ancestral Pueblos were well behind Mogollon and Hohokam development in 100 BCE, but they caught up quickly. They concentrated on maize and squash cultivation at first, adding beans and domesticated turkeys after 500 CE (Schollmeyer and Turner 2004). They hunted with spear throwers and lived in domed pole and mud stucco houses about 8 m (26 ft) in diameter. The houses had depressed clay floors, but the Ancestral Pueblo people were not yet building excavated pithouses.

Typical early Ancestral Pueblo communities were no more than clusters of three or four such simple houses. Band sizes were probably no greater than 12 to 20 people in the early years. However, this number doubled by 600 CE. Despite getting a later start in farming, the Ancestral Pueblo peoples of the Colorado Plateau region of the Southwest expanded rapidly during the cooler and wetter conditions that prevailed across the region before 1150 CE.

The Evolution of Pueblos

The Ancestral Pueblo tradition was variable, and it is defined more as everything that is demonstrably ancestral to the modern Pueblos than by any internally consistent set of shared archaeological traits. Environmental variability and the effects of distance produced the series of local Ancestral Pueblo cultures shown in Figure 6.12. These are sometimes referred to as "branches," following a scheme introduced by Gladwin in 1934 (Cordell 1997:172). Were it not for that heritage its internal diversity over both time and space might well have led archaeologists to define the Ancestral Pueblo as a series of separate cultures. On the other hand, shared traits in pottery and architecture do cross-cut the various local versions of Ancestral Pueblo culture, so archaeologists are comfortable with continuing to use a single term to describe them.

The emergence of Pueblo-like culture did not happen simultaneously across the Colorado Plateau. It is dated to 500 CE in the east and 700 CE in the west. New developments included increased farming, greater permanence of housing, the clustering of houses into hamlets and villages, and the replacement of the spear thrower by the bow and arrow. Eastern Ancestral Pueblo villages were particularly large, and some already came to feature large communal structures, "great kivas" like those built by people of the Mogollon tradition. Pottery became widely made in Ancestral Pueblo communities as these changes were unfolding.

The Pecos Classification System

The appearance of pottery provided early archaeologists with a means to define a series of ceramic phases for the Anasazi tradition, usually known as the Pecos classification system. These are traditionally named Pueblo I–V, although some archaeologists have proposed more descriptive alternate terms. The principal flaw of the Pecos classification is that it has become a developmental scheme rather than a chronological one. This is because before independent dating techniques were developed archaeologists needed to use ceramic styles for cross dating local sequences (Table 6.1). Thus Pueblo I ceramics in one part of the region were assumed to be roughly the same age as Pueblo I ceramics found in another area, and

Table 6.1 The Pecos chronology of the ancestral Pueblo (Anasazi) tradition, read from bottom to top as in a stratigraphic sequence. Dates vary from one area to another.

Periods	Approximate Dates
Pueblo V	1600 CE to present
Pueblo IV	1300 to 1600 CE
Pueblo III	1100 to 1300 CE
Pueblo II	920 to 1100 CE
Pueblo I	725–750 to 920 CE
Basketmaker III	400–500 to 725–750 CE
Basketmaker II	0 to 400–500 CE

the scheme allowed researchers to develop a comprehensive regional chronology (Cordell 1997:164–167).

Accurate tree-ring dating began a few years after the first Pecos conference. The accumulation of **dendrochronological** dates eventually showed that types that were classified as, say, Pueblo II ceramics in sites scattered across the region were not always contemporaneous. The dates assigned to any of the stages were thus only rough approximations for any of the local cultures covered by them. When dated accurately by tree rings, the western Ancestral Pueblo cultures appeared to have lagged behind the eastern ones over time. For example, whereas Pueblo I began around 700 CE in the Chaco area, it did not begin until 850 CE in the Kayenta area. Consequently, there are separate date ranges assigned to each of the Basketmaker and Pueblo developmental stages in each of the several branches.

The precision afforded by tree-ring dating made these temporal variations across space quite clear to later archaeologists, and many of them have begun substituting different phase names for the more general stage names of the Pecos scheme, or simply referring to calendar dates when describing the chronologies of local Ancestral Pueblo cultures. The latter solution seems likely to prevail in the long term.

Ancestral Pueblo Pottery

Detailed study of Ancestral Pueblo pottery and the Pecos chronology are no longer needed for dating purposes, but people remain interested in it for its aesthetic value and for technical studies. The preferred Ancestral Pueblo technique for making pottery was coiling, scraping, and polishing. Early pots were coarse, and early forms often mimicked gourd ladles. At first they were made from unwinnowed clays, adding **temper** to make the wet clays easier to work. Tempering later disappeared and potters winnowed their clays to produce much finer vessels.

Ancestral Pueblo pottery types range from plain and corrugated gray utility wares to a series of painted wares. The latter were often black-on-white, black-on-red, or polychrome painted types. All were traditionally made by the coil and scrape method. Vessels were varied and specialized after 1100 CE. Some forms, like Mesa Verde mugs (Figure 6.13), remain popular as models for modern pottery. In some parts of the region influences from potters working in the Mogollon region led to the development of oxidized types having red, yellow, and orange designs (Figure 6.14). Firing pots on top of fuel but covered so that oxygen cannot reach them leads to chemical reduction of the paints used in decoration, yielding a range of white, gray, and

Figure 6.13 Mesa Verde mugs. (Mesa Verde National Park.)

Figure 6.14 Mesa Verde oxidized bowl. (Mesa Verde National Park.)

Figure 6.15 An early shallow pithouse at Mesa Verde.

black shades. By firing the pots in ways that allow oxygen to circulate around the vessels and oxidize the paints, potters learned how to produce the brighter colors. Even a true glaze was developed by potters along the upper Rio Grande, but they never used it to coat and waterproof whole vessels. The glaze was used only as a decorative paint; ancestral Pueblos preferred porous pottery, which keep liquids cooler by allowing vessels to sweat. Modern Pueblo pottery retains both this technique and traditional painted designs, although many artists have taken their work in a variety of new directions.

Ancestral Pueblo Architecture

Ancestral Pueblo architecture began as clusters of semi-subterranean pithouses (Figure 6.15). Early floor plans were round or rounded rectangular. Later houses were built above ground, constructed from laid masonry or adobe, with contiguous square or rectangular rooms often sharing common walls. Subterranean rooms survived as ceremonial kivas even in later villages in which all habitation and storage rooms were above ground. Larger communities eventually featured great kivas, plazas, and towers. Many of these forms persist in modern Pueblo communities.

Early shallow pithouses had excavated side entrances and smoke holes above their central hearths. Later pithouses were much deeper, so deep that their cribwork roofs were at ground level or protruded only

slightly above it. Smoke holes eventually doubled as entrances, and side entrances became narrowed to become ventilator shafts. The innovation ensured the flow of fresh air into the pithouse and the flow of smoke out through the smoke hole.

The evolution from round structures to rectangular ones has been observed in many parts of the world. The earlier structures are usually associated with shared storage facilities, while the later square or rectangular ones typically have private storage rooms (Flannery 2002). This phenomenon is probably due to the demographic effects of increasing settlement size. As community numbers grow, dwelling density increases and contiguous rooms require straight common walls. At the same time the communal sharing practices of band societies are replaced by family-oriented storage strategies in tribal societies.

By 800 CE villages often had both residential pithouses and surface residences. Kivas evolved out of earlier pithouse forms. These served as meeting places for related males in what were becoming strong matrilineal societies. Great kivas were being built as larger centers of community activity in eastern Ancestral Pueblo communities by this time, but they remained absent in the west, where villages were smaller and less numerous. Kivas usually have four diagnostic features (Figure 6.16), a ventilator shaft, a deflector in front of it to prevent strong drafts, a hearth, and a **sipapu**. The last is the symbolic representation of the hole through which people emerged into the world in Pueblo myth.

Cotton appeared by 850 CE, an important introduction from Mexico. Curiously, the use of cotton did not spread to the Eastern Woodlands until after 1492. The appearance of cotton textiles in the Greater Southwest is important because it marks a decline in the need for hides to make clothing. Cotton is difficult

Ventilator Opening

Draft
Deflector

Hearth

Sipapu

Figure 6.16 Kivas exhibit standard features. There is a central hearth. Draft deflectors stand in front of ventilator shaft openings. On the other side of the hearth is the sipapu, symbolic of the hole through which humans emerged into the world according to Pueblo myth. Pilasters to hold up cribwork roofs and niches to hold special objects are often present as well. (Mesa Verde National Park)

to transform into cloth, but it makes more desirable fabrics than do native fibers and supply was not as short as it was for hides. Some specimens of cotton cloth are so finely made that they can be mistaken for lace.

Demographic Change

The Ancestral Pueblo people reached their maximum geographic expansion to the west around 1150 CE. After that environmental conditions forced the western part of the range to contract. The entire Virgin culture area was abandoned, and the century that followed saw the collapse of the Chacoan system and the continued stressing of other local cultures by environmental changes. Mesa Verde and Cibola cultures developed settlement hierarchies and regional exchange systems in the face of these stresses, replacing the Chacoans in the forefront of Ancestral Pueblo development (Figure 6.12).

A severe drought afflicted people all across the region from 1276 to 1299 CE. Dendrochronology allows us to be very sure of the dating of this climatic episode. Outermost villages collapsed first and refugees from them retreated to more central surviving communities. This increased stresses on the communities taking in refugees, which were already having their own trouble coping with the extended drought. Ancient rituals no longer seemed to work, and serious warfare broke out between Ancestral Pueblo communities as they competed for water and other increasingly scarce resources (LeBlanc 1999).

Ancestral Pueblo communities completely abandoned the San Juan River drainage around 1300 CE. People from Mesa Verde moved to the Rio Grande area, augmenting the village populations of that area. Sites in Bandelier National Monument had been in existence since 1150 CE, and occupation continued there well into the era of Spanish colonization (Kohler 2004). Chacoan people dispersed and founded new villages to the south, while Kayenta communities either merged with Tusayan Pueblos in the area where their Hopi descendants still survive, or relocated to join Mogollon villages farther south, forming multiethnic communities.

Cibola culture was concentrated in the area where their modern Zuni descendants still live. Paquimé became a major center in northern Chihuahua by 1250 CE, probably with the benefit of some immigrants from the north. It remained a major center for two more centuries (Lekson 2002).

The roughly three-century period between the abandonment of the San Juan drainage and the arrival of the Spanish in the sixteenth century is often referred to as the Pueblo IV period. During this time the Ancestral Pueblo peoples concentrated their settlements in the areas where Hopi, Zuni, and Rio Grande Pueblos still survive today. Influences from Mexico stimulated many changes in Ancestral Pueblo religion and society during this period. Because of tight tree-ring dating the timing of events in this period is better understood than are earlier Ancestral Pueblo time periods.

Mesa Verde

Mesa Verde, now a national park in southwestern Colorado, was the center of just one of several regional variants of Ancestral Pueblo early on. The Mesa Verde area was settled by 400 CE and villages subsequently spread into a variety of local ecological settings. Over time masonry replaced less permanent **jacal** walls in local architecture, and central villages came to dominate smaller subordinate ones that were scattered around them. This indicates that multivillage polities, possibly weak chiefdoms, developed here (Noble 2006).

Mesa Verde people began building and moving into blocks of apartment dwellings by 700 CE. Their villages multiplied and spread to their greatest geographic extent during 900–1150 CE. They were able to survive the warmer and drier conditions that followed that period, and the Ancestral Pueblo center of gravity actually shifted northward toward Mesa Verde. They constructed the famous Mesa Verde cliff dwellings during the 1150–1250 CE period, driven there by increasing competition amidst changing climatic conditions. As they came together into defensible cliff dwelling communities they also intensified their farming practices by constructing increasingly sophisticated water storage and distribution systems. Their population first peaked in overall size and then declined rapidly in the latter part of the thirteenth century.

Cliff Palace (Figure 6.17) is a large central community at Mesa Verde having 200 rooms and 23 kivas, a ratio of 9 to 1. The normal ratio of rooms to kivas is 12 to 1, so this suggests that Cliff Palace was special in more than just its unusually large size. Some archaeologists speculate that Cliff Palace might have been the center of a large polity that included surrounding smaller communities. Whether or not it was the center of a weak chiefdom here remains a subject of debate.

By 1300 CE the prolonged drought that beset the entire region had caused a cascade of consequences that ended with the abandonment of the Mesa Verde area (Cordell et al. 2007; Kohler et al. 2008). The surviving Mesa Verde people retreated to the south and east. Some took up residence with surviving Chacoan villages nearby. Others relocated to the upper Rio Grande Valley where they found adequate precipitation, arable soils close to villages, and broad views of their fields. The Kachina (also "Katsina" or "Katcina") Cult, which was focused on a series of over 200 supernatural beings, grew rapidly under these stressful conditions as religious movements often do. It appeared in nearly all Pueblo religious systems after their relocations and it may have served in part to integrate the amalgamating new communities.

Canyon de Chelly

Canyon de Chelly, which is located on the Navajo reservation, provides a case of Ancestral Pueblo development that parallels that of Mesa Verde. The canyon

Figure 6.17 Cliff Palace, a large community on Mesa Verde.

holds evidence of early Ancestral Pueblo development followed by a subsequent movement to cliff dwellings. The canyon was later abandoned, just as Mesa Verde was. Hunter-gatherers, the ancestors of the Navajos on whose modern reservation the canyon is located, moved in to fill the vacuum.

The appearance of Athapaskan-speaking Navajos and Apaches in the Southwest occurred too late to explain the decline of Ancestral Pueblo cultures. Their arrival in the region was more effect than cause. The decline of the Ancestral Pueblo communities was caused by the onset of hotter and drier climatic conditions, not attacks by nomadic latecomers. The early Navajos and Apaches, hunter-gatherers whose subsistence was not wiped out by the long dry spell, filled the land left largely vacant by shrinking and departing farming communities.

Rock Art

Pictographs and petroglyphs are abundant in the Desert West and they continue to attract popular attention. Many professional archaeologists avoid them because they are notoriously difficult to date and unscientific interpretations have tended to be very speculative. However, some recent successes have overcome one or both problems. The pictograph known as the "All American Man" in Canyonlands National Park, Utah, has charcoal as one of its pigments (Figure 6.18). This has allowed the pictograph to be radiocarbon dated to 1300–1375 CE (Chaffee et al. 1994).

The Chaco Phenomenon

Perhaps the most remarkable of all Ancestral Pueblo developments occurred in the Chaco region, particularly in Chaco Canyon itself. While chiefdom political organization, impressive architecture, and a regional economic system emerged in the Chaco area, the hallmarks of the Chacoan system never appeared among the western Ancestral Pueblo (Lekson 2006; Noble 2004).

The region in which Chaco culture developed is about 65,000 km^2 (25,000 mi^2). It is located in northwestern New Mexico, an area now thinly populated and seemingly remote. Like some other archaeological centers, such as the great city of Teotihuacán in Mexico, its location is hard to explain. Whether it was centered there as the result of some as yet undetermined factor or pure chance, the Chaco phenomenon arose quickly and lasted for over two centuries.

Figure 6.18 All-American Man pictograph, Canyonlands National Park.
Source: Courtesy of Tom Till Photography.

Chaco Canyon was settled around 490 CE, and it was initially not much different from other Ancestral Pueblo areas. However, by 860 CE there were many small communities in the canyon and a few larger ones. Larger communities held 100–120 households, and the total population in the early years was probably only 1,000–1,500 people. But they were just getting started.

The heyday of Chaco was 900–1125 CE, sustained by cooler and wetter conditions that favored new strains of maize. Kivas were being built by 860 CE, modeled on earlier pithouse dwellings, and matrilocal residence might have been the rule. Chacoan laborers gradually built a system of roads that radiated out to other Ancestral Pueblo centers, creating a regional web of trade and exchange between Chaco Canyon and an array of Chacoan outliers.

Local stone worked well for Chacoan masons, and perhaps it was something as simple as this that explains why the center of the Chaco phenomenon arose here rather than somewhere else. The stone splits easily into tabular slabs, which are perfect for the walls of multistory buildings. Masonry techniques and materials evolved over time as Chacoan builders got better at their craft and came to depend less on thick mud mortar. Figure 6.19 shows a simplified succession of improving bonds over time.

Chacoan villagers reached their maximum population of around 5,500 people by 1050 CE. There is no evidence of centralized government, so most archaeologists infer that it was probably organized around ritual, as is still the case among the Hopi. Despite this politically weak form of chiefdom organization, Chacoan builders managed to import 200,000 timbers for construction projects, most of them from great distances.

Pueblo Bonito

Pueblo Bonito (Figure 6.20), the most famous of the Chaco sites, is a large D-shaped apartment building that contains 800 rooms and 32 kivas (Neitzel 2003b). Its main occupation is dated by dendrochronology to 828–1150 CE. Some spaces were used during the following hundred years, but many were burned then and later (Windes 2003).

The front wall of Pueblo Bonito is oriented on a true east–west line (Figure 6.21). About 600 of the rooms were in use at any particular time in its history, others being either abandoned or not yet built. The pueblo could have housed at least 1,000 people, perhaps 1,200 at its peak, but there is no other evidence that so many people ever lived there (Neitzel 2003a).

Most kivas at Pueblo Bonito are nestled within room blocks. Two great kivas were built over the course of the eleventh and early twelfth centuries, one of them with two sunken rooms in its floor. The curved back wall of Pueblo Bonito once stood five stories high. A rock fall in January 1941 destroyed part of it.

The great house appears to have been much larger than necessary, having huge storage capacity in

Figure 6.19 Masonry evolution in Chaco Canyon, from rough stone and thick mortar (left) to dressed stones and little mortar (right).

Figure 6.20 Pueblo Bonito from the north cliff of Chaco Canyon.

Figure 6.21 Plan of Pueblo Bonito.
Source: From Stein et al 2003:51.

nonresidential rooms buried deep inside the curving rear wall (Benson et al. 2003). Pueblo Bonito was occupied for perhaps three centuries, but only 50 to 60 burials have been found associated with it. This is further evidence that the great house was larger than would have been needed to merely contain its small human population. Like the White House in Washington it was more likely a public building for the 2,000–6,000 people living elsewhere in Chaco Canyon, rather than a residential apartment building (Neitzel 2003a:148). This kind of use is supported by the ritual caches found in Pueblo Bonito. These include cylindrical vessels, human effigy vessels, and ceramic incense burners (Crown and Wills 2003).

Other large villages in the canyon include Peñasco Blanco, Hungo Pavi, Chetro Ketl, and Pueblo del Arroyo. Pueblo Bonito and Peñasco Blanco went through subsequent enlargements, probably not reaching their final sizes until around 1115 CE (Figure 6.22).

Pueblo Alto is one of a small number of big villages built above the Chaco Canyon rim. It was constructed from 1020 to 1060 CE. There are 85 rooms, but only 5 rooms were inhabited. Storerooms at Pueblo Alto opened to the outside rather than into the interior rooms and there was a huge midden of pottery. This and chert found in the midden came mostly from the Chuska area 70 km (43 mi) to the west, as had much of Chaco's lumber.

A few other smaller villages in the canyon include Wijiji, Tsin Kletzin, and Kin Kletso (Lekson 1991). All of these were built by 1100 CE in a construction effort

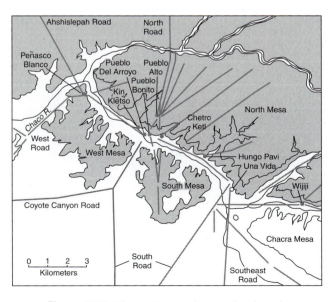

Figure 6.22 Chaco Canyon showing local roads.

that archaeologists have described as having "frenzied proportions" (Crown and Judge 1991). Roof beams were imported from great distances, many more rooms were built than were needed by the resident population, and turquoise was an important currency.

Chacoan Trade and Exchange

Chacoan communities controlled the turquoise trade by the ninth century. Chaco Canyon became a distribution hub for a system that brought in turquoise from great distances (the nearest source is 160 km or 100 mi away) and at least some of it was carried south into Mexico. The system was probably run by clan heads. This was a pattern of trading partnerships and exchange couched as gift giving that was a familiar theme across ancient North America.

Mexican goods flowed north to Chaco in exchange for turquoise. Copper bells, macaws, and conch shell trumpets from Mexico have all been found in Chacoan sites. Chacoan roads linked great houses locally and linked the canyon to at least 30 more distant outliers. Archaeologists have mapped 400 km (250 mi) so far, and there might be a total of 650 km (400 mi). Some predict that five times that total might eventually be found (Figure 6.23).

Chacoan roads are up to 12 m (40 ft) wide and very straight. One example is 95 km (59 mi) long. The roads could run dead straight because the Chacoans lacked wheeled vehicles and could overcome rock outcrops by cutting stairways in them. Roads were occasionally discontinuous and in some places there were sharp angles. Researchers have hypothesized that the roads were designed and built to facilitate pilgrimages to Chaco Canyon. This hypothesis explains several things that are otherwise not easily explained, and it has so far resisted disproof (Judge 1989; Vivian 1990). The hypothesis explains how Chacoans acquired and transported timbers, why the roads were so well built, why there is a surplus of rooms in Chacoan great houses, and why turquoise was important.

Chacoan Outliers

In addition to the many large structures in Chaco Canyon there were at least 70 outlier communities by 1115 CE. They tended to be located at 32–40-km (20–25-mi) intervals, which is a hard one-day journey on foot. Not all of them were linked by Chacoan roads, but most were linked to each other and with Chaco Canyon by signal stations on cliff tops. Many outliers mimicked the D-shaped structures of the great houses in Chaco Canyon. It appears that they might have

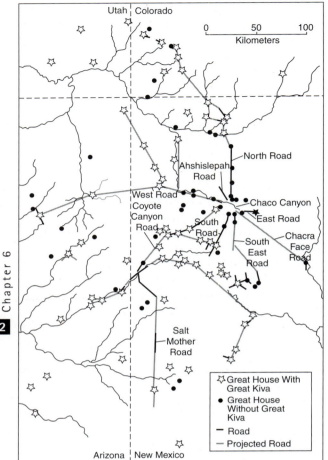

Figure 6.23 Chacoan regional roads.

taken over by migrants from Mesa Verde when climatic conditions forced them from their former homes. The migrants partitioned the large Chacoan rooms at Salmon into smaller ones like those found at Mesa Verde.

Unusual Features in Chaco Canyon

The great house called Chetro Ketl was built 825–1125 CE. It features a 30-m (98-ft) colonnade that appears to reflect Mexican Toltec architectural influence. The spaces between the columns were later filled in with masonry, making the colonnade difficult to discern but still visible. There are two great kivas at Chetro Ketl, which required 5,000 trees to roof over. The heavy cribwork and earth roofs are long gone, leaving the great kivas open to the sky. There is also a kiva tower at Chetro Ketl, an architectural feature that is found nowhere else in Chaco Canyon.

Casa Rinconada is a great kiva 19.2 m (63 ft) in diameter (Figure 6.24). It has been estimated that the cribwork and earthen roof that probably once covered it would have weighed 100 tons after being soaked by rain. This great kiva stands amidst small residences, with no associated D-shaped village. There is a peripheral bench, niches, a raised fireplace, and a clever underground entrance.

Fajada Butte is a solitary natural monument in Chaco Canyon that holds a small rock shelter containing an enigmatic spiral petroglyph (Figure 6.25). Three large stone slabs near its top enclose a small space that was probably used by shamans (Plog 1997:100–101). The slabs lie at odd angles, but claims that they were deliberately moved there by humans are doubtful. Sunlight shining through cracks between the slabs casts

supplied food to the central communities in the canyon, which would probably not have been able to sustain themselves if higher population estimates are correct.

Aztec. The outlier at Aztec was built in the early 1100s. It grew to 500 rooms and had a great kiva that was reconstructed in 1934. Among other things Earl Morris uncovered in his excavations was a 40,000-bead necklace, 23 m (75 ft) long. Warmer and drier conditions put pressure on the Chaco phenomenon in the twelfth century. The focus of Chacoan culture moved northward during 1110–1275 CE to the Aztec site.

Salmon. The Salmon outlier was built 1088–1106 CE. It is a C-shaped pueblo community containing 600–750 rooms. There is a great kiva and a tower kiva. Pottery styles found there indicate that a combined population of local people and migrants from Chaco Canyon founded it. Late in its history Salmon was

Figure 6.24 Casa Rinconada.

Figure 6.25 Fajada Butte, Chaco Canyon.

Figure 6.26 Sun dagger in an enclosure atop Fajada Butte.
Source: Copyright Solstice Project. Photo by Karl Kernberger.

slivers of light on the interior rock face. The positions of the "sun daggers" vary through the course of the year.

A shaman carved a spiral on the wall that provides a field for the daggers of sunlight. On the summer solstice a dagger of sunlight bisects the spiral moving vertically across it in the course of a few minutes (Figure 6.26). On the vernal and autumnal equinoxes the sun dagger passes right of center and a smaller dagger bisects a small secondary spiral to the left of the larger one. At the time of the winter solstice two equivalent daggers bracket the spiral. It is logical that the stone slabs and the resulting slivers of light were there first and that someone gave them greater meaning by recording their positions at key times of the year and carving the shallow spirals (Sofaer et al. 1979).

The End of the Chaco Phenomenon

Generally warmer drier conditions prevailed here after 1150 CE, as was the case across the entire Southwest. Local droughts started in 1130 CE and marginal locations became unproductive. Outliers ceased sending food to Chaco and local production was inadequate to make up the shortfall. Canyon

population began to fall and the great houses were abandoned by the early 1200s. Smaller villages survived, as did some outliers, but the larger Chaco Phenomenon collapsed.

By 1300 prolonged drought had caused the Mesa Verde area to be abandoned as well. The surviving Mesa Verde people retreated to the south and east. Some took up residence with surviving Chacoan villagers nearby.

Sinagua

The Sinagua culture of the Verde Valley in central Arizona was a secondary tradition located between the three major traditions of the region. It was made up of two cultures, Northern and Southern Sinagua, that arose around 650 CE and ended around 1400 CE (Figure 6.27). Each passed through a series of phases that have been defined by archaeologists on the basis of changing ceramic styles. The ecological context of this secondary development was partly the unusual consequence of volcanic activity in the zone lying between Hohokam and Ancestral Pueblo cultures.

The eruption of Sunset volcano in 1064–1066 drastically altered the ecology of the central Arizona region. The Verde Valley was temporarily abandoned by Indian communities after the fall of a blanket of pumice and ash. Some archaeologists argue that in the long run the ash fall actually led to better agricultural conditions and a local demographic boom after farmers returned to the devastated area. Eventually, like other cultures in the region, the Sinagua people succumbed to the hotter and drier conditions that prevailed after

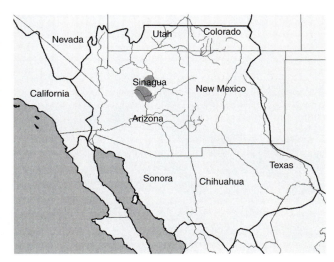

Figure 6.27 Location of Sinagua culture.

1150 CE. Their population dwindled and all Sinagua sites were abandoned by 1400 CE. The survivors added to the stream of refugees that joined communities where farming was still possible, making their own contributions to the widespread Salado culture that emerged across much of the region.

Sinagua Sites

Wupatki, which means "Tall House" in the Hopi language, is a multistory Sinagua pueblo dwelling having more than 100 rooms (Figure 6.28). Secondary structures, including two large, apparently uncovered kivalike structures, stand nearby. Wupatki was first occupied around 500 CE. The site and the valley around it were temporarily abandoned after the eruption of Sunset volcano in 1064–1066, and the site was permanently abandoned by 1225 CE.

Tuzigoot was a Sinagua site that was occupied 1000–1400 CE. It is an elongated complex of stone masonry rooms that were built along the spine of a natural outcrop in the Verde Valley. The central rooms stand higher than the others and they appear to have served public functions.

Montezuma Castle is a popular Sinagua cliff dwelling (Figure 6.29). It was occupied approximately 1125–1400 CE, its population peaking around 1300 CE. The site's dramatic setting and architecture draw tourists today.

Montezuma Castle is hopelessly misnamed, but the name probably has been attached to it too long to be abandoned. It is clearly not a castle in any traditional sense. The site is also not connected in any way with the Aztec Empire or either of the emperors named "Montezuma," or more properly "Moctezuma." Inappropriate site names like this occur in many places in the United

Figure 6.29 Montezuma Castle.

States. These are the legacy of nineteenth-century enthusiasm, a time when the discoverers of sites sometimes had too much imagination and too little information for the understanding of their discoveries.

Patayan

The major traditions of the Greater Southwest fared well before the climate changes that began around 1150 CE, and hunter-gatherers who lived at the margins of the region sometimes adopted farming, pottery, and the basics of settled life from them. One such cultural development was the Patayan tradition, which emerged among peoples living along the Colorado River on the western margin of the Southwest (Figure 6.30). The Patayan people adopted agriculture and settled life primarily from the Ancestral Pueblo and Hohokam traditions, but they never built the elaborate pueblo dwellings and ritual structures found at the region's core.

Large enigmatic intaglios occur in Patayan territory. Those near Blythe, California, are particularly notable. No one is sure whether they were made by the Patayan people or their ancestors. The figures were made by simply moving weathered rocks to the side, creating lighter patches that can best be appreciated from the air. Like the large effigy mounds of the northern Midwest, they were invested with symbolic significance that we can now only speculate about.

Figure 6.28 Wupatki in winter.

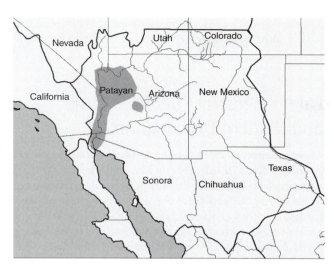

Figure 6.30 Distribution of the Patayan tradition, including the late expansion into central Arizona.

Descendants of the Patayan tradition include the Cocopa, Quechan, Halchidhoma, Mohave, Maricopa, Yavapai, Walapai, and Havasupai peoples of the Colorado Basin. The modern Havasupai people live in a spectacular setting at the bottom of a deep segment of the Grand Canyon that was long almost inaccessible except on foot or horseback. All of these speak one or another of the languages of the Cochimí-Yuman family. The descendants of the Patayan tradition spread eastward from the Colorado River in the twelfth century and later. As Ancestral Pueblo and Sinagua communities were abandoned and their inhabitants fell back into areas where agriculture was still viable, the ancestors of the Maricopas moved into a portion of the abandoned territory, as shown in Figure 6.3.

Another derivative archaeological culture called Fremont arose separately in various parts of the eastern Great Basin, in what is now Utah, beyond the regional boundary of the Greater Southwest. Fremont is discussed in Chapter 15.

The Contraction of the Greater Southwest Cultures

The environmental changes that followed 1150 CE forced new strategies upon all the peoples of the Greater Southwest. There was a temporary reprieve from 1250 to 1350 CE, but many communities had to relocate by 1450. The widespread disruption forced change upon everyone. Even communities that did not have to relocate were altered by influxes of refugees.

It is not easy for archaeologists to distinguish routine site relocation from the abandonment of a whole region and it is likely that they have too often mistaken the former for the latter (Nelson and Hegmon 2001; Nelson et al. 2006). But at the same time it is clear that large areas of the Southwest were completely vacated by agricultural villagers from the twelfth century on (Cordell 1997:365–397). The hotter and drier conditions that prevailed by then simply made farming too marginal for the communities to survive at the traditional sizes to which they had become accustomed. Recent research has shown that there was probably enough residual agricultural productivity to allow very small villages to hang on, but their populations would have been below the critical mass needed to sustain traditional ceremonies and other social customs that the Ancestral Puebloans by this time considered essential. Like most people everywhere who find themselves in such circumstances, they preferred to move on (Axtell et al. 2002).

The cycles of aggregation and dispersal in the Southwest tell us much about human behavior. Enthusiasm for sharing and collective effort appears to depend upon the perception and reality of overall well-being and long-term security. When external forces erode overall productivity and raise both immediate and long-term risks people move to smaller settlements and smaller production units. This is what happened across the Greater Southwest when scarcity reduced overall population size and prompted people to share within smaller and smaller groups. The lesson is that while there is strength in numbers, size becomes a liability when numbers cannot be sustained (Hill et al. 2004; Kohler and Gumerman 2000).

Prior to 900 CE violence in the region was primarily feuding and small-scale raiding. Between 900 and 1250 CE farming was still possible and there was relative peace, punctuated occasionally by savage episodes of warfare that were probably not yet the result of resource shortages. This was precisely the period in which the Chaco phenomenon enjoyed its heyday.

Recent research in Long House Valley has provided a detailed accounting of the demographic effects of climate change on one local population. Productive farming there drove the rise of Ancestral Pueblo population until the twelfth century. It rose sharply during 1000–1130 CE, then crashed over the next 50 years because of drought and falling groundwater levels. The population rose again after 1180, reaching a peak in 1275 before crashing a second time. After the second crash the population of the valley fell to such a low level that it was abandoned by 1300 CE. Computer modeling indicates that a few hundred Ancestral Pueblo farmers could have held on, but they chose not to. Their descendants did not simply disappear, for they are alive and well elsewhere today, the long trail of abandoned villages tracing the flowering of their ancestral traditions in the region.

The shrinking and relocation of communities and the amalgamation of many of them into new hybrid communities fostered widespread changes that archaeologists can detect in such things as new pottery styles, architectural changes, and shifts in religious symbols. One such phenomenon was the spread of new pottery styles termed "Salado," which have already been mentioned in connection with some earlier cultures (Figure 6.31). Salado styles were derived from older traditions as refugees and even whole communities relocated, merged, and adapted to new circumstances.

Salado pottery types spread rapidly across the ranges of the Hohokam and Mogollon traditions as well as some adjoining territory in the thirteenth century. The central pottery type is Gila Polychrome, which is closely related to both Pinto and Tonto Polychrome types. Salado ceramics were particularly dominant in thirteenth- and early fourteenth-century phases of the Tonto, Mimbres, and Jornada cultures of the Mogollon tradition.

Remnant cultures of the Ancestral Pueblo tradition, which were by this time living in smaller areas of northern Arizona and New Mexico, were generally not part of the Salado phenomenon. Farming conditions continued to deteriorate and the production of

Salado ceramics ceased. The culture areas in which it was manufactured were largely abandoned around 1450 CE.

Later Ancestral Pueblo and Modern Descendants

Many of today's Pueblo communities are located near the upper Rio Grande in New Mexico. They are the descendants of Ancestral Pueblo people who abandoned Mesa Verde, Chaco Canyon, and other parts of their former territory centuries ago. Some sites in this part of northern New Mexico, such as Pecos, have both long prehistoric sequences and remains dating from the Spanish colonial period.

Kuaua

Kuaua, which is located north of Albuquerque, was one of the Rio Grande communities possibly visited by the Coronado expedition of 1540–1542. Navajo hunter-gatherers were arriving in the valley in the first half of the same century. Pressure from both the Navajos and the Spanish caused the people of Kuaua to abandon the pueblo soon after 1600 CE. Excavations of a large kiva at the site have revealed very colorful murals that were painted sometime after Coronado passed through the region. Similarly striking murals have been found at Pottery Mound Pueblo southwest of Albuquerque (Schaafsma 2007).

Pecos

The site of Pecos lies east of Santa Fe, in an area near the frontier with the High Plains that was good for farming but that made them vulnerable to nomadic raiders. The pueblo was founded around 1250–1300 CE. Many Ancestral Pueblo refugees from the northwest found their way to Pecos during the first half of the fourteenth century. Marcos de Niza might have visited the town in 1539 and the Coronado expedition passed it as well. Spanish colonists subsequently built a mission church at Pecos, most of which still stands.

Puebloans revolted against Spanish rule in 1680 and the colonists fled south. After the successful revolt the Indians at Pecos constructed a traditional kiva in front of the church, an obvious symbolic rejection of Christianity (Figure 6.32). However, the community assisted the Spanish in enlarging and repairing the mission church when the colonists returned after 1700 CE (Preucel 2002).

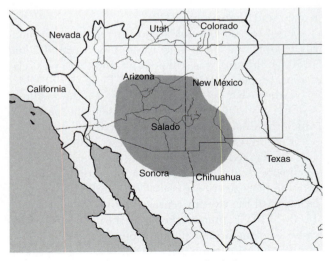

Figure 6.31 The distribution of Salado pottery.

Figure 6.32 Mission church at Pecos with later kiva in right foreground.

The location of Pecos near the western edge of the southern High Plains caused the people of the community to suffer greatly at the hands of marauding Comanches. These were nomadic Uto-Aztecan people who acquired horses from the Spanish and then abandoned hunting and gathering in the Great Basin in order to move on to the Great Plains as mounted bison hunters. They took up nomadic residence in western Texas and occasionally raided the eastern Pueblos as part of their adaptation. The Pecos population dwindled in the face of these attacks, and the pueblo was abandoned by 1838. The small number of people then resident at Pecos moved to Jemez Pueblo.

Acoma

The village Acoma is perched dramatically atop a steep-sided mesa in western New Mexico, still occupied today and probably the oldest continuously occupied community in the United States. Many immigrants from the northwest settled at Acoma in the first half of the fourteenth century. It was later one of the pueblos visited by both Fray Marcos de Niza (1539) and the Coronado expedition (1540–1542).

Acoma villagers suffered in conflict with the Spanish in 1599 CE. The village was subsequently repaired and missionized by the Spanish during the first half of the seventeenth century. The Acoma people joined in the general Pueblo revolt and evicted the Spanish in 1680, but like most other Pueblos they tolerated the return of the Spanish colonists in the early eighteenth century. A smallpox epidemic devastated Acoma in 1780 and the inhabitants suffered from encroachments by Navajos during the first half of the nineteenth century. Despite all of these setbacks, the Acoma community has survived on its mesa and in surrounding settlements below.

Modern Acoma potters are very skilled and their pottery is well known among collectors. Their work is known particularly for delicate and detailed designs on very finely designed black-on-white vessels.

Zuni

The Zunis of northwestern New Mexico derive in part from the Cibola culture of the Ancestral Pueblo tradition, in part from the Mogollon tradition. Although they are clearly related to other cultures of the Greater Southwest, their language is unique in the Greater Southwest and probably distantly related to the Penutian family. Their ancestors were among the various bands of hunter-gatherers living on the Colorado Plateau when farming, ceramic production, and settled life became available 3,000 years ago. The Zuni nation today maintains its own active archaeological program. There are several ancestral Zuni sites in and around the modern Zuni reservation that have drawn the interest of archaeologists.

Hopi

The Hopis of northeastern Arizona descend from the Little Colorado culture of the Ancestral Pueblo tradition. They speak a Uto-Aztecan language and are probably direct descendants of some of the early migrants who brought maize to the Greater Southwest from the south. Today they live mainly on or near a series of mesas in northern Arizona, surrounded by the much larger Navajo reservation.

The Kachina Cult flourished in the difficult years during which the Ancestral Pueblo villagers abandoned many of their settlements and moved to locations where farming was still possible. Kachinas remain an important part of Hopi culture and religion today, supplying inspiration for replicas that are carved from cottonwood and sold to collectors worldwide.

Arrival of the Athapaskans

The Navajos and Apaches are speakers of an Athapaskan language, a branch of the larger Nadene family of languages that moved into the region after 1500 CE. They descend from people who drifted southward from Canada, probably along the eastern edge of the Rocky Mountains.

The Navajos and Apaches were not responsible for the contraction and dislocation of Ancestral Pueblo

Figure 6.33 Traditional Navajo house (hogan).

communities, but rather moved into areas already largely abandoned by farmers. Their hunter-gatherer adaptation was better suited to the conditions that emerged after the thirteenth century in the Southwest. They spread easily into the parts of the Southwest landscape that had never been farming areas or that had been left vacant by the Puebloan farming communities. Navajo and Apache communities remain scattered across the region today.

Later Navajo culture illustrates the speed and ease with which pervasive culture change can occur (Figure 6.33). The Navajos acquired weaving and pottery making from Ancestral Pueblo teachers. They were in close contact with them before, during, and after the Pueblo revolt of 1680, when many Pueblo people took refuge with them. Cotton weaving was a men's craft among the Puebloans, but weaving became a women's craft among the Navajos. At the same time, the Navajos had acquired sheep and herding practices from the Spanish, and this made wool rather than cotton or wild fibers a favored material for weaving. The Navajos also learned to cast silver from the Spanish, and they combined this with the ancient mining of turquoise in the region to produce the jewelry for which they remain very well known. All of these adaptive changes combined with ancient philosophy and kinship practices to form the unique Navajo culture that is familiar to many people today. Meanwhile Navajo and Apache archaeologists work on their vast lands to preserve and interpret the sites they have inherited.

No other archaeological region of the United States features more sites open to public visitation, more vibrant descendant communities, or a more pervasive native influence on modern American culture. The shared archaeological heritage of the Greater Southwest is an extraordinary treasure to this region,

and like Mesoamerica it is a model to what might be possible in other regions of the continent.

Summary

1. The southwestern region of the United States and the northwestern region of Mexico can be conveniently called the "Greater Southwest."

2. Farming was probably initially carried to the region by Uto-Aztecan speakers expanding northward out of Mexico.

3. Farming spread to speakers of several other language families already resident in the Greater Southwest and three major archaeological traditions developed over time, termed the Hohokam, Mogollon, and Ancestral Pueblo traditions.

4. The cultural phenomenon centered at Chaco Canyon featured construction of many huge great houses as well as a network of roads connecting the canyon to distant outlier sites.

5. Turquoise trade to Mexico from the Greater Southwest brought copper artifacts, exotic birds, and other influences from Mesoamerica in exchange.

6. Cooler and wetter climate prevailed after 1000 BCE, making farming an attractive adaptation, but the return of warmer drier conditions after 1150 CE forced a shrinkage of human populations, warfare, and widespread settlement relocations.

7. At Mesa Verde and some other places, people responded to increased warfare by moving to defensible cliff dwellings.

8. Minor archaeological traditions called Sinagua, Patayan, and Fremont developed at the ecological margins of the region but did not survive climatic stresses after 1150 CE.

9. Salado developed as a widespread culture when drought displaced many refugees and adaptations had to change to accommodate both immigrants and changing farming conditions.

10. The ancestors of the Navajo and Apache nations moved into vacated areas after 1500 CE, where their hunting and gathering adaptations were better suited to the new prevailing conditions.

11. Modern descendants of the Ancestral Pueblo tradition currently reside mainly in northern New Mexico and Arizona.

12. Modern descendants of the Hohokam and Patayan traditions currently live in small portions of their former ranges in southern Arizona, northern Mexico, and the Colorado River valley.

Further Reading

There are many good books covering the archaeology of the Greater Southwest. Linda Cordell's *Archaeology of the Southwest* remains an excellent starting point. Stephen Plog's *Ancient Peoples of the American Southwest* is more compact and just as current. Lynne Sebastian's *The Chaco Anasazi* is a fine introduction to the Chaco phenomenon. So, too, is Noble's more recent *In Search of Chaco*. Lekson has edited *Archaeology of Chaco Canyon*, a more technical contribution, whereas Patricia Crown and James Judge have edited a comparative volume titled *Chaco & Hohokam*. Kantner's *Ancient Puebloan Southwest* is a recent general synthesis. Volumes 9 and 10 of the Smithsonian's *Handbook of North American Indians* cover the region in encyclopedic detail. There are numerous other guidebooks, syntheses, edited volumes, and books covering the crafts and histories of the living descendants of the region, virtually all of them worth consulting. Interested readers should consult the "References" section at the back of this book.

Glossary

chalchihuitl: Nahuatl word for "jewel."

dendrochronology: A technique that uses tree rings to date samples of wood found in archaeological sites. Tree-ring dating.

jacal: Wall construction featuring a stick frame with mud plaster.

kiva: A subterranean or semisubterranean room used for ceremonial purposes in the Greater Southwest.

matrilocal: Postmarital residence in which men move in with their wives' families.

sipapu: A symbolic hole found in the floor of an Ancestral Pueblo kiva.

temper: Typically sand, crushed shell, or grit added to clay to make pottery shaping and firing easier to control.

Mesoamerican Civilization

Pluralitas non est ponenda sine necessitate (Keep it simple).

William of Occam (c. 1285–1349)

Introduction

Mesoamerica is a culture area lying between the northern Mexican desert and Central America (Figure 7.1). Tribal agricultural communities that lived on tropical domesticates evolved into chiefdoms and states in this region. Olmec culture appeared early along the Gulf Coast and became a major part of the foundation of later Mesoamerican civilizations. Teotihuacán was the centerpiece of later Classic culture in the central highlands of Mexico. Monte Albán was the corresponding center in the Valley of Oaxaca. The Classic civilizations of highland Mexico were contemporaneous with the rise of Classic lowland Maya **city-states** in the Peten region and on the Yucatan Peninsula. All of them flourished but then disintegrated politically and in some cases ecologically and demographically during the course of the first millennium CE. The Mesoamerican ball game is one of the common features of Classic Mesoamerican civilization.

Mesoamerican Geography

Mesoamerica is a cultural unit more than it is a physical one. It includes everything south of the deserts of northern Mexico (from roughly the Tropic of Cancer) to western Honduras and El Salvador, a region about 900,000 km² (347,000 mi²) in size. The main division of Mesoamerica is the Isthmus of Tehuantepec. Generally speaking the archaeology west of the isthmus is culturally Mexican and that to the east of it is culturally Maya, although there are many exceptions and qualifications that will become apparent to anyone who follows references more deeply into cited publications.

Central Mexico consists of a V-shaped arrangement of two mountain ranges with a high plateau between them and flanked on both sides by coastal lowlands. The highland plateau is known as the Meseta Central, and it is bounded on the east by the Sierra Madre Oriental and on the west by the Sierra Madre Occidental. The deserts, known as the "Gran Chichimeca" after the **Chichimecs** (barbarians) who lived there, lie open to the north. At the southern end of the great V lies the natural Basin of Mexico, much of which is now covered by the vast and sprawling Mexico City.

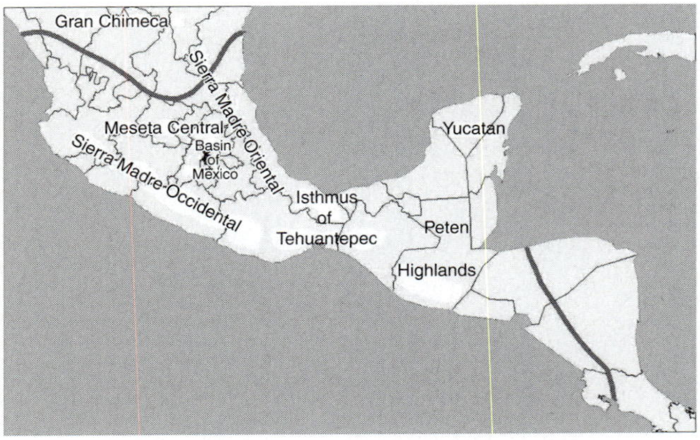

Figure 7.1 Geography of Mesoamerica.

Many of the mountains of Mesoamerica were once, and in some cases still are, active volcanoes. Examples are Popocatepetl and nearby Ixtaccihuatl, which stand just east of the Basin of Mexico. Orizaba lies dormant farther to the east while to the west the upstart Parícutin volcano burst up in a farmer's field within living memory. The earth's crust is dynamic here and earthquakes shake the region from time to time.

Climate is controlled by altitude in Mesoamerica. In the highlands summer temperatures are pleasant in the thin air and plants thrive under nearly daily thundershowers. Winters are cool and dry. Coastal lowlands are wetter, the air is heavy, and summers are very hot.

When the Spanish arrived in 1519 the Basin of Mexico was dominated by Aztecs (Mexica) and other Nahuatl-speaking peoples. West of them lived the Tarascans. Southeast of them in Oaxaca were the Zapotecs and Mixtecs. Huastecs, Totonacs, Otomis, and many others lived in large provinces along the coasts and in pockets in the highlands (Figure 7.2).

East of the Isthmus of Tehuantepec lie the highlands of Guatemala, the lowland Peten and Yucatan Peninsula to the north. These regions were mainly the domain of Maya-speaking peoples, but covering this array of related cultures with a single term should not be taken to mean that they were a homogeneous lot. A rich diversity of Maya and other groups built major centers here, in the Guatemalan highlands, and eastward to western Honduras and El Salvador.

The Guatemalan highlands are similar to those of Mexico, except that being more tropical they are not snow-covered. Forested volcanic mountains provided fertile soils for Maya farmers on a landscape that still trembles periodically. The Peten lowlands were home to most of the largest Maya ceremonial centers, which flourished until around 900 CE. Much of the region is still covered by dense tropical forest that is both hot and wet for much of the year.

The Yucatan Peninsula is a low shelf of limestone. It is wet near the Peten but drier to the north, and over much of the region **karst** features—sinkholes and caves—rather than rivers drain the landscape.

The Consequences of Plant Domestication

The domestication of plants in Mesoamerica provided the economic foundation for the development of the first complex societies in North America. As described in Chapter 4, people in highland Mexico domesticated squash, pumpkins, maize, beans, avocados, chili peppers, chocolate, cotton, amaranth, gourds, and sapotes. In several cases they domesticated two or more species of these domesticates. Several bean species were particularly important for the protein they contributed to the diet. When supplemented by dogs bred for their meat and wild deer they eventually allowed dense Mexican populations to thrive with minor amounts of protein from meat.

Although the archaeological evidence for early domestication comes primarily from the highlands (see Chapter 4), the earliest complex societies developed in the hot, wet coastal lowlands. There domesticates brought down from the highlands flourished in the rich, humid soils of cleared tropical forest, yielding two crops a year. Farmers discovered through trial and error that they could open up fields by girdling trees, cutting brush, and burning off the dead growth. Soaked by heavy rainfall and deprived of steady input of nutrients from natural forest cover, the cleared fields declined in fertility in a half dozen years, forcing farmers to constantly open new fields and allow exhausted land to recover over long fallow periods. This rotating system of cultivation is called "slash-and-burn" or **swidden** agriculture. Despite its limitations, particularly the need to have about seven times as much land lying fallow as under cultivation, lowland swidden agriculture allowed a more dense sedentary human population than had been previously possible anywhere in North America. The reliability of long-fallow cultivation made it an attractive way to make a living.

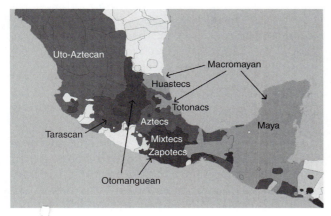

Figure 7.2 Mesoamerican language families and some major cultures in the sixteenth century.

More settled living brought with it the development of ground stone tools, weaving, and eventually pottery. The earliest pottery is not indisputably attested on sites dating much before 2000 BCE (Voorhies 1996), but sophisticated ceramics were being produced by 1600 BCE (Joyce and Henderson 2001).

Greater population density brings individuals into daily contact with ever larger numbers of other individuals. The number of one-on-one interactions soared above the 500 that most individuals are comfortable maintaining. Systems of kinship provide a framework for the multiplying interactions up to a point, but only to a point. Kinship-based systems tend to be segmentary, so when numbers get too large for a community of people to manage using kin terms alone the common solution is for the community to split, a portion hiving off and moving to a new location or the whole community breaking up into two or more relocating communities. This is the pattern of tribal societies. But investment in cleared land makes moving a less attractive option, and the general filling up of the best agricultural lands reduces the options for relocation. A relocating community cannot move easily if most or all desirable destinations are already claimed by others.

Thus population growth, settled life, and the requirements of agriculture impose constraints on burgeoning communities. Once an agricultural landscape begins to fill up its communities become circumscribed, constrained by the ecological limits of their adaptation but also hemmed in by others of like kind (Carneiro 1960). Communities that pride themselves on consensus and egalitarian principles eventually find themselves forced to accept stronger leadership and social inequalities. It is a process that has played out over and over again around the world. Tribal communities tend to become politically unstable when their populations rise above 1,000 and approach 2,000, so they must either split or innovate politically. If circumscription makes splitting impossible, then new complex polities necessarily develop.

Sooner or later material success brings increased population density and this in turn requires more social and political complexity. At first it might involve only informal representation through the leaders of residential kin groups, but eventually some kin groups acquire more members, more land, more power, or more prestige than others. Sooner or later kin group leaders come to enjoy greater wealth and status than others in their groups, maintaining their positions by providing services to the group that they would otherwise not have. Those services might be protection, management of the storage and redistribution of seasonally abundant resources, or management of religion and ideology, although an examination of historical cases indicates that some of these services were more apparent than real. The ulterior motives of elites are always self-aggrandizement, whether or not the broader populace perceives some wider benefits (Hayden and Gargett 1990). An important threshold is crossed when leaders become strong enough to ensure that their heirs inherit their positions of leadership rather than achieving it on their own.

Competition between neighboring peer polities is also a natural consequence of this process (Renfrew and Cherry 1986). Athletic and other kinds of competition have been part of human culture for thousands of years, and people have found endless ways to compete individually and as groups even as those groups have multiplied and grown. The polities that emerged on Mexico's coastal lowlands were chiefdoms, societies having permanent ritual and ceremonial centers that operated on the principle of social ranking. Chiefdoms typically have male chieftains at the highest rank, with members of their kin groups enjoying similarly high rank afforded by their close connection to the chieftain. Other kin groups and individuals within them typically hold lower ranks relative to their distance from the chiefly kin group. This was almost certainly the situation along the Gulf Coast of Mexico 1250 BCE when Olmec chiefdoms first emerged.

It makes no sense to argue that environment and technology produced Olmec civilization. Nor does it make sense to argue that Olmec civilization arose because the Olmecs wanted it to. The environment set limits and presented possibilities, without which Olmec civilization would have been impossible. But the drivers inherent in human society were also needed. There is in human societies no shortage of the drive that produces inequalities, only a shortage of opportunity. Here again we see the interplay of environment and culture that produces the things that archaeologists find remarkable.

Mesoamerican Chronology

Organizing archaeological time before the advent of radiocarbon dating depended in part upon stylistic clues from pottery and architecture to assign finds to one or another of three broad periods that followed the earlier Paleoindian and Archaic periods (Table 7.1). More important was the Maya calendar and early historical accounts. The Classic was conceived as the great 300–900 CE period in which

Box 7.1 HOW TO VISIT SITES IN MESOAMERICA

Mexico, Guatemala, Honduras, and El Salvador are strewn with large and impressive archaeological sites. There are many guidebooks, most of them useful. Some comprehensive guidebooks are loaded with information but might be too big to carry along. Some are also lacking good maps. The National Geographic Society has published several good maps. The latest of these is the *Mesoamerica Historical Reference Map*, which is sometimes out of print but which can be had on its CD compilation of maps. So too are other relevant NGS maps: *A Traveler's Map of Mexico, Archaeological Map of Middle America, Land of the Maya,* and *Visitor's Guide to the Aztec World.* The maps show most of the sites mentioned here that are open to the public, but they do not provide details about roads, and the scales are too small to help one drive to sites easily. For that the archaeotourist will require larger or more detailed maps. A good map of Mexico is available from the American Automobile Association. It is keyed to the very useful AAA Mexico TourBook, although some sites mentioned in the TourBook are missing from the map and some on the map are not mentioned in the TourBook. Archaeology is scattered among other points of interest in the TourBook, so the reader must dig for it.

The Mexican governmental Instituto Nacional de Antropología e Historia (INAH) publishes many fine guidebooks and other works. There are also, of course, many people eager to guide tourists. Guided tours often allow too little time for serious visitors to explore sites, and there is usually an obligatory detour to a souvenir shop with which the guide has a business arrangement. The adventurous can rent their own cars to drive to sites and thus avoid tourist traps and have the desired time to explore. A compromise alternative is to hire a car and a driver with price negotiated in advance and with the understanding that one is not interested in unexpected detours to souvenir shops and restaurants.

The National Museum of Anthropology in Mexico City is one of the finest of its type in the world. But the archaeology of Mexico is rich, so both states and local communities have established many regional and site-based museums as well. These are often worth visiting because the national museum cannot possibly display more than a tiny fraction of the innumerable objects that have been recovered from Mesoamerican sites. The regional museum at Jalapa is excellent, as are many others. There are over 100 museums in Mexico alone, many of them small local institutions at important sites or in major cities. The museum at Monte Albán is excellent, as one would expect, but the museum at the smaller site of San José Mogote is also worth a visit. Such local museums are often the pride of their communities and retain some of the finest artifacts. In some cases, such as at Cacaxtla, local interest began as looting but with guidance from INAH has led to the preservation and exhibit of truly spectacular things.

Mexican sites are guarded and souvenir collecting is forbidden. Petty looters and local entrepreneurs often approach tourists to offer artifacts or fakes for sale. Purchasing even a small artifact and removing it from its country of origin is illegal under both national laws and international treaties. Buying a fake, on the other hand, is harmless so long as the buyer pays what it is truly worth. INAH offers many excellent reproductions for sale.

Table 7.1 Basic mesoamerican chronology.

Period	Dates
Postclassic	900–1520 CE
Classic	300–900 CE
Preclassic (Formative)	2000 BCE–300 CE

Maya city-states, calendrics, and writing flourished in the Peten lowlands, while the impressive city-states of Teotihuacán and Monte Albán dominated the Mexican highlands. Leading up to the Classic was the Preclassic or Formative, a long 2000 BCE–300 CE period during which chiefdoms and eventually city-states developed out of earlier tribal societies. The Postclassic was the 900–1520 CE period that followed the collapse of the Classic cultures and saw the rise of warring empires, such as the Aztec Empire in the Mexican highlands and the petty city-states of the Yucatan Peninsula (López Austin and López Luján 2001; Stuart and Stuart 1993; Weaver 1981). We now know that warring was important in the Classic period as well.

The Preclassic, Classic, Postclassic sequence was a convenient way to classify archaeological cultures in a general way, and it remains a popular shorthand reference for many archaeologists today. However, by the 1950s radiocarbon dating had solved the problem of which of several possible correlations between the Maya calendar and the modern calendar was correct. It had also shown that cultural developments across Mesoamerica had not occurred in lock step, that some polities were earlier than others that were outwardly similar to them, and that political collapse was not simultaneous everywhere in the region. Refinements in radiocarbon dating have led to debates about where things fit in the traditional chronology that seem increasing beside the point. Consequently the traditional period names are used here only as convenient first approximations, not as a rigid framework.

Box 7.2 HOW TO USE MESOAMERICAN CHRONOLOGIES

Archaeological chronologies tend to have the same basic features. The problems with them are particularly apparent in Mesoamerica. Before the advent of radiocarbon and other independent dating techniques archaeologists depended upon stratigraphy and cross dating to build chronologies. The table, which shows some of the phases from two sites in the Basin of Mexico arranged in the traditional stratigraphic way with time's arrow pointing up, illustrates this. We now know that the sequence shown here began about 300 BCE and ended in 1521 CE, but the chronology could have been built without reference to calendar dates.

Mesoamerican archaeologists began by assigning finds to three broad periods, Preclassic (or Formative), Classic, and Postclassic. As their excavations yielded more detailed information they subdivided these periods and began constructing still shorter "phases" to manage chronology. Cross dating was possible when trade pieces allowed them to conclude that late Tzacualli was contemporary with Apetlac, Tenochtitlán with Chimalpa, and so on. We now have thousands of radiocarbon dates that make this procedure unnecessary, sometimes even counterproductive, but archaeologists continue to refer to traditional chronological categories as a matter of convenience.

The problem is that the practice reverses what is now a more logical procedure. The traditional procedure risks missing something important, like the fact that Mazapan ceramics come and go earlier at Teotihuacán than at Tenochtitlán. Forcing evidence into rigid boxes with invariably straight horizontal and vertical lines can also sometimes misrepresent reality. But by keeping these hazards in mind one can make use of the chronological frameworks created by archaeologists.

Period	Tenochtitlán Phases	Teotihuacán Phases
Late Postclassic	Tlatelolco Tenochtitlán	Teacalco Chimalpa
Middle Postclassic	Culhuacan/Tenayuca	Zocango Atlatango
Early Postclassic	Mazapan	Mazapan
Epiclassic	Coyotlatelco	Xometla Oxtotipac
Classic	Metepec Xolalpan Tlamimilolpa Miccaotli	Metepec Late Xolalpan Early Xolalpan Late Tlamimilolpa Early Tlamimilolpa Miccaotli
Terminal Preclassic	Tzacualli Cuicuilco V Cuicuilco IV	Apetlac Teopan Oxtotla Patlachique Tezoyuca

Figure 7.3 Colossal Olmec basalt head, Monument 3 from the San Lorenzo site.

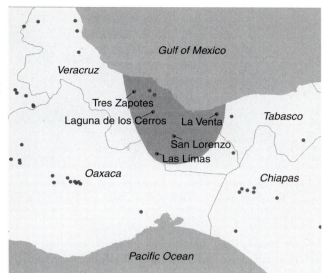

Figure 7.4 Olmec territory and key sites.

The Olmecs

Olmec culture crept into the popular literature in the 1940s, after being first discovered two decades earlier in the steamy lowlands of the Mexican Vera Cruz Coast. Matthew Stirling and other archaeologists pulled colossal helmeted heads from the swampy soil (Figure 7.3) and set them up again amidst eroded earthen mounds, mosaic pavements, and monolithic altars. Early radiocarbon dating confirmed that the remains were earlier than most known for the more complex societies of Mesoamerica, possibly as old as 1500 BCE. Stirling gave them the name "Olmec," meaning "Rubber People" in Nahuatl, the language of the much later Aztecs. We do not know what these Preclassic people called themselves.

The Olmec homeland lies on the Gulf Coast side of the Isthmus of Tehuantepec. The Tuxtla Mountains, the source of the basalt that Olmec carvers used for their colossal heads and other monuments, lie just east of Tres Zapotes in Figure 7.4.

Other similar examples of early village life have been found in other parts of Mesoamerica as well. For example, villages were established and sophisticated pottery was being manufactured in northern Honduras by 1600 BCE, and by a few centuries later there were networks of trade and exchange linking this to other similar cultures in the region (Joyce and Henderson 2001). It is easy to understand why archaeologists working outside the Olmec area have challenged the notion that the Olmecs were the mother culture of all that came later (Arnold 2003). However, recent trace element analysis of early pottery from all around Mesoamerica shows that it was manufactured in and distributed from the site of San Lorenzo in the Olmec heartland on the Gulf Coast (Blomster et al. 2005).

Furthermore, Olmec stone sculpture is abundant at San Lorenzo, La Venta, Tres Zapotes, and other heartland sites, but rarer elsewhere in Mesoamerica. All of this shows that the Olmecs truly were the primary source of Mesoamerica's first unified style and iconographic system, but unanswered questions still remain (Diehl 2005). There is no evidence of military conquest or religious proselytization, so how did Olmec influence spread? Was it a purely commercial process or trade and exchange of luxury goods between competing elites? For now the evidence favors the latter hypothesis, as it does in the Eastern Woodlands, where similar trafficking was going on at the same time.

The monumental sites of the Olmecs were ritual and ceremonial centers of chiefdoms that emerged spontaneously from a human population boom fueled by the productive cultivation of highland domesticates in a natural hothouse. Olmec country gets up to 3 m (120 in) of rain per year. Domestic plants that would not have survived a single season on their own produced abundant crops when tended by Olmec farmers.

Olmec Polities

The bulk of the Olmec population lived in individual farmsteads, simple but serviceable thatched houses and associated structures (Figure 7.5). Olmec chieftains recruited labor from the lower ranks to build ritual centers, provided in exchange for elaborate placation and manipulation of purported supernatural forces. The lower-ranking farmers that actually produced the agricultural surpluses needed to sustain the

Figure 7.5 Ordinary Olmec dwellings were probably much like these mid-twentieth-century thatched houses.

higher ranks, their lifestyles, and their building projects got the assurance of a certain future, continuity, and the occasional festival out of the bargain. It is remarkable that this worldwide pattern, which is with us still, emerged in North America in pretty much the same form as elsewhere in the world. If the North American case attests that agriculture and settled life were inevitable parts of human destiny after the close of the Pleistocene, then so too were complex polities, organized religions, and the tendency for individuals to manipulate it all for their own political and economic purposes.

Olmec polities, like all chiefdoms, lacked the diagnostic features of state organizations, which would not emerge in North America until later. Some specialists argue that the Olmec centers were already city-states, but the burden of proof is on any such hypothesis (Yoffee 2005:41). While further research may yet find convincing evidence that the Olmecs had city-states, their existence remains debatable for the time being. Chiefdoms tend to be less stable than states because they lack bureaucracies, standing armies, and distinct territorial boundaries; and although they have centralized power, they often lack clear principles of succession and can fall apart politically when leaders die. Despite these shortcomings, Olmec chiefdoms fared well for over seven centuries. Olmec chieftains developed relationships with other leaders around Mesoamerica and promoted trade in luxury goods, which they used as symbols of their rank in both life and death. Personal ornaments, figurines, and ritual paraphernalia made of Guatemalan jade moved through the trade network, as did fine ceramics. Metallurgy had begun in Peru by this time, and copper was being mined and beaten into tools and ornaments around the North American Great Lakes, but it would not appear in Mesoamerica until after 650 CE (West 1994).

Olmec Centers

San Lorenzo. San Lorenzo was the first of three great Olmec centers, and it documents the Early Olmec period that spans roughly 1500–900 BCE. Early Olmecs leveled a patch of elevated land and built a building called the "Red Palace" at the site of San Lorenzo. They also carved and set up many large basalt monuments, 10 of them being the colossal stone heads for which the Olmecs are famous. The nearest source for the basalt is 60 km (38 mi) away to the northwest, across the wet lowlands, and getting the large blocks to the site was no small task. San Lorenzo's decline about 900 BCE occurred just as the Olmec center La Venta was rising (Diehl 2004).

La Venta. La Venta rose to prominence as San Lorenzo declined and it covers the Late Olmec period from around 900 to 400 BCE. Frans Blom and Oliver La Farge investigated La Venta way back in 1926, and it continues to fascinate archaeologists today. The site was built atop a salt dome, a relatively dry sandy rise in what is otherwise low, swampy terrain. The dominant feature is Mound C-1 in Complex C, an irregular earthen mound that lacks the flat slopes of later pyramids. A series of stone monuments stand atop the platform on the south side of Mound C-1 (Bernal 1969).

The central complexes lie on an axis that deviates 8° west of true north. Complex A to the north has both massive offerings and three large serpentine mosaics laid out as gigantic geometric masks (Figure 7.6). The

Figure 7.6 Olmec stylized jaguar mask serpentine mosaic at La Venta.

axis of the site points south toward the nearest high mountain while the offerings on the north might represent the sea, which lies a few kilometers in that direction (Tate 1999).

Olmec culture contained the roots of many features of later Mesoamerican cultures. Main players in the multitude of later Mesoamerican deities were already present on Olmec culture, as demonstrated by the Las Limas Monument I, found in 1965 (Figures 7.7 and 7.8). The seated human figure has a were-jaguar baby in its lap and is decorated with the symbols for four gods, each a representation of gods known for later Mesoamerican cultures. Peter Joralemon later expanded the list of primary deities in Olmec iconography to eight (Coe 1968; Diehl 2004:101–102).

Writing systems that emerged in Maya and Zapotec cultures after 300 BCE were inspired in part by earlier Olmec writing (Houston 2006; Marcus 1992). A ceramic cylinder seal dating to about 650 BCE was recovered at San Andres, La Venta, Tabasco (Figure 7.9). The bird image on the seal is clearly connected to two glyphs by means of speech scrolls, which indicate that the glyphs were intended to represent words or phrases. The excavators specifically interpret the glyphs as representing the date 3 Ajaw in the 260-day Mesoamerican calendar. Thus the seal indicates the presence of not just writing but also of the 260-day calendar as early as 650 BCE (Pohl et al. 2002). An important feature of the San Andres glyphs is that they do not look like the concepts they are intended to reference. They are not simple picture writing, but rather abstract symbols. While they might have derived from some earlier and more literal pictures, they were by this time abstract glyphs. The difference is a hallmark of the transition from pictures to true writing.

Tres Zapotes. Tres Zapotes, the third great Olmec center, documents the last phase of the Olmec sequence, 400 BCE–400 CE, which archaeologists often refer to as the Epi-Olmec (Diehl 2004:8). The Olmecs, or at least their Epi-Olmec descendants, were already using the calendrical system that the Maya would later elaborate upon. **Stela** C at the site of Tres

Figure 7.8 The Las Limas figure, a seated Olmec adult holding a were-jaguar child and inscribed with glyphs of ancient Mesoamerican deities. *Source:* Courtesy of Michael D. Coe.

Figure 7.7 Olmec throne with seated figure at La Venta.

Figure 7.9 Olmec ceramic cylinder seal from San Andres.
Source: From Pohl et al. 2002:1985.

Zapotes, found in 1939, showed a date in the Long Count system that the Maya would later make familiar. The vigesimal (base 20) Mesoamerican system used simple dots (ones) and bars (fives) as numerals. This meant that the standard multiples went 1–20–400, rather than 1–10–100 as they do in a decimal system. The Long Count was simply a count of days beginning at a mythological starting point in the distant past using the vigesimal system. The Olmecs and later Mayas made one adjustment to the basic count. To bring the third place of the Long Count into rough correspondence with the solar calendar, they stipulated that it had 360 days rather than the 400 normally expected in vigesimal arithmetic. They did this by making a Tun equal to 18 Uinal rather than 20. The units all had names, reading from the bottom up as shown in Table 7.2.

Stela C (Figure 7.10) showed a sequence reading from the bottom up—18, 16, 6, 16—indicating that the count was for a date 18 Kin, 16 Uinal, 6 Tun, 16 Katun. The monument was broken so the crucial Baktun numeral was missing. Marion Stirling guessed that it was 7, which would produce a count of 1,125,698 days from the mythological starting point of the Long Count. Next she had to choose between alternative correlations with the Gregorian calendar that were available at the time. She chose one that gave her a date of September 3, 32 BCE. If she was right this would make

Table 7.2 Simplified long count and the Stela C date.

Long Count Structure					Stela C Inscription		
20 Katun	=	1 Bactun	=	144,000 days	[7 Bactun]	=	[1,008,000 days]
20 Tun	=	1 Katun	=	7,200 days	16 Katun	=	115,200 days
18 Uinal	=	1 Tun	=	360 days	6 Tun	=	2,160
20 Kin	=	1 Uinal	=	20 days	16 Uinal	=	320 days
		1 Kin	=	1 day	18 Kin	=	18 days

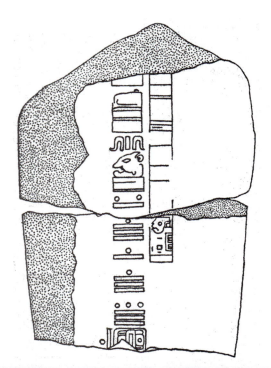

Figure 7.10 Stela C, Tres Zapotes, missing the upper portion found later, as shown in the sketch above.

Stela C the oldest date inscription in Mesoamerica known at the time.

Stirling turned out to be correct both times. The correlation she preferred was later validated by radiocarbon dating, setting the starting date to August 12, 3113 BCE in our calendar. The missing upper portion of Stela C was found 30 years after the initial discovery of the lower portion and it confirmed Stirling's guess that the Baktun numeral was seven. A slightly older inscription from the Chiapa de Corzo site has trumped Stela C, and we now know that Olmec culture was already waning long before 32 BCE. Nevertheless, this monument and the other seven monuments with the earliest Long Count dates all were found outside the Maya homeland, which makes the later Maya the inheritors of, not the inventors of, the Long Count (Diehl 2004:185–186; Justeson and Kaufman 1997).

Chalcatzingo. The Olmec system of trade and exchange linked the Olmec heartland to sources of luxury goods all over Mesoamerica, a network that laid the foundation for later complex societies. Chalcatzingo (Figure 7.11) was an Olmec outpost in the Mexican highlands, a center set at the crossroads of major trade routes (Grove 1984).

It is clear that the Olmec lords sought jade, obsidian, and other materials that we find buried with them, and we can infer that they imported pelts, feathers, and other goods that have not survived. In return they exported finished goods, with the effect that much of Olmec art is not found in the Olmec heartland but instead scattered across much of Mesoamerica (Figure 7.12). Potters at destination sites later often attempted to replicate the imports, but there is little doubt about Olmec primacy (Blomster et al. 2005). Some archaeologists even consider the Soconusco site of Cantón Carralito to have been an Olmec colony (Cheetham 2006).

Figure 7.11 The site of Chalcatzingo.

Figure 7.12 Olmec seated figure at Chalcatzingo.

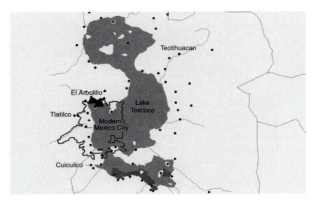

Figure 7.13 The Basin of Mexico, showing Lake Texcoco, the outline of modern Mexico City, and sites mentioned in the text.

Highland Mexico

The highland Basin of Mexico, in which modern Mexico City is located, was a region of considerable potential (see Figure 7.1). The floor of this elevated plain is just under 2,240 m (7,350 ft) high, surrounded by much higher mountains on three sides but open northward toward the desert. Before the colonial Spanish dug a canal to drain it, the centerpiece of the closed basin was a huge, brackish lake, sometimes conceptually subdivided into separately named lakes but just as often referred to in the aggregate as Lake Texcoco. The shallow lake was almost 70 km (43 mi) across from south to north. The southern part of the basin receives twice as much seasonal rainfall, so the southern end of the lake was fed by many streams and springs, which made it less brackish there than to the north. Later Aztec engineers eventually built a 13-km (8-mi) dike across the lake's waist to raise the level and freshen the water in the south and west portions of the lake (Sanders 2004).

Even without later refinements in agricultural technology the southern margin of the lake was a good place for maize farming 1600 BCE. While irrigation would be necessary in the drier northern part of the basin, the southern part was suited to productive dry farming. Lower temperature and moisture restricted farming to land near the lake, and even today farming is unproductive on upper slopes, where it is too cold, or in low-lying areas where the settling frost shortens the growing season. But here, within limits set by the environment, was an opportunity for early Mesoamerican farmers. Communities in the Basin of Mexico began producing pottery and exhibiting traces of Olmec influence during the 1350–900 BCE period. The Olmec traits disappeared during the succeeding three centuries (900–600 BCE), but the population of the valley continued to rise to around 20,000 as a distinctly highland Mexican culture developed there.

By around 100 CE there were several chiefdoms or small city-states around the Basin of Mexico, of which Teotihuacán in the northeast was one of the largest, with a population around 17,000 (Figure 7.13). The larger centers had public architecture, often terraced pyramids that supported ritual areas or temple structures.

Cuicuilco

Cuicuilco, on the southwest side of Lake Texcoco, appeared then to have the brightest future. Here the local polity built what would grow to be a large pyramid with an unusual circular footprint. Most others were square or rectangular in plan even at this early date. The earliest stages of construction in this pyramid were built of adobe. Later stages were made of rubble faced with rounded river cobbles and boulders. The stones were not dressed, so the slopes they faced had to be gradual; steeper ones would have resulted in disastrous slides.

The pyramid at Cuicuilco (Figure 7.14) grew to a diameter of 118 m (387 ft) and a height of 23 m (75 ft), after two expansion episodes that left earlier stages buried deep within. There was a large altar at the top, the last one perched atop buried earlier ones and probably once protected by a temple of wood or wattle-and-daub. By 150 BCE there were probably around 10,000 people living in the surrounding community, one-ninth of the entire population of the Basin of Mexico at the time.

Both the overall population of the region and the local one at Cuicuilco doubled again over the following century, but then disaster struck the burgeoning city-state. The nearby volcano known today as Xitli erupted, wrecking much of the community and the polity's infrastructure. Cuicuilco was already falling into ruin when Xitli erupted a second time. This time lava flowed across the city, enveloping the lower portion of the great pyramid and covering everything else. Archaeologists later chiseled through the thick lava to free the pyramid and expose the preeruption surface.

The Xitli disaster finished Cuicuilco and forced a shift in the political center of gravity in the Basin of Mexico. Teotihuacán, which had been secondary to Cuicuilco up to this point, became the center of new growth in the years leading up to 300 CE. From that beginning it grew to become the sixth largest city in the world in only three centuries.

Teotihuacán

The rise of Teotihuacán was at once unpredictable and inevitable. The communities of the Basin of Mexico in the first century BCE were like a class of kindergartners, all young and vigorous but giving no clue as to which of them was most likely to become the richest person in town. The exponential growth of Teotihuacán might not have been predicted before it happened, but surely it was inevitable that some center would grow to dominate all the others scattered around the Mexican highlands.

Teotihuacán is a Nahuatl (Aztec) name meaning "Place Where Men Become Gods" (Pérez de Lara 2005). Like everything else in this great city it was named by later people. The Pyramids of the Sun (Tonatiuh) and Moon (Metztli) almost certainly had nothing to do with those celestial bodies (Figure 7.15). The Temple of Quetzalcoatl carries its Nahuatl name because the feathered serpent dominates its façades, but we do not know what it was called by the Teotihuacános. We do know that like Quetzalcoatl, the Mesoamerican gods Tlaloc and Huehueteotl were part of the Teotihuacán pantheon.

It is still not certain which of the surviving languages of highland Mexico these people might have spoken, although the spread of cognate words for cacao and chocolate in Nahuatl and other Nahua languages around this time make this branch of Uto-Aztecan a major contender (Dakin and Wichmann 2000). Nahua words even turn up in Maya inscriptions, an indication of the cultural reach of the people of highland Mexico, and further indication that the Teotihuacános spoke a Nahua language (Macri and Looper 2003). Despite lingering uncertainties, Teotihuacán is one of the most studied ancient cities in the world, and we know much about its anonymous inhabitants.

The Pyramid of the Sun and the Temple of Quetzalcoatl were hastily excavated and stabilized in preparation for Mexico's 1910 centennial. Detailed surveys of the city and its surrounding suburbs were carried out by several teams beginning in 1960 and much of the impressive reconstruction of buildings took place at the same time (Blanton et al. 1993; Evans and Sanders 2000; Millon 1973; Parsons 1971; Parsons et al. 1982; Sanders 1986, 1987, 1994, 1995, 1996a, 1996b; Sanders and Evans 2000, 2001; Sanders et al. 1970). In

Figure 7.14 Cuicuilco pyramid, showing the original ground surface, lava layer, and modern surface.

Figure 7.15 Pyramid of the Sun and the Avenue of the Dead as seen from the Pyramid of the Moon. The Temple of Quetzalcoatl is in the distance to the right of the Pyramid of the Sun.

addition there are dozens of books that summarize what is known about Teotihuacán.

Supplying Teotihuacán. The vast lakes of the Basin of Mexico provided the opportunity for people living around them to construct productive raised beds, or **chinampas** (Figure 7.16), from swampy muck, construction that also produced channels between the beds (Armillas 1971). These in turn facilitated canoe traffic and the east transport of food produced on the chinampas. The builders of Teotihuacán could take advantage of none of this, for they were too far from the lake, and the little stream that flowed through their settlement was not sufficient for canoe traffic. As the city grew it had to be provisioned by human porters carrying food from outlying farms. Irrigation was possible on the western outskirts of the growing city, and it was practiced there until residences built by Zapotec immigrants from Oaxaca overspread the fields in 200–300 CE. This did not happen by accident, and it underscores the power of the city-state to plan and control urban growth (Nichols 1991).

Much has also been made of the disadvantages imposed by the lack of draft animals and the need to supply cities like Teotihuacán using human transport alone. Ancient Mexicans invented wheels for pull toys,

Figure 7.16 Modern chinampas in the Basin of Mexico.

but there was no good reason to scale them up for practical application. They might have used the idea to build wheelbarrows, but even these require smooth trails, and such improvements were not worth the investment. Human porters were versatile and nimble even on rough ground.

It rains here briefly nearly every day from May to October, a boon to dry farming. Irrigation was more important in the northern Basin of Mexico than in the south because rainfall was lighter there. Chinampas could be built and maintained by family groups, but irrigation required more centralized control. A large irrigation system can collapse if someone on the upstream end avoids routine maintenance and the common good requires authority and management, although smaller ones can be maintained by family groups. With adequate organization, most of what the growing city needed could be grown in the surrounding countryside. The Teotihuacános could not grow cotton this high, but they could and did import it from the Gulf lowlands, where there was vigorous production (Stark et al. 1998). As the population grew, so did the political hierarchy needed to make it all work.

Archaeologists use a series of nine phase names to keep track of the sequence at Teotihuacán. Six of these cover the period of the city's Classic heyday, from around 150 BCE to 550 CE (Box 7.2). It is not particularly useful to list them here. What is important is that by the beginning of the Common Era Teotihuacán was already the preeminent city in the Basin of Mexico. Its population rose to 80,000 as 80 to 90% of the total population of the Basin concentrated around it. Teotihuacán was transformed from a chiefdom to a city-state with the development of bureaucracy, a standing army, and a permanent ruling class, all things required to manage an urban population.

All early civilizations around the world had imposing state religions, and Teotihuacán was no exception. Priests and politicians cooperated in mutual validation, pretending to control the elements so that they could better control the populace. So successful was it that Teotihuacán boomed as a destination for religious pilgrimage at the same time as it boomed as an urban center. Rural populations in places like northern Tlaxcala 50 km (30 mi) away to the east were depleted by emigration and did not recover demographically until after the great city went into decline (Matos Moctezuma 1990).

Teotihuacán Architecture. The Teotihuacános built monumental architecture on a scale grander than anything previously seen in Mexico. They were not the first to cover their buildings with lime plaster, for it was earlier in the Maya area, but they were the first to use it extensively in the Mexican highlands. The lime appears to have been slaked away from the city at locations close to where the raw material was mined. Slaking requires plenty of wood fuel to heat the material to high temperatures, and transporting the finished lime to the city required a large amount of human energy. The plaster walls at Teotihuacán are thus another measure of the city's regional power (Barba and Frunz 1999).

Pyramid of the Moon. Saburo Sugiyama and his colleagues have dug 33.8 m (110 ft) of tunnels through the interior of the Pyramid of the Moon (Figure 7.17) in

Figure 7.17 The Pyramid of the Moon as seen from atop the Pyramid of the Sun.

order to work out its construction history, finding more than the usual amount of the unexpected along the way (Cabrera Castro and Sugiyama 1999). There were seven building stages, each covering the previous one(s), except in one case when there was heavy demolition of earlier work. The earliest was begun around 100 CE, before the Pyramid of the Sun was begun and before earlier buildings were razed to make way for the great Temple of Quetzalcoatl to the south.

The beginning of each building stage was typically marked by the sacrifice of several people. Some were outfitted with opulent jewelry, clothing, and headdresses, while others were naked, bound with their hands behind them, and in some cases decapitated. Later Aztec pyramids supported stone and masonry temples dedicated to various gods, but there is no evidence for this practice at Teotihuacán. The flat top of Stage 5 of the Pyramid of the Moon, buried deep under later construction, has a pristine plaster surface that is unblemished by any evidence of a structure. The most logical conclusion is that the square tops of these great pyramids were open ritual platforms.

Pyramid of the Sun. Construction of the much larger Pyramid of the Sun began around 150 CE (Figure 7.15). The oldest fill in it contains discarded fragments of pottery that date to the time just before that date. Only the pyramid at Cholula would eventually be bigger.

The Temple of Quetzalcoatl. The temple (Figure 7.18) was constructed inside a huge walled compound, which even today one must climb over to gain access. Earlier buildings were demolished to make way for it around 200 CE. Two hundred people, including 20 men wearing lavish decorations, were sacrificed and buried under the fill of the new building (Cabrera Castro et al. 1991). Here again the flat-topped pyramid was apparently designed as a ritual platform. The compound around it known as the Ciudadela was twice the size of a modern sports stadium, big enough to hold the entire population of the city on special occasions.

The front of the main structure was later covered by a smaller addition that covered up and preserved its elaborate façade. Archaeologists still later removed the back of the addition to expose the early façade, and the classic **talud and tablero** architecture is now one of the most popular sights in the city. Great stone masks project out from the tablero portion of each terrace. These have often been referred to as representations of Quetzalcoatl, the feathered serpent god, and Tlaloc, the rain god, but this appears to be only half right. Quetzalcoatl is obvious, and he also appears snaking along the sloping talud below the tablero. But the masks or headdresses with the donut-shaped eyes and rough skin indicate that it might represent the Primordial Crocodile god, not Tlaloc. The façade was designed to assert the power of the man who caused it to be built, and both Quetzalcoatl and the Primordial Crocodile were probably aspects of his identity (López Austin et al. 1991; Sugiyama 2005:71–86).

The Avenue of the Dead. The Avenue of the Dead is oriented 15°30′ east of true north, an alignment that points to the top of Cerro Gordo. But the direction to the top of a mountain or anything else on the horizon depends upon where one is standing, and this raises the possibility that the Teotihuacános did not orient the avenue once they had decided where to build their city, but rather built their city once they established the orientation. Ivan Šprajc (2000) presents evidence to support his conclusion that perpendicular lines that form the roughly east–west axes of the Pyramid of the Sun and the Ciudadela came first, and the Avenue of the Dead was laid out where it is once those two axes were established. The east–west axes are slightly different, and they point to spots on the horizon where the sun rises and sets on days of the year that are separated by multiples of 20 days, the basic unit of Mesoamerican mathematics and calendrics. There are also several examples of large pecked circle and cross symbols in and around Teotihuacán. These might have been surveyors' bench marks, calendars, game boards, or perhaps all three simultaneously (Aveni 1978).

The Teotihuacán mapping project produced a highly detailed description of this great city (Millon 1973). The city covers about 20 km^2 (8 mi^2), an area that compares to downtown Washington, DC (Figure 7.19).

Figure 7.18 Façade of the Temple of Quetzalcoatl, showing feathered serpents and the Primordial Crocodile.

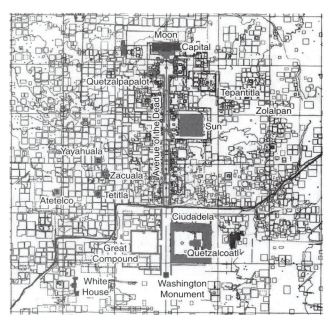

Figure 7.19 The urban core of Teotihuacán showing major structures mentioned in the text. Three buildings in Washington, DC, are superimposed to provide scale.

The archaeologists discovered that there were about 2,000 apartment complexes arrayed around the central urban core. Those that were sampled for detailed study were built to house 60 to 100 people. Multiplying these numbers and allowing for some vacancies indicates that the total population of Teotihuacán at its peak was probably between 100,000 and 150,000. William Sanders's (1996a) best estimate is 123,000. His survey data indicate that the total population of the city and its surrounding suburbs was around 145,000.

Archaeologists have excavated and reconstructed some elite residential apartment compounds such as Tetitla. More modest residences have also been explored, but all of these were typically abandoned gradually, and people moving out tend to leave little behind for archaeologists (Manzanilla and Barsba 1990). Occasionally archaeologists find Mesoamerican households that were buried suddenly under thick volcanic ash, sealing troves of evidence of everyday life (Dull et al. 2001; Plunket and Uruñuela 1998; Sheets 2000; Sheets et al. 1990). This kind urunvela bad luck for residents but good luck for archaeologists did not occur at Teotihuacán.

The Teotihuacán State. The exact nature of the Teotihuacán state continues to be the subject of debate. Most archaeologists do not doubt that Teotihuacán was a city-state, probably one with several subordinate ones linked to it. No lasting urban center of this size could have developed as a mere chiefdom, for it must have required a bureaucracy, clear succession of leadership, and some sort of standing army. It must also have had territorial boundaries, but the question then becomes how far from the ceremonial center were they set? The center was larger by far than any other of its time in Mesoamerica, but was it a spectacular city-state, the center of a vast empire like the later Aztec one, or something in between? Architecture at the site of Kaminaljuyú in the Guatemalan highlands and at some lowland Maya centers mimicked Teotihuacán. Inscriptions at the Maya centers of Tikal and Copan a thousand kilometers away mention lords from Teotihuacán. But the implications of these clues from other centers far away remain uncertain.

The Maya site of Altun Ha is even farther away from Teotihuacán, over 1,000 km (620 mi) distant. A typically Teotihuacán burial there has prompted some archaeologists to hypothesize that the city's imperial reach extended that far. But studies of the bones have shown that these were local people using some of the funerary trappings of Teotihuacán, not highland people who died far from home (White et al. 2001).

A monument at the closer site of Monte Albán in Oaxaca depicts Zapotec lords from Teotihuacán meeting with local Zapotec leaders. There appears to have been a barrio (neighborhood) of Teotihuacános at Monte Albán just as there was a Zapotec barrio at Teotihuacán, but do either of these imply political domination? The scholar consensus is probably not, at least for now.

One useful line of evidence is Thin Orange pottery, a popular trade ware at Teotihuacán. The distinctive pottery has been found throughout the city and at many other contemporaneous sites in the highlands. It was the subject of one of the earliest applications of compositional analysis in archaeology, the use of thin sections to identify mineral inclusions in the clay used to make Thin Orange. The unique mix of minerals in the raw material indicated the area of manufacture to be one or another of several localities in the mountains to the south, about a 170-km (106 mi) hike from Teotihuacán. Workshops there produced Thin Orange from 300 to as late as 750 CE (Sotomayor and Castillo Tejero 1963). Despite its importance as a trade ware at Teotihuacán, there is no evidence that the region was necessarily under the great city's political domination (Rattray 1990). Whether Teotihuacán was just a large influential center of Mesoamerican culture or the capital of the kind of sprawling political empire the later Aztecs would have is still debated.

Workshops in the city show that there were other kinds of craft specialization and that craftspeople at Teotihuacán were able to acquire a wide range of raw materials. Some made classic cylindrical tripod vessels. Two lapidary workshops contained 25 different materials, including greenstone, hematite, mica, crystal, and shell. Curiously, waste fragments of turquoise and jade were not found (Widmer 1991). The long trade routes that brought raw materials to Teotihuacán apparently did not yet extend all the way to the turquoise quarries of what is now New Mexico (Cabrero 1991; Harbottle and Weigand 1992:81).

Other things that seem conspicuously missing at Teotihuacán include writing, elaborate calendars, and ball courts. But perhaps these were not entirely absent, just not obvious. James Langley (1991) has found about 120 signs on murals and pottery at Teotihuacán that appear to comprise a simple notational system, although the elaborate calendrics of some contemporaneous cultures are still missing. There are no obvious ball courts, but surely the Teotihuacános knew some version of the game. The contemporaneous site of Cantona, which lies on the main trade route between Teotihuacán and the Gulf Coast, has dozens of ball courts. Perhaps the Avenue of the Dead was a whole string of ball courts on game day, making separate structures unnecessary.

Life in the City. The residential areas of Teotihuacán were a mix of homes and workshops. Some people managed farms outside the city, but perhaps 30% were elites or craftspeople who worked in as many as 600 workshops scattered around the city. Wealthy elite people lived in walled multifamily compounds. Several examples of this distinctive Teotihuacán residential form have been excavated and restored. One such compound could house 60 to 100 people, sometimes in splendid quarters.

The elite residents of the wealthier compounds lived amidst plastered walls decorated with beautiful painted murals. Personal adornment included elaborate costumes that have not survived but that we can reconstruct from paintings and sculptures. Individuals also subjected their incisors to elaborate filing or drilling for jade insets, all without either high-speed drills or anesthesia.

Some sections of the city were barrios (neighborhoods) for particular classes or ethnic groups, a few of which have already been mentioned. Some of them were occupied by emigrants from other parts of the highlands, often craft specialists that almost certainly spoke foreign languages (White et al. 2004). It was a cosmopolitan urban center. With a population approaching 124,000 it was certainly the largest such center in the

Americas by around 500 CE, but all of that was about to change.

The Decline of Teotihuacán. The fall of Teotihuacán occurred when the central public buildings were burned, something that typically marks conquest in ancient Mesoamerica. Teotihuacán's buildings were burned and the religious shrines within them were systematically destroyed. The timing of this disaster has been the subject of archaeological debate for many years. One problem is that radiocarbon dates on burned roof timbers date to or before the original cutting of the wood, not the time of its burning. Although later estimates have been published in the past, specialists are now focused on the sixth century as the most probable time of widespread destruction, perhaps sometime around 550 CE.

Even more difficult is the question of who was responsible for the widespread destruction. There was no shortage of potential enemies who lived within striking distance, and some archaeologists even favor home-grown internal revolt as an explanation. Palaces were burned and idols were smashed, but while the resident population dropped significantly as a result of the conflict, the city was not deserted. Many residential compounds survived the burning, but the city declined as the preeminent Mesoamerican center it had been. If outsiders were responsible they did not choose to occupy the city afterward, for there is no evidence of an alien occupation. The city-state was destroyed politically, but its population was not wiped out. The details of cause and effect remain uncertain, but archaeologists are exploring demographic and ecological changes, particularly those involving the movement of Nahuatl speakers into the Basin of Mexico from the northern desert (Manzanilla 2005).

The sudden destruction of Teotihuacán is turning out to be more typical of Mesoamerican city-states than once thought. Many Maya cities would suffer similar fates in the coming centuries. Nearer by in the highlands Xochicalco would be sacked and burned around 900 CE, and Tula would meet a similar fate around 1150 CE.

Competing City-States

Xochicalco

Xochicalco was among the competing city-states that might have contributed to the fall of Teotihuacán. The site is centered on a hilltop in the state of Morelos southwest of the modern city of Cuernavaca. It is spread across five connected and defensible hilltops. The surrounding land is not particularly good for farming, so the site was probably chosen for its access to major trade routes and its military advantages. The city-state had a population of 10,000 to 15,000 people, many of whom were engaged in craft production and long-distance trade (Hirth 2000; López Luján et al. 1995).

Xochicalco has a large and impressive ball court, but the centerpiece of the site is the Pyramid of the Plumed Serpent. The high taluds of the pyramid bear relief carvings that depict towns that paid tribute to Xochicalco as well as several seated figures that look distinctively Maya. This style is probably due to the influence of the Olmeca-Xicalanca culture, a Maya population that appears to have been resident at several sites in the highlands around this time. Another relief on the front of the pyramid depicts what appears to be the calibration of two different calendars within the coil of a feathered serpent.

Whether or not it had a hand in the destruction of Teotihuacán around 550 CE, Xochicalco suffered the same fate three and a half centuries later. Despite its protected hilltop location, around 900 CE the city was attacked and destroyed. It was abandoned and never reoccupied.

Cholula

As impressive as Teotihuacán's Pyramid of the Sun may be, there is a larger one at Cholula. The Great Pyramid of Cholula (Figure 7.20) is still used because the Spanish built a church atop it, a symbol of the religious conquest of Mexico. That makes it not just the largest pyramid in the world but also the oldest continuously occupied building in North America. The immense pyramid was tunneled by archaeologists in the twentieth century, an effort that revealed four major construction stages and at least nine minor ones. The tunnels remain open to visitors, unusually stable because the pyramid was built mainly of large adobe bricks. The initial structure was already in place by around 300 BCE, a pyramid 120 m (394 ft) on a side equipped with talud and tablero architectural elements and painted in red, black, and yellow with insect motifs. Later construction expanded the pyramid until it was 350 m (1150 ft) on a side and 55 m (181 ft) high. The architecture of Cholula was similar to that of Teotihuacán early on, but later in its long life Cholula was remodeled to look more like Gulf Coast cities, particularly El Tajín. This was probably because Cholula was occupied by the Maya-speaking Olmeca-Xicalanca at the time.

Cacaxtla

Another Olmeca-Xicalanca site is located north of Cholula in the state of Tlaxcala (Figure 7.21). This site was initially explored by local people hoping to find something that would attract tourists. When they succeeded the national government intervened to ensure that site development was done right, and the results were spectacular. Vivid murals are beautifully preserved at Cacaxtla and they reflect the Maya cultural influences.

Oaxaca

The Valley of Oaxaca 400 km (250 mi) to the southwest of the Basin of Mexico, was the setting for another variant of Mexican civilization. The Zapotecs, who are still numerous, built the great mountaintop city of Monte Albán, as well as dozens of other smaller centers around the Y-shaped valley. The Rio Salado joins the Rio Atoyac here, at an elevation that is lower than the Basin of Mexico. The valley is warm and fertile, conditions that attracted farming communities while Olmec culture was still flourishing in the lowlands to the northeast. There are 1,500 km^2 (580 mi^2) of arable land in the valley at an average elevation of 1,500 m (4,900 ft). Winter frost is very rare at that elevation and the wet season brings abundant rain from June to October.

Farmers discovered early on that climate and soil in the Valley of Oaxaca would allow for two crops a year. Irrigation prevented crop failure in years when rainfall was below average, something that might have occurred as much as 50% of the time. This in turn might have prompted the rise of the chiefdoms formed early here and that these were eventually succeeded by the development of centralized city-state government.

Figure 7.20 The great pyramid of Cholula, with pre-Hispanic architecture in the foreground and a Spanish colonial period church added to the summit.

Figure 7.21 Cacaxtla murals of a Jaguar Warrior (left)
and an Eagle Warrior (right).

San José Mogote

Prior to 500 BCE the major center in the valley was San José Mogote. Most settlements at that time were small-scale farming communities that raised maize, avocados, beans, and squash as their primary crops. Although the valley was agriculturally rich, most luxury goods had to be imported, and it was a node in the far-flung Olmec trade network. Imports included, obsidian, jade, feathers, shell, cacao, and gold. In exchange the Oaxaca people produced magnetite mirrors and pottery (Marcus and Flannery 1996).

A petroglyphic image of a slain captive at San José Mogote is associated with two glyphs, probably the individual's name and birth date in the 260-day calendar, a system that is explained later in this chapter. Other images at the nearby site of Monte Albán, long referred to as "danzantes," are very similar, and all of them probably date to the period 600 BCE to 200 CE. These early examples of Zapotec writing appear to derive from the same Olmec origins as Maya writing (Marcus 1992; Pohl et al. 2002).

Monte Albán

Monte Albán (Figure 7.22), the principal Zapotec city-state, was founded around 500 BCE and expanded by conquest beyond the Valley of Oaxaca as early as 300 BCE, before it had even consolidated its power the main valley (Spencer and Redmond 2001). These developments occurred during the heyday of Epi-Olmec

trade and exchange, so it is no surprise that Olmec influences appear in the city. San José Mogote was all but abandoned by this time and it appears likely that warfare drove the inhabitants of the valley to form a confederation and build Monte Albán as a defensive stronghold on a mountaintop at the center of the valley. The site has excellent views in all directions and it is militarily secure. There was little water and no previous occupation on the mesa where the new city was built, making it difficult to justify for any other reason (Blanton et al. 1993).

The earliest monuments at Monte Albán show clear evidence of Olmec influences. A gallery of prisoners (danzantes) in the southwest corner of the main plaza depicts dozens of sacrificial victims, not dancers at all but corpses with limbs all akimbo (Figure 7.23). Closed eyes, conspicuously missing genitals, and curlicues of flowing blood reveal the true nature of the low relief carvings. There would eventually be 320 of them, and more like them at other smaller centers around the Valley of Oaxaca.

Olmec influences fell away with time as the population of Monte Albán grew to 17,000 people. The number of small supporting communities grew from 51 to 86 and the population of the valley below topped 24,000. Like Teotihuacán, Monte Albán was a primate center, bigger by far than any of the communities around it and clearly a major city-state by 200 BCE.

The five centuries from 200 BCE to 300 CE were a period of military expansion for Monte Albán. The city-state established military garrisons as much as

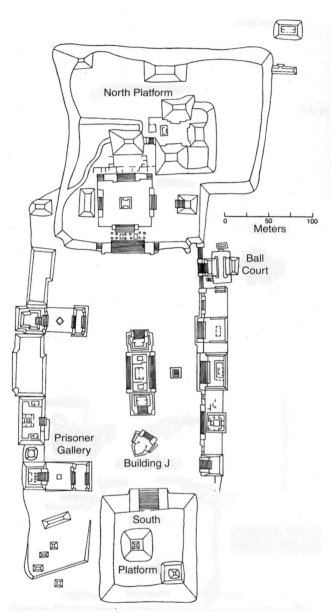

Figure 7.22 Site plan of Monte Albán.
Source: Courtesy of Joyce Marcus, University of Michigan.

Figure 7.23 Monte Albán prisoners,
often referred to as danzantes.

1995). Construction of this and other buildings on and around the main plaza proceeded as the plaza was artificially flattened. Outcrops were taken down and low spots were filled over an area the size of six modern football fields. A ball court was built at the northeastern corner of the plaza and the city had the configuration familiar to us now by around 300 CE (Figure 7.24).

Early inscriptions show that the Zapotecs at Monte Albán had calendrical notation and writing, albeit not with the elaboration seen in the Maya region. Later inscriptions show Zapotec leaders meeting with visitors wearing distinctive Teotihuacán costumes, complete with tassel headdresses that probably indicate that they were ambassadors (Marcus 1980, 1992).

The population of the city rose again to 16,500 after 300 CE, an impressive number when one remembers that all food and water apart from collected rainwater had to be hauled to the top of the mountain by human porters. The population of the valley below rose as well, and secondary centers such as Dainzu, Macuilxochitl, Tlacochahuaya, and Jalieza grew up in the political shadow of Monte Albán. Farming apparently ran into some difficulty after 500 CE, when marginal fields were abandoned and much of the population moved closer to the center. The overall population of the valley dropped, but the city continued to grow. The architectural complex known as the North Platform appears to have been an opulent but very private elite residence by this time, accessible only by way of a narrow passage and stairs. As so often happens, the progressive isolation of wealthy elites did not last. The city population of Monte Albán collapsed by over 85% after 750 CE, and the overall population in the valley declined as well. Teotihuacán had long since collapsed politically by this time, leaving a vacuum that Monte Albán and other large centers in the highlands could not fill (Blanton et al. 1993). In time

100 km (62 mi) away, an expansionist program that would have been impossible without a standing army. The hilltop population dropped by about 2000, possibly because of greater security, while the valley population continued to rise to around 40,000.

Building J, an arrow-shaped building just north of the South Platform, was once thought to be an astronomical observatory. However, inscriptions on it clearly celebrate military conquests, so archaeologists now interpret it as a military showcase (Peeler and Winter

Figure 7.24 Monte Albán from the South Platform, Building J in the foreground. The ball court is near the tree in the distant right.

Monte Albán was just another smallish city-state among several others, its main plaza largely deserted and its political dominance gone.

The rise of Zapotec culture illustrates the two-sided nature of cultural evolution. Whereas environment sets the scene, offers options, limits possibilities, and betrays human adaptation when it changes, environment alone does not determine the course of cultural evolution. The other side of the process is comprised of the drives inherent in the human species, through which individuals or sets of individuals could and did alter the course of history in its details. The details are often what fascinate archaeologists the most, and they are just as often what elude us most frequently. In our frustration at not being able to read an undeciphered glyph we come close to forgetting the more important point, that these ancient people had a form of writing. But conversely, when we focus on the discoverable we risk forgetting about the unknowns that lie beyond our reach, at least for the time being (Marcus and Flannery 1996).

Maya Civilization

Rise of the Maya in eastern Mesoamerica began by at least 3000 BCE, with the introduction of maize and manioc. By 1000 BCE Maya-speaking people equipped with Epi-Olmec agriculture, technology, and cosmology began to transform the natural environment of the Peten lowlands into a complex mosaic of forest gardens.

Patterns of raised and canalized fields that are still detectable from the air today date to this time or earlier (Pohl et al. 1996). Complex Maya societies began to emerge by 600 BCE, their growing centers probably dependent upon raised fields in some areas, and water storage in others (Scarborough and Gallopin 1991). Several Maya cities were built near hills or mountains where planners could construct reservoirs for drinking water uphill from their centers (Scarborough 1998).

Few regions exemplify the marriage between environmental opportunity and the potential of human initiative better than this one. The rich tropical forest of the Peten made many things possible given plant domesticates and the ideology of the earlier Olmecs, but it did not make them inevitable. For that we must look to the drives inherent in human culture, and the propagations of ideas (memes) that appealed to people at the time for whatever complex and now largely unknowable reasons. Without those fundamental drives complex society would not have evolved in the Peten lowlands. By the same token, no amount of ambition could have given rise to Classic Maya culture had the environment and timing not been right for it.

The Maya created a new kind of anthropogenic environment, for it was neither natural nor clear cut. The slash-and-burn or swidden techniques used by the Olmecs were used here as well. The Maya opened **milpas**, clearings in the forest for the growing of maize and other domesticates. But around them were other patches that were either former milpas lying fallow or tended but not heavily modified garden plots, where hundreds of plants used for food, fiber, and medicine were nurtured. Among these were cacao trees (*Theobroma cacao*) from which they were making chocolate as early as 600 BCE (Dakin and Wichmann 2000; Hurst et al. 2002). The garden mosaic evolved constantly, as stumps in abandoned milpas sprouted new growth, new fruit trees grew, and old ones died. The long-term cycles of such an environment meshed well with the cyclical concepts that underlay Maya notions of time and destiny.

The Peten region is low, averaging only about 200 m (660 ft) above sea level. It is hot and very wet, receiving 2–3 m (7–10 ft) of rain every year. The Peten was and still is rich in limestone and the lime necessary for both cooking and the manufacture of mortar. It was also rich in jaguar and alligator pelts, exotic bird feathers, and cacao beans. Things it lacked included obsidian, gold, and jade, all of which were imported.

Maya Trade and Exchange

Jade came only from the Montagua Valley of Guatemala. Jade is actually a range of minerals associated with serpentinite, the most important of them being jadeite and nephrite. Only jadeite is found in Mesoamerica. It was already highly valued when the Olmec system of trade and exchange was in operation and it remained so for the Classic Maya. Obsidian came from several highland sources, but most gold came by way of Central America from more distant sources.

We know that from the time of the Olmecs on there was trade and exchange of luxury goods across Mesoamerica and eventually with even more distant centers in the U.S. Southwest and the Southeast. Overland travel is well known, but the Mesoamericans also traded by canoe along the coasts. Columbus encountered them on his fourth voyage. Bartolomé de las Casas described trading canoes as long as a Spanish galley, 2.4 m (8 ft) wide, and crewed by 25 men, many of whom had their wives and children along for the ride. Jade, shark teeth, feathers, shell, stingray spines, and other luxury items were moved this way, but so too were commodities like cacao, cotton cloth, obsidian, and salt. We know from early Spanish accounts that the coastal canoe trade was controlled by wealthy lords who operated from major city-states on or near the coast. Norman Hammond (1972) and others have used obsidian from known sources to trace the inland and coastal trade routes around the Yucatan Peninsula. The native system of trade and exchange collapsed after the Spanish conquest. Epidemics devastated the populations and brought trade to a halt. When it resumed, it was under Spanish control and operated in Spanish colonial interests.

The Rise of Maya City-States

The tropical forest environment provided the means and ambition provided the inspiration for Maya civilization. It might seem to us like an improbable place for an early civilization to have flourished, but that says more about our modern prejudices than it does about the Maya. The limestone bedrock of the region was excellent building material for people having only stone tool technology. Despite occasional local setbacks, the abundance of domesticated and natural food allowed the population to grow rapidly and to high density. Chance and ambition guaranteed that eventually some families would achieve more than others. City-states emerged from earlier chiefdoms over the course of two centuries, 230–430 CE, in the Maya lowlands. The earliest dated inscription at Tikal dates to 292 CE, and its ruling dynasty claimed a founding date of 230 CE. The earliest inscription at Balakbal dates to 406 CE, while the earliest one at Calakmul dates to 431 CE. Many other city-states were also founded between 330 and 430 (Pincemin et al. 1998).

Pyramids grew in classic Mesoamerican fashion, older structures buried under ever larger ones until their tops poked through the forest canopy. They were decorated with the writing, calendrics, and religious iconography that we identify as the hallmarks of civilization. There were eventually more than four dozen city-states in the steamy Maya lowlands (Figure 7.25).

The nature of Maya polities has been clarified by the dogged work of several Maya epigraphers (specialists who study inscriptions, called **epigraphy**) who have gradually compiled dynastic lists for the best known city-states (Schele 1992). What is emerging is a picture

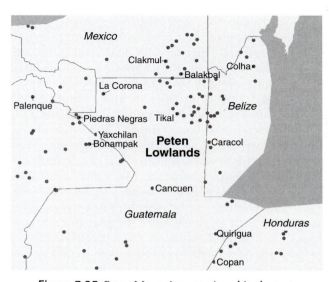

Figure 7.25 Peten Maya sites mentioned in the text.

that contrasts with the popular view that the Maya lived in peaceful theocratic city-states. Instead we see clear evidence of warfare and power politics between competing dynasties. The ambitions of local leaders drove this competition, which expressed itself in architecture and monuments that were designed to extol and make permanent the accomplishments of the lords in whose honor they were erected. Rulers are often identified according to their places in a longer dynastic succession.

Maya Writing

Maya writing took three main forms. First, hundreds of glyph inscriptions are preserved on the limestone buildings and monuments they constructed in the forest. Second, painted forms of the glyphs were put on pottery, particularly cylindrical vessels that could display elaborate scenes of historic importance. Third, Maya scribes compiled a large but unknown number of fan-folded books, which are usually referred to as **codices**. Most of those that survived until the sixteenth century were burned by Spanish religious zealots. Only 3 of the 13 indisputably pre-Hispanic books that have survived in Mesoamerica are Maya, the others being from highland Mexico (see Chapter 8). The Dresden, Madrid, and Paris Codices are known by the names of the cities where they are now housed. A fourth book, the Grolier Codex, surfaced in 1971, but many consider it a fake (Baudez 2002). Maya glyphs also turn up on many other small portable objects.

The Hauberg Stela now at Princeton University bears a Maya date equivalent to 199 CE. This is the oldest such inscription known so far for the Maya lowlands. Such monuments became common in the region by 250 CE, the date that many archaeologists prefer to set as the beginning of the Classic period. From then on elaborate full and relief carvings accompanied by date inscriptions and glyphic texts appeared on many sites. For example, a lintel in Structure 23 at Yaxchilan depicts a stunning act of self-sacrifice. A leader named Shield Jaguar holds a torch while his principal wife, Lady Xoc, draws a thorn-studded cord through a hole in her tongue.

Maya writing is more than just pictographs. Most signs refer either to whole spoken words or to specific syllables. Like Chinese characters, Maya glyphs are symbolic, sometimes contain phonemic values, and only rarely can be interpreted like simple picture writing. This means that each glyph has to be deciphered on its own terms. There is no Maya equivalent to the Rosetta Stone, no way that Maya writing can be broken all at once like a modern code. The meaning of a particular glyph is most often cracked through the long and arduous process of comparing the contexts in which it occurs. As glyph specialists discover the meanings of glyphs one at a time the larger meanings of the Maya inscriptions are increasingly well understood. They turn out not to be religious messages, but the practical information that rulers have always wanted to preserve and advertise such as the dynastic lists, the births, accessions, deaths, and military accomplishments of the people who rule (Houston 1989).

Site Q

Maya monuments have attracted both professional archaeologists and looters for many decades. Looting is still a serious problem in the region, and despite stiff laws and international agreements priceless objects still turn up on the black market. In the 1960s an extraordinary series of similar looted inscriptions began appearing on the illicit art market. Specialists were sure that they were coming from a site in the Guatemalan Peten, but no professional archaeologist knew where it was. The enigmatic site was referred to simply as "Site Q." Finally, it was announced in September 2005 that the long-sought site had been found. Marcello Canuto and a team of researchers had at last found the long-sought evidence at a center known as La Corona. The team found a panel in place in a temple platform that duplicates other Site Q hieroglyphic texts in size, style, and subject matter.

The discovery of Site Q highlights the struggle between looters and legitimate archaeologists. Without the looters the very existence of Site Q would not have been suspected in the first place, yet by removing and selling panels from the site the looters must have destroyed much valuable information. They certainly violated Guatemalan law and international treaties at the same time. Professional archaeologists argue that it would be better for sites like La Corona to remain buried and unknown than to lose their integrity to looting. Looters, and the wealthy collectors who keep them busy, claim that they are performing a public service by finding valuable artifacts and selling them at prices high enough to guarantee they will be carefully preserved. But public opinion and international law take a very different view.

Maya Architecture

Maya architecture was founded on dressed and carved limestone blocks that were stacked and mortared into lavish palaces and steep-sided terraced pyramids. Temple structures typically surmounted the towering pyramids, and these were made to look even taller through the addition of latticed roof combs. Despite their considerable architectural skills the Maya never discovered the true arch, using instead the corbelled vault. This kind of vault has an A-shaped cross section and depends upon the stacking of heavy stone counterweights atop thick walls. Only narrow rooms can be spanned by corbelled vaults, and the mass of masonry above can make buildings look top heavy in the absence of a roof comb. Temples, pyramids, platforms, palaces, ball courts, and plazas make up the cores of Maya city-state sites. Dotting the plazas are stelae, monuments designed to commemorate major events (Figure 7.26).

Like ancient Greek statues, Maya ruins are now mostly chalky white, but they were once plastered and painted dramatic colors, especially red and the famous Maya blue (Arnold et al. 2008; José-Yacamán et al. 1996). The interior murals at Bonampak are especially notable examples. Limestone weathers rapidly, so many of even the best protected Maya sites are currently at risk. Anabel Ford and many other archaeologists argue that it would be better to do less forest clearing than was standard practice in the twentieth century, leaving a canopy of trees to help protect exposed limestone block from microbial erosion.

Maya Calendars

Maya calendrics were another matter. Unlike Maya writing the systematic nature of calendrical inscriptions made it possible for scholars to crack the code in the nineteenth century (Coe 1999). The system has three main components and several minor ones. First is the Tzolkin, the 260-day ritual calendar mentioned earlier in this chapter. The second is the Haab, the 365-day solar calendar. Third is the Long Count, already described for the Tres Zapotes Stela C inscription. The Maya also

understood the cycles of the moon and Venus, and they were able to predict eclipses (Spinden 1928).

There can no longer be much doubt that the 260-day Tzolkin calendar originated as an approximation of the period of human gestation (Earle and Snow 1985). The most commonly cited medical estimate for the average time from conception to birth is 266 days, close enough to the multiple of 20 that the Maya **vigesimal** counting system preferred. The calendar worked through the permutation of 20 day names and 13 god names, not 13 units of 20 days. This is typically illustrated as two interlocking gears in books like this one, but that would imply a clocklike mechanism that the Maya did not have.

Table 7.3 shows better how this worked. Counting the two lists together the god names (represented here simply as numbers) begin to repeat after 13. The next day after the first completion of the list of 20 day names on 7 Ahaw, would be 8 Imix. The two lists run like this for 260 days, at the end of which 1 Imix comes up again and the cycle starts over (Satterthwaite 1965).

While keeping track of the Tzolkin cycles, the Maya also kept track of the solar year using the 365-day Haab calendar. This they computed by using 18 month names, 20 day names (numbered 0–19 as in modern computing), and 5 (occasionally 6) extra days to fill out the solar year. All of these elements had their own glyphs and the calendar was organized as 18 units of 20 days each rather than as a permutation like the Tzolkin calendar. The first day of the Haab calendar was 0 Pohp.

When the two calendars cycled together every day had a compound designation with four elements, such as 1 Ik 0 Pohp. The same dates fell together only every 52 years, or every 18,980 days. This was the 52-year

Figure 7.26 The Great Plaza at Tikal with temple structures and stelae.

Table 7.3 Tzolkin cycle of 20 day names shown as a permutation with the first and part of the second cycle of 13 gods.

God	Day Name	God	Day Name
1	Imix (Waterlily)	11	Chuen (Frog)
2	**Ik (Wind)**	12	**Eb (Skull)**
3	Akbal (Night)	13	Ben (Corn stalk)
4	Kan (Corn)	1	Ix (Jaguar)
5	Chicchan (Snake)	2	Men (Eagle)
6	Cimi (Death head)	3	Cib (Shell)
7	**Manik (Hand)**	4	**Caban (Earth)**
8	Lamat (Venus)	5	Etznab (Flint)
9	Muluc (Water)	6	Kawak (Storm cloud)
10	Oc (Dog)	7	Ahaw (Lord)

Calendar Round that was so important to the Maya and many other Mesoamerican cultures both then and later on. Because of the mathematics, only 52 of the 260 days of the Tzolkin can ever occur with 0 Pohp, the first day of the solar year. These are days in which the names Ik, Manik, Eb, or Caban appear, shown in bold in Table 7.3. Some later derivative calendars used these as shorthand names for the 52 solar years in the Calendar Round and avoided all the complicated details of the Classic Maya calendar.

As important as this great cycle was to the Maya, they realized that a date like 1 Imix 9 Pohp did not say anything about which cycle it was in. Such a date was incomplete in the same way that reference to the United States presidential election of '68 is incomplete. A few centuries from now people might not be sure which century such a reference is referring to. The Long Count, already briefly described for the Epi-Olmec, solved this problem by providing a linear day count to accompany the cycles of the 52-year Calendar Round. All of this information shows up frequently on Maya monuments commemorating important events. Just to be sure, the ruler of a Maya city-state would often record an important accomplishment in the Tzolkin, the Haab, and the Long Count calendars simultaneously.

Maya Art

Maya ceramics tell us much about their culture and politics. Cylindrical vessels bear courtly scenes and glyphs that commemorate important events in the lives of the elites. Specialized pieces illustrate or facilitated the taking of drugs by enema (Diamond 2001). We also know from painted vessels and inscriptions that the Maya smoked tobacco, a South American plant, but the date of its arrival remains uncertain (Robicsec 1978).

They used special spouted vessels for preparing chocolate drinks from cacao (Powis et al. 2002). We know from later sources that they preferred the drink when it was frothy, and it would have been easy to produce the desired foam by blowing into the spouts of the chocolate vessels. The same spouts then made it easy to also serve the drink. Analysis of chocolate residue from a Maya vessel recovered at Colha in northern Belize confirmed its use. Dating of the deposit from which the vessel was recovered pushed the earliest known use of chocolate back to 600 BCE (Hurst et al. 2002). Thus, chocolate was an important ritual drink in the earliest Maya monumental sites and might have been used by the Olmecs as well.

Maya religion pervaded their art, their politics, and their daily lives. Living where they did the Maya had little need of sleeves, but had they used them they would have surely worn their religion on them, for lacking sleeves they adorned nearly everything else with religious motifs. They depicted themselves laden with religious icons on stone panels, on painted murals, and on cylindrical pottery vessels. In typical Mesoamerican fashion they identified themselves with deities, often more than one at a time, and conflated deities with each other (Gillespie and Joyce 1998). Archaeologists seeking to classify images into mutually exclusive categories are often frustrated by the fluidity of ancient usage, but it made sense to cultures in which metaphor, transformation, and shifting identities were commonplace.

Major Maya City-States

Tikal

Tikal is one of the largest and today one of the most popular of Maya centers (Figure 7.27). Maya rulers of this city-state lived in opulence and presided over a center of such beauty that film and television producers find excuses to use it as a backdrop. It probably had a substantial population of around 120,000 in its domain, and its rulers may have commanded the labor and tribute of thousands more. What the average farmer got out of this deal was the assurance of water in dry years, help when it was needed, and protection from the depredations of neighboring city-states. Much of this, of course, was in the form of the intangible benefits of religious beliefs.

Tikal and other Maya centers were well connected to each other, but they were also connected to other centers in Mesoamerica. Greenish Pachuca obsidian from the Mexican highlands has been found at Tikal, indicating contacts with the great city of Teotihuacán.

Curiously, artifacts made from this exotic obsidian turn up in contexts that indicate that it was being imported by lower-ranking elites and wealthy commoners rather than by Tikal's rulers (Moholy-Nagy 1999).

The hereditary stratification at Tikal was as strongly developed as any in the Maya lowlands. The rulers were mostly male. Women are rarely depicted in Maya art at Tikal and they are underrepresented in burials, particularly elite interments. The focus on males emerged with the rise in dynastic authority at Tikal and was related to the development of the centralized city-state (Haviland 1997).

Canals and raised fields are missing around Tikal and at most other Maya centers away from northern Belize, southern Quintana Roo, and Campeche. In those parts of the domain of the Maya the groundwater lies close to the surface, and agriculture is put at risk by extremes in season inundation and desiccation. Canals are necessary for both drainage and irrigation in such circumstances, but wetland agriculture was not viable around Tikal (Pope and Dahlin 1989).

There was a political vacuum at Tikal, the so-called Tikal hiatus, from 562 to 695 CE. This followed Tikal's military defeat by Caracol. Tikal did not regain full independence for 133 years. Curiously, during this time they made heavy use of stingray spines, cone shells, and other toxic marine objects, probably for ritual reasons (Maxwell 2000).

Palenque

Palenque is a Maya center that is famous for its beautiful architecture. Maya buildings there found ways to minimize the mass of stone needed in corbelled vaulting, creating roofs that do not appear top heavy. The center is dominated by two imposing structures, the Palace, which has a spectacular reconstructed tower, and the Temple of the Inscriptions (Figure 7.28). Most

Figure 7.27 Temple of the Giant Jaguar (Temple I) at Tikal.

Figure 7.28 Temple of the Inscriptions, Palenque.

Mesoamerican pyramids were built as temple platforms, not mausoleums, but this is an exception. Archaeologists found a rock slab in the temple that covered a filled staircase, which when excavated led down to the Tomb of Pakal, one of Palenque's kings. The lid of the sarcophagus bears glyphs and the representation of a maize plant growing out of the abdomen of a recumbent man. Inside the tomb they found the remains of Pakal himself, bedecked in jade. A jade mosaic mask covered his face and jade bracelets adorned both his arms and his legs (Figure 7.29).

Occasionally city-state lords were women, but this did not change the overall pattern. Female rulers were accorded male attributes, just as males sometimes took on some feminine traits. Women thus became more masculine when they assumed roles that were typically male roles. Monuments recording the achievements of three female Maya rulers provide them with warrior titles in addition to their other identities. For example, Lady Zac Kuk (White Quetzal) ruled at Palenque for at least three years beginning in 612 CE. She abdicated in favor of her son Pakal three years later but continued to be an important force, perhaps ruling jointly with him, until her death a quarter century later (Hewitt 1999).

Copán

Copán is located in westernmost Honduras (Figure 7.30). It was smaller than Tikal, its rulers presiding over 20,000 to 25,000 subjects. Copán is best known for its extraordinary glyphic staircase, the main feature of one of its principal buildings (Fash 1991; Fash 1992; Schele 1992).

Figure 7.29 The jade funeral mask of Pakal, who was buried within the Temple of the Inscriptions at Palenque.
Source: Courtesy of the Instituto Nacional de Antropología e Historia, Mexico.

Figure 7.30 Main pyramid at Copán.
Source: Courtesy of David Webster.

It was also the setting for the eight-part *Out of the Past* television series (Webster et al. 1992; Webster et al. 1993).

The Copán ruler Waxaklajuun Ubaah K'awiil, formerly known as Eighteen Rabbit (Figure 7.31), who was portrayed on Copán Stela A in 731 CE, was the 13th successor to Yax Kuk Mo (Martin and Nikolai 2008:200). The latter was not the first ruler of Copán, but the founder of the dynasty that later rulers consistently referenced (Schele 1992:137). The city-state of Quirigua was founded as a dependency of Copán around 426 CE. The later ruler known as Buts' Tiliw rebelled against Copán's domination in 738 and Quirigua became independent during the reign of the Stela A ruler (Looper 1999). It should be no surprise that events of this kind dominate the Maya inscriptions that have been deciphered so far (Andrews and Fash 2005).

Figure 7.31 Stela at Copán depicting the ruler known as Eighteen Rabbit.
Source: Courtesy of David Webster.

The Maya Collapse

The collapse of Maya civilization occurred as the result of several factors culminating in a disastrous drought. Some important Maya centers, including Palenque, Piedras Negras, Quirigua, and Copán, stopped erecting dated monuments after 810 CE. Others, especially Tikal and others in the northern Peten, held out longer. But all of the lowland Maya sites had collapsed politically by 910 CE, a demise that marks the end of the Classic period in the region (Webster 2002).

The Debate over Cause and Effect

The search for a cause for the collapse has been muddied by the confusion of proximal and more general causes, and by the confusion of political with demographic collapse. In some cases political hierarchies collapsed but populations were left intact. In other cases whole city-states were wiped out or dispersed by warfare. In some cases there was a strong environmental component, whereas in others catastrophe came in the form of conquest from the outside or revolution from within. What is clear is that the Maya collapse was not a single event or even an orchestrated series of events, but an extended process that took at least 150 years to unfold.

There is no longer much doubt that the Maya experienced a severe and prolonged drought around 850 CE (Haug et al. 2003; Hodell et al. 2001; Shaw 2003). The effects were particularly severe in the central lowlands, where adaptive alternatives to maize agriculture were relatively few and the grandeur of city-state centers prompts even the casual observer to conclude that local elites had oversold their ability to ritually control natural forces. But things were starting to go wrong long before 850 CE. The last dated monuments in the western Peten were carved 761–810 CE. The city-states of the eastern Peten, including Belize and northeastern Honduras, collapsed next, between 811 and 860 CE. The rest succumbed 861–909 CE (Gill 1994). In several cases the local population remained in place despite the political collapse, slowly shrinking in the years that followed.

As in any ecological equation there were many competing forces and a few critical pressure points contributing to the overall collapse. Maya city-state populations had grown rapidly before the drought. The environments around many of them were stressed and degraded as demand for food increased. In many places net population growth tipped to net decline as fertility dropped a little or mortality rose a little. As general ecological stress rose, city-states fought over shrinking resources.

Warfare was nothing new to the Maya, but by the eighth and ninth centuries it was so chronic and so disruptive that their entire way of life was put at risk. The drought thus came at what was already a bad time, and the Maya lords were helpless to do much about it. The crisis required complex practical solutions, and probably more organizational skill, technical knowledge, and regional clout than any king could muster. Standing armies were available, of course, and as inappropriate as warfare might have been as a solution to the problem, then as now it might well have been the option of choice. It has always been easier (or at least quicker) to deploy armies than to develop new technologies. No doubt they also fell back on the ritual palliatives that everyone believed had worked in the past, but this was no ordinary setback. One by one the fires of civilization went out in the city-states of the Peten.

Southwestern Peten

In the southwestern Peten several city-states began fortifying their centers around 760 CE. As warfare accelerated the defenses became ever more formidable. In 2005 a team of archaeologists found the remains of nearly three dozen members of the royal family of Cancuen, all of them murdered and dumped into a shallow pool at the foot of a temple around 800 CE. The ruler, Kan Maax, and his wife were found nearby in shallow graves. Similar events occurred at many other centers over the course of a century. Within seven decades only one center was left and the area was largely depopulated (Demarest et al. 1997).

Copán

Maya cultures were changing, and archaeologists can detect it in many ways. Barbara Fash (1992) has pointed out that there was a remarkable shift in the religious and political symbolism used by the last four rulers of Copán. While rulers 13 and 14 emphasized cosmology and fertility, succeeding rulers 15 and 16 emphasized warfare. The political collapse of Copán city-state was sudden, occurring sometime between 800 and 830 CE, but for the most part the population persisted as it traditionally had for another four centuries (Freter 1992). The population was maintained at its peak during the 750–900 CE period, declining gradually after that (Webster et al. 1992). Although the collapse was sudden from the point of view of the elites and the architects, priests, and artisans they employed, it was much more gradual from the commoner's point of view. The more ecologically vulnerable parts of the valley were

abandoned first, followed by other areas as environmental degradation accelerated (Paine and Freter 1996).

Changing Symbols

Elsewhere in the Peten archaeologists often find effigy **censers** (*incensarios* or incense burners) as part of the ritual paraphernalia associated with elites prior to their political collapse. After divine kingship and the kings that enjoyed it disappeared, censers were made without images and often decorated with spikes. These were used in calendrical rituals that were associated with fire drilling while local populations persisted (Rice 1999). Generally speaking the later Maya appear to have rejected the trappings of a bygone era: the Long Count, the commemoration of rulers on monuments, even polychrome pottery. The shift in symbols marks political collapse for archaeologists.

The Yucatan Peninsula

The collapse was not as pervasive on the Yucatan Peninsula (Figure 7.32). In northwestern Yucatan the population of the city-state of Chunchucmil grew to as much as 60,000, and it was for a time a thriving center of trade. But its very success brought attacks from competitors. Chunchucmil's last major construction was a hastily built 2-km (1.25 mi) barricade that surrounded the city's core. The barricade, which was made of stone taken from nearby buildings and roads, still stands and the structures robbed to construct it were never repaired. Bruce Dahlin (2000) concludes that like other centers having such barricades, Chunchucmil was overrun and then deserted, its inhabitants annihilated or dispersed, never to return.

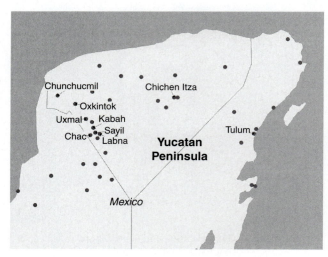

Figure 7.32 Yucatan Maya sites mentioned in the text.

There were once several large autonomous city-states in the Puuc region. They include the sites of Oxkintok, Uxmal, Chac, Sayil, Kabah, and Labna. They did not grow independently, and there was at least indirect influence on their development from as far away as Teotihuacán during 300–600 CE (Smyth and Rogart 2004). Uxmal was politically dominant over the rest during the late ninth century. However, Uxmal lost its grip by 950 CE, and as at all of the other Puuc cities grand elite activities ceased (Dunning and Kowalski 1994).

The city-states centered at the popular tourist sites of Chichén Itzá and Tulum fared better than the Peten centers. Dahlin (2002) argues that this was because people at Chichén Itzá had access to a wider range of nearby resources. Agricultural production did not suffer as much in northern Yucatan, and there were also marine resources along the coast. All of these could be secured through trade and tribute. Here political organization and military power overcame the effects of the environmental disaster.

The case of the Maya collapse provides us with an opportunity to distinguish between proximate and ultimate causation in the evolution of societies. Some archaeologists argue that a tragic event like that at Cancuen or Chunchucmil was just one event in one place, and that we cannot generalize about the Maya collapse from such particulars. Other archaeologists argue that the prolonged drought that some blame for the collapse did not begin until 850 CE and that such an explanation would be too general even if the timing were more convincing. The answer to all critics is that general ecological conditions increased stresses on Maya city-states, which allowed more specific catastrophes to do them in one at a time. Thus the collapse was like an epidemic in which each victim experienced a specific cause of death, but there was nevertheless an overall pattern to the process.

The Maya collapse was thus the sum of many things. Some city-states collapsed politically, but their populations remained in place. Others were overrun, annihilated, and completely abandoned. In still other cases refugee populations migrated to marginal locations that had not been settled previously, where they established new communities (Diamond 2005; Johnston et al. 2001; Webster 2002). In many cases local collapse might have been averted if leaders had been willing to reexamine their core values, for without that willingness they failed to solve even those problems they were able to recognize. Other fatal problems went unperceived, either because they were unprecedented and beyond the realm of prior experience or because

people who might have known better preferred stubborn denial. In the end, the inflexibility of the Maya system contributed to its own undoing.

The Mesoamerican Ball Game

The Mesoamerican ball game was an important feature of Classic Mesoamerican civilization and it left archaeological evidence in the form of ball courts at many of the major sites (Whittington 2001). Radiocarbon dates from an early ball court at a site in coastal Chiapas, Mexico, tell us that the ball game dates back to at least 1400 BCE (Hill et al. 1998). Many later Mesoamerican sites have ball courts, the grandest of which is at the Maya site of Chichén Itzá. They vary considerably in size and shape, but the typical plan is in the shape of the letter *I*, with the primary playing area being in long axis (Figure 7.33). A game called "*pelota mixteca*" survives in Oaxaca, and there are various mentions of ball games in early Spanish documents, but we are not sure exactly how it was played. It is likely that the game, like the ball courts, was quite variable over time and space, much as baseball was in the nineteenth century. Historically there appear to have been at least three major forms of the game, with an unknown number of variations (Taladoire 2003).

In most cases the game was played with a rubber ball made from one or another of the latex-producing plants found all the way from the southeastern rain forests to the northern desert (Filloy Nadal 2001). Most balls were made from the latex sap of the lowland *Castilla elastica* tree. Someone discovered that by mixing latex with sap from the vine of a species of morning glory they could turn the slippery polymers in raw latex into a resilient rubber. This in turn was molded into grapefruit-sized rubber balls having plenty of bounce (Hosler et al. 1999).

Figure 7.33 Ball court at Xochicalco.

Some ball courts, such as at Chichén Itzá and Xochicalco, had stone loops for scoring on either side of the main playing area. Others, such as those at Monte Albán and Tula, lacked them and scoring might have been done by putting the ball in the end zone. In the Aztec version points could also be awarded to the opposite team if a player failed to return the ball after only one bounce or allowed it to go out of bounds (Day 2001). Like soccer, the rules prohibited use of the hands. Players apparently had to advance the ball with their feet, legs, and hips, and there is some evidence of special padding. The stone yoke that is associated with the ball game along the Gulf Coast is probably a form of trophy that mimics hip padding. The stone yokes, *manoplas* (gauntlets), *hachas,* and *palmas* that also are associated with the ball game in that region had less obvious counterparts in ball game equipment (Scott 2001).

There are important linkages between Teotihuacán and the Gulf Coast site of Tajín, as well as between both and the mountain site of Cantona lying between them. Yet while Tajín has 16 ball courts and Cantona has 24, Teotihuacán has none (García Cook and Merino Carrión 1998). What Teotihuacán does have is at least one carved monument that might have served as a goal, raising the possibility that the great Avenue of the Dead was used to play ball games.

Much later the Aztecs demanded thousands of rubber balls in tribute from their rubber-producing province in the topical lowlands. Mexican rubber balls were traded as far north as the U.S. Southwest, where they turn up in association with Hohokam ball courts (see Chapters 6 and 8).

The Rest of Mesoamerica

Other topics and other regions in Classic Mesoamerica have to be largely ignored in a brief summary like this one. No slight is intended. For example, archaeologists and tourists have long been attracted to the major monumental sites of Mesoamerica, but there is a wealth of archaeology in other parts of Mesoamerica as well. West Mexico, a region that sprawls across Nayarit, Jalisco, Colima, Michoacan, and western Guerrero, is known for its shaft tombs and distinctive funerary pottery (Foster and Gorenstein 2000). This was also the region where the small amount of metallurgy done by the Mesoamericans got its start around 650 CE (West 1994). From there the smelting and casting of copper, gold, and silver spread to other Mexican and Maya centers. The same region has sites with public architecture in the distinctive Teuchitlan tradition,

which sometimes turns up in the form of charming ceramic models (Beekman 2000).

In addition, Maya cities were built not just in the Peten and Yucatan lowlands but also in the Guatemalan highlands. Kaminaljuyú was a large site on the outskirts of Guatemala City that is now largely destroyed by urban sprawl, but others remain under investigation. There are architectural features at Kaminaljuyú that are reminiscent of Teotihuacán, causing some archaeologists to propose that it was an outpost of that great city. That view is no longer voiced very often, but no one doubts that Kaminaljuyú was a once grand and powerful center (Kidder et al. 1946). The sudden deposition of volcanic ash around 600 CE on the site of Joya de Cerén in El Salvador preserved the evidence of daily life much as a similar eruption did at Roman Pompeii (Sheets et al. 1990).

On the Gulf Coast of northeastern Mexico the Huastec cousins of the Maya built their own thriving Classic Mesoamerican society. Their territory is closest to the U.S. Southeast, and Mexican archaeologists working in the zone between the two are increasingly finding evidence of contact around the Gulf Coast (see Chapters 9 and 11). Engraved conch shell pectorals from the Huastec homeland around modern Tampico are similar to artifacts found at the Spiro site in Oklahoma and elsewhere in the Southeast (Neurath 1994; Zaragoza Ocaña and Dávila Cabrera 1999). Eccentric flints from Oklahoma similarly have analogs in Mesoamerica (Brain and Phillips 1996; Clements and Reed 1939). Moreover, the site of Tantoc west of Tampico, which dates to around 900 CE, resembles Cahokia (Illinois) more than any Mesoamerican site (Zaragoza Ocaña 2000). Such linkages are certain to receive greater archaeological attention in the future as Mexican and U.S. archaeologists increasingly transcend political and language barriers.

Summary

1. Mesoamerica lies south of the northern desert of Mexico and extends into Central America.

2. The region has two major parts, separated by the Isthmus of Tehuantepec, and each part has highland and lowland components.

3. Tropical plants domesticated in Mesoamerica, especially maize and beans, were the foundation of agriculture there and later in other parts of the continent.

4. Olmec civilization laid the foundation for later Classic city-states and still later empires in Mesoamerica.

5. Olmec chiefdoms were nodes on a widespread trade network in luxury goods.

6. Olmec writing and calendrics were among the early developments that presaged later hieroglyphic systems of Classic Maya culture.

7. Classic cultures appeared later in highland Mexican centers and in the Maya lowlands.

8. Teotihuacán grew rapidly in the Basin of Mexico after Cuicuilco suffered the effects of a volcanic eruption.

9. A huge urban center based on state-level organization was centered at Teotihuacán, which is well known for its monumental architecture.

10. Teotihuacán declined suddenly around 550 CE, and newer centers like Xochicalco and Cholula emerged.

11. A Zapotec center formed at San José Mogote in the Valley of Oaxaca, but it was supplanted by the Classic center at Monte Albán.

12. The Monte Albán site reflects both Olmec heritage and links to the Maya region.

13. Maya city-states arose in the hot rain forest of the Peten region.

14. The Maya took writing and calendrics to levels not achieved elsewhere in Mesoamerica.

15. Of the many Classic Maya centers, Tikal, Palenque, Yaxchilan, and Copán are particularly noteworthy.

16. Maya centers collapsed politically and in some places ecologically in the Peten region during the course of the ninth century CE.

17. The Mesoamerican ball game was an important feature of many Mesoamerican centers.

Further Reading

The best recent synthesis of Mesoamerican archaeology is Susan Evans's *Ancient Mexico and Central America: Archaeology and Culture History*. An excellent summary covering the Maya and their demise is David Webster's *The Fall of the Ancient Maya: Solving the Mystery of the Maya Collapse*. Arthur Demarest's *Ancient Maya: The Rise and Fall of a Rainforest Civilization* is another. Jared Diamond provides a nice summary of societal collapse in *Collapse: How Societies Choose to Fail or Succeed,* and Schartz and Nichols have explored how such societies regenerate in their book *After Collapse*. Richard Diehl's *The Olmecs: America's First Civilization* is an excellent introduction to Mesoamerica's mother culture. A general introduction by Alfredo López Austin, Leonardo López Luján, and Bernard Ortize de Montellano is now out in both Spanish (*El Pasado Indigena*) and English (*Mexico's Indigenous Past*). The multivolume *Handbook of Middle American Indians* is no longer current but contains many fundamental chapters. Some of these and many other more specific sources can be found in the "References" section at the end of this book.

Glossary

censer: An incense burner.

Chichimec: Any of the hunter-gatherer people of northern Mexico.

chinampa: Large, raised agricultural beds in swampy land.

city-state: A state polity built around a city and its immediate environs.

codex (pl. codices): An ancient manuscript book.

epigraphy: The study of inscriptions.

karst: A limestone landscape characterized by many caves and sinkholes.

milpa: A Maya agricultural clearing.

stela (pl. stelae): A free-standing stone monument bearing inscriptions.

swidden: A form of shifting agriculture involving field rotation and long fallow periods.

talud and tablero: A Mexican architectural style featuring a flat panel (tablero) above a sloping lower wall (talud).

vigesimal: A counting system based on units of 20.

Postclassic Mesoamerica

There are forty towers at the least, all of stout construction and very lofty, the largest of which has fifty steps leading up to its base; this chief one is indeed higher than the great church of Seville.

Hernando Cortés (1962:90)

Introduction

The passing of the Classic civilizations was followed by the rise of many new city-states, some of which grew to become impressive empires. The transition began as early as 600 CE in some places. In highland Mexico the Toltec city-state arose first, followed by the Aztec one that grew into an empire. The Aztecs are better known because they survived into the sixteenth century. Their capital was Tenochtitlán, now Mexico City, which began as a pair of small city-states on a swampy island in Lake Texcoco. Aztec religion involved a complex pantheon of deities and frequent human sacrifice. Their calendars were simplified versions of those used earlier by the Classic Maya and other Mesoamericans. The Aztec Empire depended upon elaborate military expeditions, state religion, trade, and tribute, features common to empires everywhere. The empire eventually expanded to both coasts of Mexico, but failed to conquer some obstinate city-states closer to the center. Some of those unconquered enemies joined with Spanish invaders to defeat the armies of Tenochtitlán, and Mexico became a tributary of Spain by 1521.

The Postclassic Period

The period following the collapse of Classic polities in highland Mexico and the lowland Maya region and lasting until the Spanish conquest is usually referred to as the Postclassic (Figure 8.1). Of course it did not begin everywhere at once. For that matter it did not end everywhere at once either, for the Spanish conquest was a process, not a single event. In the Mexican highlands the Postclassic is usually broken into two smaller periods,

the Early Postclassic dominated by the Toltecs and the Late Postclassic by the Aztecs. These terms share the same temporal fuzziness, but they are handy and remain popular with archaeologists (Smith and Berdan 2003).

The Toltecs

The rise of the Toltecs played out in the context of ecological and demographic change that brought new people into central Mexico and put an end to the dominance of Classic city-states (Manzanilla 2005). The Toltec capital was Tula, a center on the fringe of the desert that was probably initially founded around 700 CE as a lime-producing community. Agriculture here at the northern edge of the Basin of Mexico required irrigation. With the addition of Nahuatl-speaking immigrants from farther north, forced southward by

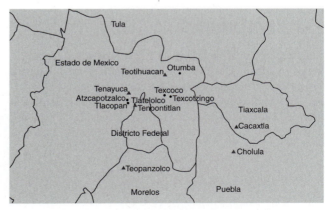

Figure 8.1 Sites of the Mesoamerican Postclassic mentioned in this chapter.

Figure 8.2 Tula. Note the colonnades and atlantid pillars atop the main pyramid.

climate change, Tula (Figure 8.2) developed into a full-blown city-state of around 60,000 people during 900–1175 CE. This was long after Teotihuacán had been burned (Mastache et al. 2002).

The architects of Tula drew upon ideas that were shared across a long strip of Mesoamerica that extended from the Basin of Mexico to the northern Yucatan Peninsula (Ringle et al. 1998). Their tastes ran to modest pyramids, ball courts, and spacious colonnaded halls. Low reliefs of jaguars, eagles, and warriors decorated the walls of their principal sites. Although a few still undeciphered glyphs have been found, written inscriptions were not their passion.

Trade and exchange expanded in the years of Tula's ascendancy. Turquoise was imported from the U.S. Southwest (Weigand 1994). Copper, shell, and even live macaws went northward in exchange.

Much information about the Toltecs survived into the colonial period as oral traditions. However, these sources are selective and highly mythologized. Historians who study **ethnohistory,** have used sources arising from oral traditions, testing them in various ways to separate dependable fact from the self-serving embroidery that such sources invariably have. What emerges is a picture with a few clear features that fill out what is known from archaeology. As we might expect, Toltec royal families were rife with political intrigue. They probably maintained standing armies and had true state organization with dual sacred and secular leadership. But there was, inevitably, conflict between these two branches of Toltec government (Davies 1977).

Under their system of government the Toltec secular leader could pass his office on to his son, while the sacred leader could not. One tradition that might be authentic tells of the sacred leader Mixcoatl, who tried to pass his office on to his son, Ce Acatl Quetzalcoatl, a man known for his opposition to human sacrifice. The secular leaders, who had a more enthusiastic attitude about human sacrifice, opposed Mixcoatl in his efforts to name his son as his successor, as well as for other reasons. The result was that Quetzalcoatl was forced into exile, moving first to Cholula and later to the Tabasco area. With this victory the secular side at Tula took over, and both militarism and human sacrifice increased as a result.

The Toltecs flourished until around 1175 CE, probably incorporating people from a variety of regional cultures. These included speakers of Nahuatl, Otomi, Huastec, Mazateco-Popoloca, and probably other languages. Tula never grew to the size of Teotihuacán, and its residential areas never had the regular compound design found at the great Classic city.

The public art at Tula reveals the Toltecs turned toward militarism and human sacrifice. Panels on the side of the main pyramid depict jaguars and eagles, the latter tearing at human hearts. A free-standing wall depicts serpents and human skulls. The main pillars of the temple atop the pyramid were sculpted to represent warriors.

The patterns established by the Toltecs would continue for another three centuries, until the coming of the Spanish. Tula fell in an early round of the cyclical warfare that eventually brought the Aztecs to prominence, but although they disappeared into history, they remained in Mexican consciousness as ancient ideals, ancestors possessed of nobility that later leaders would seek to claim as their heritage. This, too, is a characteristic of empires everywhere.

The Rise of the Aztecs

The Aztecs (Mexica) are worth studying because their society was still intact when the Spanish arrived and consequently we have documents that record sixteenth-century history as well as versions of what was then fresh oral tradition to supplement archaeological evidence (Nicholson and Kerber 1983; Solis 2004). Much of the evidence we have for the Aztec Empire and the Triple Alliance of Tenochtitlán, Texcoco, and Tlacopan (Tacuba) comes from sources written late in the sixteenth century, decades after the Spanish conquest (Berdan et al. 1994; Carrasco 1999). Gillespie (1998) has argued that the imperial alliance was concocted by later chroniclers for the glorification of native Mexican culture. An even more extreme view might be that the sources in question are little more than dubious oral propaganda that was later written down as factual history. But the lack of compelling evidence to disqualify the relevant chronicles leads most scholars to assume them to be credible so long as they survive testing by various other means (Davies 1973; Hassig 1988, 2001; Smith 1996).

The Aztecs said that they came from a mythical Aztlan "Place of the Herons" far to the north. Nineteenth-century enthusiasts looked for Aztlan in places as far removed as New Mexico and Wisconsin, but it appears more likely that the traditional roots of the Aztecs stretch only as far as the parts of northwestern Mexico where Uto-Aztecan languages are still spoken today (see Chapter 6).

There is probably no single place of origin, but rather a region from which various tribes speaking the Nahuatl language came during and following the collapse of the Toltecs around 1175 CE. The ecological reasons for their movement remain uncertain, but major demographic shifts of this kind typically occur after favorable conditions prompt population increases and subsequent unfavorable conditions force relocations. The Medieval Maximum, which produced warm conditions favorable to farmers across much of the Northern Hemisphere from 850 to 1250 CE, might have been the ultimate cause. In highland Mexico conditions were cooler and drier after 900 CE, and this led to both a drop in the levels of the lakes there and an increase in their productivity (Berres 2000). If droughts were at the same time a problem on the northern desert, then people had both carrots and sticks as reasons to relocate. Whatever the specific impetus, ancestral Aztecs were prompted to abandon the agriculturally undependable margins of the northern Mexican desert. Northern Mexico was the domain of the Chichimecs, the Nahuatl word for barbarians, and at least some of the ancestry of the later Aztecs included them.

The tribes, at least 17 of them, drifted in as three waves, along the well-worn trade roads that connected central Mexico and the U.S. Southwest. The first set settled near the large lakes of the Basin of Mexico around 1200 CE. The second wave settled in surrounding valleys of the central highlands, places like Tlaxcala, Morelos, and the Estado de Mexico around 1220 CE (Figure 8.3). The people who called themselves the Mexica were the last to arrive around 1250 CE. It was the Mexica, whom we call Aztecs, that eventually formed the core of Mesoamerica's last great pre-Hispanic empire.

By the time the Mexica arrived all the best real estate was spoken for, so they settled on an undesirable hill known as Chapultepec "Grasshopper Hill." The details are laid out in a series of contradictory rags-to-riches legends, the time line often adjusted after the fact so

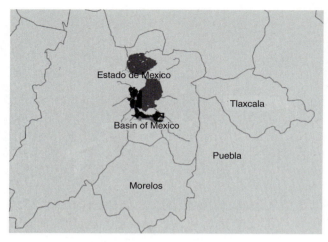

Figure 8.3 Destinations of Nahuatl-speaking migrants to the Basin of Mexico.

that major events were brought into line with solar eclipses (Aveni and Calnek 1999). And while they liked to talk about their humble origins, the ancestral Mexica were already skilled farmers and townspeople who had their own architectural style. In contrast to most earlier ones their pyramids had twin temples and double staircases. Good early examples survive at Tenayuca and Teopanzolco. The Great Temple (Templo Mayor) that was eventually built at the center of their capital of Tenochtitlán, modern Mexico City, continued in this same style through all of its expansions and renovations.

The Mexica began as subjects to various city-states in the valley, interacting with the existing powers in a complex and often sordid history, like many other dynastic histories of the time around the world. They were widely regarded as bad neighbors, mainly because of their brutal and repugnant religious practices. They fled more than once from the armies of outraged kings of nearby city-states (Figure 8.4), and they ended up retreating to an island in swampy Lake Texcoco in 1325. There they were secure and able to rebuild their fractured alliances.

It was there that the Mexica founded the cities of Tenochtitlán and Tlatelolco on an island no one else wanted. Afterward they claimed that they were led there by an eagle that landed on a cactus with a snake in its beak, a symbol that still adorns the Mexican flag. It turned out ironically to be a near-perfect location. The surrounding water provided a natural moat to deter attackers while at the same time it gave the Mexica easy canoe access to vast rich chinampas (Figure 8.5) around the island and on the southern margin of the lake (Armillas 1971; Sanders 2004). The Mexica

Figure 8.4 Basin of Mexico and the city-states of the Triple Alliance:
Tenochtitlán, Tacuba, and Texcoco.

Figure 8.5 Chinampas on the southern margin of Lake Texcoco.

eventually built a 13-km (8-mi) dike east of their island to separate the productive freshwater southern section from the more brackish northern water. The dike raised the level of the western and southern parts of the great lake and gradually freshened it. The Mexica prospered and grew in numbers, but they remained politically subservient to other stronger city-states, particularly the Tepanecs of Azcapotzalco.

A succession of six emperors from Itzcoatl to Motecuhzoma II built the empire by attacking and subjugating tributary city-states and smaller centers one at a time. It was a messy process that is not easily summarized (Figure 8.6). Acamapichtili founded a Mexica dynasty as the first tlatoani "king" of a politically independent Tenochtitlán. He and his successors engaged in the kind of dynastic intrigues that characterize monarchies throughout human history. Intermarriage with other royal lineages and claims of Toltec ancestry served them well.

A successful war made the Texcoco city-state subject to Tenochtitlán. Netzahuacoyotl was king of Texcoco in its heyday, having survived his father's death in battle and a few years of exile. Unlike the Mexica rulers his interests were in music, poetry, and the arts rather than in warfare and human sacrifice. He ordered the construction of beautiful gardens and baths on the hill of Texcotzingo east of the city-state, where tubs hewn from solid rock can still be seen (Figure 8.7).

Succeeding Mexica kings also ended the independence of Tlatelolco, the island's commercial center, and set out to systematically subjugate city-states beyond the Basin of Mexico. By 1519 they had an empire that stretched from coast to coast (Figure 8.8).

By the time the Spanish arrived in 1519 Tenochtitlán had been filled, raised, and expanded to an island city of 12–15 km² (4.6–5.8 mi²). Causeways with draw

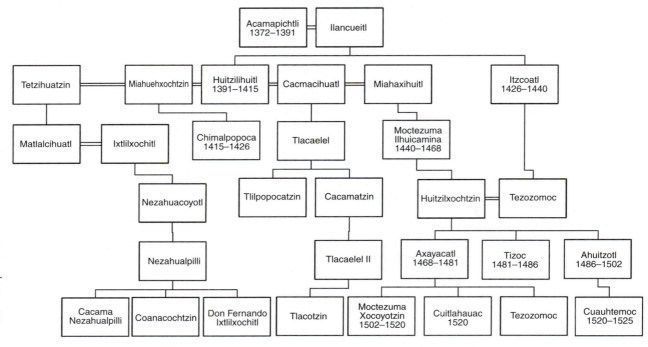

Figure 8.6 The Mexica dynasty showing the succession of Aztec emperors and their reigns.

Figure 8.7 A bath cut in solid bedrock at Texcotzingo.

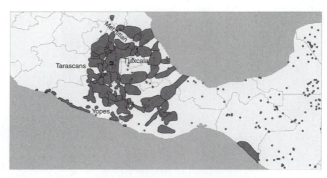

Figure 8.8 The Aztec Empire in 1519. Provinces are shown as independent units except for those in the Basin of Mexico, which have been simplified to a single unit.
Source: From Berdan et al. 1994.

bridges linked the island capital to the mainland and aqueducts brought fresh water to the city's inhabitants. About 80 buildings comprised the walled ceremonial core of the city. They included temples, palaces, dormitories, ball courts, skull trophy racks, clubhouses, and platforms for dancing and ritual combat. There were gardens and even a zoo.

From all accounts the palaces were splendid residences for the elites. They were much larger than earlier ones, and Moctezuma's residence was 2.4 hectares (6 acres) in size, dwarfing even that largest residential compound at Teotihuacán (Evans 2004). Most people lived in residential wards called "calpulli."

The conquistador Bernal Diaz del Castillo spoke for all of the astonished Spaniards under the command of Cortés. "When we saw all those cities and villages built in the water, and other great towns on dry land, and that straight and level causeway leading to [Tenochtitlán], we were astounded. These great towns and [pyramids] and buildings rising from the water, all made of stone, seemed like an enchanted vision from the tale of Amadis. Indeed, some of our soldiers asked whether it was not all a dream. . . . It was all so wonderful that I do not know how to describe this first glimpse of things never heard of, seen or dreamed of before" (Diaz del Castillo 1963:214).

Aztec Society and Empire

Aztec society was stratified, and in this case we know quite a bit about its details. The Aztec Tlatoani king and other members of the nobility formed a hereditary top rank of society. Commoners or "macehualtin" were the farmers, craft specialists, and artisans that lived in the residential calpulli of Tenochtitlán and did the work of the city. They owed both taxes and service to the lords in the noble class and in exchange they received protection and basic services. Skilled artisans could rise to high positions even if they were not of noble birth, and those that chose to become warriors could rise to quasi-noble rank through extraordinary military achievement.

Traders called "pochteca" were the richest commoners. The pochteca traveled long distances to acquire luxury goods for the nobility, and they sometimes got rich in the process. They had the right to own slaves, and this afforded them much of the lifestyle of the nobility. At the opposite end of society were the mayeque, destitute commoners who were bound to noble lords like European serfs. The lowest of the low were the tlacotin, people who had fallen into servitude through debt. The Spanish thought they were slaves, but they could own property and buy their way out of servitude if their fortunes improved. Their children were born free of debt in any case, so the idea of hereditary slavery was foreign to the Aztecs.

The Growth of Empire

The Aztec Empire grew first by Tenochtitlán's alliance with or conquest of other city-states in the Basin of Mexico. Much of what we know about its development

Box 8.1 HOW TO GET A DATE IN MESOAMERICA

The Maya Long Count is very much like our Julian period, which is a simple day count used mainly by astronomers. Joseph Scaliger was a sixteenth-century biblical scholar who invented the Julian period in 1582. This is a chronological system that is based on the consecutive numbering of days beginning with January 1, 4713 BCE. The Julian period is useful for anyone trying to manage correlations between alternative calendars because it assigns a unique serial number to every day.

There are several online programs for finding any date in our system in the Maya calendar. These can be accessed by simply searching on "Maya calendar." Most of these let the user work from either calendar to the other and to use the Julian period, Gregorian dates, the Maya Calendar Round, and the Maya Long Count. Try the program at http://www.michielb.nl/maya/calendar.html. A more colorful one can be found at http://www.pauahtun.org/Calendar/tools.html. The latter also provides correlation with the Julian period day.

Earlier in the twentieth century there were three alternative correlations of the Long Count with the Gregorian calendar, two of them having a minor range of nearly identical alternatives. They were dependent mainly upon Long Count dates that referenced astronomical events that were also dated according to the Gregorian calendar. These were revised and combined as research progressed and by midcentury the Goodman-Thompson-Martinez was preferred by most scholars. This correlation was subsequently supported by radiocarbon dates.

The later Aztec calendar was a simplified derivative version in which Nahuatl names substitute for the Maya names. The Mexica (Aztecs) did not use the Long Count, so one has to figure out which 52-year cycle any date belongs to by means of other contextual clues. An online program at http://www.azteccalendar.com/calendar-calculator.html is a good place to begin. This program provides the Julian period day, making it possible to move easily between the Aztec, Maya, Gregorian, and other calendars.

comes from fifteenth-century documents that rescued oral tradition from oblivion. These were written after 1520 by both Spanish chroniclers and Mexican authors who were literate in both Spanish and their native languages. Those of us who are not Native Americans are so accustomed to stories of royal lineages, palace intrigues, alliances formed through marriages of convenience, epic battles, and all the lust, betrayal, bravery, and deceit that goes with it all that it may escape our notice that the Aztecs and their American predecessors came to these Shakespearean ends quite independently. Here again the evidence tells us that there is something fundamentally human going on in the politics of states the world over. When Moctezuma and Cortés confronted one another in 1519, as different as their backgrounds were they recognized each other and their settings for what they were. Their cultures were not all that different despite utterly separate developmental trajectories that began thousands of years earlier.

Figure 8.8 shows the Basin of Mexico as a single unit, one of many provinces of the empire, although we know that the rise of Tenochtitlán to dominance in that relatively small theater was itself a long and complex process involving many city-state alliances and conquests. There were probably about 1.5 million people living in this core province by the time of the Spanish conquest. Arrayed around the Basin of Mexico are 55 more provinces that eventually came under the control of the Mexica of Tenochtitlán. The first Moctezuma expanded all the way to the Gulf Coast. Axayacatl and Tizoc extended it there and westward in the highlands. Ahuitzotl expanded to the Pacific Coast and eastwards toward Tehuantepec. This was, in aggregate, the Aztec Empire as it existed when the Spanish arrived.

Each outer province shown in Figure 8.8 had a provincial capital from which the Mexica wielded power over perhaps 3.33 million people (Sanders et al. 1970). Each province contained one or more formerly independent city-states, and each city-state typically had several nonstate centers and subject towns. The conquest of a provincial capital did not necessarily mean that all city-states within the province or even all the towns subject to a city-state became tributaries of the empire, and the historical record shows that it sometimes took the long-term efforts of all six emperors to finally subjugate an entire province. Frances Berdan and her colleagues (1994) have detailed this long and complex process, and their work replaces the oversimplified version found in the works of Robert Barlow (1949) and the many secondary publications that have depended upon him. The city-states that comprised a province were not necessarily contiguous,

but separated in space by other provinces or geographic barriers. That is why there are more than 55 territories shown on Figure 8.8. In addition, there were many city-states that the Mexica did not manage to conquer, despite persistent efforts. Tlaxcala and various Tarascan polities are particularly famous for having resisted conquest. Each of the hundreds of provincial capitals, cities, and towns left an archaeological site, and many of them are still imposing.

The Mexica used the techniques common to all empires to hold on to their conquests. Garrisons were installed in recalcitrant provincial centers. Hostages were taken and held for years. Some conquered city-state leaders gave their daughters in marriage to Mexica nobles and thereby survived as subject rulers. Others were executed and replaced by appointed puppet rulers. The rich complex history of the Aztec Empire is preserved in them archaeologically to some extent, but it is clear that without fifteenth-century documentation we would not be able to discern more than the crudest outlines of the processes through which Tenochtitlán came to dominate most of pre-Hispanic Mexico.

Imperial Warfare

Aztec armies typically fought as highly decorated, massed infantry units (Anawalt 1992). Warriors wore elaborate armored costumes and fought at close quarters using wooden slashing swords that were edged with razor-sharp obsidian blades. While the goal of the Aztec leaders might have been to expand the empire and acquire more tribute, the goal of the individual soldiers was to fight well and capture enemy soldiers for sacrifice. Although they had the bow and arrow, unlike most North American cultures they had retained the spear thrower (**atlatl**) and used it as a military weapon. The reason was the effectiveness of Aztec armor. Special atlatl units of the army loosed clouds of spears at opposing armies, over the heads of their own advancing infantry. The spears could penetrate armor that would have stopped arrows.

Some wars might have been largely ceremonial, or at least explained away as such if the outcome was not up to expectations. Aztec armies often attacked but rarely defeated the armies of the Tlaxcalans or the Tarascans. Contests with these city-states were called "flowery wars," spectacular war games in which neither side prevailed. Aztec soldiers went home to report that they could have beaten the Tlaxcalans if they had really wanted to, and the Tlaxcalans went home to claim invincibility. They were locked in this military stalemate when the Spanish arrived, and the result was that the Tlaxcalans joined the Spanish and made the conquest possible.

Aztec Religion

Like the formal religions of all early civilizations, the religion of the Aztecs was a powerful tradition in the service of political objectives. Archaeologists are often left with little information to interpret the symbolically charged artifacts, art, and architecture ancient civilizations left behind, but in this case we have a rich documentary record. Another problem is that modern scholars sometimes assume that the basics of later transcendental monotheistic religion also characterized early religious beliefs and practices. But the religions of early civilizations tended to pervade all aspects of daily life, and to allow for multiple deities that often interacted with one another like humans (Trigger 2003:409–443). The very human behaviors that spice up Greek mythology are typical, and they have similarly larger-than-life parallels in Aztec mythology.

The Aztecs' view of the world, like that of the Egyptians and other early civilizations, was imbued with religious overtones. It was steeped in metaphor and ordered by pervasive dualism: life–death, male–female, light–dark, fire–water, and so forth. The only simple concept was that of teotl "deity" or "sacred power," a status that they initially attributed even to the strange-looking Spanish invaders. Beyond that basic concept Aztec cosmology becomes bewilderingly complex. The crowded pantheon of gods was presided over by Ometeotl, who was both male "Ometecuhtli" and female "Omecihuatl." Other gods were often paired for one reason or another. Table 8.1 summarizes the Aztec pantheon.

Table 8.1 Simplified pantheon of principal (bold) and some minor Aztec deities.

Name	Gender	Domain	Translated Name
Celestial Gods			
Ometeotl (2)	♂ ♀	Supreme	Dual God
Tezcatlipoca	♂	Warrior	Smoking Mirror
Xiuhtecuhtli	♂	Fire	Turquoise Lord
Huehueteotl	♂	Fire	Old God
Chantico	♀	Fire	In the House
Coyolxauhqui	♀	Moon	Painted with Bells
Tecziztecatl	♂	Moon	Conch Shell Lord
Rain and Fertility Gods			
Tlaloc	♂	Rain	Rain
Chalchiuhtlicue	♂	Water	Jade Skirt
Centeotl	♂	Maize	Maize Ear God
Xochipilli	♂	Flowers	Flower Prince
Ometochtli	♂	Maguey and Pulque	Dual Rabbits
Xipe Totec	♂	Agriculture	Our Flayed Lord
Tlazolteotl	♀	Filth	Filth Goddess
Xilonon	♀	Young Maize	Young Maize Ear Doll
Xochiquetzal	♀	Beauty and Love	Flower Quetzal Feather
Coatlicue	♀	Flowers	Serpent Skirt

(*continued*)

Table 8.1 (*continued*)

Name	Gender	Domain	Translated Name
Rain and Fertility Gods			
Huehuecoyotl	♂	Lust	Old Coyote
Pahtecatl	♂	Fertility	Medicine Lord
Xololtl	♂	Twins and Monsters	Monster
Teteoinnan	♀	Earth and Fertility	Mother of Gods
Cihuacoatl	♀	Earth Mother	Woman Serpent
Cihuateteo	♀	Death in Childbirth	Woman Gods
War and Sacrifice Gods			
Tonatiuh	♂	Sun	Sun
Huitzilopochtli	♂	Warrior	Hummingbird Left
Mixcoatl	♂	War, Sacrifice, Hunting	Cloud Serpent
Mictlantecuhtli	♂	Underworld (Death)	Underworld Lord
Quetzalcoatl	♂	Creativity and Fertility	Quetzal Feather Serpent
Tlahuizcalpantecuhtli	♀	Venus	House of Dawn Lord
Mictlancihuatl	♀	Underworld (Death)	Underworld Lady
Tlaltecuhtli	♂	Earth (Death)	Earth Lord
Ehecatl	♂	Wind	Wind
Yacatecuhtli	♂	Commerce	Nose Lord

Sources: Davies 1973:306–307; Nicholson 1971:Table 3.

There were patrons for nearly every craft or profession and even gods for filth (Tlazolteotl) and lust (Huehuecoyotl). Gods listed in Table 8.1 are merely those most likely to be encountered in reading or at archaeological sites. There are literally dozens more; Henry Nicholson (1971) inventoried 129. Each was assigned a domain of jurisdiction and each had a place in the 260-day ritual calendar. Thirteen were lords of daylight, while 9 were lords of darkness. They could transform themselves from one deity to another, take alternative names, become more than one at the same time, and some were thought of as versions of others.

Aztec cosmology was thus capable of endless elaboration. For example, Ometochtli was the patron god of pulque, the alcoholic beverage made from maguey sap, but it hardly ended there. Pulque was identified with the souls of dead warriors and the stars of the night sky (Taube 1993). Each of these had other connections, so one could work through the whole cosmology by following links, much as one can today follow unexpected links through the vast Internet.

The Aztecs thought that sacrifice to the gods was required to keep the world working. The most spectacular sacrifices involved cutting beating hearts from living people, but there were also frequent sacrifices of less dramatic kind. Auto-sacrifice might involve the voluntary letting of ones own blood or some other relatively minor act. What was important was the symbolic unity of the sacrificed, the sacrificer, and the god for whom it was all being done. Probably the most astonishing of these practices was that performed in honor of Xipe Totec, "Our Lord the Flayed One." The sacrificial victim was flayed as an ear of corn might be husked and the presiding priest dressed in the flayed skin, an act that unified them both with Xipe Totec and supposedly helped with agricultural productivity (Figure 8.9).

Figure 8.9 Panel 14 from the Codex Borbonicus depicting a priest impersonating Xipe Totec. The priest wears the skin of a sacrificed victim whose hands dangle from the priest's wrists.
Sources: Courtesy of Akademishe Druck-u. Verlagsanstalt.

Figure 8.10 The Coyolxauhqui monument, Great Temple of Tenochtitlán.

Tenochtitlán

The Great Temple of Tenochtitlán was a mound of rubble under colonial buildings until 1978, but a discovery in that year changed the archaeology of Mexico City dramatically. The pyramid had been razed by the Spanish at their earliest opportunity, torn down to make way for the great cathedral that now stands across the street. In 1978 the southwest corner of the pyramid had been visible for decades in a vacant lot northeast of the cathedral, so it was clear that its destruction centuries earlier had not been complete. Rubble from the upper portions covered and protected the lower parts of the 1519 pyramid and the earlier versions of it buried within.

In 1978 electrical workers uncovered an enormous stone disk 3.25 m (10.5 ft) in diameter. The stone turned out to depict the nude dismembered body of the goddess Coyolxauhqui (Figure 8.10), and its discovery caused a sensation. It provided the impetus needed to get the Mexican government to provide the *Instituto Nacional de Anthropologia e Historia (INAH)* with a mandate to acquire all the property where the Great Temple had once stood, remove the

colonial buildings, and excavate the surviving lower portions of the temple and surrounding structures (Serrato-Combe 2001).

Archaeologists found seven major episodes of temple construction, each one covering and preserving earlier structures. The colossal weight of it all deformed the soft lake sediments on which the whole city of Tenochtitlán was built, and both the ruins of the Great Temple and the palaces surrounding it now slouch at strange angles, but all of it is currently stabilized and on view (Figure 8.11). The pyramid always had a double staircase, and at the top were two temples, the one to the north dedicated to Tlaloc and the one on the south to Huitzilopochtli. The Epoch II version was buried deeply enough to be well preserved, complete with a colorful Chacmool statue reclined in front of the Tlaloc temple.

Lavish offerings were found in several places, some having been placed on the steps of earlier structures that were covered up by additions and renovations (López Luján 2005). One life-sized pottery figure of an Eagle Warrior stands nearly 2 m (79 in) tall. Some objects were apparently made locally, but others were luxury items that came from provinces of the far-flung Aztec Empire. Most of the pieces found, including the original Coyolxauhqui stone, are now housed in the new museum constructed for that purpose on the grounds of the Great Temple. Outside visitors can now see the details of the lower portions of all seven of the

Figure 8.11 Excavated surviving portions of the Great Temple (Templo Mayor) of Tenochtitlán.

Figure 8.12 The Mexica Calendar Stone, which can be seen today in the National Museum of Anthropology in Mexico City.

nested temple structures (López Portillo et al. 1981; Serrato-Combe 2001).

Aztec Calendar and Math

Aztec calendrics and mathematics inherited the standard elements of Mesoamerican calendrics, but the Mexica modified them for their own purposes. The great calendar stone is today a national icon, the centerpiece of the National Museum of Anthropology and a common feature on Mexican coins and currency (Figure 8.12). The face of a principal god is at the center of the stone, surrounded by the movement symbol (Ollin) and four panels representing the four previous ages of the world. The next ring contains the 20 day names beginning with Cipactli (crocodile) and progressing counter clockwise. Two serpents comprise the outermost ring, their jaws meeting at the bottom and their tails separated at the top (east) by a 13-Cane numeral, which dates the carving of the stone to 1479 CE (Matos Moctezuma and Solís 2004).

The key to understanding the Mexica calendrical system is the Tonalpohualli, the 260-day ritual calendar that was equivalent to the Maya Tzolkin calendar. The two were used in the same way, by simultaneously counting off 20 day names and 13 numbers (Table 8.2). Day 1-Acatl (meaning "cane" or "reed") was followed by 2-Ocelotl "jaguar," 3-Cuauhtli "eagle," and so on through 13-Malinalli "herb" (Day 260), at which point one began again with 1-Acatl. One's birthday in

this calendar was part of one's name, and it carried with it divinatory predictions in much the same way as astrological predictions did in Europe.

The Tonalpohualli cycled with the separate solar calendar and any date in one fell on a particular date in the other every 52 years, just as in the earlier Maya calendar. However, the Mexica did not use the Long Count, so figuring out which 52-year cycle a particular date falls in depends upon archaeological or documentary context.

The Mexica used a simple method to identify solar years, which in their system probably began in early April. As it happens, if one repeatedly counts forward 365 days in the 260-day calendar one lands on one or another of only four different day names. In other words, the first day in the solar year is always on one of only four days in the ritual calendar, so these can be used in combination with the 13 numerals to name each solar year in the 52-year cycle (4 × 13 = 52). The first year of a new 52-year cycle was named for the first day in the 260-day calendar, 1-Acatl. Counting forward 365 days in the ritual calendar brings one to 2-Tecpatl. Another 365 days brings one to 3-Calli, another to 4-Tochtli, another to 5-Acatl, and so forth. Each of the four names appears just once with each of the 13 numerals. The last year in the cycle will be 13-Tochtli, by which time 52 years will have passed (Caso 1971). One can demonstrate the sequence using

Table 8.2 The Mexica Tonalpohualli, or 260-day ritual calendar shown as a permutation of twenty day names and thirteen numbers. Solar year names are shown in bold. Counting forward 365 days from the first day (1-Acatl) brings one to 2-Tecpatl. The next cycle of 365 days corresponds to 3-Calli and the next to 4-Tochtli.

Acatl	1	8	2	9	3	10	4	11	5	12	6	13	7
Ocelotl	2	9	3	10	4	11	5	12	6	13	7	1	8
Cuauhtli	3	10	4	11	5	12	6	13	7	1	8	2	9
Cozcacuauhtli	4	11	5	12	6	13	7	1	8	2	9	3	10
Ollin	5	12	6	13	7	1	8	2	9	3	10	4	11
Tecpatl	6	13	7	1	8	**2**	9	3	10	4	11	5	12
Quiahuitl	7	1	8	2	9	3	10	4	11	5	12	6	13
Xochitl	8	2	9	3	10	4	11	5	12	6	13	7	1
Cipactli	9	3	10	4	11	5	12	6	13	7	1	8	2
Ehecatl	10	4	11	5	12	6	13	7	1	8	2	9	3
Calli	11	5	12	6	13	7	1	8	2	9	3	10	4
Cuetzpallin	12	6	13	7	1	8	2	9	3	10	4	11	5
Coatl	13	7	1	8	2	9	3	10	4	11	5	12	6
Miquiztli	1	8	2	9	3	10	4	11	5	12	6	13	7
Mazatl	2	9	3	10	4	11	5	12	6	13	7	1	8
Tochtli	3	10	**4**	11	5	12	6	13	7	1	8	2	9
Atl	4	11	5	12	6	13	7	1	8	2	9	3	10
Itzcuintli	5	12	6	13	7	1	8	2	9	3	10	4	11
Ozomatli	6	13	7	1	8	2	9	3	10	4	11	5	12
Malinalli	7	1	8	2	9	3	10	4	11	5	12	6	13

a modern deck of cards because they also use four sets (suits) of 13. Table 8.3 shows 20 of the 52 possible combinations identifying specific years in the 52-year cycle and their correlations with some years in our modern Gregorian calendar that we use today.

There is more to the Mexica calendar. Each year, each 13-day period, and each day is associated with one or more gods and various prognostications. The surviving divinatory books are full of colorful guides to all of this and associated rituals. As if the puzzle were not already sufficiently complicated it turns out that different city-states in the Basin of Mexico used somewhat different calendars. The terms used were generally the same, but the starting years varied, making correlation difficult.

Native Books

Mesoamerican books do not survive in large numbers but their contents are crucial for filling out our knowledge of calendrics, ritual, religion, and history. When the Spanish arrived in Mesoamerica they found many examples of pictorial writing in the form of books called codices (singular codex). Several Mesoamerican cultures had scribes that produced unique documents in long strips, which they screen-folded, a form intermediate between the scroll form and the bound book form. The American codices were often produced with vivid color illustrations on bark paper or deer hide, and their contents were often ritual, calendrical, and quasi-historical. They were largely pictorial rather

Table 8.3 A portion of the 52-year cycle showing the Mexica year names and some equivalents in our modern calendar.

	Nahuatl	Spanish	English	Corresponding Years CE				
1	Acatl	Caña	Cane	1311	1363	1415	1467	1519
2	Tecpatl	Pedernal	Stone	1312	1364	1416	1468	1520
3	Calli	Casa	House	1313	1365	1417	1469	1521
4	Tochtli	Conejo	Rabbit	1314	1366	1418	1470	1522
5	Acatl	Caña	Cane	1315	1367	1419	1471	1523
6	Tecpatl	Pedernal	Stone	1316	1368	1420	1472	1524
7	Calli	Casa	House	1317	1369	1421	1473	1525
8	Tochtli	Conejo	Rabbit	1318	1370	1422	1474	1526
9	Acatl	Caña	Cane	1319	1371	1423	1475	1527
10	Tecpatl	Pedernal	Stone	1320	1372	1424	1476	1528
11	Calli	Casa	House	1321	1373	1425	1477	1529
12	Tochtli	Conejo	Rabbit	1322	1374	1426	1478	1530
13	Acatl	Caña	Cane	1323	1375	1427	1479	1531
1	Tecpatl	Pedernal	Stone	1324	1376	1428	1480	1532
2	Calli	Casa	House	1325	1377	1429	1481	1533
3	Tochtli	Conejo	Rabbit	1326	1378	1430	1482	1534
4	Acatl	Caña	Cane	1327	1379	1431	1483	1535
5	Tecpatl	Pedernal	Stone	1328	1380	1432	1484	1536
6	Calli	Casa	House	1329	1381	1433	1485	1537
7	Tochtli	Conejo	Rabbit	1330	1382	1434	1486	1538

than symbolic, and their contents were laid out like the storyboards used by modern filmmakers. They were mostly divinatory almanacs, the manuals used by day keepers to puzzle out the fates of people based on the signs and gods associated with crucial dates in their lives. Day keepers were consulted by new parents at the births of their children, couples at betrothal, marriage, and so on. To the Spanish, who in the sixteenth century were anything but liberal, these were the works of the devil, and impediments to Christian salvation. The books were accordingly burned in great heaps and only a few survive today.

Only 13 books predating 1519 CE are indisputably known to have survived. The Tonalamatl Aubin and the Codex Borbonicus might make the list 15, but they might also be native documents written in the sixteenth century. The Codex Becker I and the Codex Colombino are actually two fragments of the same book that ended up in different places. Only 3 Maya books are undisputed; the Codex Grolier might be a modern fake (Coe 1973; Baudez 2002). John Glass (1975) compiled an exhaustive census of 434 native Mesoamerican manuscripts, most of which postdate 1519. The parenthetical numbers in Table 8.4 refer to that inventory, which did not include the Codex Grolier. Many Mesoamerican codices have been published in facsimile form along with commentaries. These can be found using the Glass census, the electronic catalogs of major research libraries, and online inventories of book sellers. Inexpensive facsimiles of the Codices Nuttall and Borgia provide good introductions to the genre (Díaz and Rodgers 1993; Nuttall 1975).

Box 8.2 HOW TO SPOT A FAKE

There are several reasons to create a fake artifact. Principal among them is the intent to sell it as authentic for a substantial amount of money. The sale of authentic artifacts is illegal, so the faker can take comfort in the expectation of secrecy. Purchasers of looted artifacts do not want publicity so they are more easily victimized than would be the case if authentic artifacts were bought and sold publically.

Pieces made of gold, jade, turquoise, greenstone, or other valuable materials have been faked often. The rule is that if one is offered something that might be a fake it probably is. Gold or gold-plated replicas are sold legitimately by some museums, and the unscrupulous will find ways to cover or remove stamps that identify them as reproductions. Impurities in the metal that indicate modern origins can be detected in specialized labs. Microscopic analysis of metal or stone artifacts can reveal marks left by modern tools, without which the faker cannot produce pieces fast enough for the effort to be economical. Obsidian surfaces hydrate over time, and modern fakes lack this detectable layer of weathering, which is invisible to the eye but not to a well-equipped physicist.

Some artifacts are authentic but were planted either deliberately or inadvertently in deposits where they would not be expected. This is especially interesting in light of popular fascination with finds that purport to be evidence of transoceanic contacts. Usually these finds occur so far out of normal context that even the most gullible is prompted to question them. A Roman coin in a Los Angeles parking meter, a terracotta Roman head in a Mexican site, or a Norse inscription in the Midwest are all examples of "finds" that most people would reject out of hand. However, enthusiasm for some particular hypothesis sometimes clouds judgment. The Roman terracotta head has been taken seriously by some scholars, and there are many people of Norse descent who want to believe that there is more to Vikings in Minnesota than just a football team.

Some fakes are obvious and made in large amounts for the tourist trade, particularly in Mesoamerica. These modern pieces are often interesting as folk art and worth collecting as such. Authentic pieces are national patrimony, protected by international agreements, and are illegal to export. Trafficking in antiquities can be a very costly mistake.

Scholars scrutinize the surviving codices to puzzle out their arcane contents. Names and dates can be extracted from some of them, and the elaborate ritual, calendrical, and religious contents of most provide endless topics of discussion for iconographers, art historians, and ethnohistorians. The most important codices often have names derived from prior owners or current locations rather than names that relate to their American origins. Some find this objectionable, but many people and places, even "America" itself, have names that are oddly inappropriate when examined closely (Aguilera 2001; Anders and Jansen 1999; Brotherston 1995; Jansen and Pérez Jiménez 2004; León-Portilla 2003; Vail and Aveni 2004).

The Aztec Imperial Economy

The Mexica demanded and got a lot of tribute from the provinces they conquered. Each province was required to produce quotas of specific goods, and this required bookkeeping. The Codex Mendoza (Figure 8.13) provides a record of tribute items and other native documents from the early sixteenth century, showing how they kept track of land and agricultural production (Berdan and Anawalt 1992). A combination of symbols, lines, and dots made use of the zero concept and position to ascribe values, features once thought to have been limited in Mesoamerica to the Maya. The system was nearly as cumbersome as Roman numerals, which were never useful for computation. The Romans used the abacus for computation and numerals merely for notation, as we still do on cornerstones. Exactly how the Mexica computed is still uncertain, for only the notational system survives. But the evidence shows that they managed somehow (Harvey and Williams 1980).

Aztec trade and exchange was vital to the empire's island capital. The growth of the Aztec Empire was accompanied by a dramatic increase in the trade and exchange of goods that originated in the Basin of Mexico. Black-on-Red Aztec ceramics begin to appear in sites in neighboring provinces, both those tributary to the empire and those that remained independent. This pattern indicates that the trade was probably not under strong political control, for if it were the

Table 8.4 Surviving pre-1519 Mesoamerican codices. Two (*) might postdate 1519 and one (Grolier) might be a fake. Numbers refer to the Glass census.

Book	Current Location
Central Mexico Group	
Tonalamatl Aubin (15)*	Bibliothèque Nationale de France, Paris
Borbonicus (32)*	Palais Bourbon, Paris
Borgia Group (Mixteca–Puebla style)	
Borgia (33)	Vatican Library, Rome
Cospi (79)	University Library, Bologna
Fejérvàry-Mayer (118)	Free Public Museum, Liverpool
Laud (185)	Bodleian Library, Oxford
Vaticanus B (384)	Vatican Library, Rome
Vindobonensis Group (Western Oaxaca)	
Fonds Mexicain 20 (14)	Bibliothèque Nationale de France, Paris
Colombino (72)	Museum für Völkerkunde, Vienna
Becker I (27)	Museo Nacional de Antropología, Mexico City
Bodley (31)	Bodleiean Library, Oxford
Zouche-Nuttall (240)	British Museum, London
Vienna (395)	Österreichische Nationalbibliothek, Vienna
Maya Group	
Dresden (113)	Sächsische Landesbibliothek, Dresden
Madrid (187)	Museo de América, Madrid
Paris (247)	Bibliothèque Nationale de France, Paris
Grolier (fake?)	Museo Nacional de Antropología, Mexico City

Source: From Glass 1975.

goods would have gone mainly to tributary provinces (Smith 1990). The spread of ceramics manufactured in the Basin of Mexico is all the more remarkable when it is remembered that pottery is heavy, fragile, and had to be transported by human porters.

Obsidian Trade

Obsidian and things made from it can be transported more easily, so it is not surprising that that it moved farther in the flourishing post-1350 CE system of trade and exchange. Greenish obsidian from the Pachuca quarries northeast of Mexico City is particularly recognizable and easy to track archaeologically.

Pachuca obsidian has turned up as far away as Cozumel, Naco (Honduras), Chalchuapa (El Salvador), and Spiro (Oklahoma) (Barker et al. 2002; Ford et al. 1997; Smith 1990). Obsidian from other sources also found its way to sites scattered all over Mesoamerica and all of this evidence taken together allows us to trace networks of trade (Healan 1997). Some of these examples might be the result of indirect down-the-line trade rather than evidence that Aztec Pochteca traders ranged as far as Honduras and Oklahoma.

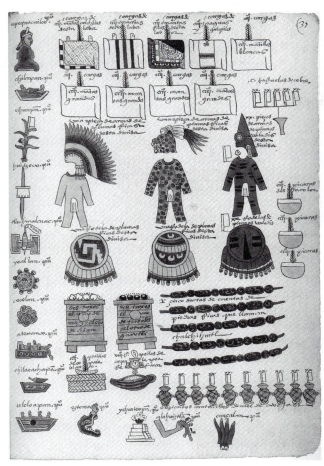

Figure 8.13 Codex Mendoza, page 37 (recto), showing tribute required of provinces in the Aztec Empire.
Source: Courtesy of the Bodlian Library, Oxford University.

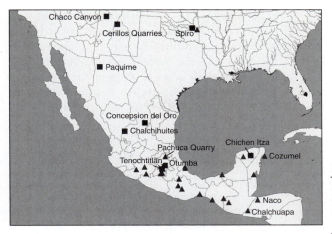

Figure 8.14 Quarry sources and destinations for Pachuca obsidian (triangles) and turquoise (squares).
Sources: Adapted from Smith 1990; Weigand 1994; Weigand and Gwynne 1982.

The Mexica clearly controlled the export of Pachuca obsidian, and we know from tribute lists that many other goods were coming into the Basin of Mexico from the outer provinces. Some goods, such as cacao, textiles, and feathers, rarely turn up in archaeological deposits, but a few durable goods do, and they often can be traced to distant sources. Jade still moved from sources in Guatemala, as it had for many centuries.

Turquoise Trade

The Mexica also obtained turquoise from the U.S. Southwest (Figure 8.14), and like obsidian it is easy to track as evidence of long-distance trade. Turquoise jewels were referred to collectively as "chalchihuitl," which the Spanish rendered as "chalchihuites." The town still called Chalchihuites was a mining center in

Zacatecas, a place named for the semiprecious stones coveted by the Mexicans. The miners at this northwestern outpost of Mesoamerica acquired their turquoise from farther north by 700 CE, using the place as an intermediary center of trade and transshipment for as long as they could, and perhaps even allowing their customers to believe that they were mining the turquoise themselves (Weigand 1968). The sources of the turquoise were mainly the Cerrillos mines in New Mexico, and the providers were the craftspeople of Chaco Canyon and the go-betweens at Paquimé (see Chapter 6) (Weigand et al. 1977).

Chalchihuites declined after 900 CE, the victim of new direct trade arrangements. It was no longer the entrepot for Southwestern turquoise, for enterprising traders could bypass Chalchihuites and trade directly with Paquimé and other centers farther north (Anawalt 1992; Carot 2000; Weigand and Gwynne 1982). Mesoamericans continued to import turquoise directly, redistributing it as finished artifacts to perhaps as far away as Chichén Itzá on the Yucatan Peninsula. The routes used were the same ones traveled by traders carrying obsidian, jade, cotton, shell, and cacao.

Copper Trade

Copper is a third material that is relatively easy to track and thus gives us insights into the workings of a much larger system of trade and exchange. The Mexica Pochteca, the adaptable long-distance traders, began moving finished copper objects from mining areas in the mountains of western Mexico to many

Mexican and Maya cities after 1300 CE. Some pieces, notably copper bells, even moved northward past Chalcihuites to the Southwest region. Copper bells having high tin content were particularly desirable for the purity of their sounds. Copper needles were sought by craftspeople and stylish but nonfunctional copper "axes" served as portable wealth (Hosler and Macfarlane 1996).

Craft Centers

The city-state of Otumba is an example of a craft center that supplied luxury goods to the burgeoning Aztec Empire. Imported turquoise was worked in Otumba's lapidary shops, along with obsidian, chert, and rock crystal (Charlton 1993; Charlton et al. 1991, 2000; Charlton et al. 1993). Tiny tiles of ground and polished turquoise were used by the thousands to decorate sculptures (Figure 8.15) and even human skulls. But although demand remained steady, disastrous droughts withered production in Chaco Canyon and Paquimé, cutting off the supply of turquoise near its sources by 1500 CE.

Commodities and Staple Foods

Aztec tribute demands also included what we would call commodities, things like blankets and bulky staple foods. They grew much of what they needed in their chinampas and transported it to market by canoe, but things like chocolate and tropical fruits had to be imported. Everything coming from beyond the shores of Lake Texcoco had to be hauled by human porters, so there had to be some maximum distance beyond which it was not economical to transport staple foods.

High-value foods like cacao beans were like other luxury goods and were taken very long distances, but maize would have been more subject to cost–benefit principles. Sanders and Santley (1983) suggested 150 km (93 mi) as the maximum distance that commodities would have been transported. Drennan (1984) and Sluyter (1993) argue that the maximum could be two or three times that far, and since we know that the Aztecs sometimes imported maize from Zempoala, almost 400 km (250 mi) away on the Gulf Coast, the maximum practical distance must have been at least that far some of the time.

Maize, beans, and the other plant domesticates of Mesoamerica were staples in the Aztec diet. Meat was scarce because only dogs and turkeys were available. By this time the ancient Mexicans had developed three distinct breeds of dogs, which varied by size and coat. At least some of them were used for food (Valadez Azúa 1999). But the inhabitants of the great city of Tenochtitlán thrived on a mix of staples grown close to home and more expensive foods imported from greater distances.

The End of Native Empires

The fall of the Aztec Empire came at the hands of a small army of Spanish adventurers who were blessed with extraordinary good luck, horses, advanced technology, willing allies, and lethal smallpox. When Hernan Cortés and his force of 500 conquistadores showed up in 1519 they went first to Zempoala, then made the long trek up into the highlands, mostly using the trade route the Zempoalans used to haul maize tribute to Tenochtitlán. Our best description of the

Figure 8.15 Aztec double-headed turquoise mosaic snake.
Source: © The Trustees of the British Museum.

expedition was written by Bernal Díaz del Castillo, one of Cortés's soldiers. Aztec emissaries, who initially thought the Spaniards were pale hairy-faced gods, tried to discourage them from continuing to Tenochtitlán. Moctezuma must have trembled with foreboding in his palace when he first heard of guns, iron armor, and soldiers mounted on horseback. Nothing like this was part of previous Mesoamerican experience.

The route of Cortés and his little army of conquistadores took them into the province of Tlaxcala, where local leaders attacked them just as they traditionally had resisted invading Aztec armies. The Spanish cavalry broke up the massed Tlaxcalan infantry and the organizational and technological advantages of the Spanish force more than made up for its numerical inferiority, at least for the time being. It did not take long for the Tlaxcalans to conclude that they would be better off allying themselves with the Spanish, who were clearly intent on moving on to Tenochtitlán. After overcoming resistance at Cholula (Figure 8.16) as well, the Spanish crossed into the Basin of Mexico through the pass between the large mountains known as Popocatepetl and Ixtacciuatl.

The Mexica grudgingly allowed the Spanish to enter Tenochtitlán, where they proved to be demanding guests. Eventually Cortés took Moctezuma prisoner. The king was killed in May 1520 and the Spanish were forced to flee the city, fighting along the causeways westward to the mainland and then around Lake Texcoco so that they could take refuge in Tlaxcala. The Spanish army had been depleted by the fighting, but they had also gained reinforcements by the addition of men from Cuba who had actually been dispatched to bring the expedition home. Cortés used his Tlaxcalan allies and

his persuasive skills to recruit Aztec tributary city-states to his side, eventually gathering a coalition large enough to assault Tenochtitlán in earnest. With infantry from Tlaxcala and elsewhere, a reinvigorated cavalry, and guns the Spanish were successful. The city fell to the forces of Cortés in August 1521, and Mexico became a tributary of the Spanish Empire.

Today's Mexicans are mindful of their Mestizo culture, a blend of the mosaic of Native American and Spanish colonial cultures. Most Mexicans are proud of this rich heritage, and protective of the monumental archaeological sites that connect them to it. One of the men with Cortés brought smallpox with him to Mexico, and the devastating epidemic he introduced caused the native Mexican population to crash early in the colonial era. Mexico recovered, of course, but cultures that grew up from the surviving communities were inevitably different from what had been Mexico before the coming of the Spanish.

The Rest of Mexico

Beyond the Aztec Empire, but quite apart from the Maya, there were several other notable Mexican cultures. It is easy to focus on the Aztec Empire and forget that there were many large and interesting polities beyond its borders. The Tarascans built and maintained a strong state to the west, resisting Aztec domination until the coming of the Spanish (Pollard 1991). Huastec and Totonac people thrived along the Gulf Coast.

Cholula and Tlaxcala

Cholula, Tlaxcala, and smaller centers nearby formed an island of independent city-states east of Mexico City that was completely surrounded by the Aztec Empire. Cholula, which had been built much earlier, was taken over by Nahuatl-speaking immigrants, relatives of the Toltecs and Aztecs. The ritual center of Cholula shifted to newer construction dedicated to Quetzalcoatl (McCafferty 1996). Hernan Cortés led his small invading army through Cholula in 1519, by then an important textile center, and the city eventually joined in the conquest of the Mexica at Tenochtitlán as described earlier (McCafferty and McCafferty 2000).

Tlaxcala was a relatively modest province north of Cholula in 1519, a confederacy of four small city-states that enjoyed productive agriculture but did not have much in the way of public architecture or raw materials for luxury goods. While the elites had their palaces, the province had been depleted of its population

Figure 8.16 Cholula, with its immense pyramid, was once a Toltec tributary and in 1519 was the scene of battles against the Spanish invaders. Spanish colonials later built a church atop the pyramid.

Figure 8.17 Polychrome vessel in the Mixteca-Puebla style.

Figure 8.18 Gold pectoral with dates from Tomb 7, Monte Albán. Note the Zapotec year date 10 Wind and the day date 2 Flint on the left and the Mixtec year date 11 House on the right.
Source: Courtesy of the *Instituto Nacional de Antropología e Historia, Mexico.*

during the centuries when major construction was going on at Cholula and Teotihuacán and migrants were moving to those and other centers from more rural areas like Tlaxcala. Thus the Nahuatl-speaking immigrants who moved into the province did not inherit any large ceremonial centers to interest modern archaeologists. Neither did they interest the Aztecs except as a potential source of food or sacrificial victims, and as a thorn in the side of their empire. Along with Cholula and a few other centers the Tlaxcalans were completely surrounded by the empire by 1500, but they remained obstinately independent. The Mexica sometimes claimed that they allowed Tlaxcala to remain independent just so a worthy enemy would be conveniently close by, but the overall strategies of the Aztec Empire suggest that they would have conquered the province if they had been able (Berdan et al. 1994).

The people of Cholula and Tlaxcala participated in the Mixteca-Puebla artistic tradition around the time of the conquest. They produced and used brilliant polychrome (Figure 8.17) pottery, some of which was shipped to Tenochtitlán for use by the Aztec nobility. The artistic styles found on the Mixteca-Puebla pottery also appear in codices that were made in the same region.

The Mixtecs

The Mixtecs of the mountains of Oaxaca came into their own following the decline of Zapotec Monte Albán, building their own centers and participating in the Mixteca-Puebla artistic tradition. Up until around 1000 CE the Mixtecs had used a calendar that was much like that of the Zapotecs. Thereafter they adopted the Toltec calendar, the form that was also used by the later Mexica.

The Mixtecs intermarried with the Zapotecs and eventually appropriated the nearly vacant site of Monte Albán (see Chapter 7). Tomb 7 at Monte Albán was later discovered by archaeologists to contain an astonishing array of lavish offerings associated with over a dozen individuals. The gold objects attracted particular attention and they are currently on display in their own secure room in the City of Oaxaca. The confused and fragmentary nature of the multiple burials indicates that Tomb 7 was used for many years, during which older remains were pushed aside or cleaned out to make room for later burials (Caso 1970; Middleton et al. 1998). The gold jewelry in Tomb 7 was made in Mixtec style using the lost wax method. One gold pectoral bears a calendrical correlation that allows us to calibrate the Mixtec calendar with the earlier Zapotec one (Figure 8.18).

The Mixtecs built residential palaces covered with intricate stone mosaic decorations. Monte Albán became a cemetery in the centuries leading up to the Spanish conquest. There were about 20 smallish city-states scattered around the Valley of Oaxaca at that time, centers that averaged about 8,000 people each. Mitla, with a population of over 10,000, was perhaps the most outstanding of them. At its core there are several palaces arranged around courtyards. These featured colonnades and perishable flat roofs that have not survived. The walls of Mitla are covered with complex stonework mosaics in elaborate geometric designs, a far cry from the bulky large-scale architecture of Classic period Mexico (Figure 8.19). Mixtec pottery similarly reflects the tastes of the Mixteca-Puebla style. Bright colors and geometric designs adorned dishes, vases, palace walls, and books alike (Figure 8.20).

The Postclassic Maya

The Maya lived in northern Yucatan and in the Guatemalan highlands after the collapse of Classic Maya city-states in the Peten (Restall 1997). Not only did the Maya thrive on the Yucatan Peninsula following the Peten collapse, there is less evidence for discontinuity there than we might have expected. The populations of the Peten region declined and there must have been at least some migration out of the region, but there was no such decline on the northern peninsula.

Chichén Itzá

Chichén Itzá was a multiethnic, cosmopolitan city-state capital for over three centuries, 700–1020 CE (Andrews 1990; Andrews et al. 2003). Evidence there indicates that most major construction occurred during the first three centuries of that period, not later as has often been thought (Ringle et al. 1998). Architectural motifs at Chichén Itzá (Figure 8.21) are very similar to those found at Tula in the Basin of Mexico, a circumstance that has long prompted archaeologists to hypothesize that Toltec elites from Tula moved to

Figure 8.20 A cup with a perching hummingbird in the Mixteca-Puebla style.
Source: Courtesy of the *Instituto Nacional de Antropología e Historia, Mexico.*

Figure 8.21 Temple of the Warriors at Chichén Itzá.

Figure 8.19 Mixtec palace at Mitla, Oaxaca.

Chichén Itzá and imposed their ideas on the local Maya. This seemed consistent with legends of the expulsion of a religious leader named Quetzalcoatl and his supporters from Tula and their migration eastward.

Figure 8.22 The ball court at Chichén Itzá as seen from the top of El Castillo.

But the motifs at Chichén Itzá turn out to be earlier than their homologs at Tula, and this has led Ringle and his colleagues to conclude that the two sites were at opposite ends of an east–west axis, along which a cult focused on the god Quetzalcoatl flourished. Quetzalcoatl, called Kukulcan by the Maya, should not be confused with the Toltec man named after him. Chichén Itzá was thus at the eastern end of a network of linked city-states, with El Tajín, Cholula, Cacaxtla, Xochicalco, and ultimately Tula at the other end in the Mexican highlands. This existed well before the expulsion of Ce Acatl Quetzalcoatl from Tula. They further propose that the cult shared by this network was responsible for the spread of the Mixteca-Puebla art style in the highlands (Ringle et al. 1998).

Hieroglyphic inscriptions that date to 800–1000 CE at Chichén Itzá include **patronymic** glyphs that are also known to have still identified important families after the Spanish arrived five centuries later. The continuity in family names refutes hypotheses that involve the replacement of older elites with new immigrant ones, leaving us with the likelihood of considerable political continuity over time on the Yucatan Peninsula. The glyphs at Chichén Itzá also indicate that powerful families enjoyed more autonomy than would be expected in a highly centralized city-state. This means that they probably had a more segmentary form of state organization (Ringle 1990).

The Yucatan Peninsula is a limestone shelf that is honeycombed with caves that carry underground rivers. Here and there the ceilings of the caverns have collapsed, producing sinkholes, classic features of Karst topography. The sinkholes were water sources for many Maya centers. Chichén Itzá has two of them,

Figure 8.23 Caracol Tower at Chichén Itzá.

called **cenotes,** one of which was used for daily water needs and the other of which was regarded as a sacred well. Archaeological dredging has recovered many artifacts from the sacred well.

At the core of Chichén Itzá are several outstanding buildings in addition to the Temple of the Warriors. The main pyramid, called "El Castillo," attracts thousands of tourists annually. Nearby is an immense ball court (Figure 8.22), the largest in Mesoamerica. Elsewhere are top-heavy corbel-vaulted structures with elaborate mosaic façades, the most striking feature of which are hook-nosed representations of Chac, the Maya rain god.

The round Caracol Tower at Chichén Itzá has long been regarded as an astronomical observatory (Figure 8.23). While some of the possible alignments of windows in the tower pinpoint astronomically significant points on the horizon, many others seem not to. The rising and setting points of the sun and Venus seem to have been especially important (Aveni et al. 1975).

Mayapan

Mayapan, which is located nearby, was probably already founded and ready to pick up the pieces when Chichén Itzá finally fell apart politically in the eleventh century (Andrews et al. 2003; Milbrath and Peraza Lope 2003). Mayapan's central feature is a small copy of El Castillo, and it is an unimpressive center compared to Chichén Itzá. The inhabitants of this late city-state built a defensive wall that enclosed about 4.2 km² (1.6 mi²). Over 4,000 structures, mostly residences, were packed into this fortified compound, enough for a population of perhaps 12,000 people.

Mayapan was just one of the last of the short-lived warring cities on the northern Yucatan Peninsula. It collapsed around 1441 CE and in the sixteenth century Spanish explorers found many small chiefdom polities in the region, none of them very large or very permanent. Local leaders were sometimes able to acquire small chiefdoms through warfare, marriage, and fortunate inheritance, but there were no permanent city-states in the region by this time. The Yucatecan Maya survived the long and sometimes difficult centuries of Spanish rule. They remain there today, many of them bilingual in Maya and Spanish, often living in the long shadows of the monuments built by their ancestors.

Highland Central America

Utatlán and other late Maya centers in the highlands of Guatemala and the state of Chiapas, Mexico, experienced a similar history. Here too larger city-states fragmented into a large number of small polities, many of them chiefdoms. The political mosaic is preserved there even today, where cultural diversity is reflected in distinctive contrasts in language and dress.

Variants of Maya culture and similar Mesoamerican cultures thrived in other parts of highland Central America, including portions of El Salvador, Honduras, and even a portion of Nicaragua. All of these were affected by epidemics, forced religious conversion, and political subjugation during the early decades of Spanish colonial rule. Maya cultures survive here as they do on the Yucatan Peninsula, modified by time and new opportunities, but still connected to their ancient heritages.

Summary

1. The Toltecs were centered at Tula, which was founded by immigrants from northern Mexico around 700 CE and collapsed in 1175 CE.

2. The Aztec Empire, which was also founded by northern immigrants, centered on an island in Lake Texcoco, which provided the capital with easy defense and convenient food supply by canoe from surrounding chinampas.

3. The history of Aztec politics is full of the palace intrigues, plots, betrayals, marriages, wars, and artistic accomplishments that characterize empires everywhere.

4. The Aztecs used warfare, trade, and guile to expand their empire to both coasts of Mexico.

5. Aztec religion featured a pantheon of dozens of deities having overlapping roles and identities.

6. The Great Temple of Tenochtitlán was deliberately destroyed by the Spanish, but excavations that began in 1978 restored the site as a central archaeological monument in Mexico City.

7. Aztec calendrics and mathematics were simpler than those of the Classic Maya, but they are better understood because of sixteenth-century records.

8. Scribes in the Aztec Empire wrote native books but only 13 of them are indisputably known to have survived Spanish efforts to eradicate them.

9. The Aztec economy featured long-distance Pochteca traders, whose connections were as far removed from Tenochtitlán as modern New Mexico, Oklahoma, and Cancun.

10. Some provinces, even a few close to Mexico City, resisted Aztec conquest and became allies of the Spanish conquistadores in the early sixteenth century.

11. Other notable cultures that flourished outside the Aztec Empire were the Tarascans, the Mixtecs, and various Maya city-states on the Yucatan Peninsula and in the Guatemalan highlands.

Further Reading

As for Chapter 7, the best recent synthesis of Mesoamerican archaeology is Susan Evans's *Ancient Mexico and Central America: Archaeology and Culture*

History. There are many other excellent sources as well, several of them being very well-produced catalogs of recent museum exhibits. These are cited along with more specific sources in the "References" section at the end of this book. The Borgia and Nuttall Codices are recommended for their sheer beauty and dramatic impact of Mesoamerican books produced in this period. Facsimiles of both are inexpensive and in print.

Glossary

atlatl: Nahuatl word for spear thrower.

cenote: A limestone sinkhole typical of Karst topography.

ethnohistory: Historical study that focuses on ethnicity.

patronymic: A name derived from that of the father or a paternal ancestor.

The Mississippians

In the center of the town and in front of the chieftain's dwellings was the temple or place of burial which the Spaniards had come to see. Here there were things admirable in grandeur, richness, curiousness and majesty—things which were strangely made and composed.

Garcilaso de la Vega

Introduction

The long, slow evolution of Archaic cultures in the Eastern Woodlands brought with it an ever more intimate knowledge of food plants, which in turn led to the domestication of some of them. During the heyday of Adena and Hopewell cultures and their widespread networks of trade and exchange people came to depend upon tubers and the starchy and oily seeds of various native plants, to the extent that some of them had become domesticates through artificial selection (see Chapter 5). But chiefdoms did not arise in the Eastern Woodlands until Mesoamerican maize was added to the regional diet. Large platform mound chiefdom centers appeared first along the rich bottomlands of the middle course of the Mississippi River. Over the course of three centuries they cropped up elsewhere in the Southeast, from the edge of the Great Plains to the Atlantic and Gulf coasts (Figure 9.1). Curiously, not all of them depended upon agriculture. The challenge to archaeologists has been to describe and explain the rise and spread of Mississippian societies, which were still thriving at the time of Hernando de Soto's 1539–1543 **entrada** (overland expedition).

Figure 9.1 The extent of Mississippian culture, showing the locations of major regional variants.

Mississippians and Mesoamericans

Several native plants were important cultigens by 750 CE, some of them having been part of the economic base of earlier Hopewell communities. The specific plants used varied from one region to another, but nearly everywhere south of the Great Lakes people depended heavily on the collection, storage, and consumption of cultivated plants. This intensification of plant use accommodated the slow steady increase in population, but nowhere did those populations reach the critical mass necessary to trigger the social and political innovations needed to convert tribal organizations into chiefdoms. That transformation would not occur until maize became a staple crop.

Whether the early platform mounds of the Eastern Woodlands were independently developed there or inspired by Mexican prototypes is still debated. The ethnography of South Texas and the northeastern states of Mexico is poorly known because it was never densely populated and because diseases swept the thin native populations from the region before most of them could be recorded. This near desert region between the Eastern Woodlands and Mesoamerica could not have supported large mound building communities.

Although travelers certainly followed trails through a long series of agricultural communities between Mesoamerica and the Southwest, they would have had to cross 1,000 km (600 mi) of dry, hostile landscape to connect Mesoamerica and the Eastern Woodlands. It was a landscape on which the Spanish castaway Álvar Núñez Cabeza de Vaca wandered all but naked for nearly eight years, from 1528 to 1536, before finding his way to Mexico City (Cabeza de Vaca 1961). Little in his description encourages archaeologists to conclude that this was ever a region that was regularly transited by traders, diplomatic delegations, or raiding parties.

Yet there are sites just south of Mexico's dry northeast that look very much like later Mississippian sites in the Eastern Woodlands. Tantoc, which is located in the eastern part of the state of San Luis Potosí, looks more like a Mississippian site than a Mesoamerican one (see Chapter 11) (Zaragoza Ocaña 2000). Perhaps more importantly, the lowland fringe around the northwestern side of the Gulf of Mexico was not as forbidding as the interior. The ancestral Huastecs of coastal northeastern Mexico may well have had connections with the Eastern Woodlands along this coastal route (see Chapter 11).

Maize spread to the Southeast from Mesoamerica sometime in the first two centuries CE. It might have come via the Southwest, but little or no evidence points in that direction. Some archaeologists once proposed that it might have been brought in by way of the Great Antilles and Florida, but the evidence from Florida has not held up well to close scrutiny. The more direct route through northeastern Mexico remains at least a viable alternative, perhaps the best one. There is clearly more for archaeologists to explore in this neglected part of North America. Whatever their origins, the new architectural forms were developed to new levels by the Mississippians and the cultures of the Gulf Coast.

The Rise of Maize Farming

Although maize spread to the Southeast sometime in the first two centuries CE, it remained a minor crop for as much as seven centuries, not becoming an immediate staple food. Early varieties of maize needed up to 200 frost-free days to mature, and for many years maize appears to have been an elite food, perhaps eaten green seasonally like modern sweet corn or reserved just for special occasions.

Maize became more than just an occasional food by 750 CE. Perhaps farmers developed more productive strains, or perhaps new cooking techniques emerged. Perhaps they found that by not eating the immature corn green but letting it ripen in the fields they gained a storable grain that would put an end to the risk of winter starvation, or perhaps people simply recognized maize as a solution to generally rising population pressure. Ecologically, maize provided both new opportunities and solutions for old problems. Whatever the specific reasons, maize changed from being a seasonal treat to being a staple crop sometime in the eighth century CE. This advance in food production laid the groundwork for a new adaptation, one that allowed a dramatic growth in community populations and triggered the formation of chiefdoms.

Farming had emerged from more generalized collecting over the centuries, a task that had long been largely the responsibility of women. Although they got help from men with the heavier work of clearing, planting, and harvesting, the labor of farming was borne mainly by women and it remained so long after the arrival of Europeans (Milner 2004:118). Thus the new adaptation was made possible largely by the labor of women.

Detecting Maize Subsistence

Carbonized remains, microscopic grains, and bone chemistry all help archaeologists detect the advent of maize diets. The archaeological detection of maize used to depend upon the lucky find of carbonized cobs or kernels in garbage deposits. Like many other plants, maize produces both distinctive pollen grains and tiny silica grains called **phytoliths** that some researchers have used to detect the plant when luck failed. Unfortunately pollen grains can migrate in the soil and maize phytoliths are difficult to distinguish from those of some other common plants, so these research strategies have not produced consistently clear results.

Fortunately, like many other tropical grasses, maize has a metabolic system that differs from that of most temperate plants. Because of its distinctive metabolism, maize absorbs carbon isotopes in slightly different proportions than do other food plants that were used in the Eastern Woodlands. Maize is termed a C4 plant, while other food plants of the Eastern Woodlands are called C3 plants to distinguish their contrasting metabolic pathways. The plant types differ in the ways they pick up and store the stable carbon isotopes ^{12}C and ^{13}C. The natural ratio in the atmosphere is about 100:1, but maize plants incorporate slightly more ^{13}C as they grow. This in turn is reflected in the bone chemistry of people having lots of maize in their diets (Gilbert and Mielke 1985). The bones of people who eat a lot of maize have slightly elevated ^{13}C levels, so archaeologists have been able to detect the shift to maize farming by observing the predicted difference in the relative levels of ^{12}C and ^{13}C in bones of people who ate little or no maize compared to those for whom it was a staple.

The dietary change can also be detected in a decline in dental health. Diets higher in sticky carbohydrates led to more rapid tooth decay. In addition, the grinding of corn into meal on grinding stones introduced powdered stone that abraded molars flat. After corn became a staple all but the youngest people were plagued with caries, lost and abraded teeth, and abscesses.

Changing Diet

Hunting remained an important source of protein, and people continued to hunt and to cultivate plants other than maize. However, the new maize staple made it possible for villages to grow and multiply, and for people to better survive winter shortages. The clearing and firing of fields had been going on for centuries, but now the practice began to transform large areas around towns into mosaics of cleared fields. Fields opened on the rich flood planes of the Mississippi and its major tributaries were virtually permanent, their fertility replenished by periodic spring flooding. Those opened in uplands left patchworks of forest, new fields, and fields recently abandoned because of falling fertility. Upland

swidden farming depended upon a ready supply of forest land to be cleared while old fields reverted to forest to regenerate their fertility. In both cases there were plenty of forest edges to attract both animals, especially deer, and edible wild plants.

It would have been helpful to Eastern Woodlands farmers had beans arrived with maize early in the first millennium, but they did not. Beans are an excellent protein source that would have reduced dependence on meat, but they did not arrive until centuries later. The reason has to do with the maturation of the bean plant, which is keyed to the number of daylight hours. Mexican beans brought north would not have flowered and borne mature fruit before the frosts of autumn because the summer days are much longer in northern latitudes than in Mexico. Mexican beans planted in New England will not flower until autumn and will bear no fruit at all. Thus it took time for beans to spread northward, their biological clocks evolving through artificial selection each step of the way. As a result, beans are rare in most but the latest Mississippian sites.

Rising population and the opportunities afforded by **oxbow lakes** in the broad midwestern flood plains also led to further intensification of fishing. Deer could not be domesticated to provide more protein from meat, and beans were still not available as a substitute, so fish were an important source of protein for Mississippian people whose diets were otherwise dominated by carbohydrates. Catfish and other species became impounded in the oxbow lakes that flanked major rivers when spring floods receded. The oxbows became natural holding ponds for the trapped fish, which Mississippians learned to exploit like fish farms (Figure 9.2).

Coincidentally, the bow and arrow became generally available from northern sources around 600–800 CE. The innovation was marked archaeologically by a sudden increase in small projectile points used to tip arrows. The new weapon allowed hunters to range widely from their homes in search of deer and to hunt smaller animals that competed for crops in the fields. The bow and arrow were also effective in warfare, which was on the increase. Rising population density increased competition for the best land, which in turn made warfare more frequent.

The Rise of Chiefdoms

Chiefdoms require three things to emerge from tribal societies. First, they need a subsistence base that is productive enough to support a class of elites and complex enough to require their authority and a ranked organizational structure. Second, they need a population base

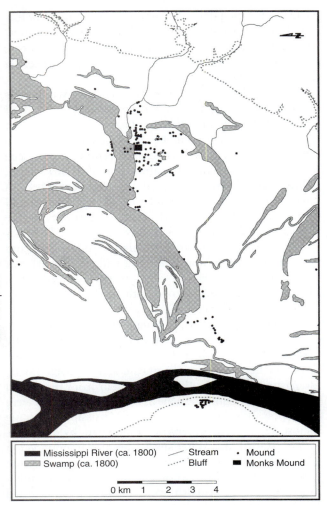

Figure 9.2 Cahokia mounds arrayed near oxbow lakes in the American Bottom just east of the Mississippi River. *Source:* Courtesy of George Milner.

Legend:
- Mississippi River (ca. 1800)
- Swamp (ca. 1800)
- Stream
- Bluff
- Mound
- Monks Mound

0 km 1 2 3 4

were flourishing in the Appalachians, eastern Texas, and along the Gulf Coast. By 1200 CE they had sprung up as far east as the Atlantic Coast, on the northern prairies of Iowa, and in northern Florida (Anderson 1999:226; Beck 2003; Milanich 1999).

Thus the rise of chiefdom societies was a natural outgrowth of the demands produced by increasing local population densities, competition for prime land, and the production of food surpluses. Stresses arose as people came to live in larger and larger communities. These involved organizational requirements for the storage and redistribution of surplus food, the management of internal political problems, and the coordinated reaction to outside threats. These were problems that could not be addressed by the simple consensus politics favored by segmental tribes, but they could be accommodated by hierarchical leadership. Earlier small tribal communities could govern themselves by broad consensus, splitting and relocating when all else failed. But the burgeoning Mississippian communities were less easily relocated, and factions within them were less willing to break away, tied as they all were to rich riverine farming lands nearby.

Size matters, and as community sizes approached 2,000 or so, the geometric growth in the number of face-to-face interactions made the everyday social and political problems increasingly difficult to resolve. A population of 1,000 people holds almost a half million potential face-to-face interactions. A population twice that size holds the potential of around four times that many face-to-face interactions. While the members of any tribal society might well appreciate a New England town meeting form of government, like any modern New England town they would find that vital processes tend to break down when the population increases above 1,000 to the vicinity of 2,000. Hierarchical leadership, tighter controls, and representative government not only solve this problem, they become imperative (Johnson 1982). In other words, chiefdoms provide an adaptive advantage when the circumstances are right.

The earlier alternative had been for a community to split into one or more smaller communities when it grew to a size that made government by consensus too unwieldy and too stressful to function. But this was possible only if geographic **circumscription** by environment or competing societies of like kind were not factors. Circumscription made fissioning and relocation impractical, so there was little choice but to move toward hierarchical leadership (Carniero 1967). Circumscription and a shortage of prime farmland were powerful forces leading to the formation of chiefdoms as well as promoting their persistence once formed. Yet despite these forces chiefdoms did collapse from time to time. The dispersal of

that is large enough, sedentary enough, and dense enough to require more organization than tribal society can provide. Third, they need innovative inspiration. It is human nature for the inspiration to appear once the requisite subsistence base is at hand, but when no model exists to emulate it might take quite a bit of pressure for it to produce political results.

In the Eastern Woodlands, the conditions for the spontaneous creation of chiefdoms emerged first in the Middle Mississippi Valley, and chiefdoms appeared there around 900 CE. Once this innovative political structure appeared there it spread to other regional populations where the same conditions already existed or were emerging. There were Mississippian chiefdoms all along the great river from Illinois to Louisiana, as well as along the lower reaches of its major tributaries, by around 1000 CE. By 1100 CE chiefdom polities communities experiencing such collapses produced a complex pattern of migrations within the Eastern Woodlands that are now difficult to trace in detail.

Variations on the Mississippian Theme

There were eventually many Mississippian chiefdoms and they left behind many town sites large and small scattered across the Eastern Woodlands, beginning around 750 CE. The primary variant was Middle Mississippian, centered on the "American Bottom" stretch of the Mississippi Valley that lies roughly between modern St. Louis and Memphis, the region where Mississippian chiefdoms first arose. Middle Mississippian spawned other regional variants as the pressures to develop chiefdom organizations developed elsewhere and people in those parts of the Southeast took inspiration from established centers. The principle secondary developments are termed South Appalachian, Plaquemine, and Caddoan Mississippian (Figure 9.1). Each of them was home to a set of related chiefdoms, each of which in turn left behind a major archaeological site surrounded by a constellation of smaller tributary sites.

The Nature of Mississippian Polities

Chiefdoms are defined minimally as sociopolitical organizations that feature two or more levels of integration. A society with a permanent chieftain and two or more subordinate family heads would qualify under this definition. Of course, much more complex chiefdoms are also known. Very complex ones have some of the features of states and in many cases they are the simplified remnants of former states (Earle 1987). Tribes can evolve into chiefdoms and states can collapse into chiefdoms.

Chiefdoms themselves tend to be unstable and subject to collapse, cycling in and out of existence because of their tendency to break up when they experience internal conflict. This kind of cyclical fissioning is common in segmentary tribes. While rarer among larger chiefdoms having much larger investments in permanent villages and towns, the effects are larger when it occurs. If circumstances make it feasible for a chiefdom to split into smaller separate polities it often will, thus spawning two or more smaller units that might persist as segmentary tribes or eventually evolve into new chiefdoms, either through internal growth or merger with other similar polities (Anderson 1990).

Mississippian chieftains were often charismatic leaders who held the allegiance of the people subordinate to them by force of their personalities as well as through whatever powers custom and precedent accorded them and their immediate subordinates. They also typically served as religious leaders, managing and sometimes exploiting the shared ideology that helped hold their polities together. Successful chiefdoms were those in which succession was managed according to some formal process, so that they did not collapse when a charismatic leader died. Failure of that process was one of the more important causes of the political collapse of chiefdoms. Not all Mississippian societies were chiefdoms, but the larger ones were. Families and larger groups moved in and out of chiefdoms as circumstances changed, for while coercion made chiefdoms stronger than tribes people could still occasionally vote with their feet.

Chieftains earned their keep by managing food surpluses, external trade, and popular ideology. So long as stored foods were available and they were able to maintain their access to surpluses they could supply the temporarily needy with critical resources. As long as religious observances were generally perceived to be working and external threats were kept at bay, chieftains were secure in their offices. Strong leaders clearly enjoyed perquisites, but modern readers often wonder what was in it for everybody else. The answer is that chieftains provided insurance for everyone except in the event of widespread catastrophe. Chiefdoms collapsed when something like warfare, drought, flooding, or the death of a leader shook public confidence.

Ironically, political collapse might also have occurred when a long period of well-being led people to conclude that the expense of leadership was no longer justified. Thus chiefdoms were inherently unstable not only because of the rare natural disaster but because like tribes they were made up of smaller units of like type. The leaders of secondary chiefdoms allied under a dominant chieftain undoubtedly looked for opportunities to break away or seize power. A central place could lose its political centrality quickly if its chieftain became ill or lost his capacity to meet the demands of his constituents.

The Archaeological Evidence

In the Southeast chieftains signaled their ranks by living in fine houses on platform mounds. Other mounds served as platforms for council houses, charnel houses, or temples, where chieftains presided over public ritual. These were typically arrayed around plazas that were the ritual centers of towns (Kidder 2004). Chieftains retained and exercised their power in part through the symbolic linkages between the mound structures. Some excavated mounds have been found to contain large deposits of animal bones and other food waste. This is evidence that feasting was one of the important activities conducted there by chieftains and other elites.

The platform mounds that are the most prominent features of Southeastern archaeological sites were often

Figure 9.3 The reconstructed site of Chucalissa in Memphis reproduces the clean, unvegetated appearance that Mississippians probably preferred.

built in stages. What we see today are usually the last editions of mounds that had long histories. Successions of leaders enlarged and resurfaced earthworks that they inherited or took over. Special clays were sometimes used to finish off a new stage, giving it a fresh new look (Figure 9.3). No doubt Mississippians would not have thought much of the grassy knolls that are now preserved in archaeological parks. Adding a new stage to a mound raised and validated the rank of the chieftain, and called upon tradition through a physical connection with the earlier mound. Sometimes that historical connection can be traced archaeologically back to a single elite residential structure under the earliest mound platform, buried under a succession of later ones. In other cases, such as at Etowah, Georgia, there is clear evidence of interruptions in the succession, as new groups took over the center after its abandonment by some earlier collapsed chiefdom (King 2003).

Some platform mounds supported **charnel houses.** These were specialized mortuary structures that were designed to contain the remains of distinguished ancestors. The charnel houses were cleaned out periodically and the accumulated human remains stored in them were taken elsewhere for burial. Such structures could hold only a small number of individuals, so it is clear that this honor and the ostentatious ritual surrounding it were reserved for elite families. The worst thing an enemy could do was to force entry to the town and defile the ancestral bones housed in the charnel house, as de Soto discovered during his entrada (de la Vega 1962).

At least some chiefdoms were led by dynastic families that were strong enough to make human sacrifice part of their burial ritual. Examples are known from the archaeological sites of Cahokia and Dickson in Illinois, as well as at some other major sites. These practices

continued into the period following European colonization and they were observed by French visitors among the Natchez, who were in turn part of the Plaquemine branch of the Mississippian phenomenon.

Just as important as the traits that set chiefdoms apart from tribal organizations are the traits of state societies that are lacking in chiefdoms. Luxury items, such as marine shell beads, were important markers of high rank in Mississippian centers, but there is no evidence that they were made by craft specialists. Crafts were turned out in households and not manufactured centrally for general redistribution. Any specialization was within the family. Thus there is no evidence for either craft specialization or for markets in which they might have been bought and sold. These important features of Mesoamerican state societies were lacking in Mississippian chiefdoms.

Demystifying Terminology

The many sources on Southeastern archaeology that are cited here and in other general works use terminology that is likely to be confusing to the uninitiated. The main source of confusion is that archaeologists have come to use period terms that were originally intended to define cultural types. "Mississippian" was originally defined as a culture type in the 1930s to distinguish the platform-mound-building chiefdoms of the Southwest and Midwest from the burial-mound-building "Woodland" tribes of the Eastern Woodlands. Both terms were converted into time periods, usually subdivided into early, middle, and late subperiods, when later dating showed that Woodland cultures were generally older than Mississippian ones. Unfortunately, the specific dates for these periods vary across the vast region of the Eastern Woodlands, making it difficult and sometimes impossible to apply them consistently everywhere. For example, the Late Woodland period in Georgia is dated to 500–1000 CE followed by the Early Mississippian, 1000–1200 CE. But in New York the Late Woodland is typically dated 1000–1500 CE and there are no Mississippian periods at all. Consequently, although the terms are convenient to use state by state, they confuse efforts to examine research questions that apply to the Eastern Woodlands as a whole. To make things worse, "Middle Mississippian" refers to the variant of Mississippian found in the middle segment of the Mississippi Valley but it is also used as a time period between Early Mississippian and Late Mississippian in other regions such as Georgia (White 2002).

Whenever possible, this book references millennia, centuries, or years BCE or CE to avoid the confusion of contradictory period names in the Eastern Woodlands. But many of the sources on which it depends do not use

Box 9.1 HOW TO INTERPRET OLDER ARCHAEOLOGICAL TERMINOLOGY

W. C. McKern proposed the terms "Woodland" and "Mississippian" as names for two culture types in 1939. Later archaeologists shifted to using the terms as time periods, often subdividing them into "early," "middle," and "late" subperiods. The Woodland and Mississippian classification of periods in the Eastern Woodlands is still widely employed, but as elsewhere on the continent the traditional period names used as a convenient form of shorthand by archaeologists have outlived their usefulness. Radiocarbon dating has rendered them obsolete.

McKern created the Midwest Taxonomic system as a means to classify archaeological cultures without reference to time at all, because most cultures known at the time could not be dated relative to one another, let alone assigned calendar dates. The Woodland "pattern" covered all the cultures that built burial mounds, along with some others that did not build mounds but had other traits in common with those that did. The Mississippian pattern covered all those cultures that built temple mounds and some associated cultures that shared their ceramic styles.

McKern subdivided these broad categories by means of several finer distinctions, one of which was "phase." The other terms are no longer important except to explain why some older publications might refer to some local "aspect" or "focus." "Phase" survived as the smaller basic unit of archaeological culture. For example, the Late Woodland period in a particular state might be defined by one or more phases.

The problem is that to serve the purpose for which they were created period names must be broadly applicable, and these are not. The Late Woodland period in Georgia spanned 500–1000 CE and was followed by the Early Mississippian, 1000–1200 CE. In the Northeast, the Late Woodland is typically dated 1000–1500 CE and there are no Mississippian periods at all. Whereas these may be convenient terms in local usage, they confuse efforts to examine questions at a larger regional scale, or to sketch the big picture in a book like this one. James Stoltman's effort to introduce an alternative scheme in 1978 failed to gain general acceptance for the same reasons. My solution is to revert to using "Woodland" and "Mississippian" as the terms were originally intended, and to refer simply to years BCE and CE or to centuries when discussing specifics. However, readers should remember that they are very likely to run into references to something like "early Late Woodland" in other archaeological publications and that such references are almost invariably meaningful only in local, state, or (occasionally) regional context.

Unfortunately, the tyranny of conventional chronology extends even to the subregional level. When little was known about Monongahela culture (c. 1050–1635 CE) of western Pennsylvania, archaeologists used a few clues from pottery typology and European trade goods to define three Monongahela periods. However, now we have dozens of excavated Monongahela sites and many dozen radiocarbon dates, and the three periods turn out to be imaginary. Earlier conclusions about this culture were not wrong given what was known at the time, but they were incomplete compared to what is known now. Archaeological science must progress not by building on past conclusions in a cumulative way, but by producing new conclusions based on all the accumulated data.

that solution. Consequently, readers should be aware that "Mississippian" is used here as a culture type, but that many of the sources cited will use that term (with modifiers such as "early" and "late") as narrowly defined period names. It is the reader's responsibility to sort out these special usages when going from this general work to specific ones dealing with state or local archaeology.

Middle Mississippian

Cahokia

Chiefdoms emerged first in the rich bottomlands of the middle course of the Mississippi known as "American Bottom," and eventually that was also where the largest

of all Mississippian towns arose. The site of Cahokia is situated in the Mississippi Valley across from the modern city of St. Louis. It was the largest of all the Middle Mississippian sites, growing to its large size by virtue of its location close to rich farmland, oxbow lakes, and trade routes for Mill Creek chert hoes and other goods. The hoes were in high demand by farmers around Cahokia as well as by farmers living around other more distant Mississippian centers. Their manufacture and distribution was an important economic activity, and Cahokia's control of that trade probably contributed to its rise as the largest Mississippian town (Figure 9.4).

Cahokia's people constructed over 100 mounds from the ninth century until the city's abandonment around 1400 CE (Figure 9.5). About half of all the fill

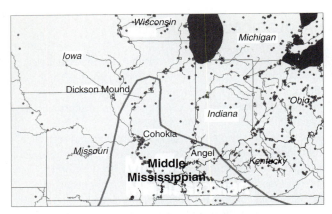

Figure 9.4 Middle Mississippian and principal sites mentioned in the text.

used in these earthworks was used to construct a single huge platform mound near the center of the town, the largest earthen structure north of Mesoamerica.

Cahokia was a center that served smaller towns in American Bottom, but despite its imposing size it probably never had more than a few thousand permanent residents (Milner 1998, 2004:135; Pauketat 2003). Archaeologists have made several efforts to estimate the size of Cahokia's population, which is difficult given the impressive number and size of the town's earthworks. Some estimates have been as high as 40,000 people, but there is no reliable evidence to indicate maximum population of more than about 6,000. This strikes many modern people as improbably small, but it must be remembered that our view of the past is skewed by the very large population sizes that came to be commonplace only in the twentieth century.

No city in the United States had a population as large as 40,000 at the time of the 1790 census. New York City had a population of 33,131 that year, and only nine other American cities and dispersed centers had populations greater than 6,000 (Table 9.1). No one doubts that these were important population centers in their time, yet they were tiny by our current standards. There are hundreds of cities larger than that in the United States today, but even at 6,000 Cahokia was the largest center north of Mexico a millennium ago. In context it was a huge center for its time.

Large towns like Cahokia were difficult to keep supplied with food in the absence of draft animals and wheeled vehicles. Waste disposal was also difficult in the absence of sanitary sewers and regular public garbage disposal. The absence of these services made all later U.S. cities unhealthy places until the cholera epidemics of the nineteenth century forced major reforms and improvements. Like all preindustrial urban centers, Cahokia was an unhealthy place that probably depended upon its social and political attractions to attract in a steady supply of new immigrants. Without immigration such towns typically have death rates too high for them to sustain their populations by new births alone.

Monks Mound. The centerpiece of Cahokia is Monks Mound, so called because a community of Trappist monks lived there for a short time after Euro-American settlement of the region. Monks mound stands 30 m (100 ft) tall and has a footprint of 5.6 hectares (13.8 acres). It contains around 622,000 m³ (814,000 yd) of earth. At first glance, most people imagine that such an immense earthwork must have required the labor of many people working many years to build, but that is not

Figure 9.5 Artist's reconstruction of Cahokia. Note that mound elevations have been exaggerated.
Source: Courtesy of Cahokia Mounds State Historic Site, painting by Lloyd K. Townsend.

Table 9.1 The two dozen largest urban areas in the United States in 1790. Were it still occupied, Cahokia would have been in the top ten with only 6000 inhabitants.

Rank	Place	Population
1	New York city, NY	33,131
2	Philadelphia city, PA	28,522
3	Boston town, MA	18,320
4	Charleston city, SC	16,359
5	Baltimore town, MD	13,503
6	Northern Liberties township, PA	9,913
7	Salem town, MA	7,921
8	Newport town, RI	6,716
9	Providence town, RI	6,380
10t	Marblehead town, MA	5,661
10t	Southwark district, PA	5,661
12	Gloucester town, MA	5,317
13	Newburyport town, MA	4,837
14	Portsmouth town, NH	4,720
15	Sherburne town (Nantucket), MA	4,620
16	Middleborough town, MA	4,526
17	New Haven city, CT	4,487
18	Richmond city, VA	3,761
19	Albany city, NY	3,498
20	Norfolk borough, VA	2,959
21	Petersburg town, VA	2,828
22	Alexandria town, VA	2,748
23	Hartford city, CT	2,683
24	Hudson city, NY	2,584

the case. The mound grew over the course of several centuries through the incremental addition of new mantles of earth. It turns out that a few hundred people could have built Monks Mound by making annual labor contributions of a couple weeks each. Neither heroic effort nor coercion was necessary for this long-term building program (Blitz and Livingood 2004; Milner 1998).

Monks Mound still stands adjacent to a large plaza, which was the venue for games and public ritual. The game of **chunky,** or some variant of it, was probably one of the most popular of these. Chunky was later documented for historic societies in the region. It was played with a pill-shaped chunky stone that was rolled across a grassy field. Young men competed by throwing spears to mark the spot where they thought the chunky stone would stop. The game tested both their judgment and their aim.

Palisade. The entire central precinct of Cahokia was surrounded by a log **palisade** that was equipped with protective bastions. The fortification was clearly intended to protect the core of the town from outside attack. In places the palisade passed through established neighborhoods, which is an indication that it was not initially part of the town plan but rather was added later in the life of the community. Residential architecture for the great majority of people consisted of square or rectangular houses constructed with wattle-and-daub walls and thatch roofs. Storage pits below ground and granaries above it provided food storage for most residents.

Woodhenges. Elsewhere in the town were secondary plazas and circular rings of posts called **woodhenges** by archaeologists. Observations from the centers of these large circles of posts allowed people to track the seasonal movements of the sun as it rose and set on the horizon. This capability was important for the timing of the agricultural cycle. Not incidentally it also would have been an important indicator of the wisdom of Cahokia's leaders, who were no doubt involved in the seasonal calendrical ritual.

Mound 72. Trade and exchange of luxury goods linked the elite leaders of major centers all across the Southeast. Mound 72 at Cahokia was found to contain clear evidence of human sacrifice. Two high-ranking males were buried there, accompanied by strings of thousands of marine shell beads. There were five pits nearby that contained the remains of dozens of sacrificed adults. Elsewhere nearby in the mound there were four men laid out together. Their heads and hands were missing, and they too appear to have been sacrificed.

Southeastern Ceremonial Complex

The highest ranking elites at Cahokia were consistently buried with symbolically charged artifacts. The symbols and the artifacts bearing them were widespread among the elite leaders of major centers across the Southeast.

Archaeologists refer to all of them together as the "Southeastern Ceremonial Complex." Some sources call it the "Southern Cult," or more rarely the "Buzzard Cult."

Trade in luxury goods connected the elites of different Mississippian centers, promoting a shared inventory of wealth and symbolism. The earlier widespread trade network of the Adena and Hopewell societies had fallen apart around 400 CE but a new one emerged connecting Mississippian centers after 1000 CE. The principal mechanism was probably down-the-line exchange between chieftains and clan leaders. Distinctive figurines and pipes (Figure 9.6) made at Cahokia have turned up in many elite Caddoan Mississippian burials, indicating a direct trade link between the two regions (Emerson et al. 2003). Perhaps chiefly delegations made long formal trips over the ancient trail system of the Eastern Woodlands as political leaders like to do the world over. Such politically motivated travel would have entailed plenty of gift exchange. In other cases, objects probably passed through many hands from their points of origin to their ultimate destinations.

Shared symbolic themes run through the Southeastern Ceremonial Complex. How these symbolic objects were interpreted and used probably varied from one part of the region to another, and not all of them are found together consistently. But it seems clear that there was a widely shared set of objects and symbols that had some standardized meanings and uses among the chiefly elites of the region. Those who were buried with these objects in death probably carried them in life, and the occurrence of very similar artifacts in widely scattered sites indicates that their meanings were widely understood.

Warfare and the importance of ancestors are primary themes in the artwork of the Southeastern Ceremonial Complex, themes that are also reflected in burial practices and defensive works at Cahokia and other Mississippian sites. Embossed copper plates and disks carved from large marine shells often depict warriors carrying trophy heads (Figure 9.7) or symbols of office. They are frequently dressed in costumes mimicking birds of prey. Wooden, ceramic, or stone statues (Figure 9.8) of humans found in Mississippian sites were probably intended to represent ancestors. These are often found buried in prominent locations, typically inside platform mounds. Minerals, crystals, bird wing fans, and rattles were also highly charged symbolic artifacts, and these too are often found with burials.

Mississippian potters made pots in the shapes of fish, ducks, beavers, turtles, and other wetland animals.

Figure 9.6 A large smoking pipe of a kneeling female figure in the Cahokia style, from Desha County, Arkansas.
Source: Courtesy of David H. Dye.

Figure 9.7 Marine shell gorget showing a warrior with forked-eye facial decoration holding a trophy head and a mace. *Source:* Courtesy of National Museum of the American Indian, Smithsonian Institution (D150853).

Figure 9.8 Two stone statues from Tennessee.
Sources: Courtesy of the Frank H. McClung Museum,
The University of Tennessee, Knoxville.

Figure 9.9 Human head effigy pot from the Rose Mound
site on the St. Francis River, Arkansas.
Source: Courtesy of David H. Dye.

Figure 9.10 Embossed face in copper with the forked-eye
motif of the Southeastern Ceremonial Complex,
height 24 cm (9.5 in). Spiro site, Oklahoma.
Source: Courtesy of the Ohio Historical Society.

These, too, were important in funerary ritual. Pots made to look like trophy heads (Figure 9.9) also have been found, but archaeologists do not agree whether these represent revered ancestors or unlucky opponents. These and other human and animal effigies were often decorated with "forked-eye" designs that might have been intended to mimic the eye pattern of some bird of prey (Figure 9.10). In some other cases eyes have lines to dots descending from them, which archaeologists have interpreted as weeping eyes.

Probably connected to the symbolic objects of the ceremonial complex was the use of "Black drink." Historic Indians in the Southeast made the ritual concoction from a species of holly (*Ilex vomitoria*). The drink is loaded with caffeine and it acts as a strong purgative, inducing vomiting, urination, and diarrhea. The Indians, particularly adult males, used it for ritual purification, often before battle (Hudson 1976).

Moundville

One of the largest and best known Mississippian sites apart from Cahokia is the Moundville site (Figure 9.11) on the Black Warrior River near Tuscaloosa, Alabama. Large platform mounds are arrayed around a plaza at the town's center (Figure 9.12). Additional mounds away from the center are smaller the more distant they are from it. This is probably a reflection of the relative

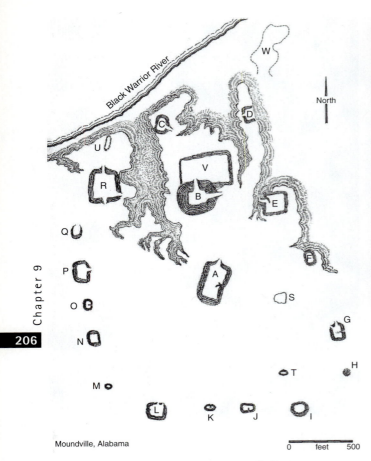

Black Warrior River

North

Moundville, Alabama

0   feet   500

Figure 9.11 Plan of the Moundville site.

Figure 9.13 The Rattlesnake Disk, a circular stone palette with the hand-and-eye motif inside intertwined rattlesnakes, 31.9 cm (12.5 in) diameter. Moundville, Alabama. *Source:* Courtesy of the University of Alabama Museums.

ranks of the extended family groups that built and maintained them (Jackson and Scott 2003).

Moundville has a total of about 29 mounds scattered across an area of 75 hectares (185 acres). The large central mound eventually reached a height of 17.5 m (57 ft), and low spots around the center of the site were filled to produce a flat surface. The life of the

Moundville community extended from the eleventh century through the sixteenth century CE (Figure 9.13).

The Black Warrior River protected the center of the town on one side and a palisade was built around the three remaining sides, encompassing the principal mounds, the plaza, and central residential areas. The palisade was rebuilt at least six times through the course of the town's six-century life.

Hernando de Soto's expedition probably visited Moundville in late 1540. The center was in decline at that time, a victim of the cycling rise and fall that affected so many chiefdoms. By the time of de Soto's visit the town was a relatively small chiefdom, one of several

Figure 9.12 Platform mound with reconstructed structure at Moundville.

in the region, and no longer a preeminent center. After a few more decades it was deserted altogether, its final days perhaps shortened by the introduction of European diseases.

Dickson Mounds

The Dickson Mounds site is a large burial complex in the Illinois River valley that contains at least 2 cemeteries, 10 superimposed burial mounds, and a platform mound. There are at least 3,000 burials in this large mortuary site, which was used from 800 to 1250 CE. The earliest burials were in burial mounds that were still being built there as late as the ninth century. Later burials were in cemeteries rather than mounds, which was common in the Mississippian tradition. The site exemplifies in one place the shift away from the earlier focus on burial mounds as the monumental foci of communities lacking large settlements to the later emphasis on platform mounds at the centers of towns. Mississippians decentralized cemeteries, making their communities rather than their burial places the centers of their lives. One group of four Mississippian people buried together at the Dickson site appear to have been sacrificed. Their heads were removed and replaced by pots (Milner 2004:133). This was not a practice that would have been common earlier.

Angel Mounds

The Angel Mounds site (Figure 9.14) was a Mississippian town in southern Indiana that was founded around 1100 CE and abandoned around 1450 CE.

The site, which overlooks the Ohio River, was the center of a major chiefdom. There are five large platform mounds and as many as seven smaller mounds surrounding two large plazas. A defensive palisade with bastions surrounded the 40-hectare (99-acre) town (Gibbon 1998:18).

The town might have contained as many as 1,000 inhabitants at its peak. There are smaller communities scattered around the lower Ohio River valley that share a distinctive pottery with the Angel site, and these appear to have been politically subordinate to the central chiefdom. It all came to an end around 1450 CE, when the Angel population, like many others around the same time, abandoned the town.

The Decline of Middle Mississippian Polities

The collapse of Middle Mississippian chiefdoms and the abandonment of many of their towns in the fifteenth century left a comparatively vacant quarter in the American Bottom portion of the Mississippi Valley, and thinner populations elsewhere across the Midwest (Cobb and Butler 2002). The reasons for the decline and disappearance of the chiefdom are uncertain, but at several centers the decline occurred in the early stages of the Little Ice Age. In addition to facing more difficult conditions for farming, the people of the Angel chiefdom and others like it were probably also pressured by the arrival of more northerly tribal farmers who were driven southward by their own crop failures. The Mississippian adaptation was probably made an

Figure 9.14 Platform mound with reconstructed structure. (Angel Mounds site, Indiana.)

untenable one by changing climate and the political and military consequences of the population shifts it created.

The inhabitants of the vacated midwestern towns broke up into smaller political units and resettled, sometimes not far from their previous centers, but occasionally more distantly. These were mainly speakers of various Siouan languages, who later moved even farther westward when they were pressured by European expansion from the East and attracted by introduction of Spanish horses from the Southwest. Nations like the historic Oto, Iowa, and Missouri were descendants of the Middle Mississippian chiefdoms, people who had adapted to changing circumstances of climate and competition from European colonists. They continued to farm when and where they could but used other evolving strategies for survival as well. Many reverted to more informal tribal social organization, and the construction of platform mounds became a thing of the past. After the arrival of Europeans, some eventually adopted horses and mounted nomadism for at least part of the year, taking advantage of the bounty of bison herds on the Great Plains for as long as they lasted.

South Appalachian Mississippian

Chiefdom political organization, public architecture featuring platform mounds, and the trappings of Mississippian ritual spread across the Southeast from the Mississippi Valley toward the Atlantic coast in the ninth and tenth centuries CE. Local populations that had reached critical densities might have evolved into chiefdoms on their own, but the Middle Mississippians provided a model that was easy to adopt, a quicker route to the same end. Some centers of what archaeologists call the "South Appalachian Mississippian" might have been established by large immigrant communities moving in from the Middle Mississippian heartland to the west. One such center was established on the Macon Plateau in central Georgia by 950 CE, earlier than elsewhere in Georgia, indicating a concerted long-distance migration (Anderson 1999). The presence of Siouan-speaking Catawbas and Tutelos in this part of the Southeast in the seventeenth century might be the result of their ancestors' relocation from farther west six centuries earlier (Figure 9.15). However, Alabama, Mississippi, and Georgia were dominated by Muskogean speakers at the time of de Soto's expedition in the sixteenth century, and many of them were also participating in the widespread Mississippian cultural tradition (Griffin 1967:185). Whether newcomers or old-timers,

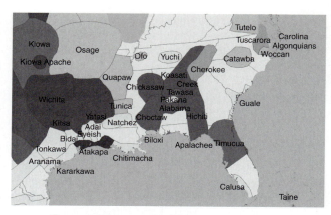

Figure 9.15 Language families and tribal areas of the Southeast around 1500 CE.

the chiefdoms of the Southeast all participated in this regional branch of Mississippian.

The South Appalachian tradition was originally defined as a regional tradition beginning with the first use of distinctive ceramics that were finished with decorated wooden paddles three millennia ago. The carved decorations on the paddles created decorative impressions on pot exteriors, which archaeologists have used to define various types. These in turn have been used to define a large number of archaeological phases for the region (Gibbon 1998:775–776).

Ocmulgee

The Ocmulgee site, also called "Macon Plateau," in central Georgia became a South Appalachian Mississippian center around 950 CE (Figure 9.16). It is located along the Ocmulgee River just outside the city of Macon and it has been protected there as a National Monument since 1936 (White 2002:66–71). Ocmulgee was occupied by a Mississippian chiefdom for the next two centuries, until around 1150 CE. The population responsible for that occupation probably migrated to the site from the Tennessee River Valley, where similar but slightly earlier pottery has been found.

Eight large platform mounds and an earth lodge were constructed at Ocmulgee during the Macon Plateau phase (950–1150 CE). The reconstructed earth lodge is a circular structure 13 m (43 ft) in diameter. The lodge had a long entrance and was probably roofed with timbers and earth, although this is still debated. Forty-seven seats were modeled into a slightly raised bench that runs around the perimeter of the round room. The part of the bench that is opposite the entrance is larger and in the shape of an eagle effigy. On it are three more seats, presumably for the principal

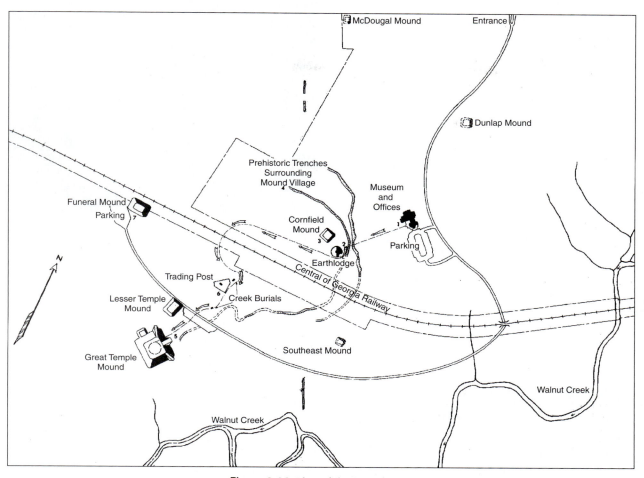

Figure 9.16 Plan of the Ocmulgee site.

leaders of the chiefdom. The modeled head of the eagle bears a forked eye, which is a common Mississippian motif.

The Ocmulgee site is very large and its mounds are unusually distant from each other, leaving room for public space and residential structures. It may be that the mounds at the southern end of the site were built and abandoned before those at the north end were begun, so like all towns this one was a work in progress that preserves archaeological evidence of its entire history (Gibbon 1998:600–601).

Ocmulgee was abandoned after 1150, but it was reoccupied by Creek Indians 1675–1725, an occupation that archaeologists term the Ocmulgee Fields phase. The de Soto expedition passed through the region in 1540, leaving destruction and disease in its wake (Figure 9.17). Towns were devastated and their residents scattered as a result. The Creek nation later formed from the remnants

of the largely Muskogean-speaking groups that survived the decades of epidemics that followed. The aggregation of refugees that reoccupied Ocmulgee in 1675 was just one of many like it in the Eastern Woodlands around this time. Like many other nations that survived these hard times the Creeks provide a case study of the formation of a new ethnicity from the fragments of older ones that fell to sizes too low to be viable as independent polities.

Etowah

The Etowah site lies along the river of the same name in northwestern Georgia. It contains six platform mounds on 21 hectares (52 acres) inside a defensive ditch. The ditch originally had an inner palisade and bastions, all designed to protect the sides of the site that were not facing the river. The largest mound at Etowah (Mound A) is 19 m (62 ft) high. The de Soto entrada

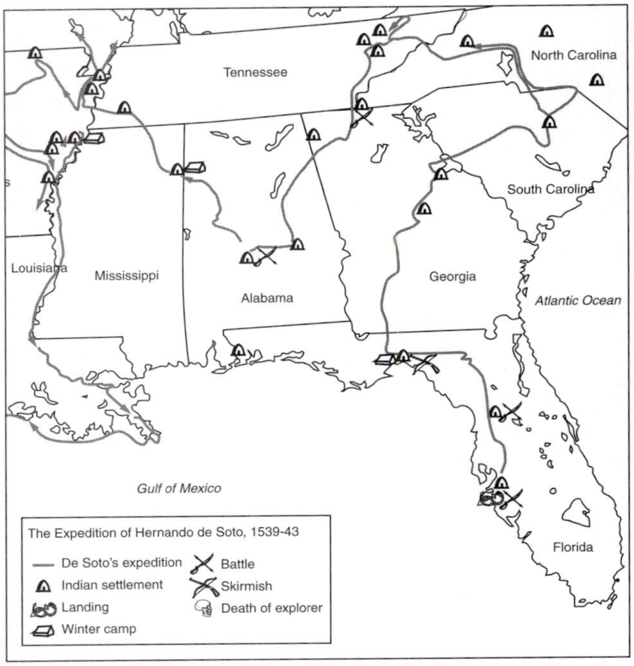

Figure 9.19 Marble statues from the Etowah site, 61 and 55.9 cm (24 and 22 in.) tall. Etowah Indian Mounds State Historic Site, Georgia.

Figure 9.17 Simplified map of the route taken by the de Soto entrada, 1539–1543 CE.

Figure 9.18 Secondary mound at Etowah as seen from the primary mound. Etowah Indian Mounds State Historic Site, Georgia.

passed through here in 1540 after first looping north-ward from central Georgia through South Carolina, North Carolina, and Tennessee in its futile search for gold.

The Etowah site is well known for spectacular finds recovered from Mound C (Figure 9.18). These included chert swords, embossed copper plates, carved shell gorgets, and an exquisite pair of marble statues (Figure 9.19). The sculptures are male and female figures sitting with their lower legs tucked under them. They reveal much about Mississippian dress and hair styles. All of the other burial offerings are fine examples of ritual objects found in the Southeastern Ceremonial Complex.

Etowah is an excellent example of a site that hosted a series of cycling chiefdoms over the course of five and a half centuries (Table 9.2). The site was occupied around 1000 by the first of three chiefdoms. This one collapsed around 1200 CE, its people de-serting the site and leaving a gap in the archaeological record. A new chiefdom took over the site around 1250, and continued until around 1375, when there was another abandonment and another gap in the record. A third chiefdom moved in around 1475 and occupied the site until 1550 CE, near the end of which time the de Soto expedition passed through. Perhaps the three occupations were repeat visits by the same evolving population, perhaps they were very different ones. Just as likely each population might have been comprised of fragments of various cycling chiefdoms.

Etowah was a different community during each of its three occupations. It was just one of several regional similar chiefdoms during the site's first occupation. After the 1200–1250 CE abandonment it was reoccu-pied and became the paramount Mississippian chief-dom in the region, no longer just one of several of the

Table 9.2 Occupations of the Etowah site.

Year	Chronology
1550	
1525	Simple Chiefdom
1500	
1475	
1450	
1425	
1400	
1375	
1350	
1325	Paramount Mississippian Chiefdom
1300	
1275	
1250	
1225	
1200	
1175	
1150	
1125	
1100	Simple Chiefdom
1075	
1050	
1025	
1000	

same kind. The second occupation had all the ritual trappings of the Southeastern Ceremonial Complex, which local elites traded and shared with others of their rank across the Southeast. The competitive linkages that maintained Etowah in the larger network of chiefdoms somehow became disrupted around 1375, and this led to the second abandonment of the site.

Etowah was reoccupied and its mounds refurbished for the last time around 1475 CE. However, this time it was once again occupied by a simple chiefdom and it was no longer a regional center. Other centers

were by this time paramount across the Southeast and Etowah never again rose to its former complexity. The last occupation ended about a decade after Hernando de Soto's visit in 1540 (King 2003).

Town Creek

With only a single platform mound, the Town Creek site in North Carolina is not large by Mississippian standards (Figure 9.20). The site was built mainly by people of the Pee Dee culture. This culture expanded into the area as early as 980 CE, bringing Mississippian traits with it. Occupation continued through various phases until 1600 CE or a little later. Pee Dee culture was just one of several cultures that participated in the South Appalachian Mississippian and interacted with one another in the region (Moore 2002:169–172).

The mound at Town Creek was built over the remains of an earlier rectangular earth lodge. The first mound stage supported a temple that was eventually destroyed by fire. The mound was then expanded and a new temple, and an east-facing ramp was built to provide easy access from the plaza. The entire site was protected by a log palisade that was built and rebuilt at least five times during the course of the town's occupation.

The Demise of the South Appalachian Mississippian

The Little Ice Age did not affect the Southeast as much as the Midwest, but the southeastern chiefdoms collapsed and dispersed in the face of devastating epidemics

Figure 9.20 Restored mound and reconstructed structure. Town Creek site, North Carolina.

that were introduced through Spanish colonial settlements. The historic Creek nation, which was actually an amalgam of refugees from various Muskogean-speaking nations that formed in the wake of that disaster, has already been mentioned. Other Muskogean refugees moved to Florida with escaped African slaves and filled the vacuum left there by the declining fortunes of the Timucuas and Calusas (see Fig. 9.15). The newcomers eventually came to be known as the Seminoles. The Cherokees, distant relatives of the Northern Iroquoians, were a politically disconnected set of 30 or 40 related but independent chiefdoms until depopulation and external threat forced the formation of their confederation (Diamond 1997:289; Hudson 1976). By the time the United States was formed the Creek and Cherokee nations, along with the Choctaws and Chickasaws, made up what were then called the "civilized tribes" of the Southeast. Their civilized status did not prevent them from being subjected to forced relocation, a practice that is unfortunately common in expanding empires. Most of them were moved to Oklahoma during the Jackson administration, and many of their descendants remain there today.

Plaquemine Mississippian

Plaquemine Mississippian culture grew out of Troyville-Coles Creek culture in the lower Mississippi Valley and surrounding territory around 1200 CE. It combined local elements with Mississippian influences to evolve into what has sometimes been characterized as a hybrid culture. But this is a characteristic of all human cultures, which always combine traditional elements with adaptive traits and practices borrowed from the outside. However one characterizes them, Plaquemine societies persisted until the late seventeenth century, well into a time when our knowledge of them is supplemented by detailed written descriptions. The best known historic

Plaquemine culture is that of the Natchez, which was described by early French explorers.

Many Plaquemine towns were reoccupied and refurbished Troyville-Coles Creek towns. Plaquemine people expanded existing platform mounds, layering them with thick new mantels of earth and constructing new secondary mounds around them. Most residents lived in small surrounding communities rather than at major centers. Major towns were occupied by elite families and their retainers, and such centers were heavily populated only during major ritual events, when people from smaller communities converged on them to take part in public events.

Unlike their Troyville-Coles Creek predecessors, Plaquemine villagers depended upon a full balanced diet of maize, beans, and squash. Squash was a regional domesticate that had been around for many centuries. Maize probably had been used previously only by elites or mainly for ritual purposes. Beans were a recent arrival from Mesoamerica that in combination with maize and squash provided an excellent source of protein. Beans relieved people of some of the need to hunt game in order to acquire necessary protein from meat. This in turn relaxed the restraint on population growth imposed by a critical resource like deer or fish. No longer was human population growth limited by the maximum size of the wild animal populations needed for food.

Emerald Mound

Emerald Mound and later Grand Village were major centers of Natchez culture. The large, flat-topped mound that is the principal public architecture at Emerald Mound was constructed around a natural hill. It stands almost 11 m (36 ft) above the surrounding terrain and it covers 3.2 hectares (8 acres), making it perhaps second in size only to Monks mound at Cahokia. Two secondary mounds sit on top of the main platform mound at this site, one at either end (Figure 9.21). There

Figure 9.21 Secondary mounds atop the main platform can be seen at the left and right. Emerald Mound, Mississippi.

were probably once four to six additional smaller mounds around the main mound at Emerald. The site was built starting around 1250 CE and remained in use until 1680 CE. It was abandoned sometime prior to the LaSalle expedition of 1682. By then the major ceremonial activities of the Natchez had been shifted to Grand Village, part of which is preserved in the modern city of Natchez, Mississippi.

Natchez

The Natchez (Naches) Indians are an excellent example of a Mississippian chiefdom in action. Indeed it is the only one for which we have detailed and reliable documentary history. The Natchez were visited by the French explorer Le Page du Pratz and others early in the eighteenth century, and we are lucky that they took time to describe what they saw (Du Pratz 1972).

Grand Village had a large open plaza with temple mounds located at each end, a typical Mississippian layout. A temple built of thick cypress logs stood on top of the bigger of the two mounds, its door facing the plaza. Three large wooden bird effigies surmounted its ridged thatch roof, and a perpetual fire burned in the outer room of the temple. The temple's inner room contained a stone statue of the first chieftain, probably not unlike the one found at Etowah, Georgia. This leader, and every subsequent leader who had followed him, was called the "Great Sun" (Figure 9.22).

Three centuries ago the then current Great Sun lived in a house on the platform mound opposite the temple across the main plaza. When any Great Sun died his house was burned, the mound was expanded and refurbished with a new mantle of earth, and a new residence was built for the next Great Sun. This was

Table 9.3 Rank inheritance in Natchez society.

Mother's Rank	Father's Rank	Child's Rank
Sun	Stinkard	Sun
Noble	Stinkard	Noble
Honored	Stinkard	Honored
Stinkard	Stinkard	Stinkard
Stinkard	Sun	Noble
Stinkard	Noble	Honored
Stinkard	Honored	Stinkard

probably how many Mississippian platform mounds had grown for centuries.

The Natchez Indians were a ranked society, a rigidly organized chiefdom in which there was little ambiguity regarding rank. The chieftain (Great Sun) and his family occupied the topmost exclusive rank of Sun. Below that rank were the Nobles, Honoreds, and Stinkards (commoners), in that order (see Table 9.3). Natchez society was strongly matrilineal, so inheritance of the Great Sun's office had to descend along female lines, thereby staying in the family. The solution was for leadership to pass from the Great Sun to his sister's son rather than his own son. This practice kept leadership within the same clan and at the same rank. Were leadership to pass to a man's own son in a matrilineal system it would necessarily pass to the clan of the younger man's mother, which for reasons of marriage restriction would normally be a different clan from that of his father.

People from the upper three ranks of Natchez society were all required to marry commoners (Stinkards). The children of these unions inherited the ranks of their mothers if their mothers had the higher rank. If a child's father was the parent holding the higher rank the child fell into the rank one step below that of the father. Table 9.3 reveals the other reason why a Great Sun could not pass his office on to his own son. The son of the Great Sun was necessarily a member of the Noble rank, a high rank but not high enough to be a legitimate Great Sun.

The Natchez system for computing social rank has interested modern mathematicians for many years. They have shown that if it were a closed system the number of people in the Sun rank would stay the same over the long term while the number of Nobles and

Figure 9.22 The Great Sun being carried in a litter, as depicted by du Pratz.

Honoreds would grow steadily. At the same time, the number of Stinkards would decline to zero over time. Like grade inflation in a modern university, the system pushed larger and larger fractions of the population up the scale over time. Consequently, to continue over the long run the system had to have a steady infusion of new Stinkards to keep that rank from dwindling to zero. In the seventeenth century these were most often refugees from other less fortunate nations in this part of the Southeast, many of which were disintegrating in the face of epidemics of European diseases.

Ambitious Natchez people could rise through the ranks through outstanding military accomplishments, the sacrifice of a child in a major ritual event, or some other notable act. Du Pratz noticed some of this at the funeral of Tattooed Serpent (Figure 9.23), who was the Great War Chief and the brother of the Great Sun at the time of his visit. The funeral featured human sacrifice of several kinds. Tattooed Serpent's chancellor, his physician, his chief domestic servant, his pipe bearer, two wives, and a volunteer noble woman were all among those that were drugged, strangled, and buried with the deceased man. The Great Sun himself was despondent over the loss of his brother and had to be dissuaded from committing suicide on the occasion.

Great Suns maintained their rank and power through a combination of fear and favoritism, favorite techniques of chieftains everywhere. Each Great Sun filled about a dozen offices with key male supporters from the higher ranks. Such systems work well as long as there is a general sense of well-being and a belief that the chieftain is successfully managing things, whether they be everyday concerns or supernatural ones. But like all chiefdoms this one was ultimately unstable and subject to catastrophic collapse. The Natchez offer just one example of how a Mississippian chiefdom was organized. There are many other possible models, and other chiefdoms may well have been quite different in their organizations, but the Natchez remain a compelling case study.

The Natchez were later decimated by epidemics and caught in colonial power struggles between the French and the English. This led to population losses that were eventually too great to be offset by the adoption of refugees from other groups. The remnants of the Natchez chiefdom were dispersed after a French attack in 1731, and they disappeared from history. Most of the survivors took refuge with the Chickasaws and other Southeastern nations and thus lost their separate ethnic identity. Their descendants survive among those nations, which were largely relocated to Oklahoma in the nineteenth century.

Caddoan Mississippian Societies

Spiro

The Caddoan variant of Mississippian developed on the southeastern Great Plains. The Spiro site in eastern Oklahoma is the centerpiece of the Caddoan Mississippian, and an important entry port for trade goods and ideas coming northward out of Mesoamerica. This variant of Mississippian was borne by speakers of Caddoan languages, whose modern descendants include the Wichita and the Caddo Indians. Like other Mississippian regional variants, this one exhibits the ritual trappings of the Southeastern Ceremonial Complex, objects and symbols that were shared by the elite leaders of chiefdoms across the Southeast at this time.

The Spiro Mound site is located on the banks of the Arkansas River in eastern Oklahoma, near Fort Smith, Arkansas. The earthworks at Spiro were built 850–1450 CE. Craig Mound, the site's centerpiece, was the only one to contain burials. Regrettably, the Pocola Mining Company was formed specifically to loot the site and during 1933–1935 looters removed thousands of artifacts made of copper, shell, stone, basketry, and

Figure 9.23 The funeral of Tattooed Serpent, as depicted by du Pratz. Note the carved birds on the roof crest and the eight sacrificial people being strangled.

Box 9.2 HOW TO VISIT MISSISSIPPIAN SITES

The biggest of all Mississippian sites is Cahokia, which can be visited across the river from St. Louis in western Illinois. The museum and interpretive center on the site is as impressive as Monks Mound, the site's massive centerpiece earthwork. Visitors should allow plenty of time to take in the interpretive center, scale Monks Mound, and visit henge and other mound features at this impressive prehistoric city, the largest north of Mexico until the late eighteenth century.

Moundville, Alabama, is maintained by the University of Alabama as another large and impressive Middle Mississippian town site. A small but well-appointed museum puts the site into meaningful context for visitors. It remains an important research center for archaeologists specializing in Mississippian archaeology.

The Dickson Mounds site can still be visited, but burials are no longer on display. Excavators left 248 burials in place and uncovered after exposure. For many years they were displayed inside a large, specially built, museum enclosure. Concern for American Indian objections to the display led to its closure in 1992, and the burials remain entombed and protected. Three excavated dwellings remain open to visitors at the site and the museum displays chronicle prehistoric life in the region.

The Angel Mound site in southern Indiana is another excellent example of a Mississippian site with both public displays and a strong research program.

The Ocmulgee site in central Georgia is a popular national monument. The largest, Mound A, is 91 m (299 ft) square at its base and 15 m (49 ft) tall. The site covers at least 70 hectares (173 acres).

The Town Creek site in North Carolina is a well-maintained and interpreted state park. The single platform mound there was completely excavated and then restored, beginning with a WPA project in 1937. The restored temple on top of the mound is a good reproduction of structures of this kind. It has been a state historic site since 1955. A charnel house (burial hut) and a minor temple building near the Little River have also been reproduced.

The Winterville site in Mississippi originally had at least 23 platform mounds. Twelve survive, including a typically dominant central mound standing 17 m (55 ft) high. There is no evidence that there was a large residential population at this and similar sites.

The Spiro site in Oklahoma originally had 12 mounds, but its centerpiece, Craig Mound, and various others were looted and destroyed by the Pocola Mining Company during 1933–1935. What remains is now reconstructed and preserved in Spiro Mounds Archaeological State Park.

There are dozens more sites open to the public across the Southeast and the Midwest. These can be found on the highway maps distributed by most states. Maps and guidebooks published by the American Automobile Association also list most of them, although a few in the guides are missing from the maps and vice versa.

textile. Engraved marine shells (Figure 9.24) are particularly notable (Phillips and Brown 1978). All of these artifacts were sold to collectors for a handsome profit. Many of the artifacts have been recovered by public institutions in the years since, but without important contextual data that would have been produced by professional excavation. Much of the physical damage to the site was repaired and many data were salvaged by the University of Oklahoma, federal agencies, and the Oklahoma Archeological Survey after the state government stopped the looting in 1936.

The elite leaders at Spiro consciously constructed pedigrees for themselves, deriving legitimacy by referencing revered ancestors. Carved wooden effigies in the Great Mortuary in Craig Mound were almost certainly meant to represent illustrious ancestors, much like the Natchez practice (Figure 9.25). Had looters not destroyed context along with various pieces of evidence they could not sell at a profit, archaeologists might well be able to say much more about the functioning of chiefdom society at Spiro and its role as a gateway town between Mesoamerica and the Eastern Woodlands.

Earthen pyramids, key domesticates, symbols, and many other features of Mississippian sites have long suggested direct contacts with Mesoamerican cities. Convincing evidence has been largely lacking, but the analysis of an obsidian artifact from Spiro has shown that it came from Mesoamerica. Trace element analysis has shown that the artifact came from the Pachuca source in the Mexican highlands, as did a couple specimens from coastal Texas (Barker et al. 2002; White and Weinstein 2008).

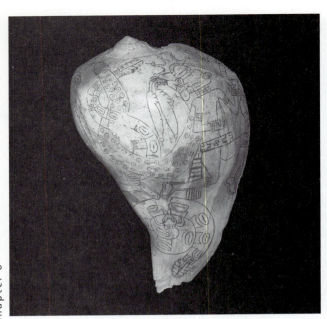

Figure 9.24 One of many engraved marine shells from Craig Mound at the Spiro site, Oklahoma.
Source: Courtesy of John Bigelow Taylor.

Figure 9.25 Red cedar mask from Craig Mound, Spiro site. The mask is equipped with deer horns and shell inserts, 28.9 cm (11.4 in.) tall.
Source: Courtesy of National Museum of the American Indian, Smithsonian Institution (T150853).

Olivella shell beads also turn up at Spiro and in other Mississippian sites. For many years these were assumed to have come from the Gulf of Mexico. Many do, but specimens of *Olivella dama*, which could only have come from the Gulf of California, have also been found at Spiro. That means that in the years around 1400 CE the people at Spiro were acquiring marine shells by way of both traders along the Gulf Coast and the Pueblo communities of the Southwest (Kozuch 2002).

Some evidence comes from even farther afield. Skulls with teeth filed in a manner common in Mesoamerica have been found at Cahokia and elsewhere in Illinois, indicating at least influence and perhaps even a few migrating individuals from highland Mexico (Griffin 1966). Many of the symbols of the Southeastern Ceremonial Complex have counterparts in Mesoamerica, particularly amongst the Huastecs of northeastern Mexico, as discussed in Chapter 11.

It is clear that we still have much to learn about Mississippian societies, their origins, and the ways in which they were linked to each other and to distant centers to the West and South. Future research is likely to show that there were many more connections between the population centers of North America than we currently appreciate. Earlier Hopewell expeditions traveled from Ohio to Yellowstone and back long before Mississippian societies arose. Aztec traders traversed the length and breadth of Mesoamerica (and conceivably beyond) when Mississippians were enjoying their heyday. De Soto and Coronado are unlikely to have been the first to undertake long-distance expeditions in the interior of North America. They are much more likely to have been just the first Europeans to make long treks through the vast interior.

Summary

1. Mississippian polities arose when the addition of maize to economic systems allowed them to grow to critical sizes.

2. Circumscription and a shortage of prime land prevented many local populations from responding to the pressures of population increase by fissioning and relocating.

3. The earliest and eventually the largest Mississippian polities developed in the American Bottom portion of the Mississippi Valley.

4. The development of Middle Mississippian was followed by secondary versions known as South Appalachian, Plaquemine, and Caddoan Mississippian.

5. Cahokia was the largest Middle Mississippian site with a population of around 6,000.

6. The Southeastern Ceremonial Complex is characterized by a set of symbols and artifact types that are found across the variants of Mississippian.

7. The rise of the South Appalachian Mississippian involved at least some migration of Siouan-speaking groups from the Midwest.

8. Mississippian polities declined in the fifteenth century, leaving a vacant area at the core of Middle Mississippian territory and thinned population elsewhere in the Midwest.

9. De Soto visited South Appalachian polities when polities in the region were already in decline.

10. French descriptions of Natchez society provide insights into Plaquemine Mississippian polities.

11. The Spiro site is a well-known Caddoan Mississippian site that was probably an entrepot between the Eastern Woodlands, Mesoamerica, and the Greater Southwest.

Further Reading

The best single recent source on the Mississippian phenomenon is George Milner's *The Moundbuilders: Ancient Peoples of Eastern North America*. It will lead to many other older and often more specific sources, including most of those cited here. Two well-illustrated museum exhibit volumes are *Ancient Art of the American Woodland Indians* and *Hero, Hawk, and Open Hand: American Indian Art of the Ancient Midwest and South*. Many of the larger sites are open to the public and offer detailed publications.

Glossary

charnel house: A building designed to hold the remains of the deceased.

chunky: An Eastern Woodlands game played with stone disks and javelins.

circumscription: Constraint on population growth imposed by surrounding populations of similar type.

entrada: A Spanish word used to describe an overland expedition.

oxbow lake: A lake formed from a segment of a river left isolated when the river changes course.

palisade: A defensive wall of large posts, also called a stockade.

phytoliths: Silica grains that form in plant cells.

swidden: A form of shifting agriculture involving field rotation and long fallow periods.

woodhenge: A circle of large posts.

The Northeastern Forests

The country is full of fine hills, open fields, very beautiful broad meadows bearing much excellent hay, which is of no use except to set fire to as an amusement when it is dry.

Gabriel Sagard, 1632

Introduction

As in every other region of North America, the peoples of the northern portion of the Eastern Woodlands worked with the constraints and the potentials of their environments and their ingenuity. The northern portion of the Eastern Woodlands (Figure 10.1) was the center of burial mound building during the heyday of Adena and Hopewell cultures (see Chapter 5). The mound builders had flourished until around 400 CE, depending in part on plant domesticates of their own creation and building far-flung trade and exchange networks.

The cultural center of gravity shifted from north to south after 400 CE as various Mississippian societies arose across the southern parts of the Eastern Woodlands. Early maize varieties that were introduced from Mesoamerica initially required long growing seasons, and beans could spread only slowly northward, plant characteristics that caused the northern forests to lapse into a cultural backwater for a few centuries (see Chapter 9). In time the more productive imported neotropical domesticates adapted and spread northward through the region, reaching the Great Lakes basin by the end of the first millennium CE.

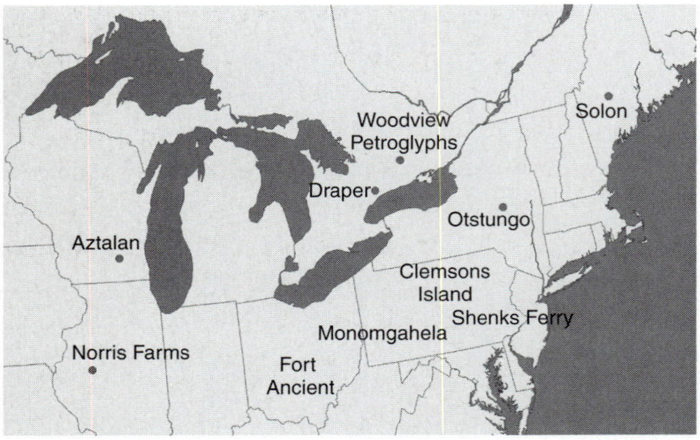

At first the peoples of the northern forests had continued with local versions of burial mound building and tribal organization, but the southward expansion of Algonquians equipped with the bow and arrow and birchbark canoe technology also redefined the region. Amidst this flow of innovations from both the south and the north Iroquoian and Siouan cultures pressed northward, encouraged by warming climate and carrying new strains of maize that grew well on upland glacial soils. By the sixteenth century CE the northern forests were populated by a mix of farmers and hunter-gatherer cultures, some of whom later became major players in the history of the colonial era, while others disappeared in the epidemics that followed settlement by Europeans.

The Rise of Farming Cultures in the Northern Woodlands

Eventually farming in the Southeast produced maize varieties that could mature in significantly fewer than 200 days. Communities that farmed with the new varieties were able to hive off and establish themselves on suitable land farther north. Subsequently they spread to the ecological limits of the new varieties, far beyond the northern fringes of Mississippian societies. The new constraint became the line of 120 frost-free days, which

Figure 10.1 The northeastern forests, showing the locations of the sites and cultures mentioned in this chapter.

today meanders through the Great Lakes region and across New England. It is no surprise that enterprising farming communities, or at least farming practices, spread northward to this new limit as domesticates adapted to shorter growing seasons emerged.

The expansion of northern farmers was further encouraged by the Medieval Maximum, a long-term warm spell that peaked around 1000 CE. Northern farming was a lucky combination of environmental opportunity, the right plant domesticates, and the human impulses we often refer to as ingenuity and enterprise.

Expansion led to population growth and competition for the best agricultural land. Over the course of a few centuries the landscape filled to near the maximum allowed by the prevailing adaptation. Deer were still a critical resource; hides were needed for clothing and meat was needed for protein. But there was a limit to how many deer the forest could provide. Even at population densities far below those of today the Indians of the northern forests were pressing the limits of sustainability, simply because a few such critical resources could not be increased or replaced by substitutes (Milner 2004:121–123).

There were also reversals of fortune. The cycle of climate change eventually led to cooler conditions, and by 1430 CE the cold episode known as the "Little Ice Age" was weighing heavily upon the northern farmers, just as it weighed upon the Mississippian polities to the south. Competition for land and other resources increased and villages increasingly relocated to defensible locations behind palisades. Shortened growing seasons forced the complete abandonment of some areas where farming had previously been possible. But for the most part the northern farmers were able to hang on. They remained scattered across the northern forests until the coming of Europeans. Some of them disappeared in the waves of epidemics that swept ahead of the newcomers in the sixteenth century, but others fared better, playing important roles in the political and military struggles of the colonial era, and leaving communities of descendants that survive to this day.

The Descendants of Hopewell

The building of burial mounds continued after 400 CE, even after Hopewell faded in its Ohio homeland. Effigy mounds continued to be built west of Lake Michigan. Simpler mounds continued to be constructed here and there from southern Ontario to northernmost Minnesota and the prairies of eastern South Dakota and Kansas (see Chapter 5).

Fort Ancient culture developed from Hopewell origins after 1000 CE back in southern Ohio. Ceremonial earthworks were redefined as fortifications by Fort Ancient architects, and their culture survived into the era when European trade goods began to reach them. Unfortunately, lethal diseases were part of the exchange as well, and these were so disastrous that we cannot be sure which if any of the surviving tribes of the Eastern Woodlands are their descendants. The Shawnees are sometimes suggested as the most likely candidates, but they were speakers of an Algonquian language, a branch of the far-flung Algic family that probably spread across the Northeast region mainly after the waning of Hopewell. The descendants of Fort Ancient were largely lost in the great dying that turned the core of the Eastern Woodlands into wilderness in the sixteenth century.

Fort Ancient culture thrived on the northern edge of the Mississippians until trade goods and diseases began to trickle in from Europe, and it is tempting to view it as derivative from the chiefdoms of the Southeast (see Chapter 9). However, there is no evidence for an elite Fort Ancient upper class, and thus no evidence of chiefdom organization. Fort Ancient leadership probably continued the big man tribal forms of the earlier Hopewell (Griffin 1992).

The Algonquian Expansion

While the introduction of new domesticates from the south led to a northward expansion of farming, there was also an early southward expansion of northerners into the Eastern Woodlands. Historical linguists have reconstructed parts of the Algonquian protolanguage from clues found in the vocabularies of various surviving daughter languages that place them in the vicinity of the lower Great Lakes region two millennia ago (Siebert 1967). Proto-Algonquian was probably spoken after about 1 CE, too late to have been the speech of some or all of the Hopewell people. It was also spoken too far north to have been the Hopewell language. The overlapping distributions of beech and tamarack (larch) trees, both known to the Proto-Algonquians, are very useful for identifying their place on the landscape of the Eastern Woodlands (Snow 1976a). The distributions of these and other plants and animals known to the Proto-Algonquians indicate that they lived around the lower Great Lakes and into northern New England at that time (Figure 10.2). This is the same time and area in which archaeologists have found Point Peninsula culture, which is identified mainly by its distinctive pottery. Archaeological and linguistic evidence all indicates that these people used wild rice, fishing gear, freshwater fish, and had tribal political organization, but that they lacked maize and did not take marine fish.

Bow and Arrow

Perhaps the most important bit of linguistic evidence is that the Proto-Algonquians had terms for the bow and arrow. Archaeological evidence also indicates that they had this new weapon by at least 600 CE and probably earlier (Blitz 1988; Fiedel 1994). They probably acquired the bow and arrow from ancestral Inuits living far to the north in Arctic Canada, who had possessed the weapon for many centuries. The bow and arrow explain why projectile point sizes were much smaller in the first millennium CE, and they partially explain why the Algonquians had an adaptive advantage and were

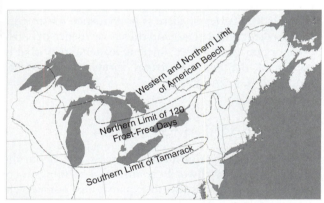

Figure 10.2 The Proto-Algonquian homeland was probably in the overlapping distributions of beech and tamarack trees.

able to spread southward into territory once dominated by Hopewell culture.

Canoes

The birchbark canoe (Figure 10.3) is probably another of their technological advantages. This light and versatile craft is perfect for the chains of lakes, rivers, and streams that thread the dense forests on flat glaciated landscapes where the northern parts of the Eastern Woodlands slowly give way to the subarctic forests of eastern Canada. For at least the last 2,000 years, trails from this transitional zone northward have been mainly short portages between water routes, places where generations of people carrying canoes beat deep paths that are still used today. Once reliable birchbark canoes were available they were the transportation mode of choice across this region.

The bark of the paper birch (*Betula papyrifera*) was used to make birchbark canoes. Contrary to much popular belief, the common chalky gray birch (*Betula populifolia*) does not provide bark that is appropriate material for canoe construction. The paper birch is a northern pioneer species. Apart from a few in the Appalachian Mountains, large specimens occur naturally today only as far south as the Pleistocene glaciers flattened the land and left a tangle of lakes and streams. In other parts of the continent where water transportation was possible people typically depended upon more cumbersome dugout canoes. The birchbark canoes by comparison were light and agile on the swift northern streams. They could be buried out of sight during the winter, carried easily across long portages, or made quickly from scratch by craftspeople with the necessary knowledge.

Figure 10.3 An Algonquian birchbark canoe.
Sources: Photographer, Michael Cullen. Courtesy of the Canadian Canoe Museum, Peterborough, Ontario.

The perishable nature of birchbark and the light wooden frames of the canoes has frustrated the attempts of archaeologists to determine when this craft was first developed. So far the best approach has been the logical elimination of alternative possibilities. Dugouts were popular before 1700 BCE in northern New England (see Chapter 5). After that, influences and perhaps immigrants appear to have had more southern origins. If birchbark canoes were one of the adaptive advantages that propelled the Algonquian expansion in the first millennium CE, then we can infer their presence in the region by that time, even in the absence of clear archaeological evidence (Snow 1980).

Around 1600 CE the Upper Great Lakes basin was inhabited primarily by speakers of Central Algonquian languages. Another branch of the family, the Eastern Algonquians, was distributed down the East Coast, from the Atlantic Provinces of Canada to coastal North Carolina. The latter distribution suggests a slow southward migratory expansion of Eastern Algonquians. This probably occurred sometime after 500 CE.

Wild Rice Gathering

Wild rice (*Zizania aquatica*) is a tall, graceful, aquatic plant that became a staple food for people living in the Great Lakes region, from northern Minnesota to New Brunswick (Britton and Brown 1923, vol. 1:168). It is most abundant in Minnesota and Wisconsin, in precisely the zone where maize agriculture is possible but too risky to be relied upon as a staple food.

The Siouan- and Algonquian-speaking peoples of the region made heavy use of wild rice in recent centuries, following practices that guaranteed its sustained productivity year after year. This required a deep understanding of the plant and its annual cycle. Harvesters pushed their birchbark canoes through thick stands of wild rice each year just before the seeds would begin to drop of their own accord. While one person paddled, another person bent the wild rice stalks over the canoe gunwale, using a stick held in one hand, striking the heads with a second stick held in the other hand. Some seeds fell back in the water, seeding the crop for the following year. But most seeds fell into the canoe, and teams of people working in pairs could harvest enough to feed their families through the long northern winter.

There are several ways to prepare wild rice. The grains were typically parched for preservation by heating them in a dry pot or tossing them in a basket or other container with hot stones. After parching, the seeds could be rubbed to remove unwanted chaff, then winnowed. After that the rice could be cooked as we do brown rice today, ground into flour, or perhaps even made to pop a bit like popcorn.

Wild rice has a natural distribution that overlaps fortuitously with the distribution of the American paper birch trees. This lucky convergence of circumstances allowed wild rice gathering to flourish in the same area where sophisticated canoe technology was most highly developed.

Algonquian Rock Art

Local archaeological sequences have revealed the details of early Algonquian adaptation to the environments of the Northeast, both interior and coastal, and this has been supplemented by their rock art, mainly petroglyphs, also found at many sites across the region. Fortunately, gaps in these lines of evidence have been partially filled by ethnographic knowledge from surviving Eastern and Central Algonquian cultures. We know that the Algonquians that lived beyond the limits of farming in southern Canada and northern New England had weak forms of tribal political organization in which leading men maintained their positions through the interconnected application of personal charisma, shamanistic power, and virility. As late as the nineteenth century these elements were still combined in male chiefs of the Penobscot **nation** in Maine (Snow 1976c).

Shamanistic power and political power were closely linked in these Algonquian cultures. People generally believed that shamans could transform themselves into animal forms while they were sleeping or lying in induced trances. The sudden appearance of a strange animal was usually interpreted as being a shaman in disguise. Fights that hunters observed between wild animals were typically interpreted as involving transformed shamans on one or both sides. Human injury or death except for drowning was typically attributed to the malevolence of shamans. The upshot of this complex of beliefs was that political power could be maintained through the subtle threat of shamanism. But it also had a positive effect for the community, for violence was conveniently displaced outside the real world and into the imaginary realm of shamanism.

Petroglyph sites preserve a record of Algonquian shamanism and associated beliefs in this northern zone between the Eastern Woodlands and the Canadian Subarctic. Some are found at sites within the bounds of this chapter, while others occur at sites covered by Chapter 14.

The Woodview petroglyphs in Ontario and the Solon petroglyphs in Maine are both excellent records

Figure 10.4 Menstruating female figure. Woodview petroglyphs, Ontario.

of the themes of shamanistic transformation and sexuality in Algonquian cultures. One large female figure at Woodview was carved over a pocket in the rock face that contained a mineral that ran red whenever it rained, making it appear that the figure was menstruating (Figure 10.4). A modern museum structure over the site now protects the petroglyphs, but at the expense of ending the occasional display of its most dynamic feature.

The Solon petroglyphs, which were carved on a rock ledge that projects into the Kennebec River in Maine, represent houses, people in canoes, birds, and other animals. But there are also many phallic males, squatting females, and disembodied phalluses and vulvas, another instance of the close association of sexuality and shamanistic power in Algonquian cultures. These linkages were still apparent in the traditional leadership of Eastern Algonquian tribes living in Maine in the nineteenth century.

Later Eastern Algonquians

The Algonquian groups of northern New England, Quebec, and the Maritime Provinces of Canada lived beyond the limits of reliable maize agriculture. So did the Ojibwa (Chippewa) and other Central Algonquian peoples living just north of the Great Lakes to the west. These more northern Algonquian peoples were all mostly dependent upon hunting and gathering in the sixteenth century. Some traded for maize with the Northern Iroquoian farming communities living just south of them, giving much-needed hides and furs in exchange. They were clearly familiar with maize and other domesticates, but the risk of crop failure was too great for them to adopt farming in this cool transitional region.

Europeans introduced the fur trade in the sixteenth century, and it was a major industry through the seventeenth century. Access to goods, including food, through trade with both Europeans and more southern native farming communities reduced the risk of starvation should crops fail. As a result, later Algonquian communities grew crops farther north than they had prior to the advent of the fur trade.

Eastern Algonquians living in Maine alternated between coastal and interior camps, depending upon the cycling of seasonal resources, sometimes congregating in larger settlements at strategic points on main rivers. These points were often at the heads of tide, choke points where migratory fish passed going to and from spawning grounds.

Eastern Algonquians in the northern woodlands lived in bark-covered houses made with frameworks of bent saplings and often covered with flattened sheets of bark. Mats or hides were also used, depending upon what was available. These **wigwam** dwellings were designed to house nuclear families or modest extended families (Figure 10.5). In a few cases people lived in multifamily longhouses, structures designed to expand as needed to hold large extended families (Snow 1980).

Figure 10.5 A typical wigwam.

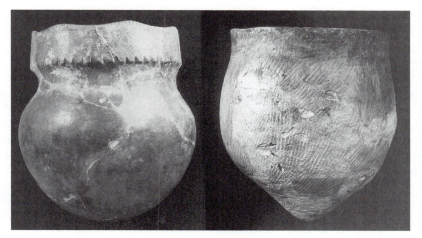

Figure 10.6 The contrasting shapes of traditional Iroquoian and Algonquian pottery relates to their uses and thermal properties. Iroquoian pots (left) are usually collared and round bottomed. Algonquian pots (right) more often have conical bottoms like this early Vinette 1 example from Milford, Connecticut. Left, 34 cm (13.5 in.) tall (Walter Elwood Museum). Right, 24 cm (9.5 in.) tall (American Indian Archaeological Institute). Resized for comparison.

Once they had spread southward along the coast many of the Eastern Algonquians living from southern New England southward adopted maize agriculture from their neighbors in the interior. This happened sometime after 800 CE. In most cases they lived in permanent villages part of the time. Some moved temporarily to summer houses near active fields in the summertime, but others dispersed while the crops ripened. Furthermore, the maritime environment is rich, so maize did not necessarily become a staple everywhere along the coast south of Maine. Archaeologists have found little evidence of maize farming in areas where fishing, shellfishing, and other forms of hunting and gathering were more productive.

Even their cooking vessels reflected the special circumstances of their adaptation (Figure 10.6). While the Northern Iroquoians in the interior made pots that were designed to withstand thermal stress on cooking fires, the more mobile Eastern Algonquians made pots that were used for more purposes than just cooking and the vessels were consequently designed to withstand mechanical stresses of rough use rather than just the thermal stress of cooking. The difference does not mean that either Northern Iroquoians or the Eastern Algonquians were trained ceramic engineers, only that potters in both groups knew from collective experience what worked best for their purposes. The southern New England adaptation, which was a loose mix of horticulture and foraging, was unusual, making archaeologists uncertain what to call it. Whether they were "mobile farmers" or "foraging horticulturalists," the later Algonquian peoples of southern New England marched to their own drummer (Chilton 2005).

Eastern Algonquians spread southward along the Atlantic coast as Iroquoians were spreading northward in the interior, cutting off the Eastern Algonquians from their Central Algonquian relatives (Figure 10.7). Some of the Algonquians that settled along the middle Atlantic coast adopted maize horticulture more aggressively than those that retained a more mixed economy.

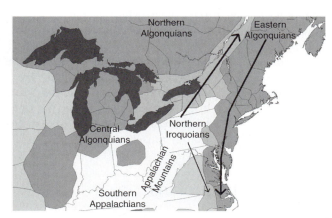

Figure 10.7 Adaptive expansions of Northern Iroquoian and Eastern Algonquian communities during the Medieval Maximum. Some Northern Iroquoians press northward while others shifted to the southeast. Eastern Algonquians expanded southward along the coast. Shown against the historic distribution of languages in the Northeast.

In those cases horticulture in turn facilitated the rise of chiefdoms in a few places in the southern part of the Eastern Algonquian range. The best known of these is the historic Powhatan chiefdom of coastal Virginia (Potter 1993).

Like all chiefdoms, the Powhatan chiefdom was an unstable one that depended upon a regular flow of both commodities and luxury goods to elite leaders. The production of these goods was managed by segmentary kin groups, and it was not so much surplus production as it was an obligatory provisioning of the political leadership by lower ranking families. Disease spread through Powhatan villages after the establishment of a Spanish mission in the area in the sixteenth century. This caused a sudden decline in the local population and the chiefdom fell apart politically (Barker 1992).

Some of the dwindling Eastern Algonquian nations hung on and survive today, whereas others disappeared from the East Coast. Communities descending from the Abenakis of northern New England persist there and in Quebec. A few, like the Penobscots of Maine, are vigorous and growing communities. Some groups in southern New England were so devastated by seventeenth-century epidemics that survivors tended to disappear into the rapidly growing immigrant communities from England. A few hung on as Native American communities, sometimes supplementing their populations by taking in former slaves of African descent.

Other nations, such as the Delawares, moved westward during the colonial era, sometimes forming multiethnic communities with other displaced easterners, sometimes reconstituting themselves as nations in lands that were temporarily beyond the reach of expanding European settlement. Many Delawares eventually moved to Indian territory beyond the Mississippi, in what is today Oklahoma. Meanwhile, several small communities that remained behind have revived, in some cases developing casino operations that have given them new wealth and restored identity. The Pequot reservation in Connecticut now houses not only one of the world's largest casinos, but also one of the world's best anthropology museums.

Northern Iroquoians

The wedge-shaped distribution of Northern Iroquoian languages between the Central and Eastern Algonquian suggests that they expanded into the region from the south, along the axis of the Appalachian Mountains, and this hypothesis is supported by archaeological and genetic evidence (Figure 10.7). Their nearest relatives are the Cherokee people of the southern Appalachians, the only surviving member of the southern Iroquoian branch of the language family. Discontinuity in the archaeological record in New York and southern Ontario suggests that the adaptive expansion of Northern Iroquoians into the area occurred early in the Medieval Maximum climatic episode a millennium ago. Speakers of Northern Iroquoian languages pushed into the Northeast along the Appalachian chain around the same time that Eastern Algonquians were expanding southward along the coast. The Iroquoians carried maize agriculture with them as their adaptive advantage and they displaced or absorbed thinner populations of Algonquian-speaking hunter-gatherers (Snow 1995b, 1996).

The Medieval Maximum lengthened the growing season in the Northeast, but there was a second attraction for farmers there as well. The glaciated soils of New York and southern Ontario were much easier to work with simple tools than were the rocky clay upland soils of the Appalachians. Iroquoian communities began hiving off and settling north of the line of maximum glaciation by 650 CE. Unglaciated central Pennsylvania was eventually abandoned by them altogether. Some Northern Iroquoians moved to the piedmont area of North Carolina, where archaeologists recognize them as the Cashie phase. The descendants of this branch of Northern Iroquoians were still living in the area during the early colonial period. But conflict with colonists and the reductions they suffered as a result of both epidemics and warfare eventually prompted them to leave. The Tuscaroras, descendants of the Cashie phase, moved north to New York early in the eighteenth century to join their Northern Iroquoian relatives there.

Northern Iroquoian Migration

Reaction to imaginary migration scenarios caused many twentieth-century archaeologists to reject migration as a significant process in the long-term adaptive processes that played out across the continent. However, this left them unable to explain the origins of the mosaic of native languages and language families across the continent as seen in Figure 10.7 and other language maps found in this book. The revival of archaeological interest in demography has removed that limitation (Anthony 1990). Adaptive expansion, migration, and epidemic decline are all among the processes of demography. Along with archaeology, genetics, historical linguistics, and a few other lines of evidence, demography has led to a better understanding of how the pattern of North American ethnicity in the sixteenth century came to be.

To understand why many archaeologists avoided discussion of migration in the late twentieth century one has to consider the excesses of earlier migration scenarios. Before the middle of the twentieth century many attempts to explain the complex mosaic of North American language and culture as it existed around 1600 CE assumed that Indian cultures were internally unchanging yet very mobile. Change in any local sequence was thus often attributed to the replacement of one culture by another migrating one, and elaborate migration scenarios were proposed in many early publications. This explains the reaction against migration hypotheses in the middle of the twentieth century. Most archaeologists rejected migration scenarios as untestable speculation, and they shifted to the assumption that migration was rare and had to be supported by strong evidence before it could be inferred. This new working assumption became deeply rooted in Iroquoian archaeology, where the *in situ* (in place) model of Iroquoian evolutionary development became the standard working hypothesis for the second half of the twentieth century (Snow 1984).

The benefit of the *in situ* model was that it simplified archaeological interpretation by removing population movement from consideration. Its disadvantage was that it robbed the study of Iroquoian adaptation of one of the major components of historical demography, population movement across space. The accumulated archaeological, linguistic, and genetic evidence no longer allows for a model that assumes a 2,000-year in-place development of the Northern Iroquoians. An ecological approach to the archaeology of North America requires that all the commonplace expressions of demographic change, including migration, must be considered.

The Timing of the Expansion

The close similarities between Northern Iroquoian languages indicate that they broke up into separate languages from a common ancestor language within the last 1,200 years. In this regard they are similar to the Romance languages of Europe, which diverged from Latin over the same period. Furthermore, vocabulary items that are common to Northern Iroquoian and can be reconstructed for Proto-Northern-Iroquoian include terms for bow and arrow, elm, hickory, and hemlock trees, maize, tobacco, and other key terms that point to a homeland in the central Appalachians, and an adaptation that already featured the bow and arrow as well as maize cultivation (Mithun 1984). There are discontinuities in the archaeological record around the time when Northern Iroquoians expanded northward, and their

adaptive expansion is also supported by genetic evidence (Malhi et al. 2001; Snow 1995b, 1996).

Upland Swidden Farming

The Northern Iroquoian expansion was facilitated by upland swidden farming techniques that required frequent moves. The farmers of the northern forests had to adopt this form of shifting agriculture because of the nature of their forest environment. They opened fields in the forest by girdling and killing trees to let the sun reach the forest floor and by burning off underbrush. There is no turf on the forest floor, so the newly opened fields had soils that were easy to work. Upland swidden farming was a successful strategy in a region where rich floodplains were in short supply (Figure 10.8). In contrast, Mississippian farmers in the Southeast often raised crops year after year on rich river bottom soils that were replenished annually by spring flooding.

The productivity of upland soil dwindles over time in the absence of fertilizer. As long as animal husbandry was not available to Indian farmers fertilizer was in very short supply. Pests also built up in cleared fields as fertility fell, so the solution was to clear additional fresh fields in the forest nearly every year. This went on as older fields were abandoned to lie fallow and revert to forest. Swidden farmers thus constantly opened new fields and abandoned older ones in order to keep productivity high.

Crops were planted in small hills mounded by hand between the skeletal trees of the dead and partially cleared forest. Men did most of the heavy clearing, and women were responsible for the planting, tending, and harvesting of crops. This was probably an outgrowth of a very ancient division of labor between hunting and gathering. More importantly, we know from ethnology that Iroquoian women also ran the affairs of the village, while the domain of men was the forest beyond the edge of the woods.

Settlement Relocations

Swidden farming also prompted periodic village relocations because new active fields tended to be opened farther and farther away from the settlements. This periodic shifting of fields and settlements forestalled the development of strong systems of land tenure. So long as there was a vast forest of uncleared upland available people did not have to fight over farmland. While Mississippian farmers vied with each other for permanent use of rich river bottomlands, the northern swidden farms competed mainly for much larger and more vaguely defined tracts of hunting territory.

Figure 10.8 Mohawk women working in a field of maize, beans, and squash.
Source: Courtesy of the New York State Museum.

Swidden farming and the lack of domesticated animals thus meant that fences and property lines were unknown in the region prior to European colonization. Swidden farmers had strong adaptive advantages over the hunter-gatherers they displaced, but they were disadvantaged in turn when they were later faced by competing farming systems transplanted from Europe. European colonists adopted American crops, but they also brought with them large domesticated animals that provided fertilizer, traction, and transportation. Furthermore, the transplanted European system required fences to separate domesticated animals from crops. Fenced fields and permanent housing led to permanent land tenure that outcompeted and displaced impermanent native swidden farmers over the long term. Eventually Northern Iroquoian farmers had no choice but to adopt at least some European animals and some European farming practices.

Until that happened, village relocations usually involved moves of only a few kilometers, but village abandonments that resulted from warfare often led to much longer migrations and resettlement. This pattern was still common in the early seventeenth century (Champlain 1907:314). Champlain noticed that while Northern Iroquoian villages moved only 1–3 leagues (5–15 km or 8–24 mi) in a normal relocation, warfare sometimes prompted moves of 40–50 leagues (over 200 km or 125 mi). Long migrations of 200 km or more followed by population growth, shorter relocations, and the budding off of new communities explains the appearance of clusters of Northern Iroquoian village sites across the region over time.

Northern Iroquoian Polities

Historic Northern Iroquoian communities were strongly matrilineal and matrilocal, much like the Pueblos of the Greater Southwest (see Chapter 6). However, Northern Iroquoian communities never had the equivalents of kivas, places for related men to come together. Instead, Northern Iroquoian men were often away from the village hunting, on diplomatic missions, or at war, especially during the warm months.

The system of nucleated Northern Iroquoian villages (Figure 10.9) and densely packed matrilocal houses suppressed internal competition between sets of related males and very effectively redirected their energies to the outside world. Smaller, less permanent, and

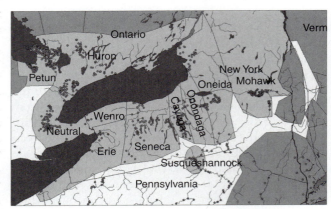

Figure 10.9 Northern Iroquoian nations (light gray) around 1630 CE. The dots are the accumulated clusters of town and village sites of the respective nations, only a few of which were occupied at any specific time.

more fractious groups of hunter-gatherers could not compete effectively with them, so it is no surprise that Northern Iroquoian villages propagated quickly across the interior Northeast after their first appearance (Divale 1984). Smaller, more mobile hunter-gatherer communities were either displaced or absorbed by the proliferating farming communities.

There was a limit to maximum village sizes because of weaknesses that were inherent in their political organizations. Villages tended to split into two or more new villages when they grew to a critical size. Not many of the early villages grew to more than a few hundred inhabitants before splitting. Stronger matrilineal household organizations eventually allowed for larger communities, but even in the sixteenth century Iroquois towns became politically unstable when their populations exceeded 1,000 and a few of them approached 2,000.

The dense, compact, semipermanent villages were possible because farming produced the necessary food. Maize and squash were staples early on and beans were added later. Beans did not become an important dietary component in the Eastern Woodlands until after 1200 CE, but beans in combination with maize eventually provided an important new source of protein that reduced dependence upon meat protein. This in turn allowed populations to grow even as changing climatic conditions began to compress village clusters into a shrinking array of suitable environments.

Northern Iroquoian Society

The Northern Iroquoians reckoned descent and clan membership through female lines and their longhouse architecture was designed to accommodate those practices. Residence after marriage was with the woman's family in a household managed by a senior woman. Accordingly, the Iroquoian longhouse was a multifamily household that could expand to accommodate more nuclear families as daughters brought home new husbands. The archaeological evidence for these social arrangements is found in the layouts of tightly packed longhouse villages and the regular internal layouts of the longhouses (Figure 10.10).

For a long time anthropologists thought that matrilocal residence and matrilineal descent were the result of the increased role of women in food production. But while reliable food production was a prerequisite for larger and more permanent villages, the relationship between settlement and the role of women was more subtle than that. Given their weak tribal organization, the densely packed Northern Iroquoian communities

Figure 10.10 The Draper site in Ontario shows the tight packing of multifamily longhouses in an unusually large village. *Source:* Courtesy of the Museum of Ontario Archeology.

would not have held together socially, politically, or demographically had they been organized along male lines. Men in residential groups tend to compete and eventually conflict with each other, and this eventually would have become so serious that the community would have fragmented, thus losing much of its competitive edge over hunter-gatherer communities in the region (Divale 1984). As it happened, the frequent settlement relocations brought about by swidden farming facilitated the periodic repackaging of household units, a process that afforded Northern Iroquoian women with opportunities to assert their organizational skills and their tranquilizing influence on the internal operations of their communities.

Longhouse Archaeology

The classic Iroquoian longhouse was a structure of variable length, about 3 fathoms (5.5 m or 18 ft) wide, and as long as it needed to be to house an extended family of related women, their husbands, and their children. A fathom is the arm span of an adult male. Each longhouse had a central aisle a fathom wide with living areas on each site. A central fire in the aisle was shared by the nuclear families on either side of the aisle. Each family had a berth for sleeping and a set of work and storage areas. Because 5 was the average size of a nuclear family, each compartment of a longhouse was about as long as it was wide and contained about 10 people on average. Some longhouses were very long, had many compartments and housed dozens of people. Even recreated shorter longhouses seem immense when one enters them.

Box 10.1 HOW TO EXPLAIN MATRILINEAL COMMUNITIES

Segmentary tribes that are dominated by males typically have patrilineal kin groups and practice patrilocal residence after marriage. That means that newly married couples tend to live with the husbands' families. Big men often arise in these circumstances and communities tend to be fractious and unstable over the long run because of competition between them and between the male kin groups they represent.

Tribes in which kin is reckoned along female lines and postmarital residence is with the woman's family are inherently more stable because matrilocal families break up groups of related males, who would otherwise tend to compete for power and reduce community cohesion. In many matrilocal tribal communities male kin groups maintain men's houses so that they have places to gather. Southwestern kivas functioned that way. The Iroquois of the northeastern forests lacked that institution, but in that case men accomplished the same end by being out of town much of the time in male kin groups that were on hunting, diplomatic, or warring expeditions.

Matrilocal tribal communities are more stable than patrilocal ones because senior women preside over lineages of related females. These are often residential units in which all of the females and unmarried males are descendants of senior females. In-marrying men are guests in such households. Men may be appointed to manage community affairs and conduct business with the outside world, but women typically keep the peace within the community.

It was long thought by many anthropologists that matrilineal systems arose because of the increased economic importance of women in tribal societies that adopted agriculture. But that does not explain the presence of matrilineal and matrilocal societies in regions where hunting and gathering prevailed and where agriculture remains ecologically impossible. A better hypothesis is that matrilineal/matrilocal societies usually arise when tribal societies migrate to new locations where external threats make larger compact (and therefore defensible) villages desirable. Larger and more densely populated villages usually need to be agricultural for them to be able to feed themselves adequately, so matrilocal societies also tend to be agricultural. But that is a misleading association between farming and matriliny that masks the true cause and effect.

Matriliny disarms the fractious male kin groups that might otherwise threaten the internal stability of large compact tribal villages. Ironically, it also redirects conflict outward from the community toward other communities. The result is that matrilineal tribal societies are often more aggressive toward outsiders and better able to expand regionally than are patrilineal ones.

The longhouses were built with frameworks of saplings and covered with large sheets of bark, typically elm bark where that tree was abundant. The archaeological evidence for the longhouses consists of lines of hearths and rows of post molds left behind by the sapling frameworks. These were clearly designed to serve as residences for a decade or two, about the amount of time separating village relocations. More permanent houses would not have been worth the investment given the demands of swidden farming, and the availability of firewood. But while they were occupied some Northern Iroquoian villages grew to be large dense communities occasionally containing dozens of longhouses.

The longhouse example illustrates the difficulty of using archaeological clues to reconstruct houses that were made of perishable materials. Figure 10.11 shows three alternative cross sections. Cross section A is taken from a drawing made by an eighteenth-century observer, the most reliable contemporary source (Bartram 1751).

Cross sections B and C are solutions followed by some modern reconstructions, neither of which conforms to the observation of the eye witness, John Bartram. Figure 10.12 shows four alternatives, modern reconstructions that each deviates from Bartram in one way or another (Snow 1997). The best modern reconstruction is in the New York State Museum, Albany. However it is in a confined space that is more easily visited than photographed.

The Little Ice Age

Northern Iroquoian villages thrived in the region until the fifteenth century, spreading into the lowlands around the St. Lawrence River and gravitating into clusters that eventually became the well-known Iroquoian nations of the colonial era. The Medieval Maximum raised the farming potential of the region while the cultural innovations of the Northern Iroquoians had provided the other half of the equation

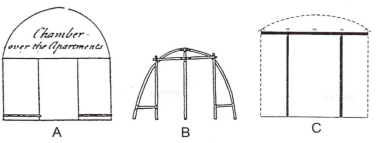

Figure 10.11 Longhouse architecture. Side walls were straight and about 3 m (10 ft) high at the eaves. Roofs were highly arched to shed snow. Longhouses were about 5.5 m (18 ft) wide.

Figure 10.12 Four reconstructed longhouses, none of them entirely successful. See Figure 10.11A for a more correct profile.

that made their adaptation a success. However, by around 1430 CE the Little Ice Age presented a new set of challenges. This environmental episode had been in the wind for decades, and by the middle of the fifteenth century farmers were facing more frequent crop failures and increasing competition for the best land. Communities that were forced to abandon marginal areas made unproductive by the shortened growing season collided with others more fortunate. The result was an increase in community sizes as some communities merged for protection. Other communities took in smaller groups of refugees with the same cumulative effect. Many communities moved to more defensible locations in the course of their periodic relocations, and protective palisades became standard features. While it might be tempting to look to other possible reasons for these settlement changes, human skeletal remains found in and around many of these communities also reveal an increase in violent deaths. It is not possible to escape the logical conclusion that warfare was on the rise.

The Formation of Confederacies

The way in which Northern Iroquoian villages propagated across the region led to the establishment of clusters of communities, which in turn differentiated into separate linguistic and political populations over time. The stresses of the Little Ice Age prompted sporadic warfare between them that gradually became endemic. Iroquoian ethnology indicates that once it began, warfare was perpetuated by an ideology of revenge. The early Northern Iroquoians believed that with the exception of drowning there was no such thing as accidental death or death by natural causes. Almost any death was attributed to the physical or magical evil doings of an enemy, even if the enemy was someone unknown. Further, the logic of Iroquoian ideology required that any death that could be blamed on an enemy had to be revenged, and this was just about all of them. The revenge ideology consequently led to a seemingly endless cycle of revenge-motivated violence.

The cycle of revenge warfare was eventually bought under control by the formation of confederacies of former enemies. Although they were very weak politically, these arrangements ended hostilies between the participating nations. There were several of them, the best known being the League of the Iroquois, a confederation of five Northern Iroquoian nations strung out across what is now the State of New York. Their alliance ended warfare between the five constituent nations, but at the same time it redirected their collective aggression outward against other nations in the region, including other Northern Iroquoian ones. The Neutral, Erie, and Huron confederacies were similar in kind, and shared their strengths and weaknesses. But of the four Northern Iroquoian confederacies only one, the League of the Iroquois, would survive to the eighteenth century, and it did so in large part by destroying the other three.

Northern Iroquoian political confederacies were the weakest possible form of chiefdom (Table 10.1). They were run by sets of representatives, typically appointed by the women of leading families in the constituent nations. There were no permanent chieftains apart from senior men who were considered to be first among equals. All decisions had to be unanimous, a requirement that led to long debates, inaction, and frequent dissolution into tribal or even smaller factions that took action on their own. Collective action was frequently impossible, a circumstance that often reduced the confederacies to little more than mutual nonaggression pacts.

The historic Northern Iroquoian confederacies formed during the course of the late sixteenth and early seventeenth centuries, each consisting of three or more previously independent nations. Their formation was marked in the archaeological record by a new surge in trade and exchange between former enemies, particularly the exchange of ceramic effigy smoking pipes. Men made and carried pipes for the smoking ritual that was so important for diplomacy and the maintenance of partnerships (Figure 10.13). It is not surprising that pipes often became gifts and found their way into deposits far from their places of manufacture (Kuhn and Sempowski 2001; Wonderly 2005).

The Petun, Wenro, and Susquehannock nations remained independent and not part of any confederacy into the seventeenth century, but they did not stand a chance in the wars of that century. European colonists offered their enemies additional alliances, political support, and a supply of firearms. With those advantages the League of the Iroquois, the best known of the Northern Iroquoian confederacies, destroyed, dispersed, or absorbed all the others within a few decades.

The archaeological evidence of the growth and development of Northern Iroquoian nations and confederacies can be tracked through large-scale demographic shifts. Hundreds of their village sites have been located, mapped, tested, and dated. A regional map (Figure 10.14) that is redrawn for each decade from 1000 CE through the colonial period shows the appearance and disappearance of communities at those sites as they built and abandoned villages in quick succession. It is likely that few large villages have been missed by archaeologists, and it is rare that the same location was occupied more than once. The demands of swidden farming kept the communities moving every decade or two, so the regional maps show a constantly changing pattern over time.

In times of peace and plenty the Northern Iroquoian villages drifted apart in the course of their periodic relocations. When they grew too large they split, and their numbers increased. When warfare forced relocation they sometimes moved great distances, as Champlain described. In hard times smaller villages often merged and fortified, and they shifted away from major trails

Table 10.1 Northern Iroquoian nations and confederacies, and their population sizes around 1630 CE. Villages were largely independent tribal societies. Nations were weak coalitions of villages and confederacies were also weakly constituted. While all of these were Iroquoian nations, only five were Iroquois proper, that is, members of the confederacy known as the League of the Iroquois or Hodenosaunee.

Confederacy	Nation	Population	
Iroquois	Mohawk	7,740	
	Oneida	2,000	
	Onondaga	4,000	
	Cayuga	4,000	
	Seneca	4,000	
	Subtotal		21,740
Huron	Arendaronon		
	Attignawantan		
	Ataronchronon		
	Attigneenongnahac		
	Tahontaenrat		
	Subtotal		21,200
Neutral	Attiragenrega		
	Ahondihronon		
	Antouaronon		
	Onguiaronon		
	Kakouagoga		
	Subtotal		24,000
Erie	Niagara		
	Cattaraugus		
	Chautauqua		
	Subtotal		13,500
Independent Nations	Petun	8,200	
	Wenro	2,000	
	Susquehannock	5,200	
	Subtotal		15,400
	TOTAL		95,840

and streams to more secure locations. Villages also came to cluster for mutual protection during times of widespread warfare, and these clusters evolved into the nations of the colonial era. Table 10.1 lists the Northern Iroquoian confederacies and independent nations, along with their probable population sizes around 1600 CE, before the advent of disastrous epidemics and genocidal warfare.

The Workings of the League of the Iroquois

The best known Northern Iroquois confederacy was known to the English as the League of the Iroquois. The confederacy is known as the Hodenosaunee (People of the Longhouse) to the Iroquois themselves, and descendant organizations still exist in New York and

Figure 10.13 A human effigy smoking pipe. Otstungo site, New York. Collections of the New York State Museum.

Ontario. The other three Northern Iroquoian confederacies probably had similar internal structures and ritual, so the League of the Iroquois is an instructive case study for understanding all of them.

The Hodenosaunee were initially a confederacy of the Mohawks, Oneidas, Onondagas, Cayugas, and Senecas, and they were sometimes referred to as the Five Nations. The Tuscaroras moved northward to join them in the early eighteenth century, forced out of their middle Atlantic homes by colonial strife. They were formally adopted by the League as a sixth nation, but they were never allowed to appoint any League chiefs. Smaller groups from other nations such as the Delawares and Tutelos were also adopted by League nations, but they were taken in as dependents, not additional constituent nations.

By the nineteenth century the affairs of the League were conducted by 50 chiefs that were appointed by clan matrons from leading families of the villages of the five nations (Table 10.2). Archaeology shows that Iroquoian villages did not cluster in the five national territories until after 1560, so that is the earliest the League could have begun forming. Like all political institutions it evolved over time, and its complete structure was not described for another three centuries, so it is difficult to assign a founding date.

The League was organized around clans and funerary ritual. Clans cross-cut national boundaries all across the Eastern Woodlands, and their origins probably lie in ancient trade networks that linked trading partners who lived far apart and spoke languages that were mutually unintelligible (see Chapter 5). The children of people belonging to the same clan were considered siblings to each other, so rules of exogamy came to be applied to clan identities over time. Early anthropologists noticed that one member of the Wolf Clan would not marry another Wolf even if they appeared to be otherwise unrelated, came from different regions, and spoke different languages. The anthropologists erroneously concluded that clans had been invented to regulate marriage because kinship and marriage in small-scale societies was what their research focused on. The true origins of clans probably go back to at least the trading partnerships of Hopewell times (Tooker 1971).

The currency of the League of the Iroquois and many other political interactions of the colonial years was marine shell wampum (Figure 10.15). Marine shell beads had been popular for centuries, but the availability of European metal tools after 1600 CE made it possible for New England Algonquian craftspeople to make small tubular beads in a standard size. These came in two colors, white from whelk columns and purple from quahog valves. Strings of beads that combined the two colors in various ways quickly became popular as symbols and memory aids in Algonquian and Iroquoian communities. As wampum beads proliferated people began weaving them into belts (Figure 10.16) having politically and religiously significant functions (Fenton 1998:224–239). These became important for the conduct of seventeenth-century colonial politics and they remain symbolically important to the Iroquois today. Wampum beads and a wide variety of glass trade beads are among the key artifacts used to date American Indian sites of the colonial era.

Iroquois clan matrons from leading families of the five constituent nations appointed male League chiefs. The fact that there was no standard number for national representation had to do with the internal politics of each of them as the confederacy evolved, not its population size. Numbers of League chiefs did not matter, for there were often vacancies due to recent deaths and the majority did not rule in any case. All decisions had to be unanimous, a rule that worked best with fewer participants than with more of them.

A new chief assumed the name and identity of one of the original 50 League chiefs who presided over the

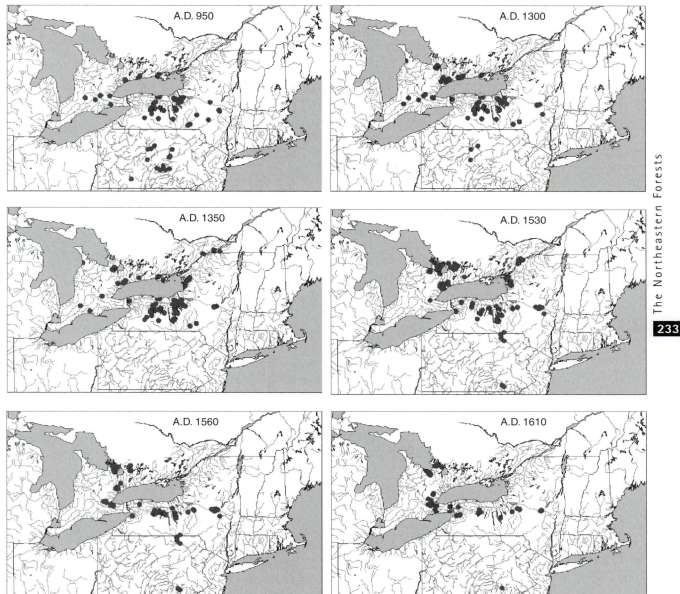

Figure 10.14 Regional maps for selected years showing the changing pattern of Northern Iroquoian sites over time.

formation of the confederacy. When a League chief died, revenge impulses were deflected by elaborate funerary rituals in which all participants offered condolences for not only the death of the deceased chief, but also for whatever other deaths might have occurred since the previous meeting. So sensitive were the traditional impulses to violence that the long ceremonies were indispensable just in case someone had died recently. Thus the Iroquois Condolence Ceremony was important not just for the assuaging of grief over the

loss of a League chief and the "raising up" of a new one in his place, but for heading off angry retributions of all kinds that might disturb the general peace between the constituent nations of the League.

The League of the Iroquois was thus a weak political alliance that existed primarily to keep internal peace, to provide occasionally for mutual defense, to facilitate occasional military offense, and to cope with European colonial expansion. The League survived the French and Indian Wars even though Iroquois warriors

Table 10.2 Hodenosaunee (League of the Iroquois) chiefs enumerated by nation and clan according to nineteenth-century sources.

Mohawk				
	Turtle		3	
	Wolf		3	
	Bear		3	
		Subtotal		9
Oneida				
	Wolf		3	
	Turtle		3	
	Bear		3	
		Subtotal		9
Onondaga				
	Bear		1	
	Beaver		2	
	Snipe		1	
	Hawk		1	
	Turtle		1	
	Wolf		1	
	Deer		2	
	Eel		3	
	Turtle		2	
		Subtotal		14
Cayuga				
	Deer		2	
	Turtle		3	
	Wolf		3	
	Snipe		2	
		Subtotal		10
Cayuga				
	Turtle		2	
	Snipe		3	
	Hawk		1	
	Bear		1	
	Wolf		1	
		Subtotal		8
		TOTAL		50

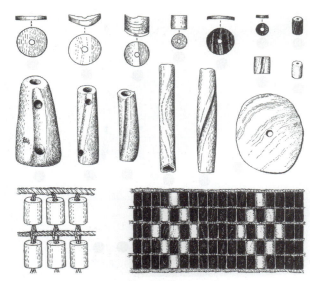

Figure 10.15 Marine shell beads (above) and seventeenth-century wampum beads (below), which were often used in strings or woven into symbolic belts.
Source: Willoughby 1935:267.

Cayugas, and Senecas were split, and their descendants own both reservations in the United States and reserves in Canada. The League of the Iroquois still exists, but in two attenuated forms on the Onondaga reservation in New York and the Six Nations reserve in Ontario.

Given the terms used in this book, the League of the Iroquois should be considered a political institution that weakly united tribal nations. It might be considered a chiefdom, but only in the weakest sense. It had a clear set of rules for succession, so robust that the League has survived, albeit in two versions. Yet although the lack of strong ranking principles facilitated its long-term survival as an institution, that same quality made the League less effective than a strong chiefdom would have been. Perhaps the Iroquois nations would have evolved into strong chiefdoms had they been able to nucleate in large permanent towns, but the demands of swidden farming kept that from happening until the American Revolution changed everything.

The Huron confederacy perhaps came closest to developing into a chiefdom with ranking and other traits common to most chiefdoms (Table 10.1). The towns and villages of the five Huron nations were clustered in and around Simcoe County, Ontario, unlike the more dispersed patterns of other Northern Iroquoian nations in the region (Fig. 10.9). They might have evolved into a single strong ranked polity in time, but they were defeated and dispersed in the course of the conflicts of the seventeenth century.

fought on both sides, but it did not survive the American Revolution as a single institution. Member nations were badly split in that conflict and many Iroquois were refugees in Ontario at its end. Virtually all Mohawks sided with the British and moved to Canada. The Oneidas mostly sided with the Americans. The Onondagas,

Figure 10.16 Central portion of the Washington Covenant Belt, which was created by Congress and conveyed to the Iroquois around the time of the War of Independence. In the collection of the Onondaga Nation.

Demographic Change and Adaptation

The effects of epidemic depopulation on many more western nations played out beyond the horizon and out of the view of literate observers, but the Northern Iroquoian experience is comparatively well documented. The crowd infections that were so devastating to American Indians had long since become common endemic diseases in Europe. Most had mutated and evolved from diseases carried by animal domesticates and other animal populations with which Old World peoples had long been in contact. Over the centuries European populations responded in part by increasing fertility to offset rising mortality from diseases such as influenza, measles, and smallpox. European social systems and subsistence practices allowed for larger numbers of children in anticipation of high childhood mortality because women were not heavily engaged in economic activities. But for Iroquoians and other northern farmers that was not a viable option. American Indian women did most of the farming, and they could not provide for their families while tending to large numbers of children. Consequently, births were limited and carefully spaced by American Indian women. It was rare for an Indian woman to have more than three children, and still more rare for her to have more than one at a time nursing. Had it been otherwise, average family size could have been larger and the Northern Iroquoian longhouses necessarily would have had a very different architecture.

We know from ethnographic records that Indian children were treasured and the death of a child prompted both grief and a desire for prompt replacement. A young mother who did not have an infant at such a time might choose to get pregnant as soon as possible. An older woman might choose to replace a lost teenager with a suitable captive brought home by a raiding party. Captives were easily incorporated into the community, and the practice became especially important later on when epidemics produced staggering losses almost overnight.

Captives were sometimes tortured and killed, but they were also routinely considered for adoption by families that had recently lost someone. Lucky captives were given the names of the people they replaced and they were expected to assume the associated identities, an expectation consistent with the passing on of League chief identities. This often worked; adopted captives often learned the language and did their best to fit in. It only seems odd to the modern reader until one recalls the compliant behavior of some twentieth-century kidnapping victims and the now well-known Stockholm syndrome. Human captives typically acquiesce to captivity if escape is impossible, and many bond with their captors.

The capacity of the Iroquois for adoption of individuals, families, larger groups, and even whole nations was the secret to their successful survival of the epidemics and wars of the colonial era. Villages that were depleted by smallpox, influenza, and other diseases were revived, not by increased births, but by the incorporation of people from defeated nations. Algonquian and Iroquoian people dislodged by expanding European settlements were also welcomed in Iroquoian communities. Many of the remnants of the three other confederacies that were destroyed by the Iroquois were taken in as refugees and quickly absorbed as adoptees. The Senecas were particularly successful using this strategy; their population was about the same size in 1776 as it was in 1630 even though the other Iroquois nations had shrunk somewhat over the same period. But even those Iroquois nations that had declined in numbers were still viable after the American Revolution, a much more adaptive outcome than the extinction experienced by so many other American Indian nations.

But what worked for one nation could not work for all of them. The problem for the northern farming cultures as a whole was that the regional native population was finite and declining. Consequently, while some groups survived and even grew, it was largely at the expense of others that were already in decline.

Under these conditions many weaker nations that were already reduced by diseases were accelerated toward extinction by raids and defections that robbed them of the healthy young people they needed to survive.

The cultural recombinations brought about by epidemics and the displacements of the colonial era also involved relocations, usually westward. Some Northern Iroquoians moved west to reconstitute themselves in new nations having new names, such as the Wyandots, Mingos, and Sandusky Senecas (Snow 1994:109–164). Reservations for all six Iroquois nations still exist in New York, but many others now have land elsewhere. The Cayuga presence in New York is very small, whereas the Senecas have several reservations and two separate governing bodies. The Onondagas still host League affairs near Syracuse, while one branch of the Oneidas operates a successful casino on reservation land in eastern New York.

The descendants of Iroquois converts to Catholicism, mostly now nominally Mohawks, survive on Canadian reserves in Quebec, while descendants of pro-British refugees of the American Revolution live mainly on Canadian reserves in Ontario. Many Oneidas migrated west to Wisconsin, and there are small reservations for other Iroquois communities in Oklahoma.

The Central Algonquians and Siouans

The Central Algonquian–speaking nations of the upper Great Lakes region adopted farming much as many of the Eastern Algonquians did. They used swidden techniques and they never gave up their hunting and gathering strategies. They lived near the northern limits of farming, and climatic cycles occasionally pushed those limits southward, forcing them to fall back on ancient food-getting practices. The expansion of displaced eastern Indians into and through this region disrupted and displaced many of these cultures, making it difficult to connect them with the archaeological traditions that went before. Expanding Europeans followed in their wakes, searching for furs, later timber, and still later farms.

The archaeology of Siouan-speaking cultures with connections to Mississippian centers is every bit as complicated. Like the Northern Iroquoians, Siouans pushed northward during the warm years of the Medieval Maximum, establishing what is known as Oneota culture. The previous occupants of the region, the builders of the effigy mound sites, withdrew northward. This might have been because their system collapsed when

Figure 10.17 Oneota culture on the northwestern fringe of Mississippian influence.

overhunting reduced critical deer populations, or it might have been more simply their inability to compete with better adapted Oneota farmers (Theler and Boszhardt 2006). Oneota eventually spread over Iowa, southern Wisconsin, and portions of adjoining states (Figure 10.17). Still later it gave rise to historic Siouan societies of the upper Midwest, many of which subsequently took to mounted nomadic lives on the Great Plains. There are many archaeological phases in this region, most of which led one way or another to various historic tribes. However, the details of those lineages are very difficult to discern archaeologically.

Oneota culture was present in southern Wisconsin by 1000 CE and it spread to the other parts of its eventual territory over the next two centuries, replacing effigy mound cultures. Oneota economy was focused on maize agriculture combined with seasonal forays to the Great Plains for bison hunting. The early Oneota villagers built burial mounds but they later shifted to burying the dead in cemeteries, a change that ended construction of earthen burial mounds in the region.

Norris Farms

One well-known Oneota mound cemetery is the Norris Farms site of west-central Illinois. The burial mounds at Norris Farms were modest piles of earth and the grave offerings that accompanied the dead in them were equally modest. This tells us that the Oneota people lived in egalitarian tribal societies lacking ranking and other traits of chiefdoms. Nevertheless, one can discern a distant connection to Mississippian practices in the details of Oneota archaeology at Norris Farms. One example was the burial of an infant with the severed hands of an adult (Milner 2004:179). One can only guess at the specific meanings of such an interment, but it is enough to say that evidence of this kind is not typical of tribal societies. It is the kind of thing one would expect to see in a chiefdom center.

Even more significantly, many of the 250 people buried at the Norris Farms site died violently. They were plagued by endemic warfare, as evidenced by arrow points embedded in bones, depression fractures in many skulls, and cut marks left in skulls. It must have been a violent and stressful time for the people of Norris Farms, perhaps the more so because they were at the leading edge of Oneota expansion into Illinois from Wisconsin around 1300 CE (Milner 2004:187). It was a frontier situation for the expanding Oneota people, and the evidence indicates that previous residents were not easily displaced.

Oneota sites are identified by their diagnostic pottery, which featured globular pots with shell tempering, strap handles, and incised designs. Like those made by Iroquois potters, pots of this kind were suited to the cooking of porridges and other foods made from maize and other plants cultivated by Oneota farmers. This, too, is consistent with cooking practices in Middle Mississippian towns.

The speakers of languages belonging to the Chiwere branch of Siouan are the most likely descendants of Oneota culture. These include the historic Winnebago, Oto, Ioway, Missouri, and Osage tribes (Gibbon 1998:612–613).

Aztalan

The site of Aztalan holds the remains of a Middle Mississippian outlier (Figure 10.18). It was discovered by Euro-American settlers along the Crawfish River between Madison and Milwaukee, Wisconsin, in 1835. Its nineteenth-century discoverers imagined incorrectly that it was the site of the ancient homeland of the Aztecs of Mexico, the fabled "Aztlan," and they accordingly gave it its inappropriate name. Later archaeological research showed that it was in fact a Middle Mississippian outlier, quite possibly a center established by migrants from Cahokia.

Aztalan was a thriving center in Oneota territory 1000–1300 CE. The Siouan-speaking Winnebago Indians who occupied southern Wisconsin are most likely the descendants of the Aztalan villagers. Aztalan was palisaded on three sides and protected by the river on the fourth. Two small, flat-topped platform mounds were built in the corners of the rectangular village that lie farthest from the river.

The Mississippian farmers at Aztalan began to have serious problems with the onset of the Little Ice Age after 1300 CE. The cold episode found them at the northern edge of the zone in which maize and other crops could be reliably grown. There were more frequent crop failures resulting from the reduced growing season, and the resulting stresses became too much for the Aztalan chiefdom to bear. The community broke up into several smaller ones and their inhabitants reverted to tribal organizations. Changing climate had forced them to depend more upon hunting and gathering and to live in more temporary settlements. It was in those communities that the Winnebagos were living when first encountered by Europeans, the chiefdoms of their ancestors all but forgotten.

Other Northerners and Other Adjustments

Some cultures probably dwindled to extinction, their survivors becoming refugees who were absorbed by luckier societies. Dynamic breakups and recombinations of all of these societies have often obscured their connections. The Cheyennes provide an informative

Figure 10.18 One of two platform mounds inside a reconstructed palisade and four bastions at the Aztalan site, Wisconsin.

example, one that we would not be able to guess from archaeological evidence alone. Like some Dakota (Siouan) groups, the Algonquian-speaking ancestral Cheyenne people were wild rice gatherers living in northern Minnesota in the seventeenth century. French fur trappers encountered them there at that time. The westward expansion of Ojibwas (Chippewas) prompted the Cheyennes to move south and to take up maize agriculture in southern Minnesota. Still later they became bison-hunting horse-mounted nomads on the Great Plains (see Chapter 12). This case and others like it illustrate the speed with which American Indian cultures could shift their adaptations and reinvent themselves. Neither the shift from wild rice to maize nor the conversion from farming to hunting appears to have been particularly traumatic for the adaptable ancestral Cheyennes even though they involved profound cultural changes.

It should not be surprising that archaeologists often have difficulty tracing the ancestry of any particular culture. Migration is typically accompanied by cultural

reinvention of the kind the Cheyennes illustrate, and the thread of continuity over time is easily lost. However, that in itself produces a discernable pattern, one in which over the larger sweep of time and space the cultures of the region appear to be transitory and disconnected. Much of this is the result of our inability to detect episodes of rapid cultural evolution in the archaeological record. This is particularly a problem for the very rapid changes that occurred after the arrival of horses. While it is comparatively easy to trace the ancestry of Northern Iroquoians, the later scramble of the northern farmers on the edge of the Great Plains left trails much harder to follow.

Epidemics and Depopulation

Lethal epidemics came later to this northern Midwest region than they did to regions of Spanish and later English colonization, but their effects were no less profound. Their later arrival was because diseases that

Box 10.2 HOW TO VISIT SITES IN THE NORTHEAST

There are many sites to visit in the region, some of which are mound sites of the sort discussed in Chapter 5. Others are later sites that are relevant to Chapter 10. Most can be found by referring to maps and guides published by the American Automobile Association. Online searches will also turn up directions and other pertinent information.

The Norton Mound Group outside Grand Rapids, Michigan, is a good example of burial mound construction. In Minnesota, I would recommend Blue Mounds State Park, Laurel Mounds, and Jeffers Petroglyphs Historic Site. New York has a few mound sites and many later Iroquoian sites, but few of them are well marked or open to the public. The Mohawk village site of Caughnawaga is just west of Fonda, New York, and it provides a rare opportunity for visitors to wander among the preserved floor plans of Iroquois longhouses.

The Lawson site near London, Ontario, and the Crawford Lake site west of Toronto offer museum exhibits as well as reconstructed longhouses on Iroquoian sites. The Kay-Nah-Chi-Wah-Nung Historical Centre preserves an Ojibwa village and burial mounds.

New England offers many good museum exhibits but few sites that offer much to see. The Mashantucket Pequot Museum at Foxwoods in eastern Connecticut is a good example. Colonial period forts can be found in several New England states, usually along the coast. Rock art can be viewed at Solon, Maine, and incidentally at a few other locations. Colonial period sites such as Plymouth Plantation, Massachusetts, Deerfield, Massachusetts, and Pemaquid, Maine, often have American Indian dimensions.

Ohio is the center of Adena and Hopewell sites, as mentioned in Chapter 5, as well as many later sites. Among the latter having good to excellent interpretive facilities are Flint Ridge, Fort Ancient, Fort Hill, and SunWatch Indian Village and Archaeological Park. Stops at these sites will lead visitors to other sites that are less well known but nonetheless important and interesting.

In Wisconsin, visitors should start with Aztalan and Lizard Mounds. Other effigy mounds can be seen at Devil's Lake State Park and Sheboygan Indian Mound Park.

These are just a few highlights. Many more sites can be found across the region by online searching. Remember at all times that collecting is both illegal and unethical. All remains belong to the landowner. In the case of publically owned lands they belong to all of us and no individual has the right to appropriate them for private use.

originated in the Old World were childhood afflictions there and they were generally not a great threat to Indians until colonists began settling complete families. This was delayed until the late sixteenth century in Virginia and until the seventeenth century in the Northeast. It was further delayed until the eighteenth and nineteenth centuries farther west (Snow and Lanphear 1988).

Once introduced in the early seventeenth century, the epidemics sometimes swept ahead of European exploration (Figure 10.19), wiping out whole communities and shattering political and social organizations before the European settlers were even aware of them (Lorant 1965:75). The whole core of the Eastern Woodlands was largely depopulated in this way. The region reverted to wilderness without Indians to fire vast expanses of forest as they had for thousands of years, or to open new fields for cultivation as they had in more recent millennia. Little wonder that leaders like Daniel Boone followed Indian trails so overgrown that they were barely traceable, into a wilderness landscape that seemed untouched by humans. Little wonder that Euro-American settlers found it difficult to attribute the impressive earthworks they found to the scattered remnant tribes they also encountered along the way. What had once been the center of Adena and Hopewell cultures, followed by Fort Ancient and others, was no man's land in the colonial era. It had taken only a few decades for large stretches of the Eastern Woodlands to revert to wilderness, long enough to erase what they had once been from living memory.

The Shawnees appear to have come out of this zone, but while they played an important role in the colonial era the precise archaeological ancestry of these Algonquian speakers remains uncertain. There were several such survivors of the chaos of colonial wars and epidemics, whose origins are now difficult or impossible to trace back in time. On the other side of the archaeological ledger are late prehistoric cultures that are well known to archaeology but which have left no known living descendants. Examples are Shenks Ferry and Monongahela cultures, which are known only from archaeology and possibly a few vague references in early documents. There are many others, in several cases cultures that would be anonymous had archaeologists not named them. They disappeared from history too early for them to get more than an occasional mention in surviving documents, too early for any survivors to be identified.

Summary

1. Expansion of farming northward was made possible by the development of maize that matured in 120 days and the onset of the Medieval Maximum climatic episode.

2. The arrival of the bow and arrow, competition for farmland and other resources contributed to the complex dynamics of life in the northern portion of the Eastern Woodlands following the demise of Hopewell.

3. Algonquian-speaking nations tended to push south into the region while Iroquoian and Siouan nations expanded northward.

4. Wild rice became a near staple where it grew wild in the Great Lakes basin.

5. Rock art reveals some features of Algonquian shamanism, which stressed transformation, power, and sexuality.

6. Upland swidden farming made Iroquoian expansion into the Northeast possible, and produced hundreds of compact matrilocal village sites.

7. Competition during the Little Ice Age produced conflict that was eventually countered in part by the formation of tribal confederacies.

8. The League of the Iroquois was a tribal confederacy that did not develop into a typical chiefdom.

9. Eastern Algonquians expanded southward along the Atlantic coast, picking up maize farming, and in Virginia becoming numerous enough to develop chiefdoms.

10. The introduction of epidemic diseases from Europe in the colonial era devastated and

Figure 10.19 Theodore de Bry's 1591 engraving (no. 20 of 43) of Native American treatment of sick individuals. *Source:* From a lost painting by Jacques le Moyne.

displaced many Eastern Woodlands societies, leading to demographic collapse and reversion of the forest to wilderness in some parts of the region.

11. Oneota was a northern derivative of Middle Mississippian that appeared southwest of the western Great Lakes.

12. A colony was established in an area west of Lake Michigan by Siouan-speaking people having origins in Middle Mississippian.

Further Reading

The *Northeast* (Vol. 15) and *Southeast* (Vol. 14) volumes of the *Handbook of North American Indians* offer descriptive sketches of the archaeology of the Eastern Woodlands as well as detailed summaries of what is know about the surviving American Indian nations of the region. Missing, of course, are ethnographic entries for the great unknown core of the region that is drained by the Ohio and Tennessee rivers. Older volumes that still provide adequate introductions are Ronald Mason's *Great Lakes Archaeology* and my own *The Archaeology of New England*. My book *The Iroquois* provides an introduction to these key players in the colonial history of the continent. All of these sources provide paths into a vast literature.

Glossary

nation: A polity or set of polities united by common language and customs.

wigwam: A dome-shaped house having a framework of bent saplings and a covering of bark or mats.

The Gulf Rim

If you desire to see me, come where I am; if for peace, I will receive you with special good will. If for war, I will await you in my town; but neither for you, nor for any man, will I set back one foot.

Quigaltam Chieftain to Hernando de Soto, 1542

Introduction

The rim of the Gulf of Mexico is a maritime environment to which Native Americans adapted in a variety of ways, a rich environment that sets it apart from the interior Eastern Woodlands to the north. Domesticates from Mesoamerica and South America led to food production and complex societies in some areas. Chiefdoms developed without agriculture in areas where natural resources were exceptionally rich. Wide water or desert gaps in the long Circum-Gulf rim restricted long-distance travel and trade between the Eastern Woodlands, Mesoamerica, and Cuba, yet there were similarities imposed by the Gulf environments (White and Weinstein 2008). The cultures of the Gulf region were among the first to be devastated by warfare, disease, and enslavement following the settlement of Cuba by Spanish colonists, the Cortés expedition to Mexico (1519), and the de Soto expedition (1539–1543) into the Southeast.

The Gulf Coast is a long, curving coastline having many indentations and considerable environmental variation, like the North American West Coast, except that it curves back on itself (see Chapter 13). A boat trip from Key West to northeastern Yucatan, staying reasonably close to land, would be 4500 km (2800 mi) long, about the same distance as a boat trip from Juneau, Alaska, to the southern tip of Baja California. Like the West Coast, what sets apart the Gulf rim from the lands lying behind it is the maritime character of the Gulf lowlands, an ecological reality that has prompted separate treatment in this chapter.

The Gulf Environment

Maritime environments are different from interior ones and those that encircle large bodies of saltwater stand apart from the inland regions at their backs. The world's greatest such region is the Mediterranean Sea and the rim of resource-rich land that surrounds it. No one doubts the importance of the Mediterranean in the development of the Classic cultures that flourished on its shores and depended upon it for food and boat transportation. North America's only comparably large marine body is the Gulf of Mexico, an expanse of water so large that it truly deserves to be called a sea. While it does not rival the Mediterranean as a stage for the rise of civilization, it does define a maritime region separate from the rest of the continent. The Gulf is nearly encircled by land, and boat travel around its rim has been possible for millennia. Yet this coastal province is not so much a single piece as it is a fragmentary residual ring made up of the maritime margins of three other regions: Mesoamerica, the Eastern Woodlands, and the Greater Antilles. Sea currents offshore make it easy to travel clockwise around the Gulf, while countercurrents closer to shore help boats along in the opposite direction. The currents are not as speedy as the inner and outer beltway rings that circulate traffic around many modern cities, but they could have facilitated boat travel (Wilkerson 2005). The extent to which such travel actually occurred has yet to be demonstrated archaeologically.

Cuba, the greatest of the Greater Antilles (Figure 11.1), lies like a loose cork in the southeastern mouth of the nearly enclosed Gulf. The first inhabitants

Figure 11.1 Map of the Gulf rim region.

familiar edge around much of the Gulf. But the Topic of Cancer separates the subtropical north from the tropical south, and crops like South American manioc could never prosper north of the line. Moreover, the south Texas and the Mexican coast north of the Tropic of Cancer is a dry zone that supported only a thin native population in 1492. Offshore the Texas barrier islands trap lagoons of hypersaline water that is up to eight times saltier than the sea and far less productive as a result.

While there are artifacts pointing to contacts across these gaps over the millennia, and the tropical crops that sustained the peoples of the Eastern Woodlands must have been brought across them as well, archaeologists remain struck by the rarity of such contacts and the failure of so many things to spread. Tobacco was carried to the Eastern Woodlands 3,000 years ago, probably by way of the Antilles (Figure 11.2). Tobacco was quickly

of the Antilles probably reached Cuba by boat, crossing 200 km (130 mi) of open ocean from the Yucatan Peninsula 6,000 years ago (4000 BCE). Sea levels were lower around the Gulf at the end of the Pleistocene, as they were elsewhere around the world. They rose toward their modern levels during the Holocene, but it was not until the rising stabilized around 4000 BCE that barrier islands and the resource-rich zones behind them could form. This made the Gulf Coast environments more attractive to hunter-gatherers after 4000 BCE, and set the stage for later developments (Widmer 2005).

Large native boats transited the gap between Yucatan and Cuba as well as the one between Cuba and Florida in the era of Spanish exploration, but the traffic was not steady enough to create cultural uniformity around the great ring of Gulf Coast lowlands. The region is not culturally uniform even today, and we should not expect it to have been so in the past. The Gulf of Mexico is a very large body of water. It is about 1,600 km (1,000 mi) across the Gulf from Tampa, Florida, to Tampico, Mexico, and the gaps between Cuba and its nearest peninsulas are 200 km (125 mi) wide.

A region as large as the Gulf of Mexico is bound to lack environmental or cultural uniformity, and in this case there are three important gaps that impeded movement around its rim. The near desert gap on land and the lowered marine productivity separating Mesoamerica from the Eastern Woodlands was a gap as formidable as the water gaps separating Yucatan, Cuba, and Florida (White 2005c:11). To be sure the sabal palm and other palms are found along most of the Gulf's coast, and no part of it is exempt from the threat of devastation in the warm months, when the Gulf turns into a cauldron of hurricanes. Barrier islands and lush mangroves are a

Figure 11.2 American Indian tobacco *(Nicotiana rustica)*. Plants are approximately 60 cm (2 ft) tall. *Source:* Courtesy of beautifulbotany.com.

adopted across North America, but although papaya and chiles also spread to Florida from the Antilles they failed to take permanent root. Cotton was important for textile weaving in the U.S. Southwest, but even though wild cotton grows in southern Florida, peoples of the Southeast made do with other fibers (Widmer 1974). Domesticated cotton was available in Mesoamerica by 1500 BCE but it was not grown in the Southeast until the colonial era (White 2005a:306–307).

Manioc might have spread part of the way with the ceramics, but turned out to be too tropical to grow in the Southeast. Apart from the ecological constraints on the spread of plant domesticates, why some things seem to have spread so easily while others did not remains an adaptation puzzle for archaeologists.

Ceramic pots are earlier in northern and western South America than elsewhere in the Americas. Fiber-tempered ceramics appear by 2500 BCE in the Southeast, earlier than in Mesoamerica (White and Weinstein 2008:236). So unless pottery was invented independently in the Southeast (and many archaeologists infer that it was), like tobacco it probably spread there by way of the islands of the Caribbean. If it did spread by that route, variability in decoration indicates that it was a spread of technology, not of a migrating population carrying it (Clark and Knoll 2005:284–288). Pottery made by a migrating population would not have differed so much from prototypes left behind.

Early Crops and Mound Building

Earthen mound building and pottery making came early to the Gulf region, but it took much longer for maize to replace native crops. In northern Louisiana the great mounds at Watson Brake (Figure 11.3) date as early as 3400 BCE and Poverty Point was built by 1600 BCE (see Chapter 5). There is no clear connection between these mound builders and those that began piling earth in the Great Lakes area a bit later. Neither is there any reason to link them directly to the Olmec mound builders of coastal Mexico, who started constructing earthen mounds there around the same time. Yet all of these people were laying similar architectural foundations, both conceptually and literally.

The lowlands around the Gulf were productive places for hunter-gatherers to make a living. The hot coast was even more productive, with its combination of terrestrial and marine plants and animals. So rich was this environment that in some places people were still living by hunting, fishing, and gathering wild foods when the first Spanish explorers encountered them. The

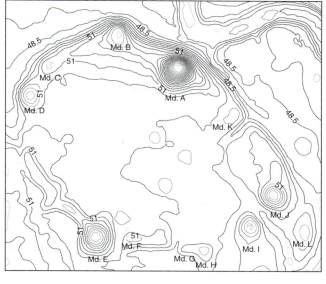

Watson Brake (16OU175)

0 10 20 30 40 50 m

N · S · W · E

Contour interval = 50 cm

Figure 11.3 Map of Watson Brake.
Source: Courtesy of Joe Saunders.

historic Calusa of the southwest coast of Florida had chiefdom polities despite lacking domesticated crops.

In contrast, the Olmecs of coastal Mexico made the most of domesticated crops (see Chapter 7), double cropping maize and other plants and laying a foundation for the rise of later Maya and Mexican states. Maize spread northward into the Eastern Woodlands and around the northern Gulf Coast sometime in the first two centuries CE. This was more than two millennia after ceramics first appeared in the Southeast, and it would be centuries more before maize became a staple there. The lesson here is that agriculture, ceramics, architecture, and chiefdom polities did not all develop or spread together. The details of the evolution of human adaptation in the region were clearly contingent upon many local factors. The more we know about the evolution of Native America societies around the Gulf Coast the clearer it is that they evolved piecemeal, something conceptually similar to mosaic evolution in biology.

Lacking the evidence we have now, many archaeologists once thought that there was a desolate gap of several centuries between the decline of Hopewell and the rise of Mississippian in the Eastern Woodlands. It is clear now that many cultures bridged that gap, among them being a few along the Gulf Coast. The important thing is not to find a bright line in time between the Hopewell tribes and later Mississippian chiefdoms, but rather to understand the several ways in which tribal societies living on local domesticates and wild resources evolved into later chiefdoms that depended mainly upon domesticates imported from Mesoamerica. A prime example is found in Troyville-Coles Creek Culture in the lower Mississippi Valley.

Troyville-Coles Creek Culture

Hopewell culture was waning in the northern Eastern Woodlands by 400 CE, and the influences that its trading network brought to the Southeast gradually disappeared. Troyville-Coles Creek culture arose in and around the lower Mississippi Valley and along the Gulf Coast as Hopewell expired, and it persisted until around 1100 CE. After that it evolved into a regional variant of Mississippian culture (see Chapter 9).

Troyville-Coles Creek towns are notable for their flat-topped mounds arranged around plazas. This was a pattern that would later become a widespread feature of Mississippian towns. Major sites near rivers usually have five to nine mounds, one of them typically much larger than the others. Smaller communities usually had no more than three mounds and many smaller hamlets and villages had none at all (Gibbon 1998:171–173).

The Troyville-Coles Creek people lived on gathered wild plants and local domesticates, and maize was of only minor importance. Acorns, persimmons, palmetto, maygrass, and squash were all more important than maize. Tobacco was cultivated as well, and protein came from deer and smaller mammals, but the bounty of the region kept maize from being adopted as a staple until as late as the thirteenth century CE (Milner 2004:153). Troyville-Coles Creek ceramics are distinctive and variable, traits that before radiocarbon dating made pottery an important dating tool for archaeologists. Good quality chert was scarce, so craftspeople either imported stone tools or depended upon bone as a material for making points.

Weeden Island, Fort Walton, and Safety Harbor Cultures

The evolution of Weeden Island culture into Fort Walton and Safety Harbor cultures in northern Florida is another case illustrating the emergence of agriculture, monumental architecture, and chiefdoms from simpler antecedents along the northeastern Gulf Coast. Many simple farming cultures persisted across the Eastern Woodlands after the collapse of the Hopewell trading network. One of these, possibly Swift Creek culture in

Alabama and Georgia, gave rise to Weeden Island culture along Florida's Gulf coast, and the lowland portions of Alabama and Georgia (Milanich 1994).

Weeden Island

Weeden Island culture (200–1000 CE) overlapped Hopewell in time (Milanich 1994:162). Like the Troyville-Coles Creek people and the builders of the Toltec Mounds in Arkansas, they were early platform mound builders, an architectural form that would later be taken to greater heights by Mississippian culture. Weeden Island had a series of at least five regional variants (Milanich 1994:155–241). The area it covered along the northeastern Gulf Coast was too large for it to have been a single culture, let alone a single polity. Some of them began to depend upon maize as a staple by 500 CE, but others delayed depending upon it until around 750. Weeden Island culture evolved into or was replaced in part of its range by Fort Walton culture by around 1000 CE.

Weeden Island villages were probably governed by tribal big men who were on the verge of becoming petty chieftains. While Weeden Island sites have some of the trappings of simple chiefdoms, they do not exhibit the elaborated traits usually associated with them. The site of Kolomoki in southwestern Georgia is a good example of a Weeden Island village with large platform mounds.

Weeden Island people also still built smaller mounds to contain graves, in the fashion of earlier Adena and Hopewell mounds. Typically a pit was dug first and cremated remains were laid in the bottom along with offerings. Rocks and clay were piled over the grave and burial mounds when finished were up to 15 m (50 ft) wide by 6 m (20 ft) high. Archaeologists sometimes find decapitated heads in the mound fill and they infer that these probably belonged to sacrificed individuals.

The McKeithen site (Figure 11.4) is a Weeden Island site in northern Florida that has three mounds laid out as points of an isosceles triangle (Milanich et al. 1997). The main axis of the triangle points toward the summer solstice sunrise. The site was occupied 200–750 CE, and the mounds were probably built in the middle of that time range. They served to support chiefly residences and temples. An elite female was buried in one of them and another mound supported a charnel house for storing the bones of the dead. The third mound was apparently used to inter and exhume bones for cleaning before their final burial. The mound structures at this site were burned around 475 CE and the mounds were given fresh mantels of sand, probably a major ritual and political event for the community.

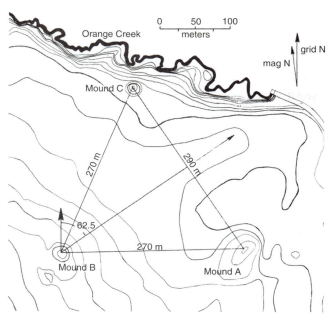

Figure 11.4 The McKeithen site, northern Florida, showing architectural alignments.
Source: Courtesy of Jerald T. Milanich.

The Crystal River site (Figure 11.5) is another site that was occupied during Weeden Island times and possibly later as well. It has several mounds, shell middens that were converted into platform mounds. There are two large limestone rocks at the site, one of which bears a crudely etched human face and torso. Some archaeologists once thought it was similar to Maya stelae found on the other side of the Gulf of Mexico. But

limestone slabs like these are common natural occurrences in this part of Florida (Milanich 1999:22–23).

Fort Walton

Fort Walton culture grew out of Weeden Island culture around 1000 CE, developing polities that were chiefdoms supported by intensive agriculture. While earlier Weeden Island farmers probably practiced swidden agriculture, planting crops in hills scattered across recently cleared fields, Fort Walton farmers planted row crops in more permanent fields (Milanich 1994:364). They also had Mesoamerican beans, which were lacking earlier. Along with maize and squash, beans became a major staple across the Southeast at this time, providing protein and thus reducing the need for meat in the diet. Sunflowers, nuts, and a wide range of other foods made for a diverse and nutritious diet.

Fort Walton communities had the beginnings of hierarchical political organization, a trait of chiefdoms. They even sported some of the symbols borrowed from the Mississippian centers in the interior of the Eastern Woodlands (Milanich 1994:364, 377).

These people had made the transition to chiefdoms, something that the ancestral Weeden Island societies had been on the verge of doing. Tropical cultigens, permanent fields, and large towns with earthworks were among the prerequisites for this jump in complexity, but such a shift also required inspiration. The first chiefdoms in the Eastern Woodlands emerged with local inspiration in the Middle Mississippi Valley around 900 CE. The idea spread, perhaps triggering similar social and political

Figure 11.5 One of two standing stones at Crystal River, inside a protective cage. The sketch to the right shows the worn petroglyph found on the stone.

Figure 11.6 The Lake Jackson site, a Fort Walton culture mound site in northern Florida.

innovations in cultures like Weeden Island earlier than they might have otherwise appeared (Anderson 1999:226). The Lake Jackson site (Figure 11.6) is a typical Fort Walton culture mound site.

Safety Harbor

Safety Harbor culture grew out of another variant of Weeden Island around 900 CE, in the area from Tampa Bay northward, but unlike Fort Walton culture the adaptation of this culture remained more reliant on wild resources. Each platform mound site was probably the center of a separate polity, in each case probably a weak chiefdom. These weak chiefdoms, which survived until Spanish colonial times, were never as complex as those of Fort Walton culture. Safety Harbor sites are generally small and dispersed, and they have produced no evidence of intensive agriculture. The central west coast of Florida was rich in wild food resources, so maize never became a major part of the Safety Harbor diet (Milanich 1994:398–399). Although Safety Harbor sites have yielded pottery, and artifacts of copper, shell, and stone that bear the symbols of the Southeastern Ceremonial Complex, they do not equal those of the more Mississippian-influenced cultures to the north and west. The Madira Bickel platform mound on the Terra Ceia site near Palmetto, Florida, is a good example.

Spanish Colonization

Spanish missionization in northern Florida led to a more intensive use of maize by the natives living there than had previously been the case (Hutchinson et al. 1998). The historic Timucuas lived in many independent polities spread over much of northern Florida. Spanish missions were planted among the Timucua villages and change came earlier to these people than to most others north of Mexico. Indeed, it was a two-way street, Spanish colonists adopting many Timucua practices just as the Timucuas absorbed many Spanish ones. They were all on their way to creating a new **creole** society of mixed ancestry in the region, but smallpox and other epidemics all but wiped out the Timucua population, putting an end to the cultural evolution of a new culture having mixed ancestry (Milanich 1996).

Southern Florida

The productivity of native plants in southern Florida was so great that the historic native peoples there never relied on maize at all. Instead they located their settlements close to concentrations of native plants that were both abundant and reliable. People in southern Florida lived seemingly at one of the ends of the earth. But although they were remote from the Mississippian developments in the interior of the continent, they were positioned to receive South American goods and ideas by way of the islands of the Caribbean. Their nonagricultural adaptation was such a successful one that it persisted after hunting and gathering had been replaced by domestic food production in much of the rest of eastern North America.

Belle Glade

There are several sites in the Belle Glade area around Lake Okeechobee that are known as "big circle" sites, the oldest of which date to the first millennium BCE. These often have large circular earthworks with attached linear ones with mounds at their ends radiating from them. Large circular ditches appear to have been designed to draw off groundwater, which otherwise would have been uncomfortably near the surface. These structures seem to point to some sort of tropical agriculture, but their nature is uncertain and will remain so until further research is done (Milanich 1998:113–122).

The evidence from the Fort Center site and others like it suggests that drained field agriculture might have been introduced across the Gulf from Mexico as early as 450 BCE. There is even some pollen evidence for the presence of maize at these sites, but it is disputed by other archaeologists (Milanich 1994:287–291). If appropriate strains of maize and the right soils had been available to these people a culture like Olmec might have emerged here. But a major commitment to farming

Box 11.1 HOW TO COPE WITH DYNAMIC ENVIRONMENTS

All environments are dynamic. Everyone is conscious of short-term changes of daily and annual cycles. Long-term changes in climate, sea levels, and vegetation are often slow shifts that people adapt to without knowing. Such changes are too slow to be noticed over the course of an individual's lifetime. But some changes are abrupt and noticeable, such as the end of the Younger Dryas 11,570 years ago, floods, hurricanes, tsunamis, tornados, landslides, forest fires, earthquakes, and volcanic eruptions. These are events that are too rare and unpredictable for any but the largest and most complex societies to prepare for, and in most environments over most of the past people simply survived as best they could and adapted as well as they could after the fact. Even today that is a favored strategy in ecozones where abrupt catastrophic change is a very low-probability event. Most people live out their lives without worrying much about any of them.

But some environments are more dynamic than others. The Gulf Coast is one such environment. In this case the dynamism is driven mainly by ocean currents and occasional hurricanes. Even after sea-level rise stabilized a few thousand years ago the coastline remained subject to constant change. Barrier islands migrate as sand is shifted by currents, prevailing winds, and periodic storms. Plants counteract these forces to some extent. Mangroves thrive along the Gulf coastline, their limbs reaching out over the water and dropping prop roots. The plants stabilize the shoreline and soil gatherers around their roots such that over time the mangroves creep out into saltwater and new land builds up under and behind them. Pioneering red mangroves are the most salt tolerant, and they lead the slow expansion across mudflats, filtering salt in their roots. Black and white mangroves follow, each with a different mechanism for disposing of salt. Hurricanes occasionally tear up stabilizing vegetation and a short-term change in sea level would upset the balance between geological and biological forces.

Prior to two centuries ago humans typically adapted to the dynamic environment of southern Florida by being flexible and opportunistic. They did not make big investments in agriculture or architecture. A similar strategy would have been appropriate if they lived in a region subject to frequent forest fires or floods.

---

appears never to have taken hold here and Belle Glade never developed beyond the big circle stage.

Archaeological sites in the Glades region are very diverse. Shell middens and earth middens mark sites where seasonal resources were gathered. Elsewhere there are burial mounds of sand or stone. Everywhere people specialized on plant, land animal, or fish resources that were locally abundant (Milanich 1994:308–311).

On the southwest coast of Florida the Key Marco site was a wet site in which artifacts of wood, fiber, and other normally perishable materials were beautifully preserved (Figure 11.7). Surviving wooden artifacts include painted and inlaid masks, tablets, plaques, and statuettes (Milanich 1994:304–308). The site was excavated over a century ago, and since then the island has been almost entirely destroyed by modern development.

Calusa

The Calusas are the best-known historic people of southern Florida. They built linear and circular shell mounds on low-lying island and mainland locations in the vicinity of Fort Myers. Some of these are over 100 m (330 ft) long, have steep sides, and are as much as 6 m (20 ft) high. The Calusas and their ancestors resided on or around these big middens, sometimes cutting artificial canals from open water to give them easy access by canoe.

The ancestral Calusahatchee culture became established after sea levels stabilized here around 700 BCE. Their subsistence shifted increasingly toward marine resources in the centuries that followed. The addition of these resources to an already rich array of terrestrial and freshwater resources made the adoption of cultivation unnecessary. Indeed, local soil and climatic conditions make agriculture impractical, probably explaining why the Olmec phenomenon was not repeated here (Widmer 1988).

By 300 CE, pressure to regulate the harvesting of a complex array of resources and to manage their redistribution led to the rise of hereditary chieftains. This is a subtropical case that is similar to that which developed on the Northwest Coast of Canada (see Chapter 13). In both cases seasonally abundant marine resources and population pressures led to the rise of chiefdoms in the absence of agriculture.

Figure 11.7 Kneeling human-feline effigy figure made of wood, 15 cm (6 in.) tall. Key Marco, Florida.
Source: Courtesy of the National Museum of Natural History.

Figure 11.8 Oblique view of Miami Circle feature, August 2000.
Source: Courtesy of the Florida Division of Historical Resources.

The Miami Circle

Archaeological testing in advance of major construction in 1998 led to the discovery of the enigmatic Miami Circle site (Figure 11.8) in downtown Miami, which serves as a good example of twenty-first-century archaeology. The site is an 11.5-m (38-ft) circle of 600 postmolds that contains 24 shallow, irregularly shaped basins. Radiocarbon dating has put its age back as far as 1,800 years ago. But this part of Miami was once heavily industrialized, and the circle features could be more recent remains that have become associated with older wood samples in the course of several episodes of construction and demolition. This is only one of the many controversies attached to this site.

While the Miami area was Tequesta Indian territory in the sixteenth century, there is little to link that or any other tribe to the site. Various stakeholders came forward during the course of the investigation carried out by cultural resource management (CRM) archaeologists. They included professional archaeologists, modern American Indian groups, state and local governments, federal agencies, developers, business interests, and citizen groups. The case illustrates both the ambiguity of many archaeological finds and the complications that arise when they become politicized. The site was purchased and preserved at great expense by Miami-Dade County, but in early 2007 it was once again threatened, this time by a collapsing sea wall.

The Northern Gulf Coast

Pensacola Culture

Pensacola culture developed in the western Florida panhandle and adjacent coastal parts of Alabama and Mississippi. It grew out of a generalized culture that was closely related to Weeden Island, but differed from it by the heavier addition of Mississippian traits adopted from interior cultures (Brown 2003). Pensacola culture shows an unusual combination of Gulf Coast and Mississippian traits. Some archaeologists also see connections with the Huastecan culture of coastal Mexico (Brose 2003).

Perhaps the best known Pensacola Culture site is the Bottle Creek site, a large site located on a low swampy island north of Mobile, Alabama. The site has at least 18 earthen mounds. Five of them are arranged around a central plaza. It was established sometime after 1100 CE, but its main occupation was from 1250 to 1550 CE. It is difficult to reach on foot and to modern people it seems like a very unlikely place to locate a ceremonial center. However, it would have been easy to access by dugout canoe, the swiftest mode of transportation available to the people who built the Bottle Creek site.

Even though the Bottle Creek site is surrounded by swamps and hidden from a distance by huge cypress trees, it was a central place. Cypress swamps typically occur near large rivers in this region, and this one lies near the confluence of the Tombigbee and Alabama rivers, where those streams become a maze of branches and bayous at the head of Mobile Bay. It was a ceremonial center for the Pensacola people, and a gateway to their society despite what seems today to have been a remote location.

Bottle Creek might have continued to be important as a sacred site as late as 1750 CE. Indian holdouts might have survived there much as the Seminoles later did in southern Florida. European artifacts were widely available at the time, but the people who held out at Bottle Creek appear to have shunned them (Brown 2003:224–226).

The Antilles

Only Cuba figures into the Circum-Gulf culture area, but to understand its role in the archaeology of North America one must also know something about the archaeology of the other islands leading back toward the South American mainland (Figure 11.1). From a South American perspective, the islands of the West Indies arc northward from the Venezuela coast and westward to the entrance of the Gulf of Mexico. The small islands of the Lesser Antilles lie like stepping stones along the east side of the Caribbean, leading to the east–west line of ever larger islands that form the Greater Antilles. The Bahama archipelago lies scattered north of the big islands, close to Florida.

The western end of Cuba lies midway between the Florida and Yucatan peninsulas in the wide mouth of the Gulf of Mexico. The train of islands leading back to the South American coast might have been the route by which tobacco, pottery, and perhaps even one strain of maize reached eastern North America. Boat traffic might also have allowed pre-Columbian exchange between Yucatan and Florida by way of Cuba. But such traffic probably was not regular, and its effects were not pervasive.

All but a few of the northern islands lie in the tropics. Summer hurricanes occasionally batter them, threatening all but those that lie near the South American coast.

Island Adaptation

Plotting all the Antilles by size and frequency produces a power curve rather than a normal curve. Figure 11.9 shows this using a log scale for island sizes in km² so that the extreme concavity of the power curve is made more linear (there are about 2.6 km² to every square mile). The sizes of islands of an archipelago, like wealth distributions and community sizes, do not usually distribute normally around a central tendency. There is only one very large land island (Cuba at 104,900 km² or 40,501 mi²) in the Antilles, just as there is only one richest person in a community or only one largest community in a region. There are a few medium-sized (or rich) cases and many very small (or poor) cases in any such distribution. In the Caribbean, Hispaniola, Jamaica, and Puerto Rico are next in size order. There are 8 more smaller islands that are each more than 1,000 km² (386 mi²) in size. There are at least 216 islands smaller than that, with the smaller size categories always having more examples than the next larger ones.

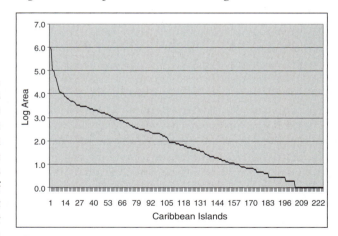

Figure 11.9 A power curve graph of 228 Caribbean islands, from the largest, Cuba, to 24 islands that are less than a tenth of a square kilometer in size. The islands are arranged by rank on the horizontal axis and their sizes are plotted according to the vertical axis.

Ecologists have used islands for many years to understand the relationships between land, plants, and animals, and anthropologists can use them similarly to understand human adaptation (MacArthur and Wilson 1967). The advantage of islands is that they are dramatically bounded and often separated from each other and mainland areas by formidable reaches of open water. A 10-km² (3.9 mi²) island is a much easier study area than is a 10-km² plot in the middle of a much larger forest. Animals do not wander on and off islands easily and most plants do not spread easily to and from islands either. The result is that islands of different sizes are often ecological containers that allow researchers to assess the effects of scale on ecological relationships. It works as well for anthropologists too.

One should expect variability to be less on smaller islands than on larger ones. Archaeologists sometimes use a measure of diversity for this purpose. The diversity measure takes into account both richness (the number of types of a certain class) and evenness (their relative proportions). If the class being considered is settlements, then one should expect there to be fewer settlements of any size and a narrower range of sizes on a small island as compared to a larger one. One should also expect to find larger primate centers on the larger island of any set of islands being considered. Human settlements in the Antilles largely conform to ecological expectations, but we learn as much or more from cases that deviate from expectations. These points are made clearer by examples below in the discussion of Taíno culture.

Peopling of the Antilles

The first people to move into the Greater Antilles did not come by way of the chain of smaller island steppingstones lying to the east, but instead probably came from the Yucatan Peninsula to the west. Their sites are found only on Cuba, Hispaniola (the island shared by Haiti and the Dominican Republic), and possibly on Puerto Rico. Similarities between stone tools found in Belize and elsewhere on the peninsula are strikingly similar to others of similar age found on Cuba and Hispaniola. The earliest of them date to around 4000 BCE (Wilson et al. 1998). Computer simulations indicate that passage by boat from Florida would have been more risky and thus less likely than passage from Yucatan (Callaghan 2003; Keegan 1994).

These early migrants lacked pottery but they must certainly not have lacked boats. Mortars and pestles or manos and metates are also missing from the earliest sites, but archaeologists are uncertain whether food

grinding implements were truly absent or if excavations have simply failed to find the evidence yet (Keegan 1994:264–265). The westernmost tip of Cuba lies 200 km (125 mi) from the nearest spot on the Yucatan Peninsula, a long distance with nothing apparent on the horizon. Of course the earliest migrants might have been propelled across the wide strait by unexpected winds and currents, ending up luckily on the shores of the largest of the islands. It was in any case a passage that must have been memorable even though we can now only try to imagine it.

Archaic Migrants

A second migratory expansion moved through the Lesser Antilles from South America after 3200 BCE, producing a series of sites that archaeologists customarily call "Archaic." The sites are marked by the absence of pottery but the presence of heavy ground-stone tools and the remains of marine foods. This wave of migrants probably came by way of Trinidad, just off the South American mainland, where there is a site containing similar artifacts that dates back to 5800 BCE. Related sites are curiously rare or absent from the southern Lesser Antilles (the Windward Islands), but present north of them in the Leeward Islands and the Greater Antilles. This suggests that movement into the more northern islands was rapid. If the spread of these people into the Antilles was rapid, it slowed once it reached the Greater Antilles. It was not until much later that traces of influence began showing up in southern Florida.

Some later Archaic West Indians made and used gouges from heavy *Strombus* shells. Similar artifacts are also found in Venezuela and Florida, but so far not often in between. This suggests that there might have been some long-distance leap-frogging migrations along the island chain (Keegan 1994:266, 269). The *Strombus* shells were a particularly useful source of raw material for tools. Unfortunately for archaeologists, many broken shells work very well as **expedient tools** without much if any additional modification. This means that it is possible to identify them certainly as tools only by collecting large samples and finding consistent patterns of deliberate breakage (O'Day and Keegan 2001).

Archaic foragers made use of many food plants, some of which were not native to the islands and had to have been introduced by humans. Thus like Archaic peoples elsewhere in the Americas, these foragers were already tending and transporting plants and their seeds, if not truly cultivating them (Berman and Pearsall 2000; Newsom 1993; Newsom and Pearsall

2000). They also hunted a variety of island animals to extinction (Keegan 2000:142). Like the Pleistocene animals of the mainland, these creatures had evolved in isolation from any human predation and were not equipped to survive it when human hunters finally arrived. The resulting new environment was probably not just anthropogenic, which can be unintentional, but the consequence of an intentional effort to replicate familiar environments in island settings. The presence of South American fruit trees and eventually guinea pigs in the Antilles is not something that can be explained away as an inadvertent and accidental byproduct of human migration. The people who brought them clearly did so intentionally.

Saladoid Culture

Pottery-making farming people carrying what archaeologists call "Saladoid" culture moved rapidly into the Lesser Antilles from South America around 500 BCE. They spread as far north as Puerto Rico, but their expansion halted there for almost a millennium (300 BCE–600 CE). They probably coexisted with Archaic peoples for a few centuries before the latter died out or were absorbed (Keegan 1994; Keegan 2000:136–138).

The adaptive expansion of Saladoid culture was probably the cumulative effect of many independent tribal groups taking advantage of opportunities offered by the islands while at the same time responding to population pressure that encouraged them to move from the mainland of South America (Siegel 1991). Most sites are near the coast, substantial villages that endured for centuries. Large extended-family houses were arranged around central plazas, which in many cases doubled as cemeteries. The people combined cultivation of manioc and sweet potatoes with plant gathering, hunting, fishing, and shellfishing. Domesticated guinea pigs were brought along and it is possible that people also domesticated the local hutia, a cat-sized rodent (Keegan 2000:141–142).

Saladoid pottery was well made and often decorated with both painted and incised designs. Adzes, gouges, and other heavy tools were made from Strombus shells as well as from fine-grained stone. Canoes, weapons, and fishing equipment were made from a variety of materials, including wood, bone, shell, and stone. Beads and ornaments were made from shell and exotic minerals. The Saladoid people traded these artifacts between islands and with the South American mainland.

Ostionoid Culture

After having not spread past Puerto Rico for centuries, pottery making finally spread through the Greater Antilles, where it defines "Ostionoid" culture (600–1200 CE). This new culture eventually spread to all the inhabitable northern islands except the Cayman Islands, which remained uninhabited until colonial times.

Monumental architecture appeared with Ostionoid culture as their simple chiefdoms replaced earlier tribal societies. Open plazas (Figure 11.10) were replaced by stone-lined ones, and ball courts and ceremonial plazas replaced plaza cemeteries as the centers of communities. Ball courts are most conspicuous in sites that were border communities. This suggests that the ball game was important for managing relations between neighboring chiefdoms, which were later called "cacicazgos" by the Spanish. Subsistence shifted as well. Maize appeared for the first time, early enough to have been the source for at least one of the strains later grown in

Figure 11.10 North wall of the Jacana site plaza.
Sources: Courtesy of David Diener and New South Associates.

the Eastern Woodlands. On some islands the pressure of long-term human population growth forced a shift from declining crabbing to the gathering of still numerous marine mollusks (Keegan 2000:152–153).

The developmental processes that characterized Mesoamerica and the Southeast occurred in the Antilles as well. Food production and settled life on the island of Puerto Rico was initially organized along traditional kinship lines. However, there was an important shift in mortuary practices, typically the most conservative of social traditions. Prior to around 600 CE the dead were buried in communal cemeteries, most probably burial grounds that were managed by large kin groups. After 600 CE burials were increasingly placed in smaller and more private places that were close to domestic quarters. Spanish descriptions of sixteenth-century practices tell us that elite people were accorded elaborate funerals consistent with this later trend. The inference to be drawn from all of this is that with the emergence of chiefdoms, leading families abandoned the earlier kin-based communal practices and focused on ancestor worship within a much more narrowly defined elite context. This is one aspect of how chiefly families dismantled a traditional tribal society that was relatively egalitarian and constructed a ranked society in which inequalities were pronounced (Curet and Oliver 1998).

The evolution from tribal society to chiefdom is also evident in changing community architecture. During the Saladoid periods tribal societies built communities around central plazas. By 700 CE villages were being equipped with formal ball courts and more structured plazas that provided emerging chieftains the spaces they needed to assert their growing elite status (Curet 1996). This appears to have made such centers both places where contests occurred and places that were themselves contested (Siegel 1999). The processes by which chieftains and their closest relatives gradually accrued power and prestige were generally the same as they were at other times and in other places. Leading families carefully managed the marriages of their children, the exercise of public ritual, and the sharing of wealth, gradually promoting themselves to ranks well above other families.

The centuries after 1200 CE also saw the production of stone collars and elbows, possibly copies of cloth pads used in the ball game, not unlike the stone yokes of the Mexican Gulf Coast in their purpose. On the other hand the objects appear to be associated with chiefly residences more than ball courts, so perhaps like stools they were mainly symbols of power (Curet 1996).

Taíno Culture

The Taínos were the historic descendants of Saladoid culture. Taíno craftspeople carved wooden "zemis" from trees they believed contained spirits (Figure 11.11). Stools and statues carved in the shapes of humans, birds, and other animals were common, but relatively few survive (Saunders and Gray 1996). Small personal or domestic zemis were fewer after 600 CE and large ones were more common. This was probably tied to the growing importance of the ancestors of chieftains and their families, who were ever more public and powerful. More paraphernalia appeared after 1200 CE, and later Spanish sources describe it as being controlled and used by chieftains, their assistants, and religious specialists (Curet 1996). Only the chieftains could take the cohoba **hallucinogen** and commune with the supernatural. Farming techniques and the environment produced a bounty that made it all possible, and the internal drivers of human nature ensured that a little inequality led to more of it.

Island geography helps us understand the historic native cultures of the Antilles, much as it helps illuminate

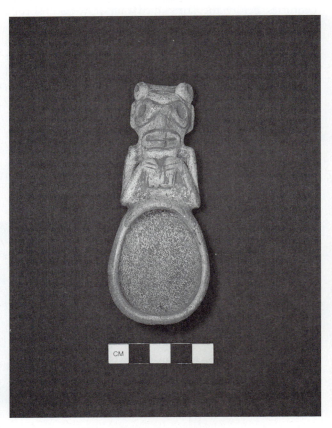

Figure 11.11 Taíno ritual spoon.
Source: Courtesy of the Matson Museum.

ecology. Most of the islands of the Caribbean are small, too small to have allowed their native populations to rise to levels that would have tested the organizational limits of tribal organization. Puerto Rico is the smallest of the four biggest islands of the Greater Antilles. We do not know from historic sources how many chiefdoms there were on Puerto Rico, but Jamaica, which is larger, had only one. We can assume for current purposes that there was also only one chiefdom on Puerto Rico in 1492.

Hispaniola is much larger. Documentary evidence indicates that there were five chiefdoms and a total population of 380,976 on Hispaniola in 1492 (Keegan 1992:112). But a population size that high would require an average of over 76,000 people per chiefdom on Hispaniola (Table 11.1). That is almost eight times higher than the theoretical maximum of 10,000 people manageable by chiefdom polities (see Chapter 1). Given the absence of evidence for state organization in the Antilles, it is likely that either the total native population on Hispaniola was closer to 50,000 or there were more chiefdoms on the island than were recorded. An intermediate alternative is that there were five chiefdoms but many more tribal societies living here and there between them. That would allow for a somewhat higher population without assuming a larger number of chiefdoms.

Generalizing further, if Hispaniola had five chiefdoms Cuba probably had about seven. If Hispaniola had a native population of nearly 381,000, then Cuba's native population probably would have been over half a million. Given the probable density of populations in the Eastern Woodlands and elsewhere in North America this too is an unbelievably high number. While this brief discussion shows that we are still far from understanding the demographics of the Antilles, island geography provides anthropology with a means to calculate much better estimates than we currently have.

The Taínos all but vanished by 1575. Their prompt demise in the face of European diseases and exploitation left many of their customs unexplained. The significance of their stools, three-pointed stones, carved monuments, and nostril bowls for inhaling hallucinogens is debated by archaeologists.

The islanders in the Lesser Antilles were part of the general theme and variations of the West Indies, but for centuries they have often been called "Caribs," a term of disparagement that was initially intended to set them apart. It now appears that all of the island people spoke languages of the Arawakan family (Keegan 1996:276–279; Wilson 1999). Those people who lived in the Lesser Antilles were ethnically similar to the Taínos of the Greater Antilles, but they lived on islands too small to allow larger populations and the formation of chiefdoms.

Whatever the Spanish called them, none of the native peoples of the Antilles lasted long. Smallpox, measles, and other European diseases destroyed the native populations there sooner than elsewhere in the Americas simply because permanent colonization was earliest there and with it came children. Lethal epidemics were childhood diseases in Europe and children who survived them were later immune as adults. European explorers were not dangerous to Indians so long as they left children at home and crews were effectively quarantined by long ocean voyages. But the Spanish colonists brought their families to the West Indies and it did not take long for epidemics to leap into Indian communities, causing high mortality rates that could not be sustained (Snow and Lanphear 1988).

Spanish domesticates then transformed the islands. They introduced horses, cattle, pigs, goats, sheep, and chickens intentionally, rats and mice unintentionally. Grapes and cereal crops did not do well, but sugarcane flourished. Maize and other American domesticates were combined with European crops that did grow well to produce a new agricultural adaptation. Other culture traits were also blended to form a new creole culture. The Spanish colonists reacted to the demographic collapse of native Indians by stepping up the importation of African slaves. By 1520 Africans were already dominating the labor force. They also contributed importantly to Spanish creole culture and African influence in the islands remains strong to this day.

The Mexican Gulf Coast

The Gulf Coast of Mexico was peripheral to both the great urban centers of the Mexican highlands and to the Classic Mayan centers of the Peten during the first

Table 11.1 Data, mostly estimates, on the Taíno chiefdoms of the Greater Antilles. Numbers of chiefdoms are derived by various inferences and are only very rough estimates.

	Area, km²	Chiefdoms
Cuba	104900	7
Hispaniola	74420	5
Jamaica	11770	1
Puerto Rico	8751	1

Box 11.2 HOW TO VISIT SITES ON THE GULF COAST

Of the Mexican sites mentioned in this chapter, El Tajín and Chichén Itzá are very popular tourist destinations and easily reached using standard guides and maps. Cuba remains out of reach for most travelers and its archaeological resources are largely undeveloped.

Caddoan Mounds State Historic Site near Alto, Texas, is the southwesternmost of Mississippian sites and it probably had connections with Huastec centers near the northeast Mexican coast to the south. Poverty Point, Louisiana, is a national monument and open to visitors. Troyville sites can be visited on the Barataria Preserve of the Jean Lafitte National Historical Park and Preserve southwest of New Orleans. Troyville itself is in the town of Jonesville, where earthworks are still visible.

The site of Kolomoki in southwestern Georgia is an excellent example of a Weeden Island village. Its main platform mound covers an area 60 x 100 m (200 x 325 ft) in size, larger than a modern football field. It was probably built after 700 CE.

The Lake Jackson site is a typical Fort Walton culture mound site. Six of the seven mounds on the site are arranged in pairs in two rows separated by a small east–west stream. The largest mound, which flanks the town plaza, is 11 m (36 ft) high and covers nearly a hectare (2.5 acres) of land.

The Crystal River site is another that was occupied during Fort Walton times and probably later as well. It has several mounds, shell middens that were converted into platform mounds. There are two large limestone rocks at the site, one of which bears a crudely etched human face and torso. Much was made of this monument when it was discovered, and some archaeologists thought it was similar to Maya stelae found on the other side of the Gulf of Mexico. That is probably a connection too distant to be credible, but others do not dismiss the possibility.

Terra Ceia is a Safety Harbor culture site, with the Madira Bickel platform mound its most prominent feature. The mound is typical of these sites, about 31 x 52 m (100 x 170 ft) at the base and 6 m (20 ft) high. It consists mainly of shell midden debris and dirt, and there is a long ramp on one side. A description from the de Soto expedition tells us that mounds like this one supported the homes of chieftains or charnel houses for the storage of ancestral bones.

These and several other Florida sites open to the public are described in detail in the guidebook titled *Indian Mounds of the Atlantic Coast*.

Figure 11.12 Pyramid of the Niches at El Tajín, Veracruz, Mexico.

millennium CE. The Mexican city of Teotihuacán had strong political and trade connections to the lowland region and the site of El Tajín (Figure 11.12) reflects its architectural influence (see Chapter 8). El Tajín lies just north of the region in which Olmec culture flourished much earlier (see Chapter 7).

Mesoamerican ball courts are frequently found in sites along the Mexican Gulf Coast, where their popularity peaked 450–700 CE. Stone yokes, *palmas*, and *hachas* are paraphernalia that were associated with the ball game, stone trophies that sometimes copied perishable equipment used by players. They wore padded yokes around their waists, but there is no evidence that they wore the stone copies. The functions of palmas and hachas are unknown, but their association with the ball game is unmistakable. The beautifully decorated stone copies might have served as athletic trophies (see Chapter 7) (Weaver 1981:345–248).

Coastal Mesoamerican ball courts inspired the construction of similar ones in the Greater Antilles. Chunky and other games played on the town plazas of the Southeast are also vaguely similar. Whereas many archaeologists argue that there is no historical connection between them, the popularity of team sports played on community fields all around the Gulf seems more than just coincidental.

Totonac Culture

Totonac potters in Veracruz produced many mold-made hollow figurines during the first millennium CE. These happy laughing faces were supplied with big grins that expose filed teeth, marks of beauty for both men and women. The region also produced small ceramic animal effigies that were equipped with axles and wheels. They were probably either toys or ritual objects. The little wheeled effigies are interesting to archaeologists because they are the only known use of wheels in the Americas before 1492. Wheels never had any practical application in the Americas because there were no animals that could have been domesticated as draft animals (Weaver 1981:250–254). Some have argued that wheelbarrows would have been handy even without draft animals. But wheelbarrows require smooth surfaces, a requirement that makes them more trouble than they are worth except over very short distances. Carts with two large wheels might have worked, but without draft animals the technological steps that might have led to them were never initiated. Humans cannot efficiently pull carts having the solid disk wheels that are the first step in technological evolution. Lighter spoked wheels could only have evolved later after some intermediate steps. Still lighter bicycle-style wheels presuppose both advanced metallurgy and the advanced engineering needed for the leap from hubs that stand on sturdy spokes to hubs that are suspended from light rims by slender metal ones. Little wonder that wheels were nonstarters for anything but toys in the Americas.

Huastec Culture

The cultures of the Mexican Gulf Coast flourished during the heyday of the Toltec Empire in the highlands, 900–1200 CE. The Huastecs lived north of the Totonacs in the northeastern corner of Mesoamerica and they have left behind distinctive ceramic styles and other art. The Huastecs had strong connections with their linguistic cousins in the Maya area and the eastern part of the Mexican Gulf Coast during the first millennium CE, but these connections were apparently severed after 900 CE and replaced by new links to the Toltecs at Tula. The new connections ran across northern Mesoamerica and perhaps northward from there. There is some evidence of Toltec influence in the U.S. Southwest and northwestern Mexico, and

Figure 11.13 Huastec shell artifacts from coastal Mexico showing similarities with shell artifacts from the Eastern Woodlands. Museo Nacional de Antropología, Mexico City.

it is reasonable to also look for links along the coast between Huastec country and the Eastern Woodlands (Weaver 1981:385–387).

Pots made in the shapes of human heads, engraved shell gorgets (Figure 11.13), fan headdresses, discoidal gaming stones, platform pipes, and sculptures of hunch-backed humans are some of the shared traits found in both the Huastec area and the Mississippian sites of the Eastern Woodlands (Zaragoza Ocaña 2005). Many symbolic motifs were also shared, including the cross-in-circle, scrolls, spirals, snakes (including feathered ones), swastikas, winged dancers, and long-nosed gods (White 2005c:19).

Pipes, and probably tobacco, are later here in Mesoamerica than in the Eastern Woodlands. Tobacco is a South American plant and its early spread to the Eastern Woodlands makes it likely that it arrived by way of the Antilles, then spread later along with smoking pipes to Mesoamerica (Griffin 1966).

The circular platform mounds at the George C. Davis site in eastern Texas look like others in the Eastern Woodlands, but they also resemble the earthen mounds on the Tantoc site in northeastern Mexico (Dávila Cabrera 2005). The Davis site is associated with ancestral Caddo Indians while Tantoc and other mound sites in the region have been associated with Huastec culture. Similarities between Caddo and Huastec have been noted by anthropologists for over a century, so this is further indication that the dry hostile country on both sides of the lower Rio Grande was not an insurmountable barrier. Archaeologists working in that area are now increasingly confident that people and ideas moved through it in both directions (Kibler 2005; Ricklis and Weinstein 2005:153).

The southeastern arc of the Circum-Gulf region is discussed in Chapter 8. Archaeological evidence from this area, particularly from the site of Chichén Itzá, indicates that there was a long, curving axis of shared art, architecture, and religion connecting that site with the central highlands of Mexico (Ringle et al. 1998). Chichén Itzá was at the end of a long network of cities that included El Tajín and various highland cities. Historical descriptions make it clear that Mesoamerican traders plied the coastal waters in their part of the Gulf, and the presence of maize and ball courts in the Antilles point to the occasional trips across open water. Indeed all three of the major gaps around the Gulf rim, the two marine ones separating Cuba and the Florida and Yucatan peninsulas, and the desert gap of southern Texas, were clearly crossed from time to time.

Long journeys by land and sea were not sufficient to turn the peoples of the Gulf into one big family. The Gulf of Mexico never had the significance for North America that the Mediterranean had (and still has) for Europe and North Africa. But they did make the Gulf region more than a North American backwater. In time archaeologists from the three modern nations that surround the Gulf will close the loops with research projects unhindered by the barriers of language, water, and politics.

Summary

1. The Gulf Coast is a rich maritime edge environment that supported the development of complex chiefdoms, sometimes in the absence of agriculture.

2. The rim of the Gulf Coast is interrupted by two major sea gaps and a desert gap, all of which restricted trade and exchange.

3. Some adaptive strategies involving tropical domesticates were possible around the southern Gulf but unworkable in cooler parts north of the Tropic of Cancer.

4. Troyville-Coles Creek culture, which featured earthworks but not maize agriculture, bridged the time gap between Hopewell and Mississippian cultures in the lower Mississippi Valley.

5. Weeden Island culture on the Gulf Coast of Florida also bridged the time gap between Hopewell and Mississippian cultures, and evolved into Fort Walton and Safety Harbor cultures, which varied in their adaptive balance of wild and domesticated foods.

6. The cultures of interior southern Florida left remains suggesting that they made a living as tropical farmers, but their use of maize is still disputed.

7. The Calusas of southern Florida had chiefdoms but depended entirely upon wild food resources.

8. The Miami Circle illustrates the emerging role of cultural resource management.

9. Pensacola culture shows some evidence of contact with Mesoamerica.

10. The first peopling of the Greater Antilles came from the Yucatan Peninsula but later waves of migrants moved along the island chain from South America.

11. Later residents of the Greater Antilles, the ancestors of the historic Taínos, had maize and ball courts.

12. The cultures of coastal Mexico were in direct contact with other Mesoamerican cultures but also had more distant connections around the Gulf Coast rim.

Further Reading

Samuel Wilson's *The Indigenous People of the Caribbean* is a good place to begin because it covers ethnology and ethnohistory as well as archaeology. William Keegan's *The People Who Discovered Columbus* is more narrowly focused on the archaeology of the Bahamas, but very usefully puts that subject into the broader context of Caribbean island ecology. A recent volume edited by Nancy White, *Gulf Coast Archaeology*, is a good place to begin exploration of the rest of the broken circle that surrounds the Gulf of Mexico. These volumes and Jerald Milanich's *Archaeology of Precolumbian Florida* are each excellent in their own right, but also provide entry points into a much larger library of books, many published by the University Press of Florida.

Glossary

creole: A culture of mixed ancestry, usually in a colonial setting.

expedient tool: A tool made quickly and without much modification of the raw material.

hallucinogen: A drug that induces hallucinations.

The Interior West

> What is life? It is the flash of a firefly in the night. It is the breath of a buffalo in the winter time. It is the little shadow which runs across the grass and loses itself in the sunset.
>
> *Crowfoot (Blackfeet), 1877*

Introduction

The western interior of North America is a set of large, arid and semiarid regions that challenge human adaptation (Figure 12.1). For most of human history the American Indians had to rely mainly on hunting and gathering to make a living. A series of long fluctuating climatic episodes that were even hotter and drier than today scorched the Interior West from 7000 to 3500 BCE. But in the last two millennia climatic conditions changed enough at times to allow other adaptations to occur such as farming, which spread up wooded river valleys of the Great Plains from sources in the Eastern Woodlands to indigenous peoples on the Great Plains. People living in the Great Basin adopted maize farming and pottery from the Pueblos of the Greater Southwest. Residents of the Plateau took on some of the cultural features of their distant relatives on the Northwest Coast. As is still the case today, the Interior West was made habitable to more than a thin population of hunter-gatherers through the introduction of transplanted technologies and societies that had developed first elsewhere.

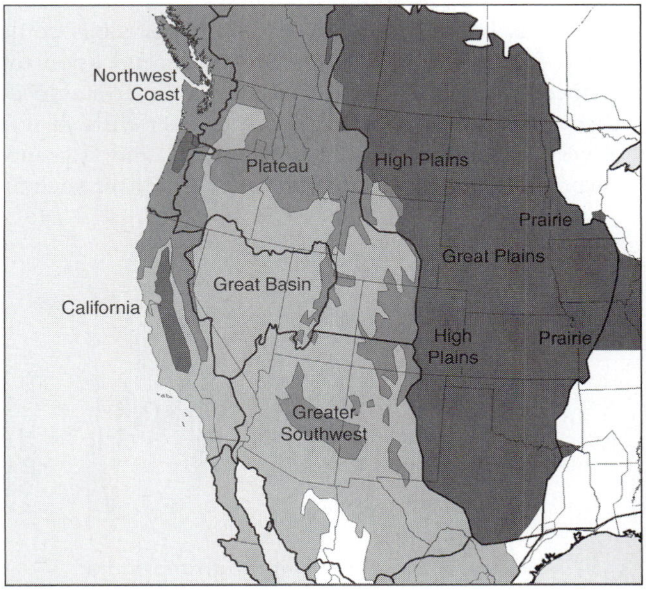

The Great Plains

The North American Great Plains region (Figure 12.2) is a vast and largely flat landscape of fire-climax grassland with riverine gallery forests and a few patches of forested uplands. The whole region tilts gently eastward,

Figure 12.1 The Interior West, including the Great Plains, the Great Basin, and the Plateau regions. Grasslands shown in dark gray.

Figure 12.2 Geography and ecology of the Great Plains.

from the foothills of the Rocky Mountains on the west to the Mississippi Valley on the east. Tributaries of the Mississippi rise in the Rockies and flow generally west to east. Fingers of forest reach up their valleys from the Eastern Woodlands, providing cover for game animals and human populations. Here and there are forested mountainous areas like the Black Hills of South Dakota that interrupt the rolling grasslands.

Even a huge and seemingly monotonous sea of grass varies from one region to another. The western portions of the region are High Plains, hotter and drier in the summer than the moister prairie that covers the eastern portions. Short grass species (wheatgrass, grama, and needlegrass) predominate on the northern High Plains. The prairie is dominated by bluestem grasses. Grama and buffalo grasses predominate on the southern High Plains, and these give way to mesquite, juniper, and oak savannas in central Texas.

Human Adaptation

There are not many plant foods for humans on the Great Plains, and herds of bison and pronghorn antelopes survive by being able to digest tough grasses. Because of the severe limitations on vegetation, a relatively large fraction of the total biomass walks around on four legs in this environment. Hunter-gatherers there have always had to depend primarily on animals for food (Bamforth 1988).

Hunter-gatherer adaptation to the Great Plains was difficult in the best of circumstances, but made more so by the erratic and unpredictable nature of temperature, rainfall, and the plant and animal resources that lived or died as a result. The whole region lies in a rain shadow cast by the Rocky Mountains. Although more rain falls in the winter than in the summer west of the Rockies in the Great Basin, the reverse is true today on the Great Plains. Yet the summer rains on the Great Plains are very spotty, randomly deluging some areas while missing others altogether.

It may seem counterintuitive, but wet summers produce more prairie fires. That is because wet summers generate more plant biomass, which inevitably dries out by fall, producing an abundance of fuel for the peak fire season in October. Thus there is more fuel for fires after wet summers than after dry ones. Prairie fires, often deliberately set by American Indians, swept unchecked across vast desiccated grasslands. The fires produced more food for herd animals in the long run and helped corral game in the short run. Any chances trees had to establish themselves away from river valleys and mountain slopes were eliminated by this

practice, which was probably common from Paleoindian times on.

The Effects of Climatic Cycling

The western Great Plains have long been generally hotter and drier than the eastern prairies, but heat and moisture have varied over time as well as over space. The whole region was significantly hotter and drier than today for three and a half millennia, 7000–3500 BCE. This long hot spell was noticed by researchers decades ago, and it often has been referred to as the "Altithermal" period (Figure 12.3). It was a 3,500-year period with at least three hot peaks in which there were near desert conditions and little human occupation across many areas of the Great Plains. The evidence for periodic burning in lake sediments is considerably less in this long period. In fact, many small lakes dried up altogether or became extremely saline during the long hot spells. Herds of bison and antelopes must have been living in smaller refuge areas in reduced circumstances, as were the human hunters that depended upon them.

Even under better climatic conditions before 7000 BCE or after 3500 BCE, bands of hunters would not have enjoyed an easy adaptation in this region. Bison herds came and went, moving more rapidly than hunters could over the huge sea of grass. Until the Spanish arrived in New Mexico and introduced horses, Indians simply lacked the ability to pursue bison efficiently. Gear was limited to what they and their dogs could carry. Before the horse they had to depend upon the chance appearance of herds and their ability to stampede them into gullies or box canyons or over cliffs. It was a very chancy way to make a living, and it is not surprising that the archaeological evidence for such an

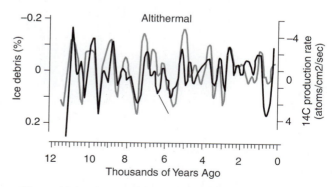

Figure 12.3 Climate cycles showing the long-term episode sometimes call the Altithermal.

Archaic adaptation to the Great Plains environment of 5,500+ years ago is thin and inconsistent.

In addition to annual cycles and very long-term changes in climate that cycle on a scale of thousands of years, there are wet–dry episodes on the Great Plains that cycle every one to two centuries. Conditions were cooler and moister after 3500 BCE, but droughts remained more intense and more frequent than today until around 1200 CE (Laird et al. 1996). Since then the drought cycle has averaged 160 years. The reasons for this cycling are still uncertain, but lake sediments preserve the evidence for it in the rising and falling frequencies of pollen, charcoal fragments, and diatoms. It is not surprising that human adaptations have cycled at the same rhythm, cultures advancing, retreating, dying out or reinventing themselves at a frequency too long to be noticed by any individual but too short to leave a clear archaeological trail over the long term.

Medium-term cycling can be detected in the historic record, when the introduction of guns and horses led to even more radical cultural change. In one case, people who were wild rice gatherers in one century became maize farmers in the next and mounted nomadic bison hunters in the one following, moving great distances and reinventing themselves each time while still hanging on to their core identities. Such a pattern of frequent radical change leaves little consistency over space and little continuity over time in the details of the archaeological record. Little wonder that Great Plains archaeology is made up of the disjointed remains of a bewildering array of complexes that flourished locally and briefly. Unlike the generalizations that can be made about the widespread and long-lived adaptations of many other parts of the continent, the one that best describes the Great Plains pattern is that it is internally both diverse and complex.

The details of adaptation presented in this chapter are intended to illustrate the complexity of Great Plains archaeology. The situation is similar to that of California (see Chapter 13), but made more difficult by two additional confounding factors not found in California. First, population density in the Great Plains region was always much thinner than in California. Second, the small populations that lived on the Great Plains were always much more mobile because they have had to respond to greater environmental instability. This means that when conditions have arisen that have been favorable for hunter-gatherers on the Great Plains, new cultures have popped up in the archaeological record, each of them having drawn upon a variety of technological, social, biological, and cultural sources that are difficult to detect. Great Plains archaeologists have paid close attention to the cycling of climate and regional ecology, which has helped them understand the timing of these adaptive episodes.

Northern Great Plains Hunter–Gatherers

The early hunter-gatherers of the Great Plains were probably not warlike because simple hunter-gatherer societies tend not to be. In contrast, complex hunter-gatherer societies tend to be more warlike and some even keep slaves. Much has been made of the warlike nature of the twentieth-century Yanomamos of South America, and they have often been cited as analogs of past hunter-gatherer societies. But Yanomamo communities were band-sized remnants of larger earlier complex horticultural societies (Fry 2005). Most of the nineteenth-century tribes and bands on the Great Plains were similarly descended from earlier horticultural societies that had operated at the tribal or chiefdom levels. They brought with them traditions of warring that were probably lacking among earlier hunter-gatherers.

For thousands of years ecological circumstances forced the various Archaic cultures of the Great Plains to depend upon individual skill and communal bison drives. Individual hunters could sometimes use stealth to sneak up on grazing bison, but it was difficult. Chasing them was simply not an option for hunters on foot. If hunters were lucky enough to encounter a bison herd near enough to an appropriate cliff or arroyo they could organize a communal hunter under the temporary leadership of some senior men. Properly organized, a band or a set of cooperating bands could engineer a bison hunt that would drive them into a trap or over a cliff, sometimes using fire (Figure 12.4).

Figure 12.4 Buffalo jump at Head-Smashed-In, Alberta.

Box 12.1 HOW TO VISIT SITES ON THE GREAT PLAINS

The best Native American site accessible to the public in South Dakota is the Mitchell Prehistoric Indian Village. Other sites that are open to the public and have interpretive signs include Fort Pierre Choteau, Fort Randall, mounds at Oakwood Lakes State Park, and prehistoric and historic sites at Hartford Beach State Park. Fort Sisseton was reconstructed by the Works Progress Administration (WPA) in the 1930s and is cared for by the State Parks Division. Sites in North Dakota include Pulver Mounds State Historic Site and Standing Rock Historic Site. The Mandan village known as On-a-Slant is preserved in Fort Abraham Lincoln State Park. Cross Ranch State Park has more such sites.

Pipestone National Monument in southwestern Minnesota was the source of red catlinite used by craftspeople further east. The route there opened the way to high-quality chert around the Knife River Indian Villages National Historic Site in North Dakota. This in turn gave them access to volcanic glass that came from Yellowstone's Obsidian Cliff in Wyoming. Each of these places is well worth a visit.

Wyoming also offers several petroglyph sites, including those of White Mountain, Killpecker, Cedar, and Pine Canyons near Rock Springs, and Castle Gardens near Riverton. Medicine Lodge State Archaeological Site offers both petroglyphs and Paleoindian remains. Legend Rock State Petroglyph Site is located north of Thermopolis.

Idaho's Weis Rockshelter, near Cottonwood, is a rare early site open to the public. Treaty Rock Historic Site in northern Idaho is historically important and also has some petroglyphs. Montana offers the Wahkpa Chu'gn Buffalo Jump as well as Paleoindian remains and petroglyphs at Medicine Lodge State Archaeological Site. Pictograph Cave State Park is located near Billings.

Arkansas's premier site is Toltec Mounds, but there are also mound sites in Parkin Archaeological State Park. Pawnee Indian Village State Historic Site offers an excavated earth lodge. Lake Scott State Park holds the Pueblo ruin known as E Cuartelejo. Oklahoma's premier site is Spiro, which still impresses despite its near devastation by looters.

Texas has many sites, including Alibates Flint Quarries National Monument, Caddoan Mounds State Historic Site, hunter-gatherer sites in Amistad National Recreation Area, petroglyphs in Seminole Canyon State Park, rock art in Hueco Tanks State Historic Site, pictographs at Paint Rock, and burial mound sites scattered around Texarcana. More mounds can be visited in Caddoan Mounds State Historic Site. Lubbock Lake Landmark is an archaeological preserve containing evidence from 12 millennia of use and occupation.

People came together under temporary leadership to plan and carry out bison drives and in the huge butchering task that followed. Willingness to obey leaders lasted only so long as it was made necessary by the demands of the communal work. Hunters sometimes built converging rows of stone cairns to funnel herds toward a trap, dead-end arroyo, or cliff. Some participants enticed or chased bison into these funnels while others, including children, waved hides to steer them. The stampeding animals were run off cliffs known as "buffalo jumps" in this way. Whole herds could be dispatched quickly, and strips of dried (jerked) meat from the butchered bison could feed families for weeks, even months. Dried meat loses most of its mass but none of its protein, allowing it to be carried easily. Communal hunts required leadership and organization, but neither was carried over as a permanent feature of the sociopolitical system. When the drive and the distribution of dried meat was over the need for leadership relaxed, and they returned to informal band organization.

Implications of Changing Point Styles

Cyclical Archaic adjustments played out from 6500 to 2000 BCE, a long period that is often called the "Middle" period by Great Plains archaeologists (Dyck and Morlan 2001:115; Frison 1998, 2001). The hallmarks of the cycling adaptations to the Holocene on the Great Plains are a series of distinctive Archaic projectile point types. Lanceolate and stemmed points went out of fashion and were replaced with smaller side-notched points as early as 7000 BCE. This might have occurred because hunters shifted to the use of smaller atlatl darts than they had previously. The earliest side-notched points belong to the Mummy Cave complex, so named for its type site in northwestern Wyoming.

During the long Middle period people lived in mobile bands that covered large territories, not unlike their Paleoindian ancestors. However, unlike the Paleoindians they appear not to have exchanged finished points made of high-quality materials. Points made from exotic raw materials are not often found in these Archaic sites. The implication is that the connubia that had characterized the mutual linkages between Paleoindian bands had been replaced on the Great Plains as they had been in the Eastern Woodlands. As thin as the overall population density must have been, it was by this time dense enough to allow people to find mutual support and marriage mates without resorting to long-distance relationships.

Housing

Life on the northern Great Plains was made difficult by seasonal temperature extremes and limited food resources. Summer houses were simple portable structures, probably skin-covered tents that could be packed up and moved. On the northwestern Great Plains and perhaps elsewhere people found rock shelters for the winter or dug pithouses, an innovation also found in the nearby Plateau region. The northern Great Plains is a region where winters are long and very cold, and survival there would have been much more difficult without warm housing (Frison 2001:135).

Changing Subsistence

Bison bones dominate archaeological assemblages in which bones have been preserved. These were probably the bones of *Bison bison occidentalis*, a now extinct subspecies or variety of bison that was slightly larger than modern bison. The bones often show butchering marks and breaks that indicate that these early Plains Indians were adept at extracting marrow from long bones.

By 3700 BCE hunters were also skilled at stalking and killing solitary animals such as mountain sheep and moose. Such skills are extraordinary, for these are very wary animals. In this case archaeologists can infer quite a bit from a few projectile points and animal bones in a site. People appear to have chosen site locations to maximize the range of plants and animals available to them at the time, resources that often pattern differently on the modern landscape. Manos and metates at many of the sites indicate that people had also found ways to extract plant foods from the environment. Wood and antler digging tools were probably used to harvest bulbs and roots such as sego lily and bitterroot.

Cooler Conditions and New Opportunities

The northern Great Plains Late period, 2000 BCE–1750 CE, followed the long cycling of extreme temperatures and drought that had prevailed earlier. Cooler and moister conditions brought about an increase in the bison herds and other game. Plains Indians continued to live in very mobile skin- or mat-covered tent communities, but larger herds brought about much more mass killing, as recorded at the buffalo jump site at Head-Smashed-In, Alberta. Trade and exchange also increased and people once again began acquiring exotic cherts from great distances. Cherts came from distant quarry sources and native copper came from the Great Lakes. All of this was probably related to the expansion of the Hopewell network of trade and exchange in the Eastern Woodlands. Hopewell traders pursued exotic raw materials through linkages that drew them farther and farther afield from their Ohio homeland. At least a few came all the way to Obsidian Cliff in northwestern Wyoming to acquire volcanic glass (see Chapter 5). It is not surprising that the Great Plains hunters living near the sources of some of these materials tapped into the emerging trade network for their own purposes.

Besant Culture

The episodic and localized character of cultural evolution on the Great Plains continued with the appearance of Besant culture in the northern part of the region around 650 BCE. Its hallmark is the Outlook point, which is small enough to have been an arrow point. The bow and arrow (Figure 12.5) was already in use far to the north, but its adoption by people on the Great Plains is usually dated to no earlier than 200 CE, over eight centuries later (Blitz 1988; Henning 2005). The Outlook point type appears to have spread in with people expanding westward from the Eastern Woodlands, along with pottery and wattle-and-daub house construction. Besant culture was a very successful bison-hunting culture, still possessed of some of the traits of Eastern Woodlands cultures. Besant traits that originated in the Eastern Woodlands included burial mounds, which in this case always included articulated bison skeletons in addition to the human burials.

Avonlea Culture

Avonlea culture appeared on the northern Great Plains around 200 CE, and they were the first Great Plains Indians to rely almost exclusively on the bow and arrow. They too were dedicated bison hunters and their adaptation lasted until 1300–1400 CE. The fate of

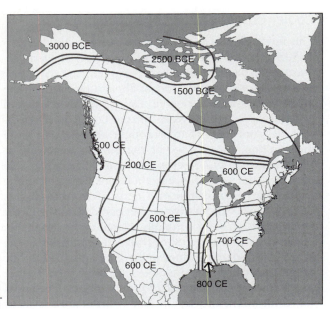

Figure 12.5 Introduction of the bow and arrow.
Source: Courtesy of John H. Blitz (1988).

Avonlea culture is disputed and there are some alternative hypotheses.

Consistent Confusion

The Medieval Maximum climatic cycle, which peaked about a thousand years ago, complicated human adaptation even more, forcing adaptive changes in some areas and probably making other areas uninhabitable. The great dunes of the Nebraska Sand Hills were active at this time, migrating ahead of the dry southwesterly winds that prevailed at the time. The dry winds did not bring the summer rainfall that comes from the Gulf of Mexico today, and northwestern Nebraska could not have been a very congenial place for a hunter-gatherer to make a living. When the warm episode ended the prevailing summer winds shifted back to the south, and the summer rains resumed. The new growth of grass stabilized the sand dunes and game became more plentiful once again (Sridhar et al. 2006).

The last thousand years on the northern Great Plains saw a greater array of archaeological complexes that culminated in various historic tribes as small local cultures adapted to the changing environment. These are distinguished from each other mainly by point types and pottery types. A sampling of them is shown in Table 12.1.

The large number of ephemeral cultures that developed on the northern margin of the Great Plains provides an even larger number of regional puzzles for archaeologists. More important to researchers who are not Great Plains specialists is the larger pattern that they all form over time and across space. Cycles of drought prevented the establishment of long-lived cultural traditions. Even after 1200 CE, when droughts settled into a less severe 160-year cycle, human adaptations waxed and waned with greater frequency than in most other parts of the continent. Thus the region is complex archaeologically, but consistently so, and that consistency allows us to draw general conclusions about the spotty and episodic nature of adaptation, cultural genesis, and abandonment. Had the Great Plains environment been stable over both time and space, the pattern would have been very different. Once again the situation invites comparison with California (see Chapter 13).

Table 12.1 A sample of late hunter-gatherer cultures from the northern Great Plains.

Culture or Complex	Location	Age
Besant	Southern Alberta	800–1850 CE
Blackduck	Minnesota and Southern Manitoba	650–1100 CE
Rainy River	Minnesota	1100–1700 CE
Selkirk	Southern Canadian Great Plains	1200–1700 CE
Devils Lake-Sourisford	North Dakota and adj. Canada	1000–1150 CE
Wanikan	Northern Minnesota	1100–1750 CE
Mortlach	Northern Great Plains	1500–1800 CE

Figure 12.6 The Bighorn Medicine Wheel, Wyoming. *Source:* Courtesy of Richard Collier, Wyoming Historic Preservation Office, Department of State Parks and Cultural Resources.

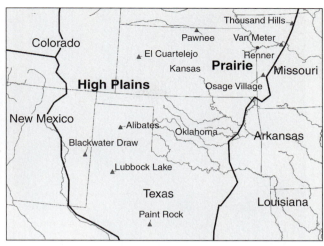

Figure 12.7 Regions and sites of the southern Great Plains.

Medicine Wheels

The Bighorn Medicine Wheel (Figure 12.6) has been a site of considerable popular interest and speculation, but its origin and function remain uncertain. This is understandable given the number and diversity of archaeological cultures in the region and the uncertainties surrounding attempts to connect any of them to later Indian nations. The feature is a ring of boulders 24 m (80 ft) in diameter that has 28 boulder spokes radiating to the ring from a central hub. Artifacts in the site indicate that it dates to recent centuries, but although it superficially resembles the layout of a Plains Sundance lodge, little of what is known of historic Great Plains Indian cultures sheds light on its purpose (Frison 1992; Liebmann 2002; Schlesier 2002).

Southern Great Plains Hunter–Gatherers

As on the northern Great Plains, the southern High Plains (Figure 12.7) experienced a much hotter and drier climate than prevails today prior to 3500 BCE, and the effects were similar. A late Paleoindian adaptation persisted there for as long as big game did, but most extinctions of large species were complete there long before the last remnants of *bison antiquus* disappeared around 6500 BCE. By that time a shift to more Archaic adaptations was already in progress in the southeastern Great Plains. As in the north, cycles of hotter and drier climate stressed and constrained human populations (Kay 1998; Vehik 2001).

The region gradually turned into a thinly populated buffer zone between other regions where human adaptation was easier. The southern Great Plains became a vast adaptive zone between the Southwest and the Southeast. This became even more so after 1500 BC. What little pottery eventually appeared in the region was derived from the Southeast. Southwestern influences are seen primarily in the form of pithouse architecture. The bow and arrow became common after 500 CE, although the atlatl remained in use in many places. Southwestern pottery eventually also began to show up in some sites around the same time.

Hunting and gathering continued as the primary adaptive strategy on the southern Great Plains up until 1450 CE. Horticulture was occasionally an option, but the environment did not allow it to take permanent root. Cooler climate and the growth of bison herds led people to hunt more on the High Plains. As on the northern Great Plains the archaeological record reveals a diversity of many local cultures. They were often short-lived. Bison hunting dominated after 1450 CE. Part of the shift was probably due to the arrival of Nadene-speaking immigrants from the north moving southward just east of the Rockies on the High Plains. Trade, conflict, and environmental stress kept cultures in flux on the southern Great Plains through the centuries leading up to contact with Europeans (Vehik 2002).

Plains Woodland Cultures

Indigenous cultures and cultures that were descended from the mound-building cultures of the Eastern Woodlands began to settle in the wooded valleys of the eastern Great Plains after 500 BCE (Figure 12.8). These were cultivators who made pottery but who, like the Adena

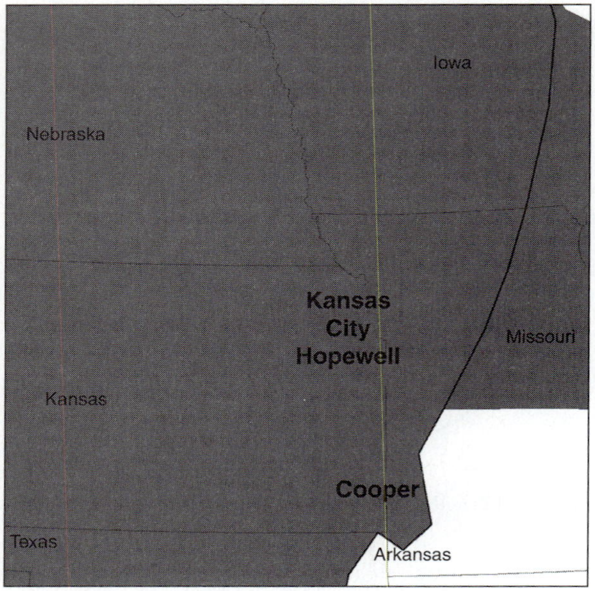

Figure 12.8 The sphere of Hopewell culture expanded westward into the eastern prairies. Kansas City Hopewellian and Cooper Hopewellian sites are both found west of the Eastern Woodlands. Notice also the eastward extension of the Prairie Peninsula in Illinois.

There are several variants on the Plains Woodland theme, all of them derived from Eastern Woodland prototypes. A form of Hopewell culture appeared at the Renner site and others around Kansas City in about 1 CE. Called "Kansas City Hopewell," it has distinctive pottery styles and impressive burial mounds containing stone-vault tombs. It is uncertain whether this culture developed locally when people adopted Hopewell traits, or if westward migrating Hopewell people brought it all with them.

Other new cultures introduced from the Eastern Woodlands include Cooper culture in northeastern Oklahoma and Valley culture of western Iowa and eastern Nebraska. They all made use of burial mounds, but their populations were thinner and their burial mounds smaller the farther west they went. There are at least 13 named and described derivative Plains Woodland archaeological cultures and variants that emerged later around 500–1000 CE. The bow and arrow were generally adopted by all of them after 500 CE, and all of them depended upon a mixture of cultivating and gathering in the river valleys, and periodic hunting on the treeless prairie away from the rivers.

So the expansion of early farming into the Great Plains region was tentative, confined to wooded river valleys, and contingent upon general climatic conditions that were not as hot and dry as they had been previously. There was probably plenty of trading and other social interaction between the newcomers and the hunter-gatherers of the Great Plains, and not much conflict. Their adaptations were complementary for the most part, and for the time being there was little to fight over here at the attenuated ends of the trails leading back to the Hopewell heartland in the Eastern Woodlands.

Plains Village Cultures

The cultures known collectively as "Plains Village" arose later as secondary developments from Mississippian culture in the Eastern Woodlands and the spread of maize agriculture. The circumstances that made the new human expansion possible were warmer climate, new crops, the bow and arrow, and the growth and eastward expansion of bison herds (Henning 2005). This second expansion of farmers up the rivers of the eastern Great Plains began as early as 850 CE. Some of them probably developed locally out of earlier Plains Woodland cultures while others were established by new migrants from the East. The new arrivals farmed small plots with maize, squash, sunflower, and a mix of other regional crops and tropical imports. They also hunted on the prairie, with pronghorn and bison being their preferred game (Steinacher and Carlson 1998; Wedel 2001).

and Hopewell people that inspired them, lacked the maize and beans that would later flourish in the Eastern Woodlands. They lived in dispersed villages of permanent circular or oval houses that were scattered along the forested courses of the western tributary streams of the Mississippi (Johnson 1998; Johnson 2001).

The hunter-gatherers that the migrants from the Eastern Woodlands encountered probably had more meat than they could consume. Fat and carbohydrates were both critical resources, which tended to be in particularly short supply in late winter and early spring. The hunter-gatherers rendered fat from bones and stored the grease with other ingredients as **pemmican,** which they made for future consumption after big hunts. But the arrival of farmers provided them with a new option. They could trade with the farmers for plant foods, solving their carbohydrate shortage and at the same time solving the farmers' meat protein shortage (Bamforth 1988). For their part, the Plains Woodland farmers solved their own critical resource problem by taking cultivation with them when they moved into the wooded valleys of the eastern Great Plains. The farmers had more options and consequently more security than did the hunter-gatherers, for they could either hunt for themselves or trade to supplement their diets with plant foods. This economic relationship persisted until the coming of horses.

Several Plains Village cultures have been described and named. The phase names of a few of them are shown in Table 12.2. The earliest Plains Village farmers lived in dispersed clusters of houses, rather than in either villages or scattered individual houses. Their houses tended to be square or rectangular, 6–7.5 m (20–25 ft) in size. In some cases they were built using wall posts with wattle-and-daub finishing. In others they used wall posts with sod and grass covering. What materials were used for roofing remains uncertain. Deep pits both inside and outside the houses served to store crops for future use.

The later Plains Village settlements were fortified and more permanent, and life within them was sedentary. But over the long term settlements first expanded westward up the river valleys of the Great Plains to the practical limit of maize horticulture, then remained there until the coming of horses and Europeans.

The arrival of Europeans eventually added another, arguably the biggest, factor to the complex and dynamic adaptive system of Plains Villagers. How they eventually evolved there into the historic tribes of the eastern Great Plains consequently remains uncertain and the subject of continuing archaeological study and debate.

Table 12.2 A sample of Plains Village phases.

Phase	Age
Nebraska	100–1250 CE
Upper Republican	1000–1350 CE
Solomon River	1000–1200 CE
Smoky Hill	1000–1350 CE
St. Helena	1350–1450 CE
Loup River (Itskari)	1100–1350 CE
Pomona	950–1350 CE
Steed-Kisker	1000–1250 CE
Great Oasis	850–1250 CE
Middle Missouri	950–1675 CE
Great Oasis	850–1100 CE
Coalescent	1300–1862 CE

For example, it has long been hypothesized that the Loup River (or Itskari) phase evolved into the Lower Loup phase. These people emerged into the historic record as the Pawnee tribes. Similarly, the related St. Helena phase people moved into the Missouri River trench to form the Coalescent tradition and their descendants probably became the historic Arikara. However, both these and alternative hypotheses are disputed (Steinacher and Carlson 1998).

Middle Missouri Origins

A very simplified scenario for just four of the Plains Village cultures is illustrative of the complex adaptations that played out on the northern Great Plains (Figure 12.9). A branch of Late Woodland farming cultures called Great Oasis appeared after 850 CE in the Missouri basin in Nebraska and Iowa, as well as in southwestern Minnesota (Tiffany and Alex 2001). Its development was influenced primarily by maize farming and by initial contact with the Middle Mississippian cultures downstream. The nearly identical Mill Creek and Lower James phases developed out of Great Oasis in the same region and persisted there until around 1350 CE. Related groups established Initial Middle Missouri villages along the river in North and South Dakota in the same period, and some archaeologists infer that they all had their roots in Great Oasis (Henning 2001, 2005).

The appearance of Initial Middle Missouri tradition villages coincided with the onset of warmer and drier climate, probably the major factor that prompted them to move up the Missouri into what are now the Dakota states. Scapula hoes, manos, and metates all point to the importance of farming. The earliest villages (969–1297 CE) were confined to the Missouri trench and western tributary valleys in South Dakota, Iowa, and western Minnesota. Late villages were confined to the Missouri trench but expanded northward into North Dakota. Still later villages (1400–1550 CE) were confined to South and North Dakota, and are referred to as the Extended Middle Missouri (Winham and Calabrese 1998; Wood, 2001).

Middle Missouri villages were typically fortified. Large, well-built semisubterranean rectangular houses were at least banked if not entirely covered with earth for insulation. The subsistence base was agriculture, with hunting and gathering on the prairie away from the village making a nearly equal contribution. The Middle Missouri tradition evolved into the historic Siouan-speaking Mandan and Hidatsa nations.

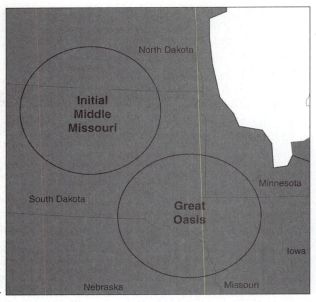
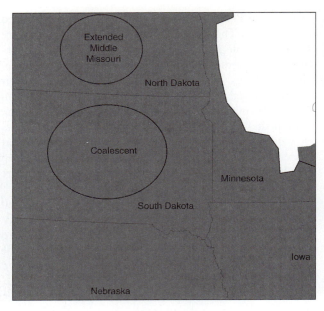

Figure 12.9 Map on the left shows the rough locations of Great Oasis and Initial Middle Missouri sites around 1000 CE. Map on the right shows the derivative Extended Middle Missouri shifted northward, with the Coalescent tradition now situated in South Dakota.

Figure 12.10 Replica Middle Missouri earth lodge.

The Coalescent Tradition

The Coalescent tradition appeared along the Missouri in northern Nebraska around 1250 CE, replacing the Middle Missouri communities that had lived there previously, then expanded into South Dakota. These villagers were immigrants from the Central Great Plains who lived in clusters of oval or squarish earth lodges (Johnson 1998; Krause 2001). In South Dakota they built ditch and palisade fortifications around their villages, an idea borrowed from the Middle Missouri villagers that lived north of them. Even those villages that lacked palisades were made up of earth lodges (Figure 12.10) that appear to have been clustered for

defensive purposes. It is clear that warfare was common in the region by this time, for there are many fortified villages belonging to the Coalescent tradition. The Crow Creek site yielded clear evidence that at least 500 villagers were killed and mutilated by unknown assailants sometime around 1300 CE.

The tradition grew and expanded rapidly during 1450–1650 CE. Villagers founded many new settlements and sometimes occupied them for only brief periods before relocating. Many of the later villages were unfortified and their earth lodges were not closely packed. Those that had palisades were not as impressively fortified as earlier villages had been, and they tended to be located in less secure frontier situations. All of this suggests that warfare was not as serious a problem as it had been earlier.

The people of the Coalescent tradition evolved into the Caddoan-speaking Arikara nation of the historic period (Figure 12.11). They flourished along the Middle Missouri in North and South Dakota along with the Siouan-speaking Mandans and Hidatsas until all of them were decimated by epidemics that reached them around 1750. Devastating smallpox epidemics came later in the nineteenth century, reducing the surviving villages even further (Betts 2006; Lehmer 2001).

What happened to the Great Oasis people in all of this is uncertain. They probably dispersed and were absorbed by Middle Missouri or Coalescent villagers. There are many other Plains Village phases that are not

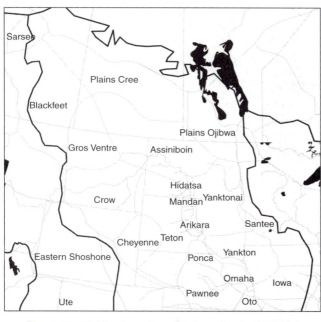

Sarsee
Plains Cree
Blackfeet
Plains Ojibwa
Gros Ventre   Assiniboin
Hidatsa
Crow   Mandan Yanktonai
Arikara   Santee
Cheyenne Teton
Eastern Shoshone   Yankton
Ponca
Omaha   Iowa
Pawnee
Ute   Oto

Figure 12.11 Northern Great Plains tribes in 1800 CE.

shown in Figure 12.9 because their origins, dates, and fates are even more uncertain.

Oneota

Oneota culture was an upper Midwest culture centered on southern Wisconsin and Iowa, and like others in the region it was related to Middle Mississippian culture (Figure 12.12). The primary carriers of Oneota culture were probably speakers of various languages of the Siouan family (Henning and Thiessen 2004). Ceramic and projectile point styles allow archaeologists to distinguish all of these phases from other similar ones. Oneota and Central Plains Villagers also dispersed around 1400 CE and the specific identities of their historic descendants are most probably several historic Siouan cultures. The rise of agricultural societies on the prairies clearly had roots in the chiefdom societies of Middle Mississippian, and at least some of them later converted to nomadic lives centered on horses and bison (Ritterbush and Logan 2000; Tiffany 2003).

Box 12.2 HOW TO VISIT SITES IN THE INTERIOR WEST

Other buffalo jumps are open to the public, but Head-Smashed-In, Alberta, is particularly well interpreted for visitors. Others include three in Montana, five in Wyoming, and several scattered around other states and provinces. However, some of these offer little interpretation.

Writing-On-Stone Provincial Park, also in Alberta, and St. Victor Petroglyphs Provincial Park in Saskatchewan are both well-interpreted rock art sites. The Jeffer Petroglyphs Historic Site in Minnesota and Pictograph Cave in Montana are also excellent rock art sites.

Pipestone National Monument in southwestern Minnesota interprets the catlinite quarry there and has an excellent display of pipes and other objects made from this popular material.

Having once reached Pipestone, Hopewell travelers were drawn further west to the chert quarries near the Knife River of North Dakota. This part of the state also boasts several late earth lodge villages that are open to the public. Knife River Indian Villages National Historic Site manages some of these. Cross Ranch and Fort Abraham Lincoln are both state parks with similar archaeological sites.

Some Hopewell craftspeople who made it as far west at the Knife River were prompted to push on to the Obsidian Cliff site in Yellowstone Park. Obsidian from this quarry has turned up in large concentrations in southern Ohio, no doubt the raw material for the person who hauled it all the way back from northwestern Wyoming.

The southern Great Plains offers fewer public sites. However, the Van Meter State Park in Missouri provides a good look at Plains Woodland remains. El Quartelejo in western Kansas is a rare Pueblo-influenced site on the High Plains. The Alibates Flint Quaries National Monument in the Texas panhandle interprets a major chert source for the region.

A majority of the public sites in the Great Basin portions of Utah and Nevada are rock art sites. Fremont Indian State Park interprets Fremont culture and the Fruita site has some interesting Fremont petroglyphs. Danger Cave is state owned, but it has yet to be developed as a well-interpreted public site.

Fort Rock Cave, Lava Island Rockshelter, Weis Rockshelter, and Treaty Rock are all worth visiting on the plateau. She Who Watches is an unusually striking example of rock art at Columbia Hills State Park, Washington, that combines petroglyphic and pictographic techniques. While open to the public it may be visited only at specified times and one should call ahead for an appointment.

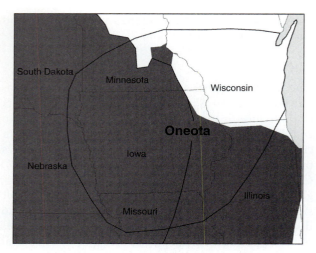

Figure 12.12 The location of Oneota culture.

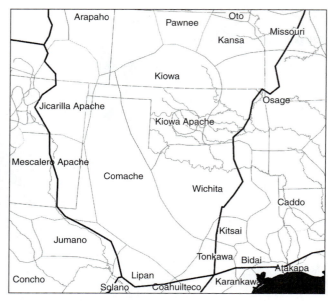

Figure 12.13 Southern Plains tribes in 1800 CE.

Southern Plains Villagers

Plains villagers also penetrated upstream from the Eastern Woodlands on the southern Great Plains by 800 CE. Their village sites are located along rivers in central Oklahoma and adjacent portions of Kansas and Texas. Some even reached the Texas panhandle and southeastern Colorado (Bell and Brooks 2001; Drass 1998). Like others north of them, these southern Plains Village people depended upon cultivation, with seasonal trips onto the plains to hunt bison and other game. Some villages were large central places surrounded by scattered houses or smaller communities, while others were more isolated and rural, but none of them had fortifications. Their houses were typically square or rectangular and built of upright posts covered with wattle-and-daub. Houses on a few Antelope Creek sites in the Texas panhandle even had contiguous rooms with common walls built of stone slabs, an architectural style that points to influences from the Pueblo communities to the southwest of them.

The fragmentary and ephemeral nature of the many hunter-gatherer cultures of the Great Plains characterizes the Southern Plains Villagers as well, and for similar reasons (Figure 12.13). The Southern Plains Village tradition is made up of many distinct archaeological phases and complexes, each separately named. The big picture is that like the later farmers of the 1930s Dust Bowl years, these Southern Plains Village people moved into marginal areas when conditions were minimally adequate, eked out a living for a time, and then abandoned their villages and either dispersed or moved downstream and eastward after 1500 CE. This chaotic movement was probably driven by their need to find more reliable water sources as the southern

Great Plains climate became drier. How these complex demographic changes eventually led to the modern Indian nations of the region remain uncertain. For example, while it is likely that the Great Bend phase evolved into the historic Wichita nation, most other ethnic origins in the region remain unknown.

The Apishapa phase villages of southeastern Colorado appear to derive from the Central Plains tradition, with less emphasis on farming and with stone architecture borrowed from the Southwest. These people did well enough in a period of higher rainfall after 1000 CE, but had to abandon the region because of drought in the fifteenth century. They might have been the ancestors of one of the historic Pawnee bands (Gunnerson 2001).

The Great Basin

The Great Basin covers 408,600 km^2 (about 157,000 mi^2). Today it is a vast arid environment, actually a mosaic of mountain ranges and 150 basins that together have no rivers draining to the outside and only a few large brackish lakes. The largest of these is the Great Salt Lake in northern Utah. During the Pleistocene the Great Salt Lake was much larger and higher than it is today, prompting scientists to name it "Lake Bonneville." There were many smaller lakes scattered about them as well (Figure 12.14).

The Pleistocene forests and lakes of the Great Basin dissipated during the Holocene, and both plant and animal species retreated up mountain slopes as

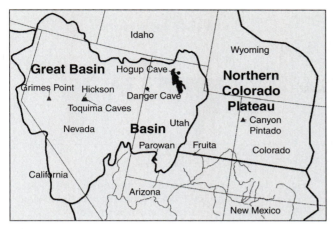

Figure 12.14 Great Basin and surrounding territory showing sites mentioned in the text and sites open to the public (triangles).

the warmer and drier conditions took over. Today rainfall is spotty and unpredictable. It never exceeds 64 cm (25 in.) per year and it is often less than 25 cm (10 in.). Desert plants can lie dormant for years until awakened by moisture. Then they flourish briefly before falling back asleep once again when the soil dries out. Hunter-gatherers moved from one resource patch to another, when they could find them, from one cool productive ridge to another when they could predict plant productivity.

Sagebrush and yucca grow on the lower flatlands, juniper, piñon, and spruce on the ridges of 160 mountain ranges that are scattered across the Great Basin. Thus there were zones of adaptation that varied by elevation and were productive at different but predictable times of the year. The piñon trees provided an important harvest of pine nuts every fall for some groups, enough to get them through the winter. Bands depended upon a mix of pine nuts, honey mesquite, screwbeans, agave (mescal), and game for survival. To document this adaptation, archaeologists have excavated several very productive dry caves in the Great Basin. Cowboy Cave, Hogup Cave, Lovelock Cave, and especially Danger Cave are all well-known sites that have produced long records of Archaic adaptation to the harsh conditions of the region (see Chapter 4).

The Great Basin was and still is even more arid than the Great Plains particularly during the extended period of hotter and drier conditions that prevailed 7000–3500 BCE. What little rain falls there today concentrates in the winter months, the reverse of the pattern of predominantly summer rainfall on the Great Plains. The result is that the Great Basin is considered one of the deserts of the Interior West, a place where farming has been difficult or impossible in most places and at most times before the coming of modern irrigation.

Archaic adaptations followed the passing of Paleoindian cultures, and simple band-level hunter-gatherer societies persisted in the Great Basin until around 400 CE (see Chapter 4). But even here there was ecological room for cultural elaboration. The Paulina Lake site in the Newberry Crater of eastern Oregon holds the earliest house structure currently known for the Great Basin, a dwelling with several hearths that dates to at least 6000 BCE (Beck and Jones 1997:194). This discovery should remind us that prehistoric peoples were innovative, and that they responded to opportunities as ecological circumstances and their knowledge allowed.

A shift in climatic conditions after 400 CE made farming without extensive irrigation a viable option in a few places. As a result of this local bands adopted farming, pottery, and associated traits from the already established farming societies living south of them (see Chapter 6).

Fremont

Fremont culture was a diverse set of at least five local farming cultures that appeared in what is now Utah around 400 CE and persisted until 1300 CE. These people were often part-time farmers who lived in scattered semisedentary farmsteads and small villages. Some switched to full-time farming when conditions were right, while others were full-time foragers. They made pottery, built and lived in permanent houses, and subsisted in part on maize farming (Adovasio 1979; Madsen and Simms 1998; Morss 1931).

The earliest Fremont sites date to around 400 CE. Some Fremont people were probably the descendants of migrants from the south. A few appear to have descended from earlier Great Plains hunter-gatherers. But most of them were most likely local hunter-gatherers who picked up agriculture and some other southwestern traits. At Hogup Cave and other sites there is no discontinuity between Fremont and earlier phases, only the addition of maize, ceramics, and a few other associated traits (Marwitt 1986). Fremont culture consequently was comprised of several variants scattered in clusters around the portion of Utah lying north of the distribution of Ancestral Pueblo sites. There are some common traits, including ceramics, clay figurines, petroglyph styles (Figure 12.15), and settlement styles, but significant variation in other traits.

Figure 12.15 Fremont petroglyphs at the Fuita site.

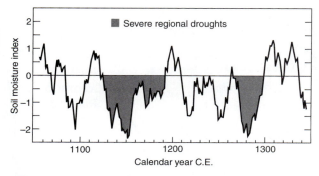

Figure 12.16 Ancient droughts in the Four Corners area. *Source:* From Kloor 2007:1543. Reprinted with permission from the American Association for the Advancement of Science.

Fremont people generally wore moccasins like their Great Basin ancestors rather than sandals like the Ancestral Puebloans. They were part-time farmers who lived in scattered semisedentary farmsteads and small villages, never entirely giving up traditional hunting and gathering for more risky full-time farming. They made pottery, built houses and food storage facilities, and raised corn, but overall they must have looked like poor cousins to the major traditions of the Greater Southwest, while at the same time seeming like aspiring copycats to the hunter-gatherers still living around them (Barlow 2002).

Maize has a metabolic chemistry that is different from that of most food plants in the Great Basin, and this leaves a chemical signature in the bones of those that depend upon it heavily for food. The bone chemistry of Fremont people has revealed that they shifted to a heavy reliance on maize after 400 CE, as expected. Perhaps more importantly, it also shows that their economies became more diverse after 850 CE, with maize being supplemented by other foods that made the key chemical signature less pronounced. However, the burials of high-status males reveal that these particular people ate more maize than did other people. They were also buried with more lavish grave offerings, indicating that social inequalities were increasing even in this remote outpost of native farming (Coltrain and Leavitt 2002).

There is great archaeological variability among Fremont sites, the consequence of their multiple local origins. Despite their marginality, the earliest Fremont sites are five centuries older than early Ancestral Puebloans.

That means that even though they were closer than other Greater Southwest traditions, the Ancestral Puebloans could not have been the initial inspiration for the development of Fremont culture. Most archaeologists conclude that Fremont culture arose mainly as the result of early Mogollon influence on Great Basin hunter-gatherers, just as Ancestral Pueblo culture did. Thus at first Fremont and Ancestral Pueblo cultures were parallel developments and only later did the continuing evolution of Ancestral Pueblo outstrip Fremont.

The Fremont tradition ended when trends toward hotter and drier climate brought droughts that forced people to abandon their settlements and their farming subsistence (Figure 12.16). Some archaeologists argue that the Fremont people had weathered earlier dry spells and were more likely uprooted by invading hunter-gatherers. But simple hunter-gatherers rarely engage in warfare and the fact remains that this was already a region that was even more marginal for farming than the Greater Southwest. Given the prevailing ecological circumstances, it is no surprise that abandonment began as early as 950 CE in northeast Utah. Fremont persisted for another four centuries around the marshlands of northwest Utah, but it too eventually disappeared altogether (Coltrain and Leavitt 2002; Kloor 2007).

It seems likely that Fremont people are among the ancestors of several modern tribes of the West, but where they went and how they became incorporated into other traditions remains largely a matter of speculation. Some of the Fremont people could have relocated to south-central Idaho, while others might be among the ancestors of the later Dismal River culture of Nebraska and Kansas. Those that had lived previously in southern Utah might have relocated southward, joining already stressed Ancestral Pueblo communities there. Still others might have been absorbed by

Numic-speaking bands of hunter-gatherers moving into the region from the southwest.

The Numic Expansion

It is curious that for the most part the Fremont farmers did not successfully revert to the hunting and gathering adaptation of their ancestors and that the region was instead overspread by the Numic branch of Uto-Aztecans (Figure 12.17). The native people encountered by the first Europeans to enter the Great Basin were not the descendants of Fremont culture, but rather the descendants of Numic migrants who spread northward and eastward across the region, at least partly after the demise of Fremont cultures (Madsen and Rhode 1994). The native inhabitants of the Great Basin all spoke closely related languages of this offshoot of the Uto-Aztecan language family. The linguistic evidence alone points to a source somewhere inside or just outside the southwestern part of the Great Basin. Their hunter-gatherer adaptation was better suited to the Great Basin during and after the onset of hotter and drier conditions of the Medieval Maximum. It might seem an easy matter to map the archaeological and linguistic records together and figure out how and when the Numic peoples spread, but it is not.

Numic speakers might have benefited technologically from the bow and arrow, but that is uncertain. They probably expanded across the Great Basin sometime after 1000 CE, but there is disagreement about the timing of the process. There is also disagreement about the key artifacts and other archaeological evidence that might be evidence of the spread. Thus while few scholars doubt that there was a Numic expansion, the details remain elusive.

The Numic peoples were very good at the high-cost exploitation of very small seeds and small animals, which explains their adaptive advantage. Consequently, they were able to live at higher population densities and on less biomass than the earlier Fremont people they replaced. The expanding Numic hunter-gatherers encountered rock art left by the previous inhabitants of the Great Basin. They added to some of it, but for the most part they appear to have left it alone. Thus the rock art of the region is largely unintelligible to historic Indian tribes. There is little in their oral traditions that can be used to interpret the rock art they inherited (Quinlan and Woody 2003).

The Great Basin Laboratory

Modern archaeologists and cultural anthropologists have focused on Numic hunter-gatherers (Figure 12.18) because even though the simplest societies are complex, they have provided crucial insights into human ecology (Grayson 1993). The Shoshones have come to be a particularly well understood example. Julian Steward (1955) discovered that there were four microenvironments used by the Shoshones that lived near the Reese River in central Nevada:

1. Upper sagebrush-grass zone
2. Pinion-juniper belt
3. Arid sagebrush flats
4. Riverine zone

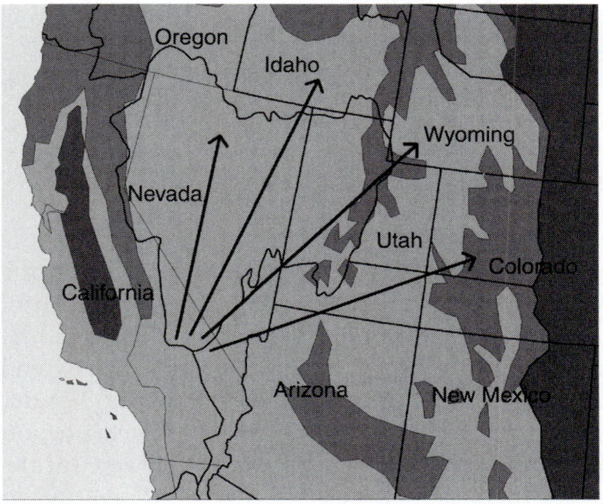

Figure 12.17 The expansion of Numic (Uto-Aztecan) people after 1250 CE.

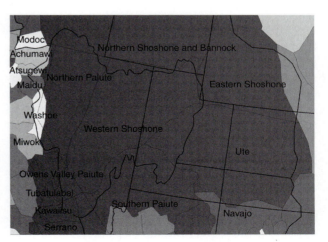

Figure 12.18 Historic tribes of the Great Basin and northern Colorado Plateau.

Figure 12.19 Shoshone summer and winter houses (wickiups).

Figure 12.20 Piñon tree and cone containing pine nuts (left).

Shoshone bands moved between these zones seasonally, relocating to productive locales as experience dictated or as news about unpredictable opportunities reached them. In the warm months their favorite game was often rabbits, which they harvested in large drives that often involved several cooperating bands. They spent their winters in camps at higher elevations near stands of piñon trees (Figures 12.19 and 12.20). They harvested pine nuts from the trees and stored them in large amounts for winter food. This adaptation was still viable in the nineteenth century and older Shoshones remembered its details long enough for anthropologists to record the information.

The Shoshones used each microenvironment for a specific set of subsistence activities, a key adaptive response in the Great Basin. This implies that there should be archaeological evidence for each of those activities. Furthermore, it should be possible to study the subsistence system using computer simulations and archaeological verification. This has turned out to be true. Over 75% of nearly 130 predictions about

Shoshone adaptation have been verified. The 25% failure rate is most likely the fault of computer modeling that still has room for improvement rather than being an indication of any shortcomings in observations or native memories of Shoshone practices (Thomas 1972).

The Plateau

The Plateau region (Figure 12.21) lies north of the Great Basin, between the Cascade Mountains on the west and the Rocky Mountains on the east. Much of the Plateau region is drained by two great rivers, the Fraser and the Columbia. Archaeologists often extend discussion of the Northwest Coast into the Plateau, and geographers have long referred to this larger region as "Cascadia." But the Plateau is kept separate for the purposes of this book because human adaptation in the region has been primarily an interior process. Like the Great Plains and the Great Basin, the Plateau was penetrated by influences from more complex societies

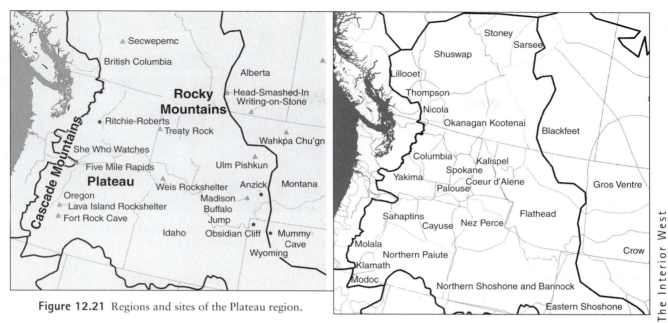

Figure 12.21 Regions and sites of the Plateau region.

Figure 12.22 Historic tribes of the Plateau region.

that flourished outside it, but it remained a region apart from them despite those influences.

The interior Plateau region is cold in winter and hot in the summer, an environment that is similar to that of the High Plains. The Cascade Mountains form a wall that keeps warmer moist air mostly to the west. When driving up the Columbia gorge and through a rare breach in that wall one is struck by how quickly the thick humid forests of the Northwest Coast give way to the dry uplands of the Plateau. Wintertime warm fronts known as Chinook winds occasionally spill across the mountains to bring sudden thaws to the Plateau region, but for the most part the climate is quite unlike that of the coast.

The distributions of language families reflect ancient linkages between the Northwest Coast and the interior Plateau (Figure 12.22). Salishan languages occur both on the coast and on the northern Plateau in Washington and British Columbia. Penutian languages are found in the Columbia River drainage of the southern Plateau and also have links to the coast. The Chinookan languages were distributed around the lower Columbia but their speakers had important trade links to the interior. Despite these connections adaptations to the Plateau environment were necessarily quite different from those that were possible along the coast.

There is little Paleoindian evidence in the Plateau region (see Chapter 3). The Richey-Roberts cache of large Clovis points at Wenatchee is the only known Clovis site in the Northwest Coast/Plateau region. It was initially discovered by a laborer laying an irrigation line in an apple orchard. Unusually large thin pairs of matched Clovis points made up the cache. The bifaces were accompanied by several bone shafts, which were probably spear foreshafts. The cache is similar to one found at the Anzic site in Montana (Ames and Maschner 1999:65).

Holocene Adaptations

Through the course of the millennia that followed the Paleoindian period adaptation for Native Americans living on the Plateau was dependent upon three key resources:

1. Migratory fish, mainly salmon
2. Edible roots
3. Large game

The presence or absence of each of these major resource groups was a strong determinant of what adaptations were possible in this region. In addition, the region has been geologically active. Dynamic environments often produce dramatic environmental changes that force humans to adjust rapidly or perish. American Indians on the Plateau adapted to an evolving landscape that sometimes featured large dramatic events that forced sudden local or even regional readaptations. The Cascade Landslide and other similarly catastrophic geological events interrupted salmon runs, a vital food source, sometimes for long periods. The huge dramatic eruption of Mount St. Helens in 1980 was similarly not a unique event for this dynamic region.

Generally speaking the cultures of the region experienced a slow evolution of technology that was associated with the harvesting of migratory fish at narrow constrictions on major rivers. Weirs, dip nets, barbed spears, and toggling harpoons all became increasingly sophisticated over time. Fishing technology did not include much use of hooks and lures. This seems odd at first glance, but Indian fishermen knew from experience that salmon usually do not take bait while migrating. Their equipment was appropriate given the nature of their prey. The bow and arrow was in use on the southern Plateau by 400–100 BCE, but it did not become popular elsewhere in the region until around 500 CE (Chatters and Pokotylo 1998:78).

Food collecting also became ever more sophisticated as people learned to identify and exploit wild plant foods that were available on the Plateau. These are by no means obvious, and they had to be discovered through trial and error. Root plants, particularly camas (*Quamasia*), were important for thousands of years (Chatters and Pokotylo 1998). The members of the Lewis and Clark expedition, whose systems had become accustomed to a high-protein diet, suffered through a long second winter of stomach disorders, during which they had to subsist primarily on this starchy and unfamiliar tuber.

Plateau Pithouse Tradition

The Plateau Pithouse tradition arose sometime after 4500 BCE along the Fraser and Thompson rivers and their main tributaries on the Canadian portion of the Plateau. The culture appears to have developed as Salishan-speaking people expanded upstream into the region from the Northwest Coast (Gibbon 1998: 663–664). The well-insulated pithouse (Figure 12.23) was an important innovation for Plateau people because they lived in a region where winter temperatures were like those of the northern Great Plains. The idea of substantial housing was not new, of course, for there were houses in eastern Oregon at least 1,500 years earlier. But this was the first time that pithouses became common on the Plateau.

The pithouse tradition developed through several phases. House pits were initially small, 4–5 m (13–16.5 ft) in diameter. They were also shallow, only 30–40 cm (12–16 in.) in depth. Some later houses were deeper and up to 20 m (66 ft) in diameter. All of them were cool in the summer and warm in the winter, a good solution for people who could afford to live in permanent homes despite being hunter-gatherers.

Figure 12.23 Reconstructed Plateau pithouse with one side left uncovered to expose the interior.

The reason that people could be reasonably sedentary was that their primary resources were migratory fish. While they hunted, foraged, and collected wild food, they did so from home bases near stream junctions or salmon fishing stations. Thus their movements to food sources from clusters of permanent pithouses were logistical, a pattern that was more highly developed on the Northwest Coast but virtually impossible for hunter-gatherers on the Great Plains. What could upset the pattern was disruption of the reliable annual run of migratory fish. Landslides can be triggered by earthquakes in this region, and big ones can change the courses of rivers and block migrating fish, sometimes for many years or even permanently. Such events occasionally did force people to undertake rapid readaptations (Hayden and Ryder 2001).

Variations in the sizes of pithouses in some late village clusters have been interpreted sometimes as indicating differentials in wealth and status. Social inequalities in these communities might have been minor as compared to much greater ones along the nearby Northwest Coast, but even a small amount of inequality would be unexpected on the Plateau (Pokotylo and Mitchell 1998:99–100). Its occurrence there, if that is what the evidence truly indicates, might be an indication of the power of cultural imitation.

Speakers of languages of the Athapaskan branch of Nadene moved on to the northern Plateau, probably within the last few centuries. The timing of their arrival is still debated, but it must have been part of the general drift of Athapaskans southward out of western Canada. Some Athapaskans continued on, moving south along the eastern front of the Rocky Mountains and reaching the Southwest around 1500 CE. Those that moved to the Plateau appear not to have reached it until after

1700 CE (Matson and Coupland 1995; Matson and Magne 2006; Pokotylo and Mitchell 1998:99).

Columbia River

Like the Fraser River to the north in British Columbia, the Columbia River was an important route between the Pacific Coast and the interior Plateau region. Salmon runs and Indian traders both moved up and down through the Columbia Gorge. The ancient lava flows used to constrain the Columbia for several kilometers where it flows through a gap in the Cascade Mountains. The resulting Five Mile Rapids made migration difficult for fish, but accordingly made fishing easy for Indians. The stretch is now a placid reservoir behind a modern dam.

Rock art at the upper end of the rapids marks the place where Indian traders met for thousands of years (Figure 12.24). Marine shell, candlefish (eulachon) oil, and other coastal goods moved upstream. In exchange, obsidian, hides, and other interior resources moved downstream to coastal communities (Ames et al. 1998).

Lewis and Clark noticed that game animals were abundant in western Montana but scarce in the Columbia Basin. What they were observing was the impact of human predation on animal populations, for the human population was more dense west of the Rockies than it was to the east of the mountains. Game animals were also relatively numerous in buffer zones between warring tribes, areas too risky for Indian hunters, but scarce closer to human settlements (Martin 1999a, 1999b).

Figure 12.24 *Tsagagalal* (She Who Watches) is the most prominent of many pictographs that adorn the jagged basalt cliffs at the upper end of the narrows of the Columbia River.

The nature of adaptation across all of the Interior West tended to be spotty and temporary over the long term, as people were repeatedly forced to readapt by environmental change that varied between being widespread, local, long term, or short-lived. Just as varied were the cultural solutions that people applied to these conditions, which they often brought with them from the outside. These highly variable circumstances produced many archaeological phenomena and therefore many puzzles to be solved. They also produced a complex mosaic of more familiar historical cultures across this vast set of regions. Nearly everywhere cultures changed quickly and dramatically when horses became widely available in the eighteenth century. But the image of the mounted Great Plains warrior in a feathered war bonnet was one that arose quickly and disappeared just as quickly, just another stage in the long dynamic history of the American Indians in the western interior.

The Horse Nomads

The mounted nomads of the Interior West are popularly the best known of all American Indian nations, but they were in fact a short-lived historical phenomenon. Hunter-gatherers in the region had long used dogs to drag travois and carry packs for their owners. Some of these nomadic groups started acquiring horses from the Spanish as early as 1660. People quickly learned how to tame and ride the horses, adapting the travois to them as well. This gave people mobility in the hunt that they had never had previously. When the Pueblos revolted against the Spanish in 1680 they confiscated thousands of Spanish horses and redistributed them to various tribes living around them (Swagerty 2001). Some, like the Utes and Shoshones, became major horse breeders and traders, helping spread them quickly to people living on or around the Great Basin and the Great Plains.

The introduction of horses from historic Spanish settlements in the Greater Southwest (see Chapter 6) eventually converted many hunting and agricultural societies to mounted nomadic cultures. Pressures from the East and the attraction of immense bison herds prompted many communities living on the fringes of the Eastern Woodlands to join those already present on the northern Great Plains. They left many tepee ring sites across the landscape of the Interior West. While some of these date to before 2000 BCE, long before horses were available, a majority of them are later, an indication of increased population size and mobility in the Late period. Tepee diameters range widely, from as little as 1.2 m (4 ft) to as much as 7.3 m (24 ft). The average is probably around 4.6 m (15 ft), a substantial tepee.

Western Indians quickly became skilled riders, using simplified equipment to hunt bison and fight from horseback. Utes acquired horses from the Pueblo and traded them to the Eastern Shoshones. They in turn distributed them to other tribes to the north and east from a center in southwestern Wyoming. Flathead and Nez Perce traders acquired horses from the Shoshones and took them to the Plateau. Crow traders, close linguistic and cultural relatives of the Hidatsa farmers living along the Missouri, brought horses there to be redistributed to neighboring Mandan and Arikara villages as well as to various Siouan tribes in that part of the northern Great Plains. Comanches left their Great Basin roots on horseback to become one of the best-known historic tribes of the southern Great Plains.

Stealing horses from neighboring tribes soon became a favorite activity of young men and a way to gain social standing. Horses multiplied and spread so rapidly that French-speaking fur traders from Quebec observed horses with Spanish brands on the northern fringes of the western Canadian Great Plains (Driver and Massey 1957:284–287).

Nearly everyone in the Interior West had horses by the end of the eighteenth century, and many nations living in the western portions of the Eastern Woodlands moved on to the Great Plains to take up bison hunting at least part of the time. Pressure from European settlers moving westward from the East Coast combined with the attractions of horse nomadism to prompt whole nations to shift their residences and their lifestyles. Guns and other trade goods added to the mix of innovations, shifting the local balance of power here and there as tribes vied to acquire weapons and mobility while denying them to their enemies.

These rapid adaptive changes produced radical shifts for many traditional societies. For example, the ancestors of the Cheyennes were wild rice gatherers settled in the woods of northern Minnesota in 1680. Only a lifetime later in 1766 some of them were maize farmers living in villages on the edge of the southern Minnesota prairie, while others of them were farming and living in earth lodges along the Sheyenne River in North Dakota, following people who had been practicing farming there since 1200 CE (Schneider 2002). A few decades later they had come together again and were living near the Black Hills of South Dakota. There they gave up farming for bison hunting and abandoned earth lodges for tepees. By the 1840s the Cheyennes were mounted Great Plains nomads (see Figure 12.11) (Moore 1987, 1996).

Many other classic Plains Indian nations were similarly late arrivals. The nomadic Crows of the High Plains were a late offshoot of the sedentary Hidatsa nation. The Arapaho, Gros Ventres, Plains Cree, Plains Ojibwa, and Blackfeet were all Algonquian-speaking nations that moved on to the Great Plains from earlier homelands in the northern woodlands. The Sioux (Lakota, Nakota, and Dakota) and Assiniboins had similarly lived earlier closer to the western Great Lakes. The Shoshone, Ute, and Comanche tribes all originated in the Great Basin (see Figure 12.13) (Gunnerson 2001).

The archaeological culture known as the Dismal River phase (1640–1730 CE) on the western Great Plains was probably left by Nadene-speaking people who moved into the region from the north, perhaps with some refugees from abandoned Fremont sites in Utah. They adopted ceramics, some farming, and permanent villages from the Caddoan-speaking Central Plains peoples east of them. They were very successful bison hunters, but they also adopted maize farming for a while. Their adaptation deteriorated when they began taking Caddoan slaves and selling them to the Spanish in New Mexico. Other Nadene speakers, ancestors of the Navajo and Apache nations, pressed on into the Southwest and became established there by 1525 CE (see Chapter 6). Many of Dismal River relatives left the Great Plains and joined the Jicarilla Apaches. Others joined the Kiowa and were later known as the Kiowa Apaches.

In short, the late archaeology of the Interior West is very complex, especially on the Great Plains. It was made so by a mosaic of shifting opportunities afforded by climate, bison, crops, horses, and available technology that caused cultures to come and go here and there with dizzying speed. This pattern continued through the first century of the existence of the United States.

The adaptation of the mounted Great Plains nomads could not last in the form that prevailed in the nineteenth century. Even the vast bison herds could not sustain the pressure of that many hunters, particularly after Europeans joined in. The Plains Indians might have evolved into pastoralists like those of central Asia had there been enough time for them to adopt cattle to replace the intractable bison, but Euro-American ranchers filled that niche too quickly. In the end, and like so many earlier cultures, the phenomenon of the mounted nomadic Indians came and went in a matter of only two centuries.

Summary

1. Both short- and long-term climatic cycling on the Great Plains, Great Basin, and interior Plateau areas led to the evolution of many short-lived cultures.

2. Medicine wheels are dramatic archaeological sites, but their purpose remains uncertain.

3. Plains Woodland cultures originating in the Eastern Woodlands moved into the Great Plains along forested river valleys.

4. Plains Woodland farmers grew crops like those that supported Hopewell culture.

5. Early Plains Village farming cultures were influenced by Mississippian cultures.

6. Plains Village communities on the Great Plains clustered along the lower reaches of major tributaries of the Mississippi.

7. The Great Basin was home to hunter-gatherers for most of the Holocene.

8. Fremont culture developed in Utah when temporary climatic conditions made it possible for local hunter-gatherers to take up cultivation and other traits from the Greater Southwest.

9. The decline of Fremont culture was followed by the expansion of Numic-speaking hunter-gatherers across the Great Basin.

10. Peoples of the Plateau region had linguistic and cultural connections to the Northwest Coast, but their environment caused their adaptations to resemble those of the northern Great Plains.

11. Pithouses built on the Plateau resembled earth lodges on the Great Plains and early dwellings in the Southwest, all of them designed to provide shelter during long, cold winters.

12. Mounted nomadic cultures developed rapidly after the introduction of the horse from Spanish colonial settlements in the Southwest.

Further Reading

Raymond Wood's edited volume titled *Archaeology of the Great Plains* is a good place to get the basic facts of Great Plains archaeology and to fill out the details of regional developments that could only be briefly sketched here. Douglas Bamforth's *Ecology and Human Organization on the Great Plains* provides a detailed look at ecology that is especially thorough in its coverage of Paleoindian and recent human adaptations. Jack Hofman provides a more detailed description of Paleoindians on the Great Plains. The Arkansas Archeological Survey Research Series includes over a dozen volumes covering the "Central and Northern Plains Overview Project" and the "Southwestern Division Overview," all funded by the Army Corps of Engineers. Key volumes from the two series are *From Clovis to Comanchero: Archeological Overview of the Southern Great Plains* and *Archaeology and Paleoecology of the Central Great Plains*. Good places to start for the archaeology of the Great Plains, the Great Basin, and the Plateau are Volumes 11–13 of the *Handbook of North American Indians*. Donald Grayson's *The Desert's Past* remains an excellent synthesis of the Great Basin. Julian Steward's *Theory of Culture Change,* which contains a key section on Great Basin adaptation, remains a classic reference in anthropology.

Glossary

pemmican: Pounded dried meat and sometimes dried fruits mixed with an equal amount of melted fat, normally stored for future use.

CHAPTER

The West Coast

You stay. I go.

Ishi, March 25, 1916

Introduction

North America's portion of the vast Pacific rim arcs from the Aleutian Islands to the coast of Mexico (Figure 13.1). The Alaskan portion is properly part of the Arctic and Subarctic regions, and dealt with in Chapter 14. Most of the Mexican and Central American portions are properly covered in Chapters 7 and 8. What lies between is the long West Coast from the Alaskan panhandle to Baja California, a long diverse maritime environment that produced some of North America's most unusual cultures.

The panhandle of Alaska and coastal British Columbia make up the deeply indented northern part of the Northwest Coast, a jagged and steep coastline, still clogged in places by mountain glaciers that reach all the way to the sea. Parts of this sinuous fringe of northwestern North America are so rugged that no modern roads parallel them. The modern environment is a temperate rain forest, kept warmer than the interior just to the east by ocean currents, wet for much of the year, and thick with giant trees and dense undergrowth.

The southern Northwest Coast spans the portions of the states of Washington and Oregon west of the Cascade Mountains. Here the coastline is straighter, and while rain forest still dominates on Washington's Olympic Peninsula, the forest of coastal Oregon is a bit drier and more subject to fire.

The California portion of the West Coast grades from tall forests in the north to chaparral and desert in the south. Finally there is the other California, the long Mexican peninsular cul-de-sac known as Baja California. It is hot and dry for its entire 1,200-km (750-mi) length. Although most of California was a mosaic of contrasting but generally productive microenvironments, particularly in the north, Baja California offered people little more than the vast interior deserts of the Great Basin and the Greater Southwest.

Agriculture was never practiced anywhere in this long coastal region before the coming of European colonists. The severe limitations imposed by the environment of Baja California did not allow native societies

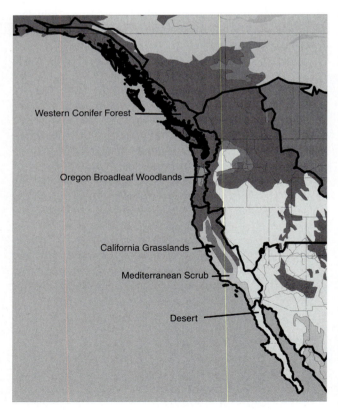

Western Conifer Forest

Oregon Broadleaf Woodlands

California Grasslands

Mediterranean Scrub

Desert

Figure 13.1 The environments of the West Coast.

there to evolve into anything more complex than band organizations. Northward through California and beyond greater natural abundance allowed for higher population densities and the emergence of tribes, but despite the region's agricultural productivity today it was not practiced there by Native Americans. Even today agriculture is less viable the farther north one travels along the Northwest Coast, yet some tribal societies there evolved into chiefdoms, a phenomenon that flummoxed early anthropologists. Except in the deserts of southern California and Baja California the West Coast was full of surprises for them, and it has taken decades of research to begin to figure it all out.

The Northwest Coast

The big picture of the Northwest Coast (Figure 13.2) is one of a naturally rich and dynamic environment that eventually became stable enough to allow hunter-gatherers to evolve more complex societies than are typically found at that subsistence level. Environmental constraints were overcome by key innovations such as cedar canoes, plank houses, slate projectile points, oil rendering, and food storage. Ranking, stratified societies, and Northwest Coast art and architecture were based on that foundation. Relatively late contact with Europeans brought epidemics later to the Northwest Coast than in many other regions, timing that helped the Northwest Coast peoples weather the effects of contact and to survive as vibrant Native American cultures to this day.

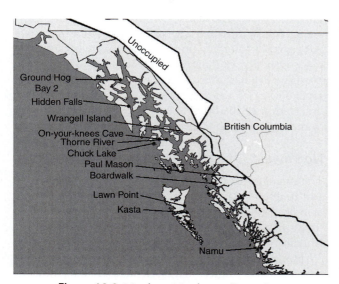

Figure 13.2 Northern Northwest Coast sites.

The mountainous coastline of Alaska and British Columbia is rugged and almost impassable on land. Lower sea levels 15,000 years ago would not have made travel much easier than it is now. Yet many archaeologists have concluded for now that there were refugia along the way and this was the most likely route taken by the first migrants from Asia to America. If so it did not become a well-worn path, for the peoples that settled in this region typically evolved in place over a long period of time.

Human beings encounter both constraints and opportunities in their environments. Technology mediates these as innovations overcome natural constraints and facilitate new opportunities. Only the mightiest of technological innovations can change some impoverished environments into places habitable by dense human populations, as Las Vegas, Nevada, illustrates. But sometimes there are uncommonly rich environments that need only a few clever innovations to facilitate the evolution of complex societies. Such was the case here.

Northwest Coast Environment

The Northwest Coast extends 2,000 km (1,250 mi) from Yakutat Bay in southeastern Alaska to northwestern California, much longer if one follows the sinuous coastline. In many places mountains leave precious little flat coastal plain for human settlement. Sites are often thus confined to a long, narrow, twisting band of suitable land sandwiched between the sea on one side and mountainous terrain on the other. This circumstance makes computation of population densities based on area almost meaningless. Northwest Coast cultures have always been strung out more like birds on a wire than like trees in a forest.

The maritime climate of the Northwest Coast has cool summers and wet, mild winters. The warm currents of the North Pacific buffer the effects of latitude and keep temperatures above freezing much of the time. The misty rain seems never to end during the winter months, but from mid-Vancouver Island south long dry spells in the summer require modern farmers to irrigate. South of British Columbia small coastal mountain ranges parallel the larger Cascade Range that separates the West Coast from the rest of the continent. Mountains force weather systems to shed their rain, creating dry climates in their lee and making the Northwest Coast environments dramatically different from those of the interior just a short distance to the east. The mountains of Vancouver Island make the mainland coast of British Columbia to the east a sunnier place that it would otherwise be.

The coastal environment is a temperate rain forest dominated by giant conifers, particularly western hemlocks, Sitka spruces, and Douglas firs. The western red cedar is less abundant but much more important to the evolution of Northwest Coast cultures. The ecological reasons for this unique forest are complex, but generally speaking the environment provides moisture and nutrients mainly in the winter, when leafless deciduous trees are dormant and unable to use them. Evergreen conifers can grow even in winter, while also tolerating the dry summer. The rarity of high winds has long favored the natural selection of large long-living trees. Species that live 500 years are common, and a few can survive for twice that long. Forest fires are rare in the moist forests of the northern coast, but they are more common to the south. While the northern coast is heavily dissected by fiords, the southern coast is straight and undissected by comparison.

Archaeologists often extend discussion of the Northwest Coast to include the interior Fraser and Columbia river basins, two great systems that drain much of the interior Plateau east of the mountains. Apart from the Klamath River in southwestern Oregon they are the only two rivers that penetrate the Cascade Mountains and link the interior to the coast along its 2,000-km (1,250-mi) extent. The upper drainages of the Fraser and Columbia rivers east of the Cascades have drier continental climates with cold winters. Because of this these interior drainages are discussed separately in Chapter 12.

Northwest Coast Resources

The West Coast teems with a vast variety of life: deer, wapiti, bears, mountain sheep, and mountain goats live in the forest; halibut, Pacific cod, and herring live in the shallow seas of the continental shelf. Hunting extended seaward just as fishing was important along inland rivers. Sea hunters took sea otters, seals, sea lions, and in some places porpoises and whales. Anadromous fish, including six species of salmon, steelhead trout, smelt, and eulachon (candlefish) (Figure 13.3) push up main rivers and coastal streams in huge numbers every year. Once dried, eulachon (*Thaleichthys pacificus*) can be burned like candles. They can also be rendered for their rich oil, which has been an important food source for thousands of years. Migratory birds and a large number of minor fish and terrestrial animals filled out the range of animal food sources available here.

The historic cultures of the Northwest Coast were extraordinary by any measure, and much archaeological effort has been expended in the search for the origins of their characteristics. There is little evidence for much

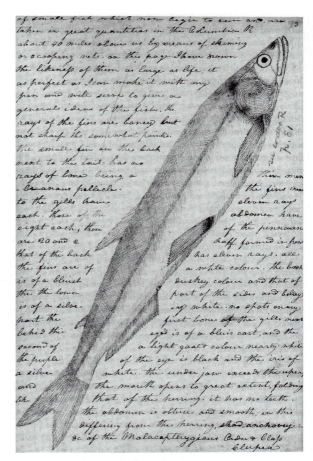

Figure 13.3 Drawing of a eulachon, made by Meriwether Lewis.
Source: Moulton (1990:434).

movement over the last seven millennia in this region, an unusual feature that appears to have allowed the languages of 11 founding populations to develop largely in place over a very long time. These peculiarities of the Northwest Coast make it reasonable to approach the archaeology of the region backward, starting with a description of the historic cultures, then jumping back to the beginning to trace their development over time.

Northwest Coast Languages

The languages of 11 ancient founder populations evolved and multiplied largely in place (Figure 13.4). Time created deep gulfs of mutual unintelligibility between many small adjacent populations over time (Thompson and Kinkade 1990). By the nineteenth century there were 39 languages belonging to the 11 families. Clusters of villages, even single villages, tended to be politically independent from others, even those that spoke the same

Figure 13.4 Language families of the Northwest Coast.

Table 13.1 Names that are common in publications are sometimes not those preferred by the modern people of Native American nations. This table provides a guide for some Canadian groups.

Nation	Sometimes Called	Language Family
Eyak	Eyak	Athapaskan
Tlingit	Tlingit	Tlingit
Haida	Haida	Haida
Nisga'a	Tsimshian	Tsimshian
Gitxsan	Tsimshian	Tsimshian
Tsimshian	Tsimshian	Tsimshian
Haisla	Kitimat	Wakashan
Haihais	Haihais	Wakashan
Heiltsuk	Bella Bella	Wakashan
Nuxalk	Bella Coola	Salishan
Ooweekeno	Kwakiutl	Wakashan
Kwakwa̱ka'wakw	Kwakiutl	Wakashan
Nuu-chan-nulth	Nootka	Wakashan
Coast Salish	Coast Salish	Salishan

or closely related languages. For simplification, anthropologists have lumped societies that were distantly related, but politically independent. Anthropologists also tend to break the long arc of coastline into Northern, Central, and Southern subdivisions, but without complete agreement about where divisions should be made (Ames and Maschner 1999:18). Some sort of subdivision is important because there are so many local cultures and there was a gradation of significant cultural differences by latitude.

Speakers of early Nadene and the probably related Tlingit languages settled on the northern part of the coast. South of them is spoken Haida, another language isolate that might be a distant member of the Nadene family, and the Tsimshianian family, a set of two or three languages. Along the central coast are the Wakashan and Salishan language families, the latter spreading eastward into the Plateau region as well.

Chimakuan, a two-language family, is isolated among others on the Washington coast. Five language families that appear to share ancient common ancestors form a mosaic along the southern coast. They are classified together by some linguists under the Penutian language phylum. Languages of the Chinookan family cluster along the lower Columbia. On the Oregon coast and in the adjacent warm Interior West of the Cascades are the perhaps distantly related Alsean, Siuslawan, and Coosan families. The Takelman family has two

representatives in the western Oregon interior. Additional Nadene languages are also found along the southern part of the Northwest Coast.

Eleven language families, with mutual connections so deep in time as to be undetectable to modern linguists, yet packed in a tight mosaic, indicate a long evolution in place. There must have been some population movement and some language extinction over six millennia, but large-scale demographic shifts do not appear to have occurred. Archaeological and biological evidence is consistent with this linguistic picture of long-term demographic continuity in the region.

The modern Indian nations of the Northwest Coast have been called by many names in recent history and frequently turn up in historical and anthropological accounts with names that their living descendants find objectionable. Preferred names are shown in Table 13.1 along with a key to identifying them in the older literature.

Historic Northwest Coast Cultures

It is helpful to examine the historic Northwest Coast cultures first before turning to the archaeological evidence for the long record leading to it. Generally speaking, the shared classic features of historic Northwest Coast culture are most strongly developed in the north and least in the southern part of the coastal region. Large cedar plank houses (Figure 13.5), totem poles, large dugout canoes, wooden boxes, and elaborate masks decorated in the distinctive art style of the region are all more dramatically present in the north. This is also the section of the Northwest Coast where marine resources are both most abundant and most variable by season.

Large villages dotted the narrow coastline, hemmed in by the ocean before them and steep mountains to their rear. Local circumstances varied, and so too did the organization of settlements and the ways in which communities organized settlement and seasonal movements. While many Northwest Coast peoples lived in large winter villages and dispersed to various short-term camps to harvest food resources through the course of the year, the Nuu-chan-nulth people of Vancouver Island also maintained summer villages where several groups might congregate. These settlements were situated to provide easy access to Pacific whaling waters off the coast (Mitchell 1990:355–356).

Historic peoples of the region harvested shellfish in huge numbers as well, leaving behind sometimes large shell middens near productive flats. It is tempting to hypothesize that shellfishing was especially im-

portant in the wintertime. However, known Heíltsuk (Bella Bella) winter villages have only minor shell middens. Neither do historic village locations necessarily coincide with places where salmon could be harvested most efficiently. All of this suggests that settlement locations were selected based on a balance of several considerations, some of them probably unknowable to us today. Canoe transportation made it possible to move to distant harvesting points easily when seasonal resources were briefly abundant, and to return almost as easily with food for long-term storage (Hobler 1990:300–301).

European Contacts

European exploration and settlement of the Northwest Coast came late compared to the rest of the continent. For three centuries after Columbus there were only sporadic visits, often by explorers who touched there only briefly before pushing on toward grander objectives. Vitus Bering came by in 1741, followed by some Spanish expeditions and James Cook in 1777. Fur traders also began stopping along the coast in the latter part of the eighteenth century, and this led to greater interest in the region on the part of both the Russians and the British. The Russians eventually established outposts at Kodiak Island, Sitka, and as far south as Fort Ross on the California coast. In the years following the American Revolution both British and American trading ships stopped along the Northwest Coast with increasing frequency, taking away loads of sea otter and other furs and leaving behind beads, guns, cloth, other trade goods, and eventually diseases.

It was not until the early nineteenth century that European expansion brought widespread change to the Indian cultures of the Northwest Coast. The sea otter was driven nearly to extinction by the 1830s, and the fur trade shifted to interior species. Somewhat later Euro-American settlers following the Oregon Trail began moving into the region, displacing Indian communities.

The native inhabitants of the Northwest Coast seemed strange to early anthropologists. Hunter-gatherers were supposed to live in small nomadic groups. Here were people who lived by hunting and gathering, yet they congregated in locally dense villages comprised of large permanent houses. Here were people who lacked the advantages of agricultural surpluses or the benefits of state organization, yet they supported lavish architecture and public art. Time would eventually reveal that they were not unique in the world, but in the nineteenth century they seemed so to many outsiders.

Figure 13.5 Reconstructed Tlingit plank clan house. Totem Bight State Historical Park near Ketchikan, Alaska, 1966.

Cycles of Abundance

The seasonality of resources was most pronounced in the north. It was no accident that while resource ownership tended to be vested in individuals along the southern part of the coast, households owned resources along the northern coast. There were good organizational reasons for this, because seasonal work varied tremendously in northern communities. For example, the eulachon run brings vast numbers of candlefish into the rivers simultaneously, requiring rapid coordinated harvest and plenty of storage capacity. The eulachon runs fail once every decade or so, but rarely twice in a row. Such failures underscore the importance of surplus production and long-term storage. The demands of storage and redistribution enhanced the importance of local households and made individual ownership a very inefficient option. Anywhere from 20 to 100 people could comprise an extended household, and this was the primary unit of production.

Household leaders controlled production, storage, and redistribution for the benefit of the whole kin group, and for that they enjoyed high rank. There were rank differentials between households as well, personified in the relative standings of their leaders. Yet at the same time there was a strong moral injunction against hoarding. Property and resources were to be used, and through that use people gained prestige and power. These practices led to broader social ranking and elaborate ceremonies that are often lumped under the term **potlatch.** Historic competitive potlatches frustrated missionaries and government officials. They also subverted the simplistic theories of nineteenth-century anthropologists, who could not explain the anomaly of wealthy hunter-gatherers.

The historic competitive potlatch ceremony, at once a feast, a lavish performance, and an ostentatious giveaway of family wealth stunned the pinched sensibilities of missionaries and government officials alike. Huge quantities of food, blankets, artwork, and other goods were given away for the enhancement of prestige and rank at these ceremonies. When the surpluses were too great to be absorbed they were flamboyantly destroyed. Piles of goods were burned and slaves were killed, all to enhance the standing of leading individuals and the groups they led. It was conspicuous consumption that rivaled the best efforts of the robber barons on the other side of the continent. That much fun and waste could not be condoned by religious and political authorities of the time, of course, and the Canadian government banned the potlatch ceremonies in 1885. The Indians

of the Northwest Coast eventually subverted efforts to suppress potlatching. The law was repealed in 1951, and modern potlatching does not feature the competitive excesses of the nineteenth century.

Northwest Coast Chiefdoms

Resources had to be both plentiful and reliable for ranking and chiefdoms to emerge. Lack of reliability would have prevented the emergence of stable ranked and inflexible societies. It is reliable and predictable abundance, not occasional abundance alone, that leads to intensification and ranking. Micmac adaptation on the Northeast Coast was much more diffuse than was that of the northern Northwest Coasters, and this ties directly to the lower reliability of maritime resources in the Micmac case (Matson 1983; Miller 1983). Little wonder that ranking and chiefdoms did not develop on the Northeast Coast.

Ranking led to some very elaborate societies, but ranking was weakly developed in some places, strongly so in others. The historic Tsimshians had strong ranking and were organized as a chiefdom rather than as a tribe (Ames 1995:171). This might have been a consequence of the introduction of European trade, which introduced new abundant and reliable resources, which in turn intensified Tsimshian ranking. In this way, European contact moved the Tsimshians closer to chiefdom organization.

On the other hand, some Northwest Coast societies appear to have developed ranking simply because their neighbors had. The region is an excellent laboratory in which to study hierarchy, which might not even be adaptive in a particular situation and still emerge (Gilman 1981). If it were perceived to be adaptive apart from resource intensification, then some societies could have adopted it before rather than after intensifying their adaptations. It is probably safe to say that hierarchy follows resource intensification in its initial independent appearance in any particular region where the available resources and technology make that possible. However, this cause–effect relationship is unambiguous only in initial independent cases. Thereafter the cause–effect relationship might be reversed, a situation similar to that seen in the Southeast and some other regions covered by this book. Such a reversal might take place if a nonhierarchical society adopts hierarchical organization based on the model of some other society with which it has contact, but in anticipation of intensifying resources. This is a general principle of human behavior to which archaeologists must be alert. It is also the principal reason why Lewis Henry Morgan and other early anthropologists were unable to apply their evolutionary schemes universally. They failed to appreciate that complex systems can be created quickly if societies (or rather the people who comprise them) perceive that they will be adaptive. This point is crucial to understanding how a system like a very hierarchical chiefdom might appear in an area where the opportunities for resource intensification seem rather marginal.

Northwest Coast Art

It was no accident that Franz Boas, the slayer of cultural theories of Morgan and others that misused the principles of biological evolution, learned much of what he knew about human culture among the Indians of the Northwest Coast (Boas 1955). The art of the Northwest Coast was the subject of one of his early works, and it is justifiably world famous. Zoomorphic designs are equally at home on cylindrical totem poles or on the flat surfaces of boxes, house façades, or Chilkat blankets (Figure 13.6). Three-dimensional forms can occur as decorations, for example bowls or spoon handles, or as portable statuettes. The shape of the eye is key, for its curves repeat in other contexts. Animals are often split and splayed and their identifying elements are sometimes rearranged to make the whole image abstract. Forms are sometimes skeletonized and there is a strong tendency to fill all the available space rather than leave an empty background.

Northwest Coast Society

Historically there were two basic social classes in most Northwest Coast societies, free people and slaves. Slaves were war captives and their descendants. Free people were often sorted further into three ranks: chiefs and chiefly families who formed an elite class, a middle rank in which people held only a few titles, and commoners who had no titles.

Northwest Coast societies were complex for hunter-gatherers and they occupied permanent settlements. But politically they never became more complex than unstable chiefdoms. Most operated at the tribal level, with the most stable unit being the extended family household. Communities organized this way could expand up to about 2,000 inhabitants, but not much higher (Ames and Maschner 1999:26). As in many other North American societies, this was the point at which tribal communities would split as the result of internal stresses. The Northwest Coast is an extraordinary region that demonstrates that

Figure 13.6 Some Northwest Coast art motifs.

complexity is not necessarily the consequence of high population density. It also demonstrates that the use of abundant marine resources does not necessarily parallel agricultural intensification (Schalk 1981:69–70). The next question to be answered is how all of this came to be.

The Geological Context

It has been helpful to first outline the nature of historic Northwest Coast cultures, because in this case first knowing something about the outcomes helps one understand the evolutionary processes that led to them. The first peopling of the Northwest Coast occurred in the context of complicated changes in the land caused by the retreat of Cordilleran glacial ice (Fedje and Christiansen 1999). The colossal weight of the ice caused isostatic depression of whole mountain ranges and their surroundings. At the same time the buildup of glacial ice on the continents took moisture from the ocean without replenishment, causing a eustatic drop in sea level. In some places depression of the land under the weight of the ice exceeded the fall in the sea level, submerging the coastline. In other places the relationship was reversed and land now submerged was above sea level at the end of the Pleistocene.

The Northwest Coast is part of the Pacific rim and like much of the rest of the rim it is also tectonically active. Flows of volcanic magma and slippages along fault lines have complicated geological history even more. Even geologically minor events, which are still frequent today, can have a major impact on human populations, given the scale at which we live. A local earthquake that is but a footnote to the grand processes of continental drift can cause productive shellfish beds to disappear, cause fishing stations to shift locations, or cause landslides to bury homes. Compounding the effects of these minor events have been major climatic cycles. The Northwest Coast has been as subject to warm and cool episodes as any other part of the continent.

The eustatic rise of sea levels at the end of the Pleistocene typically occurred at a more rapid rate than isostatic rebound of the landscape as heavy glacial ice melted, leading to temporary inundation of coastal areas that are now once again above sea level. This kind of marine transgression in southwestern British Columbia reached heights as great as a hundred meters above modern sea level before the land reemerged. The temporary inundation probably often wiped the landscape clean of archaeological evidence. Generally speaking, sea levels along the Northwest Coast approached their current levels by 3000 BCE, and since then they have presented more environmental stability and fewer big problems for human adaptation than previously.

The Evolution of Northwest Coast Forests

The forests of the region also came to take on their modern character around 3000 BCE. During the height of glaciation there were few forests of any kind north of modern Oregon, and it took time for the hemlocks, spruces, firs, and cedars of the modern forest to spread into areas that had been either glaciated or at least too cold for them (Ames and Maschner 1999:48–53). Although it took millennia for the forests of mighty trees to become established, once they were they constituted a unique environment. A giant Sitka spruce (*Picea sitchensis*) along Klootchy Creek near Seaside, Oregon, is said locally to have been the biggest tree in Oregon and the biggest Sitka spruce in the United States until it was blown down in 2007. Estimated to be over 750 years old, it stood over 63 m (206 ft) tall and had a circumference of 17 m (56 ft). Washington State claimed a co-champion having a height of 58 m (190 ft) and a circumference of 18 m (59 ft).

Washington State claims the world's largest western red cedar, the Quinault Lake Cedar on the Olympic Peninsula, which one source says is 53 m (174 ft) tall

while another gives it only 48.5 m (159 ft). Near-record firs and spruces are also found on the peninsula. The Quinault Lake Spruce is tied for the United States overall size record with a diameter of over 5 m (16 ft) and a height of just over 58 m (194 ft), but it is actually shorter than the more slender 75.6-m (248-ft) Queets spruce a few kilometers away. Two Douglas firs in the same area are assigned different heights by different sources, the largest of them being almost 90 m (295 ft.). The largest western hemlock (*Tsuga heterophylola*) on the Olympic Peninsula is not a record holder, but it stands 53 m (174 ft) tall. The upshot is that a walk through this temperate rain forest of giant trees is a humbling experience made possible only by constant maintenance of trails cut through the dense tangled undergrowth.

The Peopling of the Northwest Coast

The oldest human remains and artifacts discovered along the Northwest Coast so far come from On-Your-Knees-Cave on the northern tip of Prince of Wales Island in southeastern Alaska. These were dated to 9730–10,300 radiocarbon years BP (Fedje et al. 2004). Earlier dates from Fort Rock Cave and Wilson Butte Cave far into the interior are disputed, and the evidence for a coastal migration of very early people from Asia is only circumstantial. Consequently the earliest indisputable evidence for peopling of the Northwest Coast is no older than 11,000 BCE, and even this depends in part on inference.

There is little Paleoindian evidence in the region. The Richey-Roberts cache of large Clovis points at Wenatchee on the Plateau is the only major Clovis site known even close to the Northwest Coast. A mastodon dating to about the same time was found at the Manis site near Sequim, Washington. While there was no evidence that the mastodon had been killed by Paleoindians, Carl Gustafsen and his research team found a bone point in one of the mastodon's ribs. The point had broken off and the wound healed before the animal eventually died. The association suggests that Paleoindian hunters were in the region and that mastodons were on their prey list. But Clovis was not a coastal adaptation and the scattered fluted points in the region probably should be regarded as intrusive from the plains and the Plateau regions.

Holocene Adaptations

Archaic cultures dating to the Early Holocene (10,500–5000 BCE) on the Northwest Coast are somewhat better represented than Paleoindian ones. The problem is that sites that escaped destruction by rising sea level are probably now buried under dense rain forest vegetation, not easily found by archaeologists. Half the Nuxalk villages that were thriving in the nineteenth century were invisible by 1980, so we should not expect earlier sites to be visible or even to exist anymore (Hobler 1990:304).

An early complex of stemmed points is distributed along the Columbia River (Carlson 1990:61–62). An early Pebble Tool tradition having many local names is found to the north, around the Straits of Georgia, Juan de Fuca, and Puget Sound, as well as into the lower reaches of streams visited by migratory salmon and eulachon. The tradition also has leaf-shaped bifaces in its inventory. Roy Carlson argues that this culture had a coastal adaptation from the beginning, and that it expanded to more interior locations like The Dalles, Oregon, along major rivers. Its distant ancestor could be the Nenana complex of central Alaska. Carlson hypothesizes that this tradition ultimately led to the Salishan and Wakashan-speaking societies of the central Northwest Coast (Carlson 1990:62–69, 1996a:8–9, 1996b:216).

Microblades

The manufacture and use of microblades spread to the northern part of the Northwest Coast from Alaska during the Early Holocene. More northerly sites of the period include Ground Hog Bay 2, Hidden Falls, Thorne River, and Chuck Lake. All four lie on the Alaskan panhandle and all of them contain microblades, sometimes along with evidence that their makers exploited shellfish, fish, and terrestrial mammals. Bifaces are absent but there are unifacial chipped-stone tools.

The most important Archaic site on the central Northwest Coast is Namu. Microblades appear there around 7000 BCE, the farthest south they were made and used along the coast, apart from their sporadic appearance at some sites around the Gulf of Georgia and in caves on the slopes of Mount St. Helens. Elements of the more southerly Pebble Tool tradition also appear at Namu, so the site appears to have been at the interface of two great regional traditions. Here, too, the evidence indicates that people had a sophisticated fishing and hunting adaptation. The distribution of microblades has led many archaeologists to refer to the phenomenon as the Northwest Microblade tradition, an archaeological culture that is generally regarded as having been more than just a tool industry.

Lawn Point, Kasta, and other sites on the Queen Charlotte Islands contain evidence of the Moresby tradition, the local expression of the microblade phenomenon. Here people had to adapt to a more marine way of life. Terrestrial game was restricted to a subspecies of black bear and a now extinct dwarf caribou. Salmon was an important resource even in the Early Holocene, but eulachon was apparently absent that early (Fladmark et al. 1990:229–231; Moss et al. 2004). These and other sites of the period on the northern Northwest Coast generally lack bifaces.

Microblades largely disappeared from tool assemblages on the Northwest Coast by 4000 BCE except in a few places where they persisted along the coast of southeastern Alaska and British Columbia. Archaic sites in the southern part of the Northwest Coast feature leaf-shaped bifaces and tend to lack microblades (Ames and Maschner 1999:67–72). Thus there was cultural diversity along the northern Northwest Coast even in the early centuries of Holocene adaptation.

The Archaic peoples of the Northwest Coast were generalists that were comfortable both on the coast and in the interior, both in the forest and on the water (Ames 2002; Ames and Maschner 1999:126). There are important technological differences between sites on the coast and those in the interior; microblades appeared mainly on the coast while chipped-stone lanceolate points occur mainly in interior sites. But these differences could simply reflect different tool kits used by the same people in different circumstances. Put in its simplest possible form, the problem is whether we should think in terms of one archaeological culture in this period or two of them. In either case it is reasonably clear that the Archaic peoples of the Northwest Coast did not store large quantities of surplus food for the long term. This practice, which became very important later on, was probably discouraged by low population density and the ecologically driven need to maintain two or more seasonal residences. In other words, the Archaic peoples of this region were like most hunter-gatherers; they probably buffered food shortages by moving frequently and sharing with nearby bands. Thus salmon, for example, might have been taken in large numbers at traditional fishing stations when they were in season, and bands probably congregated in large groups at those times. But in the absence of permanent year-round settlements and long-term food storage, people reverted to other foods when the salmon runs were over.

The distribution of the early microblade sites is similar to the distribution of historic distribution of languages belonging to the Haida, Tlingit, and Athpaskan families. There is little else to go on, but this spatial distribution of related language families provides some support for the hypothesis that they are descendants of the makers of the older Denali complex. If that is true, their ancestry probably goes all the way back to the Dyuktai complex of northeastern Siberia, which was discussed in Chapters 2 and 3 (Carlson 1990:68).

Five Mile Rapids

Perhaps the most important site of the period in the southern part of the region is the Five Mile Rapids site (Figure 13.7) upstream on the Columbia River on the edge of the Plateau region. The site lies at the upper end of the Long Narrows of the Columbia (Figure 13.8), a

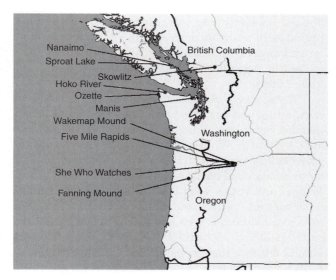

Figure 13.7 Southern Northwest Coast sites.

Figure 13.8 Columbia River, now a dam reservoir, in the vicinity of Five Mile Rapids.

65-km (40 mi) narrow gut through which salmon had to struggle upstream before the Dalles Dam submerged it all in the twentieth century. The site overlooks the first pool above the narrows in which salmon could rest after this leg of their migration, the best place for fishing on the entire river. Soon after 8000 BCE Indians began fishing in earnest here, taking huge salmon catches without specialized equipment (Cressman 1960; Strong 1976). The nearby Wakemap Mound site is similarly important.

Sites in the Portland basin west of The Dalles that date to 6000–4000 BCE contain both willow-leaf-shaped projectile points and manos and metates. Some also have produced many stone weights, sometimes inappropriately called "bolas stones." The weights were probably used with fishnets; there is no evidence that the South American bola was ever used in North America. The assemblages are further evidence that at this time people in the southern part of the region were more generally adapted than those living in the north. Grinding stones indicate that seeds and other terrestrial resources were also important parts of their diets.

The Roots of Classic Northwest Coast Culture

The cultures of the Northwest Coast developed their distinctive complex hunter-gatherer subsistence, large settled villages, social stratification, and the art style for which they are justifiably famous beginning in the Middle Holocene, 5000–1500 BCE. Marine shell middens appeared more frequently around 4400 BCE. Ocean levels and river estuaries were stabilizing around the same time. One might be tempted to attribute the absence of earlier shell middens solely to the destructive effects of rising sea levels. But isostatic rebound and tectonic uplift in some parts of the region have elevated coastal sites faster than the sea has risen, so it is not logical to conclude that all evidence of presumed earlier shellfishing has been destroyed by inundation. If they existed earlier shell middens would be preserved at least in a few uplifted areas, and indeed scattered earlier traces have been found. However, something culturally profound was going on in the region after 4400 BCE, a conclusion supported by major parallel changes on the Plateau and in California. While the growing importance of shell middens points to increased sedentism along the coast, the appearance of pit houses on the interior Plateau signals increased sedentism there too, even though stabilized sea levels cannot explain it convincingly anywhere but on the coast.

These simultaneous changes were ultimately driven by global climatic cycles. Average temperatures peaked in the northern hemisphere shortly before 5000 BCE and cooled thereafter. Cooler and wetter conditions followed until after 4000 BCE along the Northwest Coast, particularly in the summer. The temperate rain forest of the region developed as a result of the cooler and wetter conditions.

Middens and Wet Sites

The emerging environment was wetter and perhaps also more stable, allowing intertidal food resources to flourish and for Indian communities on the coast to settle into more predictable seasonal rounds. More permanent dwellings near productive tidal flats inevitably produced larger middens than ever seen previously. Heaps of discarded shell are a boon to archaeologists because their alkaline chemistry neutralizes forest acidity and facilitates the preservation of bone, antler, and other perishable materials that would otherwise dissolve over time in acidic soils.

Wood does not preserve well in middens, but fortunately the wet climate of the region has also produced boggy wet sites along the coast, and here archaeologists have found good wood preservation whether or not shell has been present. Fine examples have been found along the Hoko River. Overall the evidence indicates that the cultural evolution that led to eighteenth-century Northwest Coast culture was on track 6,000 years ago.

Middens and wet sites like those on the Hoko River are particularly productive when it comes to food remains, but it must be remembered that not everything in them was necessarily dropped there by humans. Various other predators, including eagles and other birds, occasionally contributed as well (Erlandson and Moss 2001).

Key Artifact Types and Sites

Microblades disappeared in most places on the northern coast after 4000 BCE, replaced by other kinds of chipped stone and tools of bone, antler, and ground slate. Barbed harpoons became numerous, signs that hunters were taking marine mammals and large fish at sea. Harpoon heads were designed to detach from shafts and lines attached to the heads allowed the sea hunters to tether wounded animals until they died or could be drawn near enough to the boat to be dispatched by clubs or lances.

Ground slate points accompanied bone and antler points, all of them made by similar techniques. Slate implements appeared around this time in coastal sites all around the northern hemisphere. While it is tempting to look for a common historical source for this innovation, it appears much more likely that it developed independently in many coastal regions when more settled life and marine hunting became possible. Slate can be worked using the same techniques that work well on bone and ivory. Slate points are brittle and break easily, but they are also very sharp and can penetrate the thick blubber of marine mammals. Thus the slate tools of the Northwest Coast are analogs of those found elsewhere, but not homologs sharing a common origin.

Key sites in the north are Hidden Falls and Paul Mason. The latter is an interior site that contains 12 rectangular houses that date to around 1200 BCE. Curiously, despite evidence of economic intensification and year-round use, sites like Namu and Boardwalk have produced little evidence of large permanent houses. Sea levels were still rising, so many sites of this period were probably destroyed there. Moreover, there is other evidence indicating that Namu was a permanent settlement dependent upon salmon fishing (Cannon and Yang 2006).

Wedges were in use earlier on, but the addition of celts, adzes, and heavy mauls in this period all indicate that heavy woodworking was growing in importance after 4400 BCE. While celts were hafted to serve as axes, adze blades were set with their cutting edges perpendicular to handles and used for thinning and dressing wood. Wedges and mauls were used to split straight-grained cedar logs into planks, and we can infer that these were used to build both houses and seaworthy canoes (Ames and Maschner 1999:88–93). It was probably also around this time that people started "planking" salmon, cooking the fish on thin water-soaked cedar planks, a technique borrowed by modern backyard cooks. One skeptical newspaper gourmet wondered how people who lacked sawmills could be credited with such an innovation, but they needed only wedges and mauls.

Average temperatures spiked again in the Northern Hemisphere around 3000 BCE, producing generally warmer and drier conditions. Ground-stone technology was also used to produce beads, pendants, and **labrets,** all objects that might have been used to signal rank. It is likely that we are seeing these traits in the archaeological record because social stratification, more permanent settlement, and food surpluses were emerging. The natural richness of the Northwest Coast allowed people to live year-round on permanent residential sites once their local populations were large enough and once technology and scheduling were sophisticated enough to allow exploitation of seasonal resources by specialized teams living at temporary camps. This is termed a shift from residential mobility to logistic mobility (Binford 1978), which in turn led to more complex division of labor and larger households (Ames 1985; Schalk 1981:62). A consequence of this evolving strategy was that people produced and stored food surpluses for use at other times in the seasonal round. Sociopolitical boundaries would have been necessary to distinguish those within the community having access to the surplus as opposed to others outside it who did not. The older hunter-gatherer practice of sharing with any and all had to go for the new system to be viable.

Generally speaking, the productivity of the land in the north was low compared to the southern Northwest Coast, so northern coastal communities intensified exploitation of marine resources. To the archaeologist, the evidence of this shift can be seen in:

1. Increasing site differentiation,
2. Changes in domestic organization as reflected in things such as architecture,
3. Elaboration of material culture,
4. Increasing differentiation in burials, and
5. Increasing resource intensification and storage.

Seasonal variability also eventually led to more elaborate controls on production and redistribution and consequently more dramatically pronounced social and political adaptations seen there in the nineteenth century. This included the chiefdoms that so astonished early anthropologists. Many of these innovations never spread to the Puget Sound and farther south, probably because the more southern environments did not support as much deepwater sea mammal hunting and fishing (Nelson 1990:484). Some, like the use of fish weirs, did spread south, but only after a long lag (Moss and Erlandson 1998). Of course, resource variability over time and space could also be mitigated by trade and exchange, including that which takes place at the end of a lance. Thus the elaboration of warfare and the artistic symbols of rank and power also became more pronounced in the north in the fullness of time.

If we move down the Northwest Coast to Oregon and northern California we see the archaeological signatures of hierarchy fade out because there are fewer organizational problems imposed by the environment there. In this southern part of the Northwest Coast terrestrial resources were richer, so a more diverse subsistence pattern was adopted. The lesson here may be that people will generally avoid complexity and hierarchy to the extent they can if they do not perceive any advantages. Put another way, cost–benefit considerations depend to a large extent on how one perceives both. The peoples of the southern part of the Northwest Coast were not poor relations, just people whose circumstances were different.

Late Holocene Developments

Sea levels approached their modern positions by around 1800 BCE, setting the scene for the developments of the Late Holocene, 1500 BCE–1775 CE. The exception was along the British Columbia coast, where isostatic rebound and tectonic uplift continued for several more centuries. Sea levels did not reach their modern positions there until nearly two millennia later, and the continuing instability might have postponed extensive permanent human settlement until then. Climatic cycling continued too, but having once established themselves the emerging Northwest Coast cultures were able to weather periodic changes in sea levels, temperature, and moisture. The forests of the region took on their modern character during this period, particularly the very important red cedar.

Truly permanent communities of large cedar plank houses (Figure 13.9) emerged after 1800 BCE. Large houses mean large households, often lineages of dozens of related individuals. Thus the advent of large houses also marks the rise of large household production units, with all the competition, surplus production, and ranking that development would eventually entail. Villages were typically rows of plank houses, with the highest ranking (and most imposing) households situated in the center(s) of the row(s). A single row village was usually made up of households that could reckon descent from a single ancestor. Two or more rows often indicated the same number of extended kin groups in the community, as at the Paul Mason site (Fladmark et al. 1990:238). Add the heraldic art of late totem poles and façade decorations and one has the ranking code that was understood all along the Northwest Coast in more recent centuries.

Figure 13.9 Reconstructed cedar plank houses. Museum of Anthropology, University of British Columbia.

Households tended to be matrilineal along the northern part of the coast in the nineteenth century. These social units were headed by men, but internally organized by women, making the households stable social units that competed effectively with other units of like kind. Historic households tended to be patrilineal farther south, less stable units that could become much larger quickly as dominant men acquired multiple wives, but collapse even more quickly. Not surprisingly, ranking and its elaborate symbolism was less developed here as well, because both of these things needed long-term stability.

Northwest Coast Polities

Archaeologists infer that Northwest Coast societies evolved into simple ranked societies by 1800 BCE, and that ranking became more elaborated over time. These societies eventually became stratified as well when war captives began to form an underclass of slaves. Ranked societies make distinctions between individuals that are marked by differential access to prestige, wealth, and power. Stratified societies take it a step further by defining broad mutually exclusive classes (strata). In this case there were two of them: free people and slaves. Social stratification typically does not arise in nonstate societies because kin-based societies generally lack the coercive mechanisms to maintain mutually exclusive strata. But on the Northwest Coast communities were small enough and permanent enough for the custom to arise and persist in kin-based systems.

If there were slaves then there must also have been warfare, for warfare is the means through which slaves were acquired. But when both became widespread along the Northwest Coast remains uncertain (Ames 2001). Historic Northwest Coast warfare was conducted for revenge, to capture slaves, to enhance (or salvage) prestige, and to secure critical food resources. Men also fought over women, whether it was to avenge infidelity or to capture wives. Quarrels could lead to the breakup of villages and the emigration of one or more factions, and warfare between former neighbors occasionally followed.

Centralized polities of several villages never emerged along the Northwest Coast despite the consistency one can observe within historic networks. Occasionally a particularly strong community leader would emerge as first among equals, but communities and even households remained politically independent. A chief's power base was his (occasionally her) household, and that person's prestige depended upon how productive and wealthy the household was. Because of this it was possible for a man to inherit high rank but find himself the leader of a poor household. Another man might rise to the headship of a low-ranking household that managed to accumulate great wealth and consequently significant prestige for himself. Thus it was a dynamic system in which hard work and good luck could be used to leverage higher rank for a household and its chief while sloth or ill fortune dragged another down. In the nineteenth century the mechanism for the rise and fall of household fortunes was the potlatch ceremony.

The most obvious archaeological evidence for the rise of ranking might be the first appearance of cranial deformation and labrets, but we cannot be sure that these historic symbols of rank had the same meanings when they first appeared. Cranial deformation is caused by head binding of small children, so the implication is that its use as a rank marker necessarily requires that rank was inherited at birth (ascribed) rather than earned (achieved) later on. Labrets (lip plugs) were another matter. Labrets were worn mostly, but not exclusively, by women in the nineteenth century (Moss 1999; Suttles 1990b). Unlike head deformation labrets could be acquired in later life. But in practice high-ranking youths had their lips pierced to receive small labrets at an early age, and increasingly large labrets replaced them as their wearers aged. In the eighteenth century tattooing and knobbed hats certainly indicated high rank, but this evidence rarely shows up in the archaeological record.

Late Northwest Coast Economy

Food storage was a critically important means to buffer the effects of annual cycles of natural productivity. Salmon and other migratory fish came in huge annual runs, but to take best advantage of them people had to develop technology for storage and sociopolitical procedures for redistribution. Evidence for intensified fishing comes in the form of large numbers of net sinkers and weirs, both of which indicate large-scale harvesting. The production of surplus for storage and later consumption produced the first permanent social inequalities in some parts of the region. Someone had to control storage and redistribution for the benefit of all, and that led to the emergence of lineage heads as high-ranking arbiters. Inevitably it also led to conflict, both between individuals and between communities.

Technological innovation continued as well. More complex composite harpoons were adopted to supplement simpler barbed ones. Some were made to toggle, that is, to turn sideways in a wounded sea mammal to make the point less likely to pull out when the animal tried to escape. Stone fish traps were sometimes built

Figure 13.10 Northwest Coast canoe.
Source: Museum of Anthropology,
University of British Columbia.

Figure 13.11 Bent cedar boxes.
Source: Museum of Anthropology,
University of British Columbia.

on intertidal ledges. Sole, flounders, sculpins, and other fish swam into the stone impoundments at high tide and were trapped there for easy taking when the tide went out (Hobler 1990:301; Mitchell 1990:347).

Unlike earlier houses that were sometimes round semisubterranean structures, the new plank ones were necessarily rectangular. They had to be given the heavy posts and beams and the long, rigid cedar planks from which they were constructed. Settlements of these large structures were clearly permanent, or nearly so.

Canoes allowed well-organized work parties to move temporarily to places where seasonal harvesting went on, and to bring the catch back for storage (Figure 13.10). The rise of heavy woodworking and the elaboration of harpoon technology both point to the use of large dugout canoes. While archaeologists have not yet found much direct evidence in the form of preserved canoes, there is plenty of indirect evidence. Heavy celts, adzes, and mauls must have been intended for both canoe and house construction.

Boxes made of thin kerfed and bent planks of cedar appeared as well (Figure 13.11). A single board was bent to form the sides and another was sewn on to provide a bottom. These were made in many sizes, sometimes with tops, and used for storage and cooking. Their inside corners were sealed with pitch, and hot stones were used to bring contents to a boil in the case of those used in cooking. This clever innovation filled the same functional need as pottery did in many other regions of North America. Late examples are sometimes quite large and often beautifully decorated.

There was a striking amount of technological diversity along the coast by the time of contact with Europeans. Some of this was determined by cultural choice, as in the case of surviving microblade and bipolar technologies in a few places. Some of it was determined by the availability of high-quality materials. For example, the finest celts were made of hard nephrite, but this material occurs naturally in only a few places along the coast. Consequently nephrite celts were widely traded, and substitutes of other materials, including shell, were used where the trading network did not reach (Ames and Maschner 1999:93–94). People made use of native copper for points, blades, ornaments, and tiny rivets or nails. Iron picked from flotsam on the beach was turned into knives, adzes, and awls (Davis 1990:200). Copper from the hulls of wrecked ships became raw material for the production of incised "coppers," yet another way to display rank and wealth (Figure 13.12).

The waterlogged sites at Hoko River and elsewhere have produced wood, bone, antler, and basketry artifacts that show us that Northwest Coast art and symbols of ranking were already present early in the Late Holocene. Wonderful anthropomorphic and zoomorphic artifacts were produced from 1000 BCE on (Wessen 1990).

The bow and arrow reached the region sometime between 500 and 100 BCE (Pettigrew 1990:523; Ross 1990:556). The new weapon eventually replaced the spear thrower, which disappeared from the archaeological record by 700 CE. The bow's arrival in Oregon and Washington is marked by the appearance of small narrow-necked points that were not at all like the more massive points used on spear thrower darts.

Figure 13.12 A Northwest Coast copper, probably made from sheeting taken from a wrecked ship. Alaska State Museum, Juneau.

Late Regional and Local Trends

Regional trends were complex in the Late Holocene. Local adaptations sometimes went their own ways. Climatic cycles were not extreme during the first millennium CE, but the spike known as the Medieval Maximum around 1000 CE led to warmer and drier conditions along the Northwest Coast. These conditions persisted until 1350 CE, when all of the Northern Hemisphere began to slide into the Little Ice Age. The total population size of the region might have declined somewhat as a result. Yet Indians living along the Northwest Coast weathered these long-term cycles, using their technology and social organization to buffer their effects. No doubt some communities failed in this effort while others succeeded, but differential success did not lead to dramatic large-scale population shifts. Overall there was steady growth and remarkable continuity in the region over the last 3,000 years (Ames and Maschner 1999:95; Lepofsky et al. 2005). There were probably about 150,000 people living on the Northwest Coast at first contact with Europeans (Donald 1997).

Most archaeologists working in the region conclude that generally speaking the cultures of this period did not differ much from those of the eighteenth century. But while there was continuity and cultural stability over the long term and at a regional scale, the cultures of the region were at the same time remarkably dynamic. For example, burial practices shifted away from midden burial and toward interment in cemeteries, cremation, and exposure, depending upon local dynamics. Burial mounds are rare in the West, but several were constructed around 1000 CE in southwestern British Columbia. The best known burial mound site there is Scowlitz. Burial mounds also occur along the lower Columbia and in the Willamette Valley of western Oregon. Fanning Mound, in the Willamette Valley, dates to this same period (Ames and Maschner 1999:96243). There is no evidence that any of these were derived from mound building in the Eastern Woodlands (see Chapters 5 and 9).

Warfare must have been more intense in late times than previously. Some villages were built on defensive bluffs and there is evidence of defensive fortifications in various places (Moss and Erlandson 1992). Attacks could be launched from great distances, almost always by sea. Later people on the Northwest Coast used clubs, spears, daggers, and bows and arrows, and wore helmets and armor made of wooden slats and hide. The last were tough enough to stop even European musket balls. Chipped-stone tools nearly disappeared from the tool inventory in this period, increasingly replaced by bone and antler tools. Experimentation has shown that while chipped-stone and slate points could not penetrate native armor, bone points could, and this is indirect evidence that armor was probably in use by this time. Finally, as time went on village locations in some areas shifted from spots having easy access to resources to more defensible ones with better visibility of approaches from the sea. Food harvesting might also have changed in the face of intensified warfare. Sea mammal hunting and other small-group activities declined, whereas salmon harvesting and activities that required whole communities increased. The vulnerability of smaller groups versus the security of numbers probably explains this, for there is no evidence that the abandoned resources were in decline (Maschner and Reedy-Maschner 1998).

Ozette

The most famous site along the southern Northwest Coast is Ozette at the northwestern tip of Washington (Ames 2005). The site was a Makah whaling village just south of Cape Flattery. Sometime in the early eighteenth century an earthquake caused a landslide of mud that buried part of the village, preserving houses and thousands of artifacts under wet conditions. Preservation was so good that baskets, lines, bags, harpoons, boxes, and many other items that would have normally disintegrated remained intact (Samuels 1991, 1994).

Natural erosion exposed part of the site by the 1970s and threatened to destroy the rest of it. Crews from Washington State University undertook excavation that ended up lasting an entire decade. Over 40,000 artifacts were recovered from three buried houses, and many of these are now on display nearby on the Makah reservation.

Ozette was occupied before Europeans visited the region with any frequency and before smallpox and other foreign diseases convulsed the population. Because the burial of the houses was so rapid, Ozette provides a snapshot of an instant in time that is undisturbed by either the normal cleanout that accompanies abandonment or the selectivity that typifies later looting.

Southern Northwest Coast

Cultural evolution along the lower Columbia River was interrupted by the catastrophic Cascade Landslide around 1250 CE. The side of a mountain slid into the river near the site of the modern Bonneville Dam, creating an earthen dam and a temporary reservoir. When the dam was breached the pent-up water cut down through it rapidly, causing vast flooding downstream. Virtually all previously occupied sites along the lower Columbia were abandoned and communities shifted to new locations (Figure 13.13). The remaining rubble became the Cascades of the Columbia, a stretch difficult for either canoeists or fish to navigate. Fortunately for people, that made fishing more productive in the long run. After some readjustment the communities of the lower Columbia resumed their evolution toward historic Chinook culture (Pettigrew 1990:523–525).

In the Willamette Valley the basic features of Kalapuya culture were in place by 1280 BCE (Pettigrew 1990:528). This included the exploitation of camas tubers and a wide range of seeds. Grave offerings from the Fanning mound site indicate that wealth accumulation was important here too after 300 CE. Wealth markers include ceremonial obsidian knives, whalebone clubs, ear spools, and shell ornaments. However, the huge wealth accumulations, ranking, and stratification that characterized more northerly societies in the region never developed here. The dispersed and less cyclical resources of the Willamette Valley facilitated the evolution of adaptations more like those of the Plateau and California than of the classic Northwest Coast.

California

California affords more environmental diversity than any other area of comparable size in North America (Figure 13.14). If there is a theme here it is that ancient Californians were a remarkably diverse lot, people who made their own rules, and cared not a bit about how their variability would confound later archaeologists (Jones and Klar 2007a). This has made it difficult for California archaeology to capture the attention of archaeologists working in either other regions or on

Figure 13.13 The reconstructed Cathlapotle plank house near the site of Cathlapotle, Washington. Ridgefield National Wildlife Refuge.

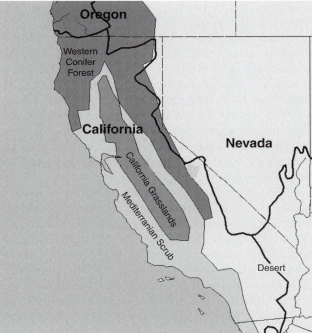

Figure 13.14 The environments of California, grossly simplified.

problems of broad general interest. However, by stepping back from the local to the regional level of analysis, one can see that the region has much to contribute to the study of cultural complexity at that scale.

California's Environment

The great Central Valley was once a large temperate grassland, home to vast herds of deer, elk, and pronghorn antelopes. The northern California coastal forest is an extension of the moist and dense Northwest Coast forest, dominated by giant redwood trees as far south as San Francisco Bay. From there south the Coast Range is covered by a mantle of chaparral and woodlands.

The reasons for California's complex pattern of microenvironments lie in the interplay of topography, latitude, altitude, prevailing winds, and ocean currents. Weather systems often move eastward across mountains and valleys. At times hot dry "Santa Ana" winds flow in a contrary direction, off the interior deserts to scorch vegetation closer to the ocean. All of these factors produce an unusually complex mosaic of small ecozones, patches of distinct plant and animal communities.

The giant redwoods of coastal California are the world's tallest trees, and getting that tall requires centuries of growth. The tallest of them is 113 m (370 ft) tall, a skyscraper in the plant kingdom. The limitation appears to be the availability of moisture and the trees' ability to pump it to needles on their uppermost branches. Redwoods are better at this than other species, although some of the giants of the Northwest Coast come close. Under ideal conditions a redwood might reach a bit higher, up to 130 m (427 ft), but it would be a stretch (Pennisi 2005). The foggy mild climate that is perfect for redwoods extended farther south during the Pleistocene, and so did the giant trees. They remain where modern conditions allow. All of the tall species of the West Coast were naturally selected for because the high winds that might blow them down are very rare in this region.

The mountains of northern California have a cooler and wetter climate than the rest of the region, more like the forests of western Oregon and Washington (Figure 13.15). The Sierra Nevada of eastern California is a high mountain range that blocks moist weather from the interior Great Basin desert. Giant sequoia trees live in scattered groves in these mountains.

The interior of California north of an east–west line running through Los Angeles is part of the Mojave Desert, whereas south of that line it is the lower Sonoran Desert. Southeastern California is included here for historical reasons, even though it is ecologically more similar to the desert Southwest.

Figure 13.15 Northern California landscape.

Along the California coast and in the Coast Range just east of it the mosaic of small microenvironments is particularly complex. These vary according to sun exposure, wind exposure, temperature, and rainfall, which can be very regular in a small area but quite different in another area not far away. This patchiness prompted the American Indian inhabitants of the region to settle into specialized local adaptations. The ecological patchwork resulted in a cultural patchwork overlying it. The resulting mosaic of small tribal areas is particularly complex in northwestern California (Figure 13.16) (Baumhoff 1978).

California's Cultural Mosaic

As was the case for the Northwest Coast, it is convenient to start with the historic cultures of California and then look backward in time. In 1492 there were no fewer than 64 mutually unintelligible languages (Figure 13.17) being spoken in native California, perhaps as many as 80 of them, in a region of only 348,000 km² (134,000 mi²). Sherburne Cook estimated the aboriginal population of California to have been 310,000±30,000, or about 10% of the total population north of the Mexican desert at that time (Cook 1978; Snow 2001). Some other regions had areas of high density but these were offset by large buffer zones of lower density. In northwestern California tribal territories of only 500–2,000 km² (190–770 mi²) were common, about the size of a typical modern U.S. county. The highest densities were located in the central valley east of San Francisco, along the coast north of that city, and along the Santa Barbara coast (Hornbeck 1983).

The more than five dozen native languages of California sort into at least six language families. The Hokan family, a hypothetical superfamily that subsumes 10 generally accepted families and isolates, might be the oldest, perhaps descended from the first coastal migrants

Figure 13.16 Reconstructed Hupa house from northwestern California.

who worked their way south along the Pacific Coast over a dozen millennia ago. Hokan language families occur scattered in the interior north, along the coast and in the southernmost part of the region. The hypothetical Penutian superfamily (which subsumes 11 families and isolates) is found along the central coast and across the vast Central Valley of California. Uto-Aztecan languages occupy the deserts of southeast California. The jam-packed northwest of California is home to three different language families, Yukian, Algonquian-Ritwan, and Nadene. The last two are tiny representatives of much larger language families, spoken by people who migrated to coastal northern California long ago, leaving their relatives behind. Mixed in them are Yukian languages, a small family with no clear ties to any other.

So many small territories and so many local adaptations have made it difficult for California archaeologists to come up with generalizations about the archaeology of their region. There are many contrasting local sequences, and most of them are identified by a vast array of peculiar artifacts, mostly decorative items made from shell or stone (Figure 13.18).

Early in the twentieth century archaeologists divided California into at least 15 districts, grouped into five regions within the state. They also defined three long periods called the Early, Middle, and Late Horizons. The term **"horizon"** as it is usually defined in archaeology is a widespread phenomenon of brief duration, usually a popular style or distinctive artifact type. The concept was

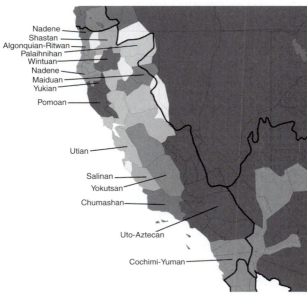

Figure 13.17 Language families of California showing the mosaic of many individual languages. Language isolates having uncertain affiliations are shown in white but not named.

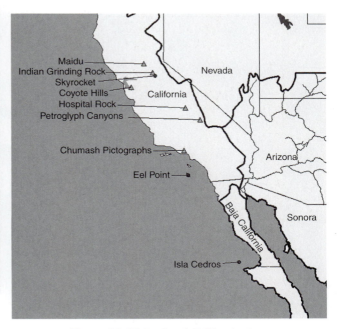

Figure 13.18 Regional California sites.

Box 13.1 HOW TO CALIBRATE RADIOCARBON DATES

Willard Libby had to assume that the amount of ^{14}C available in the atmosphere had been constant over time, and that the rate at which plants took it up had also been constant. This turned out to be almost but not quite true, with the result that radiocarbon years did not calibrate exactly with calendar years. The advent of accelerator mass spectrometry (AMS) dating made it possible for researchers to use tree-ring dating (dendrochronology) and radiocarbon dating together to measure variation in the relative proportions of ^{12}C and ^{14}C and calibrate the deviation of radiocarbon years from calendar years. This was made possible initially by bristlecone pine trees. These trees can live up to 5,000 years, and much older dead specimens still survive in the White Mountains of California. Using both the living and dead specimens, researchers were able to construct a bristlecone pine tree-ring chronology 8,000 years long. They peeled the rings from sample trees one at a time, recording the known age of each one by counting back from the outermost ring of a living tree. They then submitted the ring samples for AMS dating. This painstaking research showed that the ^{12}C:^{14}C ratio has varied slightly from year to year, and that there has been a slight long-term downward trend in the amount of ^{14}C in the atmosphere. Because of this radiocarbon dating labs generally had been reporting many older dates as younger than they should have been, considerably so for older dates. Tree rings also revealed many bumps in the calibration curve due to year-to-year variations in ^{14}C levels; however, calibration can now correct for all of these. Recent advances involving other sources of annual variation have pushed the calibration of radiocarbon dates back to 50,000 years.

The figure shows a typical calibration curve, in this case for a sample associated with mastodon (*Mammut*). The reported date of 10,395±110 is on the left-side scale, the 1-sigma range of 220 years shown in dark gray. The diagonal intercept line generated by bristlecone pine and other annual samples of known age shows variation in levels (wiggles) and error (width). Points on the radiocarbon curve on the left are reflected of the calibration curve and down to the calendar year curve (horizontal scale). Because of multiple intercepts there are three mean dates (peaks on the calendar year scale) and two 1-sigma ranges (dark gray), 10,630–10,527 and 10,451–10,005 BCE. There is a 68% chance that the true age of the sample falls in these ranges, and a 95% chance that it falls within the 2-sigma (lighter gray) ranges around the three peaks. The date range can be simplified to 10,630–10,005 BCE. These results were obtained using a standard calibration program at http://radiocarbon.pa.qub.ac.uk/calib/.

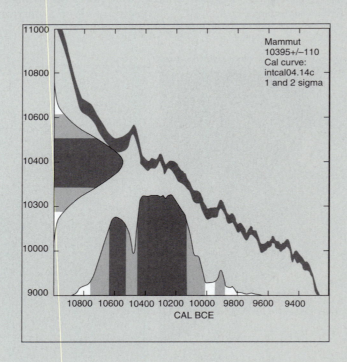

Mammut
10395+/−110
Cal curve:
intcal04.14c
1 and 2 sigma

CAL BCE

especially useful in the decades before the development of radiocarbon dating, when short-lived diagnostic styles or types were needed to calibrate local sequences with each other by cross dating. In other words, if the same short-lived diagnostic type was found at three stratified sites then researchers usually concluded that the strata in which they were found were all deposited at about the same time. However, radiocarbon dating turned this logic on its head. Archaeologists can now often date the occurrences of diagnostic items independently, and when they do they sometimes find that they appear earlier in some places and later in others. This means that instead of assuming the simultaneous deposition of key objects we can now track their spread over time and space.

The horizons defined for California are now more appropriately called "periods." The Early period began sometime after the passing of Paleoindians around 8050 BCE and did not end until after 2500 BCE. Empirical archaeological evidence is scarce for most of this long period, much of it from scattered inconspicuous sites from the latter part of the period. The San Dieguito complex in the southernmost part of the state appears to mark the beginning of this period.

As if to add to the confusion, California archaeologists often refer to a "Milling Stone Horizon," a period dating 7200–3000 BCE when hand stones and milling stones (manos and metates) are just about the only thing one finds in an archaeological deposit (Fagan 2003b:75, 94). This too is a period rather than a horizon in the strict sense, and one that is at odds with other usages in California archaeology.

Holocene Adaptations

The native people of California participated in the same process of adaptation as other early people after the beginning of the Holocene around 8050 BCE. This entailed the emergence of a regional version on an Archaic theme (see Chapter 4). Band ranges constricted, scheduled movements to traditional camp sites became regularized in a seasonal round, human modification of the landscape increased, and people focused increasingly on natural seed crops. The processing requirements of the abundant crops of seeds are what drove them to both tight scheduling and the production of milling stones. Various grasses and higher plants can be very productive, but their seeds ripen and fall in a matter of days. Successful gatherers have to know when this will occur, time their arrival at the most productive fields carefully, and mobilize effectively to harvest the seeds as quickly as possible before they drop. The sight of a band of people harvesting seeds with only shallow basketry trays

Figure 13.19 Basking elephant seals on the central California coast.

and sticks would have seemed deceptively simple to a modern observer, but the simplicity of the technique conceals complex knowledge about the environment and food processing. Harvesting quickly at just the right time was only half of it, for the seeds had to be ground into flour and in the case of acorns and some others needed special processing to make them edible.

The early Archaic peoples of coastal California appear to have subsisted primarily on seeds and shellfish (Erlandson 1994; Jones et al. 2002). Their shell middens contain milling stones for the grinding of seeds, but no evidence for harpoons, fishing tackle, or other equipment they would have needed to pursue sea mammals and large fish. They took seals, but these could have been clubbed to death on land (Figure 13.19). Deer bones indicate that they hunted terrestrial game too, so their coastal adaptation fell short of a true maritime economy (Erlandson 1994; Erlandson and Glassow 1997).

The coastline had been lower and west of its current location at the end of the Pleistocene. Along the north coast the lateral shift was small, because the water deepens quickly offshore. However, west of San Francisco Bay the continental shelf is shallow, so that the shore was distant from its current location and the bay was an estuary. Rising sea level spread eastward across the gently sloping land off San Francisco more rapidly than north of Cape Mendocino, yet still too slowly to be noticed by anybody living on the coast at the time. Eventually it rose high enough to back up through the Golden Gate and gradually turn the estuary into a bay. Off the southern California coast rising water turned the large island of Santarosae into a chain of smaller ones comprising the northern Channel Islands. Most of this happened by the end of the Early Holocene, around 6500 BCE. Sea levels rose more slowly during the Middle Holocene, and hotter drier conditions inland dried up broad shallow pluvial lakes that until then had provided game and plant foods for hunter-gatherers. The onset of the Late Holocene around 2000 BCE brought more-or-less modern climatic conditions, although continued cycling and episodes like the Medieval Maximum affected human adaptation here as they did elsewhere on the continent.

Archaic California Societies

In contrast to later cultures, the early Archaic cultures of California appear to have been generalized rather than specialized. When a region has a coast the question always arises as to whether there were distinct coastal and interior populations or the same people were moving back and forth between coastal and interior locations. The unspecialized nature of coastal sites in this early period supports the latter hypothesis. In many cases they did not have very far to travel to utilize both environments. The technological developments that would lead later to specialized cultures on the coast and in the interior were yet to come.

Although they remained hunter-gatherers rather than fishermen, the early inhabitants of southern California found a way to cross 100 km (60 mi) of ocean to San Clemente Island. Even the intermediate Santa Catalina Island is 40 km (25 mi) away. Investigation of the Eel Point site on San Clemente shows that people were living here from 6550 BCE on, a circumstance that requires us to conclude that they had substantial boats by that time (Cassidy et al. 2004; Fagan 2004). Sea levels were not yet up to modern levels, but this made the crossing of this deepwater only trivially shorter than it is now. At Eel Point these early voyagers hunted seals onshore and collected shellfish from the intertidal zone. But they also took dolphins, possibly in large numbers. Dolphins are deepwater sea mammals and their bone remains flummoxed archaeologists until Judith Porcasi and Harumi Fujita showed by analogy that hunters might have taken them regularly without elaborate fishing equipment. They noted that in places around the world where deep water is present close to shore, people have discovered that they can beach dolphins by disorienting their sensitive sonar systems. Clacking cobbles together underwater from the side of a canoe is enough to drive the animals ashore, where they can be killed by lances or clubs. Known cases from the South Pacific and the North Atlantic are only analogies, because no one proposes that they had common historical origins with California Indians. If the researchers had also found ethnographic instances of this hunting technique in southern California they might have preferred a homology hypothesis, one proposing a historical link between the Pacific Islands and California.

Not everyone is convinced by the dolphin hunting hypothesis, and it is clear that more research is needed to understand this adaptation (Glassow 2005). Eventually rising sea levels changed human or dolphin habits and people abandoned dolphin hunting around San Clemente by 1500 BCE (Porcasi and Fujita 2000). Fishing took on greater importance by that time, and people developed the hook and net technology necessary to make it work.

Although some temporary leadership would have been necessary for the organization of seed harvesting, rabbit hunting, dolphin hunting, and other collective activities, it is likely that Archaic bands were largely leaderless and egalitarian. The few burials that have been discovered contain grave offerings that make no distinction between men and women, each was as likely to be buried with a milling stone. However, Brian Fagan argues that this did not last, and that later on women tended to be buried with milling stones while men were typically buried with weapons (Fagan 2003b:98).

While theoretical models predict that people under these environmental circumstances should be expected to constantly broaden their subsistence base and to develop increasingly sophisticated ways to harvest and store seeds and the like, such was not the case. It appears that men persisted in hunting big game, even when that was a less efficient expenditure of effort. Clearly there was some resistance to evolutionary pressure to do otherwise. Hunting remained a dominant theme in rock art, and the remains of the hunt persist in the faunal remains around habitation sites. But what might seem paradoxical to us may have been nothing more than the playing out of the biological roles of men and women. Successful male hunters have always been valued more than unsuccessful ones by women in these simplest of all human societies and it should be no surprise to us to find evidence that men responded to that selective pressure (Hildebrandt and McGuire 2002).

Skyrocket

The Skyrocket site in the western foothills of the Sierra Nevada reveals that the local environment became cooler and wetter after around 3000 BCE, and this presented people with new opportunities. Grasslands interspersed with oak trees replaced the sagebrush and

Box 13.2 HOW TO DISTINGUISH ANALOGY FROM HOMOLOGY

There is nothing like a clear example to explain the difference between a couple key abstract concepts. Analogy is the principle that things that look alike probably have similar identities or functions even though they may have separate historical origins. Homology is the principle that things that have similarities that go beyond functional analogy probably share common origins.

The Chumash plank canoe allows us to make a clear distinction between analogy and homology. Seagoing canoes were developed anciently and independently in several parts of the world, including both coasts of North America. The large wooden dugouts of the Northwest Coast are analogous to similar boats elsewhere, but there is no necessary historical connection between them. They are most likely analogs lacking common origins. Human beings are ingenious and the idea of hollowing out a log to make a sturdy canoe is not one that we should expect occurred infrequently.

Fishhooks and other clues have long been cited as tantalizing clues of possible links between the people of the southern California coast and Polynesia. There are other clues of trans-Pacific contacts too, things such as bark beaters and sweet potatoes, but for now I will focus on the southern Californian case. Terry Jones and Kathryn Klar argue that there is not just one piece of evidence but several that all point to contacts between the Chumash and there relatives in the Santa Barbara region with Polynesian seafarers sometime between 400 and 800 CE. They point to Chumash canoes built of planks sewn together in Polynesian fashion, to distinctive shell fishhooks, and to two-piece bone fishhooks that also appear to have Polynesian prototypes.

There's more, because the words for plank canoe in the Chumash and neighboring Garbrielino languages appear to be loanwords borrowed from Polynesian. Thus the plank canoes of the southern California coast and Polynesia are probably homologs rather than analogs. Analogs would imply no necessary contact between California Indians and Polynesians, but homologs require it.

It would be easy to make too much of a Polynesian landing in California 1,200–1,600 years ago, which is why most archaeologists are so skeptical of such claims. If Polynesians did reach southern California their influence did not spread very far inland. There is also a long history of denigration of American Indians to be found in such claims, which too often imply that Native Americans would not have thought of building temple mounds, stone sculptures, writing, or pottery on their own. Jones and Klar imply no such thing, but rather present a strong case for homology.

We know that Polynesians found Hawaii after traveling 3,200 km (2,000 mi) across open ocean from the Society Islands, so it should not surprise us to discover that Hawaiians later stumbled across something as big as North America after sailing a similar distance eastward on fair winds in the heyday of Polynesian exploration. Only a couple centuries later the Norse touched the other coast of North America, but they too left only a faint mark on the continent.

juniper trees that had dominated during hotter drier times, and the people living on this flank of the central valley responded by making more and more use of acorns. Settlement became more substantial, and for the first time they began importing obsidian projectile points from the east and marine shells from the Pacific (Fagan 2003b:99–101). We cannot be sure what the large-scale effects on populations were through the course of these environmental changes. Some archaeologists speculate that the Hokan languages are the most ancient in the region and that the Penutian languages expanded across central California at about this time, but no one is certain (Elsasser 1978:41). If the Penutians did expand at the expense of Hokan speakers around this time they must have had some adaptive advantage that we have not yet recognized.

After 2500 BCE California people produced large numbers of shell artifacts, particularly beads and pendants of many types, which California archaeologists have used to sort out local and regional sequences (Arnold and Munns 1994). Their specialized exploitation of acorns and other seeds and greens intensified too, as people settled in and became more and more adept at exploiting the special resources of their small local areas. Acorns are a chore to collect and shell, and more labor is needed to leach the tannins from the nuts and grind them into meal. Despite the difficulty, the rise in both the number of oak trees and the number of people in California eventually led to the harvesting of over 60,000 tons of them a year. By the sixteenth century acorns were a dietary staple across much of California. To shell and grind them people developed mortars and pestles to replace manos and metates that were more generally useful for a wider range of seeds.

Acorns could be harvested once a year and the meal could be stored for months. At the same time other seeds and greens could be harvested as they always had, and hunting continued as well. Unlike on the Northwest Coast, the environment did not present difficult organizational problems. Most natural abundance came from the land, not the sea, and harvesting did not require elaborate organization, however backbreaking it might have been. Logistical harvesting problems could be managed by household groups moving comparatively short distances to food supplies, so there would have been little benefit in developing large polities.

California Tribelets

Early Californians did, however, develop social ranking in some instances. The communities were typically small, tribal in organizational type but in the low population range. As population density increased territories shrank, becoming the county-sized domains of what some anthropologists have called "tribelets." Big men who presided over chiefly families enjoyed higher ranks than others in these miniature tribes. Ethnographic accounts reveal that there were rigid social strata in some societies, including classes of chiefs, lesser elites, commoners, and slaves. Their trappings are a bewildering array of shell and stone beads and amulets (King 1978).

Any attempt to map subsistence, mortuary practices, projectile points, or house types produces a unique jigsaw puzzle mosaic unlike any of the others, adding to the difficulty encountered when trying to generalize about California archaeology. Each class of traits produces its own distinctive mosaic when mapped against the underlying mosaic of California's microenvironments. This complex pattern illustrates again the consequences of cultural evolution, which are quite different from those of biological evolution (see Chapter 1). Archaeologists can take comfort in the tendency for California's many small ancient populations to remain in place while they evolved, making changing adaptations easier to track than they would be if relocation were also a common feature, as it was on the Great Plains (see Chapter 15).

None of the abundant plants they exploited had or could develop the characteristics of domesticates even under heavy use over centuries, so the Californians remained nominally nonagricultural. At the same time they developed ever finer basketry, eventually weaving them so tightly that they were virtually waterproof. Fragile pottery was never a viable alternative to these

containers. Pomo baskets that are decorated with shell beads and bird feathers are collectors' items today, as are the many other forms made by the native Californians.

Chumash Culture

The Chumash cultures of the Santa Barbara coast are an interesting case of the rise of chiefdoms in California and possible contacts from Polynesia. There were three branches and at least six Chumash languages spoken by as many as 20,000 people when Europeans arrived (Goddard 1996:320; Shipley 1978). The Chumash probably descend from the very first Californians. At the time of first contact with Europeans the Chumash Indians had a sophisticated maritime technology, social stratification, and hereditary chiefs. The chiefs maintained their power by being simultaneously political leaders and the owners of large plank canoes, which facilitated sea mammal hunting as well as long-distance trade and exchange along the California coast. The building, maintenance, and operation of canoes required large teams, so technology and sociopolitical organization reinforced one another. That being the case, archaeologists have been interested in knowing how long such large plank canoes, and by inference hereditary chiefs, have been part of Chumash culture. Regrettably, old canoes have not been preserved. However, the chipped-stone drills and asphaltum calking needed to build them have survived archaeologically, so we now know that plank canoes were certainly being built and used by at least 700 CE (Gamble 2002). But canoes, which were still being built in the early twentieth century, must have a more ancient history than that because people were going back and forth to San Clemente Island 8,500 years ago.

New archaeological and linguistic evidences suggests the possibility that plank canoes, two-piece bone fishhooks, and words for them were transmitted to the Chumash by seafaring Polynesians around 800 CE (Jones and Klar 2005). Having reached eastern Pacific islands as remote as Hawaii around the same time (Hunt and Lipo 2006) it would not be surprising if some Polynesian voyagers missed hitting any islands and fetched up on the California shore. Chumash archaeology has long hinted at this possibility, yet many archaeologists remain quite skeptical about it. But the possibility is not far-fetched. The contact, if it occurred in California, did not have a pervasive effect on the course of North American Indian history. Whatever the origins of the plank canoe were, the taking of sea mammals gradually declined over the last few millennia, possibly because intensive hunting from canoes depressed the population (Colten and Arnold 1998).

This still leaves open the question of just what kind of canoe people were using on open water before the plank canoe came into use. A possible answer comes from Baja California, where a composite canoe with a driftwood log bottom and bundled reed sides was still being use to navigate the 23 km (14 mi) between the mainland and Isla Cedros in historic times (Des Lauriers 2005). This watercraft was sturdy and serviceable, even on open water, and it might well be a holdover from a form used elsewhere along the coast before the introduction of plank canoes.

The organizational challenges entailed by the building, maintenance, and use of large plank canoes led to the formation of Chumash chiefdoms, but the timing of this development remains debatable (Arnold and Green 2002; Gamble 2002; Gamble et al. 2002). These demands were complicated by increasing violence, as indicated by larger numbers of individuals found with projectile points embedded in their skeletons. The bow and arrow appeared in California sometime after 500 CE, and the rise in chiefdoms might have been spurred in part by an organized effort to get violence under control (Arnold 2001; Lambert and Walker 1991).

The more interior Chumash produced elaborate and colorful pictographs on the walls and ceilings of caves, which still attract visitors today (Figure 13.20). The Chumash were clearly once a large and vibrant culture, but Spanish colonists concentrated the Chumash at mission sites in the eighteenth century, where epidemics eroded their numbers over the years. Campbell Grant (1978) claimed that by 1972 there were only 40 people having Chumash ancestry remaining.

The Man Called Ishi

A man known only as "Ishi" stumbled out of the northern California mountains on August 29, 1911, probably North America's last prehistoric man. The emaciated man spoke no English or Spanish, and his short, singed hair revealed that he was in mourning. The local sheriff lodged him in a jail and called in anthropologists, who eventually determined that the man was the only surviving speaker of Yahi, a dialect of the Yana language of the Hokan family. He had been hiding out in the mountains with the remnants of his band for decades, ever since local ranchers had taken upon themselves to exterminate them.

His last living relative had died not long before, and the man simply gave himself up, an act that he probably thought would be suicidal. It was Yahi custom to never utter ones own name, and in this case the only

Figure 13.20 Chumash pictographs.
Source: Campbell Grant.

people who knew it were all dead. Names were terms of reference, not address, and as a consequence we will never know the man's name. Like most prehistoric people he remains in that sense anonymous.

A. L. Kroeber found him a home at Berkeley and everyone took to calling him "Ishi," which simply means "man" in Yahi (Figure 13.21). His health and weight returned and he gradually opened up to the anthropologists, telling them of life in his little family band. They lived as the Yahi had lived for countless centuries, unconnected to the outside world. He described his daily life, their flight from murderous ranchers, and the near catastrophe when a survey crew stumbled across their camp. Some painful memories went unspoken, but trips back to his home territory were used to fill out the details of the life of a hunter-gatherer band.

Ishi had little resistance to modern urban diseases, and within a few years he contracted tuberculosis. His life at his adopted University of California home came to an end on March 26, 1916. His last words to his academic friends were in English, "You stay, I go." There are many modern Californians of Indian descent, the inheritors of one or another of the many cultures that were once scattered across the region, Native America's most complex cultural mosaic. But Ishi was the last of his line.

Figure 13.21 The man called "Ishi," working on a leister.
Source: Copyright © Phoebe A. Hearst Museum of Anthropology and the Regents of the University of California.

Baja California

Baja California is one of the ends of the earth, a blind alley that trapped early American Indian migrants and preserved an Archaic lifestyle until the arrival of Spanish colonists (Laylander and Moore 2006). The peninsula begins and ends as a desert, a 1,200-km (750-mi) sliver of Mexico rarely more than a tenth as wide. It was and is a long, arid cul-de-sac that is separated from northwestern Mexico by the Gulf of California. Its first inhabitants were apparently closely related to the Early Holocene hunter-gatherers of southern coastal California and the Channel Islands. The people who lived on the southern cape of Baja California hunted dolphins, probably using the same techniques that archaeologists infer for dolphin hunting around San Clemente Island far to the north. Here, too, hunters with canoes could have driven the marine mammals ashore just by clacking cobbles together underwater (Porcasi and Fujita 2000). They also took seals onshore, gathered shellfish, and hunted and gathered plants and small game away from the shore, but they had little or no equipment that would cause us to call them fishermen.

Guacurians

Pinto Basin culture emerged after 8050 BCE around the shrinking playas of the interior desert of southern California, just north of Baja California. It persisted for millennia and spread southward along the coasts of the slender Baja peninsula. Styles and archaeological phase names changed over the last three millennia, but

the people of the southern peninsula remained much the same as their Pinto Basin ancestors until they were encountered by the Spanish and entered historical documents as the Guayura, Pericu, and other smaller related groups. We know very little about the Guacurian languages. Too few words survive to allow them to be classified with any of the known language families of North America. They lacked fishnets and hook-and-line equipment, just as their remote ancestors had, and took fish only with spears. They had no coiled basketry, let alone pottery, and they used simpler containers made of large leaves. They lacked the curved throwing sticks that most North American desert hunter-gatherers used to hunt rabbits. They even lacked dogs, surely a companion that their remote ancestors had.

The Guacurians were long headed (dolicocephalic), a head shape similar to that of the earliest known skeletons found in North America, and another indicator that they were isolated survivors. They were not completely isolated because they had the bow and arrow, an innovation that must have reached them only after 500 CE, when it first appeared in California (Blitz 1988). It was probably even later before the bow and arrow spread down the Baja peninsula, because the Guacurians were still using the spear thrower as well when they were first contacted (Massey 1961).

Peninsular Yumans

The Early Period culture known as San Dieguito spawned later cultures, one of which spread from southern California down the Baja peninsula, absorbing or displacing the ancestors of the Guacurians southward sometime within the last two millennia. They did not expand all the way to the end of the peninsula, so the Guacurians survived beyond them in the far south (Figure 13.22). The new people were Yuman-speaking

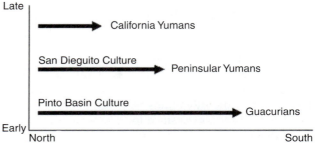

Figure 13.22 Graphic representation of the archaeological sequence for Baja California. Historic Guacurians descended from Pinto Basin culture while Peninsular Yumans descended from San Dieguito culture.

people whose language belonged to the scattered and ancient Hokan superfamily. They enjoyed an adaptive advantage, archaeologically visible as coiled basketry, hook-and-line fishing equipment, nets, and curved throwing sticks. But they too lacked pottery and dogs at first contact (Massey 1949; Rosales-López and Fujita 2000). They did have composite canoes of wood and reed, as mentioned earlier, and these might have been the kind of watercraft used by all early Californians to reach offshore islands (Des Lauriers 2005).

California Yumans

Other Yuman speakers who expanded into the northern end of the peninsula and were living there in the sixteenth century had an ever greater advantage. They possessed dogs and pottery, unlike any of the people south of them along the peninsula.

Colorful pictographs in shallow caves and rock shelters have attracted much recent attention here as they have in California. There are geometric designs, hand prints, and representations of humans, deer, mountain sheep, antelopes, mountain lions, seals, and various smaller animals (Crosby 1992; Grant 1974).

Summary

1. The distribution of several ancient language families on the Northwest Coast indicates that cultures evolved there in place over the long term, with little migration in or out of the region.

2. Chiefdoms formed on the Northwest Coast and occasionally in California in the absence of farming.

3. Northwest Coast architects learned how to make planks from cedar trees and use them in the construction of large houses and boats.

4. Several important wet sites have preserved for centuries things that would normally decay and disappear in a few years.

5. Social stratification, political innovation, art, and architecture were less elaborately developed along the southern Northwest Coast for ecological reasons.

6. The central part of the West Coast, what is now California, is a region in which agriculture is productive today, but Native American farming and pottery-making did not arise there.

7. Apart from Mesoamerica, California had the highest human population density and the most complex cultural mosaic of any region of North America in 1492.

8. California archaeology is frustratingly complex for archaeologists because of high variability in both local environments and archaeological evidence.

9. Chumash culture featured chiefdoms and the construction of large seagoing canoes, possibly due in part to contacts from Polynesia.

10. The southern part of the West Coast, Baja California, remained the desolate realm of hunter-gatherers for many millennia, preserving in its cul-de-sac the simple societies of some of the earliest migrants to the Americas.

Further Reading

The best comprehensive source for the Northwest Coast is Ames and Maschner's *Peoples of the Northwest Coast*. The Northwest Coast volume (7) of the *Handbook of North American Indians* is older but contains excellent ethnographic chapters to supplement archaeological coverage. The California volume (8) of the same series is a good place to search for specific sources, although Fagan's *Before California* provides a more current and digestible point of departure for most readers. Jones and Klar's *California Prehistory: Colonization, Culture, and Complexity* is the best starting point for serious scholars. The best starting point for Baja California is Laylander and Moore's *The Prehistory of Baja California*, which draws together chapters by several authors.

Glossary

horizon: A brief but widespread archaeological phenomenon that serves as a convenient stratigraphic marker.

labret: A plug ornament inserted in a pierced lip.

potlatch: Any of various practices of status-enhancing gift-giving or conspicuous consumption on the Northwest Coast.

The Arctic and Subarctic

The irrationality of a thing is no argument against its existence, rather a condition of it.

Friedrich Nietzsche

Introduction

The Arctic and Subarctic zones of the North American Arctic extend from Alaska, across northern Canada to Greenland (Figure 14.1). Canada is the third largest country in the world, trailing only Russia and China. Together the vast northern area covered by this chapter is almost twice the size of the rest of the continent. In addition it has always been North America's most thinly populated region, an immense archaeological venue explored by a relatively small number of hardy researchers.

Friedrich Nietzche, who is quoted above, urged us to embrace irrationality, and we might be tempted to do so when we try to understand why people would adapt to the treeless Arctic. But irrationality is not often adaptive, and irrational cultures do not survive over the long term. Consequently we must set aside suspicions that the Arctic people were inherently irra-

tional, rethink our own perceptions, and set about trying to understand the rationality of Arctic adaptation.

Many maps display the Arctic and Subarctic using Mercator projections (Figure 14.2). This is a technique for flattening the earth's curvature that exaggerates the sizes of polar regions. Mercator projections make Greenland appear to be larger than Australia even though it is not. Yet despite the fact that Greenland is classified as an island and it is actually smaller than the continent of Australia, it is nonetheless quite large.

The Arctic

The Arctic region is so vast and its archaeology is so spotty that the big picture must be described in terms of five broad stages of development. Human occupation of the Arctic was largely restricted to the productive fringes of the continent and its northern islands offshore. But despite geographic restrictions, Arctic specialists have necessarily concentrated on a sample of sites. Their work has been carried out in the contexts of differing scholarly traditions, and there have been many disagreements over how to interpret the evidence. However, Arctic archaeologists from Russia, the United States, Canada, and Denmark that have dominated archaeological research in the region have found ways to link their perspectives. They generally agree on five broad and partially overlapping stages of development, which are referred to here simply as Stages 1–5 (Dumond 1984b).

Generally speaking, Alaska was the source area for waves of northerners that repeatedly spread eastward across Arctic Canada to as far as coastal Greenland. Alaska was a center of innovation because of its environmental variability compared to the rest of

Figure 14.1 Major geographic features of the Arctic include the Bering Strait, the Aleutian Islands, the Alaska Peninsula, Kodiak Island, Point Barrow, Baffin Island, Hudson Bay, Greenland, and Newfoundland.

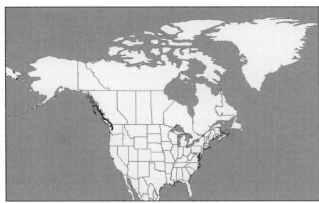

Table 14.1 Basic Arctic chronology.

Stage	Time Span
Stage 5	600 (±500)−1850 CE
Stage 4	1200 (±400) BCE−600 (±500) CE
Stage 3	2200−1200 (±400) BCE
Stage 2	5000−2200 (±300) BCE
Stage 1	15,000−5000 BCE

Figure 14.2 A Mercator projection (above) of the North American Arctic and Subarctic compared with a projection (below) that does not exaggerate the sizes of features near the pole.

the far north, and its proximity to influences from both the Northwest Coast and Asia.

Arctic Stage 1: The Earliest Evidence

Stage 1 covers the 10 millennia from 15,000 to 5000 BCE. All of the earliest indisputable archaeological evidence for humans in the region falls into this period. A few sites contain very early tools that are similar to Paleoindian artifacts found farther south in North America. Oldest among them is Swan Point. Mesa, Broken Mammoth, and the cluster of sites at which the Nenana complex has been found are younger. The Nenana complex is similar in some respects to the Clovis complex except that fluted projectile points are generally missing (see Chapter 3).

For the moment the Swan Point site holds the oldest reliably dated artifacts in Alaska, about 12,000 BCE. This was followed by the Nenana complex. Radiocarbon dates from the Mesa site suggest that it was occupied after the Younger Dryas climatic reversal of 10,850−9550 BCE, a cold episode so severe that interior Alaska appears to have been vacant of human occupation for at least a large part of it. Fluted points similar to Clovis points probably spread northward into Alaska with Paleoindian bands reoccupying the region after the Younger Dryas was over (Kunz and Reanier 1994, 1996).

Human occupation increased in the Arctic after the end of the Younger Dryas. The dominant culture from then until 5000 BCE was the American Paleo-Arctic tradition, a culture whose hallmarks were microblades, cores, bifaces, and burins. The tradition had origins in the older and more widespread tradition that some archaeologists refer to as the Beringian tradition, with roots back in Siberia's Dyuktai complex (see Chapter 2). Other similar early traditions are the Northwest Microblade tradition (see Chapter 13), the Denali complex (see Chapter 3), which are both on the mainland, and the Anangula complex of the Aleutian Islands. These are all similar archaeological phenomena, variations on a widespread theme, and simpler archaeological terminology will probably emerge in the future. In the terminology used in Europe and Asia, they all look like Mesolithic tool industries.

Arctic Stage 2: Finding Solutions

Stage 2 sites fall into the period 5000−2200 (±300) BCE. The ending date varies from place to place over three centuries, depending on local conditions. There are both interior and coastal variations on the theme of this widespread but poorly defined stage. The coastal variants include an Aleutian Island one that is found near the Anangula site. The Aleutian tradition lacks slate tools.

There are chipped-stone tools and an elaborate bone industry. Subsistence emphasized the hunting of marine mammals and ocean fishing. People lived in semisubterranean houses that were entered from the top.

Typical tool inventories of Stage 2 complexes include chipped-stone artifacts and sometimes copper artifacts where that raw material was available. Sites on Kodiak Island document the beginnings of the Ocean Bay tradition, perhaps the most clearly laid out coastal sequence known for Stage 2.

The Stage 2 interior adaptations appear to be more similar to some of the Archaic cultures found in the contiguous 48 states than to the Stage 2 coastal cultures. This has prompted archaeologists to refer to them together as "Northern Archaic" (Anderson 1968). The Onion Portage site is a key site among the many that include components falling into this broad category.

The contrast between the coastal complexes and the interior ones has led some archaeologists to propose that the Northern Archaic and not the Denali complex marks the first appearance of Nadene-speaking cultures in the interior north. If true, that would by default identify the coastal people of the same stage as Eskimo-Aleut-speakers. However, these links between archaeology and historical linguistic are speculative and thus very uncertain (Dumond, 1984b:74). What is reasonably certain is that speakers of the ancestral Nadene language(s) moved eastward from Siberia to North America sometime after the first migrants but before the ancestors of the Eskimo-Aleut peoples did. Their closest linguistic relatives still in Siberia are the Yeniseian languages, with whom they share a common ancestor language (Ruhlen 1998).

Arctic Stage 3: The Arctic Small Tool Tradition

During this period humans occupied as much of the Arctic as they ever would, spreading eastward across the Arctic to as far as Greenland and settling in wherever human adaptations were possible at all. Those living in the Aleutian Islands began their long separate evolution toward modern Aleut culture, and the split between their language and the various Eskimo languages must date to this time (Dumond 2001). The later phases of the Ocean Bay tradition, which featured polished slate implements, emerged in the Kodiak region of southwestern Alaska, but the big development was the rise and spread of the Arctic Small Tool tradition.

The Arctic Small Tool tradition developed in Alaska and spread across the American Arctic in the roughly 1,000-year period from 2200 (±300) to 1200 (±400) BCE.

This very successful adaptation to North America's most rigorous environment was certainly carried by ancestral Eskimos, and it set the basic character of all later Native American cultures in the Arctic. The tradition gets its name from the very small arrowheads, burins, side blades, microblades, and microcores left behind in sites of the period. The arrowheads probably mark the introduction of the bow and arrow into North America. The weapon spread from the Arctic to other parts of the continent over the succeeding centuries not reaching some parts of the continent until well into the first millennium CE (Blitz 1988). Some Arctic specialists prefer to remain silent on this interpretation, preferring uncertainty over speculation (Gibbon 1998:86).

The Arctic Small Tool tradition was the Arctic's first truly Eskimo culture, and its miniature tools were first discovered by their Alaskan Eskimo descendants. The tiny stone tools led some of them to speculate that they had been made by a race of little people. However, the deceptively tiny stone blades were actually used by full-sized ancestral Eskimos to edge compound tools of normal size. A bone or ivory point needed only a slot along its edge to receive a bifacial sliver of chert to serve as the hard sharp cutting edge the tool required.

The adaptation of the early Eskimos that carried the Arctic Small Tool tradition was mainly terrestrial. Although they did some seal hunting along the seasonally open coast, there is no evidence of seal hunting through the ice, a pursuit that was common much later on. Their permanent habitations tended to be built near the interior forest edge of the tundra, where caribou and migratory fish would have been plentiful. Most or all of their sites lack stone lamps for burning sea mammal oil rendered from blubber, so they probably had to stay near enough to forests to find wood for fuel at least at first (Figure 14.3) (Dumond 2005:25).

The Arctic Small Tool tradition probably spread to Alaska from northeastern Siberia, then on across the American Arctic. Its ancestral Eskimo carriers spread quickly beyond the ecological boundaries that had constrained earlier residents of Alaska, moving rapidly through the Canadian Arctic to the coast of Greenland. They hunted caribou in the interior and ventured on to the tundra as much as they could, getting better at adapting to life far beyond the tree line over time. The greatest cultural elaboration of the tradition occurred in Alaska, where it was oldest.

The Canadian variant of the Arctic Small Tool tradition is often referred to as Pre-Dorset, 2500–500 BCE, a term that anticipates the later spread of Dorset culture across the region. Pre-Dorset people eventually spread along the coast all the way to Newfoundland.

Figure 14.3 View from above of a semisubterranean house in Katmai National Park that dates to around 2000–1300 BCE. The house diameter is approximately 4 m (13 ft). Note the excavated entryway to the left.

Derivative remains of the tradition that have been found in Greenland have been labeled Independence I or Sarqaq.

There are differences from one end of this cultural continuum to the other, of course. Stemmed points in Greenland contrast with notched ones in Canada, for example. Yet there can be no doubt about the general unity of the widespread tradition, or its roots in the western end of its distribution. Little wonder that most Arctic archaeologists regard the Arctic Small Tool tradition as the cultural foundation of later Eskimo (Inuit) cultures across most of the American Arctic.

All later Eskimo cultures were known for their many clever gadgets made of bone, ivory, whale baleen, copper, leather, fiber, and stone. They used virtually any material they could get their hands on, and the origins of all this gadgetry lie in the Arctic Small Tool tradition. Curiously, recent mtDNA research on ~4,000-year-old human hair from Greenland has shown that at least some of the women in this early population were not related to either American Indians or later Eskimo and Inuit populations of the Arctic (Gilbert, Kivisild et al. 2008). This suggests that later migratory waves might have replaced this earliest widespread population rather than developing from it.

Demographic expansion tends to be along a one-way street. Ancestral Eskimos spread across the Arctic one step at a time, taking advantage of opportunities that they found on the constantly receding horizon. This kind of expansion takes a long time, and when it happens later generations tend to retain little if any knowledge about ancestral origins. When the Arctic climate became more difficult for humans after the

initial spread of the Arctic Small Tool tradition, descendant bands did not have the option of retreating back to some less hostile environment. They did not know where such a refuge might be located, and it was in any case already occupied. Rather than move, they had no option but to readapt in place as best they could. Some survived in culturally modified form, but many bands must have simply shrunk and died out.

Arctic Stage 4: Kachemak, Choris, Norton, Ipiutak, Dorset, and Old Bering Sea

The next stage of Arctic prehistory was marked by the disappearance of the Arctic Small Tool tradition. The new stage lasted from 1200 (±400) BCE to 600 (±500) CE. Survivors in Canada and Greenland evolved from Pre-Dorset and other variants of the older tradition into Dorset culture, adapting to changing conditions as best they could.

The people living in the Aleutian Island chain continued to be a culture apart from the rest. But on the Alaskan mainland there were clear breaks between the earlier Arctic Small Tool tradition communities and later ones. After 1200 BCE (give or take a few centuries) there were several derivative cultures in Alaska, each adapting to a different regional environment. Kachemak culture emerged in the Kodiak region while Norton culture developed along the coast of the Bering Sea. In northern Alaska the period saw an evolution from Choris to Norton and then to Ipiutak culture. Thus the demise of the Arctic Small Tool tradition appears to have been followed by a variety of new adaptations as survivors took alternative paths for survival.

Katchemak emerged early around the Cook Inlet on Alaska's southern coast, perhaps even in the last centuries of Stage 3. The people of this culture produced slate knives, semilunar knives (called **ulus** by modern Inuits), stone lamps, and labrets (Clark 1984:139). These items are diagnostic because they reveal that Arctic people already had some of the technology that was still crucial to the survival of their later descendants in the region as late as the twentieth century. Most notable among those key tools were their stone lamps, which must have been fueled by oil from sea mammal blubber, and which were vital to human survival beyond the tree line in the Arctic. There was too little wood north of the tree line for it to be used for fuel.

Ground slate tools and ground-stone adzes made from basalt and other fine-grained stone increased in importance in this period. Chipped-stone implements continued to be made as well, but styles and proportions varied. Labrets, some of them large lip plugs, and other ornaments became fashionable as well, and it is clear that there was much more to these cultures than mere survival.

A puzzling culture known as Old Whaling, which was probably a brief intrusion of people from Siberia, only adds to the confusion of this chaotic period of readaptation. Old Whaling was present in the fourteenth century BCE. By the last few centuries BCE Norton culture predominated as the most widespread and successful of these alternatives.

Maritime Adaptation. Generally speaking, the new adaptations involved greater dependence upon maritime resources. Choris culture emerged around Kotzebue Sound, north of the Bering Strait on Alaska's northwest coast. The tool inventory of this culture indicates that the Choris people had a broader and more varied adaptation than their predecessors (Anderson 1984). Choris sites even yield the first traces of ceramics found in the Arctic.

Norton culture was named for the Norton Sound area where it was first studied (Dumond 1984a). The Norton Eskimos used both wood and sea mammal oil for fuel. Their development of oil lamp technology freed them from the need to find wood for fuel, allowing them to live permanently on the tundra and even on the pack ice of the Arctic Ocean.

Norton hunters took small sea mammals, possibly both through holes in sea ice and from **kayaks**. These small agile boats were an important technological innovation. Larger boats that could carry whole families had yet to be developed. They also hunted caribou seasonally in the interior, but by this time terrestrial hunting was less important than maritime hunting.

Other kinds of new technology were also emerging. People made and used both men's and women's knives, the latter being semilunar implements called "ulus" by modern Eskimos (Figure 14.4). Norton people even made pottery, the earliest known in the Arctic. It was often coarse and crude, but functional (Frink and Harry 2008). It apparently derived from Choris prototypes that were in turn modeled after ceramics made in the Lena Valley of Siberia.

Ipiutak culture clearly derived from Norton culture in northern Alaska, but it was very distinct from its ancestor. Beautifully carved bone and ivory artifacts are found much more frequently in Ipiutak sites, particularly as grave offerings (Figure 14.5). Carved compound human masks, which were probably attached to wooden or leather backings, are particularly noteworthy, and these were typically buried with their owners (Figure 14.6).

Figure 14.4 Ulu or "woman's knife." The tool is grasped or hafted along the flat top and the long, sharp curved edge is used in a rocking or slicing motion. Scale is in centimeters.

Figure 14.5 Two carved ivory objects of the Ipiutak culture: a figure of a young walrus with skeletal decoration, and snow goggles. Goggles are approximately 13 cm (5 in.) long. *Source:* From Larsen and Rainey 1948:113, 125.

Figure 14.6 Ipiutak walrus ivory mask. Note the labrets on either side of the mouth opening. *Source:* From Larsen and Rainey 1948:138.

Curiously, Choris, Norton, and Ipiutak sites all lack microblades. Ipiutak also lacked pottery, slate tools, and oil lamps despite the derivation of this culture from Norton, which had these traits. The Ipiutak weapon of choice appears to have been the bow and arrow, which already had been a feature of Eskimo technology for centuries (Blitz 1988).

Ipiutak pithouses were often constructed in lines just above the beaches of coastal sites such as at Point Hope, Alaska. As sea levels fell and new beaches were created by the tides, lines of newer houses were built at lower levels. Over time this created the appearance of large villages with houses laid out along what might at first impression look like streets. Much has been made of this in short-lived speculative popular books, but the pattern was produced by cumulative effects over the long term. Ipiutak people did not live in large towns.

Old Bering Sea culture is the earliest example of a maritime adaptation like that which characterizes later Eskimo cultures across the Arctic. The technology for hunting seals, walrus, and whales from the ice and from boats was present in Old Bering Sea sites as early as 150 BCE. These people also exploited caribou and other land mammals, as well as birds and fish. The origins of Old Bering Sea, and closely related Okvik culture, appear to have been in northeast Siberia where most sites are located. But it extended to St. Lawrence Island and there are traces of it on the western coast of the Alaskan mainland (Dumond and Bland 2002; Gibbon 1998:605–606).

Dorset. Dorset culture emerged across northern Canada around 500 BCE after a cold spell drastically shrank Pre-Dorset populations. Dorset people eventually reoccupied areas across Canada and Greenland that had been abandoned by their ancestors in the face of difficult conditions during one of the prolonged cold spells of the later Holocene. Their expansion coincided with a climatic improvement and their adaptation was more sea-oriented than the earlier Pre-Dorset one had been.

Dorset people tended to live near the shore in small circular semisubterranean pithouses. They built these of whatever materials were available: stone, driftwood, whale bones, sod blocks, or some mixture of any of these materials. Their small floors were paved when appropriate materials were available and there was typically an earthen bench around the interior wall for sleeping and sitting. Short entrance tunnels were often built to provide insulation from the cold outside.

The classic snow house (igloo), which provided winter shelter where other building materials were scarce, might have been a Dorset invention. Snow houses leave few or no archaeological traces, of course, but the specialized snow knives that the Dorset people and later Thule people used do survive as evidence that snow houses were being built by this time.

They hunted caribou, musk oxen, or marine animals depending upon what was locally available. They did not have the technology for hunting sea mammals effectively on the open water. However, they did have the technology to hunt seals through breathing holes in the ice. Some modern Inuit hunters still hunted this way in the twentieth century. Patient hunters spent long hours stooped over breathing holes, watching small feathered detectors for any sign that a seal was taking air from beneath the ice. It was often a long wait, because seals maintained several breathing holes and visited any one of them only sporadically. When a seal eventually visited a hole being monitored by a hunter, the hunter plunged his harpoon downward through the hole and secured the mortally wounded seal with a line tied to the harpoon head. After that the hunter's task was to enlarge the hole so that the seal could be pulled up for butchering.

Dorset Eskimos had some important tools in their inventory but lacked some others that would be important to later Eskimos. Important parts of their kits were tools that they had invented themselves or picked up from Norton and other related cultures west of them. These included men's knives, women's knives (ulus), toggling harpoons, oil lamps, stone cooking pots, bows and arrows, fish spears, kayaks, small sleds, ice creepers, snow goggles, and some copper tools. The Dorset Eskimos also had larger boats called "umiaks" to help with transportation, which some other cultures still lacked.

Just as important as the tools they had were those that were still missing from the Dorset inventory. They lacked pottery and built-up dogsleds. The latter would be an important part of all later Eskimo adaptations.

The Dorset Eskimos were forced southward to as far as Newfoundland on Canada's east coast when a period of extended cold weather set in after 100 CE. They recovered and expanded once again during the warmer Medieval Maximum around 1000 CE, but by then there was a new Eskimo culture expanding eastward out of Alaska. Dorset culture collided with the rapidly expanding and better adapted Thule Eskimos, and by 1100 CE Dorset was overwhelmed and absorbed. Even though climatic conditions were relatively good and the Dorset Eskimos were well adapted to their environments, Thule Eskimo culture was even better adapted. Dorset culture dwindled in the face of this competition, and it disappeared as individual Dorset

Eskimos were recruited into Thule culture or, less likely, they slowly died off.

Arctic Stage 5: Thule Culture

Thule culture probably originated on the northwest coast of Alaska around 900–1000 CE. Its origins were involved somehow with the short-lived Birnirk culture of that area as well as with Norton culture. Thule Eskimos possessed or developed technology that Dorset Eskimos lacked, tools that gave them an adaptive advantage. Just as important, Thule culture emerged amidst the improved climate of the Medieval Maximum, which lubricated their adaptive expansion across the Arctic. As a result, bands of Thule Eskimos multiplied and spread rapidly eastward along the northern coasts of Alaska, Canada, and Greenland. Thule culture replaced the older cultures it encountered everywhere it spread. While still healthy, the older Dorset bands in northern Canada were unable to compete effectively with the newcomers, and they were quickly absorbed by Thule language and culture. Thule spread at a rate of at least 15 km (10 mi) per year, expanding as much as 3,200 km (2,000 mi) in only a century and a half (Figure 14.7). This rapid adaptive expansion of Thule culture was perhaps analogous to the rapid spread of Choris culture 10 millennia earlier.

Advances in harpoon technology that might have originated in the previous Stage 4 along with the development of the kayak made maritime hunting a successful strategy for Thule hunters. The toggling harpoons were designed to come apart after the tip was plunged into a sea mammal. The toggling harpoon point was attached to a long tether, and it was designed to turn sideways in the animal after it detached from the harpoon and foreshaft (Figure 14.8). The wounded animal could not pull free, but if the tether was simply tied to the gunwale of a delicate kayak, chances were that it would destroy the fragile craft in its frantic attempt to escape. The answer was yet another clever Eskimo gadget. They made large floats from seal skin and tied them midway along the harpoon point tether line. A wounded seal or walrus was thus forced to pull against the float rather than the kayak, and the hunter could simply wait for exhaustion and blood loss to do their work.

Relatives of the Thule Eskimos spread to the western and southern coasts of Alaska, where descendants speaking various languages of the Yupic branch of Eskimo-Aleut languages still live (Dumond 1965). Everywhere it went the new adaptation was oriented more toward maritime resources than any predecessor culture in the Arctic. They had both kayaks and large open boats (umiaks) for hunting and transportation. The umiaks provided transportation for whole families, food, equipment, and other supplies in months when open water was available. The closed kayak provided Thule Eskimo hunters with an ideal craft from which to hunt sea mammals with their toggling harpoons, lines, and sealskin floats.

They hunted sea mammals of all kinds, large and small, including seals and walrus. Even the bowhead whale was fair game to these skilled marine hunters. The Medieval Maximum allowed the range of the Pacific bowhead population to expand eastward into the waters around the Canadian Arctic islands, where it overlapped with the Atlantic bowheads for a few

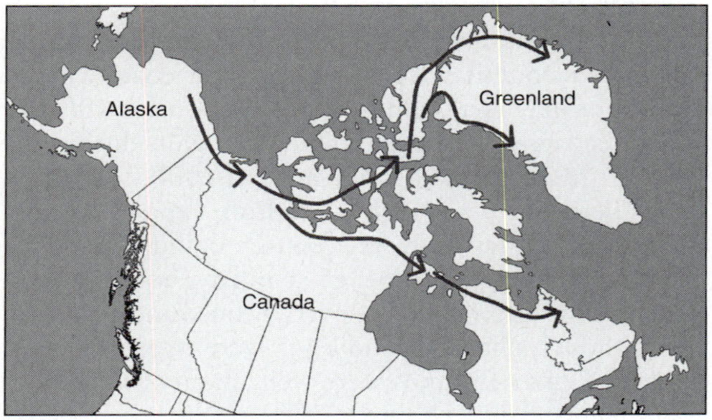

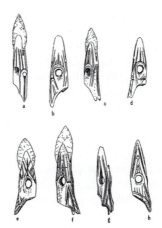

Figure 14.8 Eight antler toggling harpoon heads, four with intact stone points. All eight have basal foreshaft sockets (not visible) and holes for tethering lines to prevent a sea mammal from escaping once the tail of the head caught and turned the head sideways (toggling) inside the wound. *Source:* From Larsen and Rainey 1948:71.

Figure 14.7 The spread of Thule culture around 1000 CE.

centuries. This was probably the primary attraction for Thule hunters into and through the Canadian Arctic.

They had the soapstone lamps and multiple specialized forms of the toggling harpoons, but they also had swift new built-up dogsleds of an efficient design that is still used today (Figure 14.9). The light frameworks of standard sleds ran on iced runners of bone or ivory. Dogs were harnessed in a fanlike arc for travel across the great expanses of open sea ice, but paired in tandem for travel along narrow trails where rocks or shrubs were potential obstacles. The sled and the latter style of harnessing are still the rule for teams that compete in modern dogsled races. The success of Thule adaptation depended upon a broad range of gadgetry that included nearly everything made and used by their ancestors along with a few crucial new innovations.

Figure 14.9 Inuit dog sleds at Tree River near Coronation Gulf, Nunavut.
Source: Nunavut Photo © Canadian Museum of Civilization, photo O'Neill, 1915, image 38571LS.

Box 14.1 HOW TO INTERPRET STRATIGRAPHY

The landscape tends to accumulate sediments in some places and erode in others. Human activity contributes to both processes and nicely stratified sites occur where both natural processes and human activities produce accumulation rather than erosion. The figure is an artificial example of a site where this has occurred. The basic principle is the law of superposition, which says that generally speaking, younger deposits overlay older ones.

The original ground surface 1 defined the top of basal stratum A. That surface was modified by the excavation of a footing trench to accommodate the base of a stone wall. The space around the wall base was refilled, recreating a portion of surface 1 and producing a modified stratum that one might want to designate stratum A1, but which is left unspecified in the simplified profile.

Stratum B accumulated over time from both natural and human activity, but a new stratum (C) formed when the site was abandoned and the upper portion of the stone wall collapsed on to surface 2. Stratum C accumulated largely through natural processes. People returned to inhabit the site on surface 3, digging a large pit and throwing up a pile of dirt to form stratum D and a new surface 4. Subsequent abandonment left the site to accumulate the sediments of stratum E by natural means that filled the large pit.

People resumed living at the site on surface 5, digging small pits to anchor the posts of a house into stratum E and in one case slightly into the deeper stratum C. A larger pit found to be filled with burned soil and charcoal was clearly a fire pit. Residents of the house threw waste beyond the top of the old pile of excavated dirt, forming a midden layer above stratum E there. Both the fire pit and the midden are referred to as stratum F here.

Stratum G is the most recent stratum. It was deposited through natural processes and it contains no evidence of human activity. Notice that the relationships between strata D, E, and F on the right are not straightforward. Archaeological strata frequently depart from a flat layer-cake model. Geological strata are laid down at much larger scale and they tend to be flat, at least initially. But tectonic forces tilt, warp, or even invert geological strata over the very long term. While archaeological strata are not subject to such extreme deformation, they tend to have confusing features from the start because of the nature of human digging, filling, and other modifications.

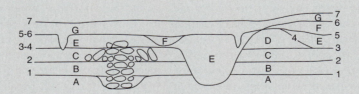

Gadgetry. Gadgetry was elaborated to an extraordinary level by the Thule Eskimos. Even the simplest tools often had clever twists, or beautiful decoration. Harness toggles, needle cases, wrist guards, wound plugs to stop the loss of valuable blood from dead game animals, harpoon heads, snow goggles, and the like all were made from clever combinations of materials and often elaborately decorated. Bone, antler, fiber, feathers, gut, skin, copper, wood, baleen, chert, and even meteoric iron were used. The long Arctic winter nights provided the time for the work that went into the production of these items, and native ingenuity provided the inspiration.

Among the clever gadgets they used are five that exemplify Eskimo ingenuity. Wolf killers were made from springs of tightly wound baleen that was encased in frozen blubber. Hungry wolves downed the blubber balls without chewing them and the sharp baleen strips sprang open upon melting in their stomachs, killing them. Hunters had only to find the carcass.

Another innovation that took advantage of animal greed was the gull hook. Gulls will snatch food out of the air, making them vulnerable to a kind of aerial fishing. Hooks thrown up at the ends of lines can be used to reel in gulls that are insufficiently cautious about what they try to eat.

A third innovation was the bird bola. Sets of strings tied together at one end and carrying weights at their other ends were thrown up into flocks of birds to entangle them and bring them down.

Fourth, the bow and arrow were already part of the Arctic tool inventory, but wood that was suitable for making strong bows was nearly impossible to find. Thule men used sinew to back their bows, providing tensile strength and power to the bow that it would not have had otherwise.

Finally, they carved snow goggles from ivory, wood, or bone. These were form fitted to the face and supplied with narrow horizontal slits. The slits cut the glare as effectively as modern darkened glass does, eliminating the hazard of snow blindness for hunters.

Thule Shelter and Subsistence. Thule houses were highly variable, reflecting both the constraints and opportunities presented by the environment on the one hand, and the cleverness of people trying to make the best of it on the other (Dawson 2001). Winter snow houses are an Eskimo cliché, of course, but like the earlier Dorset Eskimos they built houses of whatever materials came to hand. Soapstone (steatite) oil lamps were used in house interiors, less likely to break than the cruder pottery ones sometimes used by their predecessors. The lamps provided light and enough heat to drive away the chill even in winter snow houses.

Each Thule house contained a nuclear family or a small extended one. Males and females had important complementary roles in this hunter-gatherer society. Proper roles were also assigned by custom according to age, and survival of the band was difficult if any of these components were missing. Like band organizations in other times and places, Thule bands depended upon mutual support for insurance, marriage partners, and occasional cooperative undertakings. Memberships were fluid so that a band that had too many or too few males or females could split, shrink, or grow as circumstances required.

Despite their focus on maritime resources, the Thule Eskimos also pushed up rivers as far as the interior forests to fish and hunt caribou as the seasons permitted. This flexibility and breadth of adaptation served them well when the Medieval Maximum waned and the climate slid toward the Little Ice Age. The onset of colder conditions around 1400 CE rendered life in parts of the Thule range no longer viable. Even where they could still make a living Thule hunters were forced to shift emphasis away from the summertime open-water hunting of sea mammals to wintertime hunting through the sea ice. Whales disappeared and ringed seals became much more important. Some bands gave up the building and use of umiaks and large sea kayaks. There is even a story of a set of bands that shifted to a dependence upon caribou and gave up virtually all of their maritime equipment. When the new hunting pressure eventually caused the regional caribou population to crash the human population that depended upon it had no viable options to fall back on, and it too perished.

The colder conditions and more restricted hunting thus forced many Thule Eskimo bands to retreat into isolated pockets and to abandon parts of their former range. Some bands probably died out completely, whereas others survived in reduced circumstances. The Polar Eskimos, who lived in Greenland, farther north than anyone else, were isolated so long that by the nineteenth century they had no idea that other environments or even other humans existed anywhere beyond their horizon. When they were first encountered by European explorers their astonishment was complete. Environmental conditions were less rigorous outside the central Arctic and the Thule way of life has persisted in those areas into modern times.

Given the rapid spread of Thule culture from west to east across the Arctic, it is no surprise that a string of closely related modern dialects, Inuit-Inupiaq

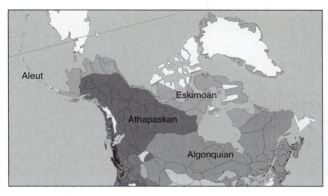

Figure 14.10 Language families of Arctic and Subarctic North America.

Figure 14.11 Norse settlements in Greenland and Newfoundland.

(Figure 14.10), is spoken by people from the Bering Sea to the east coast of Greenland (Dumond 1965). That said, however, it is also the case that a person speaking East Greenlandic will have difficulty understanding anyone speaking the Seward Peninsula Inupiaq language in Alaska. There are several Inuit-Inupiaq dialects arrayed between the two at the extreme ends of the Thule continuum, and while the divisions between them are rather arbitrarily defined, and communication is relatively easy between any two adjacent bands, they are not a single speech community. It has been a millennium since the Thule expansion, and the Little Ice Age broke communications in several places. It is no surprise that the speech of modern descendant communities has diverged over time, for it probably would have done so even in the absence of isolation.

The Norse

The Inuits of the eastern Arctic were contacted by Norse settlers, the first Europeans to find the Americas. Like the Inuit carriers of Thule culture, the Norse ventured across the North Atlantic and settled in Iceland, Greenland, and eventually Newfoundland during the Medieval Maximum (Figure 14.11).

The Norse colonized the Faroe Islands and reached Iceland by 874, probably as family groups traveling in cargo ships with all of their livestock and belongings. Many came from the Hebrides and Scotland, and most families appear to have brought Irish slaves. Finding their destinations was not as difficult as it might seem to us today. The phenomenon known as "arctic mirage" sometimes allows one to see well over the horizon. Temperature inversions sometimes allow one to see the Faroe Island from the Shetlands, Iceland from the Faroes, and Greenland from Iceland. In addition,

Figure 14.12 The Norse Oseberg ship on display. Viking Ship Museum, Oslo, Norway.

Viking sailors were in the habit of keeping ravens, which they would release when out of sight of land and then follow to the nearest landfall (Sawatzky and Lehn 1976). Norse sagas, oral traditions written down long after the events they described, recorded this process. They also preserved tales of the settlement of Greenland by around 985 CE.

The technological advantage of the Vikings is to be found mainly in their ships (Figure 14.12). All ships had clinker-built hulls, overlapping strakes joined by iron rivets such that the whole vessel had long, graceful lines. The strakes were split from curved logs, not sawn, so that none of the natural strength of the wood was lost. The hulls were light, strong, and flexible. Ships designed for war and travel were low, narrow, and fast, whereas cargo ships were higher, wider, and slower (Roesdahl 1991). Cargo ships ranged 16–25 m (53–82 ft) in length and were capable of carrying 18–38 tons.

Norse settlement concentrated around two communities, Osterbygd and Vesterbygd, the eastern and western colonies. Bands of West Greenland Eskimos were scattered near the Norse settlements and at least initially relations between the two cultures were cordial but cautious. The Norse brought their own cultural baggage with them, of course. This included agriculture and animal husbandry, both of which were minimally viable along the Greenland coast at the height of the Medieval Maximum. They built houses, barns, and Christian churches of stone, and eked out a living without resorting to an adaptation more like that of their Inuit neighbors.

Settlements in Greenland supplied furs and walrus ivory to Iceland and Norway. There were no towns or trading centers established in either Greenland or Iceland. Neither did they have kings or earls. Instead they were quasi-republics run by assemblies of chieftains. Even where their local populations were low, in the range of band or tribal societies, they maintained their traditional chiefdom form of government.

The Norse subsisted on fish, sea mammals, birds, and other game in addition to their domesticates. The shortage of grain is evident in their dentition. The Greenland Norse had heavy tooth wear, but few dental caries of the sort that typically afflict people with high-carbohydrate diets.

The Norse in America

Norse explorations farther west took them along the coasts of Baffin Island, Labrador, and Newfoundland. They eventually established another colony at the site of L'Anse aux Meadows on the northern tip of Newfoundland, apparently the "Vinland" of the Norse sagas (Figure 14.13). Helge Ingstad excavated eight turf-walled structures there in the 1960s. These included three large houses and several small outbuildings, all of them very similar to Norse structures in Greenland and Iceland. Because of internal strife and conflict with neighboring American Indians, the settlement did not last long. It was abandoned after about a decade and the settlers returned to Greenland or Iceland.

There has been much debate about Yale's Vinland map ever since its publication in 1965 (Skelton et al. 1965). The map, which supposedly dates to before Columbus, shows eastern Canada as well as Greenland. Scholarly consensus has shifted back and forth, mainly as the document's ink has passed and failed various tests of authenticity. Kristen Seaver's (2004) thorough analysis has finally shown that the Vinland map is a fraud, one almost certainly created in desperation around 1939, during the reign of Nazi Germany.

Regardless of modern forgeries, hoaxes, and misidentifications, Norse sailors apparently sailed to Labrador and elsewhere in northern Canada in search of timbers for their Greenland settlements. Norse trade goods have turned up in Inuit sites dating to 950–1450 CE. Most of these are bits of smelted iron, copper, or bronze artifacts. The last includes a bronze trader's balance, but there are also fragments of chain mail and woolen cloth. The largest concentration of Norse trade objects is on Ellesmere Island, northwest of Greenland, where Norse traders were probably in direct contact with Inuit traders.

Other trade items are more far flung and probably got to where they were found along Native American trade routes. A Norse penny that was minted between 1065 and 1080 CE was found in a site on the coast of Maine (Figure 14.14), but it now seems possible that it might have been planted there as part of a twentieth-century hoax (Gibbon 1998:565–566; Snow 1980:339).

Figure 14.13 Reconstructions of three Norse buildings at L'Anse aux Meadows, Newfoundland.
Source: ParksCanada/H.01.11.01.04(40).

Figure 14.14 Norse penny found at the Goddard site, Maine, obverse left and reverse right.
Source: Courtesy of Bruce J. Bourque.

The Demise of the Norse in North America

Trade and exchange between the Norse and the Inuits ceased around 1480 CE after the onset of the Little Ice Age. The Norse colonies in Greenland dwindled as the growing season shortened. Wheat failed to ripen and cattle were so weakened by long winters in crude barns that they had to be carried to pasture when the grass finally appeared.

The Norse settlements in Greenland withered and died out, their contact with Scandinavia long since broken. It was probably a slow sad process, as infants died with increasing frequency, young people left to seek better lives in Iceland, and remaining Norse farmers were left increasingly alone to die of old age. Some scholars find it hard to believe that such vigorous adventurers could come to such a pathetic end, and point to the trickle of Norse artifacts into eastern Canada as evidence that they might have relocated there (Seaver 2004). But that archaeological evidence more probably accumulated during the heyday of Norse settlement, for no one has found evidence of Norse settlements or burials in Canada other than the early one at L'Anse aux Meadows.

The Norse case illustrates the power of ideology in human adaptation to changing circumstances. By the time the Norse colonized Greenland they had adopted Christianity. This process began in the ninth century, and it can be observed archaeologically. Older pagan Norse in Scandinavia had tended to bury the dead with weapons and other personal belongings. Children were rare in pagan graves. Grave goods disappeared and children appeared in graves after the conversion of Norse to Christianity (Roesdahl 1991:61).

The advantage of religious conversion was that it reinforced existing institutions. The Christian religious hierarchy paralleled and supported the political hierarchy. But stubborn adherence to traditional institutions did not serve the Norse well when they were forced to confront the Little Ice Age. The Norse farmers in Greenland clung to farming, traditional gender roles, woven clothing, and Christian ideals. They refused to adopt the more adaptive forms of subsistence, division of labor, and clothing of their Inuit neighbors, whom they regarded as heathens. They paid an awful price for their stubbornness, dying out while at the same time the Inuits survived the long cold spell culturally intact.

The Subarctic

The native residents of Newfoundland that contended with the brief Norse colony at L'Anse aux Meadows were known later as the Beothuks. These people, called

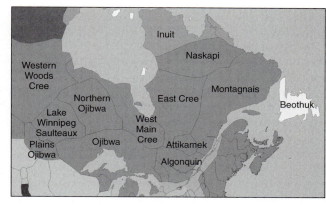

Figure 14.15 The Algonquian languages of eastern Canada. The proper classification of the Beothuk isolate is uncertain.

"Red Indians" in later historical documents, were the easternmost of the thin populations that lived scattered through the boreal forests of the Canadian Subarctic, all the way west to British Columbia and northwest as far as interior Alaska. So few words of the Beothuk language survive that linguists still debate its connections with other North American Indian languages. Beothuk was either remotely connected to the great block of Algonquian languages in the Eastern Subarctic of mainland Canada, or it was a language with a few Algonquian loanwords whose ancient connections have been lost to time (Figure 14.15).

The Beothuks lived by hunting and gathering in small bands scattered around the island of Newfoundland. They traveled by birchbark canoe when and where that was possible, and broke up into small family groups during the long, hard winters. Hunting and foraging for food were full-time pursuits that often came up short, keeping the human population very thin on the boreal forest landscape. The archaeological evidence for them is similarly thin and spotty, and this is the pattern all across the North American Subarctic.

The Eastern Subarctic lies almost entirely in Canada, mainly east of and drained by Hudson's Bay. The region is underlain by ancient bedrock that is often referred to as the Canadian Shield, and the soils of the conifer forest are both thin and acidic. The Canadian Shield is bounded on the south by the Great Lakes and on the east by the Gulf of St. Lawrence and the Atlantic Ocean. Before modern times the human population in this vast region never averaged more than about two people per 100 km^2, or about one person to every 20 mi^2.

The native peoples of the Eastern Subarctic all spoke one or another of the languages of the Algonquian branch of the Algic language family. Like the Paleo-Indians 10 millennia ago, they lived in such small bands that they had to maintain close relations over long distances in order to sustain diverse breeding populations. This phenomenon, surviving as it did into the twentieth century, has served as a model for the connubia inferred for Paleoindians. As is explained in Chapter 3, bands were embedded in connubia, abstract and overlapping social networks that had long ceased to exist south of the Subarctic.

Marriage and residence were very flexible, although women historically tended to be more mobile than men. Communication, trade, and marriage between bands in the overlapping connubia fostered widespread continuity. James Wright noted that because of that continuity, at any given date archeological culture was remarkably uniform across the entire Eastern Subarctic (Wright 1981:86). This is reflected both in the archaeological record and in the Algonquian speech of all the related bands. Eastern Subarctic people spoke a single widespread Algonquian language, but one that was so diverse that while members of a given band could communicate easily with their nearest neighbors, their speech was unintelligible to those living a thousand kilometers away. Such a loose network of dialects has been called an "L-complex" (Hockett 1958:324). The Algonquian L-complex in the Eastern Subarctic case is known as Cree-Montagnais-Naskapi, which like the continuum of Inuit languages has been rather arbitrarily divided into nine local languages by linguists.

Subarctic Subsistence

The Subarctic Algonquians subsisted primarily on woodland caribou and fish. Moose, beaver, and migratory waterfowl were also hunted. They traveled mainly along streams, particularly after they developed the birchbark canoe. Snowshoes and toboggans were also important Algonquian inventions, for they made possible travel along the frozen streams and through snowy woods in wintertime.

The environment was and still is subject to periodic forest fires. These forced hunter-gatherer bands to relocate and adapt to new conditions (Noble 1981:100). Thus the Algonquians were not adapted to a constant environment, but rather to one that was subject to periodic burning and subsequent renewal as a succession of plants and animals reappeared in the course of reforestation.

Initial Occupation

The first human inhabitants of the Eastern Subarctic probably moved into the region no earlier than 7500 BCE. The region had lain frozen under the Laurentian ice

sheet when Paleoindians spread across the rest of North America. By the time the Eastern Subarctic became habitable only unfluted lanceolate points were still being made and used, and these are the earliest artifacts found in the region. The points resemble the Agate Basin points found on the Great Plains, and they are generally classified as part of the Plano tradition. The derivative late Paleoindian culture of these first arrivals evolved into the Shield Archaic (Wright 1981:88).

Shield Archaic

The Shield Archaic is known mainly from three artifact classes: side-notched points, knives, and scrapers. Thin acidic soils in the region allow little or no preservation of bone, wood, or other organic remains, so archaeologists must infer much from small inventories of durable artifacts.

Climate sometimes drove Archaic people southward from more northerly areas and facilitated their replacement by early Eskimos. They abandoned the area northwest of Hudson Bay sometime after 1500 BCE and were replaced there by early Eskimos of the Arctic Small Tool culture. There is no evidence of contact between the two cultures, although one cannot exclude the possibility that there was some. Overall, it was a matter of one adaptation retreating from areas where changing conditions made their lifeway maladaptive, while other people whose culture was better adapted to the new conditions were drawn into the same areas (Noble 1981:100; Wright 1981:89).

Sometime in the last millennium BCE the people of the Shield Archaic began making and using pottery similar to that which is found at the same time in sites around the Great Lakes. The rest of Shield Archaic culture did not change when pottery was added, and that indicates that the new ceramic technology was adopted by these people rather than carried in by a new replacement population. The appearance of pottery has led Canadian archaeologists to call the period that follows in the Eastern Subarctic the "Initial Woodland" period. This term is used with the understanding that there was cultural continuity from Shield Archaic culture onward and no population replacement.

The Initial Woodland period in the Eastern Subarctic corresponds to what most archaeologists refer to as the "Middle Woodland" period south and east of the Great Lakes. By 600 CE there were widespread changes in the ceramics of the Canadian Initial Woodland that were sufficient to allow archaeologists to define a later ceramic period called the "Terminal Woodland" (Wright 1981:91). This period corresponds in time to what archaeologists in the northeastern United States refer to as the "Late Woodland" period. These terms illustrate again the confusion that results when the same or similar terms are used inconsistently across regions.

There are two late-named ceramic complexes that occur in sites scattered across the western part of the Eastern Subarctic. Selkirk ceramics are found in sites in northern Manitoba and Blackduck ceramics are found across southern Manitoba, northern Minnesota, and western Ontario. Selkirk pottery was made by the historic Cree Indians and Blackduck pottery was made by the Ojibwas. Pottery that turns up in the eastern part of the region appears to have been derived mainly from Iroquoian sources around the lower Great Lakes (Wright 1981:94–96).

The entire Eastern Subarctic was home to Algonquian-speaking natives when the first Europeans arrived, and the region appears to have been the source of Algonquian-speaking nations that expanded southward through the Great Lakes region and down the East Coast over the preceding 1,400 years. Many of the Algonquian languages are still spoken across the Eastern Subarctic, and there is no evidence for any other language family in the region. As mentioned earlier, the origins of Beothuk, the native language spoken in Newfoundland, is uncertain and it might have been a survival of languages spoken in the Eastern Subarctic before the arrival of Algonquians.

Algonquians apparently expanded out of the Eastern Subarctic with their adoption of the bow and arrow after 600 CE (Blitz 1988; Fiedel 1994). Some of them expanded south of the Great Lakes while the Eastern Algonquian branch spread down the Atlantic seaboard, some eventually reaching coastal North Carolina (see Chapter 10).

After 1600 CE most of the Central Algonquians died out or were pushed westward and eventually on to reservations in the Midwest. Remarkably, several of the Eastern Algonquian nations survive today in their homelands, despite the fact that they bore the brunt of initial European colonization and were in the middle of many of the colonial conflicts leading up to and including the American Revolution.

Western Subarctic

The interior portions of the Western Subarctic in Alaska and Canada were occupied by bands of Athapaskan-speaking Indians when Europeans first arrived, and they are still a major fraction of the regional population (Figure 14.16). Athapaskan languages are distributed across an ecozone that contains martens, flying

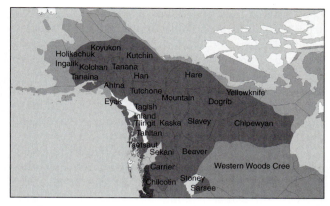

Figure 14.16 The Athapaskan languages of western Canada. The Stoney language is Siouan and Western Woods Cree is Algonquian.

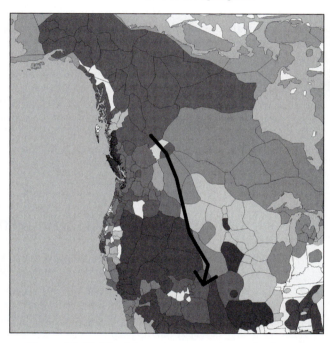

Figure 14.17 The Athapaskan expansion to the Greater Southwest against the backdrop of the historic distribution of western language families. The expansion occurred after Puebloan communities abandoned much of the region but before the arrival of Spanish colonists.

squirrels, red foxes, snowshoe hares, and wolverines. It is not surprising that cognate terms for these animals appear in Athapaskan languages and their reconstructable Proto-Athapaskan ancestor language.

Athapaskan languages are a subdivision of the larger Nadene language family, which also has branches on the Northwest Coast, the Plateau, and the northern Great Plains (Figure 14.17). Like the Algonquians in the East, the Athapaskans expanded southward relatively late. Some bands ended up in northern California, where they flourished amidst other small nations in that region (see Chapter 13). Others migrated slowly along the eastern foothills of the Rockies, eventually reaching the Southwest. They flourished there as well, moving into areas abandoned by the Pueblo Indians in the face of warming and drying conditions. Athapaskan migrants to the Southwest were ancestral to the modern Navajo and Apache nations (see Chapter 5).

Most of the later archaeology of the Western Subarctic is associated with Athapaskans, but how they came to be there is still debated. At least some of the early people that spread into North America probably moved southeastward between retreating ice sheets, as opposed to migrating southward along the Pacific Coast. The Nenana complex in Alaska probably spread through the region after 13,500 BP, giving rise to Clovis culture on the Great Plains. However, there is only the scantiest archaeological evidence for this expansion in western Canada (see Chapter 3). This was also the corridor by which the Clovis fluting technique probably spread back northwestward to Alaska. It stands to reason that the Western Subarctic must hold some of the most interesting early remains of ancient America, but most of what should be there still waits to be found.

More certain is the arrival of microblade technology in the region, which was the hallmark of a population that postdated the Paleoindians but predated the arrival of ancestral Eskimos. The Denali complex, the basic technology of the expanding Paleo-Arctic tradition, was well established in Alaska by 9000 BCE. Microblades were used with bone, antler, and wood to make sophisticated compound tools, and the origins of this technology lie in eastern Siberia. The people of the Paleo-Arctic tradition spread into the Western Subarctic from Alaska, and some archaeologists hypothesize that they were early Nadene speakers (Clark 1981). This is consistent with the observation that Nadene was the second of three waves of languages that spread to the Americas from Siberia. The last was the wave of Eskimo-Aleut languages discussed earlier in this chapter. The first was the wave that brought speech that was ancestral to all other American Indian languages.

Microblades disappeared from the archaeological record of the Western Subarctic over the course of two and a half millennia. They were often replaced in local assemblages by side-notched bifaces that probably were inspired by prototypes in the tool inventories of contemporaneous Archaic cultures located farther to the south. The transition away from microblade technology occurred as early as 2500 BCE in some places in the Western Subarctic, as late as 1 CE in others (Clark 1981:128).

The Taltheilei Shale tradition developed in the forests around Great Slave Lake and Great Bear Lake

Box 14.2 HOW TO EVALUATE NEW INFORMATION

Anyone who can read or hear is confronted daily by debates about science. These often present opposing sides in ways that leave many people not knowing what to believe. There are two major factors that are at the root of the problem. First, our primary and secondary schools do a poor job of teaching students how to evaluate opposing scientific propositions. Too often matters of fact are presented as matters of opinion. In one famous case a teacher decided that the best way to determine the sex of a dead mouse found on the playground was to have the class vote on it, and an opportunity to truly teach was lost. The second factor is that of asymmetrical debates, in which news reporters often give the views of a handful of crackpots the same weight as the unanimous opinion of the broad scientific community. Of course even Darwin and Einstein were each initially in minorities of one, but in those cases the scientific community subjected their theories to fair, honest, thorough, and repeated testing and they were soon supported by the vast majority.

The first questions to ask of any new scientific information are has it been published in an established journal, was it peer reviewed, and are there adequate references? Fairness and honesty require peer review, for only with it can we be sure that reported findings are valid, significant, and original. Error and dishonesty in science is almost always discovered and exposed by other scientists. The 1989 flap over "cold fusion" is a good example.

The process of peer review slows down publication, and it is at odds with today's demand for instant news. But history is littered with the unhappy consequences of acting on wrong information, so it is worth the wait. A useful pamphlet on how to evaluate scientific debates is available at www.senseaboutscience.org.uk/PDF/ ShortPeerReviewGuide.pdf.

Assertions made in the name of science but which violate the scientific method are referred to as pseudoscience or BS (bogus science). Most examples involve deception, dishonesty or unfair practices, and are advanced for nonscientific reasons that are often not disclosed. A current example is the argument for intelligent design in the origin of life. R. L. Park (2003) has provided us with a useful list of the Seven Warning Signs of Bogus Science. If any of the seven signs are present, the claim is probably bogus and one should start looking for other reasons to explain why the claim is being promoted.

1. The discoverer pitches the claim directly to the media.
2. The discoverer says that a powerful establishment is trying to suppress his or her work.
3. The scientific effect involved is at the very limit of detection.
4. Evidence for a discovery is anecdotal.
5. The discoverer says a belief is credible because it has endured for centuries.
6. The discoverer has worked in isolation.
7. The discoverer must propose new laws of nature to explain an observation.

Archaeology generally and North American archaeology in particular has been rife with bogus claims in the past and will probably be so in the future. Fake "petrified men" made money for their exhibitors. Fabricated claims for space aliens, Norse rune stones, Celtic monasteries, Phoenician inscriptions, and the like have likewise sold books by the carload. The Internet has turned the flow of false information into a flood. It is up to the individual reader to sort through the available information and to separate valid knowledge from bogus information.

in western Canada around 500 BCE. This tradition was directly ancestral to the modern Athapaskan cultures of the same region, but it contained no vestige of microblades (Clark 1981:118; Noble 1981:102). Most archaeologists conclude that there is no evidence for population replacement and that the loss of microblades from the Athapaskan tool inventories was simply a matter of slow technological evolution over time.

The southeastward expansion of Athapaskans from Canada's Northwest Territories began as early as 400 BCE and it continued into the historic era (Wright 1981:91–92). After 1600 CE, the movement became one of the features of the fur trade. The Western Subarctic was a primary source for furs that were shipped eastward in large freight canoes. French-speaking traders penetrated farther and farther westward from Quebec in search of furs, and the Hudson Bay Company established trading posts all over western Canada to facilitate the trade.

The success of the fur trade added incentives to Athapaskans who were already drifting south and east. They gradually replaced many Algonquian-speaking bands, who in turn retreated farther to the south and east. Intermarriage with fur traders, most of whom were operating out of eastern Canada, led to emergence of a hybrid culture in the Western Subarctic. The Meti culture, as it is called, survives today in the region.

Summary

1. The North American Arctic is such a vast region that its archaeology is best summarized in terms of five broad developmental stages.

2. Eskimo and Aleut traditions separated early and evolved differently over time.

3. Successive Eskimo adaptations tended to develop first in Alaska and then spread eastward across Canada and Greenland.

4. The first Arctic-wide Eskimo adaptation was the Stage 3, Arctic Small Tool tradition, which laid the foundation for later Arctic adaptations.

5. Dorset culture succeeded the Arctic Small Tool tradition across much of the Arctic.

6. Thule culture was the last major expansion out of Alaska, replacing Dorset and establishing the Eskimo and Inuit cultures that still survive today.

7. Alaskan Eskimo cultures were more diverse in all periods, leaving behind a variety of archaeological signatures.

8. The North American Subarctic region was dominated by Algonquian- and Athapaskan-speaking bands after the disappearance of continental glaciers.

9. Algonquian bands equipped with bows and arrows expanded southward into the Eastern Woodlands in the first millennium CE.

10. Athapaskan bands expanded southward into the Plateau, Great Plains, and eventually the Greater Southwest.

11. The dispersed band populations of the Arctic and Subarctic survived the effects of smallpox and other epidemics better than many more dense populations.

Further Reading

The best single source is Harris's *Historical Atlas of Canada*, which includes many valuable maps and text written by some of Canada's best known archaeologists.

The archaeological chapters of the Arctic and Subarctic volumes of *Handbook of North American Indians* are also very good places to start. Don Dumond's *A Naknek Chronicle* and James Wright's *Ontario Prehistory* are accessible places to start that will lead readers into the technical literature. Portions of John Hoffecker's book *A Prehistory of the North* summarize the American Arctic.

Glossary

kayak: A small closed skin boat used by an individual hunter.

ulu: A semilunar knife having its cutting edge on the curved side, often called a "woman's knife" in the Arctic.

umiak: A large open skin boat used to transport freight and family groups.

Worlds in Collision

Jugez un homme par ses questions plutôt que par ses réponses (Judge people by their questions rather than by their answers).

Voltaire (François Marie-Arouet)

"Antiquitas saeculi juventus mundi." These times are the ancient times, when the world is ancient, and not those which we account ancient *ordine retrograde*, by a computation backward from ourselves.

Francis Bacon

Introduction

The collision of the world's cultures on North American soil began in 1492 CE, over five centuries ago, and it continues today. Prior to 1492 the peoples of Eurasia and Africa had almost no clue that the continents Columbus would call "the other world" even existed. Similarly, the peoples of what would come to be called the Americas had no idea that the continents and cultures of the Eastern Hemisphere existed until their ships began to appear offshore. Yet despite their separate evolutions from small bands of hunter-gatherers to states and empires the peoples of the two worlds were remarkably similar in many fundamental ways. To understand how those similarities arose so independently is to understand the cultural evolution of all human societies. To understand how history played out after the collision of those previously independent domains is to understand cultural conflict everywhere. The desire for those insights and understandings is what frames the questions asked by modern archaeologists working in North America.

In its earliest stages the clash of cultures in North America played out as an unequal contest of arms. Europeans brought horses, guns, and steel armor, and native armies initially used traditional tactics rather than innovative ones, a conservative strategy that favored the invaders. By the time the armies of Aztec Emperor Moctezuma figured out how to throw back the Spanish invaders Cortés had recruited other nearby city-states to his banner. Worse than that for the Mexicans, immigrant Spanish children had brought smallpox with them to Cuba, and a single infected soldier was among Cortés's reinforcements in 1520. The disease spread almost unchecked through the native population, with horrendous consequences.

Smallpox and other diseases brought by Europeans and Africans ensured that the results of the coming cultural exchange would not be balanced in North America. The diseases of the Eastern Hemisphere were crowd infections that depended upon dense populations for their long-term survival. A disease like smallpox will burn itself out if it cannot find a supply of new susceptible people to infect, but too often for the good of humanity it was inadvertently carried from one local population to another. Thus the relatively dense populations of Mesoamerica suffered earlier and more severely than the smaller more scattered populations to the north of them.

Many of the diseases had jumped from populations of domesticated animals into human populations and had long since settled in as endemic childhood illnesses in Europe and Africa. In a typical population where a disease like measles was endemic all adults were immune by virtue of having had the disease as children. Only the children were susceptible, and with low body masses and strong constitutions they were usually able to survive the disease. But in the Americas none of these were endemic in 1492. Even influenza was unknown, and nobody, adult or child, was immune to any of the satanic pantheon of diseases that leaked across the Atlantic in the holds of European ships.

It was an unequal disease exchange. Of all the diseases that afflict humans, only syphilis or something similar might have originated in the Americas, and even that is uncertain. From the sixteenth century on epidemics chipped away at American Indian populations that were at least initially 100% susceptible. Especially virulent epidemics annihilated whole towns, but even lesser ones did serious damage to communities and were invariably tragic for the affected individuals. The demographic realities of the interchange were that the native populations of America declined precipitously, while burgeoning populations in Europe and Africa provided a steady supply of migrants across the Atlantic. All the rest of American history after 1492 was conditioned by this inequality.

Drugs played a role as well. The bark of the Peruvian cinchona tree produces quinine while the leaves of the coca plant produce cocaine. One is a medical miracle while the other is a modern scourge. Alcohol was produced as chicha in South America and pulque in Mesoamerica, but it was not widespread in the rest of North America until European settlers introduced it. Its effects on American Indian populations not accustomed to it produced another inequality.

The history of North America is often presented as the history of exploration by Euro-Americans, the settlement of a land largely converted to wilderness after its abandonment by decimated and dislocated Native Americans (Fisher 2004; Goetzmann and Williams 1992). Regions like central Pennsylvania had never before looked like they did when the first Euro-American settlers first squatted there. The American Indians who had long modified it with fire and hoe had been gone for decades, long enough for it to become the wilderness it had not been since the end of the Pleistocene. Little wonder that history books celebrate Daniel Boone's discovery and migration through the Cumberland Gap. The traces of the ancient Indian path he was following were by then too faint for him to see, but the trail he blazed was hardly a new one.

In some regions American Indians were missed by the worst of the initial diseases and European expeditions did not have to push through new wilderness. Coronado, deSoto, and even the much later Lewis and Clark expedition found American Indian cultures not yet ravaged by epidemics. De Soto followed well-worn trails through belts of productive farmland, moving from town to town in what was clearly not wilderness at all. These first recorded contacts often tell us much about colliding cultures before they began to substantially modify each other. The mounted tribes of the Great Plains did not exist until after the Spanish introduced horses in the seventeenth century. The mountain men of the Rockies did not exist until after Lewis and Clark in the nineteenth century. The best known nations of the Southeast did not exist until after the dislocations and reformations of the seventeenth century.

The Columbian Exchange

The two-way flow of domesticates and technology across the Atlantic after 1492 is often referred to as the "Columbian exchange." Tobacco, the first tropical plant to become widespread in North America, was an immediate hit with Europeans in the sixteenth century. Smoking was taken back to Europe and promoted there as a health benefit. Soon the Europeans were making smoking pipes from white ball clay and selling them wherever their ships went, including back in North America. The potent tobacco used by North American Indians, *Nicotiana rustica*, was replaced by the milder West Indian *Nicotiana tabacum* in Virginia's fields, and that remains the main ingredient in modern tobacco products.

Clay smoking pipes were not common in highland Mexico until the time of the Toltecs, 900–1175 CE. Inscriptions and paintings indicate that cigars or tubular pipes were smoked earlier by Classic Maya (Robicsec 1978), but smoking pipes were common in eastern North America well before that (Porter 1948; Weaver 1972:213). Tobacco is a South American plant, so if it became well established in California and the Eastern Woodlands before it did so in Mesoamerica, it was probably carried into North America either along the West Coast, by way of the islands of the Caribbean, or both. Claims have been made for smoking pipes in Olmec sites and other early contexts in Mesoamerica, but these typically reference artifacts in private collections, where dating and documentation are suspect.

In fact, so much of the archaeological evidence of smoking involves artifacts that are attractive to looters and collectors that archaeology may never be able to provide a clear history of what is arguably the worst widespread habit ever practiced by human beings. But for all that it was on the leading edge of the Columbian exchange.

Other species involved in the Columbian exchange were more benign. Domesticated plants, animals, technology, and habits good and bad flowed both ways between the Eastern and Western hemispheres from the sixteenth century on. European farmers waited impatiently for new crops to try out in their fields. Some took root but many others did not. Potatoes became an Irish staple and tomatoes became indispensable to Italian cuisine. In exchange, American Indian communities planted orchards of peach and apple trees. Colonial settlers created new American foodways based on crops and animal domesticates from all of these sources. The Pilgrims of Massachusetts quickly developed a hybrid agriculture that featured both maize and wheat, both turkeys and chickens, both squash and apples, drawing upon domesticates that were to them both new and old. It is no exaggeration to say that the cultures of North America today are hybrids that would not exist but for the fervent interactions and exchanges of the last five centuries.

American Indian Populations

The size of the native population of North America around 1500 CE has been the subject of sometimes intense scholarly debate. Attempts to estimate population sizes based on historical records have typically underestimated them because so few records predate the virulent epidemics that often swept ahead of European explorers and journalists. Crowd infections began to break out once crossing times shortened to a month and colonists began bringing their families along (Snow and Lanphear 1988). Shorter crossings and larger crews ended the effective quarantine of early voyages, and the presence of European children ensured that childhood diseases would make the journey too. Nearly everywhere the first Europeans went they inadvertently introduced diseases, then watched in horror as the communities they contacted were devastated. Local mortality rates were often catastrophic, at least 60% for smallpox alone, sometimes much more.

Using the aggregated data of specialists working all over America north of the northern boundary of Mesoamerica, Douglas Ubelaker (1988) estimated that there were about 1.9 million people living there in 1500.

But this estimate did not account for the effects of the earliest epidemics. Henry Dobyns attempted to compensate for this by making assumptions about the frequency of early epidemics, their spread, and their mortality rates (Dobyns 1983). Unfortunately, the assumptions were flawed because they did not conform to the ways in which diseases actually behave across scattered populations. Overestimation of all three variables led him to publish estimates of up to 20 million, which were both wildly exaggerated and wildly popular with the general public at the time.

The inflation of tragedy sells books, and there has been no shortage of authors willing to repeat Dobyns's estimates (Diamond 1997:211; Mann 2005). There is, however, no way to accommodate 20 million people in the living space that was available in 1500. A better approach is to first find the best estimate of the 1500 CE population densities of as many Native American cultures as possible. One or more of them are known for each of thirteen North American ecozones (Figure 15.1 and Table 15.1). By generalizing the densities within each ecozone one can generate total populations for all of them. Estimated this way the aggregate population north of Mesoamerica was most probably around 3.4 million people (Snow 2001).

The 1500 CE population of Mesoamerica is if anything even more difficult to estimate. Smallpox accompanied the Spanish conquest of the Aztec Empire in 1520 and there were multiple epidemics after 1545. Cook and Borah thought that there were at least 16 million Mesoamericans in 1531, probably many more than that (Cook and Borah 1960). But even Woodrow Borah thought that Dobyns had taken "a leap into the darkness." We have reasonably accurate census figures

Figure 15.1 Ecozones of North America north of the Mexican deserts.

Table 15.1 An ecological approach to estimating the population of North America north of the Mexican deserts in 1500 CE.

Ecozone	Cases	Sample Area	Sample Population	Sample Density	Total Area Km²	Total Population
Mediterranean Scrub	11	64,967	61,921	0.95	131,000	124,858
Boreal Forest	20	4,811,231	83,466	0.02	5,310,000	92,119
Atlantic Coniferous Forest	5	141,600	46,410	0.33	490,500	160,763
Pacific Coniferous Forest	41	480,767	197,745	0.41	1,976,000	812,752
Desert	15	1,284,534	226,923	0.18	2,613,000	461,607
Eastern Broadleaf Woodlands	34	910,825	324,984	0.36	2,955,000	1,054,349
Gulf Coast Grasslands	1	19,520	3,600	0.18	75,590	13,941
California Grasslands	2	40,690	46,465	1.14	52,050	59,437
Tundra	21	2,310,349	40,703	0.02	6,534,000	115,114
Great Plains Grasslands	0	0	0	0.18	2,925,000	526,500
Plateau Grasslands	0	0	0	0.18	54,550	9,819
Oregon Broadleaf Woodlands	0	0	0	0.18	14,650	2,637
Flooded Grasslands	0	0	0	0.18	32,050	5,769
TOTALS	150				23,163,390	3,439,665

for Mesoamerica from around 1540 CE on, from which point they show a linear decline from around 4 million to around 1 million by 1600 CE (Figure 15.2). A linear projection back to 1500 indicates that the initial population was about 5 million. This strikes some researchers as being too conservative (Sanders 1992). However, any alternative curve that is not a straight line implies a dramatic initial fall in population, after which the decline straightens out to the linear slope. Why would we assume that the slope of the decline in Figure 15.2 was different before 1540 CE from what it was after that date?

Other research shows that the shape of the curve of population decline depends upon the scale of analysis (Snow 1992). The highly convex curve that was favored by Cook and Borah for Mesoamerica and by Dobyns for the whole continent is actually demonstrable only for local or small regional populations. For example, the Mohawk population in the Northeast shows such a precipitous initial decline starting in 1634, followed by a flattening later in the century (Snow 1995a). But at the same time some other areas of North America experienced less dramatic effects and still other areas were not affected at all (Thornton 1987). It makes no sense to generalize the Mohawk catastrophe to the whole Northeast, let alone to the Eastern Woodlands or the whole continent.

Aggregation of data at the regional scale produces curves that are less convex than the one preferred by Cook and Borah. At the continental scale the curve is not a curve at all, but rather linear or nearly so (Snow 1992). This suggests that for a large subcontinental region like Mesoamerica the straight line projection in Figure 15.2 is more likely to be correct than the convex alternatives. In short, lacking evidence to the contrary we must assume that the overall slope of population

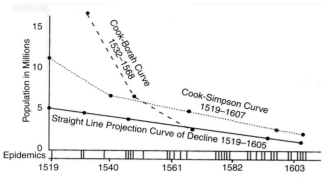

Figure 15.2 Alternative Mesoamerican population declines. *Source:* From Sanders 1992:179.

decline before 1540 CE was more or less similar to what it was after that date. There were probably about 5 million people in Mesoamerica, perhaps a few more.

Altogether North America probably had a population approaching 8.5 million in 1492. This is close to Russell Thornton's estimates and consistent with what we know about the continent's human capacity at that time (Thornton 1987; Thornton and Marsh-Thornton 1981). The long decline that followed did not bottom out until around 1890, when the American Indian population in the United States stood at only 228,000 (Thornton and Marsh-Thornton 1981:48). This was a dreadful decline no matter what the starting point might have been. Artificially inflating the initial figure does not make the accomplishments of Native North Americans any more impressive, or their devastating population decline any more tragic.

Surviving the Colonial Era

Even in the face of devastating population decline the Indians north of Mexico were able to hold their own so long as they could play the colonial powers off each other. This balancing act ended permanently at least in the East when the British expelled France from virtually all the continent with the Treaty of Paris, which concluded their war over North America in 1763. Surviving North American Indians were subjects of either England or Spain after that date, with decreasing political leverage. This did not change much as various colonies became independent from the colonial powers from the 1770s on. Fortunately for the native peoples of what is now the United States, the 1787 Constitution gives special status to American Indian nations. This provision has played a significant role in their long-term survival, as well as in the conduct of modern archaeology, as is briefly explained later in this chapter.

American Indian societies typically retreated in the face of European colonization in the first three centuries of contact. The effects of epidemics reduced their populations, and the adaptive advantages of gunpowder, steel, and state political organizations made the Europeans impossible to resist over the long term. Spanish colonial administration moved quickly to subject the native peoples of Mexico, Guatemala, and what is now the southwestern United States. The migration of Spanish colonists to North America was not heavy and there was much intermarriage with American Indians. The result was that although many native communities survived in culturally modified form, a very large fraction of the Spanish-speaking population of North America came to be made up of mestizos, people of mixed European and American Indian ancestry. Much of this is now being explored by historical archaeologists, but that burgeoning branch of the discipline is beyond the scope of this book.

History also played out differently in the United States and Canada. French-speaking colonists from Quebec frequently intermarried with American Indians, but intermarriage was rarer in the United States and western Canada. Instead, a frontier formed between Indian country and the growing English-speaking colonies of the East Coast of North America.

Conflict in the Nineteenth Century

The independent nations that arose from European colonies expanded or contracted to their current boundaries in the nineteenth century. American Indian communities either retreated in the face of this expansion or were confined to small remnants of their former territories. Western Indian tribes often ceded large amounts of land to the United States in the treaties of the nineteenth century. But they also retained large parcels as reservations. These are typically maintained today for the joint use of enrolled tribal members. Something similar unfolded in Canada, where Indian-owned lands are referred to as "reserves." Canadian reserves tend to be smaller residential communities, with their Indian residents retaining access to nearby unreserved lands. In Mexico and elsewhere in Mesoamerica native communities tended to persist much as they had for centuries, often in areas remote from centers of population and political power. Their survival was partly because their settlements and subsistence practices were more similar to those of the dominant Hispanic culture.

Generally speaking, Indian reservations in the United States were located within what already were or would become states under the terms of the U.S. Constitution, but states had no jurisdiction over them unless it was specifically conveyed by the federal government. Tribes that were located inside the boundaries of the original 13 colonies were in ambiguous circumstances throughout the nineteenth century and through much of the twentieth, because it was advantageous to the 13 founding states to consider surviving Indian communities as exempt from the provisions of the United States Constitution. Some even made their only treaties with tribes within their boundaries, believing that they were not subject to the same constitutional restrictions as the western states. Legal cases in the late twentieth century led the courts to decide that such tribes were, in fact, not exempt from the constitutional provision and laws that built upon it, a decision that has already led to several outcomes that have been advantageous to the Indians. Illegal treaties between some states and some Indian tribes have been overturned, and some other old treaties remain in question.

Overall the history of Indian relations to federal and state governments in the nineteenth century was one in which the Indians almost invariably lost land and independence (Banner 2005). The reasons for this are all contained in Figure 1.5 and discussion of it in Chapter 1. State and imperial organizations outcompete chiefdoms, tribes, and bands. When they conflict or simply do business with each other the more complex of them almost always prevails to the detriment of the less complex. It should be no surprise that Indian nations withdrew to smaller territories in the nineteenth century, or that these territories shrank as other interests whittled away at them. The destitution of many of them is well known, and some authors have even compared reservations to concentration camps. Ironically, however, it seems clear in retrospect that many Native American nations would have disappeared altogether, and individual American Indians would have vanished into the general U.S. population over time, had reservations not preserved their home bases.

Modern American Indians

Against the odds, and contrary to most expectations, American Indian cultures rebounded strongly in the twentieth century. Over 4 million people indicated that they were Native Americans in the 2000 United States national census. The number of people claiming Indian descent is undoubtedly higher than the total number of formally enrolled tribal members, but in any case it is clear that there are more American Indians in the United States today than lived in the same territory when Columbus arrived in 1492. This has been a remarkable reversal of the downward trend seen in the nineteenth century.

In 1999 Canada set off a large portion of the previously unincorporated Northwest Territories as a new province, one dominated by its scattered population of around 30,000 Inuit residents. Nunavut is the newest province of the Canadian confederation.

In twentieth-century Mexico the lands around many traditional Indian communities were converted into collective *ejidos*, but this system was abandoned by the end of the century. Indigenous communities in Mexico and Guatemala are recognized as having special status, but they do not have the reservation system of the United States or the reserve system of Canada.

The legal cases of the late twentieth century also made it clear that most recognized tribes on reservation lands in the United States were not governed by state laws. The exceptions were those cases where the federal government had explicitly turned over law enforcement on reservations to state authorities. Many things, including the regulation of gambling, are left to the states under U.S. laws. Thus many Indian reservations are not covered by state prohibitions on gambling, or prohibited from selling untaxed tobacco and gasoline. Consequently, many Indian tribes decided to open casinos and other enterprises on reservation lands as a means to generate income. Those near population centers have been quite successful, although the flow of money has sometimes also brought corruption. The Abramoff scandal of 2006 involved millions of dollars of Indian casino money and the bribery of several Washington politicians.

Many traditional American Indians have objected to the money-making schemes that reservation status has made possible. They have feared the corrupting influence of money made from selling tax-free gasoline and cigarettes as well as the larger profits coming from casinos. Their views appear in retrospect to have been accurate in several cases. On the positive side, the new Museum of the American Indian in Washington is the most recent addition to the array of units that make up the Smithsonian Institution. Part of it was financed by the recent financial successes of several contributor tribes. The opening of the new museum occasioned a parade of American Indians from all over both American continents, but especially from the United States. The new museum looks forward rather than backward in time, and its main message is that American Indian societies are alive and well in the twenty-first century.

There are hundreds of American Indian communities on and off reservations and reserves in North America. Lists of these can be found by simply searching

"Native American Nations" online. In some cases native languages are still spoken by large numbers of people. In other cases there are programs to preserve dying languages, while in many other cases their languages are already extinct. Even those communities that no longer speak native languages still preserve many native customs. These are flamboyantly expressed at periodic convocations called "powwows," at which native crafts, food, costumes, and dancing are all on display (Figure 15.3).

Some American Indians enjoy productive careers as artists. They typically blend traditional motifs and materials with more contemporary ones, and some of them have high standing in the art world. The artists of the Southwest are especially well known, but so too are individual artists from the Northwest Coast, the Northeast, and all other regions of the continent.

Figure 15.3 Tepee camp at a Lame Deer, Montana, powwow, showing both traditional and modern technology.
Source: Courtesy of Dolores and Tom Elliott.

Box 15.1 HOW TO EAT NATIVE AMERICAN FOOD

The very best way to experience Native American food is to get to Washington, DC, by whatever means available and dine at the Mitsitam restaurant at the National Museum of the American Indian. *Mitsitam* is a Delaware and Piscataway expression meaning "let's eat." The restaurant offers up an extraordinary array of dishes inspired by cuisines from all over the hemisphere, an impressive feat given that it must be done food-court style to very large numbers of visitors. The food is excellent, the service is immediate, and in my experience there is no waiting for a table.

If travel to Washington is out of the question, another alternative is to acquire the cookbook titled *Foods of the Americas: Native Recipes and Traditions* by Fernando and Marlene Divina. Their recipes have inspired the cuisine offered at Mitsitam. There are modern twists to make it easier for someone to find the necessary ingredients in most supermarkets. However, close examination of the cookbook reveals two important things. First, no modern cuisine stands alone and can get by without ingredients that would not have been available to it five centuries ago. For example, Italian cuisine makes heavy use of tomatoes, but tomatoes are South American and they were not much used in Italy until the seventeenth century. The Asian spices that are indispensable to modern American palates were not available in Europe let alone America prior to the age of exploration. The second thing that becomes obvious is that Native America contributed significantly to the foods of the world. It is difficult to imagine life today without maize, maple syrup, wild rice, tomatoes, or avocados, to name just a few.

The adventurous wishing to experience Native American food as it was before the worldwide interchange of ingredients can try eliminating non-American ingredients and substituting where necessary. Honey and maple syrup are good substitutes for refined sugar; water substitutes for milk. Native Americans had access to hickory or sunflower oil, and although they probably more often used animal fat modern cooks can be forgiven if they stay with vegetable oil.

Native American cooks did not have baking powder or baking soda five centuries ago. Neither was in wide use until the middle of the nineteenth century. Lime or ashes were used to break down corn meal and still can be, but this does not produce the leavening we have come to expect in our bread and other baked goods. An alternative is to use a yeast starter, mix it with corn meal, acorn, or other dough and allow it to rise for a few hours. Some sourdough strains have been going for a century or more and these make perfectly good starters.

Another thing that Native Americans did not have was deep-frying equipment. Fry bread made from processed flour is a popular modern Native American treat, but not something that was part of their ancient cuisine. Indeed, this and other recent additions to their diets have been blamed for soaring rates of obesity and diabetes in modern communities.

A century ago no one could have guessed that American Indians would be thriving in the twenty-first century. Well-intended officials were preaching assimilation, bureaucrats were advocating the dissolution of reservations, and even elderly Indian leaders themselves were predicting the end. It was a period in which aging Indian leaders often turned over culturally significant objects to museums because they thought that was the only way they would be preserved into the future. Anthropologists scrambled to record the details of American Indian cultures before they died out. But all of this presumed that American Indian cultures were brittle systems capable only of either staying the same or falling to pieces. In fact they were, of course, like all human cultures, dynamic and ever-changing systems that could adapt to even rapidly changing circumstances. No one can know how they will evolve from this point forward, but one way or another they will be part of whatever America is another century from now.

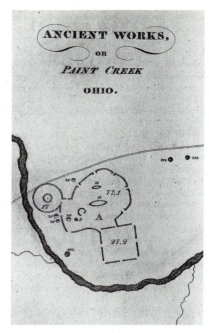

Figure 15.4 Portion of a map showing archaeological sites along Paint Creek in Ohio, published by Caleb Atwater in 1820, opposite page 145.

The Development of Archaeology

Serious archaeological interest in the origins of American Indians got a promising start with Thomas Jefferson's investigations late in the eighteenth century (see Chapter 5). But public interest soon became mired in fantasy. To understand the false starts and detours in the development of archaeology in the nineteenth century one must bear in mind the contemporaneous history of American Indians described previously. Publications that attempted to explain American Indians as the descendants of one of the lost tribes of Israel were particularly popular. Moundbuilder mythology grew up as another ingredient in the popular stew of nonsense written about American Indians in this era (Silverberg 1968). Caleb Atwater (1820), the postmaster of Circleville Ohio, wrote about the mounds in the local countryside and did a reasonably good job of separating his observations from fanciful speculation about them (Figure 15.4). But speculative conclusions were more popular than sober descriptions like Atwater's, and efforts by a few writers to give the American Indians their due were largely ignored. The result was that virtually nothing written during the half century after Jefferson's work has survived as part of the foundation for modern archaeology. It was not an era when the popular Euro-American imagination gave much time or credit to American Indians.

The situation finally improved in 1848 with the publication of Ephraim Squier and E. H. Davis's (1848)

Ancient Monuments of the Mississippi Valley by the Smithsonian Institution. Squier had been commissioned in 1845 by the American Ethnological Society to report on the mounds of Ohio. Along with Davis he surveyed and excavated mounds not just in Ohio but across much of the Eastern Woodlands. The Smithsonian had been established by Congress around the same time, and it quickly set a new scientific standard for archaeological research, which it continues to uphold today. For example, the Squier and Davis map showed many mounds and other earthworks around the city of Chillicothe, Ohio (Figure 15.5). It is hard for us to appreciate now the extraordinary difficulty Squier and Davis faced in their efforts to locate, travel to, survey, and test excavate hundreds of mounds in an era before roads and rail transportation were generally available. Squire and Davis recorded many mounds that were later razed to make way for agriculture or destroyed by treasure hunters. Their detailed maps and notes are sometimes all that remain of these important earthen monuments. Samuel Haven's *Archaeology of the United States*, which the Smithsonian also published less than a decade later, continued the new tradition of scientific rigor and a commitment to avoid speculation beyond what the available evidence could support.

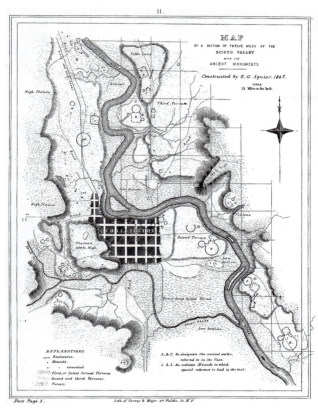

Figure 15.5 Hopewell mounds and earthworks in the vicinity of Chillicothe, Ohio, as mapped by Ephraim Squier in 1847. *Source:* From Squier and Davis 1848, facing page 3.

Figure 15.6 The Cardiff Giant, a nineteenth-century fake that still gets attention at the Farmers Museum in Cooperstown, New York.

Frauds, Fantasies, and Body Snatching

Unfortunately, the nineteenth century is also rich with archaeological fakery, fantasy, and skulduggery. Early archaeologists were beginning to discover the civilizations of Mesoamerica and map the earthen mound sites of the Eastern Woodlands, but sober reality revealed by that work seemed to not be enough. There was a "money-digger" craze during the early part of the century. A partnership between entrepreneurial con artists and gullible shovelers produced a landscape pockmarked by holes dug in search of lost Spanish and other treasures that were never found. The con artists used magic stones, divining rods, and other ridiculous occult devices to deceive themselves and their friends into believing they could get rich quick.

As the money-digging craze faded, clever entrepreneurs turned to creating fakes for fun and profit. Some of them were indeed just for fun, but then as now archaeological jokes often got out of hand. Practical jokers still often discover too late that their friends are much more gullible than expected, and the potential for socially disastrous embarrassment has led many a joker to tiptoe away from his creation with the hope that his victims will lose interest and it will all just go away (Rose 2005). Often it does not, and the prankster has to learn how to live with the consequences.

The grandest of the nineteenth-century hoaxes were the contrived "petrified" human remains that were carved, buried, then caused to be uncovered here and there around the country. The biggest of them was the 10-foot-tall Cardiff Giant (Figure 15.6), planted near Syracuse, New York, in 1868 and dug up by a couple carefully directed but unsuspecting well diggers the following year. The faker sold the crude statue for $23,000. P. T. Barnum could not acquire the original cheaply enough to suit his budget, so he made money by exhibiting a fake copy of the fake. Other fakers made other fakes, but the public appetite for them declined with time, and by the end of the century the market for petrified men was bust. The Cardiff Giant ended up at the Farmer's Museum in Cooperstown, New York, where despite the best efforts of an honest museum staff at least some casual visitors still go away thinking that it is authentic (Feder 2002; Rose 2005).

Moundbuilder mythology developed in the wake of the money diggers and the petrified man hoaxes. It was a natural outgrowth of the westward migration of Euro-American settlers. Explorers and early settlers came across thousands of earthen mounds, some of them very large and impressive burial or temple mounds described by Squier and Davis. There seemed to the newcomers that there could be no link between the mounds and the decimated Indian cultures that were still extant, some of them just barely so. There was also little inclination to attribute impressive monuments to the ancestors of people that Euro-Americans were eager to displace and if necessary to exterminate. Accordingly, the earthen monuments were attributed to a mythical lost population of moundbuilders, and in the popular imagination of the nineteenth century these folks had almost nothing to do with later American Indian cultures. The exception was that in some imaginary accounts the superior moundbuilders had been victimized by the late-arriving American Indians. Fictional accounts of moundbuilders were popular for decades, but all of them have to be understood in terms of nineteenth century America, not the millennia of American Indian history that came before that (Persuitte 2000). If the moundbuilder mythology were still popular today it would be found mainly in supermarket tabloids.

The nineteenth century was also the heyday of body snatching for fun and profit. Grave robbing was a popular pastime in nineteenth-century America. Some of it was motivated by serious science; medical professionals needed cadavers for study and training and biological anthropologists sought answers to questions about the origins of Native Americans. But neither any sensitivity to the relatives of the deceased nor even-handed respect for unmarked burials of any kind was very much in evidence. Indian burials containing grave offerings were routinely excavated for their artifacts.

The stench that rose from violated graves clung to the clothing of archaeologists longer than that of physicians, probably because the medical profession cleaned up its practices earlier than the archaeological profession did. By the time of Alfred Kroeber's work in the early twentieth century most anthropologists were at least mindful of the sensitivities surrounding the recently deceased and those in marked graves. Kroeber was outraged at the treatment of his friend Ishi's body after his death in 1916, as mentioned in Chapter 13.

The Rise of Archaeological Science

Museums in America are largely a nineteenth-century phenomenon. Cities and universities developed them for many of the same reasons that they foster football teams today. Museums were entertaining, but they were also important community status symbols when they were built. Archaeology flourished in the early museums as the revolution in stratigraphic excavation spread to America from Europe and directors sought to fill exhibit cases. Major universities like Harvard and Yale received endowments from wealthy donors to develop university museums, and many others followed their example.

Museums often focused on natural history broadly defined. At the time, most people assumed that American Indian cultures were destined to die out, so their archaeological remains were typically consigned to natural history museums, along with the remains of dodos, mammoths, stuffed bisons, and other extinct or soon-to-be-extinct creatures.

Because of their common interests in American Indians, archaeologists and ethnologists found themselves housed together in departments of anthropology in most North American museums and universities. This did not happen in Europe, where archaeology and ethnology were largely separate activities, and they developed there as separate disciplines. At larger universities Mediterranean archaeologists were also housed in classics departments, but again unlike in Europe the two groups did not have much to do with each other.

By the second half of the nineteenth century universities and colleges were burgeoning, and archaeologists scattered among them were largely following the lead of the Smithsonian. Wealthy donors endowed both the museums and expeditions to bring back things to fill their cases. Harvard University's Peabody Museum took a leadership role, but there were several others. In the same era, the Smithsonian Institution established the Bureau of American Ethnology, using supplementary congressional funding. The new bureau was headed by John Wesley Powell, the one-armed Civil War veteran who led the first boat expedition down the Colorado River. He appointed Cyrus Thomas to head the Bureau of American Ethnology (BAE) Division of Mound Exploration in 1882. A dozen years later Thomas's huge report described hundreds of sites and finally put an end to the moundbuilder mythology.

The Lure of Diffusionism

The turn of the twentieth century brought more sober archaeology, and the beginnings of a reversal in the fortunes of American Indians. Unfortunately, fundamental assumptions about the rarity of innovation in the discipline of anthropology, and lingering doubts about the ingenuity of people generally and American Indians in particular led to another protracted detour in American archaeology.

The similarity between the endpoints of cultural evolution in the Americas and those seen in other parts of the world, combined with pernicious skepticism about the innate abilities of American Indians as a whole for many years have prompted people to look across the oceans for sources of prehistoric inspiration. They have looked not for inspiration for themselves of course, but for inspiration for things archaeological that they cannot imagine the people of the Americas could have come up with on their own. Such retroactive outsourcing goes well beyond the search for rune stones by the sons of Norway or the search for Portuguese words in Algonquian languages by people who just happen to be of Portuguese extraction. Pride in one's own ancestry can sometimes outstrip rationality. But beyond that common failing, there was for many years a widespread implicit belief that cleverness is not a widespread human trait, and that any good idea most likely arose only once and then spread from its point of origin to all of the places where it was later found (Feder 2002; Williams 1991).

The assumption that people in the past were not very inventive focused attention and admiration on the presumed single origins of important developments such as writing, calendrics, pottery manufacture, and metallurgy. This made sense in the context of the industrial revolution, when the idea of brilliant inventors and patented inventions became widespread. Even slow collective processes came to be retrofitted with single inventors. The attribution of the invention of baseball to Abner Doubleday is a good example of this kind of crediting after the fact. In fact baseball developed slowly over time and in many places, eventually becoming more codified so that teams from distant locations could play each other occasionally using the same sets of rules. It was a nice gesture to honor Doubleday, a Civil War hero, but his was just one of many contributions to the game.

The result for archaeology was the diffusionist schools of interpretation, which was popular in the early twentieth century. If people were generally unimaginative and something like the invention of pottery probably occurred only once, then a reasonable task for archaeology was to track it back to its single point of origin. One could then reconstruct the way in which the idea "diffused" over time and space. This school of thought reached its height in the German "Kulturkreis" school, the model for which was concentric culture circles spreading out from a common point like ripples on the surface of a pond. But it turns out that unlike related languages that must descend from common ancestral languages, or biological traits that must have originated in single mutations, cultural traits appear independently more often and more spontaneously, and their spread does not often look much like ripples on a pond.

Certainly there are cases of unique inventions and rapid diffusion, as the origin and spread of the Ghost Dance in nineteenth-century North America illustrates. Modern fads like the spread of the hula hoop often replicate this kind of single origin and rapid spread. But many adaptive culture traits have arisen multiple times in unrelated contexts when circumstances have been right. Pottery, writing, calendars, mound building, and many other traits have all arisen independently more than once. Just as significant, inventions of this kind will almost certainly occur when the right conditions are at hand. Had Edison not invented the electric light surely someone else would have done so very soon, for once the conditions are right someone will make the connections necessary for such an invention to take place.

Outdated assumptions about the nature of innovation has a darker side. Even the people who claimed to see Egyptian writing in the walls of New England gardens probably meant no offense to American Indians, but the phenomenon is in fact more insidious in its implications. The notion that American Indians would not have come up with pyramid structures, large stone monuments, or the zero concept without inspiration from across the ocean is more than just incorrect, it is egregious. Fortunately, time and a more nobly inspired skepticism have done away with the notions that American pyramids were inspired by Egyptians, that Olmec heads came from Africa, or that Maya arithmetic had to have originated in India. Thor Heyerdahl's stunts and Erich von Däniken's lucrative hoaxes have largely faded from popular memory. The American Indians now usually get the credit they deserve.

Evidence and debate has sharpened the logic of modern archaeology. Even popular books now emphasize the role of environment in limiting or facilitating the exercise of human ingenuity, which turns out to be not just widespread but ubiquitous (Diamond 1997). If the conditions are right for mound building, people will not sit around waiting unknowingly for the idea to reach them from some distant source. Mound building will arise spontaneously in conditions like those described in Chapter 5, and it has done so several times around the world, perhaps more than once just in the Eastern Woodlands of North America. However, such an idea may well then spread to adjacent areas where conditions are close to but not quite ready for independent invention of the idea. So trait diffusion does occur, as countless examples attest, but it is not the only process at work.

All that said, some fascinating facts remain unexplained. Bark beaters and associated processes for making paper found in Mexico are remarkably similar to those found in Southeast Asia (Tolstoy 1991). Sweet potatoes that originated in South America were being grown in the Pacific islands when the first European explorers landed there. Shell fishhooks found on the coast of California appear identical to and derived from others found in Polynesia (Jones and Klar 2005). In cases like these the similarities are too numerous and too specific to be ignored. At the same time it is fair to say that none of these examples tells us that American cultures were imported (or for that matter exported) wholesale prior to 1492. These are small but intriguing puzzles that might be evidence of the occasional chance survival of a handful of castaways. Such possibilities are intriguing to us because they are at an understandable human scale. It is easy to imagine oneself as that castaway, washing up on the shore of America with little to offer in exchange for being allowed to live. Plenty of people had that experience after 1492, and most of them disappeared into the native populations, leaving not a ripple on the flow of history. But a few, like the Spaniards gone native that helped Cortes and de Soto, had an impact on the course of history, and maybe (just maybe) there were a few others like them centuries before.

The Rise of Professional Archaeology

At the beginning of the twentieth century archaeology was largely the domain of rich gentlemen, but legislation, economics, and shifts in national cultures changed everything over the decades that followed. In the United States, Theodore Roosevelt signed the Antiquities Act on June 8, 1906. The act provided for the protection of archaeological sites on federal land and authorized the president to designate important federally owned sites or regions as national monuments. Roosevelt declared 18 himself before leaving office, starting with Devils Tower, Wyoming, soon after signing the bill into law (Harmon et al. 2006).

Archaeology was still conducted mainly by universities and museums until the coming of the Great Depression, which led to a boom in field archaeology. Federal work programs like the Works Progress Administration (WPA) and the Civilian Conservation Corps (CCC) sometimes focused on archaeological excavations, which were often conducted with surprising skill and accuracy. Huge collections and records from these projects are still being analyzed by archaeologists today.

Archaeology became a growing part of many anthropology programs in colleges and universities after World War II, absorbing many professionals who had got their start in depression-era programs. Archaeology grew along with other academic disciplines when the baby-boom generation reached college age and postsecondary institutions grew rapidly in both numbers and sizes. At the same time archaeology shifted from an interest in culture history to more scientific pursuits, and this opened up additional new funding opportunities for researchers and students.

Probably the most significant recent change in American archaeology was stimulated by federal legislation requiring the mitigation of the adverse effects of any federally funded project on archaeological resources. There are several such laws, and the lead agency for archaeology, the National Park Service, has compiled them in a government publication for handy reference (Anonymous 2002). The Antiquities Act of 1906 has already been mentioned. Other milestone laws to protect archaeological resources followed, and they were all significant. However, the National Historic Preservation Act of 1966 stands out because of its broad scope and proactive approach to preservation. Section 106 of that legislation created a whole new arm of professional archaeology.

Section 106

The head of any Federal agency having direct or indirect jurisdiction over a proposed Federal or federally assisted undertaking in any State and the head of any Federal department or independent agency having authority to license any undertaking shall, prior to the approval of the expenditure of any Federal funds on the undertaking or prior to the issuance of any license, as the case may be, take into account the effect of the undertaking on any district, site, building, structure, or object that is included in or eligible for inclusion in the National Register. The head of any such Federal agency shall afford the Advisory Council on Historic Preservation established under Title II of this Act a reasonable opportunity to comment with regard to such undertaking. (Anonymous 2002:59)

This sweeping provision (note how often the word "any" is used) established a mechanism in the United States for archaeological research in anticipation of undertakings that involved any amount of federal funding, both on public and private lands. Many states followed with their own supporting legislation, which was often more stringent. Similar laws were established in Canada. In Mexico archaeology had long been in the domain of a government ministry named the Instituto Nacional de Antropología e Historia (INAH). The budget and responsibilities of INAH were similarly strengthened through the later twentieth century. Guatemala and other Mesoamerican countries tended to follow the Mexican model.

The Archaeological Resources Protection Act became U.S. law in 1979. This law went beyond mandating government agencies to protect archaeological resources to criminalizing looting on public or Indian land. Section 6 is a key provision.

> No person may excavate, remove, damage, or otherwise alter or deface or attempt to excavate, remove, damage, or otherwise alter or deface any archaeological resource located on public lands or Indian lands unless such activity is pursuant to a permit (Anonymous 2002:144).

Since the passage of these laws the archaeological profession has grown exponentially. There are probably 10,000 professional archaeologists working in the United States today, and archaeology is a billion-dollar business. Most new opportunities are not in traditional teaching posts or museum positions but rather in businesses and governmental agencies. The successes of modern archaeology have created many new careers, but they have also generated huge quantities of curated artifacts, databases, and documents. Coping with all this information and distilling it for the benefit of the public that has paid for it all now is a major new challenge for archaeology.

Another new challenge is in the proper training and preparation of the next generation of archaeologists. Most senior archaeologists came into the field when it was the domain of academics and a few government employees. All of that has changed, and the kinds of programs needed to prepare archaeologists for a profession that is increasingly nonacademic are still being developed in our colleges and universities.

Box 15.2 HOW TO PROTECT ARCHAEOLOGICAL RESOURCES

Everyone enjoys an unexpected find, and when we see a quarter on the sidewalk most of us assume that it is finders keepers. However, that is not the case with archaeological artifacts. It is illegal to remove anything from publicly owned lands because everything on them is owned collectively by us all. It is also illegal to remove anything from private land without the permission of the landowner.

Agencies that care for public property are required to inventory archaeological resources and to ensure their protection and preservation in the long term. They employ archaeologists, part of whose job it is to catalog and curate artifacts found on that property. Visitors who find things on public land are legally and ethically bound to turn them in.

Landowners and those having permission to collect from landowners are less constrained, but not entirely free to do whatever they wish. Like endangered species, unmarked graves, particularly those of American Indians, are protected by law. It is illegal to disturb them except under the terms of various federal, state, and local laws.

In cases where collecting is legal and landowners are agreeable, protection of archaeological resources is a matter of ethics. The number of projectile points that have been picked up, stored in cigar boxes or coffee cans for a few decades, then discarded is probably in the millions. Picking up a point without recording its context and providing for the preservation of both the point and its associated record is like tearing a page out of the only copy of an ancient manuscript. Archaeological resources are finite, and we owe it to future generations to act as good stewards. Unfortunately, even the most careful and responsible collector will not live forever, so we must all do what we can to ensure preservation in perpetuity. I do not assume that my heirs will necessarily treasure the past as much as I do.

No reputable archaeologist condones looting, or even the collection of artifacts in plain view for fun and profit. To discourage digging or collecting for profit professional archaeologists will decline to assign monetary value to any archaeological artifact. This may put an individual in a bind if he or she wishes to get a tax break in exchange for donation of a collection to a nonprofit institution. One solution is to calculate the accumulated costs of acquiring and curating the artifacts for tax purposes. This is how courts compute damages in looting cases, and in such cases professional assistance is available.

At a minimum, collecting carries with it the following legal and ethical requirements:

- Obtaining formal permission from the landowner.
- Making a commitment to record the precise location of each object, preferably by GPS.
- Creating a permanent recording system (paper and electronic).
- Curating artifacts under conditions that prevent deterioration.
- Planning for curation in perpetuity of both the artifacts and the records.

Archaeology and American Indians

Relations between early archaeologists and American Indians did not get off to a good start, and the search for common ground has taken many years. Denigration of American Indians, the looting of their ancestral graves, dismissal of their oral traditions, and other offenses both real and imagined plagued relations until late in the twentieth century. The Society for American Archaeology elected Arthur C. Parker, an American Indian, as its first president in 1934. Unfortunately that did not immediately lead to better relations between American Indians and archaeologists, who were mostly men and mostly of European descent. However, recent decades have brought a new diversity to the ranks of American archaeologists, and a growing fraction of their numbers is made up of people of American Indian descent. This trend, the articulation of new ethical standards, the growth of nonacademic archaeology, and the vigorous growth of archaeology as a scientific discipline are all leading to a new more inclusive and more rigorous profession.

There is a new sense of cooperation between archaeologists and American Indians at the beginning of the twenty-first century. Vitriolic dismissals of archaeological science, like Vine Deloria's assertion that the idea that "Indians came first via the Bering Strait [is] a myth with little to recommend it" are fading (Thomas 2000:xv). So, too, are positions like Robert Lowie's (1915) assertion that American Indian oral tradition is worthless as a source of information for scientific research. It turns out that oral tradition is one of several sources for testable hypotheses in archaeological science, and archaeologists are making increasing use of it. That cherished stories are sometimes disproven in the process is the price of having them taken seriously in the first place (Whiteley 2002). As more American Indians become archaeologists the perceived clash between science and oral tradition will continue to fade (Gidwitz 2007; Grier and Shaver 2008; Watkins 2003).

The Native American Graves Protection and Repatriation Act

It was common for human skeletons, including but not limited to American Indian ones, to be put on display in museums through the first three-quarters of the twentieth century. The Smithsonian Institution's National Museum of Natural History once displayed a whole wall of human skulls. As the status of American Indians rose and their version of the civil rights movement played out such exhibits were increasingly targeted by Indian activists. Exhibits of human skeletons, Indian or otherwise, gradually disappeared from museums and archaeological sites in the United States and Canada.

At the same time Native American organizations petitioned Congress for a new law protecting unmarked graves and mandating the return of human remains and sacred objects known to be affiliated with living communities. Archaeology was shifting away from excavation and toward preservation around the same time, so the two found common cause. American Indians and archaeologists working together with politicians crafted the language of the Native American Graves Protection and Repatriation Act (NAGPRA), which was signed into law in 1990. Farsighted anthropologists realized that the new law would force funding for the proper analysis and description of thousands of boxed skeletons, which was necessary to inventory them and to determine which tribes should be notified. In many cases this was something that had not been attended to for decades.

NAGPRA required that human remains that could be identified with living tribes be repatriated, along with associated grave offerings. Coverage was also extended to sacred objects, whether or not they came from graves. The law provided for creation of a committee to decide disputed claims but it left open the question of how to treat skeletal remains that were clearly American Indian but could not be identified with any particular living community. It was only a matter of time before a high-profile case would end up in the courts.

Kennewick Man

A nearly complete skeleton was found along the banks of the Columbia River near Kennewick, Washington, in July 1996. James Chatters was the first archaeologist to look at the remains and his first impression was that the features of the skull made it look more European than American Indian. He hypothesized that the individual was male and probably an early Euro-American settler. The popular press picked up the story along with the initial observation that the skeleton appeared to be "Caucasoid."

Most people still think of human variations in terms of racial categories, so the adjective "Caucasoid" was soon transformed to the noun "Caucasian" by the popular press. Further research showed that not only did the skeleton have an ancient stone point tip embedded in its pelvis, radiocarbon dating revealed that it was more than 9,000 years old. Like others of that age the Kennewick skull had features that differed from those of modern American Indians, which had prompted Chatters's comment. The popular press published pictures of the reconstructed head, which (mainly because it was bald) looked eerily like the actor Patrick Stewart. It looked like a good many bald American Indians, too. Claims came in from several quarters. A group called the Asatru Folk Assembly (Asatruans) claimed the skeleton on grounds of its supposed European ancestry. An alliance of several tribes in Oregon and Washington also filed a claim on grounds of proximity.

The case has provoked considerable discussion in the archaeological profession (Owsley and Jantz 2001; Swedlund and Anderson 1999; Thomas 2000). After additional research the Department of the Interior ruled that the skeleton should be repatriated to the Umatilla tribe and its allies. A group of professional archaeologists opposed to repatriation argued that cultural affiliation could not be demonstrated, and it filed a lawsuit to prevent it from being turned over to the confederated tribes.

The Society for American Archaeology submitted a brief as a friend of the court in which it was argued that the skeleton was clearly Native American but that it could not be affiliated with any living tribe, as required by the law. This position was on the middle ground between the claims of the plaintiffs and those of the defendants in the case. In 2004 the court held that Kennewick Man should not be repatriated because it was unaffiliated, and went further to rule that because of a flaw in the law's language the Kennewick remains could not even be regarded as American Indian.

The flaw in NAGPRA language could be fixed quickly and easily, but it might take more cases like Kennewick to clarify how unaffiliated human remains will be treated in the future (Bruning 2006). Meanwhile, a new if still uneasy alliance between professional archaeologists and American Indians is emerging, a process speeded by the entry of more Native Americans into professional archaeology. All of this is being hurried along as Americans in general and attorneys in particular find their interest in forensic archaeology to be growing rapidly. Now when a skeleton turns up along an eroding shore there are many interested parties, and a need for a new kind of archaeology.

Conclusion

The Americas were first peopled over 140 centuries ago by hunter-gatherers expanding eastward out of Siberia, equipped with speech, keen intelligence, lethal weapons, warm clothing, companion dogs, and a healthy curiosity. In most or all of those respects they were like all other humans alive at that time. The potential for much more resided unexpressed in all of them even at this early date. When the long age of Pleistocene winter finally waned a new Holocene epoch brought relatively greater stability and predictability to the world's environments. This in turn relaxed constraints on human ingenuity, and the long slowly accelerating shift to plant domesticates, animal domesticates, and larger human populations unfolded wherever natural resources allowed.

Human cleverness is not a commodity that has ever been in short supply. Nevertheless we admire adaptive new ideas, and consider them rare. We award patents and copyrights to each other; we condemn plagiarism; we prosecute counterfeiters; we celebrate innovation. We only grudgingly admit that if Walter Hunt had not invented and patented the safety pin in 1849 someone else probably would have done so in short order. That is why we also harbor the implicit assumption that humankind's greatest accomplishments have been rare occurrences, that innovations are rare, and that most of us are copycats. That is why diffusionism was once so popular.

As excessively self-deprecating as that silent assumption may be it is a useful one for the scientific process because it assigns the burden of proof in a productive way. No scientist is going to be entirely comfortable with the simple assumption that something like plant domestication arose independently in a dozen places around the world if there is any possibility that it might have arisen just once and spread to other centers. After all, what we consider the simpler (and thus preferable) of those two hypotheses is conditioned by our shared assumptions about human nature.

Given those assumptions we are fortunate to have the Americas, *an other* world in which the emergence of all those things we consider to be the traits of civilization emerged separately prior to a mere five centuries ago. The astonishing similarities between the two cultural worlds of our planet after 14 millennia of separate evolution tells us much about ourselves as a species.

Globalization is not a phenomenon of the lifetimes of people still living. It began more than five centuries ago. If it is fair to say that Columbus discovered America for Europe in 1492, then it is also fair to say that the unnamed senior American Indian in the party he introduced to the king of Portugal the following spring were the American discoverers of Europe. One day in the fall of 1492 two groups of people stood staring at each other on an island in the Bahamas, each saying in their own language something like "Who *are* those guys?" The rest is history, of course. The enthusiastic exchange of vocabulary, plants, animals, ideas, technology, and germs that followed was frenzied globalization that has continued ever since.

The sharp edges of culture contact in North America have finally dulled. If cultural differences seem never to allow everything to quite reach equilibrium, there is at least a shared sense of how differences should be resolved for the greater good. The archaeology of North America is not just for or about American Indians; these chapters have shown that it is much more than that.

I have been occasionally told by earnest and well-intentioned people that the study of the past is a waste of time. They claim that it is better to look forward than to look back, but they are wrong. Most of the colossal mistakes in human history have been made by people who have failed to learn key lessons from our past. It goes even deeper than that, because the trajectories of the past partially determine our future, and we cannot adequately predict our future without understanding our past. Archaeology is vital for our understanding of not just the origin and development of complex societies in general, but also the persistence of the many threads of cultural diversity found in the skein of modern human culture. North American archaeology is worth exploring because America before 1492 was a world too remote from today's ordinary experience to be merely imagined.

Summary

1. The European discovery of America initiated a collision between cultures that has continued for five centuries.

2. Estimates of the size of the population of North America in 1492 have varied by an order of magnitude, but a rational estimate for the number of people north of the Mexican desert is around 3.4 million.

3. There were probably about 5 million people living in Mesoamerica in 1492.

4. American Indian populations declined as they lost numbers and land, reaching a low point around the beginning of the twentieth century.

5. American Indian communities rebounded in the twentieth century.

6. Pseudoarchaeological myths about the American Indians prevailed in the early nineteenth century.

7. Professional archaeology became established in North America after the founding of the Smithsonian Institution and various large museums.

8. The federal programs of the era of the Great Depression made many contributions to archaeology.

9. The rapid growth of colleges and universities, as well as new laws promoting preservation and research, fostered many new programs in archaeology in the last third of the twentieth century.

10. Professional archaeology is an increasingly diverse field that now employs thousands of archaeologists.

Further Reading

Gordon Willey and Jeremy Sabloff provide *A History of American Archaeology,* now available in a third edition. Roger Kennedy's *Hidden Cities* covers the peculiar era of archaeological fantasy that followed Jefferson's early work. There are many good historical accounts of the collision of cultures in North America, and I recommend any of the books published by James Axtell or Francis Jennings. These will lead to the works of many other eminent ethnohistorians. Volume 4 of the *Handbook of North American Indians,* titled *History of Indian-White Relations,* will lead quickly to many specific sources.

Abbott, D. R. (editor) 2003 *Centuries of Decline during the Hohokam Classic Period at Pueblo Grande*. Tucson: University of Arizona Press.

Adovasio, J. M. 1979 The Fremont and the Sevier: Defining Prehistoric Agriculturalists North of the Anasazi, by David B. Madsen. *American Antiquity* 44(4):723–731.

Adovasio, J. M., D. J. Donahue and R. Stuckenrath 1990 The Meadowcroft Rockshelter Radiocarbon Chronology 1975–1990. *American Antiquity* 55(2):348–354.

Adovasio, J. M. and J. Pedler 2005 The Peopling of North America. In *North American Archaeology*, edited by T. R. Pauketat and D. D. Loren, pp. 30–55. Malden, MA: Blackwell.

Aguilera, C. 2001 *Códices de México*. Mexico City: Consejo Nacional de Ciencia y Tecnología.

Alley, R. B., J. Marotzke, W. D. Nordhaus, J. T. Overpeck, D. M. Peteet, R. A. Pielke Jr., R. T. Pierrehumbert, P. B. Rhines, T. F. Stocker, L. D. Talley and J. M. Wallace 2003 Abrupt Climate Change. *Science* 299:2005–2010.

Alroy, J. 2001a A Multispecies Overkill Simulation of the End-Pleistocene Megafaunal Mass Extinction. *Science* 292(5523):1893–1896.

Alroy, J. 2001b Response. *Science* 294:1459–1462.

Ames, K. M. 1985 Hierarchies, Stress, and Logistical Strategies among Hunter-Gatherers in Northwestern North America. In *Prehistoric Hunter-Gatherers*, pp. 155–180. New York: Academic Press.

1995 Chiefly Power and Household Production on the Northwest Coast. In *Foundations of Social Inequality*, edited by T. D. Price and G. M. Feinman. New York: Plenum Press.

2001 Slaves, Chiefs and Labour on the Northern Northwest Coast. *World Archaeology* 33(1):1–17.

2002 Going by Boat: The Forager-Collector Continuum at Sea. In *Beyond Foraging and Collecting: Evolutionary Change in Hunter-Gatherer Settlement Systems*, edited by B. Fitzhugh and J. Habu. New York: Kluwer Academic/ Plenum.

2005 The Place of Ozette in Northwest Coast Archaeology. In *Ozette Archaeological Project Research Report, Volume III, Ethnobotany and Wood Technology*, edited by D. L. Welchel. WSU Department of Anthropology Reports of Research, vol. 68. Seattle, WA: National Park Service.

Ames, K. M., D. E. Dumond, J. R. Glam and R. Minor 1998 Prehistory of the Southern Plateau. In *Plateau*, edited by D. E. Walker Jr., pp. 103–119. *Handbook of North American Indians*, vol. 12, W. C. Sturtevant, general editor. Washington, DC: Smithsonian Institution.

Ames, K. M. and H. D. G. Maschner 1999 *Peoples of the Northwest Coast: Their Archaeology and Prehistory*. New York: Thames and Hudson.

Anawalt, P. R. 1992 Ancient Cultural Contacts between Ecuador, West Mexico, and the American Southwest: Clothing Similarities. *Latin American Antiquity* 3(2):114–129.

Anders, F. and M. Jansen 1999 *Mexiko: Alte Handschriften beginnen zu sprechen*. Munich: Staatliches Museum für Völkerkunde.

Anderson, D. D. 1968 A Stone Age Campsite at the Gateway to America. *Scientific American* 218(6):24–33.

1984 Prehistory of North Alaska. In *Arctic*, edited by D. Damas, pp. 80–93. *Handbook of North American Indians*, vol. 5, W. C. Sturtevant, general editor. Washington, DC: Smithsonian Institution.

Anderson, D. G. 1990 Stability and Change in Chiefdom-Level Societies: An Examination of Mississippian Political Evolution on the South Atlantic Slope. In *Lamar Archaeology: Mississippian Chiefdoms in the Deep South*, edited by M. Williams and G. Shapiro. Tuscaloosa: University of Alabama Press.

1999 Examining Chiefdoms in the Southeast: An Application of Multiscalar Analysis. In *Great Towns and Regional Polities in the Prehistoric American Southwest and Southeast*, edited by J. E. Neitzel, pp. 215–241. Albuquerque: University of New Mexico Press.

Anderson, D. G. and M. K. Faught 1998 The Distribution of Fluted Paleoindian Projectile Points: Update 1998. *Archaeology of Eastern North America* 26:163–187.

Anderson, D. G. and J. C. Gillam 2000 Paleoindian Colonization of the Americas: Implications from an Examination of Physiography, Demography, and Artifact Distributions. *American Antiquity* 65:43–66.

2001 Paleoindian Interaction and Mating Networks: Reply to Moore and Moseley. *American Antiquity* 66(3):530–535.

Anderson, D. G., D. S. Miller, S. J. Yerka, J. C. Gillam and M. K. Faught 2005 Paleoindian Artifact distributions in the Southeast and Beyond. vol. 2009. University of Tennessee, Knoxville, Department of Anthropology.

Anderson, K. and T. C. Blackburn 1993 *Before the Wilderness: Environmental Management by Native Californians.* Anthropological Papers No. 40. Menlo Park, CA: Ballena Press.

Andrews, A. P. 1990 The Fall of Chichén Itzá: A Preliminary Hypothesis. *Latin American Antiquity* 1:258–267.

Andrews, A. P., E. W. Andrews and F. Robles Castellanos 2003 The Northern Maya Collapse and Its Aftermath. *Ancient Mesoamerica* 14(1):151–156.

Andrews, E. W. and W. L. Fash (editors) 2005 *Copán: The History of an Ancient Maya Kingdom.* Santa Fe, NM: SAR Press.

Anonymous 2002 *Federal Historic Preservation Laws.* Washington, DC: National Center for Cultural Resources, National Park Service.

Anthony, D. W. 1990 Migration in Archaeology: The Baby and the Bathwater. *American Anthropologist* 92:895–914.

Armillas, P. 1971 Gardens on Swamps. *Science* 174:653–661.

Arnold, D. E., J. R. Branden, P. R. Williams, G. M. Feinman and J. P. Brown 2008 The First Direct Evidence for the Production of Maya Blue: Rediscovery of a Technology. *Antiquity* 82(315):151–164.

Arnold, J. E. 2001 Social Evolution and the Political Economy in the Northern Channel Islands. In *The Origins of a Pacific Coast Chiefdom: The Chumas of the Channel Islands*, edited by J. E. Arnold, pp. 287–296. Salt Lake City: University of Utah Press.

Arnold, J. E. and T. M. Green 2002 Mortuary Ambiguity: The Ventureño Chumash Case. *American Antiquity* 67(4):760–771.

Arnold, J. E. and A. Munns 1994 Independent or Attached Specialization: The Organization of Shell Bead Production in California. *Journal of Field Archaeology* 21(4):473–489.

Arnold, P. J., III 2003 Early Formative Pottery from the Tuxtla Mountains and Implications for Gulf Olmec Origins. *Latin American Antiquity* 14(1):29–46.

Atwater, C. 1820 Description of the Antiquities Discovered in the State of Ohio and Other Western States. *Transactions and Collections of the American Antiquarian Society* 1:105–267.

Aveni, A. F. 1978 The Pecked Cross Symbol in Ancient Mesoamerica. *Science* 202:267–279.

Aveni, A. F. and E. E. Calnek 1999 Astronomical Considerations in the Aztec Expression of History. *Ancient Mesoamerica* 10(1):87–98.

Aveni, A. F., S. L. Gibbs and H. Hartung 1975 The Caracol Tower at Chichen Itza: An Ancient Astronomical Observatory? *Science* 188:977–985.

Axtell, R. L., J. M. Epstein, J. S. Dean, G. J. Gumerman, A. C. Swedlund, J. Harburger, S. Chakravarty, R. Hammond, J. Parker and M. Parker 2002 Population Growth and Collapse in a Multiagent Model of the Kayenta Anasazi in Long House Valley. *Proceedings of the National Academy of Sciences* 99:7187–7316.

Bacon, F. 1952 Advancement of Learning. In *Francis Bacon*, edited by R. M. Hutchins, pp. 1–101, vol. 30. Chicago: Encyclopaedia Britannica.

Bamforth, D. B. 1988 *Ecology and Human Organization on the Great Plains.* New York: Plenum Press.

Banner, S. 2005 *How the Indians Lost Their Land.* Cambridge, MA: Belknap Press.

Barba, L. A. and J. L. Córdova Frunz 1999 Estudios Energéticos de la Producción de Cal en Tiempos Teotihuacanos y sus Implicaciones. *Latin American Antiquity* 10(2):168–179.

Barber, R. J. 1977 Disjunct Plant Distributions and Archaeological Interpretation. *Man in the Northeast* 13:103–107.

Barker, A. W. 1992 Powhatan's Pursestrings: On the Meaning of Surplus in a Seventeenth Century Algonkian Chiefdom. In *Lords of the Southeast: Social Inequality and the Native Elites of Southeastern North America*, edited by A. W. Barker and T. R. Pauketat, pp. 61–80. Archaeological Papers of the American Anthropological Association, vol. 3. Washington, DC: American Anthropological Association.

Barker, A. W., C. E. Skinner, M. S. Shackley, M. D. Glascock and J. D. Rogers 2002 Mesoamerican Origin for an Obsidian Scraper from the Precolumbian Southeastern United States. *American Antiquity* 67(1):103–108.

Barlow, K. R. 2002 Predicting Maize Agriculture among the Fremont: An Economic Comparison of Farming and Foraging in the American Southwest. *American Antiquity* 67(1):65–88.

Barlow, R. H. 1949 *The Extent of the Empire of the Culhua Mexica.* Ibero-Americana 28 Series. Berkeley: University of California Press.

Barnowsky, A. E., P. L. Koch, R. S. Feranec, S. L. Wing and A. B. Shabel 2004 Assessing the Causes of Late Pleistocene Extinctions on the Continents. *Science* 306:70–75.

Barton, M., N. Bean, S. Dunleavy, I. Gray and A. White 2002 *Prehistoric America: A Journey through the Ice Age and Beyond.* London: BBC Worldwide Ltd.

Bartram, J. 1751 *Observations on the Inhabitants, Climate, Soil, Rivers, Productions, Animals, and Other Matters Worthy of Notice, Made by Mr. John Bartram, in His Travels from Pensilvania to Onondago, Oswego and the Lake Ontario, in Canada.* London: J. Whiston and B. White.

Baudez, C. F. 2002 Venus y el Códice Grolier. *Arqueología Mexicana* 10(55):70–79.

Baumhoff, M. A. 1978 Environmental Background. In *California*, edited by R. F. Heizer, pp. 16–24. *Handbook* of North American Indians, vol. 8, W. C. Sturtevant, general editor. Washington, DC: Smithsonian Institution.

Bayliss-Smith, T. 1978 Maximum Populations and Standard Populations: The Carrying Capacity Question. In *Social Organization and Settlement*, edited by D. Green, C. Haselgrove and M. Spriggs, pp. 129–151. British Archaeological Reports, International Series Supplement, vol. 47. Oxford: Archaeopress.

Beck, C. and G. T. Jones 1997 The Terminal Pleistocene/Early Holocene Archaeology of the Great Basin. *Journal of World Prehistory* 11(2):161–236.

Beck, R. A., Jr. 2003 Consolidation and Hierarchy: Chiefdom Variability in the Mississippian Southeast. *American Antiquity* 68(4):641–661.

Beekman, C. S. 2000 The Correspondence of Regional Patterns and Local Strategies in Formative to Classic Period West Mexico. *Journal of Anthropological Archaeology* 19:385–412.

Bell, R. E. and R. L. Brooks 2001 Plains Village Tradition: Southern. In *Plains*, edited by R. J. DeMallie, pp. 207–221. *Handbook of North American Indians*, vol. 13, W. C. Sturtevant, general editor. Washington, DC: Smithsonian Institution.

Bennett, C. H., M. Li and B. Ma 2003 Chain Letters and Evolutionary Histories. *Scientific American* 288(6):76–81.

Bennetzen, J., E. Buckler, V. Chandler, J. Doebley, J. Dorweiler, B. Baut, M. Freeling, S. Hake, E. Kellogg, R. S. Poethig, V. Walbot and S. Wessler 2001 Genetic Evidence and the Origin of Maize. *Latin American Antiquity* 12(1):84–86.

Benson, L., L. Cordell, K. Vincent, H. Taylor, J. Stein, G. L. Farmer and K. Futa 2003 Ancient Maize from Chacoan Great Houses: Where Was It Grown? *Proceedings of the National Academy of Sciences* 100(22):13111–13115.

Benz, B. F. 2001 Archaeological Evidence of Teosinte Domestication from Guilá Naquitz, Oaxaca. *Proceedings of the National Academy of Sciences* 98(4):2104–2106.

Berdan, F. F. and P. R. Anawalt 1992 *Codex Mendoza*. Berkeley: University of California Press.

Berdan, F. F., R. E. Blanton, E. H. Boone, M. G. Hodge, M. E. Smith and E. Umberger 1994 *Aztec Imperial Strategies*. Washington, DC: Dumbarton Oaks.

Berman, M. J. and D. M. Pearsall 2000 Plants, People, and Culture in the Prehistoric Central Bahamas: A View from the Three Dog Site, an Early Lucayan Settlement on San Salvador Island, Bahamas. *Latin American Antiquity* 11(3):219–239.

Bernal, I. 1969 *The Olmec World*. Berkeley: University of California Press.

Berres, T. E. 2000 Climatic Change and Lacustrine Resources at the Period of Initial Aztec Development. *Ancient Mesoamerica* 11(1):27–38.

Betts, C. M. 2006 Pots and Pox: The Identification of Protohistoric Epidemics in the Upper Mississippi Valley. *American Antiquity* 71(2):233–259.

Bever, M. R. 2006 Too Little, Too Late? The Radiocarbon Chronology of Alaska and the Peopling of the New World. *American Antiquity* 71(4):595–620.

Binford, L. R. 1978 *Nunamiut Ethnoarchaeology*. New York: Academic Press.

Birmingham, R. A. and L. E. Eisenberg 2000 *Indian Mounds of Wisconsin*. Madison: University of Wisconsin Press.

Blanton, R. E., S. A. Kowalewski, G. M. Feinman and L. M. Finsten 1993 *Ancient Mesoamerica: A Comparison of Change in Three Regions*. New Studies in Archaeology. Cambridge: Cambridge University Press.

Blitz, J. H. 1988 Adoption of the Bow in Prehistoric North America. *North American Archaeologist* 9(2):123–145.

Blitz, J. H. and P. Livingood 2004 Sociopolitical Implications of Mississippian Mound Volume. *American Antiquity* 69(2):291–301.

Blomster, J. P., H. Neff and M. D. Glascock 2005 Olmec Pottery Production and Export in Ancient Mexico Determined Through Elemental Analysis. *Science* 307:1068–1072.

Boas, F. 1955 *Primitive Art*. New York: Dover.

Bond, G., B. Kromer, J. Beer, R. Muscheler, M. N. Evans, W. Showers, S. Hoffmann, R. Lotti- Bond, I. Hajdas and G. Bonani 2001 Persistent Solar Influence on North Atlantic Climate During the Holocene. *Science* 294(5549): 2130–2136.

Bonnicksen, T. M. 2000 *America's Ancient Forests: From the Ice Age to the Age of Discovery*. New York: Wiley.

Boserup, E. 1965 *Conditions of Agricultural Growth: The Economics of Agrarian Change Under Population Pressure*. Chicago: Aldine.

Bousman, C. B., M. B. Collins, P. Goldberg, T. W. Stafford Jr., J. Guy, B. W. Baker, D. G. Steele, M. Kay, A. Kerr, G. Fredlund, P. Dering, V. Holliday, D. Wilson, W. Gose, S. Dial, P. Takac, R. Balinsky, M. Masson and J. F. Powell 2002 The Paleoindian-Archaic Transition in North America: New Evidence from Texas. *Antiquity* 76(294): 980–990.

Brain, J. P. and P. Phillips 1996 *Shell Gorgets: Styles of the Late Prehistoric and Protohistoric Southeast*. Cambridge, MA: Peabody Museum Press.

Britton, N. L. and A. Brown 1923 *An Illustrated Flora of the Northern United States, Canada and the British Possessions*, 3 vols. New York: New York Botanical Garden.

Brody, J. J. 2004 *Mimbres Painted Pottery*. Santa Fe, NM: School of American Research Press.

Brooks, A. S., J. E. Yellen, L. Nevell and G. Hartman 2005 Projectile Technologies of the African MSA: Implications for Modern Human Origins. In *Transitions Before the*

Transition: Evolution and Stability in the Middle Paleolithic and Middle Stone Age, edited by E. Hovers and S. Kuhn, pp. 233–255. New York: Kluwer Press.

Brose, D. S. 2003 Foreword. In *Bottle Creek: A Pensacola Culture Site in South Alabama*, edited by I. W. Brown, pp. xvii–xxiii. Tuscaloosa: University of Alabama Press.

Brose, D. S., J. A. Brown and D. W. Penney 1985 *Ancient Art of the American Woodland Indians*. New York: Harry N. Abrams.

Brose, D. S. and N. O. Greber (editors) 1979 *Hopewell Archaeology*. Kent, OH: Kent State University Press.

Brotherston, G. 1995 *Painted Books from Mexico: Codices in UK Collections and the World They Represent*. London: British Museum Press.

Brown, I. W. (editor) 2003 *Bottle Creek: A Pensacola Culture Site in South Alabama*. Tuscaloosa: University of Alabama Press.

Bruning, S. B. 2006 Complex Legal Legacies: The Native American Graves Protection and Repatriation Act, Scientific Study, and Kennewick Man. *American Antiquity* 71(3):501–521.

Bryan, A. L. 1969 Early Man in America and the Late Pleistocene Chronology of Western Canada and Alaska. *Current Anthropology* 10(4):339–365.

1986 Paleoamerican Prehistory as Seen from South America. In *New Evidence for the Pleistocene Peopling of the Americas*, edited by A. L. Bryan, pp. 1–14. Orono: Center for the Study of Early Man, University of Maine.

Bryan, A. L., J. Cruxent, R. Gruhn and C. Ochsenius 1978 An El Jobo Mastodon Kill at Taima-taima, Venezuela. *Science* 200:1275–1277.

Busch, L. 1994 A Glimmer of Hope for Coastal Migration. *Science* 263:1088–1089.

Butzer, K. W. 1982 *Archaeology as Human Ecology: Method and Theory for a Contextual Approach*. New York: Cambridge University Press.

Cabeza de Vaca, Á. N. 1961 *Adventures in the Unknown Interior of America*. Translated by C. Covey. Albuquerque: University of New Mexico Press.

Cabrera Castro, R. and S. Sugiyama 1999 El Proyecto Arqueológico de la Pirámide de la Luna *Arqueología* 21:19–33.

Cabrera Castro, R., S. Sugiyama and G. L. Cowgill 1991 The Templo de Quetzalcoatl Project at Teotihuacan. *Ancient Mesoamerica* 2(1):77–92.

Cabrero G., M. T. 1991 Cultura Arqueológica de Bolaños (Zacatecas y Jalisco). *Ancient Mesoamerica* 2(2):193–203.

Callaghan, R. T. 2003 Comments on the Mainland Origins of the Preceramic Cultures of the Greater Antilles. *Latin American Antiquity* 14(3):323–338.

Calvin, W. H. 2002 *A Brain for All Seasons*. Chicago: University of Chicago Press.

Campbell, L. and M. Mithun (editors) 1979 *The Languages of Native America: Historical and Comparative Assessment*. Austin: University of Texas Press.

Cannon, A. and D. Y. Yang 2006 Early Storage and Sedentism on the Pacific Northwest Coast: Ancient DNA Analysis of Salmon Remains from Namu, British Columbia. *American Antiquity* 71(1):123–140.

Cannon, M. D. and D. J. Meltzer 2004 Early Paleoindian Foraging: Examining the Faunal Evidence for Large Mammal Specialization and Regional Variability in Prey Choice. *Quaternary Science Reviews* 23:1955–1987.

Cardillo, M., G. M. Mace, K. E. Jones, J. Bielby, O. R. P. Bininda-Emonds, W. Sechrest, C. D. L. Orme and A. Purvis 2005 Multiple Causes of High Extinction Risk in Large Mammal Species. *Science* 309:1239–1241.

Carlson, R. L. 1990 Cultural Antecedents. In *Northwest Coast*, edited by W. Suttles, pp. 60–69. *Handbook of North American Indians*, vol. 7, W. C. Sturtevant, general editor. Washington, DC: Smithsonian Institution.

1996a Introduction to Early Human Occupation in British Columbia. In *Early Human Occupation in British Columbia*, edited by R. L. Carlson and L. D. Bona, pp. 3–10. Vancouver: University of British Columbia Press.

1996b The Later Prehistory of British Columbia. In *Early Human Occupation in British Columbia*, edited by R. L. Carlson and L. D. Bona, pp. 215–226. Vancouver: University of British Columbia Press.

Carniero, R. 1967 On the Relationship between Size of Population and Complexity of Social Organization. *Southwestern Journal of Anthropology* 23:234–243.

Carneiro, R. L. 1960 Slash-and-Burn Agriculture: A Closer Look at Its Implications for Settlement Patterns. In *Men and Cultures: Selected Papers of the International Congress of Anthropological and Ethnological Sciences*, edited by A. F. C. Wallace, pp. 229–234. Philadelphia: University of Pennsylvania Press.

1970 A Theory of the Origin of the State. *Science* 169:733–738.

Carot, P. 2000 Las Rutas al desierto: de Michoacán a Arizona. In *Nómadas y sedentarios en el Norte de México*, edited by M.-A. Hers, J. L. Mirafuentes, M. d. l. D. Soto and M. Vallebueno, pp. 91–112. Mexico City: Universidad Nacional Autónoma de México.

Carrasco, P. 1999 *The Tenochca Empire of Ancient Mexico: The Triple Alliance of Tenochtitlan, Tetzcoco, and Tlacopan*. Norman: University of Oklahoma Press.

Caso, A. 1970 *El Tesoro de Monte Alban*. Mexico City: Instituto Nacional de Antropología e Historia.

1971 Calendrical Systems of Central Mexico. In *Archaeology of Northern Mesoamerica, Part One*, edited by G. F. Ekholm and I. Bernal, pp. 333–348. *Handbook of Middle American Indians,* vol. 10. Austin: University of Texas Press.

Cassidy, J., L. M. Raab and N. A. Kononenko 2004 Boats, Bones, and Biface Bias: The Early Holocene Mariners of Eel Point, San Clemente Island, California. *American Antiquity* 69(1):109–130.

Cavalli-Sforza, L. L. and F. Cavalli-Sforza 1995 *The Great Human Diasporas*. New York: Addison-Wesley.

Chaffee, S. D., M. Hyman, M. Rowe, N. Coullam, A. Schreodl and K. Hogue 1994 Radiocarbon Dates on the All American Man Pictograph. *American Antiquity* 59(4):769–781.

Champlain, S. D. 1907 *Voyages of Samuel de Champlain 1604–1618*. Original Narratives of Early American History. New York: Scribner.

Chappell, J., J. Head and J. Magee 1996 Beyond the Radiocarbon Limit in Australian Archaeology and Quaternary Research. *Antiquity* 70(269):543–552.

Charlton, C. O. 1993 Obsidian as Jewelry: Lapidary Production in Aztec Otumba, Mexico. *Ancient Mesoamerica* 4(2):231–243.

Charlton, C. O., T. H. Charlton and D. L. Nichols 1993 Aztec Household-Based Craft Production: Archaeological Evidence from the City-State of Otumba, Mexico. In *Prehispanic Domestic Units in Western Mesoamerica*, edited by R. S. Santley and K. Hirth. Boca Raton, FL: CRC Press.

Charlton, T. H., D. L. Nichols and C. O. Charlton 1991 Aztec Craft Production and Specialization: Archaeological Evidence from the City-State of Otumba, Mexico. *World Archaeology* 23(1):98–114.

2000 Otumba and Its Neighbors: Ex oriente lux. *Ancient Mesoamerica* 11(2):247–265.

Chatters, J. C. and D. L. Pokotylo 1998 Prehistory: Introduction. In *Plateau*, edited by D. E. Walker Jr, pp. 73–80. *Handbook of North American Indians*, vol. 12, W. C. Sturtevant, general editor. Washington, DC: Smithsonian Institution.

Cheetham, D. 2006 The Americas' First Colony? *Archaeology* 59(1):42–46.

Childe, V. G. 1951 *Man Makes Himself*. New York: New American Library.

Chilton, E. 2005 Farming and Social Complexity in the Northeast. In *North American Archaeology*, edited by T. R. Pauketat and D. D. Loren, pp. 138–160. Malden, MA: Blackwell.

Clark, D. W. 1981 Prehistory of the Western Subarctic. In *Subarctic*, edited by J. Helm, pp. 107–129. *Handbook of North American Indians*, vol. 6, W. C. Sturtevant, general editor. Washington, DC: Smithsonian Institution.

1984 Prehistory of the Pacific Eskimo Region. In *Arctic*, edited by D. Damas, pp. 136–148. *Handbook of North American Indians*, vol. 5, W. C. Sturtevant, general editor. Washington, DC: Smithsonian Institution.

Clark, J. E. and M. Knoll 2005 The American Formative Revisited. In *Gulf Coast Archaeology: The Southeastern United States and Mexico*, edited by N. M. White, pp. 281–303. Gainesville: University Press of Florida.

Clements, F. E. and A. Reed 1939 "Eccentric" Flints of Oklahoma. *American Antiquity* 5(1):27–30.

Cobb, C. R. and B. M. Butler 2002 The Vacant Quarter Revisited: Late Mississippian Abandonment of the Lower Ohio Valley. *American Antiquity* 67(4):625–641.

Coe, M. 1999 *Breaking the Maya Code*. New York: Thames and Hudson.

Coe, M., D. R. Snow and E. Benson 1986 *Atlas of Ancient America*. New York: Facts on File.

Coe, M. D. 1968 *America's First Civilization: Discovering the Olmec*. New York: American Heritage.

1973 *The Maya Scribe and His World*. New York: Grolier Club.

Collins, M. B. 2002 The Gault Site, Texas, and Clovis Research. *Athena Review* 3(2).

Colten, R. H. and J. E. Arnold 1998 Prehistoric Marine Mammal Hunting on California's Northern Channel Islands. *American Antiquity* 63(4):679–701.

Coltrain, J. B. and S. W. Leavitt 2002 Climate and Diet in Fremont Prehistory: Economic Variability and Abandonment of Maize Agriculture in the Great Salt Lake Basin. *American Antiquity* 67(3):453–485.

Cook, S. F. 1978 Historical Demography. In *California*, edited by R. F. Heizer, pp. 91–98. *Handbook of North American Indians*, vol. 8, W. C. Sturtevant, general editor. Washington, DC: Smithsonian Institution.

Cook, S. F. and W. Borah 1960 *The Indian Population of Mexico, 1531–1610*. Ibero-Americana 31 Series. Berkeley: University of California Press.

Cordell, L. S. 1984 *Prehistory of the Southwest*. New World Archaeological Record. New York: Academic Press.

1997 *Archaeology of the Southwest*. New York: Academic Press.

Cordell, L. S., C. R. Van West, J. S. Dean and D. A. Muenchrath 2007 Climate Change, Social Networks, and Ancestral Pueblo Migration. *Kiva* 72(4):391–417.

Cortés, H. 1962 *5 Letters of Cortés to the Emperor*. Translated by J. B. Morris. New York: Norton.

Creel, D. and R. Anyon 2003 New Interpretations of Mimbres Public Architecture and Space: Implications for Cultural Change. *American Antiquity* 68(1):67–92.

Cressman, L. S. 1960 *Cultural Sequences at The Dalles, Oregon*. Transactions of the American Philosophical Society, New Series 50. Philadelphia: American Philosophical Society.

Crosby, H. W. 1992 *The Cave Paintings of Baja California: Discovering the Great Murals of an Unknown People*. San Diego, CA: Sunbelt Productions.

Crown, P. L. and W. J. Judge (editors) 1991 *Chaco & Hohokam: Prehistoric Regional Systems in the American Southwest*. Santa Fe, NM: School of American Research Press.

Crown, P. L. and W. H. Wills 2003 Modifying Pottery and Kivas at Chaco: Pentimento, Restoration, or Renewal? *American Antiquity* 68(3):511–532.

Culotta, E. 1995 Minimum Population Grows Larger. *Science* 270:31–32.

Curet, L. A. 1996 Ideology, Chiefly Power, and Material Culture: An Example from the Greater Antilles. *Latin American Antiquity* 7(2):114–131.

Curet, L. A. and J. R. Oliver 1998 Mortuary Practices, Social Development, and Ideology in Precolumbian Puerto Rico. *Latin American Antiquity* 9(3):217–239.

Dahlin, B. H. 2000 The Barricade and Abandonment of Chunchucmil: Implications for Northern Maya Warfare. *Latin American Antiquity* 11(3):283–298.

2002 Climate Change and the End of the Classic Period in Yucatan. *Ancient Mesoamerica* 13(2):327–340.

Dakin, K. and S. Wichmann 2000 Cacao and Chocolate: A Uto-Aztecan perspective. *Ancient Mesoamerica* 11(1):55–75.

Dale, V. H., C. M. Crisafulli and F. J. Swanson 2005 25 Years of Ecological Change at Mount St. Helens. *Science* 308:961–962.

Damas, D. (editor) 1984 *Arctic*, vol. 5. Washington, DC: Smithsonian Institution.

Damp, J. E., S. A. Hall and S. J. Smith 2002 Early Irrigation on the Colorado Plateau Near Zuni Pueblo, New Mexico. *American Antiquity* 67(4):665–676.

Dancey, W. S. 2005 The Enigmatic Hopewell of the Eastern Woodlands. In *North American Archaeology*, edited by T. R. Pauketat and D. D. Loren, pp. 108–137. Malden, MA: Blackwell.

Daniel, I. R., Jr. 2001 Stone Raw Material Availability and Early Archaic Settlement in the Southeastern United States. *American Antiquity* 66(2):237–265.

Darwin, C. 1959 *On the Origin of Species by Means of Natural Selection*. London: J. Murray.

Davies, N. 1973 *The Aztecs: A History*. London: Macmillan.

1977 *The Toltecs: Until the Fall of Tula*. Norman: University of Oklahoma.

Dávila Cabrera, P. 2005 Mound Builders along the Coast of the Gulf of Mexico and the Eastern United States. In *Gulf Coast Archaeology: The Southeastern United States and Mexico*, edited by N. M. White, pp. 87–107. Gainesville: University Press of Florida.

d'Azevedo, W. L. (editor) 1986 *Great Basin*, vol. 11. Washington, DC: Smithsonian Institution.

Davis, K. C. 1992 *Don't Know Much about Geography*. New York: Avon Books.

Davis, S. D. 1990 Prehistory of Southeastern Alaska. In *Northwest Coast*, edited by W. Suttles, pp. 197–202. *Handbook of North American Indians*, vol. 7, W. C. Sturtevant, general editor. Washington, DC: Smithsonian Institution.

Dawson, P. C. 2001 Interpreting Variability in Thule Inuit Architecture: A Case Study from the Canadian High Arctic. *American Antiquity* 66(3):453–470.

Day, J. S. 2001 Performing on the Court. In *The Sport of Life and Death: The Mesoamerican Ballgame*, edited by E. M. Whittington, pp. 65–77. New York: Thames and Hudson.

DeBoer, W. R. 2004 Little Bighorn on the Scioto: The Rocky Mountain Connection to Ohio Hopewell. *American Antiquity* 69(1):85–107.

Dehaene, S., V. Izard, P. Pica and E. Spelke 2006 Core Knowledge of Geometry in an Amazonian Indigene Group. *Science* 311:381–384.

de la Vega, G. 1962 *The Florida of the Inca*. Translated by J. G. Varner and J. J. Varner. Austin: University of Texas Press.

Delcourt, P. A., H. R. Delcourt, C. R. Ison, W. E. Sharp and K. J. Gremillion 1998 Prehistoric Human Use of Fire, the Eastern Agricultural Complex, and Appalachian Oak-Chestnut Forests: Paleoecology of Cliff Palace Pond, Kentucky. *American Antiquity* 63(2):263–278.

DeMallie, R. J. (editor) 2001 *Plains*, vol. 13. Washington, DC: Smithsonian Institution.

Demarest, A. A., M. O'Mansky, C. Wolley, D. Van Tuerenhout, T. Inomata, J. Palka and H. Escobedo 1997 Classic Maya Defensive Systems and Warfare in the Petexbatun Region. *Ancient Mesoamerica* 8(2):229–253.

Des Lauriers, M. R. 2005 The Watercraft of Isla Cedros, Baja California: Variability and Capabilities of Indigenous Seafaring Technology along the Pacific Coast of North America. *American Antiquity* 70(2):342–360.

Diamond, J. 1997 *Guns, Germs, and Steel*. New York: Norton.

2001 Anatomy of a Ritual. *Natural History* 7:16–20.

2004 The Astonishing Micropygmies. *Science* 306:2047–2048.

2005 *Collapse: How Societies Choose to Fail or Succeed*. New York: Viking.

Diamond, S. (editor) 1974 *In Search of the Primitive: A Critique of Civilization*. New Brunswick, NJ: Transaction Books.

Díaz del Castillo, B. 1963 *The Conquest of New Spain*. Translated by J. M. Cohen. Baltimore: Penguin Books.

Díaz, G. and A. Rodgers 1993 *Codex Borgia : A Full-Color Restoration of the Ancient Mexican Manuscript.* New York: Dover.

Diehl, R. A. 2004 *The Olmecs: America's First Civilization.* New York: Thames and Hudson.

2005 Patterns of Cultural Primacy. *Science* 307: 1055–1056.

Dikov, N. 1996 The Ushki Site, Kamchatka Peninsula. In *American Beginnings: The Prehistory and Paleoecology of Beringia,* edited by F. H. West, pp. 244–250. Chicago: University of Chicago Press.

Dillehay, T. D. 1990 *Araucania, Presente y Pasado.* Santiago de Chile: *Nómadas y sedentarios en el Norte de México.*

2000 *The Settlement of the Americas: A New Prehistory.* New York: Basic Books.

2008 Monte Verde: Seaweed, Food, Medicine, and the Peopling of South America. *Science* 320:784–786.

Dincauze, D. F. 2000 *Environmental Archaeology: Principles and Practice.* New York: Cambridge University Press.

Divale, W. 1984 *Matrilocal Residence in Pre-Literate Society.* Ann Arbor, MI: UMI Research Press.

Dobyns, H. F. 1983 *Their Number Become Thinned: Native American Population Dynamics in Eastern North America.* Knoxville: University of Tennessee Press.

Donald, L. 1997 *Aboriginal Slavery on the Northwest Coast of North America.* Berkeley: University of California Press.

Doran, G. H. (editor) 2002 *Windover: Multidisciplinary Investigations of an Early Archaic Florida Cemetery.* Tallahassee: University Press of Florida.

Doran, G. H. and D. N. Dickel 1988 Multidisciplinary Investigations at the Windover Site. In *Wet Site Archaeology,* edited by B. A. Purdy, pp. 263–289. Caldwell, NJ: Telford Press.

Doran, G. H., D. N. Dickel and L. A. Newsom 1990 A 7,290-Year-Old Bottle Gourd from the Windover Site, Florida. *American Antiquity* 55(2):354–359.

Doyel, D. E. 1991 Hohokam Exchange and Interaction. In *Chaco & Hohokam: Prehistoric Regional Systems in the American Southwest,* edited by P. L. Crown and W. J. Judge, pp. 225–252. School of American Research Advanced Seminar Series, D. W. Schwartz, general editor. Santa Fe, NM: School of American Research Press.

Drass, R. R. 1998 The Southern Plains Villagers. In *Archaeology on the Great Plains,* edited by W. R. Wood, pp. 415–455. Lawrence: University of Kansas Press.

Drennan, R. D. 1984 Long-Distance Transport Costs in Pre-Hispanic Mesoamerica. *American Anthropologist* 86:105–112.

Driver, H. E. and W. C. Massey 1957 *Comparative Studies of North American Indians.* Transactions of the American Philosophical Society, New Series 47(2). Philadelphia: American Philosophical Society.

Du Pratz, A. S. L. P. 1972 [1774] *The History of Louisiana.* Baton Rouge, LA: Claitor's.

Dull, R. A., J. R. Southon and P. D. Sheets 2001 Volcanism, Ecology, and Culture: A Reassessment of the Volcán Ilopango TBJ Eruption in the Southern Maya Realm. *Latin American Antiquity* 12(1):25–44.

Dumond, D. E. 1965 On Eskaleutian Linguistics, Archaeology, and Prehistory. *American Anthropologist* 67(5):1231–1257.

1984a Prehistory of the Bering Sea Region. In *Arctic,* edited by D. Damas, pp. 94–105. *Handbook of North American Indians,* vol. 5, W. C. Sturtevant, general editor. Washington, DC: Smithsonian Institution.

1984b Prehistory: Summary. In *Arctic,* edited by D. Damas, pp. 72–79. *Handbook of North American Indians,* vol. 5, W. C. Sturtevant, general editor. Washington, DC: Smithsonian Institution.

2001 *Archaeology in the Aleut Zone of Alaska: Some Recent Research,* vol. 58. Eugene: University of Oregon Press.

2005 *A Naknek Chronicle: Ten Thousand Years in a Land of Lakes and Rivers and Mountains of Fire.* Research/Resources Management Reports. Washington, DC: National Park Service.

Dumond, D. E. and R. L. Bland (editors) 2002 *Archaeology in the Bering Strait Region: Research on Two Continents,* vol. 59. Eugene: University of Oregon Press.

Dunham, G. H., D. L. Gold and J. L. Hantman 2003 Collective Burial in Late Prehistoric Virginia: Excavation and Analysis of the Rapidan Mound. *American Antiquity* 68(1):109–128.

Dunn, M., A. Terrill, G. Reesink, R. A. Foley and S. C. Levinson 2005 Structural Phylogenetics and the Reconstruction of Ancient Language History. *Science* 309(5743):2072–2075.

Dunning, N. P. and J. K. Kowalski 1994 Lords of the Hills: Classic Maya Settlement Patterns and Political Iconography in the Puuc Region, Mexico. *Ancient Mesoamerica* 5(1):63–95.

Durham, W. H. 1991 *Coevolution: Genes, Culture, and Human Diversity.* Stanford, CA: Stanford University Press.

Dyck, I. and R. E. Morlan 2001 Hunting and Gathering Tradition: Canadian Plains. In *Plains,* edited by R. J. DeMallie, pp. 115–130. *Handbook of North American Indians,* vol. 13, W. C. Sturtevant, general editor. Washington, DC: Smithsonian Institution.

Earle, D. and D. R. Snow 1985 The Origin of the 260-Day Calendar: The Gestation Hypothesis Reconsidered in Light of Its Use among the Quiche-Maya. In *Fifth Palenque Round Table, 1983,* edited by M. Robertson and V. Fields, pp. 241–244. San Francisco: Pre-Columbian Art Research Institute.

Earle, T. K. 1987 Chiefdoms in Archaeological and Ethnohistorical Perspective. *Annual Review of Anthropology* 16:279–308.

1991 *Chiefdoms: Power, Economy, and Ideology.* New York: Cambridge University Press.

Elena, S. F., V. S. Cooper and R. E. Lenski 1996 Punctuated Evolution Caused by Selection of Rare Beneficial Mutations. *Science* 272:1802–1804.

Elsasser, A. B. 1978 Development of Regional Prehistoric Cultures. In *California*, edited by R. F. Heizer, pp. 37–57. *Handbook of North American Indians*, vol. 8, W. C. Sturtevant, general editor. Washington, DC: Smithsonian Institution.

Ember, M. 1963 The Relationship between Economic and Political Development in Nonindustrialized Societies. *Ethnology* 2:228–248.

Emerson, T. E., R. E. Hughes, M. R. Hynes and S. U. Wisseman 2003 The Sourcing and Interpretation of Cahokia-Style Figurines in the Trans-Mississippi South and Southeast. *American Antiquity* 68(2):287–313.

Ericson, J. E. and T. G. Baugh (editors) 1993 *The American Southwest and Mesoamerica: Systems of Prehistoric Exchange*. New York: Plenum Press.

Erlandson, J. M. 1994 *Early Hunter-Gatherers of the California Coast*. New York: Plenum Press.

2002 Anatomically Modern Humans, Maritime Voyaging, and the Pleistocene Colonization of the Americas. In *The First Americans: The Pleistocene Colonization of the New World*, edited by N. G. Jablonski, pp. 59–92. Memoirs of the California Academy of Sciences, vol. 27. San Francisco: California Academy of Sciences.

Erlandson, J. M. and R. H. Colten (editors) 1991 *Hunter-Gatherers of Early Holocene Coastal California*. Los Angeles: Institute of Archaeology, University of California, Los Angeles.

Erlandson, J. M. and M. A. Glassow (editors) 1997 *Archaeology of the California Coast During the Middle Holocene*, vol. 4. Los Angeles: Institute of Archaeology, University of California, Los Angeles.

Erlandson, J. M. and M. L. Moss 2001 Shellfish Feeders, Carrion Eaters, and the Archaeology of Aquatic Adaptations. *American Antiquity* 66(3):413–432.

Erlandson, J. M., T. C. Rick, T. L. Jones and J. F. Porcasi 2007 One If by Land, Two If by Sea: Who Were the First Californians? In *California Prehistory: Colonization, Culture, and Complexity*, edited by T. L. Jones and K. A. Klar, pp. 53–62. New York: Rowman & Littlefield.

Evans, S. T. 2004 Aztec Palaces and Other Elite Residential Architecture. In *Palaces of the Ancient New World*, edited by S. T. Evans and J. Pillsbury. Washington, DC: Dumbarton Oaks.

Evans, S. T. and W. T. Sanders (editors) 2000 *The Teotihuacan Valley Project Final Report Vol. 5, The Aztec Period Occupation of the Valley, Part 1, Natural Environment, 20th Century Occupation, Survey Methodology, and Site Descriptions*, 25. University Park: Department of Anthropology, Pennsylvania State University.

Fagan, B. M. 2003a *Ancient Lives: An Introduction to Archaeology and Prehistory*. New York: Prentice Hall.

2003b *Before California: An Archaeologist Looks at Our Earliest Inhabitants*. Lanham, MD: Rowman & Littlefield.

2003c *The Great Journey: The Peopling of Ancient America*. Gainesville: University Press of Florida.

2004 The House of the Sea: An Essay on the Antiquity of Planked Canoes in Southern California. *American Antiquity* 69(1):7–16.

Farb, P. 1978 *Man's Rise to Civilization: The Cultural Ascent of the Indians of North America*, 2nd ed. New York: E. P. Dutton.

Fash, B. W. 1992 Late Classic Architectural Sculpture Themes in Copan. *Ancient Mesoamerica* 3(1):89–104.

Fash, W. L. 1991 *Scribes, Warriors and Kings*. New York: Thames and Hudson.

Feder, K. 2002 *Frauds, Myths, and Mysteries: Science and Pseudoscience in Archaeology*, 4th ed. Boston: McGraw-Hill Mayfield.

Fedje, D. W. and T. Christiansen 1999 Modeling Paleoshorelines and Locating Early Holocene Coastal Sites in Haida Gwaii. *American Antiquity* 64(1):635–652.

Fedje, D. W., Q. X. Mackie, E. J. Dixon and T. H. Heaton 2004 Late Wisconsin Environments and Archaeolgoical Visibility on the Northern Northwest Coast. In *Entering America: Northeast Asia and Beringia Before the Last Glacial Maximum*, edited by D. B. Madsen. Salt Lake City: University of Utah Press.

Fenton, W. N. 1998 *The Great Law of the Longhouse: A Political History of the Iroquois Confederacy*. Norman: University of Oklahoma Press.

Fiedel, S. J. 1994 Some Inferences Concerning Proto-Algonquian Economy and Society. *Northeast Anthropology* 48:1–11.

Fiedel, S. J. 1999a Older Than We Thought: Implications of Corrected Dates for Paleoindians. *American Antiquity* 64(1):95–115.

Fiedel, S. J. 1999b Artifact Provenience at Monte Verde: Confusion and Contradictions. *Discovering Archaeology, Special Report: Monte Verde Revisited*:1–12.

Fiedel, S. J. and C. V. Haynes Jr. 2004 A Premature Burial: Comments on Grayson and Meltzer's "Requiem for Overkill." *Journal of Archaeological Science*:121–131.

Filloy Nadal, L. 2001 Rubber and Rubber Balls in Mesoamerica. In *The Sport of Life and Death: The Mesoamerican Ballgame*, edited by E. M. Whittington, pp. 21–31. New York: Thames and Hudson.

Fisher, R. (editor) 2004 *National Geographic Historical Atlas of the United States*. Washington, DC: National Geographic Society.

Fix, A. 1999 *Migration and Colonization in Human Microevolution*. New York: Cambridge University Press.

Fladmark, K. R., K. M. Ames and P. D. Sutherland 1990 Prehistory of the Northern Coast of British Columbia. In *Northwest Coast*, edited by W. Suttles, pp. 229–239. *Handbook of North American Indians*, vol. 7, W. C. Sturtevant, general editor. Washington, DC: Smithsonian Institution.

Flannery, K. V. (editor) 1986 *Guilá Naquitz: Archaic Foraging and Early Agriculture in Oaxaca, Mexico*. Orlando, FL: Academic Press.

2002 The Origins of the Village Revisited: From Nuclear to Extended Households. *American Antiquity* 67(3):417–433.

Flannery, T. F. 2001 *The Eternal Frontier: An Ecological History of North America and Its Peoples*. New York: Atlantic Monthly Press.

Fogelson, R. (editor) 2004 *Southeast*, vol. 14. Washington, DC: Smithsonian Institution.

Ford, A., F. Stross, F. Asaro and H. V. Michel 1997 Obsidian Procurement and Distribution in the Tikal-Yaxha Intersite Area of the Central Maya Lowlands. *Ancient Mesoamerica* 8(1):101–110.

Ford, R. I. 1985 *Prehistoric Food Production in North America*. Ann Arbor: Museum of Anthropology, University of Michigan.

Foster, M. K. and S. Gorenstein 2000 *Greater Mesoamerica: The Archaeology of West and Northwest Mexico*. Salt Lake City: University of Utah Press.

Freter, A. 1992 Chronological Research at Copan. *Ancient Mesoamerica* 3(1):117–133.

Frink, L. and K. G. Harry 2008 The Beauty of "Ugly" Eskimo Cooking Pots. *American Antiquity* 73(1):103–118.

Frison, G. C. (editor) 1974 *The Casper Site: A Hell Gap Bison Kill on the High Plains*. New York: Academic Press.

1992 *Prehistoric Hunters of the High Plains*. New York: Academic Press.

1998 The Northwestern and Northern Plains Archaic. In *Archaeology on the Great Plains*, edited by W. R. Wood, pp. 140–172. Lawrence: University of Kansas Press.

2001 Hunting and Gathering Tradition: Northwestern and Central Plains. In *Plains*, edited by R. J. DeMallie, pp. 131–145. *Handbook of North American Indians*, vol. 13, W. C. Sturtevant, general editor. Washington, DC: Smithsonian Institution.

Frison, G. C. and B. Bradley 1999 *The Fenn Cache : Clovis Weapons and Tools*. Santa Fe, NM: One Horse Land & Cattle Co.

Fry, D. P. 2005 *The Human Potential for Peace: An Anthropological Challenge to Assumptions about War and Violence*. New York: Oxford University Press.

Funk, R. E. 2004 *An Ice Age Quarry-Workshop: The West Athens Hill Site Revisited*. New York State Museum Bulletin 504. Albany: New York State Education Department.

Gamble, L. H. 2002 Archaeological Evidence for the Origin of the Plank Canoe in North America. *American Antiquity* 67(2):301–315.

Gamble, L. H., P. L. Walker and G. S. Russell 2002 Further Considerations on the Emergence of Chumash Chiefdoms. *American Antiquity* 67(4):772–777.

García Cook, A. and B. L. Merino Carrión 1998 Cantona: Urbe Prehispanica el el Altiplano Central de Mexico. *Latin American Antiquity* 9(3):191–216.

Gibbon, G. (editor) 1998 *Archaeology of Prehistoric Native America: An Encyclopedia*. New York: Garland.

Gibbons, A. 1997 Monte Verde: Blessed but Not Confirmed. *Science* 275:1256–1257.

Gidwitz, T. 2007 A Different History. *Archaeology* 60(2):28–32.

Gilbert, M. T. P., D. L. Jenkins, A. Götherström, N. Naveran, J. J. Sanchez, M. Hofreiter, P. F. Thomsen, J. Binladen, T. F. G. Higham, R. M. Yohe II, R. Parr, L. S. Cummings and E. Willerslev 2008 DNA from Pre-Clovis Human Coprolites in Oregon, North America. *Science* 320:786–789.

Gilbert, M. T. P., T. Kivisild, B. Grønnow, P. K. Andersen, E. Metspalu, M. Reidla, E. Tamm, E. Axelsson, A. Götherström, P. R. Campos, M. Rasmussen, M. Metspalu, T. F. G. Higham, J.-L. Schwenniger, R. Nathan, C.-J. De Hoog, A. Koch, L. N. Møller, C. Andreasen, M. Meldgaard, R. Villems, C. Bendixen and E. Willerslev 2008 Paleo-Eskimo mtDNA Genome Reveals Matrilineal Discontinuity in Greenland. *Science* 320:1787–1789.

Gilbert, R. I. and J. H. Mielke (editors) 1985 *The Analysis of Prehistoric Diets*. New York: Academic Press.

Gill, R. B. 1994 *The Great Maya Droughts*. Austin: University of Texas Press.

Gillespie, S. D. 1998 The Aztec Triple Alliance: A Postconquest Tradition. In *Native Traditions in the Postconquest World*, edited by E. H. Boone and T. Cummins, pp. 233–263. Washington, DC: Dumbarton Oaks.

Gillespie, S. D. and R. A. Joyce 1998 Diety Relationships in Mesoamerican Cosmologies: The Case of the Maya God L. *Ancient Mesoamerica* 9(2):279–296.

Gilman, A. 1981 The Development of Social Stratification in Bronze Age Europe. *Current Anthropology* 22:1–8.

Glass, J. B. 1975 A Survey of Native Middle American Pictorial Manuscripts. In *Guide to Ethnohistorical Sources, Part Three*, edited by H. F. Cline, pp. 3–252. *Handbook of Middle American Indians,* vol. 14, R. Wauchope, general editor. Austin: University of Texas Press.

Glassow, M. A. 2005 Prehistoric Dolphin Hunting on Santa Cruz Island, California. In *The Exploitation and Cultural*

Importance of Sea Mammals, edited by G. G. Monks, pp. 107–120. Oxford, England: Oxbow Books.

Goddard, I. (editor) 1996 *Languages*, vol. 17. Washington, DC: Smithsonian Institution.

Goebel, T. 1999 Pleistocene Human Colonization of Siberia and Peopling of the Americas: An Ecological Approach. *Evolutionary Anthropology* 8(6):208–227.

Goebel, T. and M. Aksenov 1995 Accelerator Radiocarbon Dating of the Initial Upper Paleolithic in Southeast Siberia. *Antiquity* 69:349–357.

Goebel, T., W. R. Powers and N. Bigelow 1991 The Nenana Complex of Alaska and Clovis Origins. In *Clovis: Origins and Adaptations*, edited by R. Bonnichsen and K. L. Turnmire, pp. 41–79. Corvallis, OR: Center for the Study of the First Americans.

Goebel, T., M. R. Waters and M. Dikova 2003 The Archaeology of Ushki Lake, Kamchatka, and the Pleistocene Peopling of the Americas. *Science* 301:501–505.

Goebel, T., M. R. Waters and D. H. O'Rourke 2008 The Late Pleistocene Dispersal of Modern Humans in the Americas. *Science* 319:1497–1502.

Goetzmann, W. H. and G. Williams 1992 *The Atlas of North American Exploration: From the Norse Voyages to the Race to the Pole*. New York: Swanston.

Goldberg, P. and T. L. Arpin 1999 Micromorphological Analysis of Sediments from Meadowcroft Rockshelter, Pennsylvania: Implications for Radiocarbon Dating. *Journal of Field Archaeology* 26(3):325–342.

Goodman, J. 1981 *American Genesis: The American Indian and the Origins of Modern Man*. New York: Summit Books.

Goodyear, A. C. 2004 Paleoamerican Prehistory: Pre-Clovis. In *Paleoamerican Origins: Beyond Clovis*, edited by R. Bonnichsen, pp. 89–98. College Station: Center for the Study of the First Americans, Texas A&M University Press.

Grant, C. 1974 *Rock Art of Baja California*. Los Angeles: Dawson's Book Shop.

1978 Chumash: Introduction. In *California*, edited by R. F. Heizer, pp. 505–508. *Handbook of North American Indians,* vol. 8, W. C. Sturtevant, general editor. Washington, DC: Smithsonian Institution.

Gray, R. 2005 Pushing the Time Barrier in the Quest for Language Roots. *Science* 309:2007–2008.

Grayson, D. K. 1970 Statistical Inference and Northeastern Adena. *American Antiquity* 35(1):102–104.

1993 *The Desert's Past: A Natural Prehistory of the Great Basin*. Washington, DC: Smithsonian Institution Press.

2001 Did Human Hunting Cause Mass Extinction? *Science* 294(5546):1459.

Grayson, D. K. and D. J. Meltzer 2003 A Requiem for North American Overkill. *Journal of Archaeological Science* 30(5):585–593.

Greenberg, J. H. 1996 Beringia and New World Origins: I. The Linguistic Evidence. In *American Beginnings: The Prehistory and Palaeoecology of Beringia*, edited by F. H. West, pp. 525–536. Chicago: University of Chicago Press.

Greenberg, J. H., C. G. Turner II and S. L. Zegura 1986 The Settlement of the Americas: A Comparison of the Linguistic, Dental, and Genetic Evidence. *Current Anthropology* 24:477–497.

Gregory, D. A. 1991 Hohokam Settlement Patterns. In *Chaco & Hohokam: Prehistoric Regional Systems in the American Southwest*, edited by P. L. Crown and W. J. Judge, pp. 159–193. School of American Research Advanced Seminar Series, D. W. Schwartz, general editor. Santa Fe, NM: School of American Research Press.

Gremillion, K. J. 2004 Seed Processing and the Origins of Food Production in Eastern North America. *American Antiquity* 69(2):215–233.

Grier, C. and L. Shaver 2008 The Role of Archaeologists and First Nations in Sorting Out Some Very Old Problems in British Columbia, Canada. *The SAA Archaeological Record* 8(1):33–35.

Griffin, J. B. 1966 Mesoamerica and the Eastern United States in Prehistoric Times. In *Archaeological Frontiers and External Connections*, edited by G. F. Ekholm and G. R. Willey. *Handbook of Middle American Indians*, vol. 4, R. Wauchope, general editor. Austin: University of Texas Press.

1967 Eastern North American Archaeology: A Summary. *Science* 156:175–191.

1992 Fort Ancient Has No Class: The Absence of an Elite Group in Mississippian Societies in the Central Ohio Valley. In *Lords of the Southeast: Social Inequality and the Native Elites of Southeastern North America*, edited by A. W. Barker and T. R. Pauketat, pp. 53–59. Archaeological Papers of the American Anthropological Association, vol. 3. Washington, DC: American Anthropological Association.

Grove, D. 1984 *Chalcatzingo*. New York: Thames and Hudson.

Guidon, N., A. M. Pessis, F. Parenti, M. Fontugue and C. Guérin 1996 Nature and Age of the Deposits in Pedra Furada, Brazil: Reply to Meltzer, Adovasio & Dillehay. *Antiquity* 70(268):408–415.

Gumerman, G. J. (editor) 1991 *Exploring the Hohokam: Prehistoric Desert Peoples of the American Southwest*. Amerind Foundation New World Studies Series. Albuquerque: University of New Mexico Press.

Gunnerson, J. H. 2001 Plains Village Tradition: Western Periphery. In *Plains*, edited by R. J. DeMallie, pp. 234–244. *Handbook of North American Indians,* vol. 13, W. C. Sturtevant, general editor. Washington, DC: Smithsonian Institution.

Guthrie, R. D. 2003 Rapid Body Size Decline in Alaskan Pleistocene Horses before Extinction. *Nature* 426:169–171.

2004 Radiocarbon Evidence of Mid-Holocene Mammoths Stranded on an Alaskan Bering Sea Island. *Nature* 429:746–749.

Hammond, N. 1972 Obsidian Trade Routes in the Mayan Area. *Science* 178:1092–1093.

Harbottle, G. and P. C. Weigand 1992 Turquoise in Pre-Columbian America. *Scientific American* 265(2):78–85.

Hard, R. J. and J. R. Roney 1998 A Massive Terraced Village Complex in Chihuahua, Mexico, 3000 Years Before Present. *Science* 279:1661–1664.

Hare, B., M. Brown, C. Williamson and M. Tomasello 2002 The Domestication of Social Cognition in Dogs. *Science* 298:1634–1636.

Harmon, D., F. P. McManamon and D. T. Pitcaithley (editors) 2006 *The Antiquities Act: A Century of American Archaeology, Historic Preservation, and Nature Conservation*. Tucson: University of Arizona Press.

Harpending, H. C., S. T. Sherry, A. R. Rogers and M. Stoneking 1993 The Genetic Structure of Ancient Human Populations. *Current Anthropology* 34(4):483–496.

Harris, R. C. (editor) 1987 *Historical Atlas of Canada*, vol. 1. Toronto: University of Toronto Press.

Hart, D. and R. W. Sussman 2005 *Man the Hunted: Primates, Predators, and Human Evolution*. New York: Westview Press.

Hart, J. P., R. A. Daniels and C. J. Sheviak 2004 Do *Cucurbita Pepo* Gourds Float Fishnets? *American Antiquity* 69(1):141–148.

Harvey, H. R. and B. J. Williams 1980 Aztec Arithmetic: Positional Notation and Area Calculation. *Science* 210:499–505.

Hassig, R. 1988 *Aztec Warfare: Imperial Expansion and Political Control*. Norman: University of Oklahoma Press.

2001 *Time, History, and Belief in Aztec and Colonial Mexico*. Austin: University of Texas Press.

Haug, G. H., D. Günther, L. C. Peterson, D. M. Sigman, K. A. Hughen and B. Aeschlimann 2003 Climate and the Collapse of Maya Civilization. *Science* 299:1731–1735.

Haury, E. W., E. B. Sayles and W. W. Wasley 1959 The Lehner Mammoth Site, Southeastern Arizona. *American Antiquity* 25(1):2-30.

Haviland, W. A. 1997 The Rise and Fall of Sexual Inequality: Death and Gender at Tikal, Guatemala. *Ancient Mesoamerica* 8(1):1–12.

Hawkes, K. 1993 Why Hunter-Gatherers Work: An Ancient Version of the Problem of Public Goods. *Current Anthropology* 34(4):341–361.

Hayden, B. 1981 Research and Development in the Stone Age: Technological Transitions among Hunter-Gatherers. *Current Anthropology* 55(2):519–548.

Hayden, B. and R. Gargett 1990 Big Man, Big Heart?: A Mesoamerican View of the Emergence of Complex Society. *Ancient Mesoamerica* 1(1):3–20.

Hayden, B. and J. M. Ryder 2001 Prehistoric Cultural Collapse in the Lillooet Area. *American Antiquity* 56:50–65.

Haynes, C. V., Jr. 1999 Monte Verde and the Pre-Clovis Situation in America. *Discovering Archaeology, Special Report: Monte Verde Revisited*:17–19.

Haynes, G. 2002 *The Settlement of North America: The Clovis Era*. Cambridge: Cambridge University Press.

Hays, D. G. 1998 *The Measurement of Cultural Evolution in the Non-literate World*. New York: Metagram Press.

Healan, D. M. 1997 Pre-Hispanic Quarrying in the Ucareo-Zinapecuaro Obsidian Source Area. *Ancient Mesoamerica* 8(1):77–100.

Hegmon, M. 2003 Setting Theoretical Egos Aside: Issues and Theory in North American Archaeology. *American Antiquity* 68(2):213–243.

Heizer, R. F. (editor) 1978 *California*, vol. 8. Washington, DC: Smithsonian Institution.

Helm, J. (editor) 1981 *Subarctic*, vol. 6. Washington, DC: Smithsonian Institution.

Henning, D. R. 2001 Plains Village Tradition: Eastern Periphery and Oneota Tradition. In *Plains*, edited by R. J. DeMallie, pp. 222–233. *Handbook of North American Indians*, vol. 13, W. C. Sturtevant, general editor. Washington, DC: Smithsonian Institution.

2005 The Evolution of the Plains Village Tradition. In *North American Archaeology*, edited by T. R. Pauketat and D. D. Loren, pp. 161–186. Malden, MA: Blackwell.

Henning, D. R. and T. D. Thiessen 2004 Dhegihan and Chiwere Siouans in the Plains: Historical and Archaeological Perspectives, Part II. *Plains Anthropologist* 49(192):345–625.

Hewitt, E. A. 1999 What's in a Name: Gender, Power, and Classic Maya Women Rulers. *Ancient Mesoamerica* 10(2):251–262.

Highsmith, H. 1997 *The Mounds of Kashkonong and Rock River*. Fort Atkinson, WI: Fort Atkinson Historical Society and Highsmith Press.

Hildebrandt, W. R. and K. R. McGuire 2002 The Ascendance of Hunting During the California Middle Archaic: An Evolutionary Perspective. *American Antiquity* 67(2):231–256.

Hill, J. B., J. J. Clark, W. H. Doelle and P. D. Lyons 2004 Prehistoric Demography in the Southwest: Migration, Coalescence, and Hohokam Population Decline. *American Antiquity* 69(4):689–716.

Hill, J. H. 2001 Proto-Uto-Aztecan: A Community of Cultivators in Central Mexico? *American Anthropologist* 103(4):913–934.

Hill, W. D., M. Blake and J. E. Clark 1998 Ball court design dates back 3,400 years. *Nature* 392:878–879.

Hirth, K. 2000 *Ancient Urbanism at Xochicalco*, 2 vols. Salt Lake City: University of Utah Press.

Hobler, P. M. 1990 Prehistory of the Central Coast of British Columbia. In *Northwest Coast*, edited by W. Suttles, pp. 298–305. *Handbook of North American Indians*, vol. 7, W. C. Sturtevant, general editor. Washington, DC: Smithsonian Institution.

Hockett, C. F. 1958 *A Course in Modern Linguistics*. New York: Macmillan.

Hodell, D. A., M. Brenner, J. H. Curtis and T. Guilderson 2001 Solar Forcing of Drought Frequency in the Maya Lowlands. *Science* 292:1367–1373.

Hoffecker, J. F. 2005 *A Prehistory of the North: Human Settlement of the Higher Latitudes*. New Brunswick, NJ: Rutgers University Press.

Hoffecker, J. F., W. R. Powers and T. Goebel 1993 Colonization of Beringia and the Peopling of the New World. *Science* 259:46–53.

Hofman, J. L. (editor) 1996 *Archeology and Paleoecology of the Central Great Plains*, vol. 48. Fayetteville: Arkansas Archeological Survey.

Hofman, J. L., R. L. Brooks, J. S. Hays, D. W. Owsley, R. L. Jantz, M. K. Marks and M. H. Manhein (editors) 1989 *From Clovis to Comanchero: Archeological Overview of the Southern Great Plains*, vol. 35. Fayetteville: Arkansas Archeological Survey.

*Hofman, J. L. and R. W. Graham 1998 The Paleo-Indian Cultures of the Great Plains. In *Archaeology on the Great Plains,* edited by W. R. Wood, pp. 87–139. Lawrence: University of Kansas Press.

Hornbeck, D. 1983 *California Patterns: A Geographical and Historical Atlas*. Mountain View, CA: Mayfield.

Hosler, D., S. L. Burkett and M. J. Tarkanian 1999 Prehistoric Polymers: Rubber Processing in Ancient Mesoamerica. *Science* 284:1988–1991.

Hosler, D. and A. Macfarlane 1996 Copper Sources, Metal Production, and Metals Trade in Late Postclassic Mesoamerica. *Science* 273:1819–1824.

Housley, R. A., C. S. Gamble, M. Street and P. Pettitt 1997 Radiocarbon Evidence for the Late Glacial Human Recolonisation of Northern Europe. *Proceedings of the Prehistoric Society* 63:25–54.

Houston, S. D. 1989 *Maya Glyphs*. Berkeley: University of California Press.

2006 An Example of Preclassic Mayan Writing? *Science* 311:1249–1250.

Hudson, C. 1976 *The Southeastern Indians*. Knoxville: University of Tennessee Press.

Hudson, J. L. 2004 Additional Evidence for Gourd Floats on Fishing Nets. *American Antiquity* 69(3):586–587.

Hunn, E. 1994 Place Names, Population Density and the Magic Number 500. *Current Anthropology* 35:81–85.

Hunt, R. C., D. Guillet, D. R. Abbott, J. Bayman, P. Fish, S. Fish, K. Kintigh and J. A. Neely 2005 Plausible Ethnographic Analogies for the Social Organization of Hohokam Canal Irrigation. *American Antiquity* 70(3):433–456.

Hunt, T. L. and C. P. Lipo 2006 Late Colonization of Easter Island. *Science* 311:1603–1606.

Hurst, W. J., S. M. J. Tarka, T. G. Powis, F. J. Valdez and T. R. Hester 2002 Cacao Usage by the Earliest Maya Civilization. *Nature* 418:289–290.

Hutchinson, D. L., C. S. Larsen, M. J. Schoeninger and L. Norr 1998 Regional Variation in the Pattern of Maize Adoption and Use in Florida and George. *American Antiquity* 63(3):397–416.

Iltis, H. H., J. F. Doebley, R. Guzmán M. and B. Pazy 1979 *Zea diploperennis* (Gramineae): A New Teosinte from Mexico. *Science* 203:186–188.

Ingram, S. E. 2008 Streamflow and Population Change in the Lower Salt River Valley of Central Arizona, ca. A. D. 775 to 1450. *American Antiquity* 73(1):136–165.

Irwin-Williams, C. 1979 Post-Pleistocene Archaeology 7000–2000 BC. In *Southwest*, edited by A. Ortiz, pp. 31–42. *Handbook of North American Indians*, vol. 9, W. C. Sturtevant, general editor. Washington, DC: Smithsonian Institution Press.

Isenberg, A. C. 2000 *The Destruction of the Bison: An Environmental History, 1750–1920*. New York: Cambridge University Press.

Jablonski, N. G. (editor) 2002 *The First Americans: The Pleistocene Colonization of the New World*, no. 27. San Francisco: California Academy of Sciences.

Jackson, H. E. and S. L. Scott 2003 Patterns of Elite Faunal Utilization at Moundville, Alabama. *American Antiquity* 68(3):552–572.

Jansen, M. and G. A. Pérez Jiménez 2004 Renaming the Mexican Codices. *Ancient Mesoamerica* 15(2):267–271.

Jantz, R. L. and D. W. Owsley 2001 Variation Among Early North American Crania. *American Journal of Physical Anthropology* 114:146–155.

Jefferson, T. 1955 *Notes on the State of Virginia*. Chapel Hill: University of North Carolina Press.

Jennings, J. D. 1957 *Danger Cave*. Anthropological Papers no. 27. Salt Lake City: University of Utah Press.

Johnson, A. E. 2001 Plains Woodland Tradition. In *Plains*, edited by R. J. DeMallie, pp. 159–172. *Handbook of North American Indians,* vol. 13, W. C. Sturtevant, general editor. Washington, DC: Smithsonian Institution.

Johnson, C. M. 1998 The Coalescent Tradition. In *Archaeology on the Great Plains*, edited by W. R. Wood, pp. 308–344. Lawrence: University of Kansas Press.

Johnson, D. L. 1978 The Origin of Island Mammoths and the Quaternary Land Bridge History of the Northern Channel Islands, California. *Quaternary Research* 10(2):204–225.

1980 Problems in the Land Vertebrate Zoogeography of Certain Islands and the Swimming Powers of Elephants. *Journal of Biogeography* 7:383–398.

Johnson, G. 1982 Organizational Structure and Scalar Stress. In *Theory and Explanation in Archaeology: The Southampton Conference*, edited by C. Renfrew, M. J. Rowlands and B. A. Seagraves, pp. 389–422. New York: Academic Press.

Johnson, M. A. and A. E. Johnson 1998 The Plains Woodland. In *Archaeology on the Great Plains*, edited by W. R. Wood, pp. 201–234. Lawrence: University of Kansas Press.

Johnston, K. J., A. J. Breckenridge and B. C. Hansen 2001 Paleoecological Evidence of an Early Postclassic Occupation in the Southwestern Maya Lowlands: Laguna las Pozas, Guatemala. *Latin American Antiquity* 12(2):149–166.

Jones, G. T., C. Beck, E. E. Jones and R. E. Hughes 2003 Lithic Source Use and Paleoarchaic Foraging Territories in the Great Basin. *American Antiquity* 68(1):5–38.

Jones, T. L., G. M. Brown, L. M. Raab, J. L. McVickar, W. G. Spaulding, D. J. Kennett, A. York and P. L. Walker 1999 Environmental Imperatives Reconsidered: Demographic Crises in Western North America during the Medieval Climatic Anomaly. *Current Anthropology* 40(2):137–170.

Jones, T. L., R. T. Fitzgerald, D. J. Kennett, C. H. Miksicek, J. L. Fagan, J. Sharp and J. M. Erlandson 2002 The Cross Creek Site (CA-SLO-1797) and Its Implications for New World Colonization. *American Antiquity* 67(2):213–230.

Jones, T. L. and K. A. Klar 2005 Diffusionism Reconsidered: Linguistic and Archaeological Evidence for Prehistoric Polynesian Contact with Southern California. *American Antiquity* 70(3):457–484.

2007a *California Prehistory: Colonization, Culture, and Complexity*. New York: Rowman & Littlefield.

2007b Colonization, Culture, and Complexity. In *California Prehistory: Colonization, Culture, and Complexity*, edited by T. L. Jones and K. A. Klar, pp. 299–315. New York: Rowman & Littlefield.

José-Yacamán, L. Rendón, J. Arenas and M. C. Serra Puche 1996 Maya Blue Paint: An Ancient Nanostructured Material. *Science* 273:223–225.

Joyce, R. A. and J. S. Henderson 2001 Beginnings of Village Life in Eastern Mesoamerica. *Latin American Antiquity* 12(1):5–24.

Judge, W. J. 1989 Chaco Canyon-San Juan Basin. In *Dynamics of Southwest Prehistory*, edited by L. S. Cordell and G. J. Gumerman, pp. 209–261. Washington, DC: Smithsonian Institution Press.

Justeson, J. S. and T. Kaufman 1997 A Newly Discovered Column in the Hieroglyphic Text on La Mojarra Stela 1: A Test of the Epi-Olmec Decipherment. *Science* 277: 207–210.

Justice, N. D. 1987 *Stone Age Spear and Arrow Points of the Midcontinental and Eastern United States*. Bloomington: Indiana University Press.

Kaiser, J. 2002 Melting Glaciers Release Ancient Relics. *Science* 296:454–455.

Kantner, J. 2005 *Ancient Puebloan Southwest*. New York: Cambridge University Press.

Kay, M. 1998 The Central and Southern Plains Archaic. In *Archaeology on the Great Plains*, edited by W. R. Wood, pp. 173–200. Lawrence: University of Kansas Press.

Kay, M., F. B. King and C. K. Robinson 1980 Cucurbits from Phillips Spring: New Evidence and Interpretations. *American Antiquity* 45(4):806–822.

Keegan, W. F. 1992 *The People Who Discovered Columbus: The Prehistory of the Bahamas*. Gainesville: University of Florida Press.

1994 West Indian Archaeology 1: Overview and Foragers. *Journal of Archaeological Research* 2(3):255–284.

1996 West Indian Archaeology 2: After Columbus. *Journal of Archaeological Research* 4(4):265–294.

2000 West Indian Archaeology 3: Ceramic Age. *Journal of Archaeological Research* 8(2):135–167.

Kemp, B. M., R. S. Malhi, J. McDonough, D. A. Bolnick, J. A. Eshleman, O. Rickards, C. Martinez-Lebarga, J. R. Johnson, J. G. Lorenz, E. J. Dixon, T. E. Fifield, T. H. Heaton, R. Worl and D. G. Smith 2007 Genetic Analysis of Early Holocene Skeletal Remains From Alaska and Its Implications for the Settlement of the Americas. *American Journal of Physical Anthropology* 132:1–17.

Kennedy, R. 1996 *Hidden Cities: The Discovery and Loss of Ancient North American Civilization*. New York: Penguin Books.

Kennett, D. J. and B. Winterhalder (editors) 2006 *Behavioral Ecology and the Transition to Agriculture*. Berkeley: University of California Press.

Kerr, R. A. 2003 Megafauna Died From Big Kill, Not Big Chill. *Science* 300:885.

Keyser, J. D. and D. S. Whitley 2006 Sympathetic Magic in Western North American Rock Art. *American Antiquity* 71(1):3–26.

Kibler, K. W. 2005 Broader Continental Connections through the Gulf Coastal Plain of Texas. In *Gulf Coast Archaeology: The Southeastern United States and Mexico*, edited by N. M. White, pp. 197–204. Gainesville: University Press of Florida.

Kidder, A. V. 1927 Southwestern Archaeology Conference. *Science* 68:489–491.

Kidder, A. V., J. D. Jennings and E. M. Shook 1946 *Excavations at Kaminaljuyú, Guatemala*, no. 561. Washington, DC: Carnegie Institution of Washington.

Kidder, T. R. 2002 Mapping Poverty Point. *American Antiquity* 67(1):89–101.

2004 Plazas as Architecture: An Example from the Raffman Site, Northeast Louisiana. *American Antiquity* 69(3):514–532.

2006 Climate Change and the Archaic to Woodland Transition (3000–2500 cal. B.P.) in the Mississippi River Basin. *American Antiquity* 71(2):195–231.

King, A. 2003 *Etowah: The Political History of a Chiefdom Capital.* Tuscaloosa: University of Alabama Press.

King, C. 1978 Protohistoric and Historic Archaeology. In *California*, edited by R. F. Heizer, pp. 58–68. *Handbook of North American Indians,* vol. 8, W. C. Sturtevant, general editor. Washington, DC: Smithsonian Institution.

King, M. L. and S. B. Slobodin 1996 A Fluted Point from the Uptar Site, Northeastern Siberia. *Science* 273:634–636.

Kloor, K. 2007 The Vanishing Fremont. *Science* 318:1540–1543.

Kohler, T. A. (editor) 2004 *Archaeology of Bandelier National Monument: Village Formation on the Pajarito Plateau, New Mexico.* Albuquerque: University of New Mexico Press.

Kohler, T. A. and G. J. Gumerman 2000 *Dynamics in Human and Primate Societies: Agent-Based Modeling of Social and Spatial Processes.* New York: Oxford University Press.

Kohler, T. A., M. D. Varien, A. M. Wright and K. A. Kuckelman 2008 Mesa Verde Migrations. *American Scientist* 96:146–153.

Kooyman, B., M. E. Newman, C. Cluney, M. Lobb, S. Tolman, P. McNeil and L. V. Hills 2001 Identification of Horse Exploitation by Clovis Hunters Based on Protein Analysis. *American Antiquity* 66(4):686–691.

Kozuch, L. 2002 Olivella Beads from Spiro and the Plains. *American Antiquity* 67(4):697–709.

Krause, R. A. 2001 Plains Village Tradition: Coalescent. In *Plains*, edited by R. J. DeMallie, pp. 196–206. *Handbook of North American Indians,* vol. 13, W. C. Sturtevant, general editor. Washington, DC: Smithsonian Institution.

Krieger, A. D. 1964 Early Man in the New World. In *Prehistoric Man in the New World*, edited by J. D. Jennings and E. Norbeck, pp. 23–84. Chicago: University of Chicago Press.

Kroeber, A. L. 1948 *Anthropology.* New York: Harcourt, Brace.

Kuhn, R. D. and M. L. Sempowski 2001 A New Approach to Dating the League of the Iroquois. *American Antiquity* 66(2):310–314.

Kumar, S. and S. B. Hedges 1998 A Molecular Timescale for Vertebrate Evolution. *Nature* 392:917–920.

Kunz, M. L. and R. E. Reanier 1994 Paleoindians in Beringia: Evidence from Arctic Alaska. *Science* 263:660–662.

1996 Mesa Site, Iteriak Creek. In *American Beginnings: The Prehistory and Paleoecology of Beringia*, edited by

F. H. West, pp. 497–504. Chicago: University of Chicago Press.

Kuttruff, J. T., S. G. DeHart and M. J. O'Brien 1998 7500 Years of Prehistoric Footwear from Arnold Research Cave, Missouri. *Science* 281:72–75.

Lahren, L. and R. Bonnichsen 1974 Bone Foreshafts from a Clovis Burial in Southwestern Montana. *Science* 186:147–149.

Laird, K. R., S. C. Fritz, K. A. Maasch and B. F. Cumming 1996 Greater Drought Intensity and Frequency before AD 1200 in the Northern Great Plains, USA. *Nature* 384:552–554.

Lambert, P. M. and P. L. Walker 1991 Physical Anthropological Evidence for the Evolution of Social Complexity in Coastal Southern California. *Antiquity* 65:963–973.

Langley, J. C. 1991 The Forms and Usage of Notation at Teotihucan. *Ancient Mesoamerica* 2(2):285–298.

Larsen, H. E. and F. Rainey 1948 *Ipiutak and the Arctic Whale Hunting Culture.* Anthropological Papers of the American Museum of Natural History 42. American Museum of Natural History, New York.

Laylander, D. and J. Moore (editors) 2006 *The Prehistory of Baja California: Advances in the Archaeology of the Forgotten Peninsula.* Gainesville: University Press of Florida.

Leakey, L. S. B. and R. D. E. Simpson 1968 Archaeological Excavations in the Calico Mountains, California: Preliminary Report. *Science* 160:1022–1023.

LeBlanc, S. A. 1999 *Prehistoric Warfare in the American Southwest.* Salt Lake City: University of Utah Press.

Lehmer, D. J. 2001 Plains Village Tradition: Postcontact. In *Plains*, edited by R. J. DeMallie, pp. 245–255. *Handbook of North American Indians,* vol. 13, W. C. Sturtevant, general editor. Washington, DC: Smithsonian Institution.

Lekson, S. H. 1991 Settlement Pattern and the Chaco Region. In *Chaco & Hohokam: Prehistoric Regional Systems in the American Southwest*, edited by P. L. Crown and W. J. Judge, pp. 31–55. Santa Fe, NM: School of American Research Press.

2002 War in the Southwest, War in the World. *American Antiquity* 67(4):607–624.

2006 *The Archaeology of Chaco Canyon: An Eleventh-Century Pueblo Regional Center.* Santa Fe, NM: School of American Research Press, Santa Fe.

León-Portilla, M. 2003 *Códices: Los Antiguos Libros del Nuevo Mundo.* Mexico City: Aguilar.

Leonard, J. A., R. K. Wayne, J. Wheeler, R. Valadez, S. Guillén and C. Vilá 2002 Ancient DNA Evidence for Old World Origin of New World Dogs. *Science* 298:1613–1616.

Lepofsky, D., K. Lertzman, D. Hallett and R. Mathewes 2005 Climate Change and Culture Change on the Southern

Coast of British Columbia 2400–1200 cal. B.P.: An Hypothesis. *American Antiquity* 70(2):267–293.

Lepper, B. T. 2004 The Newark Earthworks. In *Hero, Hawk, and Open Hand*, edited by R. V. Sharp, pp. 73–81. New Haven, CT: Yale University Press.

Liebmann, M. 2002 Demystifying the Big Horn Medicine Wheel: A Contextual Analysis of Meaning, Symbolism, and Function. *Plains Anthropologist* 47(180):61–71.

Loendorf, L. L., C. Chippindale and D. S. Whitley (editors) 2005 *Discovering North American Rock Art*. Tucson: University of Arizona Press.

Long, A. and G. J. Fritz 2001 Validity of AMS Dates on Maize from the Tehuacán Valley: A Comment on MacNeish and Eubanks. *Latin American Antiquity* 12(1):87–90.

Looper, M. G. 1999 New Perspectives on the Late Classic Political History of Quirigua, Guatemala. *Ancient Mesoamerica* 10(2):263–280.

López Austin, A. and L. López Luján 2001 *El pasado indígena*. Mexico City: El Colegio de México.

López Austin, A., L. López Luján and S. Sugiyama 1991 The Temple of Quetzalcoatl at Teotihuacan: Its Possible Ideological Significance. *Ancient Mesoamerica* 2(1):93–105.

López Luján, L. 2005 *The Offerings of the Templo Mayor of Tenochtitlan*, Rev. ed. Albuquerque: University of New Mexico Press.

López Luján, L., R. H. Cobean and A. G. Mastache F. 1995 *Xochicalco Y Tula*. Milan: Jaca Book.

López Portillo, J., M. León Portilla and E. Matos Moctezuma 1981 *El Templo Mayor*. Mexico City: Bancomer.

Lorant, S. 1965 *The New World: The First Pictures of America*. New York: Duell, Sloan and Pearce.

Lovvorn, M. B., G. C. Frison and L. L. Tieszen 2001 Paleoclimate and Amerindians: Evidence from Stable Isotopes and Atmospheric Circulation. *Proceedings of the National Academy of Sciences* 98(5):2485–2490.

Lowie, R. 1915 Oral Tradition and History. *American Anthropologist* 17:597–599.

MacArthur, R. H. and E. O. Wilson 1967 *The Theory of Island Biogeography*. Princeton, NJ: Princeton University Press.

Macaulay, V., C. Hill, A. Achilli, C. Rengo, D. Clarke, W. Meehan, J. Blackburn, O. Semino, R. Scozzari, F. Cruciani, A. Taha, N. K. Shaari, J. M. Raja, P. Ismail, Z. Zainuddin, W. Goodwin, D. Bulbeck, H. J. Bandelt, S. Oppenheimer, A. Torroni and M. Richards 2005 Single, Rapid Coastal Settlement of Asia Revealed by Analysis of Complete Mitochondrial Genomes. *Science* 308: 1034–1036.

MacDonald, D. H. and B. S. Hewlett 1999 Reproductive Interests and Forager Mobility. *Current Anthropology* 40(4):501–523.

Macri, M. J. and M. G. Looper 2003 Nahua in Ancient Mesoamerica: Evidence from Maya Inscriptions. *Ancient Mesoamerica* 14(2):285–297.

Madsen, D. B. (editor) 2004 *Entering America: Northeast Asia and Beringia Before the Last Glacial Maximum*. Salt Lake City: University of Utah Press.

Madsen, D. B. and D. Rhode (editors) 1994 *Across the West: Human Population Movement and the Expansion of the Numa*. Salt Lake City: University of Utah Press.

Madsen, D. B. and S. R. Simms 1998 The Fremont Complex: A Behavioral Perspective. *Journal of World Prehistory* 12(3):255–336.

Mainfort, R. C. and M. L. Kwas 2004 The Bat Creek Stone Revisited: A Fraud Exposed. *American Antiquity* 69(4): 761–769.

Mainfort, R. C. J. and L. P. Sullivan (editors) 1998 *Ancient Earthen Enclosures of the Eastern Woodlands*. Gainesville: University Press of Florida.

Malhi, R. S., B. A. Schultz and D. G. Smith 2001 Distribution of Mitochondrial DNA Lineages Among Native American Tribes of Northeastern North America. *Human Biology* 73(1):17–55.

Malthus, T. 1798 *An Essay on the Principle of Population*. London: J. Johnson.

Mann, C. C. 2005 *1491: New Revelations of the Americas Before Columbus*. New York: Knopf.

Mann, D. H. and D. J. Meltzer 2007 Millennial-Scale Dynamics of Valley Fills over the Past 12,000 14C Yr in Northeastern New Mexico, USA. *Geological Society of America Bulletin* 119(11/12):1433–1448.

Mann, D. H. and D. M. Peteet 1994 Extent and Timing of the Last Glacial Maximum in Southwestern Alaska. *Quaternary Research* 42:136–148.

Manzanilla, L. (editor) 2005 *Reacomodos demográficos del Clásico al Postclásico en el centro de México*. Mexico City: Universidad Nacional Autónoma de México, Instituto de Investigaciones Antropológicas.

Manzanilla, L. and L. Barsba 1990 The Study of Activities in Classic Households: Two Case Studies from Coba and Teotihuacan. *Ancient Mesoamerica* 1(1):41–49.

Marcus, J. 1980 Zapotec Writing. *Scientific American* 242(2):50–64.

1992 *Mesoamerican Writing Systems, Propaganda, Myth, and History in Four Ancient Civilizations*. Princeton, NJ: Princeton University Press.

Marcus, J. and K. V. Flannery 1996 *Zapotec Civilization*. New York: Thames and Hudson.

Martin, P. S. 1967 Pleistocene Overkill. In *Pleistocene Extinctions: The Search for a Cause*, edited by P. S. Martin and H. E. Wright Jr. New Haven, CT: Yale University Press.

References

351

1973 Discovery of America. *Science* 179(4077):969–974.

1999a Megafauna of the Columbia Basin, 1800–1840. In *Northwest Lands, Northwest Peoples: Readings in Environmental History*, edited by D. D. Goble and P. W. Hirt. Seattle: University of Washington Press.

1999b War Zones and Game Sinks in Lewis and Clark's West. *Conservation Biology* 13(1):36–45.

Martin, S. and G. Nikolai 2008 *Chronicle of the Maya Kings and Queens*. New York: Thames and Hudson.

Marwitt, J. P. 1986 Fremont Cultures. In *Great Basin*, edited by W. L. D'Azevedo, pp. 161–172. *Handbook of North American Indians*, vol. 11, W. C. Sturtevant, general editor. Washington, DC: Smithsonian Institution.

Maschner, H. D. G. and K. L. Reedy-Maschner 1998 Raid, Retreat, Defend (Repeat): The Archaeology and Ethnohistory of Warfare on the North Pacific. *Journal of Anthropological Archaeology* 17(1):19–51.

Mason, R. J. 1962 The Paleo-Indian Tradition in Eastern North America. *Current Anthropology* 3(3):227–278.

1981 *Great Lakes Archaeology*. New World Archaeological Record. New York: Academic Press.

Masse, W. B. 1981 Prehistoric Irrigation Systems in the Salt River Valley, Arizona. *Science* 214:408–415.

Massey, W. C. 1949 Tribes and Languages of Baja California. *Southwestern Journal of Anthropology* 5(3):272–307.

1961 The Survival of the Dart-Thrower on the Peninsula of Baja California. *Southwestern Journal of Anthropology* 17:81–93.

Mastache, A. G., R. H. Cobean and D. M. Healan 2002 *Ancient Tollan: Tula and the Toltec Heartland*. Boulder: University of Colorado Press.

Matos Moctezuma, E. 1990 *Teotihuacán: The City of Gods*. New York: Rizzoli.

Matos Moctezuma, E. and F. Solís 2004 *The Aztec Calendar and Other Solar Monuments*. Mexico City: Conaculta-Instituto Nacional de Antropologia e Historia: Grupo Azabache.

Matson, R. G. 1983 Intensification and the Development of Cultural Complexity: The Northwest versus the Northeast Coast. In *The Evolution of Maritime Cultures on the Northeast and Northwest Coasts of America*, edited by R. J. Nash, vol. 11, pp. 125–148. Vancouver, British Columbia: Department of Archaeology, Simon Fraser University.

Matson, R. G. and G. Coupland 1995 *The Prehistory of the Northwest Coast*. New York: Academic Press.

Matson, R. G. and M. P. R. Magne 2006 *Athapaskan Migrations*. Tucson: University of Arizona Press.

Maxwell, D. 2000 Beyond Maritime Symbolism: Toxic Marine Objects from Ritual Contexts at Tikal. *Ancient Mesoamerica* 11(1):91–98.

Mayr, E. 1972 The Nature of the Darwinian Revolution. *Science* 176:981–989.

McCafferty, G. G. 1996 Reinterpreting the Great Pyramid of Cholula, Mexico. *Ancient Mesoamerica* 7(1):1–17.

McCafferty, S. and G. G. McCafferty 2000 Textile Production in Postclassic Cholula, Mexico. *Ancient Mesoamerica* 11(1):39–54.

McGhee, R. 1976 *The Burial at L'Anse-Amour*. Ottawa: National Museum of Man, National Museums of Canada.

Meltzer, D. J. 1995 Clocking the First Americans. *Annual Review of Anthropology* 24:21–45.

1997 Monte Verde and the Pleistocene Peopling of the Americas. *Science* 276:754–755.

1999 Human Responses to Middle Holocene (Altithermal) Climates on the North American Great Plains. *Quaternary Research* 52:404–416.

*2008 *First Peoples in the New World: Colonizing Ice Age America*. Berkeley: University of California Press.

Meltzer, D. J., J. M. Adovasio and T. D. Dillehay 1994 On a Pleistocene human occupation at Pedra Furada, Brazil. *Antiquity* 68:695–714.

Meltzer, D. J., L. C. Todd and V. T. Holliday 2002 The Folsom (Paleoindian) Type Site: Past Investigations, Current Studies. *American Antiquity* 67(1):5–36.

Merriwether, D. A. 2002 A Mitrochondrial Perspective on the Peopling of the New World. In *The First Americans: The Pleistocene Colonization of the New World*, edited by N. G. Jablonski, pp. 295–310. Memoirs of the California Academy of Sciences, vol. 27. San Francisco: California Academy of Sciences.

Middleton, W. D., G. M. Feinman and G. Molina Villegas 1998 Tome Use and Reuse in Oaxaca, Mexico. *Ancient Mesoamerica* 9(2):297–307.

Milanich, J. T. 1994 *Archaeology of Precolumbian Florida*. Gainesville: University Press of Florida.

1996 *The Timucua*. Cambridge, MA: Blackwell.

1998 *Florida's Indians from Ancient Times to the Present*. Gainesville: University Press of Florida.

1999 *Famous Florida Sites: Mount Royal and Crystal River*. Gainesville: University Press of Florida.

Milanich, J. T., A. S. Cordell, J. Vernon J. Knight, T. A. Kohler and B. J. Sigler-Lavelle 1997 *McKeithen Weeden Island: The Culture of Northern Florida, A.D. 200–900*. Gainesville: University Press of Florida.

Milbrath, S. and C. Peraza Lope 2003 Revisiting Mayapan: Mexico's las Maya Capital. *Ancient Mesoamerica* 14(1):1–46.

Miller, G. H., M. L. Fogel, J. W. Magee, M. K. Gagen, S. J. Clarke and B. J. Johnson 2005 Ecosystem Collapse in

Pleistocene Australia and a Human Role in Megafaunal Extinction. *Science* 309:287–293.

Miller, V. 1983 Social and Political Complexity on the East Coast: The Micmac Case. In *The Evolution of Maritime Cultures on the Northeast and Northwest Coasts of America*, edited by R. J. Nash, vol. 11, pp. 41–55. Vancouver, British Columbia: Department of Archaeology, Simon Fraser University.

Millon, R. (editor) 1973 *Urbanization at Teotihuacán, Mexico*. Austin: University of Texas Press.

Milner, G. R. 1998 *The Cahokia Chiefdom: The Archaeology of a Mississippian Society*. Washington, DC: Smithsonian Institution Press.

2004 *The Moundbuilders: Ancient Peoples of Eastern North America*. New York: Thames and Hudson.

Mitchell, D. 1990 Prehistory of the Coasts of Southern British Columbia and Northern Washington. In *Northwest Coast*, edited by W. Suttles, pp. 340–358. *Handbook of North American Indians*, vol. 7, W. C. Sturtevant, general editor. Washington, DC: Smithsonian Institution.

Mithun, M. 1984 The Proto-Iroquoians: Cultural Reconstruction from Lexical Materials. In *Extending the Rafters: Interdisciplinary Approaches to Iroquoian Studies*, edited by M. K. Foster, J. Campisi and M. Mithun. Albany: State University of New York Press.

Moholy-Nagy, H. 1999 Mexican Obsidian at Tikal, Guatemala. *Latin American Antiquity* 10(3):300–313.

Moore, D. G. 2002 *Catawba Valley Mississippian: Ceramics, Chronology, and Catawba Indians*. Tuscaloosa: University of Alabama Press.

Moore, J. H. 1987 *The Cheyenne Nation*. Lincoln: University of Nebraska Press.

1996 *The Cheyenne*. Cambridge, MA: Blackwell.

Moore, J. H. and M. E. Moseley 2001 How Many Frogs Does It Take to Leap Around the Americas? Comments on Anderson and Gillam. *American Antiquity* 66(3):526–529.

Morey, D. F. 1984 The Early Evolution of the Domestic Dog. *American Scientist* 82:336–347.

2006 Burying Key Evidence: The Social Bond between Dogs and People. *Journal of Archaeological Science* 33:158–175.

Morgan, L. H. 1985 *Ancient Society*. Tucson: University of Arizona Press.

Morgan, W. N. 1999 *Precolumbian Architecture in Eastern North America*. Gainesville: University Press of Florida.

Morss, N. M. 1931 *The Ancient Culture of the Fremont River in Utah*. Papers of the Peabody Museum of American Archaeology and Ethnology, Harvard University, vol. 12, no. 3. Cambridge, MA: Harvard University Press.

Moss, M. L. 1999 George Catlin among the Nayas: Understanding the Practice of Labret Wearing on the Northwest Coast. *Ethnohistory* 46(2):31–65.

Moss, M. L. and J. M. Erlandson 1992 Forts, Refuge Rocks, and Defensive Sites: The Antiquity of Warfare along the North Pacific Coast of North America. *Arctic Anthropology* 29(2):73–90.

1998 A Comparative Chronology of Northwest Coast Fishing Features. In *Hidden Dimensions: The Cultural Significance of Wetland Archaeology*, edited by K. Bernick, pp. 180–198. Vancouver: University of British Columbia Press.

Moss, M. L., D. M. Peteet and C. Whitlock 2004 Mid-Holocene Culture and Climate on the Northwest Coast of North America. In *Climatic Change and Cultural Dynamics: A Global Perspective on Holocene Transitions*, edited by D. H. Sandweiss and K. A. Maasch. San Diego, CA: Academic Press.

Moulton, G. E. (editor) 1990 *The Journals of the Lewis & Clark Expedition, November 2, 1805-March 22, 1806*. University of Nebraska Press, Lincoln.

Murdock, G. P. 1962 Ethnographic Atlas. *Ethnology* 1 and continuing.

Murdock, G. P. and C. Provost 1973 Measurement of Cultural Complexity. *Ethnology* 12:379–392.

Muro, M. 1998 New Finds Explode Old Views of the American Southwest. *Science* 279:653–654.

Naroll, R. 1956 A Preliminary Index of Social Development. *American Anthropologist* 58:687–715.

Neitzel, J. E. (editor) 1999 *Great Towns and Regional Polities in the Prehistoric American Southwest and Southeast*. Albuquerque: University of New Mexico Press.

2003a The Organization, Function, and Population of Pueblo Bonito. In *Pueblo Bonito: Center of the Chacoan World*, edited by J. E. Neitzel, pp. 143–149. Washington, DC: Smithsonian Books.

2003b *Pueblo Bonito: Center of the Chacoan World*. Washington, DC: Smithsonian Books.

Nelson, C. M. 1990 Prehistory of the Puget Sound Region. In *Northwest Coast*, edited by W. Suttles, pp. 481–484. *Handbook of North American Indians*, vol. 7, W. C. Sturtevant, general editor. Washington, DC: Smithsonian Institution.

Nelson, M. C. and M. Hegmon 2001 Abandonment Is Not As It Seems: An Approach to the Relationship between Site and Regional Abandonment. *American Antiquity* 66(2):213–235.

Nelson, M. C., M. Hegmon, S. Kulow and K. G. Schollmeyer 2006 Archaeological and Ecological Perspectives on Reorganization: A Case Study from the Mimbres Region of the U.S. Southwest. *American Antiquity* 71(3):403–432.

Neurath, J. 1994 El llamado complejo ceremonial de sureste y los posibles contactos entre Mesoamérica y la cuenca del Mississippi. *Estudios de Cultura Náhuatl* 24:315–350.

Newsom, L. A. 1993 *Native West Indian Plant Use* (Doctoral dissertation, University of Florida).

2002 The Paleoethnobotany of the Archaic Mortuary Pond. In *Windover: Multidisciplinary Investigations of an Early Archaic Florida Cemetery*, edited by G. H. Doran, pp. 191–210. Tallahassee: University Press of Florida.

Newsom, L. A. and D. M. Pearsall 2000 Spatial Trends Indicated by a Survey of Archaeobotanical Data from the Caribbean Islands. In *People and Plants in Ancient America*, edited by P. E. Minnis. Washington, DC: Smithsonian Institution Press.

Nichols, D. L., M. W. Spence and M. D. Borland 1991 Watering the Fields of Teotihuacan: Early Irrigation at the Ancient City. *Ancient Mesoamerica* 2(1):119–129.

Nichols, J. 2002 The First American Languages. In *The First Americans: The Pleistocene Colonization of the New World*, edited by N. G. Jablonski, pp. 273–293. Memoirs of the California Academy of Sciences, vol. 27. San Francisco: California Academy of Sciences.

Nichols, J. and D. A. Peterson 1996 The Amerind Personal Pronouns. *Language* 72(2):336–371.

Nicholson, H. B. 1971 Religion in Pre-Hispanic Central Mexico. In *Archaeology of Northern Mesoamerica, Part One*, edited by G. F. Ekholm and I. Bernal, pp. 395–446. *Handbook of Middle American Indians*, vol. 10, R. Wauchope, general editor. Austin: University of Texas Press.

Nicholson, H. B. and E. Q. Kerber 1983 *Art of Aztec Mexico: Treasures of Tenochtitlan*. Washington, DC: National Gallery of Art.

Noble, D. G. 2004 *In Search of Chaco: New Approaches to an Archaeological Enigma*. Santa Fe, NM: School of American Research Press.

2006 *The Mesa Verde World: Explorations in Ancestral Pueblo Archaeology*. Santa Fe, NM: School of American Research Press.

Noble, W. C. 1981 Prehistory of the Great Slave Lake and Great Bear Lake Region. In *Subarctic*, edited by J. Helm, pp. 97–106. *Handbook of North American Indians*, vol. 6, W. C. Sturtevant, general editor. Washington, DC: Smithsonian Institution.

Nuttall, Z. (editor) 1975 *The Codex Nuttall: A Picture Manuscript from Ancient Mexico*. New York: Dover.

O'Day, S. J. and W. F. Keegan 2001 Expedient Shell Tools from the Northern West Indies. *Latin American Antiquity* 12(3):274–290.

Ortiz, A. (editor) 1979 *Southwest*, vol. 9. Washington, DC: Smithsonian Institution.

1983 *Southwest*, vol. 10. Washington, DC: Smithsonian Institution.

Owsley, D. W. and R. L. Jantz 2001 Archaeological Politics and Public Interest in Paleoamerican Studies: Lessons from Gordon Creek Woman and Kennewick Man. *American Antiquity* 66(4):565–575.

Paine, R. R. and A. Freter 1996 Environmental Degradation and the Classic Maya Collapse at Copan, Honduras (A.D. 600–1250). *Ancient Mesoamerica* 7(1):37–47.

Palter, J. L. 1976 A New Approach to the Significance of the "Weighted" Spear Thrower. *American Antiquity* 41(4):500–510.

Parenti, F., M. Fontugue and C. Guérin 1995 Pedra Furada in Brazil and Its "Presumed" Evidence: Limitations and Potential of the Available Data. *Antiquity* 70(268):416–421.

Park, R. L. 2003 The Seven Warning Signs of Bogus Science. In *Chronicle of Higher Education*, pp. B20.

Parsons, J. R., E. Blumfiel, M. Parsons and D. Wilson 1982 *Prehispanic Settlement Patterns in the Southern Valley of Mexico: The Chalco-Xochimilco Region*. University of Michigan Museum of Anthropology, Memoirs 14. Ann Arbor: University of Michigan Museum of Anthropology.

Pauketat, T. R. 2001 Practice and History in Archaeology: An Emerging Paradigm. *Anthropological Theory* 1(1):73–98.

2003 Resettled Farmers and the Making of a Mississippian Polity. *American Antiquity* 68(1):39–66.

Pavelka, M. S. M. 2002 Change versus Improvement over Time and Our Place in Nature. *Current Anthropology* 43(Suppl.):S37–S44.

Peeler, D. E. and M. Winter 1995 Building J at Monte Albá. *Latin American Antiquity* 6(4):362–369.

Pennisi, E. 2005 The Sky Is Not the Limit. *Science* 310:1896–1897.

Pérez de Lara, J. 2005 Temple of the Sun. *Archaeology* 58(6):37–41.

Persuitte, D. 2000 *Joseph Smith and the Origins of the Book of Mormon*, 2nd ed. Jefferson, NC: McFarland.

Petersen, J. B. and N. A. Sidell 1996 Mid-Holocene Evidence of *Cucurbita* Sp. from Central Maine. *American Antiquity* 61(4):685–698.

Peterson, L. 1978 *A Field Guide to Edible Wild Plants*. The Peterson Field Guide Series. Houghton Mifflin Company, Boston.

Pettigrew, R. M. 1990 Prehistory of the Lower Columbia and Willammette Valley. In *Northwest Coast*, edited by W. Suttles, pp. 518–529. *Handbook of North American Indians*, vol. 7, W. C. Sturtevant, general editor. Washington, DC: Smithsonian Institution.

Phillips, P. and J. A. Brown 1978 *Pre-Columbian Shell Engravings from the Craig Mound at Spiro, Oklahoma, Part 1*. Cambridge, MA: Peabody Museum Press.

Pincemin, S., J. Marcus, L. Florey Folan, W. J. Folan, M. D. R. Domínguez Carrasco and A. Morales López 1998 Extending the Calakmul Dynasty Back in Time: A New

Stela from a Maya Capital in Campeche, Mexico. *Latin American Antiquity* 9(4):310–327.

Piperno, D. R. and K. V. Flannery 2001 The Earliest Archaeological Maize (Zea mays L.) from Highland Mexico: New Accelerator Mass Spectrometry Dates and Their Implications. *Proceedings of the National Academy of Sciences* 98(4):2101–2103.

Pitulko, V. V., P. A. Nikolsky, E. Y. Girya, A. E. Basilyan, V. E. Tumskoy, S. A. Koulakov, S. N. Astakhov, E. Y. Pavlova and M. A. Anisimov. 2004 The Yana RHS Site: Humans in the Arctic Before the Last Glacial Maximum. *Science* 303:52–56.

Plog, S. 1997 *Ancient Peoples of the American Southwest*. New York: Thames and Hudson.

Plunket, P. and G. Uruñuela 1998 Preclassic Household Patterns Preserved under Volcanic Ash at Tetimpa, Puebla, Mexico. *Latin American Antiquity* 9(4):287–309.

Pohl, M. E. D., K. O. Pope, J. G. Jones, J. S. Jacob, D. R. Piperno, S. D. deFrance, D. L. Lentz, J. A. Gifford, M. E. Danforth and J. K. Josserand 1996 Early Agriculture in the Maya Lowlands. *Latin American Antiquity* 7(4):355–372.

Pohl, M. E. D., K. O. Pope and C. Von Nagy 2002 Olmec Origins of Mesoamerican Writing. *Science* 298:1984–1987.

Pokotylo, D. L. and D. Mitchell 1998 Prehistory of the Northern Plateau. In *Plateau*, edited by D. E. Walker Jr., pp. 81–102. *Handbook of North American Indians*, vol. 12, W. C. Sturtevant, general editor. Washington, DC: Smithsonian Institution.

Pollard, H. P. 1991 The Construction of Ideology in the Emergence of the Prehispanic Tarascan State. *Ancient Mesoamerica* 2(2):167–179.

Polyak, V. J. and Y. Asmerom 2001 Late Holocene Climate and Cultural Changes in the Southwestern United States. *Science* 294:148–150.

Pope, K. O. and B. H. Dahlin 1989 Ancient Maya Wetland Agriculture: New Insights from Ecological and Remote Sensing Research. *Journal of Field Archaeology* 16:87–106.

Porcasi, J. F. and H. Fujita 2000 The Dolphin Hunters: A Specialized Prehistoric Maritime Adaptation in the Southern California Channel Islands and Baja California. *American Antiquity* 65(3):543–566.

Porter, M. N. 1948 *Pipas Precortesianas: Introducción de Chita de la Calle*. Mexico City: Acta Antropológica 3(2).

Potter, S. R. 1993 *Commoners, Tribute, and Chiefs: The Development of Algonquian Culture in the Potomac Valley*. Charlottesville: University Press of Virginia.

Powell, J. F. 1993 Dental Evidence for the Peopling of the New World: Some Methodological Considerations. *Human Biology* 65(5):799–819.

Powell-Marti, V. and P. Gilman 2006 *Mimbres Society*. Tucson: University of Arizona Press.

Powers, W. R. and J. F. Hoffecker 1989 Late Pleistocene Settlement in the Nenana Valley, Central Alaska. *American Antiquity* 54(2):263–287.

Powis, T. G., F. J. Valdez, T. R. Hester, W. J. Hurst and S. M. J. Tarka 2002 Spouted Vessels and Cacao Use among the Preclassic Maya. *Latin American Antiquity* 13(1):85–106.

Preucel, R. W. (editor) 2002 *Archaeologies of the Pueblo Revolt: Identity, Meaning, and Renewal in the Pueblo World*. Albuquerque: University of New Mexico Press.

Quinlan, A. R. and A. Woody 2003 Marks of Distinction: Rock Art and Ethnic Identification in the Great Basin. *American Antiquity* 68(2):372–390.

Railey, J. A. 1996 Woodland Cultivators. In *Kentucky Archaeology*, edited by R. B. Lewis, pp. 79–126. Lexington: University Press of Kentucky.

Rattray, E. C. 1990 New Findings on the Origins of Thin Orange Ceramics. *Ancient Mesoamerica* 1(2):181–195.

Reagan, M. J., R. M. Rowlett, E. G. Garrison, W. Dort Jr., V. M. Bryant Jr. and C. J. Johennsen 1978 Flake Tools Stratified Below Paleo-Indian Artifacts. *Science* 200:1272–1274.

Reid, J. and S. Whittlesey 1997 *The Archaeology of Ancient Arizona*. Tucson: University of Arizona Press.

Renfrew, C. and P. Bahn 2000 *Archaeology: Theories, Methods, and Practice*. New York: Thames and Hudson.

Renfrew, C. and J. F. Cherry (editors) 1986 *Peer Polity Interaction and Socio-Political Change*. Cambridge: Cambridge University Press.

Restall, M. 1997 *The Maya World*. Palo Alto, CA: Stanford University Press.

Rice, P. M. 1999 Rethinking Classic Lowland Maya Pottery Censers. *Ancient Mesoamerica* 10(1):25–50.

Richerson, P. J., R. Boyd and R. L. Bettinger 2001 Was Agriculture Impossible during the Pleistocene but Mandatory during the Holocene? A Climate Change Hypothesis. *American Antiquity* 66(3):387–411.

Rick, T. C., J. M. Erlandson and R. L. Vellanoweth 2001 Paleocoastal Marine Fishing on the Pacific Coast of the Americas: Perspectives from Daisy Cave, California. *American Antiquity* 66(4):595–613.

Ricklis, R. A. and R. A. Weinstein 2005 Sea-Level Rise and Fluctuation on the Central Texas Coast. In *Gulf Coast Archaeology: The Southeastern United States and Mexico*, edited by N. M. White, pp. 109–154. Gainesville: University Press of Florida.

Riley, C. L. 2005 *Becoming Aztlan: Mesoamerican Influence in the Greater Southwest, AD 1200–1500*. Salt Lake City: University of Utah Press.

Ringle, W. M. 1990 Who Was Who in Ninth-Century Chichen Itza. *Ancient Mesoamerica* 1(2):233–243.

Ringle, W. M., T. Gallareta Negrón and G. J. I. Bey 1998 The Return of Quetzalcoatl: Evidence for the Spread of a World Religion during the Epiclassic Period. *Ancient Mesoamerica* 9(2):183–232.

Ritterbush, L. W. and B. Logan 2000 Late Prehistoric Oneota Population Movement into the Central Plains. *Plains Anthropologist* 45(173):257–272.

Roberts, R. G., T. F. Flannery, L. K. Ayliffe, H. Yoshida, J. M. Olley, G. J. Prideaux, G. M. Laslett, A. Baynes, M. A. Smith, R. Jones and B. L. Smith 2001 New Ages for the Last Australian Megafauna: Continent-Wide Extinction About 46,000 Years Ago. *Science* 292:1888–1892.

Robicsec, F. 1978 *The Smoking Gods: Tobacco in Maya Art, History, and Religion*. Norman: University of Oklahoma Press.

Rodbell, D. T., G. O. Seltzer, D. M. Anderson, M. B. Abbott, D. B. Enfield and J. H. Newman 1999 An ~15,000-Year Record of El Niño-Driven Alluviation in Southwestern Ecuador. *Science* 283:516–520.

Roesdahl, E. 1991 *The Vikings*. Translated by S. M. Margeson and K. Williams. New York: Penguin Books.

Roosevelt, A. C., J. Douglas and L. Brown 2002 The Migrations and Adaptations of the First Americans: Clovis and Pre-Clovis Viewed from South America. In *The First Americans: The Pleistocene Colonization of the New World*, edited by N. G. Jablonski, pp. 159–235. Memoirs of the California Academy of Sciences, vol. 27. San Francisco: California Academy of Sciences.

Rosales-López, A. and H. Fujita 2000 *La antigua California prehispánica: la vida costera en El Conchalito*. Mexico City: Instituto Nacional de Antropología e Historia.

Rose, M. 2005 When Giants Roamed the Earth. *Archaeology* 58(6):30–35.

Ross, R. E. 1990 Prehistory of the Oregon Coast. In *Northwest Coast*, edited by W. Suttles, pp. 554–559. *Handbook of North American Indians*, vol. 7, W. C. Sturtevant, general editor. Washington, DC: Smithsonian Institution.

Ruddiman, W. F. 2003 The Anthropogenic Greenhouse Era Began Thousands of Years Ago. *Climatic Change* 61(3):261–293.

Ruhlen, M. 1998 The Origin of the Na-Dene. *Proceedings of the National Academy of Sciences* 95:13994–13996.

Samuels, S. R. (editor) 1991 *Ozette Archaeological Project Research Report I: House Structure and Floor Midden*, Reports of Investigations 63. Pullman: Washington State University Department of Anthropology.

1994 *Ozette Archaeological Project Research Report II: Fauna*, Reports of Investigations 66. Pullman: Washington State University Department of Anthropology.

Sanders, W. T. (editor) 1986 *The Teotihuacan Valley Project Final Report Vol. 4, The Toltec Period Occupation of the Valley; Part 1, Excavations and Ceramics*. Occasional Papers in Anthropology no. 13. University Park, PA: Department of Anthropology, Pennsylvania State University.

1987 *The Teotihuacan Valley Project Final Report Vol. 4, The Toltec Period Occupation of the Valley; Part 2, Surface Survey and Special Studies*. Occasional Papers in Anthropology no. 15. University Park, PA: Department of Anthropology, Pennsylvania State University.

1992 Ecology in Sixteenth Century Mesoamerica. *Antiquity* 66(250).

1994 *The Teotihuacan Valley Project Final Report Vol. 3, The Teotihuacan Period Occupation of the Valley; Part 1, The Excavations*. Occasional Papers in Anthropology no. 19. University Park, PA: Department of Anthropology, Pennsylvania State University.

1995 *The Teotihuacan Valley Project Final Report Vol. 3, The Teotihuacan Period Occupation of the Valley; Part 2, Artifact Analyses*. Occasional Papers in Anthropology no. 20. University Park, PA: Department of Anthropology, Pennsylvania State University.

1996a *The Teotihuacan Valley Project Final Report Vol. 3, The Teotihuacan Period Occupation of the Valley; Part 3, The Surface Survey*. Occasional Papers in Anthropology no. 21. University Park, PA: Department of Anthropology, Pennsylvania State University.

1996b *The Teotihuacan Valley Project Final Report Vol. 3, The Teotihuacan Period Occupation of the Valley; Part 4, Special Analyses, Appendices and Volume Bibliography*. Occasional Papers in Anthropology no. 24. University Park, PA: Department of Anthropology, Pennsylvania State University.

2004 The Basin of Mexico as a Habitat for Pre-Hispanic Farmers. In *The Aztec Empire*, edited by F. Solis, pp. 56–68. New York: Guggenheim Museum.

Sanders, W. T. and S. T. Evans (editors) 2000 *The Teotihuacan Valley Project Final Report Vol. 5, The Aztec Period Occupation of the Valley; Part 1, Natural Environment, 20th Century Occupation, Survey Methodology, and Site Descriptions*. Occasional Papers in Anthropology no. 25. University Park, PA: Department of Anthropology, Pennsylvania State University.

2001 *The Teotihuacan Valley Project Final Report Vol. 5, The Aztec Period Occupation of the Valley; Part 3, Syntheses and General Bibliography*. Occasional Papers in Anthropology no. 27. University Park, PA: Department of Anthropology, Pennsylvania State University.

Sanders, W. T., A. Kovar, T. Charlton and R. A. Diehl 1970 *The Teotihuacan Valley Project Final Report Vol. 1, The Natural Environment, Contemporary Occupation and 16th Century Population of the Valley*. Occasional Papers in Anthropology no. 3. University Park, PA: Department of Anthropology, Pennsylvania State University.

References

Sanders, W. T. and B. J. Price 1968 *Mesoamerica: The Evolution of a Civilization*. New York: Random House.

Sanders, W. T. and R. S. Santley 1983 A Tale of Three Cities: Energetics and Urbanization in Pre-Hispanic Central Mexico. In *Prehistoric Settlement Patterns: Essays in Honor of Gordon R. Willey*, edited by E. Z. Vogt and R. M. Leventhal, pp. 243–291. Albuquerque and Cambridge, MA: University of New Mexico Press and Peabody Museum of Archaeology and Ethnology.

Sassaman, K. E. 2005 Structure and Practice in the Archaic Southeast. In *North American Archaeology*, edited by T. R. Pauketat and D. DiPaolo Loren, pp. 79–107. Malden, MA: Blackwell.

Satterthwaite, L. 1965 Calendrics of the Maya Lowlands. In *Archaeology of Southern Mesoamerica, Part Two*, edited by G. R. Willey, vol. 3, pp. 603–631, R. Wauchope, general editor. Austin: University of Texas Press.

Saunders, J. W., R. D. Mandel, R. T. Sacier, E. T. Allen, C. T. Hallmark, J. K. Johnson, E. H. Jackson, C. M. Allen, G. L. Stringer, D. S. Frink, J. K. Feathers, S. Williams, K. J. Gremillion, M. F. Vidrine and R. Jones 1997 A Mound Complex in Louisiana at 5400–5000 Years Before the Present. *Science* 277:1796–1799.

Saunders, J. W., R. D. Mandel, C. G. Sampson, C. M. Allen, E. T. Allen, D. A. Bush, J. K. Feathers, K. J. Gremillion, C. T. Hallmark, E. H. Jackson, J. K. Johnson, R. Jones, R. T. Saucier, G. L. Stringer and M. F. Vidrine 2005 Watson Brake, A Middle Archaic Mound Complex in Northeast Louisiana. *American Antiquity* 70(4):631–668.

Saunders, N. J. and D. Gray 1996 Zemís, Trees, and Symbolic Landscapes: Three Taíno Carvings from Jamaica. *Antiquity* 70(270):801–812.

Savolainen, P., Y.-P. Zhang, J. Luo, J. Lundeberg and T. Leitner 2002 Genetic Evidence for an East Asian Origin of Domestic Dogs. *Science* 298:1610–1613.

Sawatzky, H. L. and W. H. Lehn 1976 The Arctic Mirage and the Early North Atlantic. *Science* 192:1300–1305.

Scarborough, V. L. 1998 Ecology and Ritual: Water Management and the Maya. *Latin American Antiquity* 9(2):135–159.

Scarborough, V. L. and G. G. Gallopin 1991 A Water Storage Adaptation in the Maya Lowlands. *Science* 251:658–662.

Scarry, C. M. 1993 *Foraging and Farming in the Eastern Woodlands*. Gainesville: University Press of Florida.

Schaafsma, P. (editor) 2007 *New Perspectives on Pottery Mound Pueblo*. Albuquerque: University of New Mexico Press.

Schalk, R. F. 1981 Land Use and Organizational Complexity among Foragers of Northwestern North America. In *Affluent Foragers: Pacific Coasts East and West*, edited by

S. Koyama and D. H. Thomas. Senri Ethnological Studies, vol. 9. Osaka, Japan: National Museum of Ethnology.

Schele, L. 1992 The Founders of Lineages at Copan and Other Maya Sites. *Ancient Mesoamerica* 3(1):135–144.

Schlesier, K. H. 2002 On the Big Horn Medicine Wheel: A Comment on Matthew Liebmann. *Plains Anthropologist* 47(180):61–71. *Plains Anthropologist* 47(183):387–392.

Schneider, F. 2002 Prehistoric Horticulture in the Northeastern Plains. *Plains Anthropologist* 47(180):33–50.

Schollmeyer, K. G. and C. G. Turner II 2004 Dental Caries, Prehistoric Diet, and the Pithouse-to-Pueblo Transition in Southwestern Colorado. *American Antiquity* 69(3):569–582.

Schurr, T. G. 2000 Mitchondrial DNA and the Peopling of the New World. *American Scientist* 88(3):246–253.

Scott, J. F. 2001 Dressed to Kill: Stone Regalia of the Mesoamerican Ballgame. In *The Sport of Life and Death: The Mesoamerican Ballgame*, edited by E. M. Whittington, pp. 51–63. New York: Thames and Hudson.

Seaver, K. A. 2004 *Maps, Myths, and Men: The Story of the Vinland Map*. Stanford, CA: Stanford University Press.

Sebastian, L. 1996 The *Chaco Anasazi: Sociopolitical Evolution in the Prehistoric Southwest*. New York: Cambridge University Press.

Serrato-Combe, A. 2001 *The Aztec Templo Mayor*. Salt Lake City: University of Utah Press.

Service, E. 1962 *Primitive Social Organization*. New York: Random House.

Shapiro, B., A. J. Drummond, A. Rambaut, M. C. Wilson, P. E. Matheus, A. V. Sher, O. G. Pybus, M. T. P. Gilbert, I. Barnes, J. Binladen, E. Willerslev, A. J. Hansen, G. F. Baryshnikov, J. A. Burns, S. Davydov, J. C. Driver, D. G. Froese, C. R. Harington, G. Keddie, P. Kosintsev, M. L. Kunz, L. D. Martin, R. O. Stephenson, J. Storer, R. Tedford, S. Zimov and A. Cooper 2004 Rise and Fall of the Beringian Steppe Bison. *Science* 306:1561–1565.

Sharer, R. J. and W. Ashmore 2003 *Archaeology: Discovering Our Past*, 3rd ed. New York: McGraw-Hill.

Shaw, J. M. 2003 Climate Change and Deforestation: Implications for the Maya collapse. *Ancient Mesoamerica* 14(1):157–167.

Sheets, P. D. 2000 Provisioning the Ceren Household: The Vertical Economy, Village Economy, and Household Economy in the Southeastern Maya Periphery. *Ancient Mesoamerica* 11(2):217–230.

Sheets, P. D., H. F. Beaubien, M. Beaudry, A. Gerstle, B. McKee, C. D. Miller, H. Spetzler and D. B. Tucker 1990 Household Archaeolgy at Cerén, El Salvador. *Ancient Mesoamerica* 1(1):81–90.

Shennan, S. 2000 Population, Culture History, and the Dynamics of Culture Change. *Current Anthropology* 41(5):811–835.

Shipley, W. F. 1978 Native Languages of California. In *California*, edited by R. F. Heizer, pp. 80–90. *Handbook of North American Indians,* vol. 8, W. C. Sturtevant, general editor. Washington, DC: Smithsonian Institution.

Siebert, F. T., Jr. 1967 *The Original Home of the Proto-Algonquian People*. Ottawa, Ontario, Canada: National Museum of Canada.

Siegel, P. E. 1991 Migration Research in Saladoid Archaeology: A Review. *The Florida Anthropologist* 44:79–91.

1999 Contested Places and Places of Contest: The Evolution of Social Power and Ceremonial Space in Prehistoric Puerto Rico. *Latin American Antiquity* 10(3):209–238.

Silverberg, R. 1968 *Mound Builders of Ancient America: The Archaeology of a Myth*. Greenwich, CT: New York Graphic Society.

Skelton, R. A., T. E. Marston and G. D. Painter 1965 *The Vinland Map and the Tartar Relation*. New Haven, CT: Yale University Press.

Slaughter, R. and J. Skulan 2001 Did Human Hunting Cause Mass Extinction? *Science* 294(5546):1460–1461.

Sluyter, A. 1993 Long-Distance Staple Transport in Western Mesoamerica: Insights through Quantitative Modeling. *Ancient Mesoamerica* 4(2):193–199.

Smith, B. D. 1989 Origins of Agriculture in Eastern North America. *Science* 246:1566–1571.

1997 The Initial Domestication of *Cucurbita pepo* in the Americas 10,000 Years Ago. *Science* 276:932–934.

2001a Documenting Plant Domestication: The Consilience of Biological and Archaeological Approaches. *Proceedings of the National Academy of Sciences* 98(4):1324–1326.

2001b Low-Level Food Production. *Journal of Archaeological Research* 9(1):1–43.

2001c The Transition to Food Production. In *Archaeology at the Millennium: A Sourcebook*, edited by G. M. Feinman and T. D. Price, pp. 199–229. New York: Kluwer Academic/Plenum.

2007 Niche Construction and the Behavioral Context of Plant and Animal Domestication. *Evolutionary Anthropology* 16:188–199.

Smith, M. E. 1990 Long-Distance Trade Under the Aztec Empire: The Archaeological Evidence. *Ancient Mesoamerica* 1(2):153–169.

1996 *The Aztecs*. Cambridge, MA: Blackwell.

2004 The Archaeology of Ancient State Economies. *Annual Review of Anthropology* 33:73–102.

Smith, M. E. and F. F. Berdan (editors) 2003 *The Postclassic Mesoamerican World*. Salt Lake City: University of Utah Press.

Smyth, M. P. and D. Rogart 2004 A Teotihuacan Presence at Chac II, Yucatan, Mexico: Implications for Early Political Economy of the Puuc Region. *Ancient Mesoamerica* 15(1):17–47.

Snow, D. R. 1975 The Passadumkeag Sequence. *Arctic Anthropology* 12(2):46–59.

1976a The Archaeological Implications of the Proto-Algonquian Urheimat. In *Papers of the Seventh Algonquian Conference, 1975*, edited by W. Cowan, pp. 339–346. Ottawa, Ontario, Canada: Carleton University.

1976b *The Archaeology of North America*. New York: Viking.

1976c The Solon Petroglyphs and Eastern Abenaki Shamanism. In *Papers of the Seventh Algonquian Conference, 1975*, edited by W. Cowan, pp. 281–288. Ottawa, Ontario, Canada: Carleton University.

1978 Shaking Down the New Paradigm. *Archaeology of Eastern North America* 6:87–91.

1980 *The Archaeology of New England*. New World Archaeological Record. New York: Academic Press.

1984 Iroquois Prehistory. In *Extending the Rafters: Interdisciplinary Approaches to Iroquoian Studies*, edited by M. K. Foster, J. Campisi and M. Mithun. Albany: State University of New York Press.

1992 Disease and Population Decline in Northeastern North America. In *Disease and Demography in the Americas: Changing Patterns before and after 1492*, edited by J. W. Verano and D. H. Ubelaker, pp. 177–186. Washington, DC: Smithsonian Institution Press.

1994 *The Iroquois*. The Peoples of America. Cambridge, MA: Blackwell.

1995a Microchronology and Demographic Evidence Relating to the Size of Pre-Columbian North American Indian Populations. *Science* 268:1601–1604.

1995b Migration in Prehistory: The Northern Iroquoian Case. *American Antiquity* 60(1):59–79.

1996 More on Migration in Prehistory: Accommodating New Evidence in the Northern Iroquoian Case. *American Antiquity* 61:791–796.

1997 The Architecture of Iroquois Longhouses. *Northeast Anthropology* 53:61–84.

2001 Setting Demographic Limits: The North American Case. In *Computing Archaeology for Understanding the Past*, edited by Z. Stancic and T. Veljanovski, pp. 259–261. BAR International Series, vol. 931. British Archaeological Reports, Oxford: Archaeopress.

2002 Individuals. In *Darwin and Archaeology: A Handbook of Key Concepts*, edited by J. P. Hart and J. E. Terrell, pp. 161–181. Westport, CT: Bergin and Garvey.

Snow, D. R. and K. M. Lanphear 1988 European Contact and Indian Depopulation in the Northeast: The Timing of the First Epidemics. *Ethnohistory* 35(1):15–33.

Sofaer, A., V. Zinser and R. M. Sinclair 1979 A Unique Solar Marking Construct. *Science* 206(4416):283–291.

Solis, F. (editor) 2004 *The Aztec Empire*. New York: Guggenheim Museum.

Sotomayor, A. and N. Castillo Tejero 1963 *Estudio Petrográfico de la Cerámica "Anaranjado Delgado."* Mexico City: Instituto Nacional de Antropología e Historia.

Spencer, C. S. and E. M. Redmond 2001 The Chronology of Conquest: Implications of New Radiocarbon Analyses from the Cañada de Cuicatlán, Oaxaca. *Latin American Antiquity* 12(2):182–202.

Spinden, H. J. 1928 Maya Inscriptions Dealing with Venus and the Moon. *Bulletin of the Buffalo Society of Natural Sciences* 15(1).

Šprajc, I. 2000 Astronomical Alignments at Teotihuacan, Mexico. *Latin American Antiquity* 11(4):401–415.

Squier, E. G. and E. H. Davis 1848 *Ancient Monuments of the Mississippi Valley, Comprising the Results of Extensive Original Surveys and Explorations*. Smithsonian Contributions to Knowledge, no. 1. Washington, DC: Smithsonian Institution.

Sridhar, V., D. B. Loope, J. B. Swinehart, J. A. Mason, R. J. Oglesby and C. M. Rowe 2006 Large Wind Shift on the Great Plains During the Medieval Warm Period. *Science* 313:345–347.

Stark, B. L., L. Heller and M. A. Ohnersorgen 1998 People with Cloth: Mesoamerican Economic Change from the Perspective of Cotton in South-Central Veracruz. *Latin American Antiquity* 9(1):7–36.

Steadman, D. 1995 Prehistoric Extinctions of Pacific Island Birds: Biodiversity Meets Zooarchaeology. *Science* 267:1123–1131.

Steele, D. G. and J. F. Powell 2002 Facing the Past: A View of the North American Human Fossil Record. In *The First Americans: The Pleistocene Colonization of the New World*, edited by N. G. Jablonski, pp. 93–122. Memoirs of the California Academy of Sciences, vol. 27. San Francisco: California Academy of Sciences.

Steinacher, T. L. and G. F. Carlson 1998 The Central Plains Tradition. In *Archaeology on the Great Plains*, edited by W. R. Wood, pp. 235–268. Lawrence: University of Kansas Press.

Steward, J. H. 1955 *Theory of Culture Change*. Urbana: University of Illinois Press.

Stiger, M. 2006 A Folsom Structure in the Colorado Mountains. *American Antiquity* 71(2):321–351.

Stoltman, J. B. and R. E. Hughes 2004 Obsidian in Early Woodland Contexts in the Upper Mississippi Valley. *American Antiquity* 69(4):751–759.

Storey, A. A., J. M. Ramirez, D. Quiroz, D. V. Durley, D. J. Addison, R. Walter, A. J. Anderson, T. L. Hunt, J. S. Athens, L. Huynen and E. A. Matisoo-Smith 2007 Radiocarbon and DNA Evidence for a Pre-Columbian Introduction of Polynesian Chickens to Chile. In *Proceedings of the National Academy of Sciences*, vol. 104, pp. 10335–10339. Washington, DC: National Academy of Sciences.

Straus, L. G., D. J. Meltzer and T. Goebel 2005 Ice Age Atlantis? Exploring the Solutrean-Clovis "Connection." *World Archaeology* 37(4):507–532.

Strong, E. (editor) 1976 *Wakemap Mound and Nearby Sites on the Long Narrows of the Columbia River*. Portland, OR: Binford and Mort.

Stuart, G. S. and G. E. Stuart 1993 *Lost Kingdoms of the Maya*. Washington, DC: National Geographic Society.

Sturtevant, W. C. 1975 Two 1761 Wigwams at Niantic, Connecticut. *American Antiquity* 40(4):437–444.

Sugiyama, S. 2005 *Human Sacrifice, Militarism, and Rulership*. New York: Cambridge University Press.

Suttles, W. 1990a Introduction. In *Northwest Coast*, edited by W. Suttles, pp. 1–15. *Handbook of North American Indians*, vol. 7, W. C. Sturtevant, general editor. Washington, DC: Smithsonian Institution.

1990b *Northwest Coast*, vol. 7. Washington, DC: Smithsonian Institution.

Swagerty, W. R. 2001 History of the United States Plains Until 1850. In *Plains*, edited by R. J. DeMallie, pp. 256–279. *Handbook of North American Indians*, vol. 13, W. C. Sturtevant, general editor. Washington, DC: Smithsonian Institution.

Swedlund, A. C. and D. Anderson 1999 Gordon Creek Woman Meets Kennewick Man: New Interpretations and Protocols Regarding the Peopling of the Americas. *American Antiquity* 64:569–576.

Taladoire, E. 2003 Could We Speak of the Super Bowl at Flushing Meadows?: *La pelota mixteca*, a Third Pre-Hispanic Ballgame, and Its Possible Architectural Context. *Ancient Mesoamerica* 14(2):319–342.

Tankersley, K. B. 1998 Variation in the Early Paleoindian Economies of Late Pleistocene Eastern North America. *American Antiquity* 63(1):7–20.

Tate, C. E. 1999 Patrons of Shamanic Power: La Venta's Supernatural Entities in Light of Mixe Beliefs. *Ancient Mesoamerica* 10(2):169–188.

Tattersall, I. 2001 How We Came to Be Human. *Scientific American* 285(6):56–63.

Taube, K. A. 1993 The Bilimek Pulque Vessel: Starlore, Calendrics, and Cosmology of Late Postclassic Central Mexico. *Ancient Mesoamerica* 4(1):1–15.

Taylor, K. 1999 Rapid Climate Change. *American Scientist* 87:320–327.

Taylor, R. E., C. V. Haynes Jr. and M. Stuiver 1996 Clovis and Folsom Age Estimates: Stratigraphic Context and Radiocarbon Calibration. *Antiquity* 70(269):515–525.

Theler, J. L. and R. F. Boszhardt 2006 Collapse of Crucial Resources and Culture Change: A Model for the Woodland

360

to Oneota Transformation in the Upper Midwest. *American Antiquity* 71(3):433–472.

Thomas, D. H. 1972 A Computer Simulation Model of Great Basin Shoshonean Subsistence and Settlement Patterns. In *Models in Archaeology*, edited by D. Clarke, pp. 671–704. London: Methuen.

2000 *Skull Wars*. New York: Basic Books.

Thompson, L. C. and M. D. Kinkade 1990 Languages. In *Northwest Coast*, edited by W. Suttles, pp. 30–51. *Handbook of North American Indians,* vol. 7, W. C. Sturtevant, general editor. Washington, DC: Smithsonian Institution.

Thornton, R. G. 1987 *American Indian Holocaust and Survival: A Population History Since 1492*. Norman: University of Oklahoma Press.

Thornton, R. G. and J. Marsh-Thornton 1981 Estimating Prehistoric American Indian Population Size for the United States Area: Implications of the Nineteenth Century Population Decline and Nadir. *American Journal of Physical Anthropology* 55:47–53.

Tiffany, J. A. 2003 Mississippian Connections with Mill Creek and Cambria. *Plains Anthropologist* 48(184):21–34.

Tiffany, J. A. and L. M. Alex 2001 Great Oasis Archaeology: New Perspectives from the DeCamp and West Des Moines Burial Sites in Central Iowa. *Plains Anthropologist* 46(178):1–104.

Tolstoy, P. 1991 Paper Route. *Natural History* 99(6):6–14.

Tomczak, P. D. and J. F. Powell 2003 Postmarital Residence Practices in the Windover Population: Sex-Based Dental Variation as an Indicator of Patrilocality. *American Antiquity* 68(1):93–108.

Tooker, E. 1971 Clans and Moieties in North America. *Current Anthropology* 12(3):357–376.

2003 *Understanding Early Civilizations: A Comparative Study*. New York: Cambridge University Press.

Townsend, R. F. (editor) 2004 *Hero, Hawk, and Open Hand*. New Haven, CT: Yale University Press.

Trigger, B. G. (editor) 1978 *Northeast*, vol. 15. Washington, DC: Smithsonian Institution.

Turner, C. G., II 1989 Teeth and Prehistory in Asia. *Scientific American*:88–96.

2002 Teeth, Needles, Dogs, and Siberia: Bioarchaeological Evidence for the Colonization of the New World. In *The First Americans: The Pleistocene Colonization of the New World*, edited by N. G. Jablonski, pp. 123–158. Memoirs of the California Academy of Sciences, vol. 27. San Francisco: California Academy of Sciences.

Tuross, N., M. L. Fogel, L. Newsom and G. H. Doran 1994 Subsistence in the Florida Archaic: The Stable-Isotope and Archaeobotanical Evidence from the Windover Site. *American Antiquity* 59(2):288–303.

Ubelaker, D. H. 1988 North American Indian Population Size, A.D. 1500 to 1985. *American Journal of Physical Anthropology* 77:289–294.

Vail, G. and A. F. Aveni 2004 *The Madrid Codex: New Approaches to Understanding an Ancient Maya Manuscript*. Boulder: University of Colorado Press.

Valadez Azúa, R., B. Peredes Gudiño and B. Rodríguez Galicia 1999 Entierros de Perros descubiertos en la antigua ciudad de Tula. *Latin American Antiquity* 10(2):180–200.

Van Nest, J., D. K. Charles, J. E. Buikstra and D. L. Asch 2001 Sod Blocks in Illinois Hopewell Mounds. *American Antiquity* 66(4):633-650.

Vehik, S. C. 2001 Hunting and Gathering Tradition: Southern Plains. In *Plains*, edited by R. J. DeMallie, pp. 146–158. *Handbook of North American Indians*, vol. 13, W. C. Sturtevant, general editor. Washington, DC: Smithsonian Institution.

2002 Conflict, Trade, and Political Development on the Southern Plains. *American Antiquity* 67(1):37–64.

Vilá, C., P. Savolainen, J. E. Maldonado, I. R. Amorim, J. E. Rice, R. L. Honeycutt, K. A. Crandall, J. Lundeberg and R. K. Wayne 1997 Multiple and Ancient Origins of the Domestic Dog. *Science* 276:1687–1689.

Vivian, R. G. 1990 *The Chacoan Prehistory of the San Juan Basin*. New York: Academic Press.

Voorhies, B. 1996 The Transformation from Foraging to Farming in Lowland Mesoamerica. In *The Managed Mosaic: Ancient Maya Agriculture and Resource Use*, edited by S. L. Fedick, pp. 17–29. Salt Lake City: University of Utah Press.

Walker, D. E., Jr. (editor) 1988 *Plateau,* vol. 12. Washington, DC: Smithsonian Institution.

Warner, B. G., J. J. Clague and R. W. Mathewes 1982 Conditions on the Queen Charlotte Islands, British Columbia, at the Height of the Late Wisconsin Glaciation. *Science* 218:675–677.

Washburn, W. E. (editor) 1988 *History of Indian-White Relations*, vol. 4. Washington, DC: Smithsonian Institution.

Waters, M. R. and J. C. Ravesloot 2001 Landscape Change and the Cultural Evolution of the Hohokam along the Middle Gila River and Other River Valleys in South-Central Arizona. *American Antiquity* 66(2):285–299.

Waters, M. R. and T. W. Stafford Jr. 2007 Redefining the Age of Clovis: Implications for the Peopling of the Americas. *Science* 315:1122–1126.

Watkins, J. E. 2003 Beyond the Margin: American Indians, First Nations, and Archaeology in North America. *American Antiquity* 68(2):273–285.

Weaver, M. P. 1972 *The Aztecs, Maya, and Their Predecessors: Archaeology of Mesoamerica*. Studies in Archeology. New York: Seminar Press.

1981 *The Aztecs, Maya, and Their Predecessors*. New York: Academic Press.

Webb, W. S. 1974 *Indian Knoll*. Knoxville: University of Tennessee Press.

Webb, W. S. and C. E. Snow 1974 *The Adena People*. Knoxville: University of Tennessee.

Webster, D. 2002 *Fall of the Ancient Maya*. New York: Thames and Hudson.

Webster, D., S. T. Evans and W. T. Sanders 1993 *Out of the Past: An Introduction to Archaeology*. Mountain View, CA: Mayfield.

Webster, D., W. T. Sanders and P. Van Rossum 1992 A Simulation of Copan Population History and Its Implications. *Ancient Mesoamerica* 3(1):185–197.

Webster, L. D. and M. E. McBrinn (editors) 2008 *Archaeology Without Borders: Contact, Commerce, and Change in the U.S. Southwest and Northwestern Mexico*. Boulder: University Press of Colorado.

Wedel, W. R. 2001 Plains Village Tradition: Central. In *Plains*, edited by R. J. DeMallie, pp. 173–185. *Handbook of North American Indians*, vol. 13, W. C. Sturtevant, general editor. Washington, DC: Smithsonian Institution.

Weigand, P. C. 1968 The Mines and Mining Techniques of the Chalchihuites Culture. *American Antiquity* 33(1):45–61.

1994 Observations on Ancient Mining within the Northwestern Regions of the Mesoamerican Civilization, with Emphasis on Turquoise. In *In Quest of Mineral Wealth: Aboriginal and Colonial Mining and Metallurgy in Spanish America*, edited by A. K. Craig and R. C. West, pp. 21–35. *Geoscience and Man*, vol. 33. Baton Rouge: Department of Geography and Anthropology, Louisiana State University.

Weigand, P. C. and G. Gwynne (editors) 1982 *Mining and Mining Techniques in Ancient Mesoamerica*, vol. 6 (nos. 1–2). Stony Brook: State University of New York, Stony Brook.

Weigand, P. C., G. Harbottle and E. V. Sayre 1977 Turquoise Sources and Source Analysis: Mesoamerica and the Southwestern U.S.A. In *Exchange Systems in Prehistory*, edited by T. K. Earle and J. E. Ericson, pp. 15–34. New York: Academic Press.

Wessen, G. 1990 Prehistory of the Ocean Coast of Washington. In *Northwest Coast*, edited by W. Suttles, pp. 412–421. *Handbook of North American Indians*, vol. 7, W. C. Sturtevant, general editor. Washington, DC: Smithsonian Institution.

West, R. C. 1994 Aboriginal Metallurgy and Metalworking in Spanish America: A Brief Overview. In *In Quest of Mineral Wealth: Aboriginal and Colonial Mining and Metallurgy in Spanish America*, edited by A. K. Craig and R. C. West, pp. 5–20. *Geoscience and Man*, vol. 33. Baton Rouge: Department of Geography and Anthropology, Louisiana State University.

Whalen, M. E. and P. E. Minnis 2003 The Local and the Distant in the Origin of Casa Grandes, Chihuahua, Mexico. *American Antiquity* 68(2):314–332.

Wheat, J. B. 1972 *The Olsen-Chubbuck Site: A Paleo-Indian Bison Kill*. Memoirs of the Society for American Archaeology 26.

Wheeler, R. J., J. J. Miller, R. M. McGee, D. Ruhl, B. Swann and M. Memory 2003 Archaic Period Canoes from Newnans Lake, Florida. *American Antiquity* 68(3):533–551.

White, C. D., F. J. Longstaffe and K. R. Law 2001 Revisiting the Teotihuacan Connection at Altun Ha: Oxygen-Isotope Analysis of Tomb F-8/1. *Ancient Mesoamerica* 12(1):65–72.

White, C. D., R. Storey, F. J. Longstraffe and M. W. Spence 2004 Immigration, Assimilation, and Status in the Ancient City of Teotihuacan: Stable Isotopic Evidence from Tlajinga 33. *Latin American Antiquity* 15(2):176–198.

White, M. E. 2002 *The Archaeology and History of the Native Georgia Tribes*. Gainesville: University Press of Florida.

White, N. M. 2005a Discontinuities, Common Foundations, Short-Distance Interactions, and Sporadic Long-Distance Connections around the Gulf of Mexico. In *Gulf Coast Archaeology: The Southeastern United States and Mexico*, edited by N. M. White, pp. 304–319. Gainesville: University Press of Florida.

2005b *Gulf Coast Archaeology: The Southeastern United States and Mexico*. Gainesville: University Press of Florida.

2005c Prehistoric Connections around the Gulf Coast. In *Gulf Coast Archaeology: The Southeastern United States and Mexico*, edited by N. M. White, pp. 1–55. Gainesville: University Press of Florida.

White, N. M. and R. A. Weinstein 2008 The Mexican Connection and the Far West of the U.S. Southeast. *American Antiquity* 73(2):227–277.

Whiteley, P. M. 2002 Archaeology and Oral Tradition: The Scientific Importance of Dialogue. *American Antiquity* 67(3):405–415.

Whitlam, R. 1983 Models of Coastal Adaptation: The Northwest Coast and Maritimes. In *The Evolution of Maritime Cultures on the Northeast and Northwest Coasts of America*, edited by R. J. Nash, vol. 11, pp. 109–124. Vancouver, British Columbia: Department of Archaeology, Simon Fraser University.

Whittington, E. M. (editor) 2001 *The Sport of Life and Death: The Mesoamerican Ballgame*. New York: Thames and Hudson.

Widmer, R. E. 1974 *A Survey and Assessment of Archaeological Resources on Marco Island, Collier County, Florida*. Florida Division of Archives, History, and Records Management. Copies available from 19.

1988 *The Evolution of Calusa: A Nonagricultural Chiefdom on the Southwest Florida Coast*. Tuscaloosa: University of Alabama Press.

1991 Lapidary Craft Specialization at Teotihuacan: Implications for Community Structure at 33:S3W1 and Economic Organization in the City. *Ancient Mesoamerica* 2(1):131–147.

2005 A New Look at the Gulf Coast Formative. In *Gulf Coast Archaeology: The Southeastern United States and Mexico*, edited by N. M. White, pp. 68–86. Gainesville: University Press of Florida.

Wilcox, D. R. 1991 Hohokam Social Complexity. In *Chaco & Hohokam: Prehistoric Regional Systems in the American Southwest*, edited by P. L. Crown and W. J. Judge, pp. 253–275. School of American Research Advanced Seminar Series, D. W. Schwartz, general editor. Santa Fe, NM: School of American Research Press.

Wilkerson, S. J. K. 2005 Rivers in the Sea: The Gulf of Mexico as a Cultural Corridor in Antiquity. In *Gulf Coast Archaeology: The Southeastern United States and Mexico*, edited by N. M. White, pp. 56–67. Gainesville: University Press of Florida.

Wilkes, G. 2004 Corn, Strange and Marvelous: But Is a Definitive Origin Known? In *Corn: Origin, History, Technology, and Production*, edited by C. W. Smith, pp. 3–63. New York: Wiley.

Willey, G. R. and P. Phillips 1958 *Method and Theory in American Archaeology*. Chicago: University of Chicago Press.

Willey, G. R. and J. A. Sabloff 1993 *A History of American Archaeology*, 3rd ed. San Francisco: W. H. Freeman.

Williams, B. J. 1974 *A Model of Band Society*. Society for American Archaeology Memoir 29. Society for American Archaeology.

Williams, S. 1991 *Fantastic Archaeology: The Wild Site of North American Prehistory*. Philadelphia: University of Pennsylvania Press.

Willoughby, C. C. 1935 *Antiquities of the New England Indians*. Peabody Museum of Harvard University, Cambridge.

Wilson, S. M. 1999 *The Indigenous People of the Caribbean*. Ripley P. Bullen Series. Gainesville: University Press of Florida.

Wilson, S. M., H. B. Iceland and T. R. Hester 1998 Preceramic Connections Between Yucatan and the Caribbean. *Latin American Antiquity* 9(4):342–352.

Windes, T. C. 2003 This Old House: Construction and Abandonment at Pueblo Bonito. In *Pueblo Bonito: Center of the Chacoan World*, edited by J. E. Neitzel, pp. 14–32. Washington, DC: Smithsonian Books.

Winham, R. P. and F. A. Calabrese 1998 The Middle Missouri Tradition. In *Archaeology on the Great Plains*, edited by W. R. Wood, pp. 269–307. Lawrence: University of Kansas Press.

Wobst, H. M. 1974 Boundary Conditions for Paleolithic Social Systems: A Simulation. *American Antiquity* 39:147–178.

1975 The Demography of Finite Populations and the Origins of the Incest Taboo. In *Population Studies in Archaeology and Biological Anthropology: A Symposium*, edited by A. C. Swedlund. Society for American Archaeology Memoir, vol. 30. Society for American Archaeology.

Wolverton, S. 2005 The Effects of the Hypsithermal on Prehistoric Foraging Efficiency in Missouri. *American Antiquity* 70(1):91–106.

Wonderly, A. 2005 Effigy Pipes, Diplomacy, and Myth: Exploring Interaction Between St. Lawrence Iroquoians and Eastern Iroquois in New York State. *American Antiquity* 70(2):211–240.

Wood, J. W. 1998 A Theory of Preindustrial Population Dynamics: Demography, Economy, and Well-being in Malthusian Systems. *Current Anthropology* 39:99–135.

Wood, W. R. (editor) 1998 *Archaeology on the Great Plains*. Lawrence: University of Kansas Press.

2001 Plains Village Tradition: Central. In *Plains*, edited by R. J. DeMallie, pp. 186–195. *Handbook of North American Indians*, vol. 13, W. C. Sturtevant, general editor. Washington, DC: Smithsonian Institution.

Wright, J. V. 1972 *Ontario Prehistory*. Ottawa, Ontario, Canada: National Museums of Canada. 1981 Prehistory of the Canadian Shield. In *Subarctic*, edited by J. Helm, pp. 86–96. *Handbook of North American Indians*, vol. 6, W. C. Sturtevant, general editor. Washington, DC: Smithsonian Institution.

Yesner, D. R. and G. Pearson 2002 Microblades and Migrations: Ethnic and Economic Models in the Peopling of the Americas. In *Thinking Small: Global Perspectives on Microlithization*, edited by R. G. Elston and S. L. Kuhn, pp. 133–161. Archaeological Papers of the American Anthropological Association, vol. 12. Washington, DC: American Anthropological Association.

Yi, S. and G. Clark 1985 The "Dyuktai Culture" and New World Origins. *Current Anthropology* 26(1):1–20.

Yoffee, N. 2005 *Myths of the Archaic State: Evolution of the Earliest Cities, States, and Civilizations*. New York: Cambridge University Press.

Zaragoza Ocaña, D. 2000 Interrelación de grupos cazadores-recolectores y sedentarios en la Huasteca. In *Nómadas y sedentarios en el Norte de México*, edited by M.-A. Hers, J. L. Mirafuentes, M. d. l. D. Soto and M. Vallebueno, pp. 143–150. Mexico City: Universidad Nacional Autónoma de México.

2005 Characteristic Elements Shared by Northeastern Mexico and the Southeastern United States. In *Gulf Coast Archaeology: The Southeastern United States and Mexico*, edited by N. M. White, pp. 245–259. Gainesville: University Press of Florida.

Zaragoza Ocaña, D. and P. Dávila Cabrera 1999 Un excéntrico pectoral de concha de la Huasteca Potosina. *Arqueología* 21:137–144.

References

Credits

Chapter 1

1, Fig 1.1: New York State Museum; **2**, Fig 1.2: Dean R. Snow; **5**, Fig 1.3: Dean R. Snow; **12**, Figs 1.4, 1.5: Dean R. Snow; **14**, Figs 1.6, 1.7: Dean R. Snow; **19**, Fig 1.8: DILBERT: © Scott Adams/Dist. by United Feature Syndicate. **20**, Fig 1.9: Dean R. Snow.

Chapter 2

26, Fig 2.1: Dean R. Snow; **28**, Figs 2.2, 2.3: Dean R. Snow; **29**, Figs 2.4, 2.5: Dean R. Snow; **30**, Fig 2.6: Dean R. Snow; **31**, Fig 2.7: Christy G. Turner III; **32**, Fig 2.8: Dean R. Snow; **35**, Fig 2.9: Dean R. Snow; **36**, Fig 2.10: Dean R. Snow; **37**, Fig 2.11: Dean R. Snow; **38**, Figs 2.12, 2.13: Hoffecker et al. 1993:49. Reprinted with permission from the American Association for the Advancement of Science; **39**, Fig 2.14: Dean R. Snow.

Chapter 3

41, Fig 3.1: Dean R. Snow; **44**, Fig 3.2: Dean R. Snow; **45**, Figs 3.3, 3.4: Dean R. Snow; **46**, Fig 3.5: Haury 1959:17. Reproduced by permission of the Society of American Archaeology from *American Antiquity* 25(1), 1959; **47**, Fig 3.6: David Anderson et al (2005); **48**, Fig 3.7: Dean R. Snow; **49**, Fig 3.8: King and Slobodin 1996:635. Reprinted with permission from the American Association for the Advancement of Science; **50**, Fig 3.9: Kunz and Reanier 1994:661. Reprinted with permission from the American Association for the Advancement of Science; **51**, Fig 3.10: Tom D. Dillehay; **52**, Fig 3.11: Dean R. Snow; **53**, Fig 3.12: Dean R. Snow; **54**, Fig 3.13: Dean R. Snow, Fig 3.14: Lahren and Bonnichsen 1974:149, Fig. 3. Reprinted with permission from the American Association for the Advancement of Science; **55**, Fig 3.15: Dean R. Snow; **58**, Fig 3.16: New York State Museum; Fig 3.17: (c) Image by © Han Chuanhao/XinHua/Xinhua Press/CORBIS All Rights Reserved; Fig 3.18: New York State Museum; **61**, Fig 3.19: Meltzer et al. 2002:42; **62**, Fig 3.20: Hoffecker et al. 1993:50. Reprinted with permission from the American Association for the Advancement of Science.

Chapter 4

65, Fig 4.1: Dean R. Snow; **67**, Fig 4.2: Dean R. Snow; **68**, Fig 4.3: Adapted from Britton and Brown 1923, vol. 2:625–659; **75**, Fig 4.4: Justice 1987:37, 64, 83, 87; **81**, Fig 4.5: Reproduced by permission of the Society of American Archaeology from *American Antiquity* from Danger Cave, Memoir 14, 1957; Fig 4.6: Dean R. Snow; **82**, Fig 4.7: Jones et al. 2003:31. Reproduced by permission of the Society of American Archaeology from *American Antiquity* 68(1), 2003; Fig 4.8: National Museum of Natural History, Smithsonian Institution; Fig 4.9: Dean R. Snow; Fig 4.10: Dean R. Snow; **83**, Figs 4.11, 4.12: Dean R. Snow; **84**, Fig 4.13: Dean R. Snow; **85**, Fig 4.14: Dean R. Snow; **88**, Fig 4.15: Dean R. Snow.

Chapter 5

90, Fig 5.1: Dean R. Snow; **94**, Fig 5.2: Ohio Historical Society; **95**, Fig 5.3: Jon L. Gibson; **97**, Fig 5.4: Dean R. Snow; **98**, Fig 5.5: Louise Basa; **99**, Fig 5.6: John Bigelow Taylor; Fig 5.7: Ohio Historical Society; **100**, Figs 5.8, 5.9: Dean R. Snow; **101**, Fig 5.10: Squier and Davis 1848:40; Fig 5.11: Dean R. Snow; Fig 5.12: Squier and Davis 1848:56; **102**, Fig 5.13: Dean R. Snow; **103**, Fig 5.14: Dean R. Snow; Fig 5.15: Squier and Davis 1848:opposite 66; Fig 5.16: Richard Pirko; **104**, Fig 5.17: Ohio Historical Society; **105**, Fig 5.18: Ohio Historical Society; **106**, Fig 5.19: John Bigelow Taylor; Fig 5.20: Gilcrease Museum; **107**, Fig 5.21: Squier and Davis 1848:opposite 18; **108**, Fig 5.22: Ohio Historical Society; Fig 5.23: Squier and Davis 1848:opposite 128; Fig 5.24: Dean R. Snow; **109**, Fig 5.25: National Park Service; **110**, Fig 5.26: Dean R. Snow.

Chapter 6

113, Figs 6.1, 6.2: Dean R. Snow; **114**, Fig 6.3: Dean R. Snow; **115**, Fig 6.4: Dean R. Snow; Fig 6.5: Masse 1981:410; **117**, Fig 6.6: Dean R. Snow; **118**, Fig 6.7: Dean R. Snow; **119**, Figs 6.8, 6.9 : Dean R. Snow; **122**, Fig 6.10: Dean R. Snow; **123**, Figs 6.11, 6.12: Dean R. Snow; **126**, Figs 6.13, 6.14, 6.15: Dean R. Snow; **127**, Fig 6.16: Dean R. Snow; **128**, Fig 6.17: Dean R. Snow; **129**, Fig 6.18: Tom Till Photography; **130**, Figs 6.19, 6.20: Dean R. Snow; Fig 6.21: Stein et al 2003:51; **131**, Fig 6.22: Dean R. Snow; **132**, Figs 6.23, 6.24: Dean R. Snow; **133**, Fig 6.25: Dean R. Snow; Fig 6.26: Copyright Solstice Project. Photo by Karl Kernberger. Fig 6.27: Dean R. Snow; **134**, Figs 6.28, 6.29: Dean R. Snow; **135**, Fig 6.30: Dean R. Snow; **136**, Fig 6.31: Dean R. Snow; **137**, Fig 6.32: Dean R. Snow; **138**, Fig 6.33: Dean R. Snow.

Chapter 7

140, Fig 7.1: Dean R. Snow; **141**, Fig 7.2: Dean R. Snow; **145**, Figs 7.3, 7.4: Dean R. Snow; **146**, Figs 7.5, 7.6: Dean R. Snow; **147**, Fig 7.7: Dean R. Snow; Fig 7.8: Michael D. Coe; **148**, Fig 7.9: Pohl et al. 2002:1985; **149**, Figs 7.10, 7.11: Dean R. Snow; **150**, Figs 7.12, 7.13: Dean R. Snow; **151**, Fig 7.14:

Dean R. Snow; **152**, Figs 7.15, 7.16: Dean R. Snow; **153**, Fig 7.17: Dean R. Snow; **154**, Fig 7.18: Dean R. Snow; **155**, Fig 7.19: Dean R. Snow; **157**, Fig 7.20: Dean R. Snow; **158**, Fig 7.21: Dean R. Snow; **159**, Fig 7.22: Joyce Marcus, University of Michigan; Fig 7.23: Dean R. Snow; **160**, Fig 7.24: Dean R. Snow; **161**, Fig 7.25: Dean R. Snow; **163**, Fig 7.26: Dean R. Snow; **165**, Figs 7.27, 7.28: Dean R. Snow; **166**, Fig 7.29: Instituto Nacional de Antropología e Historia, Mexico; Fig 7.30: David Webster; **167**, Fig 7.31: David Webster; **168**, Fig 7.32: Dean R. Snow; **169**, Fig 7.33: Dean R. Snow.

Chapter 8

172, Fig 8.1: Dean R. Snow; **173**, Fig 8.2: Dean R. Snow; **174**, Fig 8.3: Dean R. Snow; **175**, Figs 8.4, 8.5: Dean R. Snow; **176**, Figs 8.6, 8.7: Dean R. Snow, Fig 8.8: Berdan et al. 1994; **181**, Fig 8.9: Akademishe Druck-u. Verlagsanstalt; **181**, Fig 8.10: Dean R. Snow; **182**, Figs 8.11, 8.12: Dean R. Snow; **187**, Fig 8.13: Bodlian Library, Oxford University; Fig 8.14: Smith 1990; Weigand 1994; Weigand and Gwynne 1982; **188**, Fig 8.15: © The Trustees of the British Museum; **189**, Fig 8.16: Dean R. Snow; **190**, Fig 8.17: Dean R. Snow; Fig 8.18: Instituto Nacional de Antropología e Historia, Mexico; **191**, Fig 8.19: Dean R. Snow, Fig 8.20: Instituto Nacional de Antropología e Historia, Mexico, Fig 8.21: Dean R. Snow; **192**, Figs 8.22, 8.23: Dean R. Snow.

Chapter 9

195, Fig 9.1: Dean R. Snow; **198**, Fig 9.2: George Milner; **200**, Fig 9.3: Dean R. Snow; **202**, Fig 9.4: Dean R. Snow; Fig 9.5: Cahokia Mounds State Historic Site, painting by Lloyd K. Townsend; **204**, Fig 9.6: David H. Dye, Fig 9.7: National Museum of the American Indian, Smithsonian Institution (D150853); **205**, Fig 9.8: Frank H. McClung Museum, The University of Tennessee, Knoxville, Fig 9.9: David H. Dye, Fig 9.10: Ohio Historical Society; **206**, Figs 9.11, 9.12: Dean R. Snow, Fig 9.13: University of Alabama Museums; **207**, Fig 9.14: Dean R. Snow; **208**, Fig 9.15: Dean R. Snow; **209**, Fig 9.16: Dean R. Snow; **210**, Figs 9.17, 9.18, 9.19: Dean R. Snow; **211**, Fig 9.20: Dean R. Snow; **212**, Fig 9.21: Dean R. Snow; **213**, Fig 9.22: Dean R. Snow; **214**, Fig 9.23: Dean R. Snow; **216**, Fig 9.24: John Bigelow Taylor, Fig 9.25: National Museum of the American Indian, Smithsonian Institution (T150853)

Chapter 10

218, Fig 10.1: Dean R. Snow; **220**, Fig 10.2: Dean R. Snow, Fig 10.3: Photographer, Michael Cullen. The Canadian Canoe Museum, Peterborough, Ontario; **222**, Figs 10.4, 10.5: Dean R. Snow; **223**, Figs 10.6, 10.7: Dean R. Snow; **226**, Fig 10.8: New York State Museum, Fig 10.9: Dean R. Snow; **227**, Fig 10.10: Museum of Ontario Archeology; **229**, Figs 10.11, 10.12: Dean R. Snow; **232**, Fig 10.13: Dean R. Snow; **233**, Fig 10.14: Dean R. Snow; **234**, Fig 10.15: Willoughby 1935:267; **235**, Fig 10.16: Dean R. Snow; **236**, Fig 10.17: Dean R. Snow; **237**, Fig 10.18: Dean R. Snow; **239**, Fig 10.19: Lost painting by Jacques le Moyne.

Chapter 11

242, Fig 11.1: Dean R. Snow, Fig 11.2: beautifulbotany.com; **243**, Fig 11.3: Joe Saunders; **245**, Fig 11.4: Jerald T. Milanich, Fig 11.5: Dean R. Snow; **246**, Fig 11.6: Dean R. Snow; **248**, Fig 11.7: National Museum of Natural History; Fig 11.8: Florida Division of Historical Resources; **249**, Fig 11.9: Dean R. Snow; **251**, Fig 11.10: David Diener and New South Associates; **252**, Fig 11.11: Matson Museum **254**, Fig 11.12: Dean R. Snow; **255**, Fig 11.13: Dean R. Snow.

Chapter 12

257, Figs 12.1, 12.2: Dean R. Snow; **258**, Fig 12.3: Dean R. Snow; **259**, Fig 12.4: Dean R. Snow; **262**, Fig 12.5: John H. Blitz (1988); **263**, Fig 12.6: Richard Collier, Wyoming Historic Preservation Office, Department of State Parks and Cultural Resources, Fig 12.7: Dean R. Snow; **264**, Fig 12.8: Dean R. Snow; **266**, Figs 12.9, 12.10: Dean R. Snow; **267**, Fig 12.11: Dean R. Snow; **268**, Figs 12.12, 12.13: Dean R. Snow; **269**, Fig 12.14: Dean R. Snow; **270**, Fig 12.15: Dean R. Snow; Fig 12.16: Kloor 2007:1543. Reprinted with permission from the American Association for the Advancement of Science **271**, Figs 12.17, 12.18: Dean R. Snow; **272**, Figs 12.19, 12.20: Dean R. Snow; **273**, Figs 12.21, 12.22: Dean R. Snow; **274**, Fig 12.23: Dean R. Snow; **275**, Fig 12.24: Dean R. Snow.

Chapter 13

278, Fig 13.1: Dean R. Snow; **279**, Fig 13.2: Dean R. Snow; **280**, Fig 13.3: Moulton (1990:434); **281**, Fig 13.4: Dean R. Snow; **282**, Fig 13.5: Dean R. Snow; **284**, Fig 13.6: Dean R. Snow; **287**, Figs 13.7, 13.8: Dean R. Snow; **289**, Fig 13.9: Dean R. Snow; **291**, Figs 13.10, 13.11: Museum of Anthropology, University of British Columbia, **292**, Fig 13.12: Dean R. Snow; **293**, Figs 13.13, 13.14: Dean R. Snow; **294**, Fig 13.15: Dean R. Snow; **295**, Figs 13.16, 13.17, 13.18: Dean R. Snow; **297**, Fig 13.19: Dean R. Snow; **301**, Fig 13.20: Campbell Grant; **302**, Fig 13.21: Copyright © Phoebe A. Hearst Museum of Anthropology and the Regents of the University of California, Fig 13.22: Dean R. Snow.

Chapter 14

304, Fig 14.1: Dean R. Snow; **305**, Fig 14.2: Dean R. Snow; **307**, Fig 14.3: Dean R. Snow; **308**, Fig 14.4: Dean R. Snow, Fig 14.5: Larsen and Rainey 1948:113, 125, Fig 14.6: Larsen and Rainey 1948:138; **310**, Fig 14.7: Dean R. Snow, Fig 14.8: Larsen and Rainey 1948:71; **311**, Fig 14.9: Nunavut Photo © Canadian Museum of Civilization, photo O'Neill, 1915, image 38571LS; **313**, Figs 14.10, 14.11, 14.12: Dean R. Snow; **314**, Fig 14.13: ParksCanada/H.01.11.01.04(40), Fig 14.14 Bruce J. Bourque; **315**, Fig 14.15: Dean R. Snow; **317**, Figs 14.16, 14.17: Dean R. Snow.

Chapter 15

323, Fig 15.1: Dean R. Snow; **325**, Fig 15.2 Sanders 1992:179; **327**, Fig 15.3 Dolores and Tom Elliott; **328**, Fig 15.4: Dean R. Snow; **329**, Fig 15.5 quier and Davis 1848, facing page 3, Fig 15.6: Dean R. Snow.

Index